Allgemeiner Entschädigungsfonds – General Settlement Fund
Aicher | Kussbach | Reinisch (Hrsg. | Eds.)

Entscheidungen der Schiedsinstanz für Naturalrestitution
Decisions of the Arbitration Panel for *In Rem* Restitution

Übersetzungen/Translations: Victoria Grimes (LL.M USyd) Translation Services, Sydney, Australia; E-Mail: victoria.grimes@bigpond.com; Sarah Higgs BA (Hons); Mag. iur. Jakob Wurm EMLE, University of Vienna.
Redigiert durch die Schiedsinstanz für Naturalrestitution/Edited by the Arbitration Panel for *In Rem* Restitution.

Gedruckt mit Unterstützung des
Bundesministerium für europäische und internationale Angelegenheiten
Federal Ministry for European and International Affairs

Bibliografische Information der Deutschen Nationalbibliothek

Die Deutsche Nationalbibliothek verzeichnet diese Publikation in der Deutschen Nationalbibliografie; detaillierte bibliografische Daten sind im Internet über http://dnb.d-nb.de abrufbar.

Alle Angaben in diesem Fachbuch erfolgen trotz sorgfältiger Bearbeitung ohne Gewähr, eine Haftung der Herausgeber oder des Verlages ist ausgeschlossen.

This work is subject to copyright. All rights are reserved, whether the whole or part of the material is concerned, specifically those of translation, reprinting, broadcasting, reproduction by photocopying machine or similar means, and storage in data banks.

Copyright © 2009 Facultas Verlags- und Buchhandels AG
facultas.wuv Universitätsverlag, Berggasse 5, 1090 Wien, Österreich
Alle Rechte, insbesondere das Recht der Vervielfältigung und der Verbreitung sowie der Übersetzung, sind vorbehalten.
Titelbild: Österreichische Nationalbibliothek, Bildarchiv. Das Foto aus dem Jahr 1939 zeigt die in der Entscheidung Nr. 3/2003 antragsgegenständliche Liegenschaft. In diesem Haus im ersten Wiener Gemeindebezirk war seit der Arisierung im Jahr 1938 das Landesarbeitsamt Wien, ab 1994 das Arbeitsmarktservice Wien untergebracht.
Cover: Austrian National Library, photo archive. The photo, taken in 1939, depicts the property subject of decision no. 3/2003. Since its aryanization in 1938, first the Vienna Regional Employment office, then, from 1994, the Public Employment Service (AMS) was accommodated in this house in the first district of Vienna.
Satz und Druck: Facultas Verlags- und Buchhandels AG
Printed in Austria
ISBN 978-3-7089-0377-4 (facultas.wuv)
ISBN 978-1-84946-000-2 (Hart Publishing)

Allgemeiner Entschädigungsfonds für Opfer
des Nationalsozialismus
General Settlement Fund for Victims
of National Socialism
o.Univ.-Prof. Dr. Josef Aicher
Hon.-Prof. Dr.Dr.h.c. Erich Kussbach LL.M.
ao.Univ.-Prof. MMag. Dr. August Reinisch LL.M.
(Hrsg. | Eds.)

Entscheidungen der Schiedsinstanz für Naturalrestitution

Decisions of the Arbitration Panel for *In Rem* Restitution

Band 2 | Volume 2

Wien | Vienna 2009

HART
PUBLISHING

facultas.wuv

Contents

Introduction 6

Press Release Decision No. 8/2004 16
Decision No. 8/2004 20
Press Release Decision No. 9/2005 60
Decision No. 9/2005 62
Press Release Decision No. 24/2005 80
Decision No. 24/2005 84
Press Release Decision No. 25/2005 142
Decision No. 25/2005 146
Press Release Decision No. 26/2005 194
Decision No. 26/2005 196
Press Release Decision No. 27/2005 212
Decision No. 27/2005 216
Press Release Decision No. 28/2005 350
Decision No. 28/2005 352

Appendix

Federal Law on the Establishment of a General Settlement Fund for
Victims of National Socialism and on Restitution Measures
(GSF Law, original version: Federal Law Gazette I No. 12 /2001),
latest Version 384

Opt-In Dates of Austrian Provinces and Municipalities 412

A Select Bibliography on the Subject of *(In Rem)* Restitution 414

List of Abbreviations 418

Editors 426

Inhaltsverzeichnis

Einleitung 7

Pressemitteilung Entscheidung Nr. 8/2004 17
Entscheidung Nr. 8/2004 21
Pressemitteilung Entscheidung Nr. 9/2005 61
Entscheidung Nr. 9/2005 63
Pressemitteilung Entscheidung Nr. 24/2005 81
Entscheidung Nr. 24/2005 85
Pressemitteilung Entscheidung Nr. 25/2005 143
Entscheidung Nr. 25/2005 147
Pressemitteilung Entscheidung Nr. 26/2005 195
Entscheidung Nr. 26/2005 197
Pressemitteilung Entscheidung Nr. 27/2005 213
Entscheidung Nr. 27/2005 217
Pressemitteilung Entscheidung Nr. 28/2005 351
Entscheidung Nr. 28/2005 353

Anhang

Bundesgesetz über die Einrichtung eines Allgemeinen Entschädigungsfonds für Opfer des Nationalsozialismus und über Restitutionsmaßnahmen (Entschädigungsfondsgesetz, Stammfassung: BGBl I Nr. 12/2001), geltende Fassung 385

Opt-In von Ländern und Gemeinden 413

Auswahlbibliografie zum Themenbereich der (Natural-)Restitution 415

Abkürzungsverzeichnis 419

Herausgeber 427

Introduction

The Arbitration Panel for *In Rem* Restitution – Josef Aicher (Chairman), Erich Kussbach and August Reinisch – publishes in this second volume of the series a further seven "substantive" decisions in book form. These decisions dating from 2004 and 2005 again offer insight into the broad range of the Arbitration Panel's work and the variety of subject matters which it has to take into account during its examination of applications and its decision-making process.

In this series, only "substantive" decisions of the Arbitration Panel are published in anonymous form. "Substantive" decisions constitute those rulings which have been preceded by a detailed historical and legal examination of the circumstances of the case. The processing of these cases is generally very complex and time consuming. On the basis of the General Settlement Fund Law (GSF Law), the Arbitration Panel has developed an elaborate set of case law built up on a case by case basis.

Of the 2,152 applications (as at April 2009)[1] that have been received to date by the Arbitration Panel, thus far 285 applications have resulted in "substantive" decisions.[2] The remaining decisions are classified as "formal" and refer to those applications which, after an initial examination, did not satisfy the fundamental requirements of an application for *in rem* restitution pursuant to the GSF Law.[3]

As a result, the texts published in this series are not consecutively numbered. The publication of the "substantive" decisions is in the order of when the decisions were taken.

---

[1] Regularly updated statistical data regarding the number of received applications and decisions passed by the Arbitration Panel to date can be viewed on the homepage of the General Settlement Fund at www.nationalfonds.org, www.entschaedigungsfonds.at or www.generalsettlementfund.org.

[2] One "substantive" decision generally deals with several applications.

[3] The restriction of the area of application of an *in rem* restitution to certain publicly-owned assets with a history of seizure during the National Socialist era provides clear requirements for applications which can be examined in a first step relatively quickly both from a legal as well as an historical point of view. This applies to the establishment of the ownership situation in the year 1938 and on the legally prescribed cut off day of 17 January 2001.The question of public ownership is therefore an important criterion for the processing of an application. Applications fulfilling the requirement of public ownership at the cut off day are classified as "substantive" applications, as they require a closer legal and historical examination in terms of content. Those applications not meeting this requirement or not containing sufficient substantiation of the claimed asset are classified as "formal" applications in a first stage of the proceedings. If no objections to this classification in the form of further statements by the Arbitration Panel or supplements are made by the applicants during the course of the examination, the respective applications have to be rejected by the Arbitration Panel. The decisions of this application category are currently available on the homepage of the General Settlement Fund.

Einleitung

Mit dem zweiten Band dieser Reihe veröffentlicht die Schiedsinstanz für Naturalrestitution – bestehend aus Josef Aicher (Vorsitz), Erich Kussbach und August Reinisch – weitere sieben „materielle" Entscheidungen in Buchform. Diese Entscheidungen aus den Jahren 2004 und 2005 bieten erneut Einblick in das breite inhaltliche Spektrum der Tätigkeit der Schiedsinstanz und die Vielfalt der Themen, die sie bei ihrer Antragsprüfung und Entscheidungsfindung zu berücksichtigen hat.

In der vorliegenden Reihe werden ausschließlich „materielle" Entscheidungen der Schiedsinstanz – in anonymisierter Form – veröffentlicht. Als „materielle" Entscheidungen werden Beschlussfassungen bezeichnet, denen eine detaillierte historische und juristische Prüfung des Sachverhalts vorangegangen ist. Die Bearbeitung dieser Fälle gestaltet sich regelmäßig sehr komplex und aufwändig. Dabei hat die Schiedsinstanz auf Basis des Entschädigungsfondsgesetzes (EF-G) eine differenzierte, einzelfallbezogene Spruchpraxis ausgebildet.

Von den bisher insgesamt 2.152 (Stand: April 2009)[1] bei der Schiedsinstanz eingelangten Anträgen führten bislang 285 Anträge zu „materiellen" Entscheidungen.[2] Die übrigen bereits ergangenen Entscheidungen werden als „formell" bezeichnet und sprechen über jene Anträge ab, die nach einer Erstbegutachtung die wesentlichen Antragsvoraussetzungen für eine Naturalrestitution gemäß EF-G nicht erfüllten.[3]

Infolgedessen ist die Nummerierung der in dieser Reihe publizierten Texte nicht fortlaufend. Die Publikation der „materiellen" Entscheidungen erfolgt in der Reihenfolge ihrer Beschlussfassung.

---

[1] Regelmäßig aktualisierte statistische Daten zur Anzahl der eingelangten Anträge und der bisher getroffenen Entscheidungen der Schiedsinstanz sind auf der Homepage des Allgemeinen Entschädigungsfonds unter www.nationalfonds.org, www.entschaedigungsfonds.at oder www.generalsettlementfund.org abrufbar.

[2] Eine „materielle" Entscheidung betrifft in der Regel mehrere Anträge.

[3] Aufgrund der Beschränkung des Anwendungsbereiches von Naturalrestitution auf Vermögenswerte im öffentlichen Eigentum mit Entziehungshintergrund in der NS-Zeit liegen klare Antragsvoraussetzungen vor, die sowohl in juristischer als auch in historischer Hinsicht in einem ersten Arbeitsschritt im Allgemeinen relativ rasch überprüft werden können. Dies gilt für die Feststellung der Eigentumsverhältnisse einerseits im Jahr 1938 und andererseits am gesetzlichen Stichtag, dem 17. Jänner 2001. Das Kriterium des öffentlichen Eigentums ist somit eine wichtige Verfahrensscheide für die Antragsbearbeitung. Anträge, die die Antragsvoraussetzung des öffentlichen Eigentums zum Stichtag erfüllen, werden als „materielle" Anträge eingestuft, da sie eine nähere juristische und historische, d.h. inhaltliche Auseinandersetzung erfordern. Jene Anträge, die diese Voraussetzung nicht erfüllen oder keine hinreichende Konkretisierung des beantragten Vermögenswertes enthalten, werden in einem ersten Verfahrensstadium als „formelle" Anträge eingestuft. Sofern dieser Einstufung in der weiteren Bearbeitung keine anderen Feststellungen durch die Schiedsinstanz oder Ergänzungen durch die AntragstellerInnen entgegenstehen, müssen die betreffenden Anträge durch die Schiedsinstanz ablehnend entschieden werden. Die Entscheidungen dieser Antragskategorie sind derzeit exemplarisch auf der Homepage des Allgemeinen Entschädigungsfonds abrufbar.

All decisions on "substantive" applications by the Arbitration Panel are adopted in German. The English versions included in this volume are translations of the original German texts.

The texts of the decisions have been anonymized prior to their publication for reasons of privacy. To improve the legibility of the texts, the rules of anonymization adopted for volume I have been slightly changed. In addition, orthographical mistakes and typing errors have been rectified, abbreviations have been standardized and a gender-inclusive language has been adopted. Currencies are no longer abbreviated and placed after the amount stated (e.g. *3,000 Reichsmark* instead of *RM 3,000*). Further, in some instances references to literature relied upon in the decisions have been completed to facilitate the reader's ability to locate the same.

The wording of the texts of the decisions is, however, never changed with the exception of the anonymization. Additions and corrections in terms of contents are exclusively noted in footnotes at the relevant section to ensure the authenticity of the texts.

Press releases are issued for each decision on a "substantive" application. These precede the texts of the respective decisions in this collection of decisions to enable a quick overview of a decision's content.

The Arbitration Panel passes so-called supplementary decisions to applications (e.g. of further heirs) which it receives with regard to matters which have already been decided in proceedings.[4] With respect to volume 2 it is noted that the following supplementary decisions were passed: on 26 May 2008 *supplementary decision no. 9a/2008* regarding *decision no. 9/2005*, on 18 April 2006 *supplementary decision no. 25a/2006* regarding *decision no. 25/2005* and with respect to *decision no. 27/2005 supplementary decisions no. 27a/2006* (23 January 2006*), 27b/2007* (26 February 2007) and *27c/2008* (23 June 2008) as well as *decision no. 371/2007* (26 June 2007) which is related to the contents of decision no. 27/2005.

The Arbitration Panel also continuously publishes all "substantive" decisions und supplementary decisions together with the respective press releases in anonymous form in an online database on the homepage of the National Fund and the General Settlement Fund. Thus, all decisions made by the Arbitration Panel can be accessed via full-text search using keywords in German and English.

Furthermore, an expansion of the online database is planned for mid 2009. Apart from an expansion of its functions and contents, this database will include, amongst other things, the complete publication of all decisions, which means also the "formal" decisions and their English anonymized translations. Individual search and filter functions will also be implemented.

The procedural and operating principles of the Arbitration Panel for *In Rem* Restitution are not further expanded here. These have been described in detail in the in-

---

[4] Supplementary decisions are also published in the order of when the decisions were taken and are designated by the addition of a letter (e.g. *decision 27a/2006*).

Alle Entscheidungen der Schiedsinstanz über „materielle" Anträge ergehen in deutscher Sprache. Die in diesem Band enthaltenen englischen Versionen sind Übersetzungen der authentischen deutschen Texte.

Die Texte der Entscheidungen wurden vor ihrer Veröffentlichung aus Datenschutzgründen zunächst anonymisiert. Um die Lesbarkeit der Texte zu verbessern, wurden die Anonymisierungsregeln seit der Publikation von Band 1 leicht abgeändert. Zudem wurden in den Texten orthografische Mängel und Tippfehler behoben, Abkürzungen vereinheitlicht sowie eine Anpassung an eine gendergerechte Schreibweise vorgenommen. Währungsangaben wurden ebenfalls aufgeschlüsselt und durchgehend hinter den Summenangaben positioniert (z.B. *3.000,– Reichsmark* statt *RM 3.000,–*). Weiters wurden Angaben zu in den Entscheidungen verwendeter Literatur in Einzelfällen vervollständigt, um den LeserInnen das Auffinden derselben zu erleichtern.

In ihrem Wortlaut hingegen erfahren die Entscheidungstexte – abgesehen von der Anonymisierung – nie eine Veränderung. Inhaltliche Ergänzungen und Berichtigungen sind ausschließlich an den entsprechenden Stellen in Fußnoten vermerkt, so dass die Authentizität der Texte gewahrt ist.

Zu jeder Entscheidung eines „materiellen" Antrags werden Pressemeldungen veröffentlicht. Diese werden in der vorliegenden Entscheidungssammlung den jeweiligen Entscheidungstexten vorangestellt, um eine rasche Orientierung über den Inhalt einer Entscheidung zu ermöglichen.

Zu Anträgen (z.B. von weiteren ErbInnen), die zu schon entschiedenen Verfahrensgegenständen einlangen, werden von der Schiedsinstanz so genannte Zusatzentscheidungen getroffen.[4] Für Band 2 wird diesbezüglich darauf hingewiesen, dass zu *Entscheidung Nr. 9/2005* am 26. Mai 2008 die *Zusatzentscheidung Nr. 9a/2008* ergangen ist, zu *Entscheidung Nr. 25/2005* am 18. April 2006 *Zusatzentscheidung Nr. 25a/2006*, zu *Entscheidung Nr. 27/2005* die *Zusatzentscheidungen Nr. 27a/2006* (23. Jänner 2006*), 27b/2007* (26. Februar 2007) *und 27c/2008* (23. Juni 2008) sowie die in inhaltlichem Zusammenhang stehende *Entscheidung Nr. 371/2007* (26. Juni 2007) beschlossen wurden.

Die Schiedsinstanz veröffentlicht alle „materiellen" Entscheidungen und Zusatzentscheidungen gemeinsam mit den jeweiligen Pressemitteilungen in anonymisierter Form laufend auch auf der Homepage des Nationalfonds und Allgemeinen Entschädigungsfonds in einer Online-Datenbank. Damit können die Entscheidungen der Schiedsinstanz auch über Volltextsuche mittels Stichwörtern in deutscher und englischer Sprache abgefragt werden.

Für die Jahresmitte 2009 ist außerdem ein Ausbau der Online-Datenbank geplant. Diese wird neben einer funktionalen und inhaltlichen Erweiterung unter anderem die vollständige Veröffentlichung sämtlicher Entscheidungen, das heißt auch der „formellen" Entscheidungen und ihrer englischen Übersetzungen im anonymisier-

---

[4] Zusatzentscheidungen werden ebenfalls in der Reihenfolge ihrer Beschlussfassung veröffentlicht und sind durch die Beigabe eines Buchstabens (z.B. *Entscheidung 27a/2006*) gekennzeichnet.

troduction of volume 1.[5] In this regard, the Business Report of the National Fund and the General Settlement Fund published in October 2008 is referred to. It offers a contemporary overview of the work of both funds as well as the Arbitration Panel for *In Rem* Restitution.[6]

Several texts have been included in the appendix to volume 2. At the outset, the GSF Law in its current version as amended by Federal Law Gazette I No. 89/2008 of 2 July 2008 is reproduced. This amendment relates to Sec. 38 of the GSF Law and sets out the general conditions for an extension of the deadline for applications:

Following several extensions, the general deadline for applications for *in rem* restitution pursuant to the GSF Law expired on 31 December 2007. With the adoption of Federal Law Gazette I No. 89/2008 the legislator created the opportunity for provinces and municipalities, which resolved to opt-in in accordance with Sec. 38 of the GSF Law to have applications for *in rem* restitution of assets belonging to them examined by the Arbitration Panel,[7] to extend the deadline for applications until 31 December 2009. Thus far, the City of Vienna, the Province of Vorarlberg and the Municipalities of Mattersburg, Bad Ischl and Vöcklabruck have exercised the option to extend the deadline until the end of 2009.

Furthermore, provinces and municipalities which have not yet opted-in to the proceedings for *in rem* restitution can exercise this option until the end of 2009. After this time, such opt-in requires the consent of the Arbitration Panel. In both cases, applications can be submitted within 24 months after the regional administrative body has joined the Arbitration Panel. The respective deadlines are announced on the homepage of the General Settlement Fund. A list of the current expiration dates of the deadlines can also be found in the appendix.

Besides the list of abbreviations and the profiles of the members of the Arbitration Panel, the appendix also contains a selective bibliography regarding the topic of *in rem* restitution. It is intended to show with this summary the increased number of papers and discussions in the field of *in rem* restitution as a form of compensation.

---

[5] Allgemeiner Entschädigungsfonds/General Settlement Fund, Josef Aicher/Erich Kussbach/August Reinisch (Eds.), *Entscheidungen der Schiedsinstanz für Naturalrestitution/ Decisions of the Arbitration Panel for In Rem Restitution*, Volume 1, Vienna 2008 [bilingual, Deutsch/Englisch].

[6] Nationalfonds der Republik Österreich für Opfer des Nationalsozialismus (Ed.), *Geschäftsbericht 2007 des Nationalfonds der Republik Österreich für Opfer des Nationalsozialismus und des Allgemeinen Entschädigungsfonds für Opfer des Nationalsozialismus*. Editorial cooperation: Jürgen Schremser, Maria Luise Lanzrath, Richard Rebernik, Peter Stadlbauer, Christine Schwab, Claudia Müller, Ingeborg Gratzer and Elisabeth Leeb, Vienna 2008.

[7] Until December 2007, the City of Vienna, the Provinces of Upper Austria, Salzburg, Carinthia, Lower Austria, Styria, Vorarlberg and Burgenland as well as the Municipalities of Bad Ischl, Eisenstadt, Grieskirchen, Kittsee, Mattersburg, Purkersdorf, Oberwart, Rechnitz, Stockerau, Vöcklabruck and Wiener Neudorf have opted-in.

ten Wortlaut beinhalten. Zudem werden differenziertere Such- und Filterfunktionen implementiert.

Auf das Verfahren und die Arbeitsweise der Schiedsinstanz für Naturalrestitution wird hier nicht eingegangen, diese wurden bereits in der Einleitung zu Band 1 ausführlich dargestellt.[5] In diesem Zusammenhang wird auch auf den im Oktober 2008 veröffentlichten Geschäftsbericht des Nationalfonds und des Allgemeinen Entschädigungsfonds hingewiesen, der einen aktuellen Überblick über die Arbeit der beiden Fonds sowie der Schiedsinstanz für Naturalrestitution bietet.[6]

In den Anhang zu Band 2 wurden mehrere Texte aufgenommen. Zunächst ist die geltende Fassung des EF-G wiedergegeben, das zuletzt durch BGBl I Nr. 89/2008 vom 2. Juli 2008 geändert wurde. Diese Novellierung bezieht sich auf § 38 des EF-G und gibt die Rahmenbedingungen für eine Verlängerung der Antragsfrist vor:

Die allgemeine Antragsfrist für Naturalrestitution nach dem EF-G ist – nach mehrmaligen Verlängerungen – am 31. Dezember 2007 abgelaufen. Der Gesetzgeber hat danach mit BGBl I Nr. 89/2008 für Länder und Gemeinden, die sich gemäß § 38 EF-G zur Prüfung von Anträgen auf Naturalrestitution ihres Vermögens der Schiedsinstanz angeschlossen haben (Opt-In),[7] die Möglichkeit geschaffen, die Antragsfrist bis 31. Dezember 2009 zu verlängern. Bislang haben die Stadt Wien, das Land Vorarlberg und die Gemeinden Mattersburg, Bad Ischl und Vöcklabruck von dieser Möglichkeit der Fristverlängerung bis Ende 2009 Gebrauch gemacht.

Darüber hinaus können Länder und Gemeinden, die sich bisher noch nicht dem Naturalrestitutionsverfahren angeschlossen haben, bis Ende 2009 vom Opt-In Gebrauch machen. Danach bedarf ein solches Opt-In der Zustimmung der Schiedsinstanz. In beiden Fällen können Anträge innerhalb von 24 Monaten, nachdem sich die Gebietskörperschaft der Schiedsinstanz angeschlossen hat, eingebracht werden. Die jeweiligen Fristen werden auf der Homepage des Allgemeinen Entschädigungsfonds bekanntgegeben. Eine Liste mit den derzeitigen Fristabläufen befindet sich ebenfalls im Anhang.

Weiters enthält der Anhang neben einem Abkürzungsverzeichnis und den Kurzbiografien der Mitglieder der Schiedsinstanz eine Auswahlbibliografie zum Thema

---

[5] *Allgemeiner Entschädigungsfonds*/Josef *Aicher*/Erich *Kussbach*/August *Reinisch* (Hrsg.), Entscheidungen der Schiedsinstanz für Naturalrestitution, Band 1, Wien 2008 [zweisprachig, Deutsch/Englisch].

[6] *Nationalfonds der Republik Österreich für Opfer des Nationalsozialismus* (Hrsg.), Geschäftsbericht 2007 des Nationalfonds der Republik Österreich für Opfer des Nationalsozialismus und des Allgemeinen Entschädigungsfonds für Opfer des Nationalsozialismus. Redaktionelle Mitarbeit: Jürgen Schremser, Maria Luise Lanzrath, Richard Rebernik, Peter Stadlbauer, Christine Schwab, Claudia Müller, Ingeborg Gratzer und Elisabeth Leeb, Wien 2008.

[7] Dem Verfahren vor der Schiedsinstanz haben sich bis Dezember 2007 die Stadt Wien, die Bundesländer Oberösterreich, Salzburg, Kärnten, Niederösterreich, Steiermark, Vorarlberg und Burgenland sowie die Gemeinden Bad Ischl, Eisenstadt, Grieskirchen, Kittsee, Mattersburg, Purkersdorf, Oberwart, Rechnitz, Stockerau, Vöcklabruck und Wiener Neudorf angeschlossen.

The decisions published in volume 2 are three recommendations and four rejections which relate to properties and objects in Vienna and in the Federal Provinces of Lower Austria and Carinthia.

In decision no. 8/2004, the restitution of properties in the area of today's military training area Allentsteig and in the village Allentsteig was applied for. The Arbitration Panel had to examine whether the acquisition of properties in the course of the construction of the military training area by the German Armed Forces in 1939 constituted an act of National Socialist persecution of the vendors. The Arbitration Panel had to reject the application as – although one of the vendors was subjected to political persecution – this persecution was not causally connected to the sale of the property to the German Armed Forces and as such, a seizure of property as defined by the GSF Law had not occurred.

In decision no. 9/2005, the restitution of a property in Vienna-Hütteldorf was applied for. The Arbitration Panel examined in detail the sale negotiations between the vendor and the police administration of the German Reich of 1938. The purchase contract did not include any indication of discrimination. Also, the retrospective certification of the originally aggrieved person as being "Aryan" allowed the conclusion that there was no affiliation to a group of persons which was discriminated against by National Socialism or politically persecuted. As the Arbitration Panel was unable to establish whether the former owner was subjected to pressure or means of force, the application had to be rejected due to the lack of political persecution of the original owner of the property.

Decision no. 24/2004 contains a recommendation by the Arbitration Panel. In 1939, the German Air Force acted as "aryanizer" of the properties in question located in the Vienna suburb of Aspern which belonged to a Jewish doctor. The restitution proceedings conducted later fell under the application of the *Dritte Staatsvertragsdurchführungsgesetz* ("Third State Treaty Implementation Act"). This law contained stricter requirements for a "seizure" than those contained in the restitution acts. For this reason, the Supreme Administrative Court had rejected the restitution of the property parcels in 1963. The Arbitration Panel recommended the *in rem* restitution in this case as it confirmed the existence of a seizure of assets – in contrast to the restitution proceedings at the time – when considering the research results of the Austrian Historical Commission with respect to the Operation Gildemeester.

The Arbitration Panel also recommended the *in rem* restitution of a share of real property located in Inzersdorf in decision no. 25/2005. The property parcel in question had never previously been the subject of proceedings. As a residential building of the City of Vienna had in the meantime been erected on the property, the Arbitration Panel decided to award a comparable asset after consultation with the City of Vienna pursuant to Sec. 34 of the GSF Law.

Causal for the rejection which was pronounced in decision no. 26/2005 – as well as in decision nos. 8/2004 and 9/2005 – was the lack of a political persecution of the original property owners. The applicants had asserted that the "Yugoslavian origin" of the original owners, which was not further substantiated, had been causal for the seizure of the properties (forced sale to the German Reich Railways in Villach) dur-

Naturalrestitution. Mit dieser Zusammenschau soll auf die wachsende Anzahl von vor allem wissenschaftlichen Beiträgen und Fachdiskussionen zum Themenbereich der Naturalrestitution als Form der Entschädigungsleistung hingewiesen werden.

Bei den in Band 2 publizierten Entscheidungen handelt es sich um drei Empfehlungen und vier Ablehnungen, die Liegenschaften und Objekte in Wien und in den Bundesländern Niederösterreich und Kärnten zum Gegenstand haben.

In Entscheidung Nr. 8/2004 wurde die Rückstellung von Liegenschaften im Gebiet des heutigen Truppenübungsplatzes Allentsteig sowie im Ortsbereich Allentsteig beantragt. Die Schiedsinstanz hatte insbesondere zu prüfen, ob der Ankauf von Liegenschaften im Zuge der Errichtung des Truppenübungsplatzes durch die Deutsche Wehrmacht im Jahr 1939 eine nationalsozialistische Verfolgung der verkaufenden Parteien dargestellt hat. Da einer der Verkäufer zwar politischer Verfolgung ausgesetzt gewesen war, diese allerdings nicht im ursächlichen Zusammenhang mit dem Liegenschaftsverkauf an die Deutsche Wehrmacht stand und daher keine Vermögensentziehung im Sinne des EF-G vorlag, war der Antrag von der Schiedsinstanz abzulehnen.

In Entscheidung Nr. 9/2005 wurde die Rückstellung einer Liegenschaft in Wien-Hütteldorf beantragt. Die Schiedsinstanz unterzog bei der Entscheidungsfindung insbesondere die Verkaufsverhandlungen zwischen der Verkäuferin und der Polizeiverwaltung des Deutschen Reichs aus dem Jahr 1938 einer genauen Prüfung. Der Kaufvertrag selbst beinhaltete keine Indizien einer Diskriminierung. Auch eine nachträgliche Beurkundung, dass die ursprünglich Geschädigte „Arierin" war, ließ den Schluss zu, dass die Zugehörigkeit zu einer vom Nationalsozialismus diskriminierten oder politisch verfolgten Personengruppe nicht vorlag. Da zudem weder Druckausübung noch der Einsatz von Zwangsmitteln gegenüber der damaligen Eigentümerin festgestellt werden konnten, war der Antrag von der Schiedsinstanz mangels politischer Verfolgung der ursprünglichen Liegenschaftseigentümerin abzulehnen.

Entscheidung Nr. 24/2004 enthält eine Rückstellungsempfehlung der Schiedsinstanz. Als „Ariseur" der fraglichen Liegenschaften im Wiener Stadtteil Aspern, die einem jüdischen Arzt gehört hatten, fungierte 1939 die Deutsche Luftwaffe, daher kam beim späteren Rückstellungsverfahren das Dritte Staatsvertragsdurchführungsgesetz zur Anwendung. Dieses enthielt strengere Anforderungen für einen „Entzug" als die Rückstellungsgesetze, weshalb eine Restitution der Grundstücke vom Verwaltungsgerichtshof 1963 abgelehnt worden war. Die Schiedsinstanz empfahl in diesem Fall eine Naturalrestitution, da sie unter Berücksichtigung maßgeblicher Forschungsergebnisse der österreichischen Historikerkommission zur so genannten Gildemeester-Aktion das Vorliegen des Vermögensentzuges im Gegensatz zum seinerzeitigen Rückstellungsverfahren bejahte.

Auch in Entscheidung Nr. 25/2005 wurde von der Schiedsinstanz die Naturalrestitution eines Anteils einer in Inzersdorf gelegenen Liegenschaft empfohlen. Das fragliche Grundstück war zuvor niemals Gegenstand eines Verfahrens gewesen. Wegen einer zwischenzeitlich auf der Liegenschaft errichteten Wohnanlage der Stadt Wien entschied die Schiedsinstanz gemäß § 34 EF-G nach Konsultationen mit der Stadt Wien letztlich auf Zuspruch eines vergleichbaren Vermögenswertes.

ing the NS era. In the course of the examination of the application no evidence could be found that the origin of the former owner had played a role during the transaction with the German Reich Railways.

In decision no. 27/2005 the Arbitration Panel pronounced another recommendation. It was based on the "extreme injustice" of a prior measure. A settlement concluded between the Republic of Austria and the collection agencies in 1966 was to be examined in these proceedings. The Arbitration Panel classified this settlement as extremely unjust due to the discrepancy in value between the settlement sum and the historical estimated value of the property, as well as due to the markedly divergent interests of the collection agencies (measured against the interests of a hypothetical restitution claimant).

In decision no. 28/2005 the history of a building at Hohe Warte was examined. The property had already been restituted on 1 June 1950 pursuant to the *Erste Rückstellungsgesetz* ("First Restitution Act"). The Arbitration Panel concluded in this decision that the restitution of a property in the condition it had been in at the time of restitution – possibly even after a decrease in value – did not constitute an extreme injustice.

It is expected that this series will be continued with volume 3 of the decisions of the Arbitration Panel for *In Rem* Restitution at the beginning of 2010.

[compiled by Susanne Helene Betz]

Für die Ablehnung, die mit Entscheidung Nr. 26/2005 getroffen wurde, war – wie auch in den Entscheidungen Nr. 8/2004 und 9/2005 – das Fehlen einer politischen Verfolgung der ursprünglichen LiegenschaftseigentümerInnen ursächlich. Die AntragstellerInnen hatten angeführt, dass die nicht näher präzisierte „jugoslawische Abstammung" des ehemaligen Eigentümers kausal für den Entzug der Liegenschaften (Zwangsverkauf an die Deutsche Reichsbahn in Villach) in der NS-Zeit gewesen sei. Es fand sich jedoch im Rahmen der Prüfung des Antrags kein Hinweis darauf, dass die Abstammung des ehemaligen Eigentümers bei der Transaktion mit der Deutschen Reichsbahn eine Rolle gespielt hätte. Daraus resultierte eine ablehnende Entscheidung der Schiedsinstanz.

In Entscheidung Nr. 27/2005 sprach die Schiedsinstanz wieder eine Empfehlung aus. Diese gründete in der „extremen Ungerechtigkeit" der früheren Regelung. Zu prüfen war in diesem Verfahren ein zwischen der Republik Österreich und den Sammelstellen geschlossener Vergleich aus dem Jahr 1966, den die Schiedsinstanz sowohl aufgrund der Wertdifferenz zwischen Vergleichswert und historischem Schätzwert der Liegenschaft als auch wegen der markant abweichenden Interessenlage der Sammelstellen (gemessen an den Interessen eines hypothetischen Rückstellungswerbers) als extrem ungerecht qualifizierte.

In Entscheidung Nr. 28/2005 wurde die Geschichte eines Hauses auf der Hohen Warte geprüft. Die Liegenschaft war bereits am 1. Juni 1950 aufgrund des Ersten Rückstellungsgesetzes restituiert worden. Die Schiedsinstanz kam in dieser Entscheidung zu dem Ergebnis, dass es sich bei der Rückstellung einer Liegenschaft in jenem Zustand, in dem sie sich zum Zeitpunkt der Rückstellung befunden hat – gegebenenfalls auch nach einer Wertminderung –, um keine „extreme Ungerechtigkeit" handelt.

Band 3 der Entscheidungen der Schiedsinstanz für Naturalrestitution wird diese Reihe voraussichtlich zu Jahresbeginn 2010 fortsetzen.

[Zusammenstellung: Susanne Helene Betz]

Press Release Decision No. 8/2004

Lower Austria, Allentsteig

On 6 December 2004, the Arbitration Panel for *In Rem* Restitution rejected an application for restitution of properties located within the boundaries of the military training area Allentsteig and in the locality Allentsteig. The properties were purchased in 1939 by the German Armed Forces in the course of the construction of the military training area. One of the vendors was subjected to political persecution. According to the Arbitration Panel such persecution had no causal connection to the sale of the properties to the Armed Forces. Hence, a seizure of property as defined by the GSF law did not exist.

In her application for restitution, the applicant Hui F. asserted that all three properties were seized by the German Reich from the owners – the F. spouses and their son Anton F. – on grounds of political persecution. The German Armed Forces had instructed the *Deutsche Ansiedlungsgesellschaft* ("German Settlement Society") to purchase the concerned immovable properties in 1939 in order to construct the military training area "Döllersheim". The properties were located in the municipality Allentsteig, Lower Austria. In April 1939, the two properties belonging to the F. parents were acquired for 143,000 Reichsmark on behalf of the German Armed Forces. The properties belonging to their son had previously been acquired in March 1939 for 3,265 Reichsmark. The F. family remained in Allentsteig after the sale. Anton F. served in the German Armed Forces from 1940 and returned to Allentsteig in 1946 after being a prisoner of war. In 1949, both the F. parents as well as their son claimed the restitution of the property parcels which they had sold in 1939. In 1955, both proceedings were transferred by the Restitution Commissions which were originally in charge of the matter to the Financial Directorate Vienna. The applications for restitution were examined in accordance with the *Dritte Staatsvertragsdurchführungsgesetz* ("Third State Treaty Implementation Act") with a view as to whether the sale to the Armed Forces took place on the basis of an "unlawful application of the law" or "solely on the basis of political persecution" of the concerned persons. In both proceedings, the Financial Directorate ruled against the existence of the requirements of a seizure and dismissed the applications. The F. spouses appealed the decisions and referred to the political persecution of their son. He was treated with hostility by the NSDAP, in particular by the local group leader and mayor Fritz O. The acts of persecution had also discredited the parents who found themselves forced to sell their entire immovable property to the German Settlement Society. The application for restitution of the F. spouses was concluded by settlement with the Republic of Austria in 1961. The settlement provided for the restitution of a part of the former property which was not used for military purposes. During the 1960s and 1970s, Anton F. initiated several – ultimately unsuccessful – court proceedings which were directed at declaring the settlement of 1961 invalid and which requested the continuation of the restitution proceedings of his parents.

In its juridical appraisal, the Arbitration Panel had to examine whether political grounds for persecution were relevant for the sale of the properties to the German Armed Forces in 1939. The Arbitration Panel concluded that the construction of the military training area as such did not constitute an act of persecution and the transaction of the property purchase with the F. spouses did not include any indication for a political persecution. With respect to Anton F., the Arbitration Panel concluded that a persecution by the NS regime existed. Amongst others, this assessment could be based on the fact that Anton F. was considered a "traitor' by the local NSDAP group and that the NS district authorities also reproached him for being "politically unreliable". However, according to the Arbitration Panel, this particular acquisition of

Pressemitteilung Entscheidung Nr. 8/2004

Niederösterreich, Allentsteig

Die Schiedsinstanz für Naturalrestitution lehnte am 6. Dezember 2004 einen Antrag auf Rückstellung von Liegenschaften innerhalb des Truppenübungsplatzes Allentsteig sowie im Ortsbereich Allentsteig ab. Die Liegenschaften wurden 1939 im Zuge der Errichtung des Truppenübungsplatzes durch die Deutsche Wehrmacht angekauft. Einer der Verkäufer war politischer Verfolgung ausgesetzt. Letztere stand nach Ansicht der Schiedsinstanz aber in keinem ursächlichen Zusammenhang mit dem Liegenschaftsverkauf an die Wehrmacht. Somit lag auch keine Vermögensentziehung im Sinne des Entschädigungsfondsgesetzes vor.

In ihrem Rückstellungsbegehren erklärte die Antragstellerin Hui F., dass alle drei Liegenschaften aufgrund der politischen Verfolgung der Eigentümer – das Ehepaar F. und ihr Sohn Anton F. – durch das Deutsche Reich entzogen wurden. Der betreffende Grundbesitz wurde 1939 für die Anlage des Truppenübungsplatzes „Döllersheim" durch die von der Deutschen Wehrmacht beauftragte Deutsche Ansiedlungsgesellschaft (DAG) angekauft. Die Liegenschaften befanden sich in der niederösterreichischen Gemeinde Allentsteig. Die zwei Liegenschaften der Eltern F. wurden im Auftrag der Deutschen Wehrmacht im April 1939 für 143.000,- Reichsmark, die Grundstücke ihres Sohnes bereits im März 1939 um 3.265,- Reichsmark erworben. Die Familie F. blieb nach dem Verkauf in Allentsteig; Anton F. diente ab 1940 in der Deutschen Wehrmacht und kehrte 1946 aus der Kriegsgefangenschaft nach Allentsteig zurück. 1949 forderten sowohl die Eltern F. als auch ihr Sohn die Rückstellung ihrer 1939 verkauften Grundstücke. Beide Verfahren wurden 1955 von den zunächst zuständigen Rückstellungskommissionen an die Finanzlandesdirektion (FLD) Wien abgetreten. Die Rückstellungsanträge wurden nunmehr nach dem Dritten Staatsvertragsdurchführungsgesetz dahingehend geprüft, ob der Verkauf an die Wehrmacht aufgrund „missbräuchlicher Gesetzesanwendung" oder „lediglich auf Grund politischer Verfolgung" der Betroffenen erfolgte. In beiden Verfahren verneinte die FLD das Vorliegen der Entziehungsvoraussetzungen und wies die Anträge zurück. Das Ehepaar F. legte Berufung ein und wies auf die politische Verfolgung seines Sohnes hin. Dieser sei durch die NSDAP, namentlich den Ortsgruppenleiter und Bürgermeister Fritz O., angefeindet worden. Die Verfolgungshandlungen hätten auch die Eltern in Misskredit gebracht, so dass sie sich gezwungen sahen, ihren ganzen Grundbesitz an die DAG zu veräußern. Der Rückstellungsantrag des Ehepaars F. wurde 1961 durch einen Vergleich mit der Republik Österreich beendet, der die Rückgabe eines militärisch nicht genutzten Teils des ehemaligen Grundbesitzes vorsah. In den 1960er und 1970er Jahren strengte Anton F. – erfolglos – mehrere Gerichtsverfahren an, die unter anderem auf eine Annullierung des Vergleichs von 1961 und eine Fortsetzung des elterlichen Rückstellungsverfahrens zielten.

In ihrer rechtlichen Beurteilung hatte die Schiedsinstanz zu prüfen, ob politische Verfolgungsgründe für den Verkauf der Liegenschaften an die Deutsche Wehrmacht im Jahr 1939 maßgeblich waren. Die Schiedsinstanz gelangte zur Ansicht, dass die Anlage des Truppenübungsplatzes per se keine Verfolgung darstellt und dass auch die Abwicklung des Liegenschaftsankaufs gegenüber dem Ehepaar F. keine Anhaltspunkte für eine politische Verfolgung enthält. In Bezug auf Anton F. hielt die Schiedsinstanz eine Verfolgung durch das NS-Regime für erwiesen. Diese Einschätzung konnte sich u.a. darauf stützen, dass A. in den Augen der NSDAP-Ortsgruppe als „Verräter" galt und ihm auch von Seiten der NS-Bezirksbehörden seine „politische Unzuverlässigkeit" vorgehalten wurde. Allerdings stand nach Ansicht der

property by the Armed Forces was not causally connected to the relevant discriminations. The immovable property of Anton F. would have anyhow been claimed by the Armed Forces. In addition, the implementation of the sale was carried out in a manner which did not indicate any discriminatory treatment of Anton F. For this reason, the Arbitration Panel also concluded that a seizure of property had not occurred.

For use by media; not legally binding upon the Arbitration Panel for In Rem Restitution.

Schiedsinstanz der konkrete Grundstückserwerb durch die Wehrmacht in keinem ursächlichen Zusammenhang mit den betreffenden Diskriminierungen. Der Grundbesitz von Anton F. wäre ohnehin von der Wehrmacht angefordert worden. Auch die Durchführung des Verkaufs erfolgte in einer Weise, die keine diskriminierende Behandlung des Anton F. erkennen ließ. Aus diesem Grund lag für die Schiedsinstanz auch keine Vermögensentziehung vor.

Zur Verwendung durch die Medien bestimmter Text, der die Schiedsinstanz nicht bindet.

Arbitration Panel for *In Rem* Restitution

Decision number 8/2004

The Arbitration Panel for *In Rem* Restitution (Chairman Dr. Josef Aicher, university professor, and Dr.Dr.h.c. Erich Kussbach LL.M., retired ambassador and honorary professor, as well as MMag. Dr. August Reinisch LL.M, university professor, as Members) decided on 6 December 2004 in the legal matter of Hui F. regarding *in rem* restitution of the properties register number ("EZ") X1, cadastral district ("KG") Allentsteig, and EZ X2 and X3, KG Allentsteig:

The application for *in rem* restitution of the properties is rejected.

Reasons:

1. Submission by the Applicant

In the application of 12 June 2003, the applicant sought the restitution of the properties EZ X1, X2 and X3 belonging to land register KG Allentsteig. The applicant substantiated her application as follows:

Hui F. was the adoptive daughter of Josef F., born on 1 January 1910. Josef F. together with his brother Anton F. had been the heir to the estate of his parents, Josef and Franziska F. Upon his brother's death, Josef F. inherited his estate.

The F. family had owned a farm in Allentsteig which it had had to sell on 27 March 1939/22 April 1939 to the German Reich (*Wehrmacht*, "German Armed Forces") as the military training area Döllersheim was to be erected there. (Since the conclusion of the sale, the purchase contract has been lost. However, enclosed with the application is a notice by the *Deutsche Ansiedlungsgesellschaft* ("German Settlement Society"). The purchase contract was originally included with the notice.)

At this point in time, the properties EZ X2 and X3, KG Allentsteig still belonged to Josef (Sr.) and Franziska F. Each of them owned 50 %. Due to the parents' severe illness, a transfer of the property to the son, Anton F., had already been planned. The applicant did not know whether this transfer had failed due to the forced sale or whether Josef F. (Jr.)'s assertion was true that Anton F.'s acquisition of the properties had been impossible due to the fact that he had been denied a certificate of political harmlessness.

The third property, EZ X1, KG Allentsteig, had already been owned by Anton F. when the forced sale was carried out.

Anton F. was critically opposed to the Nazi regime. However, he had neither belonged to any other party, nor had he been in any other way politically active or had participated in the resistance. He had presumably made critical comments in public several times which had led to the refusal to issue him a certificate of political harmlessness, which he would have needed to work as a baker.

Furthermore, his hunting license and his gun license had been revoked since he had been classified as politically unreliable. After some years with the German Armed Forces, he had again sought to be issued a gun license. This had again been denied for reasons of "political unreliability".

A medical certificate dated 11 October 1959 existed, according to which Anton F. had been treated for pains in the lower back between the middle of 1938 and spring of 1939. The pa-

Schiedsinstanz für Naturalrestitution

Entscheidungsnummer 8/2004

Die Schiedsinstanz für Naturalrestitution beschließt am 6. Dezember 2004 durch den Vorsitzenden o.Univ.-Prof. Dr. Josef Aicher und die Schiedsinstanzmitglieder Honorarprofessor Dr.Dr.h.c. Erich Kussbach LL.M., Botschafter i.R. und ao.Univ.-Prof. MMag. Dr. August Reinisch LL.M. in der Rechtssache Hui F. wegen Naturalrestitution der Liegenschaften Einlagezahl (EZ) X1, Katastralgemeinde (KG) Allentsteig und EZ X2 und EZ X3, KG Allentsteig:

Der Antrag auf Naturalrestitution der Liegenschaften wird abgelehnt.

Begründung:

1. Vorbringen der Antragstellerin

Mit dem Antrag vom 12. Juni 2003 begehrte die Antragstellerin die Rückstellung der Liegenschaften EZ X1, Grundbuch (GB) KG Allentsteig und EZ X2 und EZ X3, Grundbuch KG Allentsteig. Die Antragstellerin begründete ihren Antrag wie folgt:

Hui F. sei die Adoptivtochter von Josef F., geb. 1. Jänner 1910. Josef F. sei wiederum gemeinsam mit seinem Bruder Anton F. Erbe seiner Eltern Josef und Franziska F. gewesen. Nach dem Tode des Bruders habe Josef F. diesen beerbt.

Die Familie F. habe eine Landwirtschaft in Allentsteig besessen, die sie am 27. März 1939 bzw. 22. April 1939 an das Deutsche Reich (Wehrmacht) habe verkaufen müssen, da dort der Truppenübungsplatz Döllersheim errichtet wurde. (Der Kaufvertrag sei inzwischen verloren gegangen, dem Antrag ist jedoch eine Mitteilung der Deutschen Aussiedlungsgesellschaft [DAG] beigelegt, welcher ursprünglich der Kaufvertrag beigelegt war.)

Die Liegenschaften EZ X2 und EZ X3, KG Allentsteig, hätten zu diesem Zeitpunkt noch Josef sen. und Franziska F. je zur Hälfte gehört, eine Übergabe an den Sohn Anton F. sei wegen schwerer Erkrankung der Eltern bereits geplant gewesen. Ob diese am Zwangsverkauf scheiterte oder ob die Behauptung von Josef F. jun., Anton F. sei es wegen der Verweigerung eines politischen Unbedenklichkeitszeugnisses unmöglich gewesen, Liegenschaftseigentum zu erwerben, zutrifft, sei der Antragstellerin nicht bekannt.

Die dritte Liegenschaft EZ X1, KG Allentsteig habe sich zum Zeitpunkt des Zwangsverkaufes bereits im Eigentum von Anton F. befunden.

Anton F. sei dem Nazi-Regime kritisch gegenübergestanden. Er habe jedoch weder einer anderen Partei angehört noch sei er sonst irgendwie politisch tätig oder am Widerstand beteiligt gewesen. Wahrscheinlich habe er sich des Öfteren in der Öffentlichkeit kritisch geäußert, so dass ihm die Ausstellung einer politischen Unbedenklichkeitsbescheinigung, die er für die Ausübung des Bäckerberufes gebraucht hätte, verweigert worden sei.

Weiters seien ihm sein Jagdschein und sein Waffenschein entzogen worden, da er als politisch unzuverlässig eingestuft worden sei. Nach einigen Jahren bei der Wehrmacht habe er sich wieder um die Ausstellung eines Waffenscheines bemüht, dies sei wieder wegen „politischer Unzuverlässigkeit" verweigert worden.

Es gebe eine ärztliche Bestätigung vom 11. Oktober 1959, wonach eine Behandlung von Anton F. von Mitte 1938 bis Frühjahr 1939 wegen Schmerzen in der Lendenkreuzgegend stattgefunden habe, die der Patient auf Misshandlungen (Fußtritte), „die er während einer Unter-

tient had explained that those pains had been caused by abuse (i.e. being kicked), "which he had suffered during an investigation by the *Gestapo* ["Secret State Police"] in St. Pölten in July 1938." On 1 July 1965, an official certificate as defined by the *Opferfürsorgegesetz* ("Victims Welfare Act") had been issued to Anton F. On 19 July 1978, a 50 % reduction in Anton F.'s ability to carry out gainful employment had been determined with the explanation: "of which at the most 20 % are connected to the abuse which was imposed on you in the course of the political persecution."

After the war, the family had initiated restitution proceedings. On 4 July 1960, the Financial Directorate for Vienna had rejected the application for restitution. The appeal proceedings had been concluded with a settlement. In this settlement, the Republic of Austria had committed to the restitution of certain property parcels of EZ X2, which had not been situated within the boundaries of the military training area. Apparently, in 1961, there had been persons renting and using these property parcels. If this had also been the case prior to 1945, then this would be another indication that a seizure on the grounds of persecution had taken place. In return, the F. family committed to paying 55,000 Schilling. All claims for restitution were supposed to be considered as settled and paid with this settlement. The final sentence of the settlement had read as follows:

> "Regardless of this, it remains at the liberty of the claimants for restitution or their legal successors to claim, on the basis of a possible future legal regulation, properties not restituted with this settlement and previously owned by them, and concerning which restitution proceedings were pending."

2. Submission by the Federal Government

On 15 June 2004, the Republic of Austria represented by the State Financial Procurator's Office submitted a statement. At the beginning of this statement, a detailed summary of the facts was presented.

The former EZ X1, X2 and X3 of KG Allentsteig were the subject of the application. These properties had been sold to the German Reich (German Armed Forces – Treasury – Army) in 1939. The proceeds of the sale had been at the free disposal of the vendors.

Subsequently, the statement dealt with the involvement of the F. family in National Socialism. Before 1938, the F. family had sympathized with National Socialism. In 1934, Anton F. had been arrested in connection with so-called paper firecracker attacks. The fact was that during the course of his arrest he had named the initiators of the attacks as well as the location of a National Socialist arms cache. Due to this testimony, Anton F. was treated as a traitor by the National Socialists after the *Anschluss*. The other members of the F. family had also been subjected to reprisals.

During the course of the construction of the military training area Döllersheim the German Settlement Society together with Anton F. and his parents signed the previously mentioned purchase contracts.

In 1949, Anton F. had filed an application for restitution with the Restitution Commission. By decision of 22 May 1958, the application for restitution had been rejected.

On 1 June 1949, the spouses Josef and Franziska F. had filed an application for restitution regarding EZ X2 and X3, KG Allentsteig. These proceedings had resulted in a settlement between the applicants and the Republic of Austria, according to which parts of the properties which had been transferred to the German Reich had been restituted in exchange for the refund of the purchase price of 55,000 Schilling. According to the documents, the background

suchung durch die Gestapo in St. Pölten im Juli 1938 erlitten hatte", zurückgeführt habe. Anton F. sei am 1. Juli 1965 eine Amtsbescheinigung iSd Opferfürsorgegesetzes (OFG) ausgestellt worden. Am 19. Juli 1978 sei eine 50 %ige Minderung der Erwerbstätigkeit festgestellt worden mit der Ausführung: „Davon entfallen maximal 20 % auf die durch Misshandlungen im Verlauf der politischen Verfolgung Ihnen zugefügten Schädigungen."

Die Familie habe nach dem Krieg ein Rückstellungsverfahren angestrengt. Die Finanzlandesdirektion (FLD) Wien habe am 4. Juli 1960 den Antrag auf Rückstellung abgewiesen. Das Berufungsverfahren sei mittels Vergleich beendet worden. Die Republik habe sich darin zur Rückstellung einzelner Parzellen der EZ X2, die nicht vom Truppenübungsplatz umfasst waren, verpflichtet. Anscheinend habe es 1961 Mieter und Benützer dieser Grundstücke gegeben. Wenn dies auch schon vor 1945 so gewesen sei, so wäre dies ein weiteres Indiz für eine verfolgungsbedingte Entziehung. Die Familie F. habe sich im Gegenzug verpflichtet, 55.000,– Schilling zu bezahlen. Mit diesem Vergleich sollten alle Ansprüche auf Rückstellung als verglichen und bereinigt gelten. Der Schlusssatz des Vergleiches habe gelautet:

„Dessen ungeachtet bleibt es den Rückstellungswerbern bzw. deren Rechtsnachfolgern unbenommen, auf Grund einer allfälligen künftigen gesetzlichen Regelung Ansprüche für die durch diesen Vergleich nicht rückgestellten und ihnen ehedem gehörigen Grundstücke, über die ein Rückstellungsverfahren anhängig war, aus dem Titel des Schadenersatzes zu stellen."

2. Vorbringen der Bundesregierung

Am 15. Juni 2004 brachte die Republik Österreich, vertreten durch die Finanzprokuratur, eine Stellungnahme ein. Eingangs wurde in dieser Stellungnahme eine ausführliche Sachverhaltszusammenfassung vorgebracht.

Gegenstand des Antrages seien die ehemaligen EZ X1, X2 und X3 der KG Allentsteig. Diese seien 1939 an das Deutsche Reich (Wehrmacht-Fiskus-Heer) verkauft worden. Der Kaufpreis sei den VerkäuferInnen zur freien Verfügung gestanden.

In weiterer Folge ging die Stellungnahme auf das Verhältnis der Familie F. zum Nationalsozialismus ein. Vor 1938 habe die Familie F. mit dem Nationalsozialismus sympathisiert. 1934 sei Anton F. im Zusammenhang mit so genannten Papierbölleranschlägen verhaftet worden. Tatsache sei, dass er im Zuge seiner Haft den Urheber der Anschläge genannt und die Lage eines NS-Waffenlagers bekannt gegeben habe. Aufgrund dieser Aussage sei Anton F. nach dem „Anschluss" von den Nationalsozialisten als Verräter behandelt worden. Die übrigen Mitglieder der Familie F. seien ebenfalls Repressalien ausgesetzt gewesen.

Im Zuge der Errichtung des Truppenübungsplatzes Döllersheim habe die DAG mit Anton F. und dessen Eltern die zuvor dargestellten Kaufverträge abgeschlossen.

Anton F. habe 1949 bei der Rückstellungskommission einen Rückstellungsantrag eingebracht. Mit Bescheid vom 22. Mai 1958 sei der Rückstellungsantrag abgewiesen worden.

Bezüglich der EZ X2 und EZ X3 der KG Allentsteig hätten die Ehegatten Josef und Franziska F. am 1. Juni 1949 einen Rückstellungsantrag gestellt. Es sei in diesem Verfahren zu einem Vergleich zwischen den AntragstellerInnen und der Republik Österreich gekommen, nach welchem Teile der dem Deutschen Reich übereigneten Grundstücke gegen Rückerstattung des Kaufpreises von 55.000,– Schilling zurückgestellt worden seien. Als Hintergrund für diesen Vergleich gehe aus den Akten hervor, dass sich die vom Vergleich erfassten Grundstücke außerhalb des Truppenübungsplatzes befanden, so dass hier die Anwendbarkeit des § 1 Drittes Staatsvertragsdurchführungsgesetz (3. StVDG) in Frage zu stellen gewesen sei.

to this settlement was that the properties subject of the settlement were situated outside the military training area. In this case the applicability of para. 1 of the *Dritte Staatsvertrags-durchführungsgesetz* ("Third State Treaty Implementation Act") would have had to be challenged.

Being the legal successor to his parents, Anton F. had also filed an action with the Constitutional Court against the Republic of Austria, which had been dismissed by the Constitutional Court on 11 June 1965. By statement of 3 January 1966, Anton F. sought the continuation of the restitution proceedings. This application had been dismissed by decision of the Federal Ministry of Finance. A complaint against this directed to the Supreme Administrative Court had been rejected as being without merit.

On 10 March 1969, Anton F. had filed an action with the Regional Court for Civil Matters Vienna against the Republic of Austria and sought a declaratory judgment which ruled that item 5 of the aforementioned settlement was null and void. The action had been rejected by the Regional Court for Civil Matters. The decision had been confirmed by the decision of 19 November 1969 by the Higher Regional Court for Civil Matters Vienna as well as by the decision of 26 May 1970 by the Supreme Court.

Through a further action for damages, Anton F. had sought compensation from the Republic of Austria for a total of 180,000 Schilling. Finally, by decision of 30 June 1977 the Supreme Court had rejected this action.

Regarding the conditions defined in the *Entschädigungsfondsgesetz* ("General Settlement Fund Law", GSF Law) the State Financial Procurator's Office stated that the presented documents showed that all properties subject of the application had been dealt with in an official decision or in a prior settlement (EZ X3 and EZ X2).

A recommendation by the Arbitration Panel to the Federal Government suggesting the restitution of the properties in question to the previous owners would require in the present case that this settlement or the official decisions would have represented an extreme injustice. In principle, the applicant must demonstrate the existence of an extreme injustice. In the present case, no submissions regarding this matter have been made.

With regard to the political persecution, the Financial Procurator's Office explained the following: Since the predecessors of the applicant had not belonged to a group of persons which was discriminated against during National Socialism, it has to be examined whether an actual discriminatory act of persecution was present. Only the seizure could be considered to be such an act.

However, the seizure in itself did not represent an act of persecution. In order to be able to meet the definition of persecution, the seizure must have been an act by the National Socialist regime which was intended to persecute the aggrieved person. However, the construction of the military training area Döllersheim had not been directed against the families affected by the associated procurement of land. It had not been employed as a measure of repression.

It cannot be clearly established from the present documents whether the predecessors of the applicant had actually been subjected to political persecution and, if this were to be the case, resulting in the applicant's eligibility to file applications in accordance with the GSF Law. This question can, however, be set aside since the way the purchase was conducted did not differ in comparison to other instances where procurement of land for purposes of the German Armed Forces took place. A standardized contract had been used. In the present case, both purchase contracts had been exempt from fees, charges and taxes. In one contract – divergent from the text of the standardized contract – "down payments" for the benefit of the

Anton F. habe auch als Rechtsnachfolger nach seinen Eltern eine Klage gegen die Republik Österreich beim Verfassungsgerichtshof (VfGH) eingebracht, welche von diesem mit Beschluss vom 11. Juni 1965 zurückgewiesen worden sei. Mit Schriftsatz vom 3. Jänner 1966 habe Anton F. die Fortsetzung des Rückstellungsverfahrens begehrt. Dieser Antrag sei mit Bescheid des Bundesministeriums für Finanzen (BMF) zurückgewiesen worden. Eine dagegen an den Verwaltungsgerichtshof (VwGH) gerichtete Beschwerde sei als unbegründet abgewiesen worden.

Am 10. März 1969 habe Anton F. gegen die Republik Österreich beim Landesgericht für Zivilrechtssachen (LGfZRS) Wien Klage erhoben und die Feststellung begehrt, dass Punkt 5 des vorzitierten Vergleiches wegen Nichtigkeit rechtsunwirksam sei. Die Klage sei vom LGfZRS Wien abgewiesen worden, das Urteil sei durch das Urteil des Oberlandesgerichts (OLG) Wien vom 19. November 1969 sowie das Urteil des Obersten Gerichtshofes (OGH) vom 26. Mai 1970 bestätigt worden.

Mit einer weiteren Klage habe Anton F. von der Republik Österreich die Zahlung von insgesamt 180.000,– Schilling aus dem Titel des Schadenersatzes begehrt. Diese Klage sei letztendlich vom OGH mit Urteil vom 30. Juni 1977 rechtskräftig abgewiesen worden.

Hinsichtlich der Voraussetzungen nach dem Entschädigungsfondsgesetz (EF-G) brachte die Finanzprokuratur vor, dass es sich aus den vorliegenden Unterlagen ergebe, dass sämtliche antragsgegenständlichen Grundstücke Gegenstand einer behördlichen Entscheidung oder Gegenstand eines früheren Vergleiches (EZ X3 und EZ X2) gewesen seien.

Eine Empfehlung der Schiedsinstanz, die Bundesregierung möge die gegenständlichen Liegenschaften an die früheren Eigentümer zurückstellen, würde im gegenständlichen Fall voraussetzen, dass dieser Vergleich bzw. die behördlichen Entscheidungen eine extreme Ungerechtigkeit dargestellt hätten. An sich sei die extreme Ungerechtigkeit vom Antragsteller darzutun. Im vorliegenden Fall liege kein diesbezügliches Vorbringen vor.

Hinsichtlich der politischen Verfolgung führte die Finanzprokuratur wie folgt aus: Da die Rechtsvorgänger der Antragstellerin nicht einer vom Nationalsozialismus diskriminierten Personengruppe angehört hätten, sei hier zu untersuchen, ob eine tatsächliche diskriminierende Verfolgungshandlung vorliege. Und hier könne bloß die Entziehung in Betracht kommen.

Der Entzug für sich alleine stelle jedoch noch keine Verfolgungshandlung dar. Diesem müsse, um dem Begriff der Verfolgung entsprechen zu können, zumindest ein davor liegender Wille des nationalsozialistischen Regimes vorangehen, welcher die Verfolgung der Geschädigten bezweckt haben könnte. Die Anlage des Truppenübungsplatzes Döllersheim sei jedoch nicht gegen die von der damit einhergehenden Landbeschaffung betroffenen Familien gerichtet gewesen. Sie sei nicht als Mittel der Repression eingesetzt worden.

Wenngleich sich aus den vorliegenden Unterlagen nicht mit Klarheit beantworten lasse, ob die Rechtsvorgänger der nunmehrigen Antragstellerin tatsächlich einer politischen Verfolgung ausgesetzt gewesen seien und letztere daher antragsberechtigt nach dem EF-G sei, könne dies hier auf sich beruhen, zumal auch die Kaufvertragsmodalitäten als solche nicht auf eine unterschiedliche Behandlung gegenüber anderen Maßnahmen zur Landbeschaffung zum Zwecke der Wehrmacht hinweisen würden, sei doch eine Vertragsschablone zur Anwendung gekommen. Im vorliegenden Fall seien beide Kaufverträge gebühren-, stempel- und steuerfrei gewesen. In einem Vertrag seien – abweichend vom Standardtext – zugunsten der VerkäuferInnen „Abschlagszahlungen" vor der grundbücherlichen Durchführung für die Beschaffung eines Ersatzgrundstückes oder zur Sicherung des Lebensunterhaltes der VerkäuferInnen ermöglicht worden. Die Ausstellung des politischen Unbedenklichkeitszeugnisses für

vendors had been made possible prior to the incorporation of the title in the land register, for the procurement of a substitute property or for meeting the vendors' living expenses. The issue of the certificate of political harmlessness for Anton F. and a subsequent property transfer to him would not have changed anything since he also would have had to sell the properties necessary for the military training area or they would have been expropriated in exchange for an adequate compensation.

Subsequently, the only issue that had been criticized by the vendors regarding the remuneration was that an additional "business transfer fee" was only paid for "two years even though four years would have been the usual". The argument regarding the improper application of laws in the present case may only be put forward in connection to the properties situated outside the military training area. However, these exact properties had been restituted pursuant to the settlement in exchange for the refund of the purchase price.

With respect to the possible property seizure, the Financial Procurator's Office stated that the signing of a purchase contract for the purpose of averting the threat of an expropriation, which would have been possible under the legal situation at that time (hence was not based on misuse) and further would have been connected to adequate compensation, did not represent a seizure of property. Hence, regarding the properties situated in the area of the military training area, no property seizure as defined by the GSF Law occured, even if the predecessors of the applicant had otherwise been subjected to acts of persecution due to their political views.

With regard to the possible "extreme injustice", the Financial Procurator's Office elaborated that it remained to be examined whether the settlement which was concluded by the predecessors with the Republic of Austria could represent an extreme injustice as defined by the GSF Law. This settlement resulted in the restitution to the claimants of one part of the property. The part in question had been sold to the German Settlement Society by the previous owners and had not been situated within the boundaries of the military training area Döllersheim. However, an extremely unjust disadvantage had not been substantiated by the applicant or her predecessors. Further, there was no indication that the settlement had not met the essential principles of the relevant applicable law or that there had been a discrepancy in value between the true value of the properties and the settlement sum.

Hence, in regard to all properties, the prerequisites for a recommendation for restitution of the properties to the applicant were not fulfilled.

As a result, on behalf of the Federal Government the Financial Procurator's Office filed an application for the rejection of the present applications for *in rem* restitution.

3. Evidence

Evidence was taken by reviewing the following documents enclosed with the application for *in rem* restitution:

Various letters by Josef F., letter by Anton F., birth certificate of Anton F., death certificate of Josef F., decision by the District Court Gmunden, file number 6 A 771/00a, certificate of inheritance, District Court Gmunden, Anton F., decision by the District Court Gmunden of 18 April 1988, birth certificate Josef F., historical land register extract EZ X1, KG Allentsteig, historical land register extract EZ X3 KG Allentsteig, historical land register extract EZ X2 KG Allentsteig, decision by the Financial Directorate of 22 May 1958, settlement of 9 November 1961, decision by the district administrator of the district Zwettl of 25 May 1939, letter by the district administrator of the district Zwettl of 13 December 1939, decision by the

Herrn Anton F. und eine nachfolgende Übergabe des Besitzes an ihn hätte nichts geändert, da auch er die für den Truppenübungsplatz erforderlichen Grundstücke hätte veräußern müssen bzw. diese gegen entsprechende Entschädigung enteignet worden wären.

Es sei in weiterer Folge von den VerkäuferInnen hinsichtlich des Entgelts lediglich bemängelt worden, dass „eine Geschäftsablöse nur für 2 Jahre" zusätzlich geleistet worden sei, „obwohl für 4 Jahre üblich war". Das Argument der missbräuchlichen Rechtsanwendung könne im vorliegenden Fall allein hinsichtlich der außerhalb des Truppenübungsplatzes gelegenen Grundstücke ins Treffen geführt werden; genau diese Grundstücke seien aber mit Vergleich gegen Rückerstattung des diesbezüglichen Kaufpreises rückübereignet worden.

Bezüglich der etwaigen Vermögensentziehung brachte die Finanzprokuratur vor, dass der Abschluss eines Kaufvertrages zur Abwendung einer drohenden Enteignung, die nach der damaligen Rechtslage möglich gewesen wäre (d.h. nicht missbräuchlich erfolgte) und darüber hinaus mit einer angemessenen Entschädigung verbunden gewesen wäre, keine Vermögensentziehung darstelle. Sohin liege hinsichtlich der auf dem Areal des Truppenübungsplatzes gelegenen Grundstücke keine Vermögensentziehung im Sinne des EF-G vor, selbst wenn die RechtsvorgängerInnen der Antragstellerin im Übrigen wegen ihrer politischen Anschauungen Verfolgungshandlungen ausgesetzt gewesen sein sollten.

Hinsichtlich der etwaigen „extremen Ungerechtigkeit" führte die Finanzprokuratur aus, dass zu prüfen bleibe, ob der Vergleich, den die RechtsvorgängerInnen mit der Republik Österreich abgeschlossen haben, eine extreme Ungerechtigkeit im Sinne des EF-G darstellen könne. Aufgrund dieses Vergleiches sei jener Teil des von den früheren EigentümerInnen an die DAG verkauften Grundstückbestandes, welcher nicht innerhalb der Grenzen des Truppenübungsplatzes Döllersheim gelegen habe, an die AntragstellerInnen zurückgegeben worden. Eine extrem ungerechte Benachteiligung hätten die Antragstellerin und ihre RechtsvorgängerInnen jedoch nicht dargelegt. Überdies weise nichts daraufhin, dass der Vergleich nicht mit den wesentlichen Grundsätzen der sachlich anwendbaren Gesetzesgrundlagen übereingestimmt habe oder dass eine Wertdiskrepanz zwischen dem wahren Wert der Liegenschaften und der Vergleichssumme zulasten der AntragstellerInnen vorliege.

Hinsichtlich sämtlicher Liegenschaften lägen sohin die Voraussetzungen für eine Empfehlung, die Liegenschaften der Antragstellerin zu übergeben, nicht vor.

Die Finanzprokuratur stellte sohin für die Bundesregierung den Antrag, die Schiedsinstanz für Naturalrestitution möge die vorliegenden Anträge auf Naturalrestitution ablehnen.

3. Beweise

Beweise wurden erhoben durch Einsichtnahme in folgende, dem Antrag auf Naturalrestitution beigelegte Dokumente:

Diverse Schreiben des Josef F., Schreiben des Anton F., Geburtsurkunde Anton F., Sterbeurkunde Josef F., Beschluss des Bezirksgerichts (BG) Gmunden, GZ 6 A 771/00a, Einantwortungsurkunde, BG Gmunden, Anton F., Beschluss des BG Gmunden vom 18. April 1988, Geburtsurkunde Josef F., historischer Grundbuchsauszug EZ X1, KG Allentsteig, historischer Grundbuchsauszug EZ X3, KG Allentsteig, historischer Grundbuchsauszug EZ X2, KG Allentsteig, Bescheid der FLD vom 22. Mai 1958, Vergleich vom 9. November 1961, Bescheid des Landrates des Landkreises Zwettl vom 25. Mai 1939, Schreiben des Landrates des Landkreises Zwettl vom 13. Dezember 1939, Bescheid des Landeshauptmanns (LH) in Niederdonau vom 15. Jänner 1940, Bescheid des Landrates des Landkreises Zwettl vom 18. April 1944, Schreiben der Gauleitung Niederdonau vom 10. Oktober 1940, Abschrift der Beilage zu Zl.

head of the provincial government Niederdonau of 15 January 1940, decision by the district administrator of the district of Zwettl of 18 April 1944, letter by the *Gauleitung* ("NS regional administration") Niederdonau of 10 October 1940, copy of the supplement to file number 273.665-32/61 (Federal Ministry of Finance, dept. 34), letter by the German Settlement Society of 10 May 1939, notification on the result of the hearing of evidence, department of the Upper Austrian provincial government of 19 July 1978, letter by the consultant Dr. Franz H. of 11 October 1959, copy of a savings book of Josef and Franziska F., number 18804, copy of a savings book of Anton F., number 16100, copy of a savings book of Josef and Franziska F., number 18806, correspondence of Josef F. – Federal Ministry of Finance/Financial Procurator's Office, 31 May 1999 until 19 August 1999 (submitted later by the applicant on 5 August 2004), restitution settlement Financial Directorate – W. Scholarship Foundation 28 April 1959 (two pages in copied form, submitted later by the applicant on 11 August 2004), letter by the Federal Ministry of Finance of 13 June 1984 as well as the reply by Anton F. of 28 July 1984 (submitted later by the applicant, supplement to her letter of 30 August 2004), statement regarding the rejection of the claim of Anton and Josef F. of 18 July 1976; regarding compensation claim 39 b Cg 287/74 (submitted later by the applicant, supplement to her letter of 30 August 2004).

The following documents were obtained by the Arbitration Panel as supplementary documentation:

Austrian State Archives, Department Archives of the Republic, record group 06: Financial Directorate file[1] 1-3 VR-V 2444/57 (Josef (Sr.) and Franziska F.): assignment decision of 1 February 1957, notification of application of 10 July 1957, land register entry of 10 July 1957, land register decision of 24 July 1957, submission by Dr. S. of 19 September 1957, letter by Josef F. of 26 September 1957, decision by the Financial Directorate of 28 March 1958, appeal of 16 April 1958, presentation report to the Federal Ministry of Finance of 23 April 1955, addendum by Dr. S. of 2 May 1958, report to the Federal Ministry of Finance, decision of appeal by the Federal Ministry of Finance of 12 September 1958, submission by Dr. S. of 3 November 1958, letter by the Federal Buildings' Administration II Vienna of 23 January 1958, letter to the Federal Buildings' Administration II Vienna of 30 January 1959, letter by Anton F. of 15 February 1959, hearing announcement, letter by Dr. S. of 19 February 1959, minutes of hearing of 18 March 1959, letter by the district administrator of the district Zwettl of 13 December 1939, letter by the district administrator of the district Zwettl of 25 May 1939, decision by the district administrator of the district Zwettl of 18 April 1944, decision of 15 January 1940, letter by Josef F. of 19 March 1959, record of 14 April 1959, letter by the Financial Directorate of 14 April 1959, letter to the Federal Ministry of Finance of 11 May 1959, letter by the tax office Zwettl of 15 May 1959, letter by the tax office Zwettl of 2 June 1959, record of 1 June 1959, letter to the Financial Procurator's Office of 5 June 1959, statement by the Financial Procurator's Office of 9 June 1959, memo to the Financial Procurator's Office of 18 June 1959, statement by Dr. S. of 25 June 1959, letter to the local authorities of Allentsteig of 25 June 1959, letter by the Township of Allentsteig of 3 August 1959, letter by Josef F. of 26 October 1959, official decision of 10 February 1960, memo to the Financial Procurator's Office of 22 October 1960, first record of 24 February 1960, second record of 24 February 1960, third record of 24 February 1960, file memo of 25 February 1960, memoranda to the parties, report to the head of department of 8 March 1960, statement by the Financial Procurator's Office of 29 February 1960, letter to the local authorities of Schwarzenau of 14 March 1960, statement by Dr. S. of 2 March 1960, letter by the *Gaupersonalamt* ("NS regional personnel department") of 10 October 1940,

---

[1] Supplementation at the time of going to press: Financial Directorate registry number 24513.

Schiedsinstanz für Naturalrestitution – Entscheidung Nr. 8/2004

273.665-32/61 (BMF, Abt. 34), Schreiben der DAG vom 10. Mai 1939, Verständigung vom Ergebnis der Beweisaufnahme, Amt der OÖ. Landesregierung, vom 19. Juli 1978, Schreiben des Primar Dr. Franz H. vom 11. Oktober 1959, Kopie eines Sparkassenbuches Josef und Franziska F., Nr. 18804, Kopie eines Sparkassenbuches Anton F., Nr. 16100, Kopie eines Sparkassenbuches Josef und Franziska F., Nr. 18806, Korrespondenz Josef F. – BMF/Finanzprokuratur, 31. Mai 1999 bis 19. August 1999 (von Antragstellerin am 5. August 2004 nachgereicht), Rückstellungsvergleich FLD – W. Stipendienstiftung 28. April 1959 (zwei Seiten in Kopie, durch Antragstellerin am 11. August 2004 nachgereicht), Schreiben des BMF vom 13. Juni 1984 sowie Antwortschreiben Anton F. vom 28. Juli 1984 (nachgereicht durch Antragstellerin, Anlage zu ihrem Brief vom 30. August 2004), Stellungnahme zur Abweisung des Klagebegehrens durch Anton und Josef F. vom 18. Juli 1976; betr. Schadenersatzklage 39 b Cg 287/74 (nachgereicht durch Antragstellerin, Anlage zu ihrem Brief vom 30. August 2004).

Folgende Dokumente wurden als ergänzende Dokumentation durch die Schiedsinstanz eingeholt:

Österreichisches Staatsarchiv (ÖStA), Archiv der Republik (AdR), Abteilung 06: FLD-Akt[1] 1-3 VR-V 24442/57 (Josef sen. und Franziska F.): Abtretungsbeschluss vom 1. Februar 1957, Antragsmeldung vom 10. Juli 1957, Grundbuchseingabe vom 10. Juli 1957, Grundbuchsbeschluss vom 24. Juli 1957, Eingabe Dr. S. vom 19. September 1957, Schreiben des Josef F. vom 26. September 1957, Bescheid der FLD vom 28. März 1958, Berufung vom 16. April 1958, Vorlagebericht an das BMF vom 23. April 1955, Nachtrag des Dr. S. vom 2. Mai 1958, Bericht an das BMF, Berufungsbescheid des BMF vom 12. September 1958, Eingabe des Dr. S. vom 3. November 1958, Schreiben der Bundesgebäudeverwaltung II Wien vom 23. Jänner 1958, Schreiben an die Bundesgebäudeverwaltung II Wien vom 30. Jänner 1959, Schreiben des Anton F. vom 15. Februar 1959, Verhandlungsausschreibung, Schreiben des Dr. S. vom 19. Februar 1959, Verhandlungsschrift vom 18. März 1959, Schreiben des Landrates des Kreises Zwettl vom 13. Dezember 1939, Schreiben des Landrates des Kreises Zwettl vom 25. Mai 1939, Bescheid des Landrates des Kreises Zwettl vom 18. April 1944, Bescheid vom 15. Jänner 1940, Schreiben des Josef F. vom 19. März 1959, Niederschrift vom 14. April 1959, Schreiben der FLD vom 14. April 1959, Schreiben an das BMF vom 11. Mai 1959, Schreiben des Finanzamtes Zwettl vom 15. Mai 1959, Schreiben des Finanzamtes Zwettl vom 2. Juni 1959, Niederschrift vom 1. Juni 1959, Schreiben an die Finanzprokuratur vom 5. Juni 1959, Äußerung der Finanzprokuratur vom 9. Juni 1959, Note an die Finanzprokuratur vom 18. Juni 1959, Äußerung des Dr. S. vom 25. Juni 1959, Schreiben an das Gemeindeamt in Allentsteig vom 25. Juni 1959, Schreiben der Stadt Allentsteig vom 3. August 1959, Schreiben des Josef F. vom 26. Oktober 1959, Amtsverfügung vom 10. Februar 1960, Note an die Finanzprokuratur vom 22. Oktober 1960, 1. Niederschrift vom 24. Februar 1960, 2. Niederschrift vom 24. Februar 1960, 3. Niederschrift vom 24. Februar 1960, Aktenvermerk vom 25. Februar 1960, Noten an die Parteien, Bericht an den Dienststellenleiter vom 8. März 1960, Stellungnahme der Finanzprokuratur vom 29. Februar 1960, Schreiben an das Gemeindeamt Schwarzenau vom 14. März 1960, Äußerung des Dr. S. vom 2. März 1960, Schreiben des Gaupersonalamtes vom 10. Oktober 1940, 1. Niederschrift vom 30. März 1960, 2. Niederschrift vom 30. März 1960, Bestätigung des Dr. H. vom 11. Oktober 1959, Noten an die Finanzprokuratur, Antrag des Dr. S. vom 12. April 1960, Schreiben der Finanzprokuratur vom 8. April 1960, Rückziehung des Antrages vom 23. Mai 1960, Bescheid der FLD vom 4. Juli 1960 (S. 5 des Bescheids wird in zwei weiteren Kopien durch die Antragstellerin am

---

[1] Ergänzung zum Zeitpunkt der Drucklegung: FLD Registraturnummer 24513.

first record of 30 March 1960, second record of 30 March 1960, confirmation by Dr. H. of 11 October 1959, memoranda to the Financial Procurator's Office, application by Dr. S. of 12 April 1960, letter by the Financial Procurator's Office of 8 April 1960, withdrawal of the application of 23 May 1960, decision by the Financial Directorate of 4 July 1960 (the applicant submitted later two further copies of page 5 of the decision on 5 and 11 August 2004; one copy with notes made by Anton F.; one copy with the registry notes by the Federal Ministry of Finance), appeal of 28 July 1960, letter of 8 July 1960, appeal by Josef F. of 24 July 1960, memorandum to the Federal Ministry of Finance of 5 August 1960, settlement of 9 November 1961, land register entry of 11 December 1960, letter by Dr. V. of 20 August 1963, power of attorney of 19 August 1963, letter to the Financial Directorate Vorarlberg of 30 August 1963, letter by the Financial Directorate of 28 October 1963;

Financial Directorate file[2] 1-2 VR-V 21009/56 (Anton F.): Assignment decision of 13 September 1956, land register extract, notification by the Financial Directorate of 6 December 1956, land register entry of 30 November 1956; statement by Dr. S. of 23 August 1957, decision by the Financial Directorate, VR-V 21009/56, RK 212/49 (Anton F.): Letter by the Financial Directorate of 30 January 1975, claim for restitution of 29 June 1949, letter to the District Court Allentsteig of 11 June 1949, decision by the District Court Allentsteig of 28 July 1949, three decisions by the Restitution Commission established with the Regional Court for Civil Matters Vienna of 2 August 1949, letter by the representative *in absentia* of 18 August 1949, decision by the Restitution Commission established with the Regional Court for Civil Matters Vienna of 17 November 1949;

Financial Directorate file registry 24543: Letter by Anton F. of 6 November 1964, file overview of 12 November 1964, decision by the Federal Ministry of Finance of 8 June 1966, letter by Anton F. of 26 January 1967, letter by the Financial Directorate of 31 January 1967, letter by the Federal Ministry of Finance of 6 February 1967, Supreme Administrative Court decision file number 1113/66-2, letter by the Federal Ministry of Finance of 20 February 1962, letter to the Federal Ministry of Finance of 19 February 1962;

Financial Directorate file registry 24543/II (Josef (Sr.) and Franziska F.): Application of 29 June 1949, power of attorney of 2 November 1956, letter to the District Court Allentsteig, decision by the District Court Allentsteig of 28 July 1949, three decisions by the Restitution Commission of 2 August 1949, letter by the representative *in absentia* of 18 August 1949, decision of the Restitution Commission of 17 November 1949, declaration for joinder by the Financial Procurator's Office, submission by Dr. T. of 7 February 1951, submission by Dr. T. of 3 January 1951, application by Dr. S. of 31 July 1956, submission of a certified power of attorney of 9 November 1956, letter by the Restitution Commission of 23 November 1956, application by the Financial Procurator's Office of 12 January 1957.

Austrian State Archives, Department Archives of the Republic, record group 02: Registry Archives of the Republic 40/A 1950 /GZ.22.672 2a/ 50 (regarding RK 212/49 Anton F.): Petition to the Allied Council via the Federal Chancellary; Application to the Allied Council for the approval of the conduct of the proceedings regarding the restitution of assets to Anton F., dated 8 February 1950, with supplements copied from restitution proceedings 1949; Regional files regarding Fritz O.'s, Josef F. (Sr.)'s, Josef F. (Jr.)'s and Rudolf Sa.'s NSDAP membership registry Archives of the Republic, Federal Ministry for Interior Affairs GA number 280.934; 90/596; 90/598; 416/582.

District Court Zwettl, land register department: Facsimile of 16 February 2004, purchase contract Anton F./German Reich (EZ X1) of 27 March 1939, purchase contract Josef and

---

[2] Supplementation at the time of going to press: Financial Directorate registry number 21403.

5. bzw. 11. August 2004 nachgereicht; eine Kopie mit Anmerkung Anton F.; eine Kopie mit Registraturvermerken des BMF), Berufung vom 28. Juli 1960, Schreiben vom 8. Juli 1960, Berufung des Josef F. vom 24. Juli 1960, Note an das BMF vom 5. August 1960, Vergleich vom 9. November 1961, Grundbuchseingabe vom 11. Dezember 1960, Schreiben des Dr. V. vom 20. August 1963, Vollmacht vom 19. August 1963, Schreiben an die FLD Vorarlberg vom 30. August 1963, Schreiben der FLD vom 28. Oktober 1963;

FLD-Akt[2] 1-2 VR-V 21009/56 (Anton F.): Abtretungsbeschluss vom 13. September 1956, Grundbuchsauszug, Meldung der FLD vom 6. Dezember 1956, Grundbuchseingabe vom 30. November 1956; Äußerung des Dr. S. vom 23. August 1957, Bescheid der FLD, VR-V 21009/56, RK 212/49 (Anton F.): Schreiben der FLD vom 30. Jänner 1975, Rückstellungsantrag vom 29. Juni 1949, Schreiben an das BG Allentsteig vom 11. Juni 1949, Beschluss des BG Allentsteig vom 28. Juli 1949, drei Beschlüsse der Rückstellungskommission beim LGfZRS Wien vom 2. August 1949, Schreiben des Abwesenheitskurators vom 18. August 1949, Beschluss der Rückstellungskommission beim LGfZRS Wien vom 17. November 1949;

FLD-Akt Registraturnummer 24543: Schreiben des Anton F. vom 6. November 1964, Aktenübersicht vom 12. November 1964, Bescheid des BMF vom 8. Juni 1966, Schreiben des Anton F. vom 26. Jänner 1967, Schreiben der FLD vom 31. Jänner 1967, Schreiben des BMF vom 6. Februar 1967, Verwaltungsgerichtshoferkenntnis Zl 1113/66-2, Schreiben des BMF vom 20. Februar 1962, Schreiben an das BMF vom 19. Februar 1962;

FLD-Akt Registraturnummer 24543/II (Josef sen. und Franziska F.): Antrag vom 29. Juni 1949, Vollmacht vom 2. November 1956, Schreiben an das BG Allentsteig, Beschluss des BG Allentsteig vom 28. Juli 1949, drei Beschlüsse der Rückstellungskommission vom 2. August 1949, Schreiben des Abwesenheitskurators vom 18. August 1949, Beschluss der Rückstellungskommission vom 17. November 1949, Beitrittserklärung der Finanzprokuratur, Eingabe durch Dr. T. vom 7. Februar 1951, Eingabe durch Dr. T. vom 3. Jänner 1951, Antrag des Dr. S. vom 31. Juli 1956, Vorlage einer beglaubigten Vollmacht vom 9. November 1956, Schreiben der Rückstellungskommission vom 23. November 1956, Antrag der Finanzprokuratur vom 12. Jänner 1957.

ÖStA, AdR, Abteilung 02: Registratur AdR 40/A 1950 /GZ.22.672 2a/ 50 (betr. RK 212/49 Anton F.) Ansuchen beim Alliierten Rat via Bundeskanzleramt (BKA): Antrag an den Alliierten Rat auf Zustimmung zur Durchführung des Verfahrens zur Rückstellung von Vermögen an Anton F., 8. Februar 1950, mit Beilagen in Abschrift aus Rückstellungsverfahren 1949; Gauakten betr. NSDAP-Mitgliedschaft von Fritz O., Josef F. sen., Josef F. jun., Rudolf Sa. – Registratur AdR, BMI GA Zl. 280.934; 90/596; 90/598; 416/582.

BG Zwettl, Abteilung GB: Fax vom 16. Februar 2004, Kaufvertrag Anton F./Deutsches Reich (EZ X1) vom 27. März 1939, Kaufvertrag Josef und Franziska F./Deutsches Reich (EZ X2) vom 22. April 1939, Beschluss des Anerbengerichts Allentsteig vom 24. August 1939.

Amt der oberösterreichischen (OÖ) Landesregierung, Opferfürsorgeakt Anton F.: Schreiben der OÖ Landesregierung vom 6. April 2004, Bescheid des Amtes der OÖ Landesregierung vom 3. Mai 1966, Bericht an den Herrn LH vom 18. Oktober 1965, Bescheid des Amtes der OÖ Landesregierung vom 12. Juli 1965, Schreiben von Rechtsanwalt (RA) V. an die Opferfürsorge-Abteilung der OÖ Landesregierung vom 29. April 1965, Diktat (unvollständig) von M. 1939, Niederschrift der Aussage des Zeugen Franz C. vom 7. September 1964, Zeugenaussage von Dr. Franz H. vom 16. Dezember 1964, Zeugenaussage von Anton B. vom

---

[2] Ergänzung zum Zeitpunkt der Drucklegung: FLD Registraturnummer 21403.

Franziska F./German Reich (EZ X2) of 22 April 1939, decision by the *Anerbengericht* ("court for matters relating to the inheritance of farming estates") Allentsteig of 24 August 1939.

Office of the Upper Austrian provincial government, Victims Welfare file Anton F., letter by the Upper Austrian provincial government of 6 April 2004, decision by the office of the Upper Austrian provincial government of 3 May 1966, report to the head of the provincial government of 18 October 1965, decision by the office of the Upper Austrian provincial government of 12 July 1965, letter by the lawyer V. to the Department for Victims Welfare of the Upper Austrian provincial government of 29 April 1965, dictation (incomplete) by M. 1939, minutes of the statement by the witness Franz C. of 7 September 1964, testimony by Dr. Franz H. of 16 December 1964, testimony by Anton B. of 19 November 1964, letter by the lawyer V. to the head of the provincial government of Upper Austria regarding the examination of the witness Josef B. of 27 August 1964, letter by the lawyer V. to the head of the provincial government of Upper Austria of 16 October 1963, decision of the Federal Ministry for Social Administration of 26 July 1963, information by the District Commission Zwettl regarding an assignment (Federal Ministry for Social Administration to the District Commission Zwettl of 17 April 1961) of 29 May 1961, Dr. K. to department 23 of 21 November 1962, expert opinion Anton F. of the General Hospital Linz (Prim. Doz. K. Huber) of 1 February 1962, letter by the District Commission Gmunden to the office of the Upper Austrian provincial government (undated), testimonial by Josef F. of 19 May 1961, Federal Ministry for Social Administration to the office of the Upper Austrian provincial government of 17 April 1961, local authority Laakirchen to the District Commission Gmunden of 2 July 1959, local authority Laakirchen to the District Commission Gmunden of 20 July 1959, local authority Laakirchen to the District Gmunden of 31 August 1959, objection by Anton F. to the office of the Upper Austrian provincial government of 6 May 1959, decision by the Upper Austrian provincial government of 24 April 1959, letter by Anton F. of 16 March 1959, letter by the Concentration Camp Association to the office of the Upper Austrian provincial government of 10 April 1959, copy of the letter by the NSDAP regional administration Niederdonau to "Pg." (*Parteigenosse*, "party member") Josef F. (undated), decision of the Zwettl district administrator to Anton F. of 25 May 1939, letter by the Zwettl district administrator to Anton F. of 13 December 1939, decision of 15 January 1940 by the head of the provincial government in Niederdonau regarding the suspension of the hunting license, decision by the Zwettl district administrator of 18 April 1944, police certificate of conduct for Anton F. (undated), confirmation by the District Commission Gmunden of 26 March 1959, birth certificate and certificate of baptism of Anton F. of 24 January 1947, right of abode certificate for Anton F. of 26 February 1959.

District Court Zwettl, land register KG Allentsteig: land register copy EZ X2 and EZ X3, copy of the land register regarding house number Z (extracts).

Land surveyor's office Gmünd, Department Zwettl: plans of the 1961 boundaries of the military training area, plans no. 1869 Allentsteig.

Civil litigation files[3]: File no. 22 Cg 52/69 (nullity suit against item 5 of the settlement of 9 November 1961) and file no. 39b Cg 287/74 (action for damages amounting to 180,000 Schilling), appeal dated 6 February 1970 Anton F./lawyer Dr. S., rejection of the appeal by the Supreme Court, decision of 26 May 1970, statement of claim Anton F./lawyer Dr. V., 12 April 1974, appeal answer by the Financial Procurator's Office, 2 June 1974, appeal dated 25 August 1976 Anton F./ lawyer Dr. V.

---

[3] Supplementation at the time of going to press: Files located at the State Financial Procurator's Office (Wien, 1., Singerstraße 17–19).

19. November 1964, Schreiben des RA V. an den LH für OÖ betr. Zeugeneinvernahme des Josef B. vom 27. August 1964, Schreiben des RA V. an den LH für OÖ vom 16. Oktober 1963, Bescheid des Bundesministeriums für soziale Verwaltung vom 26. Juli 1963, Auskunft der Bezirkshauptmannschaft (BH) Zwettl zu umseitigem Auftrag (Bundesministerium für soz. Verwaltung an BH Zwettl vom 17. April 1961) vom 29. Mai 1961, Dr. K. an Abteilung 23 vom 21. November 1962, Gutachten Anton F. des AKH Linz (Prim. Doz. K. Huber) vom 1. Februar 1962, Schreiben des BH Gmunden an das Amt der OÖ Landesregierung (ohne Datum), Zeugenaussage des Josef F. vom 19. Mai 1961, Bundesministerium für soziale Verwaltung an das Amt der OÖ Landesregierung vom 17. April 1961, Gemeindeamt Laakirchen an die BH Gmunden vom 2. Juli 1959, Gemeindeamt Laakirchen an die BH Gmunden vom 20. Juli 1959, Gemeindeamt Laakirchen an die BH Gmunden vom 31. August 1959, Einspruch des Anton F. an das Amt der OÖ Landesregierung vom 6. Mai 1959, Bescheid der OÖ Landesregierung vom 24. April 1959, Schreiben des Anton F. vom 16. März 1959, Schreiben des KZ Verbandes an das Amt der OÖ Landesregierung vom 10. April 1959, Abschrift des Schreibens der NSDAP-Gauleitung Niederdonau an „Pg." Josef F. (ohne Datum), Bescheid des Landrates Zwettl an Anton F. vom 25. Mai 1939, Schreiben des Landrates Zwettl an Anton F. vom 13. Dezember 1939, Bescheid des LH in Niederdonau betr. Jagdscheinentzug vom 15. Jänner 1940, Bescheid des Landrates des Kreises Zwettl vom 18. April 1944, Polizeiliches Führungszeugnis für Anton F. (ohne Datum), Bescheinigung der BH Gmunden vom 26. März 1959, Geburts- und Taufschein des Anton F. vom 24. Jänner 1947, Heimatrechts-Bescheinigung für Anton F. vom 26. Februar 1959.

BG Zwettl, historisches Grundbuch KG Allentsteig: Grundbuchskopie EZ X2 und EZ X3, Grundbuchskopie Haus Nr. Z (Auszüge).

Vermessungsamt Gmünd, Dienststelle Zwettl, Mappenpläne: Mappenpläne 1961 Grenzen des Truppenübungsplatzes, Mappenpläne 1869 Allentsteig.

Zivilprozessakten[3]: AZ 22 Cg 52/69 (Klage auf Nichtigkeit des Punkts 5 im Vergleich 9. November 1961) u. AZ 39b Cg 287/74 (Schadenersatzklage in Höhe 180.000,– Schilling), Revisionsschrift Anton F./RA Dr. S. vom 6. Februar 1970, Abweisung der Revision durch OGH, Urteilsschrift vom 26. Mai 1970, Klageschrift Anton F./RA Dr. V., 12. April 1974, Klagebeantwortung Finanzprokuratur, 2. Juni 1974, Berufungsschrift Anton F./RA Dr. V., 25. August 1976.

„Deutsche Dienststelle für die Benachrichtigung der nächsten Angehörigen von Gefallenen der ehemaligen deutschen Wehrmacht", Berlin, Auskunft zu Anton F. vom 1. Juli 2004.

4. Festgestellter Sachverhalt

Anton F. wurde am 3. Februar 1908 als Sohn von Josef F. sen., geb. 18. Juli 1877, und Franziska F., gebürtige Me., geb. 26. Februar 1881, geboren.

Josef F. jun. wurde am 2. Februar 1910 als Sohn von Josef F. sen., geb. 18. Juli 1877, und Franziska F., gebürtige Me., geb. 26. Februar 1881, geboren.

Die Liegenschaft EZ X1, KG Allentsteig, bestehend aus den Grundstücken Y1 Acker, Y2 Wald und Y3 Wald, stand seit 24. Februar 1937 im Eigentum des Anton F. Diese Liegenschaft wurde mit Kaufvertrag vom 27. März 1939 an das Deutsche Reich, Wehrmacht Fiskus Heer, verkauft und dieser Eigentumsübergang grundbücherlich einverleibt.

---

[3] Ergänzung zum Zeitpunkt der Drucklegung: Akten einliegend bei der Finanzprokuratur (Wien, 1., Singerstraße 17–19).

"Deutschen Dienststelle für die Benachrichtigung der nächsten Angehörigen von Gefallenen der ehem. dt. Wehrmacht" ("German Office for the Notification of Next-of-Kin of Members of the Former German Armed Forces who were Killed in Action"), Berlin, information regarding Anton F., 1 July 2004.

4. Established Facts

Anton F. was born on 3 February 1908 as the son of Josef F. (Sr.), born on 18 July 1877, and Franziska F., née Me., born on 26 February 1881.

Josef F. (Jr.) was born on 2 February 1910 as the son of Josef F. (Sr.), born on 18 July 1877, and Franziska F., née Me., born on 26 February 1881.

Since 24 February 1937, the property EZ X1, KG Allentsteig, comprising the property parcels Y1 field, Y2 forest and Y3 forest, was owned by Anton F. This property was sold pursuant to the purchase contract of 27 March 1939 to the German Reich, German Armed Forces Treasury Army. This transfer of ownership was incorporated in the land register.

Since 4 October 1910, the property EZ X3, KG Allentsteig, comprising the property parcels Y4 barn, Y5/3 field and Y5/2 field, was owned by Josef (Sr.) and Franziska F. This property was sold pursuant to the purchase contract of 22 April 1939 to the German Reich, German Armed Forces Treasury Army. This transfer of ownership was incorporated in the land register.

Since 26 September 1903, the property EZ X2, KG Allentsteig comprising the property parcels Y6/2, Y7, Y8, Y9, Y10, Y11, Y12, Y13, Y14, Y15, Y16, Y17, Y18, Y19, Y20, Y21, Y22, Y23, Y24, Y25, Y26/1, Y26/2, Y27, Y28/1, Y28/2, Y29, Y30, Y31, Y32, Y33, Y34, Y35, Y36, Y37, Y38, Y39, Y40, Y41, Y42/2, Y43/1, Y44, Y45, Y46, Y47, Y48, Y49, Y50, Y51, Y52, Y53/1, Y54/1, Y55/1, Y56/1, Y57/1, Y57/2, Y58, Y60/1, Y60/2 was owned by Josef (Sr.) and Franziska F. This property was sold to the German Reich pursuant to the purchase contract of 22 April 1939, German Armed Forces Treasury Army. This transfer of ownership was incorporated in the land register.

The vendors Anton F., Josef (Sr.) and Franziska F. received the proceeds from the sale to their free disposal.

The reasons for withdrawing the catering concession for the military training area from the F. bakery could not be established.

The Directorate for Security of Lower Austria described Anton F. as a "keen supporter of the NSDAP". In 1934, Anton F. was brought to the Wöllersdorf detention camp because he was involved in prohibited political activity. There, Anton F. informed the authorities of another illegal National Socialist, Rudolf Sa., who was in possession of firearms and explosives. Rudolf Sa. was held under arrest between 1934 and 1938 for illegal political (National Socialist) activity.

Anton F.'s brothers, Josef and Leopold, were also illegal National Socialists and members of the *SA (Sturmabteilung*, "Storm Division"). After the *Anschluss* Josef F. (Sr.) and his son Josef F. renewed their NSDAP memberships. This was endorsed by the local group leadership, namely Fritz O.

In 1937 before the *Anschluss*, Josef (Sr.) and Franziska F. wanted to transfer their property to their son Anton F. due to health reasons.

In 1938, the mayor and local group leader O. ordered Josef F. (Sr.) to leave Allentsteig. The pestering and threats carried out by the party had also complicated the financial situation of

Schiedsinstanz für Naturalrestitution – Entscheidung Nr. 8/2004

Die Liegenschaft EZ X3, KG Allentsteig, bestehend aus den Grundstücken Y4 Scheuer, Y5/3 Acker und Y5/2 Acker, stand seit 4. Oktober 1910 im Eigentum des Josef sen. und der Franziska F. Diese Liegenschaft wurde mit Kaufvertrag vom 22. April 1939 an das Deutsche Reich, Wehrmacht Fiskus Heer, verkauft und dieser Eigentumsübergang grundbücherlich einverleibt.

Die Liegenschaft EZ X2, KG Allentsteig, bestehend aus den Grundstücken Y6/2, Y7, Y8, Y9, Y10, Y11, Y12, Y13, Y14, Y15, Y16, Y17, Y18, Y19, Y20, Y21, Y22, Y23, Y24, Y25, Y26/1, Y26/2, Y27, Y28/1, Y28/2, Y29, Y30, Y31, Y32, Y33, Y34, Y35, Y36, Y37, Y38, Y39, Y40, Y41, Y42/2, Y43/1, Y44, Y45, Y46, Y47, Y48, Y49, Y50, Y51, Y52, Y53/1, Y54/1, Y55/1, Y56/1, Y57/1, Y57/2, Y58, Y60/1, Y60/2, stand seit 26. September 1903 im Eigentum des Josef sen. und der Franziska F. Diese Liegenschaft wurde mit Kaufvertrag vom 22. April 1939 an das Deutsche Reich, Wehrmacht Fiskus Heer, verkauft und dieser Eigentumsübergang grundbücherlich einverleibt.

Die Kaufsummen erhielten die VerkäuferInnen Anton F., Josef sen. und Franziska F. zur freien Verfügung.

Es konnte nicht festgestellt werden, aus welchen Gründen der Bäckerei F. die Lieferkonzession an den Truppenübungsplatz entzogen wurde.

Anton F. wurde von der Sicherheitsdirektion Niederösterreich als „eifriger Anhänger der NSDAP" bezeichnet und wegen verbotener parteipolitischer Betätigung 1934 ins Anhaltelager Wöllersdorf verbracht. Dort wurde von Anton F. ein weiterer illegaler, dort angehaltener Nationalsozialist, Rudolf Sa., den Behörden im Zusammenhang mit Waffen- und Sprengstoffbesitz bekannt gemacht. Rudolf Sa. saß wegen illegaler politischer (nationalsozialistischer) Betätigung 1934 bis 1938 in Haft.

Auch Anton F.s Brüder Josef und Leopold waren illegale Nationalsozialisten, außerdem Mitglieder der SA. Nach dem „Anschluss" erneuerten Josef F. sen. und sein Sohn Josef F. ihre NSDAP-Mitgliedschaften. Dies erfolgte mit Befürwortung der Ortsgruppenleitung, namentlich Fritz O.

Josef sen. und Franziska F. wollten ihren Besitz aus gesundheitlichen Gründen bereits vor dem „Anschluss" im Jahr 1937 an ihren Sohn Anton F. übergeben.

Josef F. sen. wurde ab 1938 vom Bürgermeister und Ortsgruppenleiter O. aufgefordert, Allentsteig zu verlassen. Die Nachstellungen und Drohungen von Parteiseite haben auch die wirtschaftliche Existenz von Josef sen. und Franziska F. in Allentsteig erschwert. Das Ehepaar F. hat daraufhin einen Umsiedlungsantrag gestellt, welcher durch die Kreisbauernschaft Allentsteig mit der Begründung abgelehnt wurde, dass die dem Ehepaar F. verbleibende Bäckerei und Gastwirtschaft lebensfähig seien. Josef sen. und Franziska F. stellten danach nochmals einen Umsiedlungsantrag, da ihnen durch Ortsgruppenleiter O. nahegelegt wurde, die Stadt zu verlassen. Dieser Antrag wurde dann genehmigt.

Vom Landrat des Landkreises Zwettl wurde Anton F. mittels Bescheid vom 25. Mai 1939 der Bezirks-Jahresjagdschein entzogen, nachdem er ihm einen Monat zuvor, am 24. April 1939, ausgestellt worden war. Als Begründung wurde angeführt, dass „auf Grund Ihres politischen Vorlebens ein einwandfreies staatsbürgerliches Verhalten nicht mehr zu erwarten ist. Ihr bisheriges Verhalten lässt besorgen, dass Sie die öffentliche Sicherheit gefährden, weshalb die Versagung [...] ausgesprochen werden musste." Gemäß § 23 Waffengesetz wurde über Anton F. mit Bescheid des Landrates vom 13. Dezember 1939 auch das Verbot ausgesprochen, Schusswaffen zu erwerben, zu besitzen oder zu führen. Etwaige in seinem Besitz sich befindliche Waffen als auch Munition würden entschädigungslos eingezogen werden.

Josef (Sr.) and Franziska F. in Allentsteig. Consequently, the couple F. made an application for resettlement. This application was rejected by the district farming community Allentsteig on the grounds that the bakery and restaurant still remaining with couple F. were sufficiently viable. Subsequently, Josef (Sr.) and Franziska F. filed another application for resettlement as the local group leader O. urged them to leave the city. This application was then granted.

By decision of 25 May 1939, the district administrator of the district Zwettl withdrew Anton F.'s annual district hunting license. The license had been issued to Anton F. one month earlier on 24 April 1939. The cited reason for this withdrawal was: "due to your political past, good citizenly behavior is not to be expected. Your previous behavior leaves it to be expected that you may endanger public security, and for this reason the refusal [...] had to be given." Pursuant to para. 23 of the *Waffengesetz* ("Weapons Law") of 13 December 1939, by decision of the district administrator it was decided that Anton F. was prohibited to acquire, own or carry firearms. Any arms as well as ammunition found in his possession would be confiscated without compensation.

Anton F. appealed against the first decision. However, the appeal was not granted. The reason given was that the examination by the state police concluded that Anton F. "does not possess the political reliability required for the granting of a hunting license." In 1944, when Anton F. again applied for an annual district hunting license, the application was not granted for the same reasons.

Anton F. was unfit for work from mid-1938 to spring 1939. He told his physician, Dr. Franz H., that the pains in the lower-back were as a result of being abused (i.e. being kicked). Anton F. also told him that he had suffered this abuse in St. Pölten in July 1938 while being examined by the Secret State Police.

On 10 October 1940, the regional administration Niederdonau confirmed in writing to Josef F. (Sr.) that it was not able to issue a certificate of political harmlessness for his son Anton F. In this letter Josef F. (Sr.) was addressed as a "Pg." (party member).

On 16 April 1940, Anton F. was drafted by the German Armed Forces. Until 16 August 1943 he served in bakery companies, then in the headquarters of the tank regiment 36 and until 6 November 1944, again in the bakery company. From 6 November 1944 until 13 February 1946 he was a (western allied) prisoner of war. In 1941, he turned lance corporal, in 1944 senior lance corporal. After his captivity, Anton F. returned to Allentsteig.

On 1 June 1949, Anton F. submitted an application to the Restitution Commission established with the Regional Court for Civil Matters Vienna, External Senate with the District Court Krems/Donau, in accordance with the *Dritte Rückstellungsgesetz* (Third Restitution Act), for the restitution of the property EZ X1, KG Allentsteig. By final and binding decision of 13 September 1956, file no. Rk 212/49-8, pursuant to para. 31 (1) and para. 43 (5) of the *Erste Staatsvertragsdurchführungsgesetz* ("First State Treaty Implementation Act"), these proceedings were transferred to the Financial Directorate for Vienna, Lower Austria and Burgenland and were continued in accordance with the *Zweite Rückstellungsgesetz* ("Second Restitution Act").

Anton F.'s application was rejected by decision of the Financial Directorate for Vienna dated 22 May 1958. The rejection was explained as follows:

"The claimant's argument that the property had been seized for the preparation of offensive warfare for military purposes, and that hence this qualified as an incorrect application of the law, is not applicable. Rather, the construction of military training areas does not represent a typical National Socialist measure but a process possible in all states. In this case, this process was based on the law of 29 March 1935, *RGBl.* ("Reich Law Gazette") I., page 467,

Schiedsinstanz für Naturalrestitution – Entscheidung Nr. 8/2004

Gegen den ersteren Bescheid erhob Anton F. Berufung, der jedoch keine Folge gegeben wurde. Als Grund wurde angeführt, dass die staatspolizeiliche Überprüfung ergeben habe, dass Anton F. „die für die Erlangung eines Jagdscheines erforderliche politische Zuverlässigkeit" nicht besitze. Auch einem neuerlichen Antrag Anton F.s auf einen Bezirks-Jahresjagdschein im Jahr 1944 wurde aus ebendiesen Gründen keine Folge gegeben.

In der Zeit von Mitte 1938 bis Frühjahr 1939 war Anton F. arbeitsunfähig. Er gab gegenüber seinem behandelnden Arzt, Primar Dr. Franz H. an, die Schmerzen in der Lendenkreuzgegend seien auf Misshandlungen, wie Fußtritte, zurückzuführen, die er, Anton F., während einer Behandlung durch die Gestapo in St. Pölten im Juli 1938 erlitten habe.

Die Gauleitung Niederdonau bescheinigte Josef F. sen. am 10. Oktober 1940, nicht in der Lage zu sein, für dessen Sohn Anton F. ein Unbedenklichkeitszeugnis ausstellen zu können. In diesem Schreiben wurde Josef F. sen. mit „Pg." (Parteigenosse) bezeichnet.

Anton F. ist am 16. April 1940 zur Wehrmacht einberufen worden und diente bis zum 16. August 1943 in Bäckerei-Kompanien, danach in der Stabskompanie des Panzer-Regiments 36, dann bis 6. November 1944 wieder in einer Bäckerei-Kompanie. Vom 6. November 1944 bis 13. Februar 1946 war er in (westalliierter) Kriegsgefangenschaft. Er wurde 1941 zum Gefreiten, 1944 zum Obergefreiten befördert. Anton F. kehrte nach seiner Kriegsgefangenschaft nach Allentsteig zurück.

Am 1. Juni 1949 beantragte Anton F. bei der Rückstellungskommission beim LGfZRS Wien, Außensenat beim Kreisgericht Krems/Donau, gemäß dem Dritten Rückstellungsgesetz (3. RStG) die Rückstellung der Liegenschaft EZ X1, KG Allentsteig. Mit rechtskräftigem Beschluss vom 13. September 1956, GZ. Rk 212/49-8, wurde dieses Verfahren gemäß § 31 Abs 1 und § 43 Abs 5 des Ersten Staatsvertragsdurchführungsgesetzes (1. StVDG) an die FLD für Wien, Niederösterreich und Burgenland abgetreten und nach dem Zweiten Rückstellungsgesetz (2. RStG) fortgesetzt.

Mit Bescheid der FLD Wien vom 22. Mai 1958 wurde der Antrag Anton F.s abgewiesen. Die Abweisung wurde dahingehend begründet, dass

„das Argument des Antragstellers, dass die Liegenschaft für die Vorbereitung eines Angriffskrieges zu militärischen Zwecken enteignet wurde und daher in diesem Vorgang eine missbräuchliche Gesetzesanwendung liege, nicht greift. Vielmehr ist in der Anlage von Truppenübungsplätzen keine typisch nationalsozialistische Maßnahme zu erblicken, sondern ein in allen Staaten möglicher Vorgang, welcher in diesem Falle auf das Gesetz vom 29. März 1935, RGBl I, Seite 467, in der Fassung des 12. April 1938, RGBl I, Seite 387, gestützt, vor sich ging. Ob für die Zwecke der Wehrmacht erworbene Grundstücke dann auch de facto für militärische Zwecke verwendet wurden, ist irrelevant. Entscheidend ist, dass das Deutsche Reich diese für die Anlegung des Truppenübungsplatzes Döllersheim erworben hat und der Erwerb aufgrund eines Gesetzes erfolgte. Eine missbräuchliche Anwendung desselben aber konnte der Antragsteller in keiner Richtung glaubhaft machen. Eine politische Verfolgung ist nicht behauptet worden."

Josef sen. und Franziska F. stellten am 29. Juni 1949 den Antrag auf Rückstellung der Liegenschaften EZ X2, KG Allentsteig und EZ X3, KG Allentsteig an die Rückstellungskommission beim LGfZRS Wien, Außensenat beim Kreisgericht Krems. Als Abwesenheitskurator für das Deutsche Reich wurde Johann La. am 28. Juli 1949 bestellt. Die Rückstellungskommission wies am 17. November 1949 die RückstellungswerberInnen an, die Zustimmung der Alliierten Kommission in Österreich zur Durchführung des Rückstellungsverfahrens einzuholen. Am 3. Jänner 1952 zogen die RückstellungswerberInnen ihren Antrag

last modified on 12 April 1938, Reich Law Gazette I., page 387. Whether the properties, which had been acquired for the purposes of the German Armed Forces, were then actually used for military purposes is irrelevant. It is decisive that the German Reich acquired these properties for the purpose of construction of the military training area Döllersheim and that the acquisition happened on the basis of a law. The applicant could, however, in no manner substantiate a misuse of this law. A political persecution has not been asserted."

On 29 June 1949, Josef (Sr.) and Franziska F. filed an application with the Restitution Commission established with the Regional Court for Civil Matters Vienna, External Senate with the District Court Krems, for the restitution of the properties EZ X2, KG Allentsteig and EZ X3, KG Allentsteig. On 28 July 1949, Johann La. was appointed as a representative *in absentia* for the German Reich. On 17 November 1949, the Restitution Commission instructed the claimants for restitution to procure the approval of the Allied Commission in Austria for the conduct of the restitution proceedings. On 3 January 1952, the claimants for restitution withdrew their application concerning the property parcels Y44, Y45, Y46, Y47 and Y8, all located in EZ X2, land register Allentsteig as these were no longer owned by the German Reich. On 6 March 1957, pursuant to para. 43 (5) of the First State Treaty Implementation Act, the proceedings were transferred to the Financial Directorate for Vienna. On 19 September 1957, Dr. S., the representative of the claimants for restitution, filed a submission with the Financial Directorate for Vienna, in which he submitted that "the laws valid at the time were incorrectly applied" and that the claimants for restitution had been forced to sell some parcels due to political persecution. This submission was supplemented by Josef (Sr.) and Franziska F. on 26 September 1957. Both claimants for restitution maintained that the political persecution of their son, Anton F., had had an impact on their entire family. By decision of 28 March 1958, the Financial Directorate for Vienna dismissed the application for restitution. On 16 April 1958, the claimants for restitution filed an appeal against this decision. This application was dismissed by the Financial Directorate for Vienna by decision of 4 July 1960 with reference to the regulations in the Third State Treaty Implementation Act. Josef (Sr.) and Franziska F. filed an appeal against this decision with the Federal Ministry of Finance. On 12 September 1958, the Federal Ministry of Finance issued an appeal decision, in which the challenged decision was repealed and referred back to the authority of first instance for a renewed hearing and the issue of a new decision. During the course of these proceedings, the Federal Buildings' Administration II Vienna announced the construction of a war memorial on the property parcels Y57/2 and Y58. During the following months of the year 1959, Josef F., Josef B., Franz M., Franz W., Barbara G., Anton F., Josef F. (Sr.), Franz Wu., Hubert Mei. as well as Rudolf Sa. were questioned regarding the circumstances of the property acquisitions concerning the F. family. According to statements by Franz M., a witness during the restitution proceedings of Josef (Sr.) and Franziska F., Anton F. "was considered as a traitor after the *Anschluss* among members of the NSDAP."

Barbara G. testified that she broke off her engagement to Anton F. due to anonymous letters, in which it was written that her fiancé would lose his property and that he would be deported to a detention camp. Adding to this, the local group leader O. informed G.'s father that he no longer wanted to have the family in Allentsteig and that Anton F. would no longer own anything. According to some testimonials, Anton F.'s political ostracism also had an impact on his parents. Franz M. testified "that the F [...] family was avoided by the members of the NSDAP due to the son, Anton F[...]'s betrayal." According to statements by Anton F., Fritz O. forbade the operators of the army canteen to continue buying products from the restaurant and the F. bakery, which was "a heavy economical loss". In addition, regarding their parents' persecution the two F. sons testified: "from 1938 until 1945, my parents were no longer po-

hinsichtlich der Grundstücke Y44, Y45, Y46, Y47 und Y8, alle einliegend der EZ X2, GB Allentsteig, zurück, da diese nicht mehr im Eigentum des Deutschen Reichs waren. Am 6. März 1957 wurde das Verfahren gemäß § 43 Abs 5 des 1. StVDG an die FLD Wien abgetreten. Dr. S., Vertreter der RückstellungswerberInnen, brachte am 19. September 1957 eine Eingabe bei der FLD Wien ein, in welcher dieser vorbrachte, dass „die damals geltenden Gesetze missbräuchlich angewendet wurden" und dass die RückstellungswerberInnen auch aufgrund politischer Verfolgung zur Veräußerung einiger Parzellen genötigt worden seien. Diese Eingabe wurde am 26. September 1957 von Josef sen. und Franziska F. ergänzt. Die beiden RückstellungswerberInnen hielten dabei fest, dass sich die politische Verfolgung ihres Sohnes Anton F. auf die gesamte Familie ausgewirkt habe. Mit Bescheid vom 28. März 1958 wurde der Rückstellungsantrag durch die FLD abgewiesen. Gegen diesen Bescheid erhoben die RückstellungswerberInnen am 16. April 1958 Berufung. Dieser Antrag wurde von der FLD Wien mit Bescheid vom 4. Juli 1960 unter Hinweis auf die Bestimmungen des 3. StVDG abgewiesen. Gegen diesen Bescheid erhoben Josef sen. und Franziska F. Berufung an das BMF. Am 12. September 1958 erließ das BMF einen Berufungsbescheid, in welchem der angefochtene Bescheid behoben und zur neuerlichen Verhandlung und Erlassung eines neuen Bescheides an die Behörde erster Instanz verwiesen wurde. Im Zuge dieses Verfahrens wurde von der Bundesgebäudeverwaltung II Wien bekannt gegeben, dass auf den Grundstücken Y57/2 und Y58 ein Kriegerdenkmal errichtet werden sollte. In den folgenden Monaten des Jahres 1959 wurden Josef F., Josef B., Franz M., Franz W., Barbara G., Anton F., Josef F. sen., Franz Wu., Hubert Mei. sowie Rudolf Sa. zum Hergang der Liegenschaftsankäufe gegenüber der Familie F. einvernommen. Laut Angaben von Franz M., Zeuge im Rückstellungsverfahren Josef sen. und Franziska F., galt Anton F. „nach dem Anschluss in den Reihen der Mitglieder der NSDAP als Verräter".

Barbara G. sagte aus, dass sie ihre Verlobung mit Anton F. aufgrund von anonymen Briefen gelöst habe, in welchen stand, dass ihr Verlobter seinen Besitz verlieren und in ein Anhaltelager kommen werde. Auch der Ortsgruppenleiter O. habe dem Vater von Frau G. mitgeteilt, dass er die Familie nicht mehr in Allentsteig haben wolle und Anton F. nichts mehr besitzen werde. Nach einigen ZeugInnenaussagen habe sich die politische Ächtung des Anton F. auch auf seine Eltern ausgewirkt. Franz M. sagte aus, „dass die Familie F[…] wegen des Verrates des Sohnes Anton F[…] in Allentsteig von den Mitgliedern der NSDAP gemieden wurde". Nach Angaben von Anton F. habe Fritz O. den BetreiberInnen der Heereskantine verboten, weiterhin Waren von der Gastwirtschaft und der Bäckerei F. zu beziehen, was ein „schwerer wirtschaftlicher Verlust" gewesen sei. Zur Verfolgungssituation ihrer Eltern sagten die beiden Söhne F. außerdem aus: „1938 bis 1945 wurden meine Eltern nicht mehr politisch verfolgt" (Anton F.) und „meinen Eltern hat man niemals mit einer Verschickung in ein Konzentrationslager gedroht" (Josef F.).

Rudolf Sa. verweigerte die Aussage bezüglich der Entlassungsgründe von Anton F. aus dem Anhaltelager Wöllersdorf. Des Weiteren gab er an, sich an die Ereignisse zwischen 1934 und 1945 nicht erinnern zu können.

Am 9. Juni 1959 brachte die Finanzprokuratur eine Äußerung ein. In dieser wurde vorgebracht, dass

„die Antragsteller, welche zufolge ihres Alters das Gastwirtschafts- und Bäckereigewerbe persönlich nicht mehr ausüben konnten und welche zugeben mussten, dass der Ertrag der Gastwirtschaft seit der NS-Machtergreifung sehr zurückgegangen ist, am Eigentum dieses, vom Deutschen Reich nichtbeanspruchten Restbesitzes wirtschaftlich nicht mehr interessiert waren."

litically persecuted" (Anton F.) and "my parents had never been threatened with being sent to a concentration camp" (Josef F.).

Rudolf Sa. denied testifying in regard to the reasons for Anton F.'s release from the detention camp Wöllersdorf. Further, he stated that he could not remember the occurrences that happened between 1934 and 1945.

On 9 June 1959, the Financial Procurator's Office filed a submission. In it, it argued that

"the applicants, who due to their age were no longer able to personally carry on the restaurant and bakery and who had to admit that the proceeds from the restaurant had very much diminished since the assumption of power by the National Socialists, were no longer economically interested in the ownership of the remaining property, which had not been claimed by the German Reich."

Whereupon, in a counter statement Dr. S. on behalf of the applicants for restitution stated the following: "In no manner have these proceedings shown that we ever even had any intention to sell. It was only proven that we have been practically forced to sell due to the persecutions." On 4 July 1960, the Financial Directorate issued the decision in which the application for restitution was again dismissed. On 28 July, the claimants for restitution again appealed this decision.

Subsequently, the parties entered into settlement negotiations. During the course of these negotiations, department 34 of the Federal Ministry of Finance welcomed an amicable solution since a restitution by decision seemed to be unfavorable and a rejection of the appeal could in any case be challenged in the Supreme Administrative Court because the properties had not been used by the German Armed Forces, nor had they been used by the federal army. On 9 November 1961, the Republic of Austria, represented by the State Financial Procurator's Office, and Josef and Franziska F. concluded a settlement during negotiations before the Federal Ministry of Finance. The settlement set out that the Republic of Austria would restitute to the claimants for restitution the parcels number Y6/2, Y7, Y42/2, Y43/1, Y57/2, Y58, which at the time were part of the EZ X2, KG Allentsteig and that the claimants would pay an amount of 55,000 Schilling:

"Therewith all reciprocal claims coming from the title of the purchase price refund and from the compensation for expenditures are settled and paid. With this settlement all pending claims made in proceedings before the Financial Directorate for Vienna, Lower Austria and Burgenland, which have been decided by the Directorate in its decision of 4 July 1960, file number VR-V 20.156-33/60 (then Restitution Commission established with the Regional Court for Civil Matters Vienna, External Senate with the District Court Krems file no. Rk 213/49), especially those claims regarding restitution of further property parcels, are paid and settled. Apart thereof, the applicants for restitution, or their legal successors, are at liberty to file claims based on possible future legal regulation under the title of compensation regarding properties not restituted by this settlement and previously belonging to them, concerning which restitution proceedings were pending."

In 1964, Anton F. represented by his lawyer Dr. Theodor V., filed a suit against the Republic of Austria with the Constitutional Court pursuant to para. 137 of the Federal Constitution Law (regarding public law claims concerning property law). The suit claimed an unencumbered transfer of EZ X3, *in eventu* payment of 76,000 Schilling as well as *in eventu* the adjudication by the Federal State that the settlement of 9 November 1961 was null and void. On 11 June 1963, this claim was dismissed.

On 3 January 1966, Anton F., as the heir to Josef (Sr.), and Franziska F., filed an application with the Federal Ministry of Finance for the continuation of the restitution proceedings

In einer Gegenäußerung brachte daraufhin Dr. S. für die RückstellungswerberInnen Folgendes vor: „Es ist in keiner Weise im Verfahren zu Tage getreten, dass wir überhaupt je solche Veräußerungsabsichten hatten, sondern nur bewiesen worden, dass wir durch die Verfolgungen praktisch zur Veräußerung gezwungen wurden." Am 4. Juli 1960 erging der Bescheid der FLD, in welchem der Antrag auf Rückstellung neuerlich abgelehnt wurde. Gegen diesen Bescheid wurde wiederum durch die RückstellungswerberInnen am 28. Juli Berufung erhoben.

Daraufhin kam es zu Vergleichsverhandlungen. Im Zuge derselben wurde von der Abt. 34 des BMF eine vergleichsweise Regelung begrüßt, da eine bescheidmäßige Rückstellung unopportun erschien und eine Abweisung der Berufung allenfalls beim VwGH bekämpft werden konnte, da die Liegenschaften weder von der Deutschen Wehrmacht benutzt worden waren noch vom Bundesheer verwendet wurden. Am 9. November 1961 schlossen die Republik Österreich, vertreten durch die Finanzprokuratur, und Josef und Franziska F. in einer Verhandlung vor dem BMF einen Vergleich. Dieser Vergleich beinhaltete, dass die Republik Österreich die Parzellen Nr. Y6/2, Y7, Y42/2, Y43/1, Y57/2, Y58, damals einliegend in der EZ X2, KG Allentsteig, an die RückstellungswerberInnen zurückstellt werde und diese den Betrag von 55.000,– Schilling bezahlen:

„Damit sind sämtliche gegenseitigen Ansprüche aus dem Titel der Kaufpreiserstattung und des Ersatzes für Aufwendungen verrechnet und verglichen. Mit diesem Vergleich sind alle im Verfahren vor der Finanzlandesdirektion für Wien, Niederösterreich und Burgenland anhängig gemachten Ansprüche, die von dieser mit Bescheid vom 4. Juli 1960, Zl VR-V 20.156-33/60, entschieden wurden (seinerzeit Rückstellungskommission beim LGfZRS Wien, Außensenat beim Kreisgericht Krems GZ. Rk 213/49), insbesondere solche auf Rückstellung weiterer Grundstücke, verglichen und bereinigt. Dessen ungeachtet bleibt es den Rückstellungswerbern bzw. deren Rechtsnachfolgern unbenommen, auf Grund einer allfälligen künftigen gesetzlichen Regelung Ansprüche für die durch diesen Vergleich nicht rückgestellten und ihnen ehedem gehörigen Grundstücke, über die ein Rückstellungsverfahren anhängig war, aus dem Titel des Schadenersatzes zu stellen."

1964 brachte Anton F. über seinen Rechtsvertreter Dr. Theodor V. beim Verfassungsgerichtshof eine Klage gegen die Republik Österreich nach Art. 137 Bundes-Verfassungsgesetz (B-VG) (betr. vermögensrechtliche öffentlich-rechtliche Ansprüche) ein. Das Klagebegehren lautete auf lastenfreie Übertragung der EZ X3, in eventu auf Zahlung von 76.000,– Schilling sowie in eventu auf Anerkennung der Nichtigkeit des Vergleichs vom 9. November 1961 durch den Bund. Am 11. Juni 1964 wurde diese Klage abgewiesen.

Am 3. Jänner 1966 brachte Anton F. als Erbe von Josef sen. und Franziska F. beim BMF einen Antrag auf Fortsetzung des Rückstellungsverfahrens hinsichtlich der EZ X3, KG Allentsteig ein. Dieser Antrag wurde mit Bescheid vom 8. Juni 1966 zurückgewiesen. Gegen diesen Bescheid wurde durch Anton F. wiederum Beschwerde beim VwGH erhoben. Der VwGH wies am 24. November 1966 die Beschwerde als unbegründet ab.

Anton F. unternahm es, in zwei Klagen 1969 und 1974 den Punkt 5 des Vergleichs von 1961 auf zivilrechtlichem Wege beim LGfZRS Wien anzufechten und – wegen Unmöglichkeit einer Rückstellung in natura – Schadenersatz einzufordern. In beiden Verfahren wurden die Klagen des Anton F. mit Endurteil des OGH sowie des OLG abgewiesen.

Am 16. März 1959 suchte Anton F. um Zuerkennung eines Opferausweises gemäß § 4 OFG an. In der Begründung gab er an, dass sein Einkommen durch politische Verfolgungsmaßnahmen länger als 3 ½ Jahre um mehr als die Hälfte vermindert gewesen sei. Die Übernahme des elterlichen Besitzes sei ihm wegen nicht erteilter „Politischer Unbedenklichkeitser-

regarding EZ X3, KG Allentsteig. By decision of 8 June 1966 this application was dismissed. Anton F. subsequently filed a complaint against this decision with the Supreme Administrative Court. On 24 November 1966, the Supreme Administrative Court dismissed the complaint as being without merit.

In two civil suits, in 1969 and in 1974 respectively, Anton F. appealed against item 5 of the settlement of 1961 before the Regional Court for Civil Matters Vienna and claimed financial compensation due to the impossibility of restitution in kind. In both proceedings, the claims by Anton F. were dismissed with final judgment by the Supreme Court and the Higher Regional Court for Civil Matters.

On 16 March 1959, Anton F. applied for a victim's identification card in accordance with para. 4 of the Victims Welfare Act. In his reasoning he stated that his income had been reduced by more than 50 % for more than three and half years due to political persecution. The takeover of the parental property had been rendered impossible for him due to the fact that he had not been conferred a "certificate of political harmlessness" and for this reason he had also not been able to marry. He had "subsequently suffered income and property losses".

On 24 April 1959, this request was rejected by a decision "since the stated damages do not represent damages as defined by letter d of para. 1 (2) of the Victims Welfare Act". Anton F. appealed against this decision. By decision of 26 July 1963, the Federal Ministry for Social Affairs did not grant F.'s appeal of 6 May 1959 against the rejection of his application for a victim's identification card on 24 April 1959. It is stated in the explanation that neither letter c – reduction of the ability to work by at least 70 % due to health problems – nor letter d – income reduced by at least 50 % for at least three and a half years when compared to the time before the start of the persecution – is fulfilled.

On 6 September 1961, Anton F. applied for compensation of income as defined by para. 14b of the Victims Welfare Act.

On 16 October 1963, Anton F. filed an application for the issue of an official confirmation in accordance with para. 4 of the Victims Welfare Act.

By decision of 12 July 1965, this request was granted and an official confirmation as defined by para. 1 (1) of the Victims Welfare Act was issued. Hence, his health problems, which according to his statements were caused by the Secret State Police's abuse, were recognized. According to the reasons stated in the decision it could be assumed as proven "that due to your political activity against the illegal NSDAP in July 1938 you have been severely abused by the Secret State Police in St. Pölten to such an extent that you have suffered a subsequent reduction of at least 50 % of your ability to work for a period of more than six months." Concerning this matter, in a report of 18 October 1965 to the head of the provincial government of Upper Austria, it was noted

"that the issue of an official confirmation by the higher office based on the claimant's health problems also took place in a very obliging manner since the hard-won evidence would have equally allowed a rejection. However, due to the present lack of evidence the decision was made in favor of the claimant."

The application of September 1961 for compensation of income pursuant to para. 14b of the Victims Welfare Act was dismissed by decision of 3 May 1966. This decision was explained as follows: The prevention of the takeover of the parental property does not meet the requirements of the cited para. 14b of the Victims Welfare Act. Even though it may be possible that this prevention generated a financial loss, still "the attainment of a higher income had the damaging measure not taken place cannot be taken into consideration".

klärung" verunmöglicht worden und er habe deshalb auch nicht heiraten können. Er sei „in der Folge an Vermögen und Einkommen schwer geschädigt worden".

Am 24. April 1959 erfolgte die Ablehnung dieses Ansuchens per Bescheid, „da die angegebenen Schäden keine Schädigung i. S. des § 1 Abs 2 lit. d. OFG darstellen". Hiegegen erhob Anton F. Berufung. Mit Bescheid vom 26. Juli 1963 gab das Bundesministerium (BM) für Soziales der Berufung F.s vom 6. Mai 1959 gegen die Ablehnung seines Opferausweis-Gesuchs am 24. April 1959 nicht statt. In der Begründung heißt es, dass weder der Tatbestand lit. c – durch Gesundheitsschäden bewirkte Verminderung der Erwerbsfähigkeit um mindestens 70 % – noch der Tatbestand lit. d – um mindestens die Hälfte vermindertes Einkommen gegenüber der Zeit vor Einsetzen der Verfolgungsmaßnahme während wenigstens 3 ½ Jahren – erfüllt werde.

Am 6. September 1961 suchte Anton F. um Einkommensentschädigung i. S. von § 14b OFG an.

Am 16. Oktober 1963 erfolgte ein Ansuchen Anton F.s um Ausstellung einer Amtsbescheinigung nach § 4 OFG.

Per Bescheid vom 12. Juli 1965 wurde diesem Ansuchen stattgegeben und eine Amtsbescheinigung i.S.d. § 1 Abs 1 OFG ausgestellt. Seine laut Aussage durch Gestapo-Misshandlung erlittenen Gesundheitsschäden wurden hiemit anerkannt. Laut Begründung des Bescheides könne es als erwiesen angenommen werden, „dass Sie wegen Ihrer politischen Betätigung gegen die illegale NSDAP im Juli 1938 durch die Gestapo in St. Pölten so schwer misshandelt wurden, dass Sie in der Folge eine mindestens 50 %ige Minderung ihrer Erwerbsfähigkeit durch mehr als 6 Monate erlitten haben." Hierzu wird in einem Bericht an den LH von Oberösterreich vom 18. Oktober 1965 festgehalten,

„dass auch die Ausstellung einer Amtsbescheinigung auf Grund der Gesundheitsschädigung des Antragstellers vom ho. Amte in sehr entgegenkommender Weise erfolgte, da die mühsam erbrachten Beweise ebenso gut eine Ablehnung zugelassen hätten. Wegen des vorliegenden Beweisnotstandes wurde aber zugunsten des Antragstellers entschieden."

Das Ansuchen um Einkommensentschädigung nach § 14b OFG vom September 1961 wurde per Bescheid vom 3. Mai 1966 abgewiesen. Begründet wurde dies folgendermaßen: Die Verhinderung der Übernahme des elterlichen Besitzes könne nicht dem Tatbestand des zitierten § 14b OFG unterstellt werden. Auch wenn ein finanzieller Verlust durch diese Verhinderung erfolgt sein sollte, so könne dennoch „die Erzielung eines größeren Einkommens für den Fall des Unterbleibens der schädigenden Maßnahme nicht in Betracht gezogen werden".

Josef F. sen. verstarb am 10. Mai 1961 in Allentsteig. Anton F. verstarb am 4. November 1987. Dessen gesamter Nachlass wurde dem erblasserischen Bruder Josef F. jun. zur Gänze eingeantwortet. Josef F. jun. verstarb am 18. August 2000 und wurde seine Adoptivtochter Hui F. abhandlungsbehördlich ermächtigt, über die erblichen Guthaben zu verfügen. Mangels eines Nachlassvermögens fand eine Verlassenschaftsabhandlung nicht statt.

Die Ab- und Zuschreibungen der einzelnen beantragten Grundstücksnummern stellen sich seit 1938 folgendermaßen dar:

Y6/2 und Y7 werden am 21. Juli 1964 der EZ X2 abgeschrieben und mit diesen die neue EZ X4 dieses GB eröffnet. Diese EZ steht heute im Privateigentum. Diese zwei Grundstücke wurden mittels Vergleich zurückgestellt.

Arbitration Panel for *In Rem* Restitution – Decision No. 8/2004

Josef F. (Sr.) died on 10 May 1961 in Allentsteig. Anton F. died on 4 November 1987. His entire estate was inherited pursuant to a certificate of inheritance by his brother Josef F. (Jr.). Josef F. (Jr.) died on 18 August 2000. His adoptive daughter Hui F. was officially authorized to dispose of the inheritable assets. A processing and settlement of the estate was not performed due to the lack of estate assets.

Since 1938, the partitioning and merger of the individual property parcel numbers subject of this application are as follows:

On 21 July 1964, Y6/2 and Y7 are partitioned off from EZ X2 and form the new EZ X4. Today, this EZ is privately owned. These two properties were restituted by settlement.

On 7 January 1947, Y8 is partitioned off from EZ X2 and merged into EZ X5. According to the current land register this property parcel number now forms part of EZ X6. This EZ is privately owned.

Y9, Y12, Y13 and Y14 are deleted due to their incorporation with property parcel number Y61/2. Today, this property parcel number forms part of EZ X7, which is privately owned.

Y11 is deleted due to its incorporation with property parcel number Y62. According to the cadastral map, this property parcel number now forms part of EZ X8 and within this EZ is located within property parcel number Y19/1. This EZ is owned by the Republic of Austria (Military Administration).

Y16, Y17 and Y18 are deleted due to their incorporation with property parcel number Y63. According to the cadastral map, this property parcel number now forms part of EZ X8 and within this EZ is located within property parcel number Y19/1. This EZ is owned by the Republic of Austria (Military Administration).

On 5 February 1969, Y10, Y15, Y19, Y24, Y25, Y26/1, Y26/2, Y27, Y28/1, Y28/2, Y31, Y32, Y33, Y37, Y38, Y52, Y53/1, Y54/1, Y55/1 and Y56/1 are partitioned off from EZ X2 and merged into EZ X9 of this land register.

According to the cadastral map, the property parcel numbers Y24, Y25, Y26/1, Y26/2, Y27, Y28/1, Y28/2, Y31, Y32 and Y33 of this EZ now form part of EZ X8 and within this EZ are located within property parcel number Y64/2. The property parcel numbers Y15, Y37 and Y19 form part of EZ X8, however, are located within property parcel number Y19/1. The property parcel numbers Y10 and Y52 form part of EZ X8, however, are located within property parcel number Y65/1. Y53/1, Y54/1, Y55/1 and Y56/1 form part of EZ X8. However, they are recorded as property parcel number Y70. This EZ is owned by the Republic of Austria (Military Administration). The property parcel number Y38 forms part of EZ X7, however, it is located within property parcel number Y66/1. Today, this EZ is privately owned.

Y20 and Y21 form today part of property parcel number Y68/1. Today, this property parcel number forms part of EZ X8. This EZ is owned by the Republic of Austria (Military Administration).

Y22 is deleted due to its incorporation with property parcel number Y67. Today, this property parcel number forms part of property parcel number Y68/1. Today, this property parcel number forms part of EZ X8. This EZ is owned by the Republic of Austria (Military Administration).

Y23 is deleted due to its incorporation with property parcel number Y69. Today, this property parcel number forms part of property parcel number Y70/1. Today, this property parcel number forms part of EZ X8. This EZ is owned by the Republic of Austria (Military Administration).

Schiedsinstanz für Naturalrestitution – Entscheidung Nr. 8/2004

Y8 wird am 7. Jänner 1947 der EZ X2 abgeschrieben und der EZ X5 dieses GB zugeschrieben. Laut aktuellem GB befindet sich diese Grundstücksnummer nunmehr innerhalb der EZ X6. Diese EZ steht in Privateigentum.

Y9, Y12, Y13 und Y14 werden infolge Vereinigung mit der Grundstücksnummer Y61/2 gelöscht. Diese Grundstücksnummer befindet sich heute innerhalb der EZ X7, diese befindet sich im Privateigentum.

Y11 wird infolge Vereinigung mit Grundstücksnummer Y62 gelöscht. Laut Mappenplan befindet sich diese Grundstücksnummer nunmehr innerhalb der EZ X8, hier innerhalb der Grundstücksnummer Y19/1. Diese EZ befindet sich im Eigentum der Republik Österreich (Heeresverwaltung).

Y16, Y17, Y18 werden infolge Vereinigung mit der Grundstücksnummer Y63 gelöscht. Laut Mappenplan befindet sich diese Grundstücksnummer nunmehr innerhalb der EZ X8, hier innerhalb der Grundstücksnummer Y19/1. Diese EZ befindet sich im Eigentum der Republik Österreich (Heeresverwaltung).

Y10, Y15, Y19, Y24, Y25, Y26/1, Y26/2, Y27, Y28/1, Y28/2, Y31, Y32, Y33, Y37, Y38, Y52, Y53/1, Y54/1, Y55/1, Y56/1 werden am 5. Februar 1969 von der EZ X2 abgeschrieben und der EZ X9 dieses GB zugeschrieben.

Die Grundstücksnummern Y24, Y25, Y26/1, Y26/2, Y27, Y28/1, Y28/2, Y31, Y32, Y33 dieser EZ befinden sich laut Mappenplan nunmehr innerhalb der EZ X8, hier innerhalb der Grundstücksnummer Y64/2. Die Grundstücksnummern Y15, Y37 und Y19 befinden sich innerhalb der EZ X8 jedoch in Grundstücksnummer Y19/1. Die Grundstücksnummern Y10, Y52 befinden sich innerhalb der EZ X8 jedoch in Grundstücksnummer Y65/1. Y53/1, Y54/1, Y55/1, Y56/1 befinden sich innerhalb der EZ X8 jedoch in Grundstücksnummer Y70. Diese EZ befindet sich im Eigentum der Republik Österreich (Heeresverwaltung). Die Grundstücksnummer Y38 befindet sich innerhalb der EZ X7 jedoch in Grundstücksnummer Y66/1. Diese EZ befindet sich heute im Privateigentum.

Y20, Y21 liegen heute innerhalb der Grundstücksnummer Y68/1. Diese Grundstücksnummer ist heute innerhalb der EZ X8. Diese EZ befindet sich im Eigentum der Republik Österreich (Heeresverwaltung).

Y22 wird infolge Vereinigung mit Grundstücksnummer Y67 gelöscht. Diese Grundstücksnummer liegt heute innerhalb der Grundstücksnummer Y68/1. Diese Grundstücksnummer ist heute innerhalb der EZ X8. Diese EZ befindet sich im Eigentum der Republik Österreich (Heeresverwaltung).

Y23 wird infolge Vereinigung mit Grundstücksnummer Y69 gelöscht. Diese Grundstücksnummer liegt heute innerhalb der Grundstücksnummer Y70/1. Diese Grundstücksnummer ist heute innerhalb der EZ X8. Diese EZ befindet sich im Eigentum der Republik Österreich (Heeresverwaltung).

Y29, Y30 befinden sich heute innerhalb der Grundstücksnummer Y64/3.

Y34, Y35 werden infolge Vereinigung mit der Grundstücksnummer Y71 gelöscht. Laut Mappenplan befindet sich diese Grundstücksnummer nunmehr innerhalb der EZ X8, hier innerhalb der Grundstücksnummer Y72. Diese EZ befindet sich im Eigentum der Republik Österreich (Heeresverwaltung).

Y36 wird infolge Vereinigung mit Grundstücksnummer Y73 gelöscht. Diese Grundstücksnummer liegt heute innerhalb der Grundstücksnummer Y72. Diese Grundstücksnummer ist heute innerhalb der EZ X8. Diese EZ befindet sich im Eigentum der Republik Österreich (Heeresverwaltung).

Y29 and Y30 form today part of property parcel number Y64/3.

Y34 and Y35 are deleted due to their incorporation with property parcel number Y71. According to the cadastral map, this property parcel number now forms part of EZ X8 and within this EZ is located within property parcel number Y72. This EZ is owned by the Republic of Austria (Military Administration).

Y36 is deleted due to its unification with property parcel number Y73. Today, this property parcel number forms part of property parcel number Y72. Today, this property parcel number forms part of EZ X8. This EZ is owned by the Republic of Austria (Military Administration).

On 8 December 1941, Y40 is partitioned off from this EZ and merged into EZ X10. Today, this property parcel forms part of EZ X11. This EZ is privately owned.

Y42/2: Today, according to the electronic land register, this property parcel forms part of EZ X12. Today, this property is privately owned.

Y43/1: Today, according to the electronic land register, this property forms part of EZ X12. Today, this property is privately owned.

On 16 August 1943, Y44 and Y45 are partitioned off from this EZ. The EZ X13 is introduced in its place in the land register. The property parcel number Y44 is divided into Y44/1, Y44/2 and Y44/3. Today, Y44/1 forms part of EZ X13. Y44/2 forms part of EZ X14 and Y44/3 forms part of EZ X15. Y45 forms part of EZ X13. All EZ are privately owned.

Y46: This property parcel forms part of EZ X16. This EZ is privately owned.

Today, Y47 forms part of EZ X17. Today, this EZ is privately owned.

Y48, Y49, Y50 and Y51 are deleted due to their incorporation with property parcel number Y74. According to the cadastral map, this property number now forms part of EZ X8, and within this EZ is located with property parcel number Y19/1.

On 2 July 1964, Y57/1 and Y42/2 are partitioned off this EZ. The EZ X12 is introduced in its place in the land register.

On 2 July 1964, Y57/2 and Y58 are partitioned off this EZ. The EZ X18 is introduced in its place in the land register.

Y60/1 and Y60/2 are deleted due to their incorporation with property parcel number Y75. Today, Y60/1 forms part of property parcel number Y70/1. Today, Y60/2 forms part of property parcel number Y53/1. Today, these property parcel numbers form part of EZ X8.

For the sake of completeness, the Arbitration Panel notes that the property parcel numbers Y42/2, Y43/1, Y6/2, Y7, Y58, Y57/2, Y45, Y44, Y8, Y46, Y47 and Y40 were not located on the territory of the planned military training area at the time of the sale.

5. Consideration of Evidence

The established facts are based on the presented unobjectionable documents, the open land register, the report of the Austrian Historical Commission and the submissions by the applicant.

The findings that Anton F. was interrogated and abused by the Secret State Police in St. Pölten are based on Anton F.'s statement of 16 October 1963 which was made during the victims welfare proceedings. There is some circumstantial evidence concerning these facts also in the restitution proceedings as well as in the proceedings before the victims' welfare department after 1945. In his statement of 29 May 1961, the contemporary witness, Franz M.,

Y40 wird am 8. Dezember 1941 aus dieser EZ abgeschrieben und der EZ X10 dieses GB zugeschrieben. Dieses Grundstück befindet sich heute innerhalb der EZ X11. Diese EZ ist im Privateigentum.

Y42/2: Dieses Grundstück befindet sich heute laut elektronischem GB in der EZ X12. Diese Liegenschaft befindet sich heute im Privateigentum.

Y43/1: Dieses Grundstück befindet sich heute laut elektronischem GB in der EZ X12. Diese Liegenschaft befindet sich heute im Privateigentum.

Y44 und Y45 werden am 16. August 1943 dieser EZ abgeschrieben und hierfür die EZ X13 dieses GB eröffnet. Die Grundstücksnummer Y44 wird in Y44/1, Y44/2 und Y44/3 geteilt. Y44/1 ist heute Teil der EZ X13, Y44/2 ist heute Teil der EZ X14 und Y44/3 ist heute Teil der EZ X15. Y45 ist Teil der EZ X13. Sämtliche EZ befinden sich im Privateigentum.

Y46: Dieses Grundstück befindet sich in der EZ X16. Diese EZ befindet sich im Privateigentum.

Y47 befindet sich heute innerhalb der EZ X17. Diese EZ befindet sich heute im Privateigentum.

Y48, Y49, Y50, Y51 werden infolge Vereinigung mit der Grundstücksnummer Y74 gelöscht. Diese Grundstücksnummer befindet sich laut Mappenplan nunmehr innerhalb der EZ X8, hier innerhalb der Grundstücksnummer Y19/1.

Y57/1 und Y42/2 werden am 2. Juli 1964 dieser EZ abgeschrieben und mit der neuen EZ X12 dieses GB eröffnet.

Y57/2 und Y58 werden am 2. Juli 1964 dieser EZ abgeschrieben und mit der neuen EZ X18 dieses GB eröffnet.

Y60/1, Y60/2 werden infolge Vereinigung mit der Grundstücksnummer Y75 gelöscht. Y60/1 liegt heute innerhalb der Grundstücksnummer Y70/1. Y60/2 liegt heute innerhalb der Grundstücksnummer Y53/1. Diese Grundstücksnummern sind heute innerhalb der EZ X8.

Der Vollständigkeit halber stellt die Schiedsinstanz fest, dass sich die Grundstücksnummern Y42/2, Y43/1, Y6/2, Y7, Y58, Y57/2, Y45, Y44, Y8, Y46, Y47 und Y40 zum Zeitpunkt des Verkaufes nicht auf dem Gebiet des geplanten Truppenübungsplatzes befunden haben.

5. Beweiswürdigung

Der festgestellte Sachverhalt gründet sich auf die vorgelegten unbedenklichen Urkunden, das offene GB, den Bericht der Historikerkommission und das Vorbringen der Antragstellerin.

Die Feststellung, dass Anton F. von der Gestapo in St. Pölten einvernommen und misshandelt wurde, gründet sich auf die Aussage des Anton F. am 16. Oktober 1963 im Opferfürsorge-Verfahren und es finden sich einige Indizien auf diesen Sachverhalt auch in den Rückstellungsverfahren sowie im Verfahren vor der Opferfürsorge-Behörde nach 1945. Der Zeitzeuge Franz M. hielt in seiner Aussage vom 29. Mai 1961 fest, dass in Allentsteig von einer Einvernahme Anton F.s bei der Gestapo die Rede war, außerdem sei auch anlässlich einer Parteiveranstaltung vom stellvertretenden Ortsgruppenleiter Dr. Kö. gesagt worden, dass „Anton F[...], der Verräter, wieder da sei und dafür eine Tracht Prügel bekommen hat und längere Zeit damit zu tun haben wird". Weiters gründet sich diese Feststellung auf das schlüssige Protokoll des Anton F. behandelnden Arztes Dr. Franz H. im Jahr 1959.

Die Annahme einer diskriminierenden Behandlung des Anton F. durch örtliche Vertreter des NS-Regimes erscheint nicht zuletzt durch die vom Betroffenen angegebene Motivierung

noted in his account that in Allentsteig there was talk about an interrogation of Anton F. by the Secret State Police. Besides this, during a party event the deputy local group leader, Dr. Kö., said that "Anton F[…], the traitor, was back again and he had been beaten for this and he would be aware of this for some time." These findings are further based on the conclusive protocol of 1959 by the physician who treated Anton F., Dr. Franz H.

The assumption of a discriminatory treatment of Anton F. by the local representatives of the NS regime seems conclusive when considering the motivations for his ostracism, which were stated by him as the affected person. According to Anton F.'s statements of 18 March 1959, made during the restitution proceedings regarding Josef (Sr.) and Franziska F., the assaults on his person by the Secret State Police as well as the attribution of "political unreliability" are to be seen as a revenge by local members of the NSDAP for occurrences which took place in 1934. During this period, Anton F. was imprisoned in the detention camp Wöllersdorf where he informed the police authorities about an illegal arms-cache of the NSDAP. The occurrences of 1934 are confirmed by historical documents in the Austrian State Archives. Anton F.'s interpretation that the local NSDAP, namely the local group leader O. and the NSDAP member Sa., took revenge for the "betrayal" of 1934 seems to be plausible, not least because of the fear expressed by Anton F. in as early as 1934, that his statements would – should they become known – endanger him.

Further indications of Anton F.'s "political ostracism" can also be gathered from several letters addressed to Anton F. by local authorities and party offices of the NS state, in which he is denied the issue of a local hunting licence as well as the possession of arms and ammunition. In these letters, the official prohibitions are justified with the "political unreliability" of the applicant Anton F. According to a letter of 15 January 1940 by the office of the provincial government Niederdonau, such assessment was established on the basis of an "examination by the state police".

The findings that Josef (Sr.) and Franziska F. wanted to hand over their property to their son Anton F. due to health reasons before the *Anschluss* in 1937, is taken from the appeal letter of 24 July 1960 by Anton and Josef F. (Jr.) to the Federal Ministry of Finance.

The comments about the "political pressure" on Josef and Franziska F. result from statements by Anton F. of 20 July 1959 during the victims' welfare proceedings as well as from the files regarding the restitution proceedings before the Financial Directorate after 1945: The submission of 26 September 1957 by Josef (Sr.) and Franziska F. and the testimonies of 14 April 1959 by Franz M., Barbara G. and Franz W.

The findings that Anton F.'s father as well as his brothers Josef (Jr.) and Leopold were members of NS party organizations are based upon several statements made during the restitution proceedings, especially on Josef F.'s statement of 18 March 1959. Additionally, the NSDAP memberships of Josef F. (Sr.) and his son Josef F. before and after 1938 can be verified by NSDAP personnel files from the holdings of the NS regional files. In a letter by the regional administration Niederdonau of 10 October 1940, Josef F. (Sr.) is addressed as "Pg." – party member of the NSDAP. According to Anton F.'s statements of 6 November 1963 made during the restitution proceedings regarding Marie L., his brother Josef at the instigation of the NSDAP local group leadership had performed political espionage services in one concrete case after 1938.

Statements by the claimants for restitution made in their claims of 29 June 1949 as well as in the submission of 26 September 1957 addressed to the Financial Directorate, verify that the vendors, Anton F., Josef (Sr.) and Franziska F., actually received the proceeds from the sale and in the case of Josef (Sr.) and Franziska F. could actually deposit it with the *Länderbank* Vienna.

seiner Ächtung schlüssig: Gemäß Aussagen von Anton F. im Rückstellungsverfahren Josef sen. und Franziska F. vom 18. März 1959 seien die Übergriffe auf seine Person seitens der Gestapo sowie die Zuschreibung „politischer Unzuverlässigkeit" als Revanche örtlicher NSDAP-Mitglieder für einen Vorgang im Jahr 1934 zu sehen, als Anton F. im Anhaltelager Wöllersdorf inhaftiert war und den Polizeibehörden Angaben über ein illegales Waffenlager der NSDAP machte. Der Vorgang aus dem Jahr 1934 lässt sich durch historische Dokumente im Österreichischen Staatsarchiv erhärten. Auch Anton F.s Deutung, dass sich die örtliche NSDAP, namentlich Ortsgruppenführer O. und der NSDAP-Angehörige Sa., für den „Verrat" 1934 revanchierten, erscheint plausibel, nicht zuletzt durch die bereits 1934 geäußerte Befürchtung Anton F.s, sich durch seine Angaben, sollten sie bekannt werden, großer Gefahr auszusetzen.

Weitere Hinweise auf eine „politische Ächtung" des Anton F. ergeben sich auch aus mehreren Schreiben von lokalen Behörden und Parteistellen des NS-Staates an Anton F., in welchen diesem sowohl die Ausstellung eines Bezirksjagdscheines verweigert als auch Waffen- und Munitionsbesitz verboten wird. In den Korrespondenzen werden die behördlichen Verbote mit der „politischen Unzuverlässigkeit" des Ansuchenden Anton F. begründet; eine Einschätzung, welche sich lt. Schreiben der Landeshauptmannschaft Niederdonau vom 15. Januar 1940 aufgrund „staatspolizeiliche(r) Überprüfung" ergeben habe.

Die Feststellung, dass Josef sen. und Franziska F. ihren Besitz aus gesundheitlichen Gründen bereits vor dem „Anschluss", im Jahr 1937 an ihren Sohn Anton F. übergeben wollten, ist der Berufungsschrift Anton und Josef F. jun. an das BMF vom 24. Juli 1960 entnommen.

Die Ausführungen hinsichtlich des „politischen Drucks" auf Josef und Franziska F. ergeben sich aus Aussagen von Anton F. am 20. Juli 1959 im Opferfürsorge-Verfahren sowie aus Akten zu den Rückstellungsverfahren vor der FLD nach 1945: Der Eingabe Josef sen. und Franziska F. vom 26. September 1957 und den Zeugenaussagen durch Franz M., Barbara G. und Franz W. vom 14. April 1959.

Die Feststellungen, dass der Vater von Anton F. wie auch seine Brüder Josef jun. und Leopold Mitglieder von NS-Parteiorganisationen waren, gründen sich auf mehrere Aussagen in den Rückstellungsverfahren, insbesondere die Aussage des Josef F. vom 18. März 1959. Die NSDAP-Mitgliedschaften des Josef F. sen. und seines Sohnes Josef F. vor und nach 1938 lassen sich zudem durch NSDAP-Personen-Formulare aus dem Bestand der Gauakten belegen. In einem Schreiben der Gauleitung Niederdonau vom 10. Oktober 1940 wird Josef F. sen. als „Pg." – Parteigenosse der NSDAP – tituliert. Nach Aussage von Anton F. im Rückstellungsverfahren Marie L. vom 6. November 1963 hat sein Bruder Josef auf Veranlassung der NSDAP-Ortsgruppenleitung nach 1938 in einem konkreten Fall politische Spitzeldienste geleistet.

Dass die VerkäuferInnen Anton F., Josef sen. und Franziska F. die Kaufsummen tatsächlich erhalten haben und – im Falle des Josef sen. und der Franziska F. – bei der Länderbank Wien einlegen konnten, beruht auf Aussagen der RückstellungswerberInnen in ihren Anträgen vom 29. Juni 1949 sowie in der Eingabe an die FLD vom 26. September 1957.

Die Feststellungen hinsichtlich der Lieferkonzession gründen sich auf die vorliegenden Dokumente aus den Rückstellungsverfahren. Ein zeitgenössischer dokumentarischer Beleg zu diesem Vorgang findet sich nicht. Es bleibt fraglich, inwieweit es der Ortsgruppenleitung überhaupt möglich war, eine „Entziehung" der Kantinenlieferaufträge der Familie F. zu bewirken, wie seitens der RückstellungswerberInnen behauptet wurde. Es bleibt auch offen, ob und inwieweit ein Wegfall von Lieferungsaufträgen, so sehr er als benachteiligend und un-

The findings regarding the catering concession are based on the documents presented during the restitution proceedings. A contemporary documental proof concerning this occurrence cannot be found. It remains doubtful how far it was even possible for the local group leadership to bring about a "withdrawal" of the F. family's canteen catering orders as was asserted by the applicants for restitution. It also remains open whether and in how far the cessation of delivery orders – however much it was experienced as disadvantageous and unjustified – was based on non-politically motivated measures by the military administration.

6. Juridical Appraisal

1. Hereditary Title

In accordance with Sec. 27 (2) of the GSF Law, applying *mutatis mutandis* the provisions of the (Austrian) General Civil Code, heirs are eligible to file an application. The applicant is the adoptive daughter of Josef F. Josef F. is the heir to his brother Anton F. Anton F. and Josef F. are the sons of Josef (Sr.) and Franziska F. The Arbitration Panel assumes that in accordance with the afore-cited provision, the proof of the legal hereditary title is sufficient for the eligibility to file applications, if no stronger reasons for appeal are presented. The applicant is the adoptive daughter of a descendant or heir of the originally aggrieved person, hence, his legal heiress. Evidence denying this hereditary title was not presented. Due to the established hereditary title, the Arbitration Panel regards the applicant as eligible to file applications.

2. Persecution

Pursuant to Sec. 27 of the GSF Law, persons and their heirs are eligible to file an application if one of the listed reasons for persecution – namely political grounds, grounds of origin, grounds of religion, sexual orientation, physical or mental handicap or accusations of so-called asociality – applies or if they left the country to escape such persecution. The listing of the reasons for persecution is exhaustive and, as apart from the National Fund Law, does not contain any further elements on which the applicant could base her submission.

A persecution on political grounds of an aggrieved person can also exist if the originally aggrieved person belonged to a group of persons which was discriminated against by National Socialism (for example, organized ideological opponents of National Socialism) or if he/she was actually subjected to discriminatory actions or to acts of persecution by being counted amongst the group of persons affected by the discriminatory intent of the relevant measure.

None of the originally aggrieved persons belong to a group of persons discriminated against by National Socialism.

It has to be differentiated between the persecution of Josef and Franziska F. and the persecution of Anton F. when trying to establish whether discriminatory actions were actually carried out.

In contemporary documents as well as in documents generated from restitution proceedings after 1945, indications are found which support the claim of Anton F.'s political persecution.

The abovementioned documents and the corresponding recollections of contemporary witnesses allow one to draw the conclusion that during the phase of National Socialism between 1938 and 1945, Anton F. was actually subjected to discriminatory actions in such a manner that he was repeatedly subjugated to the arbitrariness and violent measures of the National Socialist regime. As such, it can be assumed that Anton F. was politically persecuted. Also, a

gerechtfertigt erlebt wurde, in nicht politisch motivierten Handlungen der Heeresverwaltung begründet war.

6. Rechtliche Beurteilung

1. Erbrecht

Gem. § 27 Abs 2 EF-G sind ErbInnen in sinngemäßer Anwendung der Bestimmungen des Allgemeinen Bürgerlichen Gesetzbuches (ABGB) antragsberechtigt. Die Antragstellerin ist die Adoptivtochter des Josef F. Josef F. ist der Erbe seines Bruders Anton F. Anton F. und Josef F. sind die Söhne von Josef sen. und Franziska F. Die Schiedsinstanz geht davon aus, dass nach der vorzitierten Bestimmung der Nachweis des gesetzlichen Erbrechts, wenn nicht stärkere Berufungsgründe dargetan werden, für die Antragsberechtigung ausreichend ist. Die Antragstellerin ist die Adoptivtochter eines Deszendenten bzw. Erben der ursprünglich Geschädigten, somit deren gesetzliche Erbin. Es wurde kein diesem Erbrecht entgegenstehender Nachweis vorgelegt. Hiermit sieht die Schiedsinstanz die Antragsberechtigung der Antragstellerin aufgrund des nachgewiesenen Erbrechts als gegeben an.

2. Verfolgung

Gemäß § 27 EF-G sind Personen und deren ErbInnen antragsberechtigt, wenn einer der aufgelisteten Verfolgungsgründe, nämlich Verfolgung aus politischen Gründen, aus Gründen der Abstammung, Religion, Nationalität, sexuellen Orientierung, aufgrund einer körperlichen oder geistigen Behinderung oder aufgrund des Vorwurfes der so genannten Asozialität, vorliegt bzw. diese das Land verlassen haben, um einer solchen Verfolgung zu entgehen. Die Aufzählung der Verfolgungsgründe ist taxativ und enthält im Unterschied zum Nationalfondsgesetz keine weiteren Tatbestände, auf die die Antragstellerin ihr Begehren stützen könnte.

Eine Verfolgung des Geschädigten aus politischen Gründen kann auch dann gegeben sein, wenn der ursprünglich Geschädigte einer vom Nationalsozialismus diskriminierten Personengruppe (i.e. organisierte weltanschauliche Gegner des Nationalsozialismus) zugehörig, oder wenn er tatsächlich diskriminierenden Handlungen unterworfen oder einer Verfolgungshandlung ausgesetzt war, indem er dem von der diskriminierenden Zielsetzung der jeweiligen Maßnahme gemeinten Personenkreis zugerechnet wurde.

Keiner der ursprünglich Geschädigten gehört einer vom Nationalsozialismus diskriminierten Personengruppe an.

Hinsichtlich der Frage, ob tatsächlich diskriminierende Handlungen gesetzt wurden, ist einerseits zwischen der Verfolgung des Josef und der Franziska F. und der Verfolgung des Anton F. zu unterscheiden.

In Bezug auf Anton F. finden sich sowohl in zeitgenössischen Dokumenten als auch in jenen zu den Rückstellungsverfahren nach 1945 Hinweise, welche die Behauptung einer auf seine Person bezogenen politischen Verfolgung abstützen.

Die oben genannten Dokumente und diesbezüglichen ZeitzeugInnenerinnerungen lassen den Schluss zu, dass Anton F. während der NS-Phase 1938 bis 1945 tatsächlich diskriminierenden Handlungen derart ausgesetzt war, dass er persönlich der Willkür und den Gewaltmitteln des NS-Regimes wiederholt unterworfen wurde. Insofern kann eine politische Verfolgung des Anton F. als gegeben angenommen werden. Auch wird eine Verfolgung des Anton F. durch die Sachverhaltsfeststellung der Bundesregierung außer Streit gestellt.

persecution of Anton F. is seen as indisputable by the establishment of facts by the Federal Government.

Regarding the examination of the persecution of Franziska and Josef. (Sr.), the handed down indications of such actions are not as conclusive as in Anton F.'s case.

The handed down contemporary documents, i.e. the files regarding the property sale to the German Settlement Society as well as a letter by the regional administration Niederdonau to Josef F. (Sr.), do not indicate that Anton F.'s parents were politically discriminated against in the same way as Anton F.

Indications of a possible political persecution of Anton F.'s parents can be found in the restitution proceedings before the Financial Directorate after 1945. The claimants for restitution as well as their sons and further interrogated contemporary witnesses declare that Anton F.'s parents were also affected by the political ostracism of their son. The "political pressure" and the "total discrimination by the local population" starting from their son's persecution had an effect on the entire family.

The F. family's restaurant was avoided and the deliveries from the restaurant to the army canteen were prevented. Finally, the parents, under "extreme political pressure", saw themselves forced to sell the properties situated within the planned military training area as well as the local properties to the German Settlement Society.

How far the earlier mentioned "political pressure" also represents a persecution as defined by the GSF Law is to be established on the basis of the presented documents as well as in the light of the contemporary knowledge about persecution and confiscation practices by the National Socialist state.

The only concrete indications of a possible discriminatory action against Anton F.'s parents are related to the withdrawal of a catering concession as well as to the seizure of the properties. However, according to the view of the Arbitration Panel, seizures *per se* do not necessarily have to represent acts of persecution. If a person does not belong to any persecuted group and if this person was not actually subjected to discriminatory actions, a seizure would qualify as a political persecution if it was shown to be plausible that the seizure was a deliberate act by the National Socialist regime and its representatives whose intention in carrying out the act was to persecute an individual.

Neither their local living conditions, as recalled in the restitution proceedings after 1945, nor the present contemporary files dating from the National Socialist phase indicate a clear political intent to persecute in regard to Josef (Sr.) and Franziska F. and to the entire F. family. The relevant statements are too contradictory to allow one to derive the existence of a persecution during which the mentioned persons were subjected to the arbitrariness and the violent measures of the National Socialist regime.

In the restitution proceedings, contradictory statements are found regarding the question whether Josef (Sr.) and Franziska F. were actually subjected to political persecution by representatives of the National Socialist state after 1938. On the one hand, in the victims welfare proceedings Anton F. stated that Josef (Sr.) and Franziska F. were subjected to "continuous threats, harassment and boycott". The witness Franz M. stated during the restitution proceedings "that the F[…] family was shunned by the NSDAP members in Allentsteig because of their son, Anton F[…]'s betrayal." On the other hand, in their statements of 18 March 1959, Anton F. as well as Josef F. noted that between 1938 and 1945 their parents "were no longer politically persecuted" and that they "have never been threatened with a concentration camp". From further statements made during the restitution proceedings as well as from contempo-

Hinsichtlich einer zu prüfenden Verfolgung von Franziska und Josef sen. F. sind die überlieferten Hinweise auf entsprechende Handlungen nicht von derselben Schlüssigkeit wie im Fall des Anton F.

Die überlieferten zeitgenössischen Dokumente, das sind die Unterlagen zum Liegenschaftsverkauf an die DAG sowie ein Schreiben der Gauleitung Niederdonau an Josef F. sen., geben keinen Hinweis darauf, dass die Eltern von Anton F. in ähnlicher Weise wie dieser politisch diskriminiert wurden.

Anhaltspunkte für eine mögliche politische Verfolgung der Eltern von Anton F. finden sich in den Rückstellungsverfahren vor der FLD nach 1945. Sowohl die RückstellungswerberInnen als auch ihre Söhne sowie weitere einvernommene ZeitzeugInnen geben an, dass auch die Eltern von Anton F. durch die politische Ächtung ihres Sohnes in Mitleidenschaft gezogen wurden. Der auf sie ausgeübte „politische Druck" bzw. die „völlige Diskriminierung durch die Ortsbevölkerung" habe sich, von der Verfolgung ihres Sohnes ausgehend, auf die gesamte Familie ausgewirkt.

Das Gasthaus der Familie F. sei gemieden worden, die Lieferungen der Gastwirtschaft an die Heereskantine seien unterbunden worden, schließlich hätten sich die Eltern unter dem „schwersten politischen Druck" gezwungen gesehen, nicht nur die innerhalb des geplanten Truppenübungsplatzes gelegenen, sondern auch die innerörtlich gelegenen Grundstücke an die DAG zu verkaufen.

Inwieweit nun der besagte „politische Druck" auch eine Verfolgung im Sinne des EF-G darstellt, ist anhand der vorliegenden Dokumente sowie im Lichte der gegenwärtigen Kenntnisse zur Verfolgungs- und Entziehungspraxis im NS-Staat zu prüfen.

Die einzigen Konkretisierungen hinsichtlich einer möglicherweise diskriminierenden Handlung gegenüber den Eltern von Anton F. beziehen sich auf den Entzug einer Lieferkonzession sowie die Entziehung der Liegenschaften. Nach Auffassung der Schiedsinstanz können allerdings in Entziehungen per se noch keine Verfolgungshandlungen erblickt werden. Gehört eine Person keiner verfolgten Personengruppe an und ist sie auch nicht tatsächlich diskriminierenden Handlungen unterworfen gewesen, so kann einer Entziehung dann politische Verfolgungsqualität zukommen, wenn sie als Ausdruck einer personenbezogenen Verfolgungsabsicht des nationalsozialistischen Regimes (bzw. seiner Vertreter) plausibel gemacht würde.

Weder lässt sich aus der örtlichen Lebenssituation, wie sie in den gegenständlichen Rückstellungsverfahren nach 1945 geschildert wurde, noch aus den vorliegenden zeitgenössischen Akten der NS-Phase eine deutliche politische Verfolgungsabsicht in Bezug auf die Personen Josef sen. und Franziska F. bzw. die Familie F. im Ganzen ersehen. Die entsprechenden Angaben sind zu widersprüchlich, um daraus eine Verfolgung ableiten zu können, im Zuge derer die besagten Personen der Willkür und den Gewaltmitteln des NS-Regime unterworfen worden wären.

Zur Frage, ob Josef sen. und Franziska F. nach 1938 tatsächlich einer politischen Verfolgung durch VertreterInnen des NS-Staates ausgesetzt waren, finden sich in den Rückstellungsverfahren einander widersprechende Aussagen. Einerseits wurde von Anton F. im Opferfürsorge-Verfahren festgehalten, dass Josef sen. und Franziska F. „dauernden Drohungen, Schikane und Boykott" ausgesetzt waren und wurde vom Zeugen Franz M. im Rückstellungsverfahren ausgesagt „dass die Familie F[...] wegen des Verrates des Sohnes Anton F[...] in Allentsteig von den Mitgliedern der NSDAP gemieden wurde"; andererseits hielten sowohl Anton F. als auch Josef F. in ihren Aussagen vom 18. März 1959 fest, dass ihre Eltern 1938

rary documents dating prior to 1945, namely NSDAP personnel files (regional files), it has become known that Josef F. (Sr.) and his sons had joined the NSDAP before the *Anschluss* and/or that they supported the illegal National Socialist movement. Anton F. also supported the illegal National Socialist movement. Further, the files of the regional personnel department prove that after the *Anschluss* Josef F. (Sr.) as well as his son Josef F. renewed their membership which had existed prior to 1938. The renewal took place in October 1938 with the explicit recommendation by the local group leadership, namely by Fritz O.

With respect to the property seizure it can firstly be noted that the construction of the military training area as such as well as the associated sale and purchase proceedings, cannot be regarded as the expression of a desire to persecute the concerned property owners. Also, in Josef (Sr.)'s and Franziska F.'s case, the sale took place according to normal procedures. This conclusion can be drawn when inspecting the files. The incorporation of those properties of EZ X2, which were situated outside the military training area in the central local area of Allentsteig may indicate a possibly discriminatory treatment of the F. vendors. It seems that after the purchase in 1939 these properties were not used for military purposes. Some of these parcels were sold to private owners after the purchase by the German Armed Forces. According to statements by Josef (Sr.) and Franziska F., they were forced to sell the properties located within the village due to the political pressure from the local NSDAP.

This assessment is inconsistent with other circumstances and facts:

The property sale took place during a relatively early phase of the resettlement during which realistic purchase prices were established and for the most part replacement properties were available. The purchase price of 143,000 Reichsmark awarded to the vendors as well as the fact that the proceeds from the sale actually did reach the vendors and were entered with the *Länderbank* Vienna suggests a thoroughly customary course of this transaction. According to statements by the applicants for restitution, in 1945 the proceeds from the sale were still in the account.

There is no further conclusive evidence for the repeated claim that the sale of the properties situated outside the military training zone, took place only on account of pressure by the local NSDAP.

It must be noted that the local NSDAP was not responsible for the selection of suitable properties for acquisition and for the realization of the purchases. Rather, the German Settlement Society as well as the military administration had this responsibility. Also, the purchase of properties within the village formed part of the purchases which the German Settlement Society had carried out for the army. The F. family's properties were not the only ones affected by this. Based on the present sources and literature, especially concerning the acquisition activities of the German Settlement Society within the Municipality of Allentsteig, a coincidence of interests of the NSDAP and the German Settlement Society or of the military administration cannot be established. It is more likely that the contrary would have been the case: The municipal representatives of Allentsteig, namely mayor O., feared that considerable economic losses would be caused by the construction of the military training area as well as by the associated acquisitions of the properties situated in the Allentsteig area. Contemporary sources show that in 1942 mayor O. directed a list for payment to the Reich Treasury (Army) which set out the lost business tax. The F. family's restaurant and bakery is also to be found among the businesses listed by O., for which the unpaid business tax was to be settled.

Even if it can be assumed that when the exact borders within the local area were created and/or substitute properties were identified local arrangements had been made between representatives of the German Settlement Society, party offices and the NS district farming com-

bis 1945 „nicht mehr politisch verfolgt" waren bzw. dass ihnen „nie mit dem KZ gedroht" wurde. Aus weiteren Aussagen im Rückstellungsverfahren sowie aus zeitgenössischen Dokumenten vor 1945, namentlich NSDAP-Personalakten (Gauakten) ist bekannt geworden, dass Josef F. sen. und seine Söhne vor dem „Anschluss" der NSDAP beigetreten waren bzw. die illegale NS-Bewegung unterstützten; letzteres trifft auch auf Anton F. zu. Aus den Akten des Gaupersonalamtes ist überdies nachgewiesen, dass sowohl Josef F. sen. wie auch dessen Sohn Josef F. ihre vor 1938 bestehende Mitgliedschaft nach dem „Anschluss" erneuerten. Letzteres erfolgte mit ausdrücklicher Befürwortung durch die Ortsgruppenleitung noch im Oktober 1938, namentlich durch Fritz O.

Hinsichtlich der Liegenschaftsentziehung kann zunächst festgehalten werden, dass die Anlage des Truppenübungsplatzes als solche sowie die daran anknüpfenden Verkaufs- bzw. Ankaufsvorgänge nicht als Ausdruck eines Willens gelten können, die betroffenen GrundstückseigentümerInnen zu verfolgen. Auch der Verkaufsvorgang im Falle Josef sen. und Franziska F. erfolgte den Akten nach zu schließen in üblicher Weise. Auf eine möglicherweise diskriminierende Behandlung der Verkäufer F. könnte der Einbezug jener Grundstücke der EZ X2 hinweisen, welche außerhalb des Truppenübungsplatz im zentralen Ortsbereich von Allentsteig lagen. Für diese Grundstücke scheint nach Ankauf 1939 keine militärische Verwendung erfolgt zu sein und wurden einige dieser Parzellen auch nach dem Ankauf durch die Wehrmacht an private Eigentümer weiterveräußert. Laut Aussagen von Josef sen. und Franziska F. waren sie zu den Verkäufen der im Ort gelegenen Grundstücke durch den politischen Druck der örtlichen NSDAP gezwungen.

Dieser Einschätzung stehen andere Umstände entgegen:

Der Liegenschaftsverkauf erfolgte in einer relativ frühen Phase der Aussiedlung, während welcher reale Kaufpreise erlegt wurden und weitgehend Ersatzgrundstücke zur Verfügung standen. Der den VerkauterInnen zugesprochene Kaufpreis von 143.000,– Reichsmark sowie der Umstand, dass die Kaufsumme den VerkäuferInnen tatsächlich zugekommen ist und bei der Länderbank Wien verbucht werden konnte, spricht eher für einen durchaus üblichen Ablauf dieser Transaktion. Nach Angaben der RückstellungswerberInnen befand sich die Kaufsumme 1945 noch auf dem Konto.

Für die wiederholte Behauptung, dass der Verkauf der außerhalb des Truppenübungsplatzes gelegenen Grundstücke nur auf Druck der örtlichen NSDAP erfolgte, finden sich keine weiteren schlüssigen Belege.

Es ist festzuhalten, dass für die Ausscheidung anzukaufender Liegenschaften und die Durchführung der Ankäufe nicht die örtliche NSDAP, sondern die DAG sowie die Heeresverwaltung zuständig waren. Auch der Ankauf innerörtlicher Liegenschaften war Bestandteil der von der DAG vorgenommenen Ankäufe für das Heer. Die Liegenschaften der Familie F. waren nicht die einzigen, die davon betroffen waren. Gerade in Bezug auf die Ankaufstätigkeit der DAG im Bereich der Gemeinde Allentsteig kann aufgrund vorliegender Quellen und Literatur keine Interessenkoinzidenz von NSDAP und DAG bzw. Heeresverwaltung festgestellt werden. Es dürfte eher das Gegenteil der Fall gewesen sein: Die Gemeindevertretung von Allentsteig, namentlich Bürgermeister O., befürchteten erhebliche wirtschaftliche Einbußen durch die Anlage des Truppenübungsplatzes sowie die damit verbundenen Liegenschaftsankäufe im Ortsgebiet Allentsteig. Aus zeitgenössischen Quellen ergeht, dass Bürgermeister O. im Jahr 1942 zur Abgeltung entgangener Gewerbesteuern eine entsprechende Aufstellung an den Reichsfiskus (Heer) richtete. Unter den von O. aufgelisteten Betrieben, deren nicht mehr erbrachte Gewerbesteuer abzugelten war, finden sich auch Gastwirtschaft und Bäckerei der Familie F.

munity, the conclusion can be drawn that each purchase of properties which were situated outside of the military training area meant a financial expense for the army. This expense had to be explained objectively – at least by the German Settlement Society. It seems rather unlikely that during the property acquisition the army (military district command Vienna) would have been influenced by political considerations and/or by a desire to extract revenge on a local level.

It must be noted that even if the district farming community together with the local NSDAP informally or prior to a regular application procedure, was responsible for the assessment of the suitability for resettlement, they dismissed an initial "application for resettlement" by Josef (Sr.) and Franziska F. since the remaining bakery and restaurant were considered "viable". Only a second application for resettlement was later approved.

Also the statement which was repeatedly made by the claimants for restitution, Josef (Sr.) and Franziska F., saying that they had been pressured to sell, among other things, due to their son Anton F.'s politically restricted economic freedom and freedom to conduct business transactions, can be questioned. On account of the presented documents, it has to be assumed that the means for the economic management as well as the F. parents' financial situation had already been very restricted due to "non-political" reasons: their personal health situation and the sale of almost the entire farm, which was situated within the military training area. According to the statement made by Josef F. (Jr.) during the restitution proceedings of 18 March 1959, his parents had already thought about handing over their property in 1937/38 since, for health reasons, they regarded themselves as incapable of running the property.

Neither the construction of the military training area as such, nor the way the property purchases with regard to (Sr.) and Franziska F. were carried out, point to a persecution which was directed at the owners.

Hence, a persecution for political reasons of Josef and Franziska F. as defined by Sec. 27 of the GSF Law did not exist.

As such, the application for restitution of the properties EZ X3 and X2 KG Allentsteig was to be rejected.

3. Public Property

a) "Federal Property"

The prerequisite of "publicly-owned property" regarding the historical property EZ X1 KG Allentsteig of Anton F. is fulfilled since on 17 January 2001 the property was owned by the Republic of Austria.

b) Seizure on the Basis of one of the listed Grounds for Persecution

In accordance with Sec. 28 (1) item 1 of the GSF Law the property must have been seized from the previous owner between 12 March 1938 and 9 May 1945 for the above-mentioned grounds for persecution.

Hence, the main question is whether the seizure of the property EZ X1 KG Allentsteig was adequately connected to the persecution of Anton F. or whether the seizure only took place because the properties were located within the boundaries of the planned military training area.

The seizure in itself does not show a connection to the persecution. The persecution and seizure of the property have to be at least causally connected. Hence, a seizure has to be the expression of a persecution. The construction of a military training area and the associated necessary property purchases as such do not allow one to conclude a connection of this kind.

Selbst wenn angenommen werden kann, dass bei der genauen Grenzziehung im Ortsgebiet bzw. hinsichtlich der vorzusehenden Ersatzgrundstücke örtliche Absprachen der DAG-Vertreter mit Parteistellen und der NS-Kreisbauernschaft erfolgten, ist davon auszugehen, dass jeder Ankauf von außerhalb des Truppenübungsplatzes gelegenen Grundstücken eine finanzielle Aufwendung des Heeres bedeutete und diese – jedenfalls von Seiten der DAG – sachlich zu begründen war. Dass sich das Heer (Wehrkreiskommando Wien) durch politische Rücksichten bzw. Revanchebedürfnisse lokaler Provenienz beim Grundstückskauf hätte leiten lassen, erscheint eher unwahrscheinlich.

Selbst wenn die Kreisbauernschaft informell bzw. im Vorfeld eines regulären Antragsverfahrens und in Verbindung mit der örtlichen NSDAP für die Einschätzung der Eignung zur Aussiedlung zuständig war, ist festzuhalten, dass sie einen ersten „Umsiedlungsantrag" von Josef sen. u. Franziska F. abgelehnt hat, da die verbliebene Bäckerei und Gastwirtschaft „lebensfähig" gewesen seien. Erst ein zweiter Umsiedlungsantrag ist dann genehmigt worden.

Auch die wiederholt getroffene Feststellung der RückstellungswerberInnen Josef sen. und Franziska F., dass sie sich unter anderem aufgrund der politisch eingeschränkten Erwerbs- und Geschäftsfreiheit ihres Sohnes Anton F. zum Verkauf an die DAG genötigt sahen, kann hinterfragt werden. Aufgrund der vorliegenden Dokumente ist anzunehmen, dass das Vermögen zur Wirtschaftsführung und die Ertragslage der Eltern F. bereits durch „unpolitische" Gründe sehr eingeschränkt war: Durch ihre eigene gesundheitliche Verfassung sowie durch den Verkauf nahezu der gesamten Landwirtschaft innerhalb des Truppenübungsplatzes. Nach Aussage von Josef F. jun. im Rückstellungsverfahren vom 18. März 1959 überlegten seine Eltern bereits 1937/38, ihren Besitz zu übergeben, da sie sich zu dessen Bewirtschaftung aus gesundheitlichen Gründen nicht mehr in der Lage sahen.

Weder die Anlage des Truppenübungsplatzes als solche noch die Durchführung der Liegenschaftsankäufe in Bezug auf Josef sen. und Franziska F. geben Aufschluss über eine auf die EigentümerInnen abzielende Verfolgung.

Eine Verfolgung aus politischen Gründen von Josef und Franziska F. iSd § 27 EF-G lag daher nicht vor.

Der Antrag auf Rückstellung der Liegenschaften EZ X3 und X2, KG Allentsteig war daher abzulehnen.

3. Öffentliches Vermögen

a) „Bundeseigentum"

Hinsichtlich der historischen Liegenschaft EZ X1, KG Allentsteig des Anton F., ist die Voraussetzung des „öffentlichen Eigentums" erfüllt, da das Grundstück am 17. Jänner 2001 im Eigentum der Republik Österreich stand.

b) Entzug aus einem der aufgezählten Verfolgungsgründe

Gemäß § 28 Abs 1 Z 1 EF-G muss die Liegenschaft zwischen 12. März 1938 und 9. Mai 1945 den früheren EigentümerInnen aus oben genannten Verfolgungsgründen entzogen worden sein.

Die Hauptfrage ist daher, ob die Entziehung der Liegenschaft EZ X1, KG Allentsteig in adäquatem Zusammenhang mit der Verfolgung des Anton F. stand oder ob die Entziehung nur wegen der Lage der Liegenschaften im Raum des geplanten Truppenübungsplatzes erfolgte.

Regarding the construction of the military training area Döllersheim, possibly even regarding the *Gesetz über die Landbeschaffung zum Zwecke der Wehrmacht (GBlÖ. 313/38)* ("Law on Land Procurement for purposes of the German Armed Forces" [Austrian Law Gazette 313/38]), it must be explained that the goal of the above-mentioned National Socialist law as well as the construction of the military training area Döllersheim was not directed against the aggrieved parties, but served the purposes of war preparation. The construction of the military training area renders the aggrieved persons as victims of National Socialist injustice. However, the construction of the military training area did not serve the seizure of properties for political reasons as defined by the GSF Law.

All of Anton F.'s properties were situated within the boundaries of the planned military training area and had to be sold by him regardless of a persecution of the originally aggrieved person. Also, the sale was carried out in such a manner that a discriminatory treatment of the vendor cannot be concluded. As such, a connection between the sale and Anton F.'s persecution does not exist.

Hence, the application for restitution of the property EZ X1, KG Allentsteig was to be rejected.

Dr. Josef Aicher, university professor, Chairman
Dr.Dr.h.c. Erich Kussbach, LL.M., honorary professor and retired ambassador
MMag. Dr. August Reinisch, LL.M., university professor

Der Entzug für sich alleine zeigt noch keinen Zusammenhang mit der Verfolgung. Vorliegen muss zumindest ein ursächlicher Zusammenhang zwischen Verfolgung und Liegenschaftsentzug, sohin eine Entziehung, die der Verfolgung Ausdruck verleiht. Aus der Anlage eines Truppenübungsplatzes und den damit notwendig werdenden Liegenschaftsankäufen als solchen kann nicht auf einen derartigen Zusammenhang geschlossen werden.

Hinsichtlich der Anlegung des Truppenübungsplatzes Döllersheim, eventuell sogar des Gesetzes über die Landbeschaffung zum Zwecke der Wehrmacht (GBlÖ 313/38) ist auszuführen, dass die Zielsetzung obgenannten nationalsozialistischen Gesetzes als auch die Errichtung des Truppenübungsplatzes Döllersheim sich nicht gegen die Geschädigten richteten, sondern der Kriegsvorbereitung dienten. Die Anlage des Truppenübungsplatzes macht die Geschädigten zu Betroffenen nationalsozialistischen Unrechts, diente aber nicht zum Entzug von Liegenschaften aus politischen Gründen im Sinne des EF-G.

Sämtliche Grundstücke des Anton F. lagen innerhalb des geplanten Truppenübungsplatzes und mussten deshalb unabhängig von einer Verfolgung des ursprünglichen Geschädigten durch diesen verkauft werden. Auch die Durchführung des Verkaufes erfolgte in einer Weise, die auf keine diskriminierende Behandlung des Verkäufers schließen lässt. Daher liegt ein Zusammenhang zwischen dem Verkauf und der Verfolgung des Anton F. nicht vor.

Der Antrag auf Rückstellung der Liegenschaft EZ X1, KG Allentsteig war daher abzulehnen.

o.Univ.-Prof. Dr. Josef Aicher, Vorsitzender
Honorarprofessor Dr.Dr.h.c. Erich Kussbach LL.M., Botschafter i.R.
ao.Univ.-Prof. MMag. Dr. August Reinisch LL.M.

Press Release Decision No. 9/2005[1]

Vienna, Hütteldorf

On 7 June 2005, the Arbitration Panel for *In Rem* Restitution rejected an application for restitution of a property owned by the Federation (Bundesimmobiliengesellschaft m.b.H.) in Vienna-Hütteldorf. According to the Arbitration Panel there were no indications for a political persecution of the original owners of the property.

In March 1938, Marie M.-A. was the sole owner of the 54,000 m^2 property on which a late baroque palace with several agricultural buildings was located. Pursuant to the purchase contract of 7 July and the addendum of 15 September 1938 Marie M.-A. sold the property, which was heavily encumbered with several liens, to the "*Reichsführer-SS* and the Head of the German Police (Police Administration)" for a total of 580,000 Reichsmark. At the end of the war, the French occupying powers took over the property and set up the French High Commissioner's office in the building.

In March 1954, the three joint heirs of Marie M.-A., Heinrich M.-A. (Jr.), Maria B. and Flora P., submitted written waivers. In these waivers they confirmed that the property in question had been duly sold pursuant to a purchase contract with the German Reich (Police Administration), the "purchase contract was concluded voluntarily without any pressure or other manipulations", the agreed purchase price had reflected the true value of the property and the purchase price had been paid, although late, in its entirety. The heirs further stated that they would not assert any claims against the purchaser or his/her legal successor resulting from an earlier legal entitlement to restitution. In the course of the implementation of the *Staatsvertrag* ("State Treaty") of 1955, the ownership title to the property passed to the Republic of Austria in August 1957. The grandson of Marie M.-A. applied for the restitution of the property.

In its juridical appraisal, the Arbitration Panel had to examine if the originally aggrieved person was politically persecuted as defined in Sec. 27 of the GSF Law. The purchase contract did not include any exceptional clauses and otherwise corresponded to the standard and unobjectionable purchase contracts. Also, the retrospective certification of the originally aggrieved person as being "Aryan" allows – in the view of the Arbitration Panel – the conclusion that there was no *per se* affiliation to a group of persons which was discriminated against by National Socialism or politically persecuted. As the Arbitration Panel was unable to establish whether Marie M.-A. was subjected to pressure or means of force, this circumstance could not be considered as an actual discriminatory action. Hence, the application was to be rejected due to the lack of persecution of the original owner.

For use by media; not legally binding upon the Arbitration Panel for In Rem Restitution.

---

[1] See also *decision number 9a/2008* in conjunction with this decision.

Pressemitteilung Entscheidung Nr. 9/2005[1]

Wien, Hütteldorf

Die Schiedsinstanz für Naturalrestitution lehnte am 7. Juni 2005 den Antrag auf Rückstellung einer im Eigentum des Bundes (Bundesimmobiliengesellschaft m.b.H.) stehenden Liegenschaft in Wien-Hütteldorf ab. Nach Ansicht der Schiedsinstanz lagen keine Hinweise auf eine politische Verfolgung der ursprünglichen Liegenschaftseigentümer vor.

Die mit einem spätbarocken Schloss und mehreren Wirtschaftsgebäuden bebaute, 54.000 m^2 große Liegenschaft befand sich im März 1938 im Alleineigentum von Marie M.-A. Mit Kaufvertrag vom 7. Juli und Nachtrag vom 15. September 1938 verkaufte Marie M.-A. die mit mehreren Pfandrechten schwer belastete Liegenschaft an den „Reichsführer-SS und Chef der Deutschen Polizei (Polizeiverwaltung)" zu einem Gesamtkaufpreis von 580.000,– Reichsmark. Bei Kriegsende übernahm die französische Besatzungsmacht die Liegenschaft und errichtete in dem Gebäude das französische Hochkommissariat.

Im März 1954 gaben die drei Miterben nach Marie M.-A., Heinrich M.-A. jun., Maria B. und Flora P., schriftliche Verzichtserklärungen ab. In diesen bestätigten sie, dass die gegenständliche Liegenschaft im Jahr 1938 durch ordnungsgemäßen Kaufvertrag mit dem Deutschen Reich (Polizeiverwaltung) verkauft worden sei, „der Kaufvertrag ohne jeglichen Zwang oder sonstige Beeinflussung freiwillig abgeschlossen wurde", der vereinbarte Kaufpreis dem wahren Wert des Objekts entsprochen und der Kaufpreis zwar verspätet, aber zur Gänze ausbezahlt worden sei. Die Erben gaben weiters an, keinerlei Ansprüche aus dem Titel einer Rückstellung gegen den Käufer oder deren Rechtsnachfolger zu stellen. Im Zuge der Umsetzung des Staatsvertrags von 1955 ging das Eigentumsrecht an der Liegenschaft im August 1957 an die Republik Österreich über. Der Enkel von Marie M.-A. beantragte die Rückstellung der Liegenschaft.

In ihrer rechtlichen Beurteilung hatte die Schiedsinstanz zu prüfen, ob eine politische Verfolgung der ursprünglich Geschädigten im Sinne des § 27 Entschädigungsfondsgesetz vorliegt. Der Kaufvertrag beinhaltete keine außergewöhnlichen Vertragsklauseln und entsprach auch sonst den unbedenklichen Kaufverträgen. Auch die nachträgliche Beurkundung, dass die ursprünglich Geschädigte „Arierin" war, lässt nach Ansicht der Schiedsinstanz den Schluss zu, dass die Zugehörigkeit zu einer vom Nationalsozialismus diskriminierten oder politisch verfolgten Personengruppe nicht per se vorgelegen hat. Da die Schiedsinstanz nicht feststellen konnte, ob Marie M.-A. einer Druckausübung oder dem Einsatz von Zwangsmitteln ausgesetzt war, konnte dieser Umstand nicht als tatsächlich diskriminierende Handlung gewertet werden. Der Antrag war somit mangels Verfolgung der ursprünglichen Eigentümerin abzulehnen.

Zur Verwendung durch die Medien bestimmter Text, der die Schiedsinstanz nicht bindet.

---

[1] Zu dieser Entscheidung siehe auch *Entscheidung Nr. 9a/2008*.

Arbitration Panel for *In Rem* Restitution

Decision number 9/2005[1]

The Arbitration Panel for *In Rem* Restitution (Chairman Dr. Josef Aicher, university professor, and Dr.Dr.h.c. Erich Kussbach LL.M., retired ambassador and honorary professor, as well as MMag. Dr. August Reinisch LL.M, university professor, as Members) decided on 7 June 2005 in the legal matter of Dr. Rudolf P., represented by Mag. Ewald Scheucher, regarding *in rem* restitution of the property L.-straße 429, register number ("EZ") X1 and EZ X2, cadastral district ("KG") Hütteldorf:

The application for *in rem* restitution of the property is rejected.

Reasons:

1. Submission by the Applicant

1 In the application of 28 May 2003, the applicant sought the restitution of the property L.-straße 429, EZ X1 and EZ X2, KG Hütteldorf and asserted the following:

2 On 12 October 1894, the property located at house 49, L.-straße 429, Vienna XIV. had been jointly purchased from the E. brothers by Dr. Heinrich M.-A. (Sr.) and his wife Marie M.-A., née Po., each of them taking a 50 % share. Pursuant to the purchase contract of 8 January 1929, Marie M.-A. had purchased EZ X1 from her husband, making her the sole proprietor of the estate.

3 In 1938, the property including the house had not been sold voluntarily but under duress. During the negotiations with the representatives which were authorized by the *Reichsführer-SS* Himmler, it had transpired that the property parcel was needed for the construction of police barracks. Significant psychological stress had been imposed through the presence of several SS-men. On the last day of the negotiations, the negotiators had become impatient and had made threatening remarks. For this reason, Dr. Heinrich M.-A. (Sr.), realizing what would happen to him and his wife if he did not surrender to Himmler's will, had yielded to the pressure. He had finally agreed to the sale. The applicant states that he had received this information from his mother Flora P., the daughter of Dr. Heinrich (Sr.) and Marie M.-A. She had been present several times during the negotiations and in addition she had been continuously informed by Dr. Heinrich M.-A. (Sr.).

4 Further, the applicant states that he had belonged to the so-called *Studentenfreikorps* ("Student Free Corps"). For this reason, the *Gestapo* ("Secret State Police") had been monitoring him since members of this organization had been persecuted in 1938 and some had also been arrested. On 4 September 1938, the applicant had been arrested by the Secret State Police, had then been brought to the headquarters in the Hotel "Metropol" and had been interrogated for hours. On 7 September 1938, he had been released under the condition that he remain in daily contact, having to report over a time span of several weeks.

5 In the statement submitted by the applicant on 4 April 2005, the foregoing submissions were repeated and it was emphasized that it was made unmistakably clear to the M.-A.-

---

[1] See also *decision number 9a/2008* in conjunction with this decision.

Schiedsinstanz für Naturalrestitution

Entscheidungsnummer 9/2005[1]

Die Schiedsinstanz für Naturalrestitution beschließt am 7. Juni 2005 durch den Vorsitzenden o.Univ.-Prof. Dr. Josef Aicher und die Schiedsinstanzmitglieder Honorarprofessor Dr.Dr.h.c. Erich Kussbach LL.M., Botschafter i.R. und ao.Univ.-Prof. MMag. Dr. August Reinisch LL.M. in der Rechtssache Dr. Rudolf P., vertreten durch Mag. Ewald Scheucher, wegen Naturalrestitution der Liegenschaft L.-straße 429, Einlagezahl (EZ) X1 und EZ X2, Katastralgemeinde (KG) Hütteldorf:

Der Antrag auf Naturalrestitution der Liegenschaft wird abgelehnt.

Begründung:

1. Vorbringen des Antragstellers

Mit dem Antrag vom 28. Mai 2003 begehrte der Antragsteller die Rückstellung der Liegenschaft L.-straße 429, EZ X1 und EZ X2, KG Hütteldorf und brachte wie folgt vor: 1

Die Liegenschaft Wien XIV., L.-straße 429, Haus 49 sei am 12. Oktober 1894 von Dr. Heinrich M.-A. sen. und seiner Ehefrau Marie M.-A., geborene Po. gemeinschaftlich je zur Hälfte von den Brüdern E. gekauft worden. Mit Kaufvertrag vom 8. Jänner 1929 habe Marie M.-A. von ihrem Ehemann die EZ X1 gekauft, wodurch sie Alleineigentümerin des Anwesens geworden sei. 2

Im Jahr 1938 sei das Grundstück samt Haus nicht freiwillig, sondern unter Zwang verkauft worden. Bei den Verhandlungen mit den von Reichsführer-SS Himmler Beauftragten habe sich herausgestellt, dass die Parzelle für den Bau einer Polizeikaserne benötigt werde. Durch die Anwesenheit mehrerer SS-Leute sei großer psychischer Druck ausgeübt worden. Am letzten Tag der Verhandlungen seien die Verhandler ungeduldig geworden und hätten Drohungen ausgesprochen. Aus diesem Grund habe sich Dr. Heinrich M.-A. dem Druck gebeugt, als ihm klar geworden sei, was seiner Frau und ihm bevorstünde, wenn er sich nicht dem Willen Himmlers fügen würde, und habe schließlich eingewilligt. Der Antragsteller gibt an, diese Informationen von seiner Mutter Flora P., der Tochter von Dr. Heinrich sen. und Marie M.-A., erhalten zu haben. Diese sei bei den Verhandlungen öfters anwesend gewesen und zudem von Dr. Heinrich M.-A. ständig informiert worden. 3

Weiters gibt der Antragsteller an, dem so genannten Studentenfreikorps angehört zu haben und dadurch ins Visier der Geheime Staatspolizei (Gestapo) geraten zu sein, da Mitglieder dieser Vereinigung 1938 verfolgt und zum Teil inhaftiert worden seien. Der Antragsteller sei am 4. September 1938 von der Gestapo verhaftet, in die Zentrale im Hotel „Metropol" gebracht und stundenlang verhört worden. Am 7. September 1938 sei er mit der Auflage entlassen worden, täglich zur Verfügung zu stehen, was ein mehrere Wochen langes Melden bedeutet habe. 4

---

[1] Zu dieser Entscheidung siehe auch *Entscheidung Nr. 9a/2008.*

family, who had refused to sell the property, that a continuing refusal would result in arrest and persecution of the married couple. In order to protect himself, his wife and his family members, who were *österreichtreu* ("loyal to Austria"), Dr. M.-A. (Sr.) had signed the purchase contract in the presence of the SS-representatives.

6	Further, it was stated that Heinrich M.-A. (Jr.), the applicant's uncle, had been the only family member who prior to 1938 had been a committed National Socialist, that he had also been a member of the NSDAP and that he had been allegedly arrested for a short time after the end of the war in Salzburg. For these reasons, the waiver which had been declared by Heinrich M.-A. (Jr.) on 17 March 1954, according to which the purchase contract signed in 1938 had been signed "without force or other influencing actions", had been given solely to protect his interests. A request for restitution by the applicant's uncle due to political persecution of his family would have subjected him to an intensive scrutiny, something he could not have been interested in 1954.

2. Evidence

7	Evidence was taken by reviewing the documents enclosed with the application for *in rem* restitution.

8	The following documents were obtained by the Arbitration Panel as supplementary documentation:

9	Austrian State Archives of the Republic, Federal Ministry of Finance and Asset Protection box 3929 M.-A.; Austrian State Archives, Financial Directorate file no. 30402, box I-VI, M.-A.; Austrian State Archives, presidential chancellary no. 16.154/35, post number 17.838; Austrian State Archives, Federal Investigation Bureau file no. 379.485-G.D.4/35 and file no. 367.761-G.D. 4/35; Austrian State Archives, Federal Ministry of Justice 33.325/49 criminal case of Heinrich M.-A. and Karl R. on account of para. 8, 10, 11 of the *Verbotsgesetz* ("Prohibition Act") and para. 6 *Kriegsverbrechergesetz* ("War Criminals Act"); Austrian State Archives, Archives of the Republic, file no. 53267 *(Gauakt)* Heinrich M.-A.; Austrian State Archives, Property Transaction Office Ind.-A. 382, part I-III, B. Mineral Oil Ltd.; Austrian State Archives, Collection Agency, notices no. 1534 and 1535 as well as a letter of refusal no. 1100 and 1101; entries regarding M.-A. and Heinrich M.-A. & Co. in: *Lehmann 1938* and *Lehmann 1938 protokollierte Firmen* (Lehmann 1938 Registered Companies) and *Lehmann 1940 Branchenverzeichnis* (Lehmann 1940 Classified Directory); Municipal Department 8 Vienna Municipal and Regional Archives, *Vermögensentziehungs-Anmeldungsverordnung* ("Ordinance on the Notification of Seized Property") 14th district, 513; Municipal Department 8 Vienna Municipal and Regional Archives, processing and settlement of the estate 13 A 276/44 Marie M.-A.; Municipal Department 8 Vienna Municipal and Regional Archives, processing and settlement of the estate 13 A 235/45 Heinrich M.-A.; Federal Archives, Berlin, R 2 (Reich Ministry of Finance) file no. 11371 (takeover of the Austrian Federal Police and Gendarmerie to the Reich budget 1938–1939), file no. 31690 (buildings register of the *Ordnungspolizei* [regular police force of Nazi Germany], file no. 12202 (subsidy for the City of Vienna for the employment of the *Ordnungspolizei* in Austria 1939); Berlin Federal Archives, NS 3 (SS-Central-Office for Economy and Administration) file no. 20 (acquisition and rental of properties and buildings 1938–1945);

Literature

10	Copies from the report by the Historical Commission (ed.), Ulrike Felber et al., *Eigentumsänderungen in der österreichischen Industrie 1938–1945*/part I, *Branchen- und Fall-*

In dem am 4. April 2005 vom Antragsteller eingebrachten Schriftsatz wurde das bisherige Vorbringen wiederholt und betont, dass der Familie M.-A., die sich geweigert habe, die Liegenschaft zu verkaufen, unmissverständlich klar gemacht worden sei, dass eine fortgesetzte Weigerung Haft und Verfolgung für das Ehepaar nach sich ziehen würde. Um sich, seine Gattin und seine österreichtreu eingestellten Familienmitglieder zu schützen, habe Dr. M.-A. sen. den Kaufvertrag in Anwesenheit von SS-Leuten unterzeichnet.

Weiters wurde angegeben, dass Heinrich M.-A. jun., der Onkel des Antragstellers, als einziges Familienmitglied schon vor 1938 überzeugter Nationalsozialist, auch NSDAP-Mitglied und angeblich nach Kriegsende in Salzburg kurzfristig inhaftiert gewesen sei. Aus diesen Gründen sei die Verzichtserklärung, die Heinrich M.-A. jun. am 17. März 1954 abgegeben habe, derzufolge der 1938 abgeschlossene Kaufvertrag „ohne Zwang oder sonstige Beeinflussung" abgeschlossen wurde, ausschließlich interessengeleitet gewesen. Ein Rückstellungsbegehren durch den Onkel des Antragstellers wegen politischer Verfolgung seiner Familie hätte zu einer näheren Auseinandersetzung mit seiner Person geführt, an welcher er 1954 kein Interesse hätte haben können.

2. Beweise

Beweise wurden erhoben durch Einsichtnahme in die dem Antrag auf Naturalrestitution beigelegten Dokumente.

Folgende Dokumente wurden als ergänzende Dokumentation durch die Schiedsinstanz eingeholt:

Österreichisches Staatsarchiv (ÖStA), Archiv der Republik (AdR) Bundesministerium für Finanzen/Vermögenssicherung (BMF/VS) Karton 3929 M.-A.; ÖStA, Finanzlandesdirektion (FLD) Akt 30402, Karton I–IV, M.-A.; ÖStA, Präsidialkanzlei Zl. 16.154/35, Nachzahl 17.838; ÖStA, Bundeskanzleramt (BKA) Zl. 379.485-G.D.4/35 und Zl. 367.761-G.D. 4/35; ÖStA, Bundesministerium für Jusitz (BMJ) 33.325/49 Strafsache gegen Heinrich M.-A. und Karl R. wegen §§ 8, 10, 11 Verbotsgesetz (VG) und § 6 Kriegsverbrechergesetz (KVG); ÖStA, Archiv der Republik (AdR), Gauakt 53267 Heinrich M.-A.; ÖStA, Vermögensverkehrsstelle (VVSt) Ind.-A. 382, Teil I–III, B. Mineralöl A.G.; ÖStA, Sammelstelle (SSt), Meldungen Nr. 1534 und 1535 sowie Negativbescheid Nr. 1100 und 1101; Einträge zu M.-A. bzw. Heinrich M.-A. & Co. In: „Lehmann 1938" bzw. „Lehmann 1938 protokollierte Firmen" und „Lehmann 1940 Branchenverzeichnis"; MA 8 Wiener Stadt- und Landesarchiv (WStLA), Vermögensentziehungs-Anmeldeverordnung (VEAV) 14., 513; MA 8 WStLA, Verlassenschaftsabhandlung 13 A 276/44 Marie M.-A.; MA 8 WStLA, Verlassenschaftsabhandlung 13 A 235/45 Heinrich M.-A.; Bundesarchiv Berlin (BAB), R 2 (Reichsfinanzministerium) Akt 11371 (Übernahme der österreichischen Bundespolizei und -gendarmerie auf den Reichshaushalt 1938–1939), Akt 31690 (Bautenverzeichnis der Ordnungspolizei), Akt 12202 (Zuschuss an die Stadt Wien für den Einsatz der Ordnungspolizei in Österreich 1939); BAB, NS 3 (SS-Wirtschafts- und Verwaltungshauptamt) Akt 20 (Erwerb und Vermietung von Grundstücken und Gebäuden 1938–1945);

Literatur zu den Feststellungen

Kopien aus dem Bericht der Historikerkommission: Ulrike *Felber* et al., Eigentumsänderungen in der österreichischen Industrie 1938–1945/Teil I. Branchen- und Falldar-

darstellungen/part II, (= Publications of the Austrian Historical Commission. Online version) Vienna 2002[2].

11   Report by the Historical Commission (ed.), Felber et al., *Eigentumsänderungen in der österreichischen Industrie 1938–1945*/part I. *Branchen- und Falldarstellungen*/part II (= Publications of the Austrian Historical Commission. Online version) Vienna 2002; Franz Xaver Woeber, *Anmerkungen. Die M[...] von und zu A[...] Eine genealogische Studie*. 2 volumes, Vienna 1898; Ingrid Spitzbart, *Johannes Brahms und die Familie M[...]-A[...] in Gmunden und Wien*, Gmunden 1997; August M. zu A., *Lebensbilder des Stammherrn der Wiener Familie M[...]-A[...] Josef Maria Ritter vom M[...] zu A[...]*, Vienna 1907; Georg Clam Martinic, *Österreichisches Burgenlexikon. Burgen und Ruinen, Ansitze, Schlösser und Palais*. Including color photographs by Gerhard Trumler. First Edition, Linz 1991; Bundesdenkmalamt (ed.), Districts X–XIX and XXI–XXIII. Edited by Wolfgang Cerny, Ingrid Kastel et al., Vienna. 1997 (= Dehio Vienna. *Die Kunstdenkmäler Österreichs*); Walter Wiltschegg, *Die Heimwehr. Eine unwiderstehliche Volksbewegung?* Vienna 1985 (= Studies and Sources on Austrian Contemporary History, vol. 7).

12   Internet sites: www.archaeologie-wien.at [29 June 2004]; www.e[...]h[...]wien.at [26 May 2004]; www.burgen-austria.com [26 June 2004].

3. Established Facts

a) Development from 1911 until 1945

13   The applicant Dr. Rudolf P. was born on 27 November 1911 as the son of Flora P., née M.-A.

14   Flora P., born on 15 July 1888, Marie B., born on 7 April 1887, and Heinrich M.-A. (Jr.), born on 22 June 1896, were the children of Dr. Heinrich Josef Vinzenz M.-A (Sr.), born on 1 December 1856, and his wife Marie M.-A., née Po., born on 16 May 1861.

15   Pursuant to the purchase contract of 29 January 1895, Dr. Heinrich (Ritter von) M. (zu) A. and Marie von M. (zu) A. purchased from the estate of the E. family the property EZ X1 and X2, KG Hütteldorf located at L.-straße 429 in 1140 Vienna. The incorporation of the ownership title of Marie and Heinrich von M. zu A., each 50 %, into the land register was performed on 26 February 1895.

16   Pursuant to the purchase contract of 27 December 1928, Marie M.-A. purchased from her husband Heinrich his 50 % share of the property which comprised the parcels Y1 construction site, Y2 garden, Y3 and Y4 construction site, Y5 and Y6 garden, with a total size of 5.3428 ha, for a total of 250,000 Schilling. In consequence she became the sole proprietor of the estate located at L.-straße 429, Vienna 14. (EZ X1 and X2).

17   Until 1938, a total of eight priority notices regarding a lien in the amount of 380,000 Crowns were recorded in the land register of property EZ X2. From 1935 on, a lien amounting to 32,000 Schilling for the benefit of the *Österreichische Sparkasse* and a security of 6,400 Schilling were added and recorded in the land register. These two liens existed until

---

[2]   Supplementation at the time of going to press: From 2002 to 2003, this text could be found under http://www.historikerkommission.gv.at/deutsch_home.html and was published in 2004 as: Ulrike Felber, Peter Melichar, Markus Priller, Berthold Unfried, Fritz Weber, *Ökonomie der Arisierung*. Part 1: *Grundzüge, Akteure und Institutionen* Vienna (Oldenbourg) 2004 (= Publications of the Austrian Historical Commission, vol. 10/1).

stellungen/Teil II (= Bericht der Österreichischen Historikerkommission, Onlineversion) Wien 2002.[2]

Ulrike *Felber* et al., Eigentumsänderungen in der österreichischen Industrie 1938– 1945/Teil I. Branchen- und Falldarstellungen/II (= Bericht der Österreichischen Historikerkommission, Onlineversion) Wien 2002; Franz Xaver *Woeber*, Anmerkungen. Die M[...] von und zu A[...] Eine genealogische Studie. 2 Bände, Wien 1898; Ingrid *Spitzbart*, Johannes Brahms und die Familie M[...]-A[...] in Gmunden und Wien, Gmunden 1997; *August M. zu A.*, Lebensbilder des Stammherrn der Wiener Familie M[...]. Josef Maria Ritter vom M[...] zu A[...] Wien 1907; Georg Clam *Martinic*, Österreichisches Burgenlexikon. Burgen und Ruinen, Ansitze, Schlösser und Palais. Mit Farbfotografien von Gerhard *Trumler*, 1. Aufl. Linz 1991; Bundesdenkmalamt (Hg.), Bezirke X bis XIX und XXI bis XXIII. Bearbeitet von Wolfgang *Cerny*, Ingrid *Kastel* et al., Wien 1997 (= Dehio Wien. Die Kunstdenkmäler Österreichs); Walter *Wiltschegg*, Die Heimwehr. Eine unwiderstehliche Volksbewegung? Wien 1985 (= Studien und Quellen zur österreichischen Zeitgeschichte, Band 7). 11

Internetseiten: www.archaeologie-wien.at [29. Juni 2004]; www.e[...]h[...]wien.at [26. Mai 2004]; www.burgen-austria.com [26. Juni 2004]. 12

3. *Festgestellter Sachverhalt*

a) Verlauf in den Jahren 1911 bis 1945

Der Antragsteller Dr. Rudolf P. kam am 27. November 1911 als Sohn von Flora P., geb. M.-A. zur Welt. 13

Flora P., geboren am 15. Juli 1888, Marie B., geboren am 7. April 1887 und Heinrich M.-A. jun., geboren am 22. Juni 1896, waren die Kinder von Dr. Heinrich Josef Vinzenz M.-A. sen., geboren am 1. Dezember 1856, und seiner Ehefrau Marie M.-A., geb. Po., geboren am 16. Mai 1861. 14

Mit Kaufvertrag vom 29. Jänner 1895 erwarben Dr. Heinrich (Ritter von) M. (zu) A. und Marie von M. (zu) A. aus dem Besitz der Familie E. die Liegenschaft EZ X1 und X2 der KG Hütteldorf in 1140 Wien, L.-straße 429. Die grundbücherliche Einverleibung des Eigentumsrechts für Marie und Heinrich von M. zu A. je zur Hälfte erfolgte am 26. Februar 1895. 15

Mit Kaufvertrag vom 27. Dezember 1928 erwarb Marie M.-A. von ihrem Ehegatten Heinrich den Hälfteanteil der Liegenschaft, bestehend aus den Parzellen Y1 Bauarea, Y2 Garten, Y3 und Y4 Bauarea, Y5 und Y6 Garten im Gesamtausmaß von 5,3428 Hektar um insgesamt 250.000,– Schilling und wurde damit Alleineigentümerin des Anwesens in Wien 14., L.-straße 429 (EZ X1 und X2). 16

Bis zum Jahr 1938 waren auf der Liegenschaft EZ X2 insgesamt acht Vormerkungen zu einem Pfandrecht auf den Betrag von 380.000,– Kronen angemerkt. Ab 1935 kam ein Pfandrecht der Österreichischen Sparkasse in der Höhe von 32.000,– Schilling und eine Kaution 17

---

[2] Ergänzung zum Zeitpunkt der Drucklegung: Dieser Text war von 2002 bis 2003 unter http://www.historikerkommission.gv.at/deutsch_home.html abrufbar und wurde 2004 veröffentlicht als: Ulrike *Felber*, Peter *Melichar*, Markus *Priller*, Berthold *Unfried*, Fritz *Weber*, Ökonomie der Arisierung. Teil 1: Grundzüge, Akteure und Institutionen Wien (Oldenbourg) 2004 (= Veröffentlichungen der Österreichischen Historikerkommission, Band 10/1).

the signing of the purchase contract with the "*Reichsführer-SS und Chef der Deutschen Polizei (Polizeiverwaltung)*" (Reichsführer-SS and Chief of the German Police [Police Administration]) on 7 July/15 September 1938."

18   On 2 December 1938, due to a receipt of cancellation of 17 November 1938, the lien of the Sparkasse in the land register and – on application – the last notice regarding the lien of 380,000 Crowns of 6 July 1938 were cancelled. Through this, the property EZ X2 became unencumbered.

19   From March 1929 until the signing of the purchase contract (receipt of cancellation of 28 October 1938) a lien in the amount of 190,000 Schilling was also recorded as an encumbrance to the property EZ X1. The property EZ X1 also became unencumbered on 2 December 1938.

20   Pursuant to the purchase contract of 7 July/15 September 1938 Marie M.-A., represented by her lawyer Dr. Karl W., sold the property EZ X1 (property parcels Y2/1, Y5/1 and Y6/1) and EZ X2 (property parcels Y1, Y2/2, Y5/2 and Y6/2) with a total size of 54,000 m^2 to the "*Reichsführer-SS* and Chief of the German Police (Police Administration)" represented by the "Inspector of the *Ordnungspolizei*" of the Vienna Department for Administration and Law for a total purchase price of 580,000 Reichsmark. The incorporation of the ownership title of the "German Reich (Police Administration)" into the land register took place on 11 July/8 October 1938.

21   Later (on 15 September 1938), the total size of the purchased object of "54,000 m^2, more or less" was inserted in para. 1 of the purchase contract. In this addendum Marie M.-A. stated that in accordance with *GBlÖ* ("Austrian Law Gazette") No. 103/38 she was "Aryan". The payment conditions were prescribed in para. 2 of the contract. According to these, a partial amount of 250,000 Reichsmark was supposed to be paid to the vendors within 14 days of the incorporation in the land register "for the purpose of being released from any encumbrances"; the balance of 330,000 Reichsmark was supposed to be paid "after the certificate of the release from encumbrances was produced". This release from encumbrances was registered in the land register on 2 December 1938. The second partial amount was also paid to Marie M.-A. However, it could not be established when this payment was made.

22   It can be assumed that several SS-men were present during the sales discussions which took place beforehand. However, it could not be established whether the purchasers pressured Marie M.-A. and/or her husband, Dr. Heinrich M.-A. (Sr.), in order to force the signing of the purchase contract. Also, it was not possible to establish how the sales discussions had been initiated. Further, it could not be established whether the vendors belonged to a political opposition movement or whether they were politically active in any other way.

23   The applicant, and grandson of the aggrieved party, was arrested by the Secret State Police on 4 September 1938 for being suspected of participating in an illegal reactionary organization and for danger of conspiracy. The applicant was released again on 7 September 1938.

24   At least during the years 1933 and 1934, Dr. Rudolf P. was a member of the Student Free Corps, a student movement in Vienna. This movement was founded in 1922 and was a uniformed military unit which was mainly made up of student fraternity members. From 1934, the Student Free Corps did not admit Jews as members. As requirements for admittance, para. 5 of the regulations of this student movement included "German ethnicity" and

Schiedsinstanz für Naturalrestitution – Entscheidung Nr. 9/2005

von 6.400,– Schilling hinzu und wurde im Grundbuch angemerkt. Diese beiden Pfandrechte blieben bis zum Abschluss des Kaufvertrages mit dem „Reichsführer-SS und Chef der Deutschen Polizei (Polizeiverwaltung)" vom 7. Juli bzw. 15. September 1938 aufrecht.

Am 2. Dezember 1938 wurde im Grundbuch einerseits aufgrund einer Löschungsquittung vom 17. November 1938 das Pfandrecht der Sparkasse sowie andererseits auf Antrag die letzte Anmerkung betreffend das Pfandrecht von 380.000,– Kronen vom 6. Juli 1938 gelöscht. Damit wurde die Liegenschaft EZ X2 lastenfrei. 18

Auf der EZ X1 lastete von März 1929 bis zum Abschluss des Kaufvertrages (Löschungsquittung vom 28. Oktober 1938) ebenfalls ein Pfandrecht lautend auf den Betrag von 190.000,– Schilling. Auch die Liegenschaft EZ X1 wurde am 2. Dezember 1938 lastenfrei. 19

Marie M.-A., vertreten durch ihren Rechtsanwalt (RA) Dr. Karl W., verkaufte mit Kaufvertrag vom 7. Juli und 15. September 1938 die Liegenschaft EZ X1 (Grundstücksparzellen Y2/1, Y5/1 und Y6/1) und EZ X2 (Grundstücksparzellen Y1, Y2/2, Y5/2 und Y6/2) mit insgesamt 54.000 m^2 an den „Reichsführer-SS und Chef der Deutschen Polizei (Polizeiverwaltung)", vertreten durch den „Inspekteur der Ordnungspolizei" vom Amt für Verwaltung und Recht in Wien, zu einem Kaufgesamtpreis von 580.000,– Reichsmark. Die grundbücherliche Einverleibung des Eigentumsrechts erfolgte mit 11. Juli bzw. 8. Oktober 1938 für das „Deutsche Reich (Polizeiverwaltung)". 20

Im Kaufvertrag wurde in § 1 nachträglich (am 15. September 1938) das Gesamtausmaß des Kaufobjekts mit „54.000 m^2 mehr oder weniger" eingefügt. In diesem Nachtrag erklärte Marie M.-A. gemäß dem Gesetzblatt für das Land Österreich (GBlÖ) 103/38, „Aricrin" zu scin. Unter § 2 des Vertrages wurden die Zahlungsmodalitäten festgelegt. Demnach sollte ein Teilbetrag von 250.000,– Reichsmark binnen 14 Tagen nach grundbücherlicher Durchführung „zwecks Lastenfreistellung" an die Verkäuferin zur Auszahlung gelangen, der Rest von 330.000,– Reichsmark „nach erbrachtem Nachweis der Lastenfreistellung". Diese Lastenfreistellung wurde am 2. Dezember 1938 im Grundbuch eingetragen. Auch der zweite Teilbetrag wurde an Marie M.-A. ausbezahlt. Es konnte jedoch nicht festgestellt werden, wann diese Auszahlung erfolgt ist. 21

Von einer Anwesenheit mehrerer SS-Leute bei den im Vorfeld geführten Verkaufsgesprächen kann ausgegangen werden. Es konnte jedoch nicht festgestellt werden, ob seitens der Käufer Druck auf Marie M.-A. bzw. auf ihren Ehemann Dr. Heinrich M.-A. sen. ausgeübt wurde, um den Kaufvertragsabschluss herbeizuführen. Auch konnte nicht festgestellt werden, wie es zu der Anbahnung der Verkaufsgespräche gekommen ist. Weiters konnte nicht festgestellt werden, ob die Verkäufer einer politischen Oppositionsbewegung angehört haben oder sich in anderer Weise politisch betätigt haben. 22

Der Antragsteller und Enkel der Geschädigten wurde am 4. September 1938 von der Gestapo wegen Verdachts der Teilnahme an einer illegalen reaktionären Organisation und wegen Verabredungsgefahr verhaftet. Am 7. September 1938 wurde der Antragsteller wieder freigelassen. 23

Dr. Rudolf P. war zumindest in den Jahren 1933/34 Mitglied des „Studentenfreikorps", einer Studentenverbindung in Wien. Diese wurde 1922 gegründet und stellte eine uniformierte, militärische Einheit dar, die sich vor allem aus Burschenschaftern rekrutierte. Seit 1934 nahm der „Studentenfreikorps" keine Juden mehr auf. § 5 der Dienstordnung dieser Studentenverbindung beinhaltete als Aufnahmevoraussetzung die „deutsche Volkszugehörigkeit" und die „arische Abstammung bis ins dritte Glied". Gleichzeitig galt das Stu- 24

"Aryan descent, traceable at least three generations back". At the same time, the Student Free Corps was considered an elite unit of the *Heimwehr* ("Home Guard"). In 1933 and 1934, the fraternity enjoyed its greatest expansion. During 1935 and 1936, its membership decreased as National Socialism grew stronger in the universities. In 1936, this fraternity dissolved.

25   In 1934, the applicant participated as a *Schutzkorpsjäger* ("Fighter of the Defense Corps") in the violent battles around the city of Steyr. In 1935, he was awarded the bronze merit medal by President Wilhelm Miklas.

26   The applicant did not assert a connection concerning time and content between his arrest by the Secret State Police and the sale of the property in July with addendum of 15 September 1938. Such a connection could not be established.

b) Further Developments since 1945

27   The transfer of the property in question from the administration of the Police Directorate Vienna to the sovereign administration of the Financial Directorate for Vienna, Lower Austria and Burgenland was carried out on 1 July 1948. In 1945, the property had been seized as former German property and used by the French occupying powers. Initially, the rent which had been determined by the City of Vienna, the property taxes, the duties and running costs were paid for the use of the property.

28   In February 1949, the French occupying powers inquired with the Federal Ministry of Finances whether the property in question would be under fiduciary administration only until it was to be restituted under the framework of the Austrian restitution legislation to the previous owner, Marie M.-A.

29   This inquiry was forwarded to the building administrator, Maria V., with the instructions to announce the following to the rent accounting office of the French military government concerning the property located at L.-straße 429:
– pursuant to the purchase contract of 7 July/15 September 1938, the property located at L.-straße 429–435, Vienna XIV. had been purchased from the previous owner, Maria M.-A., by the German Reich (Police Administration). For this reason it was covered by the *Dritte Rückstellungsgesetz* ("Third Restitution Act");
– since the restoration of the Republic of Austria, the property was no longer public property but was merely regarded as restitution property which is held in trust by an Austrian authority. This authority will terminate the administration after the restitution to a party entitled to restitution.
– the transfer of the property from the police administration to the administration of the Financial Directorate which had taken place pursuant to the Decree by the Ministry for Asset Protection and Economic Planning of 17 February 1948, represented an act of solely administrative nature;
– a building administrator had been instructed to perform all administrative tasks arising from the administration of the property.

30   In a letter by the Financial Directorate to the accounting office of the French military authority of 6 September 1950 it was explicitly pointed out that even though the German Reich (Police Administration) appeared as the owner of the property in the land register, Marie M.-A., being the aggrieved owner according to the restitution legislation, was entitled to file restitution claims with the responsible authority. In accordance with the *Behördenüberleitungsgesetz* ("Authority Transition Act"), the Financial Directorate held in trust the property until the restitution decision had become final and binding.

dentenfreikorps als Eliteeinheit der Heimwehr. Die Verbindung hatte ihren größten Zulauf in den Jahren 1933 und 1934. Mit dem Erstarken des Nationalsozialismus an den Hochschulen in den Jahren 1935/36 verringerte sich ihre Mitgliederzahl. 1936 löste sich diese Studentenverbindung auf.

1934 hat der Antragsteller als Schutzkorpsjäger bei den heftigen Kämpfen um die Stadt Steyr teilgenommen. Dafür wurde ihm 1935 vom Bundespräsidenten Wilhelm Miklas die bronzene Verdienstmedaille verliehen. 25

Ein zeitlicher oder inhaltlicher Zusammenhang zwischen der Verhaftung des Antragstellers durch die Gestapo und dem Verkauf der Liegenschaft im Juli mit Nachtrag vom 15. September 1938 wurde vom Antragsteller nicht behauptet und konnte nicht festgestellt werden. 26

b) Weiterer Verlauf ab 1945

Die Übernahme der gegenständlichen Liegenschaft aus der Verwaltung der Polizeidirektion Wien in die hoheitliche Verwaltung der FLD für Wien, Niederösterreich und das Burgenland erfolgte am 1. Juli 1948. Die Liegenschaft war bereits seit 1945 von der französischen Besatzungsmacht als ehemaliges Deutsches Eigentum beschlagnahmt und benutzt worden. Für die Benutzung des Objekts wurden zunächst auch der von der Stadt Wien festgesetzte Mietzins, die Grundsteuern, die Abgaben und Betriebskosten bezahlt. 27

Bereits im Februar 1949 wurde seitens der französischen Besatzungsmacht beim BMF angefragt, ob die gegenständliche Liegenschaft nur solange in treuhändischer Verwaltung stünde, bis dieselbe im Rahmen der österreichischen Rückstellungsgesetzgebung an die frühere Eigentümerin Marie M.-A. zurückgegeben würde. 28

Diese Anfrage wurde an die Gebäudeverwalterin Maria V. weitergeleitet und diese angewiesen, bezüglich der Liegenschaft L.-straße 429 der Mietzinsverrechnungsstelle der französischen Militärregierung bekanntzugeben, dass 29
– die Liegenschaft Wien XIV., L.-straße 429–435 durch Kaufvertrag vom 7. Juli bzw. 15. September 1938 durch das Deutsche Reich (Polizeiverwaltung) von der früheren Eigentümerin Maria M.-A. gekauft worden sei und aus diesem Grund unter das Dritte Rückstellungsgesetz (3. RStG) falle;
– seit der Wiederherstellung der Republik Österreich die Liegenschaft auch kein Staatseigentum mehr darstelle, sondern lediglich als Rückstellungsgut in treuhändiger Verwaltung einer österreichischen Behörde stehe, die die Verwaltung nach erfolgter Rückstellung an einen Rückstellungsberechtigten beenden werde;
– die Übergabe der Liegenschaft von der Polizeiverwaltung in die Verwaltung der FLD, die gemäß dem Erlass des Bundesministeriums für Vermögenssicherung und Wirtschaftsplanung (BMVS) vom 17. Februar 1948 erfolgt sei, lediglich eine verwaltungstechnische Maßnahme darstelle;
– mit der Durchführung aller sich bei der Verwaltung der Liegenschaft ergebenden administrativen Arbeiten eine Gebäudeverwalterin beauftragt worden sei.

In einem Brief der FLD an die Verrechnungsstelle für die französische Militärbehörde vom 6. September 1950 wurde ausdrücklich darauf hingewiesen, dass zwar im Grundbuch das Deutsche Reich (Polizeiverwaltung) als Eigentümer der Liegenschaft aufscheine, aber Marie M.-A. im Sinne der Rückstellungsgesetzgebung als geschädigte Eigentümerin berechtigt sei, bei der zuständigen Stelle Rückstellungsansprüche geltend zu machen. Die FLD verwalte im Sinne des Behördenüberleitungsgesetzes treuhänderisch die Liegenschaft so lange, bis ein Rückstellungsbescheid in Rechtskraft erwachsen sei. 30

31 Towards the end of 1951, the French occupying powers notified the Financial Directorate that the payment of the fees for the use of the property was being terminated on 1 December 1951. The stated reason for this was that the property was under German ownership and that in accordance with French orders, no rent or fees for the use of the property were to be paid. From 1952 on, only the property taxes and duties were still being paid for the property. As a result of the presented reasons, the Federal Ministry of Finance endeavored to convince the French occupying forces to release the property in order to use it productively.

32 For a short time, the French High Commissioner pursued the idea of renting the property to situate the French embassy there. However, soon this idea was discarded since amongst other things, considerable structural and sanitary repairs would have been necessary.

33 The facts of the case had to be established during the course of the clarification of the legal relationships and for the purpose of establishing whether the heirs of the former owner, Marie M.-A., sought to commence restitution proceedings for the property.

34 In the Federal Ministry of Finance's Property Control Department 4, it was recalled that the M.-A. family claimed that it had not voluntarily sold the property but that due to the expected refund of the purchase price (approximately 600,000 Reichsmark), it would not make an application for restitution for the time being. In a report by the Federal Ministry of Finance of 3 December 1953, it was noted that the M.-A. family "according to information by the High Commissioner did not seek restitution." Further, in a statement of 19 December 1953 by Maria B.-L., Marie M.-A.'s daughter, it said that an application for restitution would not be submitted due to the lack of necessary funds for the refund of the purchase price of the time.

35 On 9 January 1954, Ida M.-A., the niece of the previous owner, explained to the Police Directorate Vienna, Department 1, the course of the property sale. According to her statement, the property was not sold to the German Reich (Police Administration) under duress, or for political or racial reasons. During this period of time in the year 1938, the M.-A. family had experienced financial problems and had been happy to be able to sell this large asset, which had been difficult to dispose of. Hence, according to the statement by Ida M.-A. this was not an act of "aryanization".

36 In addition, Marie M.-A.'s son, Heinrich (Jr.), had been interrogated by the Police Directorate Vienna regarding the property in question. On 30 January 1954, he stated that he had been well informed in this matter and that hence he was able to confirm that the sale of the property in 1938 had not taken place under duress rather according to the rules and that it did not represent an act of aryanization.

37 In March 1954, Marie M.-A.'s three joint heirs, Heinrich M.-A. (Jr.), Maria B. and Flora P., submitted written waivers. In these waivers, they confirmed that the property in question had been sold to the German Reich (Police Administration) in 1938 by a duly executed purchase contract. As joint heirs, they were able to declare that "the purchase contract was concluded voluntarily without any force or any other influence". Further, the value agreed upon in the contract corresponded to the actual value of the asset and the purchase price had been paid late but in full. Further, the heirs agreed not to claim restitution from the purchaser or their legal successors.

38 A connection concerning time or content between the waiver declared by Heinrich M.-A. (Jr.) and the legal proceedings, which were initiated against him in 1949 due to the vi-

Ende 1951 erstattete die französische Besatzungsmacht der FLD die Mitteilung, dass 31
die Zahlung der Benützungsentschädigung mit 1. Dezember 1951 eingestellt werde. Als
Grund dafür wurde angegeben, dass sich die Liegenschaft im Deutschen Eigentum befände und dafür nach französischen Verfügungen kein Mietzins bzw. keine Benützungsentschädigung gezahlt werde. Ab 1952 wurden nur noch die Grundsteuern und Abgaben für
die Liegenschaft gezahlt. Aus den dargelegten Gründen bestand nun seitens des BMF das
Bestreben, die französische Besatzungsmacht zur Freigabe der Liegenschaft zu bewegen,
um sie nutzbringend zu verwerten.

Kurzzeitig verfolgte das französische Hochkommissariat die Idee, die Liegenschaft für 32
die Unterbringung der französischen Botschaft zu mieten; diese wurde jedoch schon bald
wieder verworfen, da unter anderem an der Liegenschaft erhebliche bauliche und sanitäre Instandsetzungsarbeiten notwendig gewesen wären.

Im Zuge der Ordnung von Rechtsverhältnissen und zum Zweck der Feststellung, ob 33
seitens der ErbInnen nach der ehemaligen Eigentümerin Marie M.-A. ein Rückstellungsverfahren für die Liegenschaft angestrebt werde, musste der Sachverhalt geklärt werden.

In der Vermögenssicherungs-Abteilung 4 des BMF war erinnerlich, dass die Familie 34
M.-A. behauptete, nicht freiwillig verkauft zu haben, aber wegen der zu erwartenden Kaufpreisrückzahlung (rund 600.000,– Reichsmark) vorläufig ein Rückstellungsantrag noch
nicht gestellt werde. In einem Bericht des BMF vom 3. Dezember 1953 wurde festgehalten, dass die Familie A. „nach Informationen des Hochkommissars keine Rückstellung begehre". Des Weiteren gab Maria B.-L., die Tochter von Marie M.-A., in einer Aussage vom
19. Dezember 1953 an, dass ein Rückstellungsantrag aus Mangel an notwendigen Mitteln
zur Rückerstattung des seinerzeitigen Kaufpreises nicht gestellt werden würde.

Am 9. Jänner 1954 erörterte Ida M.-A., die Nichte der vormaligen Eigentümerin, bei 35
der Polizeidirektion Wien, Abteilung 1, den Verlauf des Liegenschaftsverkaufs. Laut ihrer
Aussage wurde die Liegenschaft L.-straße 429 nicht unter Zwang oder aus politischen oder
rassischen Gründen an das Deutsche Reich (Polizeiverwaltung) verkauft. Die Familie M.-
A. habe sich zu dieser Zeit, im Jahr 1938, in finanziellen Schwierigkeiten befunden und
sei froh gewesen, dieses große Objekt, das schwer zu verkaufen gewesen sei, veräußern
zu können. Nach Angabe von Ida M.-A. lag somit kein Arisierungsakt vor.

Auch der Sohn von Marie M.-A., Heinrich jun., wurde über den Verkauf der gegen- 36
ständlichen Liegenschaft von der Polizeidirektion Wien befragt. Am 30. Jänner 1954 gab
dieser an, in dieser Angelegenheit bestens informiert gewesen zu sein und somit bestätigen zu können, dass der Verkauf der Liegenschaft im Jahr 1938 nicht unter Zwang, sondern ordnungsgemäß durchgeführt worden sei und keinen Arisierungsakt dargestellt habe.

Im März 1954 gaben die drei MiterbInnen nach Marie M.-A., Heinrich M.-A. jun., 37
Maria B. und Flora P., schriftliche Verzichtserklärungen ab. In diesen bestätigten sie, dass
die gegenständliche Liegenschaft im Jahr 1938 durch ordnungsgemäßen Kaufvertrag mit
dem Deutschen Reich (Polizeiverwaltung) verkauft worden sei. Sie seien als MiterbInnen
in der Lage zu erklären, dass „der Kaufvertrag ohne jeglichen Zwang oder sonstige Beeinflussung freiwillig abgeschlossen wurde". Des Weiteren habe der im Vertrag vereinbarte Gegenwert dem tatsächlichen Wert des Objektes entsprochen und der Kaufpreis sei
zwar verspätet, aber zur Gänze ausbezahlt worden. Die ErbInnen gaben weiters an, keinerlei Ansprüche aus dem Titel einer Rückstellung gegen den Käufer oder deren Rechtsnachfolgerinnen zu stellen.

Ein zeitlicher oder inhaltlicher Zusammenhang der von Heinrich M.-A. jun. abgege- 38
benen Verzichtserklärung mit dem Gerichtsverfahren, das 1949 gegen ihn wegen Versto-

olation of the Prohibition Act in accordance with para. 8, 10, 11 and para. 6 of the War Criminals Act could not be established. The proceedings pursuant to para. 6 of the War Criminals Act were discontinued in the same year pursuant to para. 109 of the *Strafprozessordnung* ("Criminal Procedure Law").

39 Since it was now clarified that no restitution claims would be filed and after the French occupying powers had released the property, the attempt of the Financial Directorate to productively utilize the property led to the signing of an indefinite rental contract with the "*Österreichische Eh.-gesellschaft*" on 7 July 1955. The agreed monthly rental was 2,728 Schilling, excluding running costs and property taxes.

40 The unproblematic conclusion of the rental contract was possible since Article 22 item 11 of the *Staatsvertrag* ("State Treaty") of 15 May 1955, *BGBl.* ("Federal Law Gazette") No. 152/55, in conjunction with para. 11 of the *Erste Staatsvertragsdurchführungsgesetz* ("First State Treaty Implementation Act") Federal Law Gazette No. 165/56 led to the *ex lege* transfer of the property to the Republic of Austria.

41 On 15 March 1956, the "*Österreichische Eh.-gesellschaft*" was dissolved. Its legal successor, the "*E. H.-ges.m.b.H.*", assumed the obligations under the contract.

42 On 27 August 1957, on account of an application by the State Financial Procurator's Office, no. 54441-2/57 of 24 August 1957, the ownership title to the property in question was transferred to the Republic of Austria. Since the government had no need for the property, it was initially intended to sell it. The Financial Directorate was instructed to carry out a public tender and to establish the market value.

43 During the course of these events several expert opinions were provided. However, these had differing results. An alternative offer was prepared after the offer by the "*E. H.-ges.m.b.H.*" as well as the offer by the City of Vienna were far below the value verified in the expert opinion commissioned by the Federal Ministry of Finance. This alternative offer represented a "relatively favorable solution" for the Federation. Hence, the Federal Ministry of Finance decided not to sell the property but rather to confer a right to build to the tenant.

44 This right was conferred to the "*E. H.-ges.m.b.H.*" after the signing of the property development contract on 16 June 1959 for a duration of 70 years (until 2030). The right to build was recorded in the land register for EZ X2, where new buildings were planned and for the already built on parcels Y2/1 and Y3 of EZ X1 (which during the course of these events were merged in to EZ X2 in 1959). Additionally, a right of first refusal regarding the property EZ X2 was incorporated for the benefit of the "*E. H.-Ges.m.b.H.*" These notifications were recorded in the land register on 7 May 1960.

45 The property in question was owned on 17 January 2001 and is still federally owned (*Bundesimmobiliengesellschaft m.b.H.*) today.

4. Consideration of Evidence

46 The established facts are based on the submitted unobjectionable documents, the open land register, the reports by the Historical Commission, archive material researched by the Arbitration Panel and the submission by the applicant.

47 Contradictory statements exist regarding the question of whether or not duress had been exercised during the sale. The applicant merely referred to statements made by his mother according to which pressure had been exercised by the SS-men during the sales negotiations. Further proof in this regard does not exist. However, at the same time the waivers

ßes gegen das VG gem. §§ 8, 10, 11 und wegen § 6 KVG eingeleitet und hinsichtlich § 6 KVG in demselben Jahr gemäß § 109 Strafprozessordnung (StPO) zurückgestellt wurde, konnte nicht festgestellt werden.

Nachdem nun klargestellt war, dass keine Rückstellungsansprüche geltend gemacht werden würden und nachdem die französische Besatzungsmacht die Liegenschaft freigegeben hatte, führte der Versuch der FLD, die Liegenschaft nutzbringend zu verwerten, am 7. Juli 1955 zum Abschluss eines unbefristeten Mietvertrages mit dem Verein „Österreichische Eh.-gesellschaft". Als Mietzins wurden 2.728,– Schilling monatlich exklusive Betriebskosten und Grundsteuern vereinbart. 39

Der problemlose Abschluss des Mietvertrages war deshalb nun möglich, da aufgrund des Art. 22 Z 11 des Staatsvertrages vom 15. Mai 1955, Bundesgesetzblatt (BGBl) 152/55, in Verbindung mit § 11 des 1. Staatsvertragsdurchführungsgesetzes (1. StVDG BGBl 165/56) die Liegenschaft ex lege auf die Republik übergegangen war. 40

Am 15. März 1956 wurde der Verein „Österreichische Eh.-gesellschaft" aufgelöst. Sein Rechtsnachfolger, die „E. H.-ges.m.b.H." trat in den Vertrag ein. 41

Am 27. August 1957 wurde aufgrund eines Antrages der Finanzprokuratur, Zl. 54441–2/57 vom 24. August 1957 im Grundbuch das Eigentumsrecht an der gegenständlichen Liegenschaft für die Republik Österreich einverleibt. Da an der Liegenschaft kein staatlicher Bedarf bestand, wurde zunächst eine Veräußerung beabsichtigt und die FLD beauftragt, eine öffentliche Ausschreibung durchzuführen und den Verkehrswert zu ermitteln. 42

Im Zuge dessen wurden mehrere Schätzgutachten erstellt, die jedoch zu unterschiedlichen Ergebnissen führten. Nachdem sowohl das Angebot der „E. H.-ges.m.b.H.", als auch jenes der Stadt Wien weit unter dem Schätzwert des vom BMF in Auftrag gegebenen Kontrollgutachtens lagen, wurde ein Alternativvorschlag ausgearbeitet, der für den Bund eine „relativ günstige Lösung" darstellte. Das BMF beschloss daher, die gegenständliche Liegenschaft nicht zu verkaufen, sondern der Bestandnehmerin ein Baurecht einzuräumen. 43

Dieses wurde der „E. H.-ges.m.b.H." nach Unterzeichnung des Baurechtsvertrages vom 16. Juni 1959 für eine Dauer von 70 Jahren (bis 2030) ausgestellt. Das Baurecht wurde für die EZ X2, wo Neubauten geplant waren, und für die bereits bebauten Parzellen Y2/1 und Y3 der EZ X1 (die im Zuge dessen im Jahr 1959 der EZ X2 zugeschrieben wurden) im Grundbuch eingetragen. Zusätzlich wurde der „E. H.-ges.m.b.H." ein Vorkaufsrecht an der Liegenschaft EZ X2 einverleibt. Diese Anmerkungen wurden am 7. Mai 1960 im Grundbuch eingetragen. 44

Die gegenständliche Liegenschaft befand sich zum Stichtag am 17. Jänner 2001 und steht bis heute im Eigentum des Bundes (Bundesimmobiliengesellschaft m.b.H.). 45

4. Beweiswürdigung

Der festgestellte Sachverhalt gründet sich auf die vorgelegten unbedenklichen Urkunden, das offene Grundbuch, die Berichte der Historikerkommission, seitens der Schiedsinstanz recherchierte Archivalien und das Vorbringen des Antragstellers. 46

Hinsichtlich der Frage, ob beim Verkauf Zwang ausgeübt wurde, liegen widersprüchliche Angaben vor. Der Antragsteller berief sich lediglich auf Angaben seiner Mutter, wonach bei den Verkaufsverhandlungen Druck seitens der SS-Leute ausgeübt worden ist. Weitere Beweise hiezu liegen nicht vor. Gleichzeitig sind jedoch die von den MiterbInnen, Heinrich M.- A. jun., Marie B.-L. und Flora M.-A. abgegebenen Verzichtserklärungen als 47

declared by the joint heirs, Heinrich M.-A. (Jr.), Marie B.-L. and Flora M.-A., as well as the statement by the niece, Ida M.-A., are to be considered. These expressly state that pressure was not applied during the sale of the property. These waivers were declared before an authority (police). Hence, they have a higher degree of authenticity.

48 In addition, an indirect pressure exercised upon Marie M.-A., which might have resulted from the fear of the persecution of her grandson due to his past involvement with the Student Free Corps, cannot be assumed since the sale of the property had been carried out prior to the arrest of Rudolf P. The applicant also does not establish a connection between the sale of the property and Marie M.-A.'s concern for her grandson's arrest.

49 Regarding a possible political persecution of the originally aggrieved person, it was not possible to arrive at any findings since neither pieces of information were provided nor was it possible to retrieve any.

50 The finding that there was no connection between the arrest of the applicant by the Secret State Police and the sale of the property is based upon the lack of evidence that the purchaser had in any way influenced the vendor regarding the sale.

51 Since neither the documents nor the submissions by the applicant allowed for the determination of a connection between the waiver declared by Heinrich M.-A. (Jr.) and the legal proceedings initiated against him in 1949 and discontinued in the same year, such a connection could not be established.

5. Juridical Appraisal

5.1 Right to Inherit

52 In accordance with Sec. 27 (2) of the *Entschädigungsfondsgesetz* ("General Settlement Fund Law", GSF Law), applying *mutatis mutandis* the provisions of the (Austrian) General Civil Code heirs are eligible to file applications. The Arbitration Panel assumes that according to the aforementioned provision the proof of the legal right to inherit – provided no stronger reasons for appeal are presented – is sufficient for the eligibility to file applications. Along with his siblings, Huberta Maria B. and Floriane P., the applicant is a descendant of the originally aggrieved person and hence a legal heir. Evidence conflicting with this right to inherit has not been presented. On the basis of the established right to inherit, the Arbitration Panel recognizes the eligibility of the applicant to file an application.

5.2 Public Property

Property of the Federation

53[3] In accordance with Sec. 28 (1) item 3 of the GSF Law, the term "publicly-owned property" comprises properties which on 17 January 2001 were exclusively and directly owned by the Federation or any legal person under public or private law wholly owned, directly or indirectly, by the Federation. On 17 January 2001, the property was owned by the *Bundesimmobiliengesellschaft m.b.H.* The only member of this legal person is the Republic of Austria, represented by the Federal Ministry of Economics and Labor. Hence, the Federation has the exclusive control of the company. As such, the prerequisite of the sole ownership by the Federation can be regarded as fulfilled.

---

[3] In the original text of this decision margin notes 53–57 were omitted due to a technical error.

auch die Aussage der Nichte, Ida M.-A. zu berücksichtigen. Diese stellen ausdrücklich fest, dass beim Liegenschaftsverkauf kein Druck ausgeübt wurde. Diese Verzichtserklärungen wurden vor einer Behörde (Polizei) abgegeben. Es kommt ihnen daher eine erhöhte Beweiskraft zu.

Auch eine mittelbare Druckausübung auf Marie M.-A., die aus Angst vor Verfolgung 48 ihres Enkels aus seiner Studentenfreikorpsvergangenheit resultieren hätte können, kann nicht angenommen werden, da der Liegenschaftsverkauf vor der Verhaftung von Rudolf P. stattgefunden hat und auch vom Antragsteller kein Bezug hergestellt wird zwischen dem Liegenschaftsverkauf und der allenfalls befürchteten Verhaftung.

Im Bezug auf eine mögliche politische Verfolgung der ursprünglich Geschädigten 49 konnten keine Feststellungen getroffen werden, da diesbezügliche Informationen weder beigelegt noch eruierbar waren.

Die Feststellung, dass zwischen der Verhaftung des Antragstellers durch die Gestapo 50 und dem Verkauf der Liegenschaft kein Zusammenhang bestanden hat, gründet sich auf den Mangel von Hinweisen, dass von der Seite der Käufer diesbezüglich auf die Verkäuferin Einfluss genommen worden ist.

Da weder aus den Unterlagen noch aus dem Vorbringen des Antragstellers ein Zusam- 51 menhang zwischen der durch Heinrich M.-A. jun. abgegebenen Verzichtserklärung und dem 1949 gegen ihn eingeleiteten und in demselben Jahr zurückgestellten Gerichtsverfahren eruierbar gewesen ist, konnte ein solcher auch nicht festgestellt werden.

5. Rechtliche Beurteilung

5.1 Erbrecht

Gemäß § 27 Abs 2 Entschädigungsfondsgesetz (EF-G) sind ErbInnen in sinngemäßer 52 Anwendung der Bestimmungen des Allgemeinen Bürgerlichen Gesetzbuches (ABGB) antragsberechtigt. Die Schiedsinstanz geht davon aus, dass nach der vorzitierten Bestimmung der Nachweis des gesetzlichen Erbrechts, wenn nicht stärkere Berufungsgründe dargetan werden, für die Antragsberechtigung ausreichend ist. Der Antragsteller ist neben seinen Geschwistern Huberta Maria Be. und Floriane P. ein Deszendent der ursprünglich Geschädigten, somit ein gesetzlicher Erbe. Es wurde kein diesem Erbrecht entgegenstehender Nachweis vorgelegt. Hiermit sieht die Schiedsinstanz die Antragsberechtigung des Antragstellers aufgrund des nachgewiesenen Erbrechts als gegeben an.

5.2 Öffentliches Vermögen

Bundeseigentum

Gemäß § 28 Abs 1 Z 3 EF-G umfasst der Begriff „öffentliches Vermögen" Liegen- 53[3] schaften, welche sich am 17. Jänner 2001 ausschließlich und unmittelbar im Eigentum des Bundes oder einer unmittelbar oder mittelbar im Alleineigentum des Bundes stehenden juristischen Person des öffentlichen oder privaten Rechts befanden. Die Liegenschaft befand sich zum Stichtag und steht bis heute im Eigentum der Bundesimmobiliengesellschaft.m.b.H. Die einzige Gesellschafterin dieser juristischen Person ist die Republik Österreich, vertreten durch das Bundesministerium für wirtschaftliche Angelegenheiten.

---

[3] In der Entscheidungsurschrift wurde hier aufgrund eines technischen Gebrechens irrtümlich mit der Randzahl 58 fortgesetzt.

Arbitration Panel for *In Rem* Restitution – Decision No. 9/2005

5.3 Persecution

54 Pursuant to Sec. 27 of the GSF Law, persons and their heirs are eligible to file an application if one of the listed grounds for persecution exists, namely persecution on political grounds, on grounds of origin, religion, nationality, sexual orientation, of mental or physical handicap or of accusations of so-called asociality, or if they left the country in order to escape such persecution. The list of the grounds for persecution is exhaustive and does not contain any further elements which could be used by the applicant to support his claim.

55 A persecution of the aggrieved person on political grounds can exist if the originally aggrieved person was a member of a group of persons which was discriminated against by the National Socialists (that is an organized ideological opponent of National Socialism), or if he/she actually was subjected to discriminatory actions or subjected to an act of persecution by being counted as part of the circle of persons to which the respective measure with the discriminatory goal was applied.

56 In June 1938, the originally aggrieved person sold the property in question to the German Reich (Police Administration). The purchase contract did not contain any exceptional clauses and also otherwise corresponded to other standard and unobjectionable purchase contracts. Also, the retrospective certification of the originally aggrieved person as being "Aryan" allows the conclusion that there was no affiliation to a group of persons which was discriminated against by National Socialism.

57 Since it could not be established whether Marie M.-A. was subjected to pressure or the application of means of force, this circumstance cannot be viewed as an actual discriminatory action and hence as a ground for persecution in the sense of a political persecution.

58 Hence, a persecution on political grounds of Marie M.-A. pursuant to Sec. 27 of the GSF Law did not exist.

59 The application for restitution of the property L.-straße 429, EZ X1 and EZ X2, KG Hütteldorf, was to be rejected.

Dr. Josef Aicher, university professor, Chairman
Dr. Dr. h. c. Erich Kussbach, LL.M., honorary professor and retired ambassador
MMag. Dr. August Reinisch, LL.M., university professor

Die alleinige Verfügungsbefugnis dieses Unternehmens steht somit dem Bund zu. Damit kann die Vorbedingung des Alleineigentums des Bundes als erfüllt angesehen werden.

5.3 Verfolgung

Gemäß § 27 EF-G sind Personen und deren ErbInnen antragsberechtigt, wenn einer der aufgelisteten Verfolgungsgründe, nämlich Verfolgung aus politischen Gründen, aus Gründen der Abstammung, Religion, Nationalität, sexuellen Orientierung, aufgrund einer körperlichen oder geistigen Behinderung oder aufgrund des Vorwurfes der sogenannten Asozialität, vorliegt bzw. diese das Land verlassen haben, um einer solchen Verfolgung zu entgehen. Die Aufzählung der Verfolgungsgründe ist taxativ und enthält keine weiteren Tatbestände, auf die der Antragsteller sein Begehren stützen könnte.

Eine Verfolgung der Geschädigten aus politischen Gründen kann dann gegeben sein, wenn die ursprünglich Geschädigten einer vom Nationalsozialismus diskriminierten Personengruppe (i.e. organisierte weltanschauliche GegnerInnen des Nationalsozialismus) zugehörig oder wenn sie tatsächlich diskriminierenden Handlungen unterworfen oder einer Verfolgungshandlung ausgesetzt waren, indem sie dem von der diskriminierenden Zielsetzung der jeweiligen Maßnahme gemeinten Personenkreis zugerechnet wurden.

Im Juni 1938 verkaufte die ursprünglich Geschädigte die gegenständliche Liegenschaft an das Deutsche Reich (Polizeiverwaltung). Der Kaufvertrag beinhaltete keine außergewöhnlichen Vertragsklauseln und entsprach auch sonst den unbedenklichen Kaufverträgen. Auch die nachträgliche Beurkundung, dass die ursprünglich Geschädigte „Arierin" war, lässt den Schluss zu, dass die Zugehörigkeit zu einer vom Nationalsozialismus diskriminierten Personengruppe nicht vorgelegen hat.

Da nicht festgestellt werden konnte, ob Marie M.-A. einer Druckausübung oder dem Einsatz von Zwangsmitteln ausgesetzt war, kann dieser Umstand nicht als tatsächlich diskriminierende Handlung und somit als Verfolgungsgrund im Sinne einer politischen Verfolgung gewertet werden.

Eine Verfolgung aus politischen Gründen von Marie M.-A. im Sinne des § 27 EF-G lag daher nicht vor.

Der Antrag auf Rückstellung der Liegenschaft L.-straße 429, EZ X1 und EZ X2, KG Hütteldorf war abzulehnen.

o.Univ.-Prof. Dr. Josef Aicher, Vorsitzender
Honorarprofessor Dr.Dr.h.c. Erich Kussbach LL.M., Botschafter i.R.
ao. Univ.-Prof. MMag. Dr. August Reinisch LL.M.

Press Release Decision No. 24/2005

Vienna, former Aspern Airport

On 20 September 2005, the Arbitration Panel for *In Rem* Restitution recommended the restitution of a property in Aspern owned by the City of Vienna. The Arbitration Panel arrived at this conclusion after considering the relevant research results of the Austrian Historical Commission regarding the so called "Operation Gildemeester".

In March 1938, the property subject of this application was owned by the Jewish attorney-at-law Dr. Dagobert R. The R. family, including the current applicant, joined the so called emigration operation Gildemeester in August 1938. The purpose of Operation Gildemeester, which was limited to Vienna and Graz, was to organize the emigration of needy persons who were not members of the Jewish Community but were considered Jews under the Nuremberg Laws. For this reason wealthy Jews were supposed to entrust the banking house *Krentschker & Co.*, which was appointed trustee for this operation by the NS authorities, with their entire assets. The trustee was responsible for the administration and utilization of the assets while a certain percentage of these assets was to be earmarked for financing the emigration operation. In return the contributors to the fund – approximately 100 Jewish families with around 300 depositors – hoped to quickly liquidate their assets and to receive preferential treatment upon emigration.

In April 1940, two years after joining Operation Gildemeester, Dr. Dagobert R. signed the purchase contract concluded with the German Reich regarding the property in which the German Air Force was interested due to the planned extension to the runway of the Vienna-Aspern Airport. Dr. Dagobert R. was deported to Theresienstadt with his wife in 1942. He died there in October 1943.

In 1947, the heirs of Dr. Dagobert R., including the current applicant, initiated restitution proceedings. As the property, which was located in the Soviet zone, was considered "German property", it was necessary to obtain the Soviets' consent for the opening of restitution proceedings. Due to the lack of such consent, the proceedings could only be continued and finalized after the conclusion of the State Treaty. Following the rejection of the claim for restitution by the lower instances under application of the *Dritte Staatsvertragsdurchführungsgesetz* ("Third State Treaty Implementation Act"), the Supreme Administrative Court also confirmed conclusively this legal opinion in October 1963. The decisive factor for the bodies in charge of the restitution at the time was that Dr. Dagobert R. had personally signed the purchase contract with the Air Force. The Arbitration Panel had to examine in detail these negative decisions as a re-opening of previously decided cases is – according to the GSF Law – only possible in exceptional cases.

The Arbitration Panel has the legal obligation to consider the reports of the Austrian Historical Commission during its decision making process. In its decision, it follows the study by Venus/Wenck, *Die Entziehung jüdischen Vermögens im Rahmen der Aktion Gildemeester* (Vienna 2004). In this study, the involvement of the NS regime and the transfers of assets which had taken place in the course of the Operation Gildemeester was described for the first time comprehensively. In doing so, the true character of the operation was revealed. On the basis of the occurrences at the time of joining the Operation Gildemeester which have been documented sufficiently for this particular case, the Arbitration Panel views the existence of a seizure already in the transfer of Dr. Dagobert R.'s assets to the trustee, the banking house

Pressemitteilung Entscheidung Nr. 24/2005

Wien, ehemaliges Flugfeld Aspern

Die Schiedsinstanz für Naturalrestitution hat am 20. September 2005 die Rückstellung einer der Stadt Wien gehörenden Liegenschaft in Aspern empfohlen. Die Schiedsinstanz kommt zu diesem Ergebnis unter Berücksichtigung maßgeblicher Forschungsergebnisse der österreichischen Historikerkommission zur so genannten „Gildemeester-Aktion".

Die beantragte Liegenschaft befand sich im März 1938 im Eigentum des jüdischen Rechtsanwaltes Dr. Dagobert R. Die Familie R., darunter auch die jetzige Antragstellerin, trat im August 1938 der so genannten Auswanderungsaktion Gildemeester bei. Diese auf Wien und Graz konzentrierte Aktion hatte den Zweck, die Auswanderung von bedürftigen Personen zu organisieren, die nicht Mitglieder der Israelitischen Kultusgemeinde waren, nach den Nürnberger Gesetzen aber als Juden galten. Dazu sollten wohlhabende Juden ihr gesamtes Vermögen dem von den NS-Behörden für die Aktion bestellten Treuhänder, dem Bankhaus Krentschker & Co., zur Verwaltung und Verwertung übergeben, wobei ein bestimmter Prozentsatz dieses Vermögens zur Finanzierung der Auswanderungsaktion bereitzustellen war. Als Gegenleistung versprachen sich die Fondsbeiträger – etwa 100 jüdische Familien mit rund 300 Einzahlenden – eine beschleunigte Vermögensliquidierung und bevorzugte Behandlung bei der Auswanderung.

Im April 1940, zwei Jahre nach Beitritt zur Aktion Gildemeester, unterzeichnete Dr. Dagobert R. einen mit dem Deutschen Reich geschlossenen Kaufvertrag über die Liegenschaft, an der die deutsche Luftwaffe wegen der geplanten Erweiterung des Rollfeldes beim Flughafen Wien-Aspern interessiert war. Dr. Dagobert R. wurde mit seiner Ehefrau 1942 nach Theresienstadt deportiert, wo er im Oktober 1943 starb.

Im Jahr 1947 wurde durch die Erben nach Dr. Dagobert R., darunter die jetzige Antragstellerin, das Rückstellungsverfahren eingeleitet. Da die in der Sowjetzone gelegene Liegenschaft als „Deutsches Eigentum" galt, war eine Zustimmung von sowjetischer Seite zur Durchführung des Verfahrens erforderlich. Mangels einer solchen Zustimmung konnte das Verfahren erst nach Abschluss des Staatsvertrages fortgesetzt und beendet werden. Nachdem der Rückstellungsanspruch von den unteren Instanzen unter Anwendung des Dritten Staatsvertragsdurchführungsgesetzes abgewiesen worden war, bestätigte auch der Verwaltungsgerichtshof im Oktober 1963 endgültig diese Rechtsansicht. Für die damaligen Rückstellungsinstanzen war der Umstand entscheidend, dass Dr. Dagobert R. den Kaufvertrag mit der Luftwaffe persönlich unterschrieben hatte. Die Schiedsinstanz musste sich im Detail mit diesen ablehnenden Entscheidungen auseinandersetzen, da ein Aufrollen bereits entschiedener Fälle nach dem Entschädigungsfondsgesetz nur in Ausnahmefällen möglich ist.

Die Schiedsinstanz hat den gesetzlichen Auftrag, Befunde der österreichischen Historikerkommission bei ihrer Entscheidungsfindung zu berücksichtigen. Sie folgt in ihrer Entscheidung der Studie von *Venus/Wenck*, Die Entziehung jüdischen Vermögens im Rahmen der Aktion Gildemeester (Wien 2004). Darin wurden die Involvierung des NS-Regimes und die stattgefundenen Vermögensverschiebungen im Rahmen der Gildemeester-Aktion erstmals umfassend dargestellt und damit der wahre Charakter der Aktion offengelegt. Aufgrund der für den konkreten Fall ausreichend dokumentierten Vorgänge beim Beitritt zur Aktion Gildemeester sieht die Schiedsinstanz bereits mit der Übergabe des Vermögens von Dr. Dagobert R. an den Treuhänder, das Bankhaus Krentschker & Co., den Vermögensentzug als gegeben

Krentschker & Co.. Thereupon, Dr. Dagobert R. was deprived of even the slightest degree of freedom of contract. As the seizure of assets in the framework of the Operation Gildemeester only took place due to the NS persecution, the provisions of the Third State Treaty Implementation Act do not prevent a restitution.

For use by media; not legally binding upon the Arbitration Panel for In Rem Restitution.

an. Dr. Dagobert R. war ab diesem Zeitpunkt jegliche vertragliche Gestaltungsfreiheit genommen. Da der Vermögensentzug durch die Aktion Gildemeester lediglich aus Gründen der NS-Verfolgung eingetreten ist, stehen auch die Bestimmungen des Dritten Staatsvertragsdurchführungsgesetzes einer Rückstellung nicht entgegen.

Zur Verwendung durch die Medien bestimmter Text, der die Schiedsinstanz nicht bindet.

Arbitration Panel for *In Rem* Restitution

Decision number 24/2005

The Arbitration Panel for *In Rem* Restitution (Chairman Dr. Josef Aicher, university professor, and Dr.Dr.h.c. Erich Kussbach LL.M., retired ambassador and honorary professor, as well as MMag. Dr. August Reinisch LL.M., university professor, as Members) decided on 20 September 2005 in the legal matter Rosa W. regarding *in rem* restitution of the property in Oberen Lehen, Aspern, register numbers ("EZ") X1, X2 and X3 (all formerly EZ X4), cadastral district ("KG") Eßling:

1. The restitution of the property parcels Y1/1, Y1/2, Y1/7, Y1/8, Y1/9, Y1/53 (a sub-divided area of the original property parcel Y1/53), Y1/54 and Y1/58, all constituent parts of EZ X1, KG Eßling; of the property parcels Y1/10, Y1/11, Y1/12, Y1/13, Y1/14 and Y1/15 contained in the property parcels Y1/35 and Y1/59, EZ X1, KG Eßling as well as the property parcels Y1/52 and Y1/53 (a sub-divided area of the original property parcel Y1/53) contained in the property parcel Y2, EZ X2, KG Eßling, is recommended.

2. The application for restitution of the property parcel Y1/5, EZ X3, KG Eßling, is rejected.

Reasons:

1. Submission by the Applicant

1   On 27 October 2002, the applicant Rosa W. applied for *in rem* restitution of the undeveloped property lot in Oberen Lehen, Aspern, EZ X4 (EZ X1). The City of Vienna had been the owner of the property on 17 January 2001. This claim had never previously been conclusively decided or settled by agreement by an Austrian court or administrative body. The property had been seized for religious reasons from Dr. Dagobert R., last residing at H.-straße 14, 1020 Vienna. The applicant was the heiress of Dr. R.

2   Additionally, in her earlier application for compensation of 5 June 2002 to the General Settlement Fund, the applicant, among other things, provided the following information under the property category "immovable property" in the field "cadastral district": "Esslingen Y1/1, Y1/2, Y1/5, Y1/7, Y1/8, Y1/9, Y1/10, Y1/11, Y1/12, Y1/13, Y1/14, Y1/15 and Y1/53". This property had already been the subject of Austrian court proceedings and/or administrative proceedings but the decision at that time had been extremely unjust. The remaining submission by the applicant corresponds with her statements of 27 October 2002.

2. Submission by the City of Vienna

3   On 5 January 2005, the City of Vienna commented on the application and on the documents researched by the Arbitration Panel as follows:

4   The property had been sold on 19 April 1940 by Dr. Dagobert R. to the German Reich – Reich Treasury (Aviation) for 16,835.30 Reichsmark. The purpose of this acquisition had been to facilitate the expansion of the Aspern airport ("Aspern Air-Base Project"). At the same time, numerous other property parcels in the area had also been acquired for this reason.

Schiedsinstanz für Naturalrestitution

Entscheidungsnummer 24/2005

Die Schiedsinstanz für Naturalrestitution beschließt am 20. September 2005 durch den Vorsitzenden o.Univ.-Prof. Dr. Josef Aicher und die Schiedsinstanzmitglieder Honorarprofessor Dr.Dr.h.c. Erich Kussbach LL.M., Botschafter i.R. und ao.Univ.-Prof. MMag. Dr. August Reinisch LL.M. in der Rechtssache Rosa W. wegen Naturalrestitution der Liegenschaft in der Oberen Lehen, Aspern, Einlagezahlen (EZ) X1, X2 und X3 (alle ehemals EZ X4), Katastralgemeinde (KG) Eßling:

1. **Die Rückgabe der Grundstücke Y1/1, Y1/2, Y1/7, Y1/8, Y1/9, Y1/53 (als Teilfläche des ursprünglichen Grundstückes Y1/53), Y1/54 und Y1/58, alle Bestandteil der Grundbuchseinlage X1, KG Eßling, der in die Grundstücke Y1/35 und Y1/59, Grundbuchseinlage X1, KG Eßling, einbezogenen Grundstücke Y1/10, Y1/11, Y1/12, Y1/13, Y1/14 und Y1/15 sowie der in das Grundstück Y2, Grundbuchseinlage X2, KG Eßling, einbezogenen Grundstücke Y1/52 und Y1/53 (als Teilfläche des ursprünglichen Grundstückes Y1/53) wird empfohlen.**
2. **Der Antrag auf Rückgabe des Grundstücks Y1/5, Grundbuchseinlage X3, KG Eßling, wird abgelehnt.**

Begründung:

1. Vorbringen der Antragstellerin

Die Antragstellerin Rosa W. beantragte am 27. Oktober 2002 Naturalrestitution einer unbebauten Liegenschaft in der Oberen Lehen, Aspern, mit der EZ X4 (EZ X1). Die Stadt Wien sei am 17. Jänner 2001 Eigentümerin der Liegenschaft gewesen. Diese Forderung sei niemals zuvor durch österreichische Gerichte oder Verwaltungsbehörden endgültig entschieden oder einvernehmlich geregelt worden. Die Liegenschaft sei Dr. Dagobert R., zuletzt wohnhaft in der H.-straße 14 in 1020 Wien, aus religiösen Gründen entzogen worden. Die Antragstellerin sei Erbin von Dr. R.

Darüber hinaus machte die Antragstellerin bereits in ihrem Antrag auf Entschädigung durch den Allgemeinen Entschädigungsfonds vom 5. Juni 2002 in der Vermögenskategorie „Immobilien" im Feld „Katastralgemeinde" unter anderem folgende Angaben: „Esslingen Y1/1, Y1/2, Y1/5, Y1/7, Y1/8, Y1/9, Y1/10, Y1/11, Y1/12, Y1/13, Y1/14, Y1/15 u. Y1/53". Diese Liegenschaft sei bereits Gegenstand eines österreichischen Gerichtsverfahrens bzw. eines verwaltungsbehördlichen Verfahrens gewesen, wobei die damalige Entscheidung sehr ungerecht gewesen sei. Im Übrigen deckt sich das Vorbringen der Antragstellerin mit ihren Angaben vom 27. Oktober 2002.

2. Vorbringen der Stadt Wien

Die Stadt Wien nahm am 5. Jänner 2005 zum Antrag und zu den von der Schiedsinstanz recherchierten Unterlagen wie folgt Stellung:

Die Liegenschaft sei am 19. April 1940 von Dr. Dagobert R. zu einem Preis von 16.835,30 Reichsmark an das Deutsche Reich – Reichsfiskus (Luftfahrt) verkauft worden. Zweck dieses Ankaufes sei die Vergrößerung des Flugplatzes Aspern („Projekt Fliegerhorst Aspern") gewesen, weshalb zur gleichen Zeit auch zahlreiche andere Grundstücke in der Umgebung angekauft worden seien.

5 In 1940, on the occasion of the merger with property parcel number Y3/4, the EZ X1, KG Eßling had been established. As before, the owner had been the Reich Treasury (Aviation).

6 The property EZ X4, KG Eßling had been incorporated into EZ X1, KG Eßling on 21 March 1942. At the time of the incorporation, EZ X4, KG Eßling had consisted of the property parcels Y1/1, Y1/2, Y1/5, Y1/7, Y1/8, Y1/9, Y1/10, Y1/11, Y1/12, Y1/13, Y1/14, Y1/15, Y1/52, Y1/53, Y1/54 and Y1/58.

7 In 1964, the ownership title regarding the property EZ X1, KG Eßling, had been incorporated into the land register for the Republic of Austria (Federal Buildings Administration II). This had happened on the basis of Article 22 of the *Staatsvertrag* ("State Treaty") and of para. 11 (1) of the *Erste Staatsvertragsdurchführungsgesetz* ("First State Treaty Implementation Act") of 25 July 1956, *BGBl.* ("Federal Law Gazette") No. 165/1956.

8 In 1983, due to a land-exchange contract of 13 April 1981, the ownership title to EZ X1, KG Eßling had been incorporated for the City of Vienna.

9 On 12 March 1981, the City of Vienna had sold the property parcel Y1/5, EZ X1, KG Eßling to Gerda and Max H. Finally, in 1993 the property parcel Y1/52 as well as a subdivided area of property parcel Y1/53 – in each case with the incorporation into property parcel Y2 – had been merged to form part of EZ X2, KG Eßling.

10 Regarding the property subject of this application, restitution proceedings had been pending, which had finally been concluded by the decision of 10 October 1963 by the Supreme Administrative Court. Initially, Dagobert R. had appeared as the claimant in these proceedings, having been the original owner. In 1948, his daughters Friederike O. and Rosa W. had entered into the proceedings as his legal successors. The Supreme Administrative Court had judged the case on the basis of para. 1 (2) of the *Dritte Staatsvertragsdurchführungsgesetz* ("Third State Treaty Implementation Act"), Federal Law Gazette No. 176/1957:

11 The existing military need and the location and connection to the expansion project for the Aspern airport had been the sole reason for the acquisition of the property by the German Reich. The purchase price of 16,835.30 Reichsmark, which had been determined in the purchase contract of 1940, was paid entirely by the *Luftgaukommando* ("Air-District Commando") and had been transferred for safekeeping to the banking house *Krentschker & Co.* in Vienna, which had been appointed as a trustee by the State Commissioner for Private Enterprises regarding the properties of the vendor. The property parcel subject of the restitution proceedings was located in the middle of the area that had been acquired by the Reich Treasury (Aviation) during the National Socialist period for the purpose of expanding the Aspern airfield. Thus, political considerations had been irrelevant for the acquisition of the property parcels. Property owners who had never been subjected to political (racial) persecution had also been forced to sell their property. It therefore seemed to be out of the question that the owner had been forced to sell solely for reasons of political persecution. Procedures adopted for the implementation of the acquisition which had also been linked to the political (racial) persecution, such as the agreed deposit of the purchase price with a trustee do not alter the fact that the acquisition proceeded in compliance with the laws prevailing at the time.

12 The City of Vienna drew the following conclusions from this decision: According to decision no. 1/2003 of the Arbitration Panel for *In Rem* Restitution, the seizure of a prop-

Schiedsinstanz für Naturalrestitution – Entscheidung Nr. 24/2005

Die Grundbucheinlage X1 der KG Eßling sei im Jahr 1940 anlässlich der Zuschreibung des Grundstücks mit der Nummer Y3/4 eröffnet worden. Eigentümer sei auch hier der Reichsfiskus (Luftfahrt) gewesen. 5

Die Liegenschaft mit der EZ X4 der KG Eßling sei am 21. März 1942 in die Grundbucheinlage X1 der KG Eßling einbezogen worden. Zum Einbeziehungszeitpunkt habe die EZ X4, KG Eßling aus den Grundstücken Y1/1, Y1/2, Y1/5, Y1/7, Y1/8, Y1/9, Y1/10, Y1/11, Y1/12, Y1/13, Y1/14, Y1/15, Y1/52, Y1/53, Y1/54 und Y1/58 bestanden. 6

Im Jahre 1964 sei ob der Liegenschaft mit der EZ X1, KG Eßling, das Eigentumsrecht für die Republik Österreich (Bundesgebäudeverwaltung II) einverleibt worden. Dies sei aufgrund des Art. 22 des Staatsvertrages (StV) und des § 11 (1) des Ersten Staatsvertragsdurchführungsgesetzes (1. StVDG) vom 25. Juli 1956, Bundesgesetzblatt (BGBl) Nr. 165/1956 geschehen. 7

Im Jahre 1983 sei aufgrund eines Tauschvertrages vom 13. April 1981 an der Grundbucheinlage X1, KG Eßling, das Eigentumsrecht für die Stadt Wien einverleibt worden. 8

Am 12. März 1981 habe die Stadt Wien das Grundstück mit der Nummer Y1/5, Grundbucheinlage X1 der KG Eßling, an Gerda und Max H. verkauft. Im Jahr 1993 seien schließlich das Grundstück Nr. Y1/52 sowie eine Teilfläche des Grundstückes Nr. Y1/53 – jeweils unter Einbeziehung in das Grundstück Nr. Y2 – zur Grundbucheinlage X2 der KG Eßling zugeschrieben worden. 9

Bezüglich der gegenständlichen Liegenschaft sei ein Rückstellungsverfahren anhängig gewesen, welches mit dem Erkenntnis des Verwaltungsgerichtshofes (VwGH) vom 10. Oktober 1963 endgültig beendet worden sei. Als Antragsteller sei in diesem Verfahren zunächst Dagobert R. als ursprünglicher Grundstückseigentümer aufgetreten. Im Jahr 1948 seien seine Töchter Friederike O. und Rosa W. als seine Rechtsnachfolgerinnen in das Verfahren eingetreten. Der VwGH habe den Fall anhand des § 1 Abs 2 des Dritten Staatsvertragsdurchführungsgesetzes (3. StVDG), BGBl Nr. 176/1957, beurteilt: 10

Für den Erwerb des Grundstücks durch das Deutsche Reich seien allein der hierfür gegebene militärische Bedarf bzw. die Lage und Zugehörigkeit zu dem Projekt der Vergrößerung des Flugplatzes Aspern maßgebend gewesen. Der im Kaufvertrag von 1940 festgelegte Kaufpreis in der Höhe von 16.835,30 Reichsmark sei zur Gänze vom Luftgaukommando bezahlt worden und zu treuen Händen des vom Staatskommissar in der Privatwirtschaft bezüglich der Vermögenschaften des Verkäufers bestellten Treuhänders, des Bankhauses Krentschker & Co. in Wien, überwiesen worden. Das rückstellungsverfangene Grundstück habe sich inmitten jenes Gebietes befunden, das während der NS-Zeit zum Zwecke der Vergrößerung des Flugfeldes Aspern vom Reichsfiskus Luftfahrt erworben worden sei. Demnach hätten politische Momente bei der Erwerbung der Grundstücke keine Rolle gespielt. Auch niemals der politischen (rassischen) Verfolgung ausgesetzt gewesene Eigentümer von Grundstücken seien zur Veräußerung ihres Grundbesitzes verhalten worden. Daher erscheine es ausgeschlossen, dass der Eigentümer lediglich aufgrund politischer Verfolgung zur Veräußerung genötigt worden sei. Daran vermögen auch Modalitäten in der Durchführung des Erwerbsvorganges, die mit der politischen (rassischen) Verfolgung im Zusammenhang gestanden seien, wie der vereinbarte treuhändige Erlag des Kaufpreises nichts zu ändern und der Erwerbsvorgang entspreche den damaligen Gesetzen. 11

Aus diesem Erkenntnis zog die Stadt Wien folgende Schlüsse: Nach der Entscheidung 1/2003 der Schiedsinstanz für Naturalrestitution sei der Entzug einer Liegenschaft für sich allein noch keine Verfolgungshandlung. Dem Entzug müsse ein davor liegender Wille des nationalsozialistischen Regimes vorangehen, welcher die Verfolgung des Geschädigten 12

erty alone does not constitute an act of persecution. The seizure would have to be preceded by the intention of the National Socialist regime to persecute the aggrieved person. This intention to persecute would have to be evident by means of an act of force. It was to be taken from the Supreme Administrative Court's decision that the property in question represented part of an area which had been assigned to a large project of the German Armed Forces, i.e. the building of the Aspern air-base. The acquisition of contiguous properties had been necessary for the realization of this project. Hence, the basis for the transactions in question, which the then owner had been forced to comply with, was not motives (political reasons, origin, religion, etc.) as described in Sec. 28 (1) item 1 of the *Entschädigungsfondsgesetz* ("General Settlement Fund Law" – GSF Law). The only concern had been the realization of the project of the German Armed Forces. For this reason, an act of persecution in accordance with Sec. 28 (1) item 1 of the GSF Law did not exist.

13   Also, the conclusion of the restitution proceedings with the above-mentioned decision of the Supreme Administrative Court in principle did not allow an *in rem* restitution. Exceptions to this principle are only allowed in particular specific cases. The Arbitration Panel must unanimously reach the conclusion that such a decision constituted an extreme injustice according to Sec. 28 (1) item 2 of the GSF Law. It was not evident from the application that the existence of an extreme injustice had been asserted.

14   Nevertheless, the City of Vienna was already dealing with this problem: Up to now, the Arbitration Panel had explained that a previous decision of an Austrian court or administrative body was regarded extremely unjust if it was based on a decision-making process which indicated that the statutory basis of the decision had been applied unobjectively to the disadvantage of the aggrieved person and that therefore the aggrieved person had been grossly disadvantaged. By its own admission, the Arbitration Panel was not authorized (referring to decision no. 3/2003 regarding para. 31 (1) of the First State Treaty Implementation Act) to examine general legal regulations with a view to a possible extreme injustice. The same holds true with respect to para. 1 of the Third State Treaty Implementation Act.

15   No indications of an extreme injustice could be inferred from the submitted documents. On the one hand, the "Aspern Air-Base Project", part of which concerned the property subject of the application, was well documented. On the other hand, after considering restitution proceedings of other properties, the conclusion could not be drawn that in the W. case, legal regulations had been interpreted to the disadvantage of the claimants. The Supreme Administrative Court had also dealt with restitution proceedings of adjacent properties and had expressed the above-mentioned arguments in a consistent and logical manner. The application of the Third State Treaty Implementation Act by the Supreme Administrative Court had been carried out in a justifiable manner.

16   According to the decisions nos. 3/2003 and 4/2004, an overly long duration of proceedings can be a criterion for the existence of an extreme injustice, however, this could not be applied to proceedings which were concluded by a decision. Shorter proceedings would not have altered the negative decision. Furthermore, the entry into force of the Third State Treaty Implementation Act (Federal Law Gazette No. 176/1957) had been a prerequisite for the decision.

17   In its submission of 9 September 2005, the City of Vienna initially supplemented its statement concerning the properties subject of the application. The 14,612 m^2 area of the property parcels which had been sold by Dr. R. on 19 April 1940 corresponded exactly with the area of the property parcels which the City of Vienna had acquired from the Republic of Austria on 13 April 1981. The property parcels Y1/10, Y1/11, Y1/12, Y1/13, Y1/14 and

bezwecke. Dieser Verfolgungszweck müsse im Zwangsakt seinen Ausdruck finden. Dem Erkenntnis des VwGH sei zu entnehmen, dass die gegenständliche Liegenschaft Teil eines Gebietes darstelle, das einem Großprojekt der Wehrmacht gewidmet gewesen sei: der Errichtung des Fliegerhorstes Aspern. Zur Realisierung dieses Projektes sei der Erwerb von Liegenschaften in einem zusammenhängenden Areal notwendig gewesen. Grundlage der gegenständlichen Transaktionen, zu denen der seinerzeitige Eigentümer verhalten worden sei, seien damit nicht Motive, wie sie im § 28 (1) Z 1 Entschädigungsfondsgesetz (EF-G) angeführt sind (politische Gründe, Abstammung, Religion, etc.), sondern es sei um die Umsetzung eines Wehrmachtsprojektes gegangen. Daher liege eine Verfolgungshandlung gemäß § 28 Abs 1 Z 1 EF-G nicht vor.

Außerdem spreche das mit oben erwähntem Erkenntnis des VwGH abgeschlossene Rückstellungsverfahren grundsätzlich gegen eine Naturalrestitution. Eine Ausnahme von diesem Grundsatz werde nur in besonderen Einzelfällen gemacht. Die Schiedsinstanz müsse einstimmig zur Auffassung gelangen, dass eine solche Entscheidung eine extreme Ungerechtigkeit gemäß § 28 Abs 1 Z 2 EF-G darstelle. Aus dem Antrag sei nicht ersichtlich, dass das Vorliegen einer extremen Ungerechtigkeit behauptet worden sei.   13

Dennoch gehe die Stadt Wien bereits jetzt auf diese Problematik ein: Bisher habe die Schiedsinstanz ausgeführt, dass eine frühere Entscheidung eines österreichischen Gerichtes oder einer Verwaltungsbehörde insbesondere dann als extrem ungerecht angesehen werde, wenn sie auf einer Entscheidungsfindung beruht, die darauf hindeutet, dass gesetzliche Entscheidungsgrundlagen objektiv unvertretbar zu Lasten des Geschädigten angewendet worden seien und der Geschädigte dadurch grob benachteiligt worden sei. Die Schiedsinstanz sei nach eigenen Angaben nicht dazu berufen (Hinweis auf Entscheidung 3/2003 betreffend § 31 Abs 1 des 1. StVDG), generelle gesetzliche Regelungen auf eine etwaige extreme Ungerechtigkeit zu prüfen. Dies habe auch für § 1 des 3. StVDG zu gelten.   14

Aus den vorliegenden Unterlagen ergäben sich keine Anhaltspunkte für eine extreme Ungerechtigkeit. Einerseits sei das Projekt „Fliegerhorst Aspern", dessen Teil die verfahrensgegenständliche Liegenschaft sei, gut dokumentiert, und andererseits gelange man auch aus den Rückstellungsverfahren bezüglich anderer Liegenschaften nicht zu dem Ergebnis, dass im Fall W. gesetzliche Bestimmungen zu Lasten der AntragstellerInnen ausgelegt worden seien. Der VwGH habe sich nämlich auch mit Rückstellungsverfahren benachbarter Liegenschaften befasst und die bereits dargestellten Argumente in einheitlicher und nachvollziehbarer Weise zum Ausdruck gebracht. Die Anwendung des 3. StVDG durch den VwGH sei in vertretbarer Weise erfolgt.   15

Das Kriterium der überlangen Verfahrensdauer, das nach den Entscheidungen 3/2003 und 4/2004 das Vorliegen einer extremen Ungerechtigkeit eines Vergleiches indizieren kann, könne auf ein mit Entscheidung abgeschlossenes Verfahren nicht angewendet werden. Auch eine kürzere Verfahrensdauer hätte nichts an der abschlägigen Entscheidung geändert. Überdies sei für die Entscheidung in der Sache das Inkrafttreten des 3. StVDG (BGBl Nr. 176/1957) Voraussetzung gewesen.   16

In ihrer Stellungnahme vom 9. September 2005 ergänzte die Stadt Wien zunächst ihr Vorbringen zu den antragsgegenständlichen Liegenschaften. Das Flächenausmaß der von Dr. R. am 19. April 1940 verkauften Grundstücke stimme mit dem Flächenausmaß der von der Stadt Wien von der Republik Österreich am 13. April 1981 erworbenen Grundstücke – 14.612 m^2 – exakt überein. Die Grundstücke mit den Nrn. Y1/10, Y1/11, Y1/12, Y1/13, Y1/14 und Y1/15 mit einer Gesamtfläche von 2.553 m^2 seien zur Tagebuchzahl 5647/1986 mit dem Grundstück Nr. Y1/35 vereinigt worden. Gleichzeitig sei das vergrößerte Grundstück Nr. Y1/35 in die Grundstücke Nr. Y1/35 und Nr. Y1/59 unterteilt worden. Die Flä-   17

Y1/15 with a total area of 2,553 m² had been combined with property parcel Y1/35 under the daily file number 5647/1986. At the same time, the enlarged property parcel Y1/35 had been subdivided into property parcels Y1/35 and Y1/59. Today, the area of property parcel Y1/35 amounts to 12,727 m²; the area of Y1/59 amounts to 4,451 m². Property parcel Y1/52 with an area of 81 m² and a sub-divided area of property parcel Y1/53 with an area of 8 m² have been merged to form daily file number 5316/1992 of EZ X2 (public property), KG Eßling and have been combined with property parcel Y2. Regarding this property parcel, N.-E.-Straße was designated a public road; an *in rem* restitution could not take place as Sec. 34, sentence 2 of the GSF Law would have to be observed. The remaining property parcel Y1/53 was still registered under EZ X1, KG Eßling, and had an area of 703 m².

18 Regarding the request of the Arbitration Panel for a statement on the "Operation Gildemeester", the City of Vienna initially compiled a general submission on its organization and course of events. According to the City of Vienna, a conclusive historic assessment and evaluation of "Operation Gildemeester" as a forced seizure could not be achieved even after studying the book Theodor Venus/Alexandra-Eileen Wenck, *Die Entziehung jüdischen Vermögens im Rahmen der Aktion Gildemeester*, as this particular subject was left unresolved by the authors. In the introduction on page 24, the authors themselves cited Charles Ka., the head of the Foreign Exchange Department of the Jewish Community in Vienna, as an example of the vagueness of a possible assessment and the objective difficulties. He commented on the operation as follows:

> "'Operation Gildemeester' was a mysterious matter placed in the no-man's-land between the *Gestapo* ["Secret State Police"] and welfare. I don't think that in this case one can speak of compulsion, but with the help of 'Operation Gildemeester', the people hoped for a quicker emigration than with the help of the Community."

19 From a legal point of view, the assessment by the Supreme Administrative Court was to be adhered to as the personal conclusion of the contract by Dr. R. on 19 April 1940 showed that only by joining "Operation Gildemeester" a seizure in the meaning of the restitution laws did not exist. No sales trustee had been appointed in compliance with the *Verordnung über den Einsatz jüdischen Vermögens* ("Ordinance on the Use of Jewish Property") of 3 December 1938. The file of the Reich Governor in Vienna, Higher Administration for Settlement, also indicated that Dr. R. himself was active as a vendor. A letter from the banking house *Krentschker & Co.*, which referred to its role as a trustee in "Operation Gildemeester", had been answered by a letter dated 13 November 1940 from the Administration for Settlement. In this letter, it was stated that an appointment of a trustee of this kind concerning agricultural land was ineffective. On 11 January 1941, Dr. R. had gone to see the authority in person. On 21 January 1941, he had lodged a successful legal appeal against the imposition of a general reduction of 20 % of the value established in the expert valuation so that, in consequence, the full price of 16,835.50 Reichsmark had been transferred to the (frozen) account of the banking house *Krentschker & Co.*

20 A comparison of the two decisions by the Supreme Administrative Court, one of 29 November 1962, file number 272/60, and one of 10 October 1963 regarding the property in question, showed that the decision of 10 October 1963, which had been issued about one year later, did not make any reference to the decision passed in 1962. This would seem to suggest that the Supreme Administrative Court itself assumed differing circumstances: In the facts, which served as a basis for the decision made in 1962, the *Deutsche Wirtschaftsprüfungs- und Treuhandgesellschaft* ("German Audit and Trust Company") had been appointed as a trustee by means of an executive order of 29 January 1940 by the *Abwick-*

che des Grundstücks Nr. Y1/35 betrage heute 12.727 m², jene des Grundstücks Nr. Y1/59 4.451 m². Das Grundstück Nr. Y1/52 im Ausmaß von 81 m² und eine Teilfläche des Grundstücks Nr. Y1/53 im Ausmaß von 8 m² seien zur Tagebuchzahl 5316/1992 der Grundbuchseinlage X2 (öffentliches Gut), KG Eßling, zugeschrieben und mit dem Grundstück Nr. Y2 vereinigt worden. Bezüglich dieses Grundstücks liege eine Widmung als öffentliche Straße vor („N.-E.-Straße"); eine Naturalrestitution könne nicht erfolgen, sondern es müsse § 34 2. Satz EF-G beachtet werden. Das restliche Grundstück Nr. Y1/53 liege heute noch in der Grundbuchseinlage X1, KG Eßling, ein und habe eine Fläche von 703 m².

Zu der am 20. Juli 2005 durch die Schiedsinstanz aufgetragenen Stellungnahme zur Gildemeester-Aktion erstattete die Stadt Wien zunächst ein allgemeines Vorbringen zu deren Organisation und Ablauf. Nach Ansicht der Stadt Wien gelinge eine abschließende geschichtliche Beurteilung bzw. Bewertung der „Gildemeester-Aktion" dahingehend, ob es sich um eine zwangsweise Entziehung handle auch nach Studium des Werkes Theodor *Venus*/Alexandra-Eileen *Wenck,* Die Entziehung jüdischen Vermögens im Rahmen der Aktion Gildemeester, nicht, da dieser Punkt auch von den Autoren offen gelassen werde. Die Autoren selbst würden in der Einleitung auf Seite 24 Charles Ka., Leiter der Devisenabteilung der Israeltischen Kultusgemeinde (IKG) in Wien, als Beispiel für die Unschärfen einer möglichen Beurteilung und die objektiven Schwierigkeiten dafür zitieren, der die Aktion folgendermaßen einschätze: 18

„Die ,Aktion Gildemeester' war eine mysteriöse Angelegenheit im Niemandsland zwischen Gestapo und Wohlfahrt. Ich glaube nicht, dass man von Zwang reden kann, aber die Leute versprachen sich eine schnellere Auswanderung mit Hilfe der ‚Aktion Gildemeester' als durch die Kultusgemeinde."

Aus rechtlicher Sicht sei der Beurteilung des VwGH zu folgen, da der persönliche Abschluss des Kaufvertrages durch Dr. R. am 19. April 1940 zeige, dass allein durch den Beitritt zur „Aktion Gildemeester" keine Entziehung im Sinne der Rückstellungsgesetze vorliege. Es sei kein Veräußerungstreuhänder gemäß der Verordnung über den Einsatz jüdischen Vermögens vom 3. Dezember 1938 bestellt worden. Auch aus dem Akt des Reichsstatthalters in Wien, Obere Siedlungsbehörde, gehe hervor, dass Dr. R. selbst Tätigkeiten als Verkäufer setzte. Ein Schreiben des Bankhauses Krentschker & Co., in dem dieses auf seine Rolle als Treuhänder der „Aktion Gildemeester" verweise, sei von der Siedlungsbehörde mit Schreiben vom 13. November 1940 dahingehend beantwortet worden, dass eine derartige Treuhandbestellung in Bezug auf landwirtschaftlich genutzte Flächen unwirksam sei. Am 11. Jänner 1941 habe Dr. R. persönlich bei der Behörde vorgesprochen. Am 21. Jänner 1941 habe er ein erfolgreiches Rechtsmittel gegen die Festlegung eines allgemeinen Abschlages von 20 % auf den im Schätzgutachten ermittelten Wert eingelegt, sodass der, laut Schätzgutachten, volle Preis von 16.835,50 Reichsmark auf das (Sperr)konto des Bankhauses Krentschker & Co. überwiesen worden sei. 19

Ein Vergleich der beiden Erkenntnisse des VwGH, jenes vom 29. November 1962, Zl. 272/60, und des vom 10. Oktober 1963 zur antragsgegenständlichen Liegenschaft, zeige, dass sich in der rund ein Jahr später ergangenen Entscheidung vom 10. Oktober 1963 kein Hinweis auf die Entscheidung aus dem Jahr 1962 finde. Dies lege den Schluss nahe, dass der VwGH selbst von einem unterschiedlichen Sachverhalt ausgegangen sei: In dem dem Erkenntnis aus dem Jahr 1962 zugrundeliegenden Sachverhalt sei durch die Abwicklungsstelle der Vermögensverkehrsstelle (VVSt) Wien mit Dekret vom 29. Jänner 1940 die Deutsche Wirtschaftsprüfungs- und Treuhandgesellschaft auf Grund der Verordnung über den Einsatz jüdischen Vermögens vom 3. Dezember 1938 zum Treuhänder bestellt worden. Der Abschluss des Kaufvertrages sei am 14. März 1941 durch die Wirtschaftsprüfungs- und Treuhandgesellschaft als Vertreter des Eigentümers erfolgt. 20

lungsstelle ("Processing and Settlement Office") of the *Vermögensverkehrsstelle* ("Property Transaction Office") Vienna, on the basis of the Ordinance on the Use of Jewish Property of 3 December 1938. The purchase contract had been concluded on 14 March 1941 by the German Audit and Trust Company, which represented the owner.

21 With respect to the facts that are to be presently considered, the banking house *Krentschker & Co.* did not act a sales trustee in accordance with the Ordinance on the Use of Jewish Property of 3 December 1938. Dr. R. himself had been the vendor on 19 April 1940.

22 In the view of the Supreme Administrative Court, in the first case, the seizure had taken place at the time of the appointment of the trustee and not only when the purchase contract was concluded on 14 March 1941. In the case of Dr. R., the seizure had only occurred after the conclusion of the purchase contract, and therefore in direct connection with a project of the German Armed Forces. "Operation Gildemeester" itself did not represent an obligation to surrender property. Hence, on account of para. 1 (2) of the Third State Treaty Implementation Act, a seizure of property, which could have given rise to claims for restitution, did not exist.

23 Regarding the question of extreme injustice, the City of Vienna submitted the following supplementary statement: Compensation for losses caused by the payment of discriminatory taxes had been provided for by the *Abgeltungsfonds* ("Compensation Fund"), which was established by law in 1961. In all cases in which Gildemeester-participants had filed claims, claims for the compensation of discriminatory taxes had also been filed. On page 497/498, Venus/Wenck referred to the fact that in the case of family R. all three entitled heirs had died prior to the compensation payment, resulting in the remaining compensation being returned to the fund. However, this was not logical and contradicted what was recorded in the file. The heirs of the original owner, Dr. Dagobert R., were his two daughters Friederike O. and Rosa W. Additionally, in 1963 Bertha R. had renounced – before the Compensation Fund – all payments compensating losses of her husband's assets in favor of her two daughters. Friederike O. had died on 30 March 1963. Her sister, the applicant, was alive.

24 Rosa W. had been awarded a so-called original payment of 120,601.74 Schilling by the Compensation Fund. At least 49,839.11 Schilling of this amount had been disbursed. Rosa W. had been actively involved in the proceedings; she had also lodged an appeal against the decision. The property parcels subject of the application also appeared in the files of the Compensation Fund. Therefore, it appeared that discriminating taxes also concerning this property had been covered by the compensation. For this reason, Rosa W. had already received compensation, also concerning the property losses of her father Dr. Dagobert R., through the Compensation Fund. As a result, an *in rem* restitution in accordance with Sec. 28 (1) item 2 second case of the GSF Law is precluded since the stated injustice had already been compensated.

3. Established Facts

25 The applicant was born on 24 June 1906 as the daughter of Dr. Dagobert (aka David) and Bertha R.

26 Dr. Dagobert R. was born on 17 October 1865 and died on 17 October 1943 in the concentration camp Theresienstadt. Bertha R. was born on 13 April 1871 and died on 11 November 1967 in Bondi, Australia.

27 Besides the applicant, the spouses R. had another daughter, Friederike O., née R., divorced F., born on 7 May 1898. Friederike O. died on 30 March 1963 in Vienna. Friederike O. has no direct descendants.

Im hier zu beurteilenden Sachverhalt sei das Bankhaus Krentschker & Co. kein Veräußerungstreuhänder gemäß der Verordnung über den Einsatz des jüdischen Vermögens vom 3. Dezember 1938. Der Verkäufer am 19. April 1940 sei Dr. R. selbst gewesen. 21

Nach Ansicht des VwGH sei im ersten Fall der Vermögensentzug zum Zeitpunkt der Treuhandbestellung eingetreten – und nicht erst zum Zeitpunkt des Kaufvertragsabschlusses am 14. März 1941. Im Fall R. sei die Entziehung erst durch den Vertragsabschluss – und damit in direktem Zusammenhang mit einem Wehrmachtsprojekt – eingetreten. Die Gildemeester-Aktion selbst stelle keinen Zwang zur Vermögensaufgabe dar. Daher liege aufgrund von § 1 Abs 2 des 3. StVDG auch keine Vermögensentziehung vor, die zu Rückstellungsansprüchen hätte führen können. 22

Zur Frage der extremen Ungerechtigkeit erstattete die Stadt Wien folgendes ergänzendes Vorbringen: Durch den 1961 gesetzlich eingerichteten so genannten Abgeltungsfonds seien Entschädigungen für Verluste, die durch die Entrichtung diskriminierender Steuern entstanden waren, vorgesehen worden. In allen Fällen, in denen Gildemeester-TeilnehmerInnen Anträge gestellt hätten, seien auch Anträge auf Entschädigung für diskriminierende Steuern gestellt worden. Wenn in *Venus/Wenck*, Seite 497/498, darauf hingewiesen werde, dass im Falle der Familie R. vor Abschluss der Auszahlung alle drei berechtigten ErbInnen verstorben seien, sodass der Rest der Entschädigung an den Fonds zurückgefallen sei, so sei dies nicht nachvollziehbar und widerspreche der Aktenlage. ErbInnen des ursprünglichen Grundeigentümers Dr. Dagobert R. seien seine beiden Töchter Friederike O. und Rosa W. Im Jahre 1963 habe Bertha R. gegenüber dem Abgeltungsfonds zudem auf alle Zuwendungen für Vermögensverluste nach ihrem Gatten zugunsten ihrer beiden Töchter verzichtet. Friederike O. sei am 30. März 1963 verstorben, ihre Schwester Rosa W., die Antragstellerin, sei am Leben. 23

Rosa W. sei vom Abgeltungsfonds eine so genannte ursprüngliche Zuwendung von 120.601,74 Schilling zugesprochen worden. Davon seien zumindest 49.839,11 Schilling ausbezahlt worden. Rosa W. sei in das Verfahren aktiv involviert gewesen, sie habe auch ein Rechtsmittel gegen die Entscheidung erhoben. Die gegenständlichen Grundstücke würden auch in den Akten des Abgeltungsfonds aufscheinen. Es liege daher nahe, dass diskriminierende Abgaben auch betreffend diese Liegenschaft in die Entschädigung einbezogen worden seien. Daher habe Rosa W. durch den Abgeltungsfonds bereits eine Entschädigung – auch was Vermögensverluste ihres Vaters Dr. Dagobert R. betreffe – erhalten. Damit sei eine Naturalrestitution gemäß § 28 Abs 1 Z 2 2. Fall EF-G ausgeschlossen, da bereits eine Entschädigung für das geschehene Unrecht geleistet worden sei. 24

3. Festgestellter Sachverhalt

Die Antragstellerin wurde am 24. Juni 1906 als Tochter von Dr. Dagobert (auch David) und Bertha R. geboren. 25

Dr. Dagobert R. wurde am 17. Oktober 1865 geboren und verstarb am 17. Oktober 1943 im Konzentrationslager Theresienstadt. Bertha R. wurde am 13. April 1871 geboren und verstarb am 11. November 1967 in Bondi, Australien. 26

Neben der Antragstellerin hatte das Ehepaar R. eine weitere Tochter, Friederike O., geborene R., geschiedene F., geboren am 7. Mai 1898. Friederike O. verstarb am 30. März 1963 in Wien. Friederike O. hat keine direkten Nachkommen. 27

Der Nachlass von Dr. Dagobert R. wurde am 7. Dezember 1948 je zur Hälfte seinen beiden Töchtern Friederike O. und der Antragstellerin Rosa W. eingeantwortet, nachdem Bertha R. die Erbschaft ausgeschlagen hatte. 28

28   On 7 December 1948, the estate of Dr. R. was devolved to his daughters Friederike O. and the applicant Rosa W, each receiving one half after Bertha R. had relinquished the inheritance.

29   On 10 May 1963, the inheritance of Friederike O. was devolved in its entirety to her nephew George W., Bondi, Australia. He is the son of the applicant. On 27 October 2002, George W. had assigned to Rosa W. all restitution claims to which he was legally entitled as the legal successor to Friederike O.

30   On 12 March 1938, Dr. Dagobert R., resident of H.-straße 14/9, 2nd District, Vienna, member of the Jewish Community, was the owner of EZ X4, KG Eßling, juridical district Groß-Enzersdorf. This property consisted of the property parcels Y1/1, Y1/2, Y1/5, Y1/6, Y1/7, Y1/8, Y1/9, Y1/10, Y1/11, Y1/12, Y1/13, Y1/14, Y1/15, Y1/52, Y1/53 and Y1/54. On 24 March 1938, the property parcel Y1/6 had been changed to Y1/58.

31   In August 1938, Dr. Dagobert R. and his wife Bertha, their daughters Rosa W. and Friederike F. and their spouses Otto W. and Karl F. joined "Emigration Operation Gildemeester" in order to be able to rapidly emigrate and to pay the taxes prescribed by the National Socialist regime (Reich Flight Tax, Jewish capital levy) by means of the liquidation of their assets.

32   The purpose of Operation Gildemeester, which was limited to the conurbations of Vienna and Graz, was to organize, finance and accelerate the emigration of needy persons who were not members of the Jewish Community but were considered Jews pursuant to the Nuremberg Laws. For this reason wealthy Jews were supposed to entrust banking house *Krentschker & Co.* with their entire assets. On 30 May 1938, the State Commissioner for Private Enterprises had appointed the banking house *Krentschker & Co.* to be the trustee during this operation. The trustee was to be responsible for the administration and utilization of the assets while a certain percentage (usually 10 %) of these assets were to be earmarked for financing the emigration operation. The relationship between the beneficiary and the trustee was recorded in a so-called "trust protocol" and in an inventory regarding the property to be entrusted. Finally, admission to Operation Gildemeester occurred within the framework of regular meetings between Dr. Erich Ra., who was the legal adviser of the operation, and representatives of the Secret State Police. In total, approximately 100 Jewish families with around 300 depositors joined the operation. The peak time for joining Operation Gildemeester was during the period from May 1938 to March 1939.

33   On 19 August 1938, Dr. Dagobert and Bertha R., Rosa and Otto W. as well as Friederike and Karl F., the latter personally, the others through a representative, in the presence of Moritz K. as the representative of the banking house *Krentschker & Co.*, Vienna I., Bösendorferstrasse 2, stated the following before Dr. Erich Ra., trainee lawyer in Vienna I., S.-ring 8:

> "I. We have instructed the banking house *Krentschker & Co.* to assume our entire assets in order to hold them in trust and for utilization. We will provide the details on the acquisition of the assets by the banking house *Krentschker & Co.* to the best of our knowledge and belief. The inventory, which will be drawn up by the banking house *Krentschker & Co.*, will be added to this statement. […] We have given the banking house *Krentschker & Co.* the power-of-attorney and have explicitly authorized it to be served tax law notices on our behalf, especially concerning the Reich Flight Tax for the Territory of Austria. Also, to give in our name legally binding declarations to the tax authorities, thus also to the Reich Flight Tax office for the territory of Austria.

Der Nachlass von Friederike O. wurde am 10. Mai 1963 zur Gänze ihrem Neffen George W., Bondi, Australien, dem Sohn der Antragstellerin, eingeantwortet. George W. hat am 27. Oktober 2002 alle ihm als Rechtsnachfolger nach Friederike O. zustehenden Restitutionsansprüche an Rosa W. abgetreten.

Dr. Dagobert R., wohnhaft in der H.-straße 14/9 im 2. Wiener Gemeindebezirk, Angehöriger der israelitischen Religionsgemeinschaft, war am 12. März 1938 Eigentümer der Grundbuchseinlage X4, KG Eßling, Gerichtsbezirk Groß-Enzersdorf. Diese Liegenschaft bestand aus den Grundstücken Y1/1, Y1/2, Y1/5, Y1/6, Y1/7, Y1/8, Y1/9, Y1/10, Y1/11, Y1/12, Y1/13, Y1/14, Y1/15, Y1/52, Y1/53 und Y1/54. Am 24. März 1938 wurde die Grundstücksnummer Y1/6 in Y1/58 abgeändert.

Dr. Dagobert R. und seine Ehefrau Bertha, ebenso wie ihre Töchter Rosa W. und Friederike F. samt deren Ehegatten Otto W. und Karl F., traten im August 1938 der „Auswanderungsaktion Gildemeester" bei, um rasch auswandern und die vom nationalsozialistischen Regime vorgeschriebenen Steuern (Reichsfluchtsteuer, Judenvermögensabgabe) durch Liquidierung ihres Vermögens bezahlen zu können.

Die auf die Ballungsräume Wien und Graz beschränkte Aktion Gildemeester hatte den Zweck, die Auswanderung von bedürftigen Personen, die nicht Mitglieder der IKG waren, nach den Nürnberger Gesetzen aber als Juden galten, zu organisieren, zu finanzieren und zu beschleunigen. Dazu sollten vermögende Juden ihr gesamtes Vermögen dem durch den Staatskommissar in der Privatwirtschaft am 30. Mai 1938 für diese Aktion bestellten Treuhänder, das Bankhaus Krentschker & Co., zur Verwaltung und Verwertung übergeben, wobei ein bestimmter Prozentsatz dieses Vermögens (im allgemeinen 10 %) zur Finanzierung der Auswanderungsaktion bereitzustellen war. Das Verhältnis zwischen Treugeber und Treuhänder wurde in einem so genannten Treuhandprotokoll und in einer Inventarliste über das zu übergebende Vermögen festgehalten. Die Aufnahme in die Aktion Gildemeester erfolgte schließlich im Rahmen von regelmäßigen Besprechungen zwischen dem Rechtsberater der Aktion Dr. Erich Ra. und Vertretern der Gestapo. Insgesamt nahmen etwa 100 jüdische Familien mit einer Gesamtzahl von rund 300 Fondsbeiträgern an der Aktion teil. Der zeitliche Schwerpunkt des Beitritts zur Aktion Gildemeester fiel in den Zeitraum von Mai 1938 bis März 1939.

Am 19. August 1938 gaben Dr. Dagobert und Bertha R., Rosa und Otto W. sowie Friederike und Karl F., letzterer persönlich, alle anderen durch einen Vertreter, vor Dr. Erich Ra., Rechtsanwaltsanwärter in Wien I., S.-ring 8 in Anwesenheit von Moritz K. als Vertreter des Bankhauses Krentschker & Co., Wien I., Bösendorferstraße 2, Folgendes zu Protokoll:

„I. Wir haben dem Bankgeschäft Krentschker & Co. den Auftrag erteilt, unser gesamtes Vermögen treuhändig zur Verwaltung und Verwertung zu übernehmen. Die Angaben zur Vermögensübernahme durch das Bankgeschäft Krentschker & Co. werden wir nach bestem Wissen und Gewissen machen. Die Inventuraufnahme, welche das Bankgeschäft Krentschker & Co. anfertigen wird, wird diesem Gedenkprotokoll angeschlossen werden. [...] Wir haben das Bankgeschäft Krentschker & Co. ausdrücklich bevollmächtigt und ermächtigt, steuerrechtliche Zustellungen, insbesondere solche der Reichsfluchtsteuer für das Land Oesterreich für uns entgegenzunehmen und in rechtsverbindlicher Weise für uns den Steuerbehörden, somit auch der Reichsfluchtsteuerstelle für das Land Oesterreich gegenüber Erklärungen abzugeben.

II. [...] Aus den übernommen Vermögenswerten hat das Bankgeschäft Krentschker & Co. unsere sämtlichen Verbindlichkeiten zu decken. Hiezu gehören insbesondere

II. [...] The banking house *Krentschker & Co.* is to cover our obligations in their entirety from the assumed assets. Reich Flight Tax and other taxes particularly form part of this. Further, the banking house *Krentschker & Co.* is to place at our disposal an amount of ... [sic!] 125,000 Reichsmark (in letters: Reichsmark one hundred twenty five thousand) with the Jewish Community, for the acquisition of 2,000 English Pounds (Capitalist Certificate). Furthermore, the banking house *Krentschker & Co.* is to place at our disposal those amounts that are necessary to cover our living expenses, namely a total of 1,500 Reichsmark (in letters: Reichsmark one thousand five hundred) per month, the expenses and costs connected to our departure including an amount of 14,000 Reichsmark (in letters: Reichsmark fourteen thousand) to purchase equipment, for possible charges including the approval for transfer of jewelry, carpets, furniture (old property) and above-mentioned equipment (new property); as well as finally providing the means for the expenses of Dr. Camillo von L[...].

III. [...] The remaining surplus after the costs and expenses of the banking house *Krentschker & Co.* including the costs for the legal consultation of the banking house *Krentschker & Co.* have been covered is to be paid to the Gildemester Fund or to the administrator of the emigration-relief operation Gildemester.

IV. To cover the costs of the banking house *Krentschker & Co.* including their legal consultation we offer   % (in letters: percent) of the net property at the time of the registration with Operation Gildemester. [...] We are depositing with Dr. Hugo We[...], attorney in Vienna I., S[...]-ring 8, as the representative of the banking house *Krentschker & Co.*, the notarized proxies, in the names of Dr. Hugo We[...] and Dr. Erich Ra[...], Vienna, on and request the mentioned persons to make decisions for us, which will be deemed necessary by the trustee, and to submit all legally binding declarations and carry out all acts, which are necessary to put our entire property at the disposition of the banking house *Krentschker & Co.*"

34   The transfer of the assets of the families R., F. and W. to the banking house *Krentschker & Co.* took place on 23 August 1938. The fiduciary transfer of the property ownership to the banking house *Krentschker & Co.* was recorded in a supplement to the above-mentioned inventory as follows:

"[...] On the basis of the inventory carried out by myself, (us), I am, (we are), the owners of the following properties: [*Followed by a listing of the properties*]. I (we) ask you to take these in trust and to appoint an administrator that suits you. Further, I (we) ask you to try to sell the above-mentioned properties and to either transact this sale yourself or through a broker that suits you. I (we) authorize you to make all decisions regarding the aforementioned properties, including to be able to incur encumbrances. [...]"

35   On 14 November 1938, Dr. Dagobert and Bertha R., Rosa W. and Friederike F. issued the following memorandum of debt – quoted (in parts) – and reached the following mortgage agreement – also quoted (in parts) – with the banking house *Krentschker & Co.*:

36   "[...] We, the undersigned Berta R[...], Dr. David, also known as Dagobert R[...], Rosa W[...] and Friederike F[...] owe jointly and severally to the banking house *Krentschker & Co.*, rec. general partnership in Vienna I., Börsendorferstrasse 2, a loan amounting to 150,000 Reichsmark [...] and undertake to pay this amount entirely and in cash, but in the meantime to pay 5 % interest yearly from 21 September 1938. For the purpose of securing our above-mentioned debt in the amount of 150,000 Reichsmark including 5 % interest since 21 September 1938, I [...] Dr. David, aka Dagobert, R[...] pledge the following properties, which are owned by me: EZ [X5], KG Sechshaus with

Reichsfluchtsteuer und sonstige Steuern. Weiters hat uns das Bankhaus Krentschker & Co. einen Betrag von .... [sic!] RM 125.000 (in Worten Reichsmark einhundertfünfundzwanzigtausend) zum Ankauf von engl. Pfund 2.000 (Kapitalistenzertifikat) bei der Kultusgemeinde in Wien zur Verfügung zu stellen. Ferners [sic!] sind uns vom Bankgeschäft Krentschker & Co. die zum Lebensunterhalt notwendigen Beträge und zwar insgesamt RM 1.500,– (in Worten: Reichsmark eintausendfünfhundert) monatlich, die zur Bezahlung mit unserer Ausreise verbundenen Spesen und Kosten einschliesslich eines Betrages von RM 14.000,– (in Worten: Reichsmark vierzehntausend) für Ausrüstungszwecke, allfälliger Auflagen einschliesslich der Transferbewilligung von Schmuck, Teppichen, Möbel (Altbesitz) und obenerwähnter Ausrüstungsgegenstände (Neubesitz) wie schliesslich die Mittel für das Expensar des Herrn Dr. Camillo von L[...], bereitzustellen.

III. [...] Ein sodann verbleibender Überschuss ist nach Deckung der Kosten und Spesen des Bankgeschäftes Krentschker & Co. einschliesslich der Kosten der advokatorischen Beratung des Bankgeschäftes Krentschker & Co. an den Gildemesterfonds oder an den Vermögensträger der Auswanderungshilfsaktion Gildemester zur Einzahlung zu bringen.

IV. Zur Abdeckung der Kosten des Bankgeschäftes Krentschker & Co. oncl. [sic!] der advokatorischen Beratung derselben bieten wir   % (in Worten: Prozent) des Nettovermögens im Zeitpunkt der Anmeldung zur Gildemester-Aktion an. [...] Wir erlegen bei Herrn Dr. Hugo We[...], Rechtsanwalt in Wien I., S[...]ring 8 als dem Vertreter des Bankgeschäftes Krentschker & Co. die notariell beglaubigte [sic!] Vollmachten, lautend auf die Herren Dr. Hugo We[...] und Dr. Erich Ra[...], Wien, am   und stelle [sic!] an die genannten Herren das Ersuchen, für uns Verfügungen zu treffen, die der Treuhänder als notwendig bezeichnen wird und alle rechtsverbindlichen Erklärung [sic!] abzugeben und Handlungen zu setzen, die notwendig sind unser gesamtes Vermögen zur Disposition des Bankgeschäftes Krentschker & Co. zu stellen."

Die Übergabe des Vermögens der Familien R., F. und W. an das Bankhaus Krentschker & Co. erfolgte am 23. August 1938. Die treuhänderische Übertragung des Liegenschaftsbesitzes an das Bankhaus Krentschker & Co. wurde in einer Ergänzung zur oben erwähnten Inventur folgendermaßen festgehalten:

„[...] Auf Grund der von mir, (uns), unterfertigten Inventur bin ich, (sind wir), Eigentümer folgender Liegenschaften: [*Es folgt die Aufzählung der Liegenschaften*]. Ich wir ersuche(n) Sie dieselben in Treuhand zu übernehmen und einen Ihnen genehmen Verwalter zu bestellen. Ich wir ersuche(n) Sie weiters um den Verkauf obiger Liegenschaften bemüht zu sein und diesen Verkauf entweder selbst oder durch einen Ihnen genehmen Vermittler tätigen zu wollen. Ich wir ermächtige(n) Sie bezüglich vorgenannter Liegenschaften alle Verfügungen zu treffen, insbesondere aber Belastungen vornehmen zu können. [...]"

Am 14. November 1938 stellten Dr. Dagobert und Bertha R., Rosa W. und Friederike F. folgenden (auszugsweise) wiedergegebenen Schuldschein aus und schlossen mit dem Bankhaus Krentschker & Co. folgenden (ebenfalls auszugsweise) wiedergegebenen Pfandbestellungsvertrag:

„[...] Wir endesgefertigten Berta R[...], Dr. David auch Dagobert R[...], Rosa W[...] und Friederike F[...] schulden zur ungeteilten Hand dem Bankhaus Krentschker & Co., prot. offene Handelsgesellschaft in Wien I., Bösendorferstrasse 2, für einen Darlehensbetrag von RM 150.000,– [...] und verpflichten uns, diesen Betrag voll und bar zu bezahlen, in der Zwischenzeit aber seit dem 21. September 1938 mit 5 % jährlich zu

Arbitration Panel for *In Rem* Restitution – Decision No. 24/2005

the house S[…]-strasse O. no. 73, EZ [X6], KG Brigittenau with the house K[…]-strasse O. no. 61, half of which is owned by me, and the property EZ [X4], KG Esslingen; […] and we give our explicit consent that without our knowledge and agreement, on the grounds of this promissory note, the simultaneous lien for the claim of 150,000 Reichsmark […] including the 5 % interest incurred since 21 September 1938 for the benefit of the banking house *Krentschker & Co.* rec. general partnership in Vienna I., Bösendorferstrasse 2, namely recorded in land register […] as a main security and […] in EZ [X4], KG Esslingen, […] as a subsidiary security, can be incorporated at any time. […]. We authorize the banking house *Krentschker & Co.*, Vienna I., Bösendorferstrasse 2, as our trustee, to submit to the land register an application for incorporation of the above-mentioned lien and to lodge any relevant legal appeals, as well as to regulate and implement any matters regarding associated charges. […] The spouses Dr. David, aka Dagobert, R[…] and Bertha R[…], as well as Rosa W[…] and Friederike F[…] are Jews."

37   Whether this loan amount was disbursed or not, and in what form, cannot be established.

38   On 2 March 1940, the lien of 75,000 Reichsmark was incorporated as a subsidiary security for the benefit of the banking house *Krentschker & Co.*, KG Eßling, after the approval of the mortgage contract by the Property Transaction Office on 3 May 1939, and by the *Devisenstelle* ("Foreign Exchange Board") Vienna on 7 June 1939. The property EZ X7, KG Leopoldstadt, which was the property of Friederike F., served as a main security of the simultaneous mortgage.

39   On 24 November 1938, in the presence of Dr. Erich Ra., the same seven parties involved in the statement of 19 August 1938 recorded the following amendment to the agreement of 19 August 1938:

"The following has been agreed between the parties: I. Taking the change of factual and legal circumstances into consideration, the process (see particularly position II) of the statement) which was established in the statement of 19 August 1938, proves to be unfeasible. Dr. Dagobert (David) R[…] and his wife, Mrs. Bertha R[…], will for the time being not leave the country, so that the payment of the Reich Flight Tax for the designated persons is not applicable. The amount in Reichsmark, which was deposited with the Jewish Community in Vienna by the banking house *Krentschker & Co.* for the purpose of acquiring a Capitalist Certificate by Dr. R[…] and his wife, will be made available for a certificate of this kind to be used by Otto W[…] and his family. The expenses so far incurred by the banking house *Krentschker & Co.* will be offset against the complete assets which were handed over to the trust. Further, these assets will be used to cover the 10 % levy to the Gildemeester Fund and the expenses for the trustee. The levy as well as the expenses are calculated on the basis of the net assets at the time of transfer. The remaining part of the assets, in accordance with the legal and administrative regulations, is at the sole disposal of Dr. R[…] and his wife to cover their domestic living expenses."

40   Friederike and Karl F. left Austria on 15 December 1938, the applicant and her husband Otto W. left on 17 February 1939. The reason why Dr. Dagobert and Bertha R. did not leave the country or could not leave the country cannot be established.

41   On 15 December 1938, Dr. Dagobert R. issued a declaration of assets, which reflected the amendments regarding the inventory rendered on 15 July 1938 (as at 27 April 1938) and included the following:

verzinsen. Zur Sicherung unserer obenangeführten Schuld im Betrage von RM 150.000.– samt 5 % Zinsen seit 21. September 1938 bestelle ich [...] Dr. David auch Dagobert R[...] die mir eigentümlich gehörigen Liegenschaften Einlage Z. [X5] Katastralgemeinde Sechshaus mit dem Haus S[...]strasse O. Nr. 73, die mir zur Hälfte gehörige Liegenschaft Einlage Z. [X6] Katastralgemeinde Brigittenau mit dem Haus K[...]strasse O. Nr. 61 und die mir gehörige Liegenschaft Z. [X4] Katastralgemeinde Eßlingen zum Pfand; [...] und erteilen unsere ausdrückliche Einwilligung, dass auf Grund dieses Schuldscheines das Simultanpfandrecht für die Forderung von 150.000,– RM [...] samt 5 % Zinsen seit 21. September 1938 zu Gunsten des Bankgeschäftes Krentschker & Co. prot. offene Handelsgesellschaft in Wien I., Bösendorferstraße 2 und zwar in Einlage [...] als Haupteinlage und [...] auf der Liegenschaft Einlage Z. [X4] Katastralgemeinde Eßlingen, [...] als Nebeneinlage ohne unser ferneres Wissen und Einvernehmen jederzeit einverleibt werden kann. [...] Wir ermächtigen das Bankgeschäft Krentschker & Co., Wien, I., Bösendorferstrasse 2 als unseren Treuhänder, zur Einbringung des Grundbuchsgesuches um Einverleibung des obenerwähnten Pfandrechtes und zur Einbringung aller damit im Zusammenhang stehenden Rechtsmittel sowie zur Regelung und Durchführung aller damit verbundenen Gebührensachen. [...] Die Ehegatten Dr. David auch Dagobert R[...] und Bertha R[...], sowie die Frauen Rosa W[...] und Friederike F[...] sind Juden."

Ob und in welcher Form dieser Darlehensbetrag ausbezahlt wurde, kann nicht festgestellt werden. 37

Nach Genehmigung des Pfandbestellungsvertrages durch die Vermögensverkehrsstelle am 3. Mai 1939 und der Devisenstelle Wien vom 7. Juni 1939 wurde am 2. März 1940 das Pfandrecht auf der Grundbuchseinlage X4, KG Eßling, zugunsten des Bankhauses Krentschker & Co. für eine Forderung von 75.000,– Reichsmark als Nebeneinlage einverleibt. Als Haupteinlage der Simultanhypothek diente die sich im Eigentum von Friederike F. befindliche Liegenschaft mit der EZ X7, KG Leopoldstadt. 38

Am 24. November 1938 gaben dieselben sieben Beteiligten des Protokolls vom 19. August 1938 vor Dr. Erich Ra. folgende Änderung der Vereinbarung vom 19. August 1938 zu Protokoll: 39

„Zwischen den Parteien wurde folgendes vereinbart: I. Mit Rücksicht auf die geänderte Rechts- und Sachlage erweist sich das im Gedenkprotokoll vom 19. August 1938 festgelegte Programm (siehe insbesondere Punkt II) des Gedenkprotokolles) als undurchführbar. Herr Dr. Dagobert (David) R[...] und dessen Gattin, Frau Bertha R[...], werden zunächst nicht ausreisen, sodass die Errichtung der Reichsfluchtsteuer für die Genannten entfällt. Der Reichsmarkbetrag, welcher vom Bankgeschäft Krentschker & Co., für den Erwerb eines Kapitalistenzertifikates durch Herrn Dr. R[...] und Gattin bei der Kultusgemeinde Wien erlegt wurde, wird für ein solches Zertifikat, welches durch Herrn Otto W[...] und Familie benützt werden soll, zur Verfügung gestellt. Die vom Bankhaus Krentschker & Co., bisher gemachten Aufwendungen werden mit der Einheit des gesamten in Treuhand übergebenen Vermögens verrechnet; ferner wird dieses Vermögen zur Deckung der 10%igen Abgabe an den Gildemeester-Fonds und der Kosten des Treuhänders herangezogen. Die Abgabe sowie die Kosten errechnen sich von einer Bemessungsgrundlage nach dem reinen Vermögen im Zeitpunkt der Übergabe. – Der sodann verbleibende Rest des Vermögens steht Herrn Dr. R[...] und Gattin zur Deckung ihres Lebensunterhaltes im Inlande nach Maßgabe der gesetzlichen und behördlichen Vorschriften allein zur Verfügung."

"On 19 August 1938, together with my wife Bertha R[…], I transferred all assets to the banking house *Krentschker & Co.*, Vienna I., Habsburgergasse 2 in return for the obligation of paying all of my liabilities and taxes, putting at my disposal the necessary means for living costs, paying the expenses for my leaving the country, making my departure as rapid as possible and finally placing the possible remainder at the disposal of the Gildemeester Fund, from which the expenses for the migration of impecunious Jews are being paid. Hence, I do not own any property and also did not own it on 12 November 1938. […]"

42   On 19 April 1940, Dr. Dagobert R., as "vendor" signed a purchase contract with the Reich Treasury (Aviation) concerning the property EZ X4, KG Eßling, consisting of the above-mentioned properties, for 16,835.30 Reichsmark. The Air-District Commando 17, Vienna, appeared as the representative of the Reich Treasury. The price for a single square meter of the total of 14,612 m^2 ranged from 0.60 to 1.90 Reichsmark. Certain provisions of the purchase contract read as follows:

"4. The purchase price is due on […]. The payment is to be transferred for safekeeping to the banking house *Krentschker & Co.* Vienna I., Bösendorferstrasse no. 2, appointed by the State Commissioner for Private Enterprises in regards to the assets of the vendor.
[…]
7. The present contract will only become legally binding upon the approval by the Ministry of Agriculture in Vienna, Higher Administration for Settlement and the Foreign Exchange Board.
8. […] With reference to the tariff post 102:f of the General Fee Tariff 1925, *RGBl.* ("Reich Law Gazette") No. 208/25, in connection with para. 2 (2) of the *Landbeschaffungsgesetz für Zwecke der Wehrmacht* ("Law on Land Procurement for Purposes of the German Armed Forces") of 29 March 1935, 12 April 193? [sic] Reich Law Gazette I p. 467/387, it is noted that the Reich Treasury (Aviation), after inspection of the object of purchase, would have had the right to expropriate. Therefore, the present legal transaction is exempted from all fees, stamp-duties and taxes. […]"

43   This property was acquired in connection with the extension to the runway of the Vienna-Aspern Airport planned by the German Air Force. It had been put into operation as an airport for amateur pilots in 1912 and in the late 1920s had been extended into an amateur and commercial airport. Until March 1938, Austrian air combat forces were also stationed in Aspern. Initially, the airport stayed in operation during the war. Additionally, a temporary school for instrument flight (1940) was established there, as well as the air ambulance service 17 (1945). Various planes of the German Air Forces were also being kept there. Towards the end of the war, Aspern served predominantly as a maintenance center for the German carrier Lufthansa.

44   The western border of property parcel Y1/5 was approximately 350 m away from the eastern border of the airport. Hundreds of small property parcels had been acquired from more than 50 persons and unified in newly established register numbers for the purpose of extending the airport. During the time they belonged to the air force, these properties were not rearranged but merely re-designated.

45   On 10 June 1940, the Air-District Commando XVII submitted the purchase contract to the Processing and Settlement Office of the Property Transaction Office for approval. On 18 June 1940 the Processing and Settlement Office forwarded the application of the Air-District Commando to the department of Higher Administration for Settlement located at

Friederike und Karl F. verließen Österreich am 15. Dezember 1938, die Antragstellerin und ihr Ehemann Otto W. am 17. Februar 1939. Warum Dr. Dagobert und Bertha R. nicht ausreisten bzw. nicht ausreisen konnten, kann nicht festgestellt werden. 40

Am 15. Dezember 1938 errichtete Dr. Dagobert R. ein Vermögensbekenntnis, das die Veränderungen gegenüber dem am 15. Juli 1938 abgegebenen Vermögensverzeichnis (nach dem Stand vom 27. April 1938) wiedergab und auszugsweise folgenden Inhalt hat: 41

„Ich habe am 19.8.1938 gemeinsam mit meiner Ehegattin Bertha R[...] alle Aktiven dem Bankgeschäft Krentschker & Co., Wien I. Habsburgerg. 2 übertragen, gegen die Verpflichtung alle Passiven und Steuern für mich zu bezahlen, bis zu meiner Ausreise die notwendigen Mittel für den Lebensunterhalt zur Verfügung zu stellen, die Spesen meiner Ausreise zu bezahlen und meine Ausreise mit aller tunlichen Beschleunigung zu ermöglichen und dafür den allfälligen Rest dem Gildemeesterfond aus welchem die Kosten für die Abwanderung mitteloser Juden gedeckt werden, zur Verfügung zu stellen. Ich besitze daher keinerlei Vermögen und besass ein solches auch am 12. November 1938 nicht. [...]"

Am 19. April 1940 unterzeichnete Dr. Dagobert R. als „Verkäufer" den Kaufvertrag mit dem Reichsfiskus (Luftfahrt) über die Liegenschaft mit der EZ X4, KG Eßling, bestehend aus den oben genannten Grundstücken, zu einem Preis von 16.835,30 Reichsmark. Als Vertreter des Reichsfiskus trat das Luftgaukommando 17, Wien, auf. Die einzelnen Quadratmeterpreise der insgesamt 14.612 m² lagen zwischen 0,60 und 1,90 Reichsmark. Einzelne Bestimmungen des Kaufvertrages lauten auszugsweise: 42

„4. Der Kaufpreis ist [...] fällig. Der Erlag erfolgt zu treuen Händen des vom Staatskommissar in der Privatwirtschaft bezüglich der Vermögenschaften des Verkäufers bestellten Treuhänders, d. i. das Bankhaus Krentschker & Co. Wien 1., Bösendorferstraße Nr. 2.
[...]
7. Der vorliegende Vertrag tritt erst in Rechtswirksamkeit, wenn er vom Ministerium für Landwirtschaft in Wien, Obere Siedlungsbehörde und von der Devisenstelle genehmigt wird.
8. [..] Mit Bezug auf Tarifpost 102:f des Allgemeinen Gebührentarifes 1925, RGBl 208/25, in Verbindung mit § 2 (2) des Landbeschaffungsgesetzes für Zwecke der Wehrmacht vom 29.3.1935, 12.4.193? [sic] RGBl I S. 467/387, wird festgestellt, dass dem Reichsfiskus (Luftfahrt) in Ansehung des Kaufgegenstandes das Recht der Enteignung zugestanden wäre. Das gegenständliche Rechtsgeschäft ist daher von allen Gebühren, Stempelgebühren und Steuern befreit. [...]"

Der Erwerb dieser Liegenschaft stand im Zusammenhang mit der geplanten Erweiterung des Rollfeldes des Flughafens Wien-Aspern durch die deutsche Luftwaffe. Er war 1912 als Sportflughafen in Betrieb genommen und in den späten 20er-Jahren zum Sport- und Verkehrsflughafen ausgebaut worden. Bis März 1938 gelangten in Aspern auch österreichische Luftstreitkräfte zur Stationierung. In den Kriegsjahren blieb der Verkehrsbetrieb zunächst aufrecht, außerdem wurden dort zeitweilig eine Blindflugschule (1940) sowie der Sanitätsflugdienst 17 (1945) untergebracht und verschiedene Flugzeugtypen der deutschen Luftwaffe abgestellt. Zu Kriegsende diente Aspern dann der Deutschen Lufthansa vor allem als Wartungsbasis. 43

Die westliche Grundstücksgrenze der Parzelle Y1/5 befand sich etwa 350 m von der östlichen Flugplatzgrenze entfernt. Zur Erweiterung des Flughafens wurden Hunderte von kleinen Grundstücken von mehr als 50 Personen aufgekauft und in neu begründeten Ein- 44

the Ministry for Agriculture which had jurisdiction over these applications. Initially, the Higher Administration for Settlement was a department of the Ministry for Agriculture. After its dissolution in late 1940, the Higher Administration for Settlement was relocated to the respective Reich Governor and was responsible for processing aryanizations of agricultural property. Purchase contracts concerning agricultural land were submitted to them by the Property Transaction Office or the contracting parties for approval. On 10 October, the banking house *Krentschker & Co.* urged the Higher Administration for Settlement to approve the purchase contract. Among other things, the bank pointed out that it acted as the trustee of Dr. Dagobert R., who had entrusted the bank with his property for administration and utilization. Further, he and his wife were supposed to leave the country in the near future on the instructions of the Secret State Police. The purchase price was needed for the payment of the travel expenses and other obligations.

46   In its written reply to the banking house *Krentschker & Co.,* dated 13 November 1940, the Higher Administration for Settlement, among other things, pointed out the following:

> "Regarding your letters of 10. [...] /X.1940, you inform the Higher Administration for Settlement [...] that by means of a notification from the State Commissioner for Private Enterprises that you have been appointed as the trustee of the property of Dr. Dagobert Israel R[...] regarding the sale Dr. Dagobert R[...] – Air-District Commando XVII. [...]. Hereunto, I must inform you that this appointment as trustee made by the Property Transaction Office is not valid, as, in accordance with para. 17 (3) of the Ordinance of 3./XII.1938, only the Higher Administration for Settlement is responsible for the appointment of trustees for agricultural property. If you wish to implement the contract, you have to apply for a special appointment from the Higher Administration for Settlement. [...] I [Dr. M[...] from the Higher Administration for Settlement] will have the Dr. Dagobert R[...]/Air-District Commando XVII. contract processed as soon as possible. Because the present copy of the valuation does not indicate the name of the author of the expert opinion, the completion of this file could not occur until now. I therefore request you to add the missing information. Upon receipt of your message I will immediately proceed to the processing of your file [...]".

47   The banking house *Krentschker & Co.* used the services of the real estate office Ri. & Co. for the administration and utilization of the entrusted property. The two companies' partners had a close personal interaction. The two partners from *Krentschker & Co.*, Moritz K. and Kurt P., were silent partners of Ri. & Co. Ri. & Co. arranged the purchase contract concerning the transaction R./Air-District Commando and ensured that the necessary expert valuations were obtained. The valuation report, which was provided by the municipal administration of the Region Vienna on 14 December 1940, identified a market value of 16,503.80 Reichsmark. On 15 January 1941, the *Preisbildungsstelle* ("Pricing Authority"), which was established with the Reich Governor in Vienna, made the following statement to the Higher Administration for Settlement regarding the purchase price:

> "I [Dr. Ph[...] from the Pricing Authority] consider the agreed purchase price [...], which is still within the range of the *Preisstop-Verordnung* ("Price Freeze Decree"), as tenable. Without a doubt though, the price represents the maximum possible regarding the price authorized by the Price Freeze Decree for the property parcels in question. In order to infer a reasonable market value, a deduction of 20 % would need to be applied to the total estimated value identified by the municipal administration for all applicable properties resulting in a reasonable market value of 13,250 Reichsmark for the property parcels in question."

lagezahlen vereinigt. Diese Grundstücke wurden während ihrer Zugehörigkeit zur Luftwaffe nicht umgestaltet, sondern lediglich umgewidmet.

Am 10. Juni 1940 reichte das Luftgaukommando XVII den Kaufvertrag bei der Abwicklungsstelle der Vermögensverkehrsstelle zur Genehmigung ein. Am 18. Juni 1940 trat die Abwicklungsstelle den Antrag des Luftgaukommandos zuständigkeitshalber an das Ministerium für Landwirtschaft, Obere Siedlungsbehörde, ab. Die Obere Siedlungsbehörde war zunächst ein Amt des Landwirtschaftsministeriums, nach dessen Auflösung Ende 1940 des jeweiligen Reichsstatthalters, und war für die Abwicklung von Arisierungen bei landwirtschaftlichem Grundbesitz zuständig. Ihr wurden Kaufverträge betreffend Agrarflächen zur Genehmigung von der Vermögensverkehrsstelle oder den Vertragspartnern übermittelt. Am 10. Oktober urgierte das Bankhaus Krentschker & Co. bei der Oberen Siedlungsbehörde die Genehmigung des Kaufvertrages. Die Bank wies unter anderem darauf hin, dass sie als Treuhänder von Dr. Dagobert R. agiere, der ihr sein Vermögen zur treuhändigen Verwaltung und Verwertung übergeben habe. Er und seine Frau sollten überdies nach Weisung der Geheimen Staatspolizei in nächster Zeit ausreisen, wobei man den Kaufpreis zur Bestreitung der Ausreisekosten und seiner sonstigen Verbindlichkeiten benötige.

45

In ihrem Antwortschreiben an das Bankhaus Krentschker & Co. vom 13. November 1940 wies die Obere Siedlungsbehörde unter anderem auf Folgendes hin:

46

„Zu Ihren Briefen vom 10. [...] /X.1940 geben Sie an die Obere Siedlungsbehörde [...] bekannt, dass Sie durch einen Bescheid des Staatskommissars in der Privatwirtschaft vom 30./III.1938 zum Treuhänder des Vermögens des Dr. Dagobert Israel R[...], in der Verkaufsangelegenheit Dr. Dagobert R[...] – Luftgaukommando XVII., [...] ernannt wurden. Hiezu habe ich Ihnen bekanntzugeben, dass diese Bestellung zum Treuhänder von Seite der Vermögensverkehrsstelle unwirksam ist, da lediglich zur Berufung eines Treuhänders für landwirtschaftlichen Besitz gemäss § 17, Abs.3 der Verordnung vom 3./XII.1938, allein die Obere Siedlungsbehörde zuständig ist. Sofern Sie die Abwicklung durchführen, müssten Sie um eine besondere Bestellung bei der Oberen Siedlungsbehörde einreichen. [...] Den Vertrag Dr. Dagobert R[...]-Luftgaukommando XVII werde ich [gemeint ist Dr. M[...] von der Oberen Siedlungsbehörde] baldmöglichst zur Durchführung bringen. Die Erledigung dieses Aktes konnte bisher nicht erfolgen, weil aus der aufliegenden Abschrift der Schätzung nicht hervorgeht, wer der Verfasser des Gutachtens ist. Ich bitte Sie, das Fehlende daher nachzutragen. Ich werde nach Übermittlung Ihrer Nachricht den Akt unverzüglich bearbeiten [...]".

Das Bankhaus Krentschker & Co. bediente sich bei der Verwaltung und Verwertung des treuhänderisch übernommenen Liegenschaftsvermögens des Realitätenbüros Ri. & Co. Es bestand zwischen beiden Unternehmen eine enge personelle Verzahnung auf Gesellschafterseite. Die beiden Gesellschafter von Krentschker & Co., Moritz K. und Kurt P., beteiligten sich als stille Gesellschafter an Ri. & Co. Im Zusammenhang mit der Transaktion R. – Luftgaukommando vermittelte Ri. & Co. den Kaufvertrag und sorgte für die Einholung der notwendigen Schätzgutachten. Der am 14. Dezember 1940 erstellte Schätzungsbefund der Gemeindeverwaltung des Reichsgaues Wien wies einen Verkehrswert von 16.503,80 Reichsmark aus. Die beim Reichsstatthalter in Wien eingerichtete Preisbildungsstelle nahm am 15. Jänner 1941 unter Bezugnahme auf diesen Schätzungsbefund gegenüber der Oberen Siedlungsbehörde zur Höhe des Kaufpreises auszugsweise wie folgt Stellung:

47

„Ich [gemeint ist Dr. Ph[...] von der Preisbildungsstelle] erachte den vereinbarten Kaufpreis [...] noch im Rahmen der Preisstop-Verordnung für vertretbar. Er stellt jedoch zweifelsohne die Höchstgrenze des nach der Preisstop-Verordnung für die ge-

Arbitration Panel for *In Rem* Restitution – Decision No. 24/2005

48 On 11 January 1941, Dr. Dagobert R. personally urged the Higher Administration for Settlement to issue an approval decision since he wanted to leave Vienna for Shanghai as quickly as possible. He feared that this route would soon be blocked.

49 The Reich Governor in Vienna, Higher Administration for Settlement, approved the purchase contract by decision of 6 January 1941. However, this decision was only issued on or after 15 January 1941 with reference to para. 8 of the Ordinance on the Use of Jewish Property of 3 December 1938, Reich Law Gazette I p. 1709. Among others, the following entry is to be found in the subject heading of the approval: "*Entjudung* ("Dejewification") Dr. Dagobert Israel R[…]". Considering the statement of the Pricing Authority, the decision contained the following conditions:

> "1. On the basis of para. 15 (1) of the Ordinance on the Use of Jewish Property, the vendor is ordered to pay the amount of 3,583.30 Reichsmark as an *Ausgleichsumlage* ("compensatory levy") for the benefit of the German Reich to the local tax office within three weeks.
> 2. The balance of the purchase price of 13,250 Reichsmark is to be transferred to an account which is registered under the name of the vendor at a foreign exchange bank located in the *Ostmark*, and which can be disposed of only with the approval of the Foreign Exchange Board Vienna, Department for Supervision I., Teinfaltstr. 4."

50 On 21 January 1941, Dr. Dagobert R. filed a complaint against this ruling. It would have been necessary to provide reasons for the approval being conditional. The Ordinance of 3 December 1938 was aimed at balancing the difference between the appropriate price and the agreed price. In this case, however, the agreed price was also the correct price. The completed purchase contract had been presented to him by the Air-District Commando only for signature. The Municipality Vienna had also calculated the same price. Hence, the prerequisites for the imposition of the condition were missing. He had been forced to leave the country in the nearest future. The proceeds from the sale were to be used for his departure.

51 On 21 January 1941, the Reich Governor in Vienna, Higher Administration for Settlement, informed the banking house *Krentschker & Co.* of the approval, dated 6 January 1941, of the purchase contract, and of the complaint by Dr. R. against the ruling. At the same time, the authority pointed out the following:

> "Upon production of the ruling before the Air-District Commando XVII, by which you have been appointed by the State Commissioner as trustee for the administration and utilization of the property of Dr. Dagobert R[…], you will receive the proceeds from the transaction."

52 On 3 February 1941, the Reich Minister for Nutrition and Agriculture granted the complaint by Dr. Dagobert R. and amended the ruling of 6 January so that the payment of the compensatory levy of 3,585.30 Reichsmark was cancelled and not replaced. Hence, the agreed purchase price of 16,835.30 Reichsmark was to be paid in full to the account of a foreign-exchange bank mentioned above under section 2 of the ruling. In an "explanation" conveyed exclusively to the Reich Governor, Higher Administration for Settlement Vienna, the Reich Minister explained, among other things, the following:

> "The agreed purchase price of 16,835.30 Reichsmark is based […] on an estimate by the municipal administration Vienna […]. It seems questionable to aim for a reasonable market value in this situation. But it is also by no means acceptable to […] establish the reasonable market value by proposing a general deduction of 20 %. […] A deduction of 20 % also seems to be too high since generally the reasonable market value

genständlichen Grundstücke zulässigen Preises dar. Um auf den mässigen [sic!] Verkehrswert zu kommen, wäre von dem von der Gemeindeverwaltung für alle in Betracht kommenden Liegenschaften ermittelten Gesamtschätzwert noch ein Abschlag von 20 v.H. zu machen, so dass sich als mässiger [sic!] Verkehrswert für die gegenständlichen Grundstücke ein Betrag von rund RM 13.250,– ergeben würde."

Am 11. Jänner 1941 urgierte Dr. Dagobert R. persönlich bei der Oberen Siedlungsbehörde die Ausstellung des Genehmigungsbescheides, da er Wien so rasch als möglich in Richtung Shanghai verlassen wollte. Er befürchtete allerdings eine baldige Sperre dieser Route. 48

Der Reichsstatthalter in Wien, Obere Siedlungsbehörde, genehmigte den Kaufvertrag mit Bescheid vom 6. Jänner 1941 – tatsächlich erlassen jedoch erst am oder nach dem 15. Jänner 1941 – unter Bezugnahme auf § 8 der Verordnung über den Einsatz des jüdischen Vermögens vom 3. Dezember 1938, Reichsgesetzblatt (RGBl) I S. 1709. In der Betreffzeile des Bescheides findet sich unter anderem folgender Eintrag: „Entjudung Dr. Dagobert Israel R[…]". Unter Berücksichtigung der Stellungnahme der Preisbildungsstelle enthielt der Bescheid folgende Auflagen: 49

„1. Auf Grund des § 15, Abs. 1 der Verordnung über den Einsatz des jüdischen Vermögens, wird dem Verkäufer aufgetragen, den Betrag von RM 3.583.30 als Ausgleichsumlage zugunsten des Deutschen Reiches innerhalb 3 Wochen an das zuständige Finanzamt einzuzahlen.
2. Der restliche Kaufpreis von RM 13.250.— ist auf ein auf den Namen des Verkäufers lautendes Konto bei einer in der Ostmark geführten Devisenbank einzuzahlen, über das nur mit Genehmigung der Devisenstelle Wien, Ueberwachungsabteilung I., Teinfaltstr. 4 verfügt werden darf."

Am 21. Jänner 1941 erhob Dr. Dagobert R. Beschwerde gegen diesen Bescheid. Da im Bescheid eine Einschränkung der Genehmigung erfolgt sei, hätte er einer Begründung bedurft. Die Verordnung vom 3. Dezember 1938 bezwecke die Differenz zwischen dem angemessenen Preis und dem vereinbarten Preis auszugleichen. Hier sei aber der vereinbarte Preis auch der richtige. Der fertige Kaufvertrag sei ihm vom Luftgaukommando nur zur Unterschrift vorgelegt worden. Auch die Gemeinde Wien habe denselben Preis errechnet. Es fehlten daher die Voraussetzungen zur Vorschreibung einer Auflage. Er sei gezwungen, in allernächster Zeit auszuwandern. Der Kaufpreis solle für seine Ausreise verwendet werden. 50

Am 21. Jänner 1941 informierte der Reichsstatthalter in Wien, Obere Siedlungsbehörde, das Bankhaus Krentschker & Co. von der Genehmigung des Kaufvertrages, datiert mit 6. Jänner 1941, und von der Beschwerde Dr. R.s gegen diesen Bescheid. Gleichzeitig wies die Behörde auf Folgendes hin: 51

„Bei Vorweis des Bescheides beim Luftgaukommando XVII mit dem Sie durch den Staatskommissar zum Treuhänder für die Verwaltung und Verwertung des Vermögens von Dr. Dagobert R[…] bestellt wurden, werden Sie den Gegenwert der aus dem Kaufabschluss resultiert, erhalten."

Der Reichsminister für Ernährung und Landwirtschaft gab der Beschwerde von Dr. Dagobert R. am 3. Februar 1941 statt und änderte den Bescheid vom 6. Jänner dahingehend ab, dass die festgesetzte Ausgleichszahlung von 3.585,30 Reichsmark ersatzlos aufgehoben wurde. Der vereinbarte Kaufpreis von 16.835,30 Reichsmark war daher in voller Höhe an die oben in Punkt 2 des Bescheides genannte Stelle zu zahlen. In einer nur an den Reichsstatthalter, Obere Siedlungsbehörde, Wien, übermittelten „Begründung" führte der Reichsminister unter anderem Folgendes aus: 52

will be only around 10 % lower than the full market value. But this fact can be disregarded here since the proceeds from the sale serve to finance the emigration of the complainant. The circular decree of 8 November, no. VIII 17267/39 refers to the consideration of the personal circumstances of the Jewish vendor in the determination of the reasonable market value. Thus, the Higher Administration for Settlement is authorized to disregard the imposition of a compensatory levy in order to not question the emigration of the Jews, which after all is the purpose of all aryanization measures. The advantage, which devolves upon every Jewish vendor through this, is small as the proceeds have to be used for the fulfillment of the various obligations caused by the emigration and in accordance with the stipulated provisions, the Jewish vendor has no opportunity to transfer the remaining cash assets abroad. Due to these considerations, the imposition of the condition of the payment of the compensatory levy could be refrained from."

53 Following the presentation of the purchase contract of 19 April 1940, the ruling of the Reich Governor in Vienna – Higher Administration for Settlement of 6 January 1941 and the decision of 3 February 1941 of the Reich Minister for Nutrition and Agriculture, the Land Register Court Groß-Enzersdorf recorded the ownership title of the Reich Treasury (Aviation) to the property EZ X4, KG Eßling on 22 May 1941.

54 On 23 July 1941, the amount of 16,835.30 Reichsmark was transferred to the restricted-access secure account "Dr. David and Mrs. Berta R[…], Vienna" set up with the banking house *Krentschker & Co.*, with the designation "Comp. Air-District Commando".

55 On 21 March 1942, EZ X4, KG Eßling, was merged to form EZ X1, KG Eßling, opened on 6 September 1940, also under the ownership of the Reich Treasury (Aviation).

56 The property, which was still under the registered ownership of the applicant after she had left the country, serves as an example of the sale of properties owned by emigrated Gildemeester-participants by the entrusted banking house *Krentschker & Co.* as follows: On 22 October 1940, the banking house *Krentschker & Co.* applied for the approval of the purchase contract concerning EZ X8, KG Ober St. Veit, with the property department of the State Administration of the Region Vienna, Processing and Settlement Office. Extracts from the application had the following content:

> "On the basis of the decision of the State Commissioner for Private Enterprises of 30 May 1938, file no. W 2310/Bi/Hl/1938, we have been entrusted with the administration and utilization of the property of emigrating and wealthy Jews through the 'Gildemeester emigration relief-operation for Jews'. Rosa Sara W[…] has joined this operation and has entrusted us with the administration and utilization of her property. With the purchase contract of 21 October 1940, the above-mentioned person […] has sold […] the property belonging to her. […] As trustees, we apply for the approval of this purchase contract."

The purchase contract was signed by Dr. Erich Ra. on behalf of the applicant. Dr. Ra. acted on account of a power-of-attorney issued in his name by the applicant on 24 August 1938, in which the right to sell the above-mentioned property is specified. The applicant herself had not participated in this transaction. In particular, she could not influence the date of sale, the purchase price, or the choice of the purchasers.

57 On 9 October 1942, Dr. Dagobert R. and his wife Bertha were deported to Theresienstadt. Dr. Dagobert R. died there on 17 October 1943. This day was recorded as the date of death in the death declaration of the Regional Court for Civil Matters Vienna of 1 December 1947.

Schiedsinstanz für Naturalrestitution – Entscheidung Nr. 24/2005

„Der vereinbarte Kaufpreis von 16.835.30 RM beruht [...] auf einer Schätzung der Gemeindeverwaltung Wien [...]. Bei dieser Sachlage auf einen mässigen [sic!] Verkehrswert abzukommen, erscheint bedenklich. Es ist jedoch auch keineswegs angängig, [...] den mässigen [sic!] Verkehrswert in der Weise zu ermitteln, dass ein allgemeiner Abzug von 20 % in Vorschlag gebracht wird. [...] Ein Abzug von 20 % erscheint auch zu hoch zu sein, da im allgemeinen der mässige [sic!] Verkehrswert nur etwa 10 % unter dem vollen Verkehrswert liegen wird. Es kann aber vorliegend hiervon abgesehen werden, da der Verkaufspreis zur Finanzierung der Auswanderung des Beschwerdeführers dient. Auf die Berücksichtigung der persönlichen Verhältnisse des jüdischen Veräusserers bei der Ermittlung des mässigen [sic!] Verkehrswertes, ist bereits in dem Rd.Erlass vom 8.November Nr. VIII 17267/39 hingewiesen. Der Oberen Siedlungsbehörde ist hierdurch die Befugnis gegeben, von Ausgleichszahlungen abzusehen, um die Auswanderung der Juden, die letzten Endes das Ziel aller Arisierungsmassnahmen [sic!] ist, nicht in Frage zu stellen. Der Vorteil, der hiedurch dem jüdischen Veräusserer zufällt, ist gering, da der Verkaufserlös zur Erfüllung mannigfacher Verpflichtungen aus Anlass der Auswanderung verwandt werden muss und der jüdische Veräusserer nach der getroffenen Regelung keinerlei Möglichkeiten hat, ein verbleibendes Barguthaben nach dem Ausland zu transferieren. Aus diesen Erwägungen heraus konnte vorliegend die Auflage der Ausgleichszahlung in Fortfall kommen."

Unter Vorlage des Kaufvertrages vom 19. April 1940, des Bescheides des Reichsstatthalters in Wien – Obere Siedlungsbehörde vom 6. Jänner 1941 und der Entscheidung des Reichsministers für Ernährung und Landwirtschaft vom 3. Februar 1941 trug das Grundbuchsgericht Groß-Enzersdorf am 22. Mai 1941 auf der Liegenschaft mit der EZ X4, KG Eßling, das Eigentumsrecht für den Reichsfiskus (Luftfahrt) ein. 53

Am 23. Juli 1941 langte der Betrag von 16.835,30 Reichsmark mit der Widmung „Vgtg. w/Luftgaukommando" auf dem beschränkt verfügbaren Sicherungskonto „Herrn Dr. David u. Frau Berta R[...], Wien" beim Bankhaus Krentschker & Co. ein. 54

Die Grundbuchseinlage X4, KG Eßling, wurde am 21. März 1942 der am 6. September 1940 eröffneten, ebenfalls im Eigentum des Reichsfiskus (Luftfahrt) stehenden Grundbuchseinlage X1, KG Eßling, zugeschrieben. 55

Anhand einer sich nach der Ausreise noch im grundbücherlichen Eigentum der Antragstellerin befindlichen Liegenschaft wird der Verkauf des von den ausgereisten Gildemeester-Teilnehmern treuhänderisch übergebenen Liegenschaftsbesitzes durch das Bankhaus Krentschker & Co. im Folgenden exemplarisch dargestellt: Das Bankhaus Krentschker & Co. richtete am 22. Oktober 1940 einen Antrag auf Genehmigung des Kaufvertrages zur Grundbuchseinlage X8, KG Ober Sankt Veit, an die Staatliche Verwaltung des Reichsgaues Wien, Abwicklung der Vermögensverkehrsstelle, Abteilung Liegenschaften. Dieser Antrag hatte auszugsweise folgenden Inhalt: 56

„Durch den Bescheid des Staatskommissars in der Privatwirtschaft vom 30. Mai 1938, Zl.W 2310/Bi/Hl/1938, sind wir als Treuhänder für die Verwaltung und Verwertung des Vermögens der im Rahmen der ‚Gildemeester Auswanderungshilfsaktion für Juden' auswandernden vermögenden Juden bestellt worden. Rosa Sara W[...] ist dieser Aktion beigetreten und hat uns ihr Vermögen zur treuhändigen Verwaltung und Verwertung übergeben. Durch den Kaufvertrag vom 21.Okt 1940 hat die Obengenannte [...] das ihr gehörige Grundstück [...] verkauft. [...] Wir stellen als Treuhänder den Antrag auf Genehmigung dieses Kaufvertrages."

Der Kaufvertrag wurde namens der Antragstellerin von Dr Erich Ra. unterfertigt. Dr. Ra. handelte aufgrund einer durch die Antragstellerin am 24. August 1938 zu seinen Guns-

58   In the so-called list of assets of Jews evacuated to the eastern territories of 9 October 1942, the following statements were given regarding Dr. R. under category "c) frozen accounts and savings books": "Frozen account *Krentschker & Co.*, 1st District, Schubertring 3, 80,000 Reichsmark". Next to it the handwritten comment can be found "seized by Central Office".

59   By request of the Central Office for Jewish Emigration in Vienna of 5 January 1943, between 11 and 16 January 1943 the banking house *Krentschker & Co.* transferred an amount of 81,210 Reichsmark from the secure account held for the R. couple to the special account "Resettlement of Jews" of the Central Office for Jewish Emigration Vienna, account no. 29803, set up with the *Länderbank* Vienna Corporation. On 15 January 1943, the banking house *Krentschker & Co.* informed the Central Office for Jewish Emigration that all assets of the spouses R. had been transferred.

60   The special account "Resettlement of Jews" was a collective account, to which the seized properties of several hundred deported people had been credited. The Central Office for Jewish Emigration which was directly under the control of the Inspector of the *Sicherheitspolizei* ("Security Police") and the *Sicherheitsdienst* ("Security Service") of Vienna, had the exclusive right of disposal over this account.

61   With the collection decision of 16 February 1943 by the Secret State Police, State Police, Central Office Vienna, the entire movable and immovable assets as well as all rights and claims of Dr. Dagobert and Bertha R. were seized for the benefit of the German Reich. Further, it was ordered that the utilization and administration of these assets fell under the competence of the Chief Finance President Vienna-Lower Danube. Subsequently, on 11 January 1944, the Chief Finance President Vienna-Lower Danube issued a letter to the banking house *Krentschker,* in which he asked for the closure of the secure account in the name of R. and for the transfer of the credit balance to the cheque account Vienna no. 51 of the Higher Finance Pay Office. On 17 January 1944, in its reply to this letter, the banking house *Krentschker* pointed out that the assets of the spouses R. had already been transferred to the above-mentioned special account "Resettlement of Jews" in January 1943.

62   On 18 September 1947, Bertha R., having been appointed representative *in absentia* of her husband Dr. Dagobert R., filed a claim for the restitution of the property EZ X4, KG Eßling, with the Restitution Commission installed at the Regional Court for Civil Matters Vienna. The application was directed against the Reich Treasury (Aviation). In extracts, the application had the following content:

"Until 19 April 1940, Dr. Dagobert R[…] was the sole owner of the above-mentioned property. Due to the pressure caused by the circumstances after the assumption of power by the National Socialists, he had to have the entire property sold below its true value by the appointed trustee, banking house *Krentschker & Co.* This happened on account of the ruling of the Reich Governor Vienna and the decision of the Reich Minister for Nutrition and Agriculture. […]"

63   On 4 November 1950, after a representative *in absentia* had been appointed by the Guardianship Court for the adverse party in November 1947, the Restitution Commission informed both parties that for the continuation of the restitution proceedings, in accordance with Article 1 and Article 5 (IV) of the Second Control Agreement of 28 June 1946, a written agreement by the Allied Commission in Austria was to be procured by the claimant through the Federal Chancellary, a liaison office of the Allied Council. The restitution proceedings could not be continued until this agreement had been procured.

ten ausgestellten Vollmacht, in der das Recht zur Veräußerung der obengenannten Liegenschaft ausdrücklich genannt wird. Die Antragstellerin selbst war an dieser Transaktion nicht beteiligt; insbesondere konnte sie weder auf den Zeitpunkt des Verkaufes, die Höhe des Kaufpreises noch die Auswahl der Käufer einen Einfluss nehmen.

Am 9. Oktober 1942 wurden Dr. Dagobert R. und seine Frau Bertha nach Theresienstadt deportiert. Dr. Dagobert R. verstarb dort am 17. Oktober 1943. Dieser Tag wurde in der Todeserklärung des Landesgerichtes für Zivilrechtssachen (LGfZRS) Wien vom 1. Dezember 1947 als Todeszeitpunkt festgestellt. 57

Im so genannten Vermögensverzeichnis in die Ostgebiete evakuierter Juden vom 9. Oktober 1942 wurden für Dr. R. in der Rubrik „c) Sperrkonten und Sparkassenbücher" folgende Angaben gemacht: „Sperrkto Krentschker u. Co., 1., Schubertring 3, RM 80.0000,-" Daneben findet sich der handschriftliche Vermerk „von Centralstelle eingezogen". 58

Über Aufforderung der Zentralstelle für jüdische Auswanderung in Wien vom 5. Jänner 1943 überwies das Bankhaus Krentschker & Co. von ihrem für das Ehepaar R. geführten Sicherungskonto zwischen dem 11. und 16. Jänner 1943 einen Betrag von 81.210,– Reichsmark auf das Sonderkonto „Juden-Umsiedlung" der Zentralstelle für jüdische Auswanderung Wien, Kontonr. 29803, bei der Länderbank Wien A.G. Das Bankhaus Krentschker & Co. teilte der Zentralstelle für jüdische Auswanderung am 15. Jänner 1943 mit, dass damit sämtliche Werte der Eheleute R. überwiesen seien. 59

Das Sonderkonto „Juden-Umsiedlung" war ein Sammelkonto, auf dem die eingezogenen Vermögen mehrerer Hundert deportierter Personen gutgeschrieben wurden. Die Verfügungsberechtigung darüber oblag ausschließlich der Zentralstelle für jüdische Auswanderung, einer dem Inspekteur der Sicherheitspolizei und des Sicherheitsdienstes Wien unterstellten Dienststelle. 60

Mit Einziehungserkenntnis der Geheimen Staatspolizei, Staatspolizeileitstelle Wien vom 16. Februar 1943 wurden das gesamte bewegliche und unbewegliche Vermögen sowie alle Rechte und Ansprüche von Dr. Dagobert und Bertha R. zugunsten des Deutschen Reiches eingezogen. Weiters wurde angeordnet, dass die Verwertung und Verwaltung dieser Vermögenswerte in die Zuständigkeit des Oberfinanzpräsidenten (OFP) Wien-Niederdonau falle. Der Oberfinanzpräsident Wien-Niederdonau richtete daraufhin am 11. Jänner 1944 ein Schreiben an das Bankhaus Krenschtker mit der Bitte um Schließung des auf den Namen R. lautenden Sicherungskontos und Überweisung des Guthabens auf das Postscheckkonto Wien Nr. 51 der Oberfinanzkasse. In der Beantwortung dieses Schreibens am 17. Jänner 1944 wies das Bankhaus Krentschker daraufhin, dass die Vermögenswerte der Eheleute R. bereits im Jänner 1943 auf das oben erwähnte Sonderkonto „Juden-Umsiedlung" geflossen seien. 61

Am 18. September 1947 brachte Frau Bertha R. als bestellte Abwesenheitskuratorin für ihren Ehemann Dr. Dagobert R. bei der beim LGfZRS Wien eingerichteten Rückstellungskommission einen Antrag auf Restitution des Grundstückes mit der EZ X4, KG Eßling ein. Der Antrag richtete sich gegen den Reichsfiskus (Luftfahrt). Er enthielt auszugsweise folgendes Vorbringen: 62

„Herr Dr. Dagobert R[…] war bis zum 19.4.1940 Alleineigentümer obengenannter Liegenschaft. Unter dem Druck der Verhältnisse nach der Machtübernahme durch den Nationalsozialismus musste er die ganze Liegenschaft weit unter dem wahren Wert auf Grund des Bescheides des Reichsstatthalters Wien und der Entscheidung des Reichsministers für Ernährung und Landwirtschaft durch den bestellten Treuhänder, das Bankhaus Krentschker & Co. verkaufen lassen. […] "

Arbitration Panel for *In Rem* Restitution – Decision No. 24/2005

64 Pursuant to the Second Control Agreement of 28 June 1946, the respective occupying power was assigned the right of disposal over German Property. It required prior written consent of the Allied Council. The consent requirement was handled differently by the four occupying powers. Apart from a few exceptions, the Soviet occupying power did not permit restitution proceedings regarding German Property. The reason for this approach was that the Soviet occupying power regarded German Property as "German External Assets" as defined by the Potsdam Agreement of 2 August 1945. When a request for approval regarding the opening of restitution proceedings concerning German Property was submitted, the Soviet representatives in the relevant control committees regularly adopted a negative stance.

65 From 1 November 1947, EZ X1, KG Eßling, was under the administration of the Soviet occupying power as so-called German Property.

66 A notice of assent from the Allied Commission was not submitted by the claimant. On 29 July 1952, the State Financial Procurator's Office on behalf of the Republic of Austria submitted its declaration for joinder to the restitution proceedings. The 'public interest' requirement was that property parcels subject of this application were likely to pass into the ownership of the Republic of Austria on the basis of the State Treaty and that they be would used by the Republic for important public purposes.

67 Subsequently, the Restitution Commission labeled the file several times with the note *DE* (= *Deutsches Eigentum* "German Property"). On 2 August 1956, after the representative *in absentia* for the Reich Treasury had presented two applications for the resumption of proceedings, one in September 1955 and one in June 1956, the Restitution Commission assigned the proceedings, referring to Sec. 31 (1) of the First State Treaty Implementation Act to the Financial Directorate for Vienna, Lower Austria and Burgenland.

68 In June 1957, both heirs of Dr. Dagobert R., his daughters Friederike O. and Rosa W., joined the proceedings as claimants.

69 In response to an inquiry by the Financial Directorate for Vienna, Lower Austria and Burgenland regarding the utilization of the proceeds from the sale, the banking house *Krentschker & Co.* stated on 22 January 1958, that the proceeds of 16,853.30 Reichsmark concerning the property in question had been received by them on 23 July 1941 and were then transferred to the restricted-access secure account of Dr. Dagobert and Bertha R. Various payments had then been made from this account.

70 On 1 March 1958, the claimants presented a comprehensive submission on the matter of the seizure of the property in view of the provisions of the Third State Treaty Implementation Act. Essentially, it explained that Dr. Dagobert R., as a Jewish lawyer, had been forced to sell the property solely for political reasons. He had been brought before the Reich Governor in Vienna by SA men. There, he had been ordered to immediately assign the property to the Reich Treasury. The proceeds from the sale were supposed to be transferred to a frozen foreign exchange account which was to be opened for him.

71 On 3 November 1959, a hearing took place at the Financial Directorate, in which Dr. Alfred O. and the attorney-at-law Dr. Heinrich B. participated as representatives of the claimants. Dr. O., husband of the claimant Friederike O., testified as a witness at the time. He stated that he only knew about the contemporary occurrences by hearsay. His statement corresponded in essence with the submission by the claimants of 1 March 1958. The claimants abstained from the hearing of further witnesses and of the parties.

72 On 19 November 1959, the State Financial Procurator's Office, in excerpts, made the following statements:

Schiedsinstanz für Naturalrestitution – Entscheidung Nr. 24/2005

Nach der pflegschaftsgerichtlichen Bestellung eines Abwesenheitskurators für den Antragsgegner im November 1947 informierte die Rückstellungskommission beide Parteien am 4. November 1950, dass gemäß Art. 1 und Art. 5 Abs IV des 2. Kontrollabkommens vom 28. Juni 1946 zur Durchführung des Rückstellungsverfahrens vom Antragsteller die schriftliche Zustimmung der Alliierten Kommission in Österreich im Wege des Bundeskanzleramtes – Verbindungsstelle zum Alliierten Rate – einzuholen sei. Vor Beibringung dieser Zustimmung könne das Rückstellungsverfahren nicht fortgesetzt werden. 63

Nach dem 2. Kontrollabkommen vom 28. Juni 1946 fiel die Verfügung über Deutsches Eigentum der jeweiligen Besatzungsmacht zu und bedurfte der vorherigen schriftlichen Zustimmung des Alliierten Rates. Die Bewilligungspflicht wurde von den vier Besatzungsmächten unterschiedlich gehandhabt. Die sowjetische Besatzungsmacht ließ Rückstellungsverfahren bezüglich Deutschen Eigentums bis auf wenige Ausnahmen nicht zu. Der Grund für diese Haltung lag darin, dass die sowjetische Besatzungsmacht das Deutsche Eigentum als „German External Assets" im Sinne des Potsdamer Abkommens vom 2. August 1945 erachtete. In den betreffenden Kontrollgremien nahmen die sowjetischen Vertreter regelmäßig eine ablehnende Haltung ein, wenn Genehmigungsgesuche betreffend die Einleitung von Rückstellungsverfahren zu Deutschem Eigentum vorgelegt wurden. 64

Die Grundbuchseinlage X1, KG Eßling, stand ab 1. November 1947 als so genanntes Deutsches Eigentum unter der Verwaltung der sowjetischen Besatzungsmacht. 65

Eine Zustimmungserklärung der Alliierten Kommission wurde von der antragstellenden Partei nicht vorgelegt. Am 29. Juli 1952 erklärte die Finanzprokuratur im Namen der Republik Österreich den Beitritt zum Rückstellungsverfahren. Das öffentliche Interesse sei darin gelegen, dass die gegenständlichen Grundstücke aufgrund des StV voraussichtlich in das Eigentum der Republik Österreich übergehen und von dieser für wichtige öffentliche Zwecke verwendet werden sollten. 66

Die Rückstellungskommission kalendierte den Akt in der Folge mehrmals mit dem Vermerk DE (= Deutsches Eigentum). Nach zwei durch den Abwesenheitskurator für den Reichsfiskus eingebrachten Fortsetzungsanträgen im September 1955 und im Juni 1956 trat die Rückstellungskommission am 2. August 1956 das Verfahren unter Hinweis auf § 31 Abs 1 des 1. StVDG der Finanzlandesdirektion (FLD) für Wien, Niederösterreich und das Burgenland ab. 67

Im Juni 1957 traten die beiden Erbinnen nach Dr. Dagobert R., seine Töchter Friederike O. und Rosa W., auf Antragstellerinnenseite in das Verfahren ein. 68

Auf Anfrage der FLD für Wien, Niederösterreich und das Burgenland zur Verwendung des Kaufpreises teilte das Bankhaus Krentschker & Co. am 22. Jänner 1958 mit, dass der Erlös von 16.853,30 Reichsmark betreffend die gegenständliche Liegenschaft am 23. Juli 1941 bei ihnen eingelangt und auf das beschränkt verfügbare Sicherungskonto von Dr. Dagobert und Bertha R. erlegt worden sei. Von diesem Konto seien dann diverse Zahlungen geleistet worden. 69

Am 1. März 1958 erstatteten die Antragstellerinnen ein umfangreiches Vorbringen zum Entzug der Liegenschaft im Hinblick auf die Bestimmungen des 3. StVDG. Im Wesentlichen wurde dabei ausgeführt, dass Dr. Dagobert R. als jüdischer Rechtsanwalt lediglich aus politischen Gründen genötigt worden sei, die Liegenschaft zu verkaufen. Er sei von SA-Leuten dem Reichsstatthalter in Wien vorgeführt worden und habe dort den Auftrag erhalten, die Liegenschaft unverzüglich an den Reichsfiskus abzutreten. Der Kaufpreis sollte dabei auf ein für ihn zu eröffnendes Devisensperrkonto erlegt werden. 70

"The acquisition by the German Reich, Reich Treasury (Aviation) of the property parcels belonging to the estate inventory of the former EZ [X4], KG Eßling, by means of the purchase contract of 19 April 1940, was in no way causally connected to the landowner belonging to a racially persecuted group of persons. Solely the location of the site was relevant for the acquisition of these property parcels, which had to be incorporated in the grounds of the airfield due to the expansion of the airport Aspern. […] Also, the fact that the purchase price, which was agreed upon in the purchase contract of 19 April 1940, was to be paid to the trustee appointed by the State Commissioner for Private Enterprises for the assets of the vendor does not change anything […]."

73 On 11 October 1960, the claimants replied to the statement of the State Financial Procurator's Office. They did not particularly address the arguments of the State Financial Procurator's Office regarding the location of the property but emphasized that the property acquisition had been coerced using then usual means of exerting pressure on racially persecuted persons and that the vendor had never received a fraction of the purchase price for his free disposal. An investigation into the motive for the property seizure was unnecessary as in any case, their father had lost his property during National Socialism without receiving compensation, and the purchase contract was to be regarded as void even if the surrounding properties had been sold on the basis of valid purchase contracts.

74 On 16 October 1960, the claimants supplemented this statement with the following:

"The land was expropriated by the air force for air force purposes. […] The purpose of this expropriation was to strengthen the fighting ability of the National Socialist Air Force for the purpose of the National Socialists' final victory. […] The other landowners were compensated by the National Socialist regime with other property parcels or money. Dr. R[…], however, had never received even a penny because everything had to be handed over to the trustee who, very trustworthily, administered it into his own pocket."

75 On 27 October 1960, the Financial Directorate for Vienna, Lower Austria and Burgenland issued the ruling. The authority dismissed the application. With reference to the prerequisites for the existence of a seizure stipulated in para. 1 (2) of the Third State Treaty Implementation Act, the Financial Directorate explained its decision as follows:

76 "However, the statements by the restitution claimants […] are not sufficient to prove the existence of one of the two stated prerequisites for the assumption of an actual seizure. Dr. Dagobert R[…] fell under the scope of the National Socialist racial legislation after the German occupation of Austria and subsequently, he is to be regarded as a persecuted person. However, a causal link between this fact and the acquisition of the land could not be proven."

77 The testimony of the witness Dr. O., according to which his father-in-law had been forced to conclude the contract amid threats, was regarded as a misunderstanding by the authority:

"It is true that originally, during the conclusion of the contract, a compensatory levy had been imposed by the Reich Governor in Vienna, Higher Administration for Settlement. However, the relevant decision was cancelled by the Reich Ministry for Nutrition and Agriculture, after Dr. Dagobert R[…] had personally filed a complaint with the Ministry to the effect that the vendor was not limited by any kind of restriction regarding the purchase price. In the case of a forced sale by means of threat, the vendor, without a doubt, would have neither dared lodge an appeal, nor would he have had any kind

Am 3. November 1959 fand eine mündliche Verhandlung bei der FLD statt, an der Dr. Alfred O. und Rechtsanwalt Dr. Heinrich B. als Vertreter der Antragstellerinnen teilnahmen. Dr. O., Ehegatte der Antragstellerin Friederike O., sagte dabei als Zeuge aus. Er gab an, dass er die damaligen Ereignisse nur vom Hörensagen kenne. Seine Aussage deckte sich im Wesentlichen mit dem Vorbringen der Antragstellerinnen vom 1. März 1958. Die Antragstellerinnen verzichteten auf die Einvernahme weiterer Zeugen und der Parteien.

Die Finanzprokuratur nahm am 19. November 1959 dazu auszugsweise wie folgt Stellung:

„Die Erwerbung der zum Gutsbestand der ehemaligen EZ. [X4] KG. Essling gehörigen Grundstücke durch das Deutsche Reich, Reichsfiskus Luftfahrt mit Kaufvertrag vom 19. April 1940 stand in keinerlei ursächlichem Zusammenhang mit der Zugehörigkeit des Grundeigentümers zu einer rassisch verfolgten Personengruppe. Maßgeblich für diese Erwerbung war allein die örtliche Lage dieser Grundstücke, welche anlässlich der Erweiterung des Flugplatzbereiches Aspern in das Fluggelände einbezogen werden mussten. [...] Hieran vermag auch der Umstand nichts zu ändern, dass der im Kaufvertrag vom 19. April 1940 ausbedungene Kaufpreis zu Handen des vom Staatskommissär in der Privatwirtschaft bezüglich der Vermögenschaften des Verkäufers bestellten Treuhänders zu bezahlen war [...]."

Am 11. Oktober 1960 replizierten die Antragstellerinnen auf die Äußerung der Finanzprokuratur. Sie gingen darin nicht im Speziellen auf die Argumente der Finanzprokuratur hinsichtlich der Lage des Grundstückes ein, sondern betonten, dass der vorliegende Liegenschaftserwerb mit den damals üblichen Druckmitteln gegenüber rassisch verfolgten Personen erzwungen worden sei und dass der Verkäufer keinen Bruchteil des Kaufpreises je zur freien Verfügung erhalten habe. Eine Suche nach dem Motiv der Vermögensentziehung scheine vernachlässigbar, ihr Vater hätte im Nationalsozialismus auf jeden Fall seinen Grundbesitz ohne eine Gegenleistung verloren, und der Kaufvertrag sei auch dann als nichtig zu betrachten, wenn umliegende Liegenschaften mit gültigen Kaufverträgen seinerzeit veräußert wurden.

In Ergänzung dieser Stellungnahme brachten die Antragstellerinnen am 16. Oktober 1960 noch Folgendes vor:

„Der Grund wurde von der Luftwaffe für Zwecke der Luftwaffe enteignet. [...] Der Zweck dieser Enteignung war die Vergrößerung der Schlagkraft der nationalsozialistischen Luftwaffe zum Zwecke des nationalsozialistischen Endsieges. [...] Die anderen Grundeigentümer wurden vom nationalsozialistischen Regime durch andere Grundstücke oder geltlich entschädigt. Dr. R[...] hat jedoch nie auch nur einen Pfennig erhalten, weil Alles dem Treuhänder übergeben werden musste, der sehr treu für seine Tasche verwaltet hat."

Am 27. Oktober 1960 erließ die FLD für Wien, Niederösterreich und das Burgenland den Bescheid. Die Behörde wies den Antrag ab. Unter Bezugnahme auf die Entziehungstatbestände in § 1 Abs 2 des 3. StVDG begründete sie ihre Entscheidung auszugsweise wie folgt:

„Die Ausführungen der Rückstellungswerberinnen [...] sind jedoch nicht geeignet, das Vorhandensein einer der beiden angeführten Voraussetzungen für die Annahme eines Entziehungstatbestandes darzulegen. Dr. Dagobert R[...] fiel wohl nach der deutschen Besetzung Österreichs unter die Bestimmungen der ns. Rassengesetzgebung und ist zufolge dieser als verfolgte Person anzusehen; doch konnte keine Kausalität zwischen dieser Tatsache und dem Grunderwerb nachgewiesen werden."

of success in doing so. Therefore, it is to be assumed that the process of the legal transaction was not influenced by the racial persecution of Dr. R[…]."

78 The administrative body explained the following about the location of the property parcel:

"[…] it has to be pointed out that the German Reich has purchased further properties for the purpose of the expansion of the airport, evidently with the aim of expanding the airport facilities in accordance with the relevant technical requirements. The distance from the original airport border amounts to approximately 350 m. Therefore, it is clear that solely the military requirements and the property's location and connection to the area needed for the planned construction were factors which led to the purchase by the German Reich."

79 Regarding the free disposal of the proceeds from the sale it was explained:

"Where the claimants for restitution assert that the proceeds were not received for free disposal, this circumstance is not essential for the assessment of the legal transaction at that time: According to the information of 22 January 1958 provided by the banking house *Krentschker & Co.*, the purchase price of 16,853.30 Reichsmark determined in the purchase contract was paid by the Air-District Commando in its entirety. A possible seizure of a part of this amount at a later point in time can be ignored for the assessment of the case in question."

80 On 18 November 1960, both claimants filed an appeal against this decision. They produced a submission that essentially had the same wording as in the first instance, applied for the questioning of Bertha R. and suggested a review of the constitutionality of para. 1 of the Third State Treaty Implementation Act. During the appeal proceedings, the claimants produced an affidavit rendered by Bertha R. about the seizure at the time. The contents of this affidavit cannot be established.

81 On 2 February 1961, the Federal Minister of Finance issued the appeal decision. He did not grant the appeal and confirmed the decision of the Financial Directorate. In the explanation of the appeal decision he argued, with reference to the Third State Treaty Implementation Act, that solely the location of the claimed properties – in the middle of the area which had been purchased by the Reich Treasury for the purpose of expanding the airport – made it evident that political considerations had not played a part in the acquisition. Other local landowners who had never been subjected to a political (racial) persecution also had to sell property parcels to the Reich Treasury (Aviation). With reference to the comment "dejewification of Dr. Dagobert R." on the approval decision of the purchase contract in question, the Federal Minister remarked that "it is completely clear" that "this decision is in no way connected to the purchase *intention* of the Reich Treasury (Aviation). Rather, the issuing of this decision was merely a consequence of the prevailing regulations on the sale of Jewish property at the time." In addition, the compensatory levy that was at first determined in the decision was cancelled after a complaint by the vendor. "This had evidently happened because this had not been a dejewification as defined by the relevant legal provisions at that time."

82 The Federal Minister of Finance assumed, as did the court of first instance, that the asserted threats against Dr. Dagobert R. made by SA men were actually a misunderstanding. It seemed out of the question that the Reich Treasury (Aviation) let party organizations carry out sales transactions. It had always been possible for the Reich Treasury to acquire properties by way of expropriation. Moreover, the successful appeal by Dr. Dagobert R.

Die Aussage des Zeugen Dr. O., dass sein Schwiegervater unter Drohungen zum Vertragsabschluss gezwungen worden sei, wurde von der Behörde als Missverständnis gesehen:

„Wohl war ursprünglich im Zuge des Vertragsabschlusses vom Reichsstatthalter in Wien, Obere Siedlungsbehörde, eine Ausgleichsumlage zur Vorschreibung gelangt, doch wurde der diesbezügliche Bescheid auf Grund einer von Dr. Dagobert R[...] persönlich an das Reichsministerium f. Ernährung und Landwirtschaft eingebrachten Beschwerde von diesem Ministerium aufgehoben, sodass bezüglich des Kaufpreises der Verkäufer keiner wie immer gearteten Beschränkung unterlag. Im Falle eines durch Drohung erzwungenen Kaufabschlusses hätte der Verkäufer jedoch zweifellos weder die Einbringung eines Rechtsmittels gewagt noch hiebei einen Erfolg erzielt. Es ist somit anzunehmen, dass die Modalitäten des Rechtsgeschäftes von der rassischen Verfolgung Dr. R[...] unbeeinflusst blieben."

Zur Lage des Grundstücks führte die Behörde Folgendes aus:

„[...] muß darauf verwiesen werden, dass das Deutsche Reich für die Vergrößerung des Flugplatzes noch weitere Liegenschaften erworben hat, offenbar in dem Bestreben, die Flugplatzanlagen dem jeweiligen technischen Stand entsprechend erweitern zu können; die Entfernung von der ursprünglichen Flugplatzgrenze beträgt ca. 350 m. Es ist somit offensichtlich, dass für den Erwerb durch das Deutsche Reich allein der hiefür gegebene militärische Bedarf bzw. ihre Lage und Zugehörigkeit zu dem für die geplante Anlage benötigten Areal massgebend waren."

Zur freien Verfügbarkeit des Kaufpreises:

„Wenn die Rückstellungswerber geltend machen, dass der Kaufpreis nicht zur freien Verfügung gelangt wäre, so ist auch dieser Umstand für die Beurteilung des seinerzeitigen Rechtsgeschäftes nicht wesentlich: Lt. Auskunft des Bankhauses Krentschker u. Co. vom 22. Jänner 1958 wurde der im Kaufvertrag festgelegte Kaufpreis von RM 16.853,30 zur Gänze vom Luftgaukommando bezahlt; eine allfällige spätere Entziehung eines Teiles dieses Betrages kann für die Beurteilung des gegenständlichen Falles unbeachtet bleiben."

Am 18. November 1960 erhoben die beiden Antragstellerinnen Berufung gegen diesen Bescheid. Sie erstatteten im Wesentlichen ein gleichlautendes Vorbringen wie in der 1. Instanz, beantragten die Einvernahme von Bertha R. und regten eine Prüfung der Verfassungsmäßigkeit von § 1 des 3. StVDG an. Während des Berufungsverfahrens legten die Antragstellerinnen eine von Bertha R. abgegebene eidesstattliche Erklärung über den seinerzeitigen Entziehungsvorgang vor. Der Inhalt dieser Erklärung kann nicht festgestellt werden.

Am 2. Februar 1961 erließ der Bundesminister für Finanzen den Berufungsbescheid. Er gab der Berufung keine Folge und bestätigte den Bescheid der FLD. In der Begründung des Berufungsbescheides führte er unter Bezugnahme auf das 3. StVDG aus, dass allein schon aus der Lage der begehrten Grundstücke – inmitten des Gebietes, das für die Flughafenerweiterung vom Reichsfiskus erworben worden war – ersichtlich sei, dass politische Momente bei der Erwerbung keine Rolle gespielt hätten. Auch weitere dortige GrundbesitzerInnen, die niemals einer politischen (rassischen) Verfolgung unterworfen gewesen seien, hätten Grundstücke an den Reichsfiskus (Luftfahrt) veräußern müssen. Zu dem Vermerk „Entjudung Dr. Dagobert R." auf dem Genehmigungsbescheid zum fraglichen Kaufvertrag merkte der Bundesminister an, dass „es vollkommen klar" sei, dass „dieser

Arbitration Panel for *In Rem* Restitution – Decision No. 24/2005

regarding the compensatory levy resulted in the possibility to transfer the entire purchase price to the appointed trustee, the banking house *Krentschker & Co*. This entirely complied with the provisions of the time and was not connected to the intention of the Reich Treasury (Aviation) to purchase the property.

83 With regard to the alleged unconstitutionality of the Third State Treaty Implementation Act, the Minister of Finance referred to the decision of the Constitutional Court of 25 March 1960, B 406/59-13, which had confirmed the constitutionality of this law.

84 On 22 March 1961, the claimants for restitution filed an appeal against this decision of the Minister of Finance with the Supreme Administrative Court. In the reasons for their appeal the claimants asserted the illegality of the content of the decision and its illegality due to the violation of procedural regulations since essential facts had been assumed contrary to the contents of the file as well as the fact that these facts needed to be supplemented.

85 With reference to the first point of complaint, the claimants asserted that particularly para. 31 (1) and para. 43 (5) of the First State Treaty Implementation Act were unconstitutional as these regulations were in breach of Article 83 of the *Bundesverfassungsgesetz* ("Federal Constitution Law") as well as non-specified regulations of the European Convention on Human Rights. Also, the Third State Treaty Implementation Act, particularly Article I (1), was unconstitutional since it repealed Article 26 (1) of the State Treaty, an Article embodied in the Constitution. The provisions regarding restitution established in the State Treaty would for the most part be invalidated by the Third State Treaty Implementation Act. Additionally, the Third State Treaty Implementation Act violated the *Grundsatzgesetz der Republik Österreich* ("Basic Law of the Republic of Austria") from 1945.

86 The second point of complaint was elaborated by the claimants as follows:

"The appeal decision by the Ministry of Finance is unlawful because the Ministry assumes that the words 'expropriation of Jewish property' had been based on a ruling by the Higher Administration for Settlement. The words 'for the purpose of expropriation of Jewish property' are written on the purchase contract, which was forced upon Dr. R[…] […] This clearly shows that this purchase contract represented an expropriation of Jewish property. […] In addition, the assumption that the oft mentioned incident with the SA men had something to do with the release of the purchase amount is wrong. […] However, it is certain […] that the SA men entered the apartment of Dr. R[…] and amid threats ordered him to come immediately to the Higher Administration for Settlement to conclude the purchase contract. Hence, it is not a 'supposed controversy' or a 'wrong assumption', as claimed by the Ministry of Finance and the Financial Directorate, but a given fact testified under oath, that everything took place as described above. This, as well as the notation 'expropriation of Jewish property' on the *purchase contract*, unequivocally shows that this matter was a violent confiscation. The fact that on this occasion it was noted that the vendor was not permitted to dispose of the proceeds from the sale but was coerced to deposit it into a frozen account is actually irrelevant. […]".

87 On 4 September 1963, the Minister of Finance issued his rejoinder, in which he referred, with regard to the submission by the complainants, to the grounds for the decisions by the lower administrative bodies. He also pointed out the established juridical practice of the Supreme Administrative Court, especially the decisions no. 577/62, no. 634/60 and no. 717/60, which were applicable to the case at issue.

Bescheid in keinerlei Zusammenhang mit der Erwerbs*absicht* des Reichsfiskus Luftfahrt steht. Die Erlassung dieses Bescheides war vielmehr lediglich die Folge der damals geltenden Bestimmungen über die Veräußerung jüdischen Liegenschaftsbesitzes." Außerdem sei die im Bescheid zunächst festgelegte Ausgleichszulage nach Beschwerde des Verkäufers schließlich aufgehoben worden. „Dies offenbar deshalb, weil es sich hiebei eben um keine Entjudung im Sinne der damaligen diesbezüglichen gesetzlichen Bestimmungen gehandelt hat."

Der Finanzminister ging wie die 1. Instanz davon aus, dass es sich bei der behaupteten 82 Bedrohung von Dr. Dagobert R. durch SA-Leute um einen Irrtum handle. Es scheine ausgeschlossen, dass der Reichsfiskus Luftfahrt Verkaufsaktivitäten durch Parteiorganisationen ausführen ließ. Er habe jederzeit die Möglichkeit gehabt, Grundstücke auf dem Enteignungswege zu erhalten. Überdies habe die erfolgreiche Beschwerde Dr. Dagobert R.s gegen die Ausgleichszulage dazu geführt, dass der gesamte Verkaufspreis an den bestellten Treuhänder, das Bankhaus Krentschker & Co. überwiesen werden konnte. Dies entspräche durchaus den damaligen Bestimmungen und es bestünde kein Zusammenhang mit der Erwerbsabsicht des Reichsfiskus Luftfahrt.

Hinsichtlich der behaupteten Verfassungswidrigkeit des 3. StVDG verwies der Fi- 83 nanzminister auf das Erkenntnis des Verfassungsgerichtshofes vom 25. März 1960, B 406/59-13, mit dem die Verfassungsmäßigkeit dieses Gesetzes bestätigt worden war.

Am 22. März 1961 erhoben die Rückstellungswerberinnen gegen den Bescheid des Fi- 84 nanzministers Beschwerde an den VwGH. Als Beschwerdegründe wurden Rechtswidrigkeit des Bescheidinhaltes und Rechtswidrigkeit wegen Verletzung von Verfahrensvorschriften, da der Sachverhalt in wesentlichen Punkten aktenwidrig angenommen worden sei und er überdies der Ergänzung bedürfe, geltend gemacht.

Zum ersten Beschwerdepunkt brachten die Rückstellungswerberinnen zunächst vor, 85 dass insbesondere §§ 31 Abs 1 und 43 Abs 5 des 1. StVDG verfassungswidrig seien, da diese Bestimmungen sowohl gegen Art 83 Bundes-Verfassungsgesetz (B-VG) als auch gegen nicht näher genannte Bestimmungen der Europäischen Menschenrechtskonvention verstoßen würden. Auch das 3. StVDG, in concreto Art. I Abs 1, sei verfassungswidrig, da er den in der Verfassung verankerten Art. 26 Abs 1 des StV außer Kraft setze. Die dort festgelegten Wiedergutmachungsbestimmungen würden durch das 3. StVDG zum größten Teil wertlos gemacht werden. Zudem verstoße das 3. StVDG gegen das „Grundsatzgesetz der Republik Österreich aus dem Jahre 1945".

Den zweiten Beschwerdegrund führten die Rückstellungswerberinnen auszugsweise 86 wie folgt aus:

„Der Berufungsbescheid des Finanzministeriums ist rechtswidrig, weil das Ministerium annimmt, daß die Worte „Enteignung von Judenvermögen" auf einen [sic!] Bescheid der Oberen Siedlungsbehörde gestanden seien. Die Worte: „Zwecks Enteignung von Judenvermögen" stehen auf dem Dr. R[…] aufgezwungen Kaufvertrag. [...] Daraus geht eindeutig hervor, dass es sich bei diesem Kaufvertrag um Enteignung von Judenvermögen gehandelt hat. [...] Rechtswidrig ist ferner die Annahme, daß die schon öfter erwähnte Szene mit den SA-Männern sich auf die Freigabe des Kaufbetrages bezogen hat. [...] Feststeht jedoch, [...] daß SA-Männer in die Wohnung des Dr. R[…] eindrangen und ihn unter Drohungen aufforderten, sofort zum Abschluß des Kaufvertrages zur Oberen Siedlungsbehörde zu kommen. Es ist also keine „angebliche Kontroverse" oder „irrtümliche Annahme" wie das Finanzministerium und die FLD es behaupten, sondern eine durch Eid belegte feststehende Tatsache, daß sich alles so ab-

88 With the decision of 10 October 1963, the Supreme Administrative Court rejected the complaint on the merits. Initially, the Supreme Administrative Court dealt with the interpretation of para. 1 (2) of the Third State Treaty Implementation Act:

"As the Supreme Administrative Court has repeatedly [...] explained in [...] its decisions of 24 January 1963, no. 634/60 and 1717/60, in accordance with the original wording and the natural meaning of the Third State Treaty Implementation Act, acquisitions by the German Reich for military reasons are supposed to be treated differently than the other transfers of property connected to the National Socialist assumption of power. The reason for this is that generally for the acquisition of these properties the owner as such was not of importance but rather the location of the property and its suitability for the military purposes of the German Reich. Also, concerning the question of whether in particular cases a seizure in the meaning of the restitution laws is to be assumed, the deciding factor is supposed to be the location of the property and its relative location to training areas and airports or, in general, other military objects, while disregarding the political persecution."

89 With reference to the appeal, the Supreme Administrative Court stated the following:

"According to these principles, the concerned authority was in any case authorized to conclude that these properties, which were needed for the expansion of the Aspern airport, would have been claimed for purposes of the German Armed Forces, regardless of whether they had belonged to the politically persecuted Dr. Dagobert R[...] or any other person. This seems to also exclude that the owner, as was asserted, was urged to sell *merely* due to political persecution. Hence, the process adopted *for the implementation* of the acquisition which was connected to the political (racial) persecution, such as the payment of the proceeds from the sale to the trustee appointed by the State Commissioner for Private Enterprises, the banking house *Krentschker & Co.*, agreed in item 4 of the purchase contract and the transfer of the proceeds from the sale to a frozen foreign exchange account, which had been ordered by the Reich Governor in Vienna, Higher Administration for Settlement in his ruling of 6 January 1941 did not justify the existence of a seizure as defined in para. 1 (2) of the Third State Treaty Implementation Act. The conclusion of the purchase contract of 19 April 1940 by Dr. Dagobert R[...] in person shows that the banking house *Krentschker & Co.* is not a sales trustee in accordance with para. 2 of the Ordinance on the Use of Jewish Property of 3 December 1938, *DRGBl.* ("German Reich Law Gazette") I p. 1709."

But in cases in which the claimed seizure was brought about by a legal transaction, an abusive application of the then existing laws is – according to the juridical practice of the Supreme Administrative Court – out of the question.

90 Regarding the assertion of procedural errors, it stated the following:

"Considering the legal situation and the circumstances, the complainants' assertion of procedural errors proves to be irrelevant, particularly their accusation that contrary to the contents of the file the concerned authority had wrongly assumed that the comment 'Dejewification Dr. Dagobert R[...]' had been located on the Higher Administration for Settlement's decision and not on the purchase contract of 19 April 1940, as well as that the incident involving the SA men was related to the release of the proceeds from the sale and not to the order to come to the Higher Administration for Settlement to finalize the purchase contract. The political persecution of Dr. Dagobert R[...] is also not disputed by the concerned authority. However, the Higher Administration for Settlement in accordance with para. 8 of the Ordinance on the Use of Jewish Property had to

gespielt hat, wie oben beschrieben wurde. Es geht daraus sowie auch aus dem Aufdruck „Enteignung von Judenvermögen" am *Kaufvertrag* unzweideutig hervor, daß es sich um eine gewaltsame Konfiskation gehandelt hat. Daß bei dieser Gelegenheit auch über die Nichtzurverfügungstellung des Kaufbetrages, sondern seine zwangsweise Hinterlegung auf ein Sperrkonto gesprochen wurden, ist eigentlich unerheblich. [...]".

Am 4. September 1963 erstattete der Finanzminister seine Gegenschrift, in der er hinsichtlich des Vorbringens der Beschwerdeführerinnen auf die Begründungen der Bescheide der Vorinstanzen verwies. Im Übrigen wies er auf die ständige Judikatur des VwGH hin, insbesondere auf die Erkenntnisse Zl. 577/62, Zl. 634/60 und Zl. 717/60, die auf den gegenständlichen Fall anwendbar seien.

87

Mit Erkenntnis vom 10. Oktober 1963 wies der VwGH die Beschwerde als unbegründet ab. Der VwGH setzte sich zunächst mit der Auslegung von § 1 Abs 2 des 3. StVDG auseinander:

88

„Wie der Verwaltungsgerichtshof bereits wiederholt [...] in seinen Erkenntnissen vom 24. Jänner 1963, Zl. 634/60 und 1717/60 ausgeführt hat [...] sollen nach dem klaren Wortlaut und dem natürlichen Sinne des 3. Staatsvertragsdurchführungsgesetzes Erwerbungen des Deutschen Reiches für militärische Zwecke anders als die sonstigen Vermögensübertragungen im Zusammenhang mit der nationalsozialistischen Machtübernahme behandelt werden, da für den Erwerb dieser Grundstücke im allgemeinen nicht die Person des Eigentümers, sondern die Lage des Grundstückes und seine Eignung für militärische Zwecke des Deutschen Reiches maßgebend war. Auch für die Beantwortung der Frage, ob im einzelnen Falle nach § 1 des 3. Staatsvertragsdurchführungsgesetzes eine Entziehung im Sinne der Rückstellungsgesetze anzunehmen ist, soll nach der klaren Absicht des Gesetzgebers (§ 6 ABGB) die örtliche Lage des Grundstückes und der räumliche Zusammenhang mit Übungs- und Flugplätzen oder sonstigen militärischen Objekten im allgemeinen unter Hintansetzung der politischen Verfolgung von ausschlaggebender Bedeutung sein."

Zum Beschwerdefall nahm der VwGH wie folgt Stellung:

89

„Nach diesen Grundsätzen war die belangte Behörde bei Grundstücken, die zur Erweiterung des Flugplatzes Aspern benötigt wurden, jedenfalls berechtigt, den Schluss zu ziehen, dass diese Grundstücke für Zwecke der Wehrmacht auch in Anspruch genommen worden wären, gleichgültig, ob sie dem politisch verfolgten Dr. Dagobert R[...] oder irgendeiner anderen Person gehört hätten. Damit erscheint es aber auch bereits ausgeschlossen, dass der Eigentümer, wie behauptet, *lediglich* aufgrund politischer Verfolgung zur Veräußerung genötigt worden ist. Daher vermögen auch Modalitäten *in der Durchführung* des Erwerbsvorgangs, die mit der politischen (rassischen) Verfolgung im Zusammenhang standen, so der im Pkt. 4 des Kaufvertrages vereinbarte Erlag des Kaufpreises zu treuen Handen des vom Staatskommissar in der Privatwirtschaft bezüglich der Vermögenschaften des Verkäufers bestellten Treuhänders Bankhaus Krentschker & Co. bzw. der im Bescheid des Reichsstatthalters in Wien, Obere Siedlungsbehörde, vom 6. Jänner 1941 angeordnete Erlag des Kaufpreises auf ein Devisensperrkonto keinen Entziehungstatbestand nach § 1 Abs. 2 des 3. Staatsvertrasdurchführungsgesetzes zu begründen. Beim Bankhaus Krentschker & Co. handelt es sich, wie sich aus dem persönlichen Abschluß des Kaufvertrages vom 19. April 1940 durch Dr. Dagobert R[...] ergibt, nicht um einen Veräußerungstreuhänder gemäß § 2 der Verordnung über den Einsatz jüdischen Vermögens vom 3. Dezember 1938, DRGBl I S. 1709."

approve the contract. However, the contract was concluded by the Reich Treasury (Aviation), Air-District Commando XVII as purchaser, represented by the air-district director, further represented by the senior executive officer S[…]."

91 Regarding the question of the constitutionality of para. 31 (1) and para. 43 (5) of the First State Treaty Implementation Act and Article I para. 1 of the Third State Treaty Implementation Act, the Supreme Administrative Court replied that "the Constitutional Court has already discussed the matter in numerous decisions […] and reached the conclusion that the provisions do not give rise to concern with regards to their constitutionality."

92 On 11 December 1961, Rosa W., as the heiress to her father Dr. Dagobert R., claimed before the Compensation Fund, among other things, an account balance held with the banking house *Krentschker & Co.* of 111,091.51 Reichsmark and the payment of 28,400 Reichsmark Jewish capital levy. On 23 July 1941, 16,835.30 Reichsmark had been transferred to this account by the Air-District Commando for the property EZ X4. The Compensation Fund recognized 91,266.90 Reichsmark of that claim as being the account balance which had been transferred in 1943 from the banking house *Krentschker & Co.* to the special account "Resettlement of Jews" of the Central Office for Jewish Emigration as a loss of assets in the category "assets on bank accounts". The remaining balance of Rosa W.'s claim of 19,824.65 Reichsmark comprised firstly the amount still owing by Dr. Dagobert R. to the Jewish Community in Vienna, which had been transferred by the Community to the special account at the end of 1943. This amount had not been taken into consideration by the Compensation Fund. Secondly, the difference comprised the proceeds from the sale of securities, which were taken into consideration in the category "securities". An amount of 22,001.04 Reichsmark was recognized as a Jewish capital levy payment. Having taken into consideration further losses in the category "securities", the compensation payment by the Compensation Fund to Rosa W. totaled 120,601.74 Schilling (so-called original allocation). Initially, this amount was reduced to 35 % of the actual loss (so-called adjusted allocation) in accordance with the statutes of the Compensation Fund. Hence, the amount was reduced to 42,210.60 Schilling. Rosa W. received the entire amount and later, in 1965 and 1966, two supplementary payments of 7,839.11 Schilling each. Hence, all in all 57,888.82 Schilling were disbursed.

93 Rosa W. filed appeals – provided for in the statutes of the Compensation Fund – against the non-adjudication of an amount of 17,613.35 Reichsmark. The adjudication committee as well as the board of trustees turned down the appeals.

94 Bertha R. applied for compensation concerning her payment of the Jewish capital levy amounting to 37,400 Reichsmark. The Compensation Fund awarded an amount of 29,000 Schilling. This amount was paid in its entirety to Bertha R. and/or her heiress Rosa W. Compensation of further losses claimed by her in the categories "balance in bank accounts" were rejected by the Compensation Fund due to insufficient substantiation of the confiscation. Regarding the losses asserted by her in the category "cash", the Compensation Fund established that these were losses of assets of her husband Dr. Dagobert R. Also in this case, the Compensation Fund could not pay an allocation to her, since Bertha R. had forgone all allocations regarding the losses of her husband for the benefit of her daughters Rosa W. and Friederike O.

95 On 29 December 1964, the ownership title to EZ X1, KG Eßling, was incorporated into the land register for the Republic of Austria (Federal Buildings Administration II) in reference to Article 22 of the State Treaty and para. 11 (1) of the First State Treaty Imple-

In solchen Fällen aber, wo die behauptete Entziehung durch ein Rechtsgeschäft herbeigeführt wurde, könne nach der Rechtsprechung des VwGH eine missbräuchliche Anwendung damals bestandener Gesetze an sich nicht in Frage kommen.

Zur Verfahrensrüge führte er aus: 90

„Bei dieser Rechts- und Sachlage, erweist sich die Verfahrensrüge der Beschwerdeführerinnen, insbesondere der von ihnen unter dem Gesichtspunkt der Aktenwidrigkeit gemachte Vorwurf, die belangte Behörde habe zu Unrecht angenommen, daß der Vermerk ‚Entjudung Dr. Dagobert R[…]' sich auf dem Bescheid der Oberen Siedlungsbehörde und nicht auf den Kaufvertrag vom 19. April 1940 befunden haben, sowie daß die Szene mit den SA-Leuten sich auf die Freigabe des Kaufpreises und nicht auf die Aufforderung, zum Abschluß der Kaufvertrages zur Oberen Siedlungsbehörde zu kommen, bezogen habe, als unwesentlich. Die politische Verfolgung des Dr. Dagobert R[…] wird auch von der belangten Behörde nicht bestritten. Die Obere Siedlungsbehörde hatte allerdings gemäß § 8 der Verordnung über den Einsatz jüdischen Vermögens den Vertrag zu genehmigen. Abgeschlossen wurde der Kaufvertrag auf Seite des Käufers jedoch vom Reichsfiskus Luftfahrt, Luftgaukommando XVII, vertreten durch den Luftgauintendanten, dieser vertreten durch Regierungsrat S[…]"

Zur Frage der Verfassungsmäßigkeit der §§ 31 Abs 1 und 43 Abs 5 des 1. StVDG und 91
Art. I § 1 des 3. StVDG erwiderte der Verwaltungsgerichtshof, dass „sich der Verfassungsgerichtshof bereits in mehreren Erkenntnissen [...] damit befasst habe und zu dem Ergebnisse gelangt sei, dass die Bestimmungen in verfassungsrechtlicher Hinsicht unbedenklich seien."

Am 11. Dezember 1961 machte Rosa W. als Erbin nach ihrem Vater Dr. Dagobert R. 92
beim Abgeltungsfonds unter anderem Kontoguthaben beim Bankhaus Krentschker & Co. in der Höhe von 111.091,51 Reichsmark und die Bezahlung von 28.400 Reichsmark Judenvermögensabgabe (JUVA) geltend. Auf diesem Konto war am 23. Juli 1941 die Summe von 16.835,30 Reichsmark für die Liegenschaft EZ X4 vom Luftgaukommando eingelangt. Der Abgeltungsfonds anerkannte von dieser Forderung 91.266,90 Reichsmark als jenes Kontoguthaben, das 1943 vom Bankhaus Krentschker & Co. auf das Sonderkonto „Judenumsiedlung" der Zentralstelle für jüdische Auswanderung überwiesen worden war als Vermögensverlust in der Kategorie „Guthaben auf Bankkonten". Der Differenzbetrag zu Rosa W.s Forderung – 19.824,65 Reichsmark – bezog sich einerseits auf den Restbetrag eines Erlages Dr. Dagobert R.s bei der IKG Wien, der Ende 1943 seitens der Kultusgemeinde auf das Sonderkonto überwiesen worden war. Dieser Betrag wurde vom Abgeltungsfonds nicht berücksichtigt. Andererseits handelte es sich um Verkaufserlöse für Wertpapiere, die in der Kategorie „Wertpapiere" Berücksichtigung fanden. Als JUVA-Zahlung wurde ein Betrag von 22.001,04 Reichsmark anerkannt. Unter Berücksichtigung von weiteren Verlusten in der Kategorie „Wertpapiere" betrug die Höhe der Entschädigungsleistung seitens des Abgeltungsfonds an Rosa W. insgesamt 120.601,74 Schilling (so genannte ursprüngliche Zuwendung). Gemäß den Statuten des Abgeltungsfonds wurde dieser Betrag zunächst auf 35 % des tatsächlichen Verlustes (so genannte berichtigte Zuwendung), also auf 42.210,60 Schilling, herabgesetzt. Rosa W. erhielt diesen Betrag zur Gänze sowie zwei spätere Aufzahlungen von je 7.839,11 Schilling in den Jahren 1965 und 1966 – gesamt daher 57.888,82 Schilling – ausbezahlt.

Gegen die Nichtzuerkennung eines Betrages von 17.613,35 Reichsmark erhob Rosa W. 93
die in den Statuten des Abgeltungsfonds vorgesehenen Einsprüche. Sowohl die Zuerkennungskommission als auch das Kuratorium entschieden über die Rechtsbehelfe abschlägig.

mentation Act. On 30 June 1983, EZ X1 passed into the ownership of the City of Vienna; this was due to a land-exchange agreement signed with the Republic of Austria.

96 On 17 January 2001, the ownership status for the property subject of this application was as follows:

97 The property parcels with the numbers Y1/1, Y1/2, Y1/7, Y1/8, Y1/9 and Y1/53 (as part of the original property parcel; see below margin note 100), Y1/54 and Y1/58 were part of EZ X1, KG Eßling, which was under the ownership of the City of Vienna.

98 On 30 January 1984, the property parcel Y1/5 was partitioned off the property EZ X3, KG Eßling. This register number belonged equally to Gerda and Max H.

99 On 14 October 1986, the property parcels with the numbers Y1/10, Y1/11, Y1/12, Y1/13, Y1/14 and Y1/15 (in addition to other property parcels) were incorporated into the property parcel Y1/35, which had been subdivided on the same day into the property parcels Y1/35 and Y1/59. Both property parcels were part of EZ X1, KG Eßling and were under the ownership of the City of Vienna.

100 On 25 February 1993, a subdivided area of the property parcels Y1/53 and Y1/52 (in addition to other property parcels) was partitioned off EZ X2, KG Eßling. The merger and incorporation into property parcel Y2, which belonged to this register number took place on 28 April 2003. EZ X2, KG Eßling was under the ownership of the City of Vienna. At the cut off day and still currently it is designated as public property (public traffic thoroughfare).

4. Evidence

101 Evidence was taken by reviewing the following documents enclosed with the application for *in rem* restitution: Otto W.'s and Rosa R.'s marriage certificate of 29 July 1934, issued in Vienna, 1st District, Seitenstettengasse 4, registry office of the Jewish Community; birth certificate of Rosa W., registry office of the Jewish Community; copy from the land register regarding EZ X4 from 1947; letter dated 10 May 1939 from the banking house *Krentschker & Co.* to Rosa W. concerning Operation Gildemeester; marriage certificate of Dr. Dawid [sic!] R. and Bertha He., issued by the registry office of the Jewish Community on 23 January 1936; minutes taken from memory of 19 August 1938 by Dr. Erich Ra. regarding the trusteeship by the banking house *Krentschker & Co.* of the assets of the family R.; letter by the Jewish Community – foreign exchange information office of 9 February 1939 to Dr. Dagobert R. concerning the visa-cancellation in two passports for Palestine; minutes taken from memory of 24 November 1938 by Dr. Erich Ra. regarding the amendment of an agreement referred in the minutes taken from memory of 19 August 1938; list of assets of Dr. Dagobert R. of 2 January 1942 prepared by the banking house *Krentschker & Co.* with information concerning a "restricted access secure account" of Dr. David and Berta R.; letter of 6 December 1952 by the Austrian *Länderbank* to Friederike O.; letter of 8 June 1956 by Rosa W., Friederike O. and Bertha R. to the German Embassy in Australia; property notice sheet (excerpt) of 24 October 1955 regarding EZ X1, KG Eßling.

102 The following documents were produced as case documentation by the *In Rem* project of the Historical Commission: Case documentation by the Historical Commission (Edith Leisch-Prost, Verena Pawlowsky, Harald Wendelin, *In Rem* project – City of Vienna), documentation on the Aspern air-base (together with notifications of the relevant seized properties and the Financial Directorate file 23664 [Marie Mi.]).

Schiedsinstanz für Naturalrestitution – Entscheidung Nr. 24/2005

Bertha R. beantragte beim Abgeltungsfonds für von ihr bezahlte JUVA-Forderungen von 37.400,– Reichsmark als Ersatz. Der Abgeltungsfonds sprach einen Betrag von 29.000,– Schilling zu. Dieser Betrag wurde zur Gänze an Bertha R. bzw. an ihre Erbin Rosa W. ausbezahlt. Weitere von ihr beantragte Verluste in der Kategorie „Guthaben auf Bankkonten" wurden vom Abgeltungsfonds wegen mangelnder Glaubhaftmachung der Konfiskation abgelehnt. Bezüglich der von ihr in der Kategorie „Bargeld" geltend gemachten Verluste stellte der Abgeltungsfonds fest, dass es sich hierbei um Vermögensverluste des Ehegatten Dr. Dagobert R. handelte. Nachdem Bertha R. bezüglich der Verluste ihres Ehegatten auf alle Zuwendungen zugunsten ihrer Töchter Rosa W. und Friederike O. verzichtete hatte, konnte der Abgeltungsfonds auch hier an sie keine Zuwendung gewähren. 94

Am 29. Dezember 1964 wurde ob der Grundbuchseinlage X1, KG Eßling, unter Hinweis auf Art. 22 des StV und § 11 Abs 1 des 1. StVDG das Eigentumsrecht für die Republik Österreich (Bundesgebäudeverwaltung II) einverleibt. Am 30. Juni 1983 ging diese Grundbuchseinlage aufgrund eines mit der Republik Österreich abgeschlossenen Tauschvertrages in das Eigentum der Stadt Wien über. 95

Am 17. Jänner 2001 ergaben sich für die antragsgegenständliche Liegenschaft folgende Eigentumsverhältnisse: 96

Die Grundstücke mit den Nummern Y1/1, Y1/2, Y1/7, Y1/8, Y1/9, Y1/53 (als Teilfläche der ursprünglichen Parzelle, siehe unten Rz 100), Y1/54 und Y1/58 waren Teil der sich im Eigentum der Stadt Wien befindlichen Grundbuchseinlage X1, KG Eßling. 97

Das Grundstück Y1/5 war am 30. Jänner 1984 nach der Liegenschaft mit der EZ X3, KG Eßling abgeschrieben worden. Diese Grundbuchseinlage befand sich je zur Hälfte im Eigentum von Gerda und Max H. 98

Die Grundstücke mit den Nummern Y1/10, Y1/11, Y1/12, Y1/13, Y1/14 und Y1/15 (neben weiteren Grundstücken) waren am 14. Oktober 1986 in das Grundstück Y1/35 einbezogen worden, das am selben Tag in die Grundstücke Y1/35 und Y1/59 geteilt worden war. Beide Grundstücke waren Teil der Grundbuchseinlage X1, KG Eßling und befanden sich im Eigentum der Stadt Wien. 99

Eine Teilfläche des Grundstückes Y1/53 und das Grundstück Y1/52 (neben anderen Grundstücken) waren am 25. Februar 1993 nach der Grundbuchseinlage X2, KG Eßling abgeschrieben worden. Die Zuschreibung zu dieser Einlage und die Einbeziehung in das zu dieser Einlage gehörende Grundstück Y2 erfolgten am 28. April 2003. Die Grundbuchseinlage X2, KG Eßling befand sich im Eigentum der Stadt Wien. Sie wies zum Stichtag und weist bis dato eine Widmung als öffentliches Gut (Öffentliche Verkehrsfläche) aus. 100

4. Beweise

Beweis wurde erhoben durch Einsichtnahme in folgende dem Antrag auf Naturalrestitution beigelegten Dokumente: Trauungszeugnis Otto W. und Rosa R. vom 29. Juli 1934, ausgestellt Wien, I., Seitenstettengasse 4, Matrikelamt der IKG; Geburtszeugnis der Rosa W., Matrikelamt der IKG; Grundbuchsabschrift zur EZ X4 aus 1947; Schreiben des Bankhauses Krentschker & Co. an Rosa W. betreff Gildemeester-Aktion vom 10. Mai 1939; Trauungszeugnis von Dr. Dawid (sic) R. und Bertha He., Matrikelamt der IKG, ausgestellt am 23. Jänner 1936; Gedächtnisprotokoll vom 19. August 1938 von Dr. Erich Ra. betreff die treuhändige Verwaltung des Vermögens der Familie R. durch das Bankhaus Krentschker & Co.; Schreiben der IKG – Devisen-Auskunftsstelle vom 9. Februar 1939 an Dr. David R. betreff die Streichung von Visa für Palästina in zwei Reisepässen; Gedenkpro- 101

103 The following documents were obtained by the Arbitration Panel as supplementary documentation: Files from the Austrian State Archives, Archives of the Republic, record group 06, finances: inventory immovable German Property, Vienna environs, box 6A, extracts on Aspern airport; files from the Property Transaction Office Vienna Lg. ("property") 4172, volume II, Lg. 3346; Lg. 823; list of assets no. 44423 of Dr. Dagobert R. of 15 July 1938 including enclosures I. and II.; files from the Financial Directorate: file 24289 Dagobert R., file 14832 W. Rosa and Otto (excerpts); files from the Compensation Fund on the R. and W. family 2180/5, 2181/5, 2182/5, 2183/5, 1542/5 (excerpts); file from the Assistance Fund on Berta R. (excerpts); copy of the file note of the Federal Ministry of Finance department 34 on Dagobert R.; files of the Ministry of Finance box 6597; entry for EZ X4, KG Eßling in the real-estate card-index of the Austrian State Archives: 1325/II, A. 1354/A R. Dagobert, register number X4, 'negative' according to the land register; entry for EZ X1, KG Eßling in the real-estate card-index of the Austrian State Archives: "EZ [X1], 'positive', KG Eßling (former register number [X9] – merged into EZ [X1]), Anton Re[…], 1230 W[…]-gasse 1; EZ [X9] Donaufeld belonged to Leopold Bl[…] and co-owner. A 1/3 share was restituted to the other owners by the Financial Directorate VR.V 5576-/2/50. 'Negative'; field 1/1; Leopoldau, according to the purchase contract of 07 November 1939 to (aryanizer) Reich Treasury (Aviation). Antonia G[…], 1160 Vienna, D[…]-gasse 29; EZ [X1] (originally [X10]), KG Eßling; confiscator: German Reich – purchase contract of 28 April 1939. Application for restitution of the property rejected by decision of 28 June 1956 as not representing a typical National Socialist measure but a confiscation for the purposes of aviation"; Austrian State Archives, Archive of the Republic, Supreme Administrative Court, file on decision no. 496/61; Austrian State Archives, Archive of the Republic, Reich Governor Vienna – Higher Administration for Settlement, file A. W. 206.

104 Files from the Vienna Municipal and Regional Archives, files regarding the Ordinance on the Notification of Seized Property: files on Berta R. and Dagobert R.; Friederike F./Friederike O., Rosa W.; restitution files: 2 RK 62/65 (G., procedure concerning neighboring property), 2 RK 118/56 (Re., procedure concerning neighboring property), 2 RK 112/65 (T., procedure concerning neighboring property), 2 RK 124/56 (Kä., procedure concerning comparable property); estate documentation Dagobert R. 8 A 281/48.

105 Historical land register: EZ X4, KG Eßling including certificates (daily file number 2540/36, 98/16) and EZ X1, KG Eßling including certificates (daily file number 1677/1940, 5911/64, 123/60, 1391/39); C-sheet regarding EZ X7, land register Leopoldstadt (excerpt) and related certificates on daily file number 10952/1939.

106 Land register excerpts on EZ X1, X2 and X3, all KG Eßling.

107 Plans of the MA 37, building inspection department, City of Vienna on EZ X1, KG Eßling; plans of the surveyor's office Vienna regarding the property area of EZ X4, KG Eßling.

108 Literature: Theodor Venus and Alexandra-Eileen Wenck, *Die Entziehung jüdischen Vermögens im Rahmen der Aktion Gildemeester. Eine empirische Studie über Organisation, Form und Wandel von „Arisisierung" und jüdischer Auswanderung in Österreich 1938–1941*, Vienna (Oldenbourg) 2004 (= Publications of the Austrian Historical Commission, vol. 20/2); Walter Schroeder, *Flugfelder in der Ostmark 1938–1945*; Judith Wita, *Die Geschichte des Flughafen Wien*, Vienna 2003, thesis; History Museum of the City of Vienna (ed.), *Aspern. Von der Steinzeit zum Motorenwerk*, Vienna 1981; Wolfram Lenotti, *Mehr als ein Landeplatz,* Vienna 1988; Othmar Tuider, *Die Wehrkreise XVII und XVIII*.

tokoll vom 24. November 1938 von Dr. Erich Ra. betreff eine Abänderung der Vereinbarung festgehalten im Gedenkprotokoll vom 19. August 1938; Vermögensaufstellung von Dr. Dagobert R. vom 2. Jänner 1942, aufgestellt vom Bankhaus Krentschker & Co. mit Angaben über ein „beschränkt verfügbares Sicherungskonto" von Dr. David und Berta R.; Schreiben der Österreichischen Länderbank an Friederike O. vom 6. Dezember 1952; Schreiben an die Deutschen Botschaft in Australien von Rosa W., Friederike O. und Bertha R. vom 8. Juni 1956; Grundbesitzbogen (Auszug) betreff die EZ X1, KG Eßling vom 24. Oktober 1955.

Folgende Dokumente wurden als Falldokumentation durch das IN-REM-Projekt der Historikerkommission beigebracht: Falldokumentation der Historikerkommission (= Edith Leisch-Prost, Verena Pawlowsky, Harald Wendelin, Projekt IN REM – Stadt Wien), Dokumentation über Fliegerhorst Aspern (mit Vermögensentziehungs-Anmeldungsverordnungen (VEAV) der entsprechenden Grundstücke und FLD-Akt 23664 [Marie Mi.]). 102

Folgende Dokumente wurden als ergänzende Dokumentation durch die Schiedsinstanz eingeholt: Akten aus dem Österreichischen Staatsarchiv (ÖStA), Archiv der Republik (AdR), Bestandsgruppe 06, Finanzen: Bestand unbewegliches deutsches Eigentum, Wien Umgebung Karton 6A, Auszüge zum Flughafen Aspern; Akten der VVSt Wien Lg. 4172 Band II, Lg. 3346, Lg. 823; Vermögensverzeichnis Nr. 44423 von Dr. Dagobert R. vom 15. Juli 1938 samt Anlage I. und II.; Akten der FLD: FLD Akt 24289 Dagobert R., FLD Akt 14832 W. Rosa und Otto (Auszüge); Abgeltungsfondsakten der Familie R. und W. 2180/5, 2181/5, 2182/5, 2183/5, 1542/5 (Auszüge); Hilfsfondsakt Berta R. (Auszüge); Kopie des Aktenvermerks der Kartei BMF (Bundesministerium für Finanzen) Abt. 34 zu Dagobert R.; Akten des BMF Karton 6597; Eintrag in der Immobilienkartei des ÖStA für EZ X4, KG Eßling: 1325/II, A. 1354/A R. Dagobert, EZ X4, laut GB negativ; Eintrag in der Immobilienkartei des ÖStA für EZ X1, KG Eßling: „EZ [X1], positiv, KG Essling (alte EZ [X9] – der EZ [X1] zugeschrieben), Anton Re[…], 1230 W[…]-gasse 1; Die EZ [X9] Donaufeld gehörte Leopold Bl[...] und Mitbesitzer. 1/3 Anteil von FLD VR. V 5576-/2/50 an die anderen Besitzer zurückgestellt. Negativ; Acker 1/1; Leopoldau, lt. Kaufvertrag 07.11.1939 an (Ariseur) Reichsfiskus (Luftfahrt). G[...] Antonia, 1160 Wien D[...]-gasse 29; EZ [X1] (ursprünglich [X10]), KG Essling; Entzieher: Deutsches Reich – Kaufvertrag vom 28.04.1939. Antrag auf Rückstellung der Liegenschaft mit Erkenntnis vom 28.06.1956 zurückgewiesen, da keine typische nationalsozialistische Maßnahme, sondern Enteignung für Zwecke der Luftfahrt"; ÖStA, AdR, VwGH, Akt zum Erkenntnis Zl. 496/61; ÖStA, AdR, Reichsstatthalter Wien – Obere Siedlungsbehörde, Akt A.W. 206. 103

Akten aus dem Wiener Stadt- und Landesarchiv, Akten nach der VEAV: VEAV Akten zu Berta R. und Dagobert R.; Friederike F. bzw. Friederike O., Rosa W.; Rückstellungsakten: 2 RK 62/65 (G., Verfahren betreffend benachbarte Liegenschaft), 2 RK 118/56 (Re., Verfahren betreffend benachbarte Liegenschaft), 2 RK 112/65 (T., Verfahren betreffend benachbarte Liegenschaft), 2 RK 124/56 (Kä., Verfahren betreffend vergleichbare Liegenschaft); Verlassenschaftsdokumentation Dagobert R. 8 A 281/48. 104

Historische Grundbücher: EZ X4, KG Eßling samt Urkunden (Tagebuchzahl 2540/36, 98/16) und EZ X1, KG Eßling samt Urkunden (Tagebuchzahl 1677/1940, 5911/64, 123/60, 1391/39); C-Blatt zur EZ X7, Grundbuch Leopoldstadt (Auszug) und bezughabende Urkunden zur Tagebuchzahl 10952/1939. 105

Grundbuchsauszüge zu EZ X1, EZ X2 und EZ X3, alle KG Eßling. 106

1938–1945, Vienna 1975; Hans Witek, „*Arisierungen*" *in Wien. Aspekte nationalsozialistischer Enteignungspolitik 1938–1940*, in: Emmerich Tálos, Ernst Hanisch, Wolfgang Neugebauer and Reinhard Sieder (eds.), *NS-Herrschaft in Österreich. Ein Handbuch*, Vienna 2000, at 795 ff.

109 Decisions: Decision of the Supreme Administrative Court of 29 November 1962, no. 272/60.

110 Electronic sources: excerpts from the database on the project entitled "Collection of Names of the Austrian Holocaust Victims" by the Documentation Center of Austrian Resistance, Vienna.

5. Consideration of Evidence

111 Contradictory evidence was produced regarding the reasons Dr. Dagobert and Bertha R. did not or could not leave the country. On the one hand, the applicant states that her father had been in the hospital most of the time, at least from 1938 onwards and that he had been deported from the hospital to a concentration camp. This would seem to suggest that Dr. Dagobert R. could no longer leave the country due to health reasons. The serious health problems suffered by Dr. R. are also documented in a legal appeal which was filed by the applicant in 1963 against the decision by the Compensation Fund. According to this, he had to endure eight operations connected to prostate hypertrophy and incontinence. On the other hand, in a letter to Dr. Ka. dated 27 November 1938, Dr. R. states that during a discussion, director K. had demanded that he would definitely refrain from leaving the country as in staying, he [meaning the bank director, comm. by the Arbitration Panel] would no longer have to pay the Reich Flight Emigration Tax. Here, it can only be assumed that financial problems had prevented him from leaving the country. The meaning of the letter can no longer be unambiguously established. However, the personal visit by Dr. R. to the Higher Administration for Settlement in January 1941 shows that he still made an effort to leave the country. Accordingly, Dr. R. could not have been continuously bedridden.

112 On the one hand, the reasons for joining Operation Gildemeester can be inferred from the motives described in Theodor Venus/Alexandra-Eileen Wenck, *Die Entziehung jüdischen Vermögens im Rahmen der Aktion Gildemeester*, volume 20/2 of the publications of the Austrian Historical Commission (refer to p. 144 f: "[…] being able to assure an unrestricted departure from Austria"; p. 159 "[…] that then I would be under his protection [meant here is Dr. Ra[…], comm. by the Arbitration Panel] and I would not be arrested anymore […]"), which spurred wealthy Jews to join Operation Gildemeester. These motives are confirmed in an undated letter by the applicant directed to the General Settlement Fund:

> "We heard of Operation Gildemeester and joined it; as you can read in my notes, there was no other way of getting out. […] The expenses incurred due to taxes and obligations, which were imposed on us, were very high; the way out of this was Gildemeester […]."

113 The facts on the surrender of the properties are based on the letter dated 29 August 1938 by the applicant to the banking house *Krentschker & Co*. A letter to this effect by Dr. Dagobert R. could not be found anymore. However, the Arbitration Panel is convinced that Dr. Dagobert R. had to have written a similar letter to the banking house *Krentschker & Co*. concerning his property, especially after taking into consideration the detailed description in Venus/Wenck, at 151–154, of the course of events regarding the admission to Operation

Mappenpläne der Magistratsabteilung (MA) 37, Baupolizei, Stadt Wien zur EZ X1, KG Eßling; Pläne des Liegenschaftsgebietes EZ X4, KG Eßling des Vermessungsamtes Wien. 107

Literatur zu den Feststellungen: Theodor *Venus* und Alexandra-Eileen *Wenck*, Die Entziehung jüdischen Vermögens im Rahmen der Aktion Gildemeester. Eine empirische Studie über Organisation, Form und Wandel von „Arisierung" und jüdischer Auswanderung in Österreich 1938–1941, Wien (Oldenbourg) 2004 (= Veröffentlichungen der Österreichischen Historikerkommission, Band 20/2); Walter *Schroeder*, Flugfelder in der Ostmark 1938–1945; Judith *Wita*, Die Geschichte des Flughafen Wien, Wien Dipl. Arbeit, 2003; Historisches Museum der Stadt Wien (Hg.), Aspern. Von der Steinzeit zum Motorenwerk, Wien 1981; Wolfram *Lenotti*, Mehr als ein Landeplatz, Wien 1988; Othmar *Tuider*, Die Wehrkreise XVII und XVIII. 1938–1945, Wien 1975; Hans *Witek*, „Arisierungen" in Wien. Aspekte nationalsozialistischer Enteignungspolitik 1938–1940. In: Emmerich *Talos*, Ernst *Hanisch*, Wolfgang *Neugebauer* and Reinhard *Sieder* (Hg.), NS-Herrschaft in Österreich. Ein Handbuch, Wien 2000, S. 795 ff. 108

Entscheidungen: Erkenntnis des VwGH 29. November 1962, Zl. 272/60 109

Elektronische Quellen: Auszüge aus der Datenbank zum Projekt „Namentliche Erfassung der österreichischen Opfer des Holocaust" des Dokumentationsarchiv des österreichischen Widerstandes (DÖW), Wien. 110

5. Beweiswürdigung

Zu den Gründen, warum Dr. Dagobert und Bertha R. nicht ausreisten bzw. nicht ausreisen konnten, liegen einander widersprechende Beweise vor. Einerseits gibt die Antragstellerin an, ihr Vater sei zumindest ab 1938 zum größten Teil im Spital gewesen und sei auch aus dem Spital abgeholt und ins Konzentrationslager verschleppt worden. Dies würde den Schluss nahelegen, dass Dr. Dagobert R. aus gesundheitlichen Gründen nicht (mehr) ausreisen konnte. Auch in einem Rechtsbehelf, den die Antragstellerin 1963 gegen die Entscheidung des Abgeltungsfonds erhob, wird auf schwerwiegende gesundheitliche Probleme von Dr. R. hingewiesen. Danach habe er insgesamt acht Operationen wegen Prostatahypertrophie und Blasenschwäche erdulden müssen. Andererseits gibt Dr. R. in einem Schreiben an einen Herrn Dr. Ka. vom 27. November 1938 an, dass Direktor K. bei einer Besprechung seinen definitiven Verzicht auf eine Ausreise verlangt habe, weil damit für ihn (gemeint ist damit der Bankdirektor, Anm. der Schiedsinstanz) die Notwendigkeit der Bezahlung der Reichsfluchtsteuer entfalle. Man kann hier nur vermuten, dass ein finanzieller Engpass die Ausreise verhindert hat. Die genaue Bedeutung dieses Schreibens lässt sich nicht mehr eindeutig erschließen. Im Übrigen zeigt aber die persönliche Vorsprache von Dr. R. vor der Oberen Siedlungsbehörde im Jänner 1941, dass er sich nach wie vor um seine Ausreise sehr bemüht hat. Demgemäß kann Dr. R. nicht ständig bettlägerig gewesen sein. 111

Die Gründe für den Beitritt zur Gildemeester-Aktion ergeben sich einerseits aus den in Theodor *Venus* und Alexandra-Eileen *Wenck*, Die Entziehung jüdischen Vermögens im Rahmen der Aktion Gildemeester, Band 20/2 der Veröffentlichungen der Österreichischen Historikerkommission, geschilderten Motiven (vergleiche S. 144f: „[...] ungehinderte Ausreise aus Österreich sicherstellen zu können", S. 159: („[...] dass ich dann unter seinem Schutz [gemeint ist Dr. Ra[...], Anm. der Schiedsinstanz] stehe und nicht mehr verhaftet [...] würde"), die vermögende Juden dazu bewogen hat, der Gildemeester-Aktion beizutreten. Diese Motive werden in einem von der Antragstellerin an den Allgemeinen Entschädigungsfonds gerichteten undatierten Schreiben bestätigt: 112

Gildemeester and the handing over of the trust estate. It would not seem understandable to the Arbitration Panel if such a declaration would not have been requested from Dr. Dagobert R.

114 The fact that the statement of the Pricing Authority of 15 January 1941 was already taken into consideration in the decision by the Higher Administration for Settlement dated 6 January 1941 concerning the purchase contract between R. and the Air Force is only an ostensible contradiction and is a result of the following: It is traceable from the administrative file of the Reich Governor in Vienna, Higher Administration for Settlement, concerning the sale of the above-mentioned property, that the statement of the Pricing Authority had been taken into consideration during the issue of the ruling. Nevertheless, in the facts, the date of 6 January 1941 is retained, as this date is stated in all official documents as the date of the issue of the ruling.

115 As for the rest, the established facts are based on certificates produced by the applicants, the land register, the reports of the Historical Commission, and archive material researched by the Arbitration Panel.

6. Juridical Appraisal

116 Dr. Dagobert R., the person affected by the loss of assets, was persecuted by the National Socialist regime for reasons of origin; he was a Jew according to the Nuremberg Laws. The applicant is the universal successor to Dr. Dagobert R. and hence pursuant to Sec. 27 (2) of the GSF Law eligible to file applications.

117 The universal successor to the second heiress of Dr. Dagobert R., Friederike O., is George W. The latter has assigned all of his claims for restitution to the applicant through the assignment agreement of 27 October 2002. There is no provision to be found in the GSF Law, which would invalidate such an assignment, which is permissible according to the regulations of civil law (para. 1396 and the following paragraphs of the [Austrian] General Civil Code). Hence, the applicant herself is eligible to assert claims for *in rem* restitution of Dr. Dagobert R.

118 Regarding the property parcels Y1/1, Y1/2, Y1/5, Y1/7, Y1/8, Y1/9, Y1/10, Y1/11, Y1/12, Y1/13, Y1/14, Y1/15, Y1/52, Y1/53, Y1/54, and Y1/58, owned by Dr. Dagobert R. on 12 March 1938 (all contained in EZ X4, KG Eßling on the named date), forming part of the application, property Y1/5 – now contained in EZ X3, KG Eßling – was under private ownership on 17 January 2001, the date relevant for the assessment of ownership status. As a result, the requirement of "publicly-owned property" is not met as stipulated in Sec. 28 (1) item 3 of the GSF Law and Sec. 38 of the GSF Law in connection with the resolutions of those territorial authorities, which provide for a joining to ("opt in") part 2 of the GSF Law. Therefore, already for this reason, the application for *in rem* restitution concerning this property parcel had to be rejected.

119 According to the established facts, all other property parcels that are applied for were under the ownership of the City of Vienna on 17 January 2001. Pursuant to Sec. 38 of the GSF Law in connection with the resolution of 27 June 2001 by the Municipal Council Vienna the prerequisite of "publicly-owned property" required for a restitution is fulfilled. Where the City of Vienna asserts – in regard to the property areas relevant for the restitution, which are contained in EZ X2, KG Eßling – that a restitution *per se* is impossible, this assertion need not be followed. Although the property was designated as a public street through an administrative act, this does not preclude the obligation for restitution (Supreme

„Wir hörten von der Gildemesteraktion und schlossen uns dort an, wie Sie aus meinen Aufzeichnungen ersehen werden gab es kein normales entkommen [sic!]. [...] Die Ausgaben an Steuern und Verpflichtungen, die uns auferlegt wurden waren sehr gross, der Ausweg war Gildemester [...]."

Die Feststellungen zur Übergabe der Liegenschaften gründen sich auf das Schreiben der Antragstellerin an das Bankhaus Krentschker & Co. vom 29. August 1938. Von Dr. Dagobert R. konnte ein solches Schreiben nicht mehr aufgefunden werden. Die Schiedsinstanz ist jedoch davon überzeugt, dass Dr. Dagobert R. – sein Liegenschaftseigentum betreffend – ein gleichlautendes Schreiben an das Bankhaus Krentschker & Co. richten musste. Dies insbesondere unter Berücksichtigung des in *Venus/Wenck*, S. 151–154, detailliert beschriebenen Ablaufes der Aufnahme in die Gildemeester-Aktion und der Übergabe des Treuhandvermögens. Der Schiedsinstanz erschiene es nicht nachvollziehbar, wenn man von Dr. Dagobert R. eine solche Erklärung nicht verlangt hätte.

Dass die Stellungnahme der Preisbildungsstelle vom 15. Jänner 1941, im bereits mit 6. Jänner 1941 datierten, zum Kaufvertrag R. – Luftwaffe ergangenen Bescheid der Oberen Siedlungsbehörde Berücksichtigung fand, ist nur ein scheinbarer Widerspruch und ergibt sich aus Folgendem: Dem Verwaltungsakt des Reichsstatthalters in Wien, Obere Siedlungsbehörde, betreffend den Verkauf der oben genannten Liegenschaft ist nachvollziehbar zu entnehmen, dass die Stellungnahme der Preisbildungsstelle bei der Bescheiderlassung Berücksichtigung fand. In den Feststellungen wird demgegenüber trotzdem der 6. Jänner 1941 beibehalten, da dieses Datum in allen offiziellen behördlichen Schriftstücken als Datum der Bescheiderlassung genannt wird.

Im Übrigen gründet sich der festgestellte Sachverhalt auf die von der Antragstellerin vorgelegten Urkunden, das Grundbuch, die Berichte der Historikerkommission und seitens der Schiedsinstanz recherchierte Archivalien.

6. Rechtliche Beurteilung

Der durch den Vermögensverlust betroffene Dr. Dagobert R. wurde aus Gründen der Abstammung – er war Jude nach den Nürnberger Rassegesetzen – vom nationalsozialistischen Regime verfolgt. Die Antragstellerin ist Gesamtrechtsnachfolgerin von Dr. Dagobert R. und daher gemäß § 27 Abs 2 des EF-G antragsberechtigt.

Universalsukzessor nach der zweiten Erbin von Dr. Dagobert R., Friederike O., ist George W. Dieser hat mit Zessionsvertrag vom 27. Oktober 2002 alle ihm daraus zustehenden Restitutionsansprüche an die Antragstellerin abgetreten. Dem EF-G ist keine Bestimmung zu entnehmen, die eine derartige nach den Bestimmungen des bürgerlichen Rechtes [§§ 1396 ff Allgemeines bürgerliches Gesetzbuch (ABGB)] jedenfalls zulässige Abtretungsvereinbarung ungültig machen würde. Die Antragstellerin ist damit allein legitimiert, Ansprüche auf Naturalrestitution nach Dr. Dagobert R. geltend zu machen.

Hinsichtlich der vom Antrag umfassten, sich am 12. März 1938 im Eigentum von Dr. Dagobert R. befindlichen Grundstücke Y1/1, Y1/2, Y1/5, Y1/7, Y1/8, Y1/9, Y1/10, Y1/11, Y1/12, Y1/13, Y1/14, Y1/15, Y1/52, Y1/53, Y1/54 und Y1/58 (zum genannten Datum alle innenliegend in der Grundbuchseinlage X4, KG Eßling) stand das Grundstück Y1/5 – nunmehr innenliegend in der Grundbuchseinlage X3, KG Eßling – am für die Beurteilung der Eigentumsverhältnisse maßgeblichen Stichtag 17. Jänner 2001 im Privateigentum. Da somit kein „öffentliches Vermögen" gemäß § 28 Abs 1 Z 3 EF-G bzw. § 38 EF-G iVm den Beschlüssen jener Gebietskörperschaften, die einen Beitritt zu Teil 2 des EF-G vorsehen, vorliegt, war der Antrag auf Naturalrestitution hinsichtlich dieses Grundstücks schon aus diesem Grund abzulehnen.

Arbitration Panel for *In Rem* Restitution – Decision No. 24/2005

Court decision no. 72/65 including further references). For cases of this kind, Sec. 34 of the GSF Law provides for the possibility that after consultation with the relevant authority, a comparable property may be awarded.

120   In accordance with Sec. 32 (1) of the GSF Law, the Arbitration Panel is not to decide claims that were previously decided by Austrian courts or administrative bodies. A decision of this kind exists due to the negative decision of 10 October 1963 of the Supreme Administrative Court. The law permits a digression from such a decision in cases where the prior decision represents an extreme injustice or if the claim had been rejected for lack of evidence – this evidence not having been accessible to the applicant, but now being accessible.

121   Further, the GSF Law includes the instructions to take relevant findings by the Austrian Historical Commission into consideration during the decision-making process (Sec. 30 leg. cit.). In this connection, the Arbitration Panel refers to the material published by the Austrian Historical Commission including, Theodor Venus and Alexandra-Eileen Wenck, *Die Entziehung jüdischen Vermögens im Rahmen der Aktion Gildemeester. Eine empirische Studie über Organisation, Form und Wandel von „Arisisierung" und jüdischer Auswanderung in Österreich 1938–1941*, Vienna (Oldenbourg) 2004 (= Publications of the Austrian Historical Commission, vol. 20/2). The aforementioned findings contain evidence which demands a revised evaluation of Operation Gildemeester. This evidence was not accessible at the time, which also explains why the applicant had considered the purchase contract for the property in question during the restitution proceedings as a seizure and was not able to substantiate it specifically (see above margin note 62). Hence, the Arbitration Panel assumes that the elements of Sec. 32 (2) item 2 of the GSF Law are fulfilled for the following reasons:

122   Until now, Operation Gildemeester has received little attention in historical research. It was difficult to correctly evaluate the true character of this Janus-headed operation: On the one hand, authority and helper in the looting of Jewish property; on the other hand, a helping hand to speed up Jewish emigration. Only Charles Ka. is to be mentioned here with his evaluation given in 1967; he was the head of the Foreign Exchange Department of the Jewish Community in Vienna in 1938 and had been in contact with Gildemeester participants. After World War II, Ka. was engaged in the compensation practice of persecuted Jews for property losses during the NS regime: "'Operation Gildemeester' was a mysterious matter situated in no-man's-land between the Secret State Police and welfare. I don't think that in this case one can speak of compulsion, but with the help of 'Operation Gildemeester', the people hoped for a quicker emigration than with the help of the Community." (Venus/Wenck, at 22–24).

123   In contrast, the report of the Historical Commission by Venus/Wenck has disclosed for the first time in a stringent manner the history of the development, the practical implementation, the involved persons, the involvement of the National Socialist regime, the property transfers and, above all, the institutionalized nature of Operation Gildemeester. The extensive influence of the National Socialist state is particularly illustrated by the following points:

• The appointment of the banking house *Krentschker & Co.* as trustee of Operation Gildemeester was carried out by the State Commissioner for Private Enterprises, who at the same time was the head of the Property Transaction Office. The main function of this office, established in May 1938, was, on the one hand, the receipt and administration of the property notices, which were to be submitted by Jewish citizens. On the other hand, the office was in charge of approving the sale and leasing of companies if Jews were in-

Alle anderen beantragten Parzellen befanden sich nach den getroffenen Feststellungen am 17. Jänner 2001 im Eigentum der Stadt Wien. Gemäß § 38 EF-G iVm dem Beschluss des Gemeinderates Wien vom 27. Juni 2001 ist damit die für eine Rückstellung erforderliche Voraussetzung „öffentliches Vermögen" erfüllt. Wenn die Stadt Wien bezüglich der in der Grundbuchseinlage X2 der KG Eßling einliegenden rückstellungsrelevanten Grundstücksflächen vorbringt, dass eine Rückstellung per se ausgeschlossen ist, so ist dem nicht zu folgen. Die durch Verwaltungsakt ausgesprochene Zweckwidmung der Liegenschaft als öffentliche Straße steht einer Rückstellungspflicht dem Grunde nach nicht entgegen (Oberster Gerichtshof [OGH] SZ 72/65 mit weiteren Nachweisen). Für Fälle dieser Art sieht § 34 EF-G die Möglichkeit vor, dass nach Konsultation mit der entsprechenden Instanz ein vergleichbarer Vermögenswert zugesprochen wird. 119

Gemäß § 32 Abs 1 EF-G hat die Schiedsinstanz nicht über solche Forderungen zu entscheiden, die bereits zuvor von österreichischen Gerichten oder Verwaltungsbehörden entschieden wurden. Eine solche Entscheidung liegt mit dem ablehnenden Erkenntnis des VwGH vom 10. Oktober 1963 vor. Ein Abgehen von einer solchen Entscheidung erlaubt das Gesetz in jenen Fällen, wenn die frühere Entscheidung eine extreme Ungerechtigkeit darstellt oder der Anspruch aus Mangel an Beweisen abgelehnt wurde, diese Beweise der AntragstellerIn nicht zugänglich waren, nunmehr aber zugänglich sind. 120

Das EF-G enthält weiters den Auftrag, relevante Befunde der österreichischen Historikerkommission bei der Entscheidungsfindung zu berücksichtigen (§ 30 leg. cit.). Die Schiedsinstanz weist in diesem Zusammenhang auf die Veröffentlichungen der Österreichischen Historikerkommission hin. Dazu gehört Theodor *Venus* und Alexandra-Eileen *Wenck*, Die Entziehung jüdischen Vermögens im Rahmen der Aktion Gildemeester. Eine empirische Studie über Organisation, Form und Wandel von „Arisierung" und jüdischer Auswanderung in Österreich 1938–1941, Wien (Oldenbourg) 2004 (= Veröffentlichungen der Österreichischen Historikerkommission, Band 20/2). Der vorstehend zitierte Befund enthält Beweise, die zu einer anderen Bewertung der Aktion Gildemeester zwingen. Diese Beweise waren damals nicht zugänglich, woraus sich auch erklärt, dass die Antragstellerinnen im Rückstellungsverfahren die Entziehung im Kaufvertrag zur gegenständlichen Liegenschaft gesehen hatten und nur unspezifisch darauf hinweisen konnten (siehe dazu oben Rz 62). Die Schiedsinstanz geht daher davon aus, dass der Tatbestand des § 32 Abs 2 Z 2 EF-G erfüllt ist. Dies aus folgenden Gründen: 121

Die Aktion „Gildemeester" fand in der bisherigen zeithistorischen Forschung wenig Beachtung. Man tat sich schwer, den Charakter dieser janusköpfigen Aktion – hier Instanz und Helfer beim Raub jüdischen Vermögens, da Hilfestellung zur beschleunigten jüdischen Auswanderung – richtig einzuschätzen. Es soll hier nur Charles Ka. mit seiner Einschätzung aus dem Jahr 1967 zu Wort kommen, der 1938 als Leiter der Devisenabteilung der IKG Wien mit Gildemeester-Teilnehmern in Kontakt gestanden war und nach dem Zweiten Weltkrieg in die Entschädigungspraxis von verfolgten Juden für Vermögensverluste während des NS-Regimes eingebunden war: „Die Aktion ‚Gildemeester' war eine mysteriöse Angelegenheit im Niemandsland zwischen Gestapo und Wohlfahrt. Ich glaube nicht dass man von Zwang reden kann, aber die Leute versprachen sich eine schnellere Auswanderung mit Hilfe der ‚Aktion Gildemeester' als durch die Kultusgemeinde." (*Venus/Wenck*, S. 22–24.) 122

Demgegenüber hat erstmals der Historikerkommissionsbericht von *Venus/Wenck* die Entstehungsgeschichte, die praktische Durchführung, die beteiligten Personen, die Involvierung des nationalsozialistischen Regimes, die stattgefundenen Vermögensverschiebungen und vor allem den institutionalisierten Charakter der Gildemeester-Aktion in strin- 123

volved in legal transactions of that kind. Hence, the main task of the Property Transaction Office was the implementation and approval of "Aryanizations" (compare with Hans Witek, *"Arisierungen" in Wien. Aspekte nationalsozialistischer Enteignungspolitik 1938–1940*, in: Emmerich Tálos, Ernst Hanisch, Wolfgang Neugebauer and Reinhard Sieder (editors), *NS-Herrschaft in Österreich. Ein Handbuch*, Vienna 2000, at 795 ff.). The National Socialist regime used a bank during Operation Gildemeester in order to assure a "proper" registration, administration and utilization of those property assets that were to be alienated. (Venus/Wenck at 131). There were two reasons why the banking house *Krentschker & Co.*, which until that moment in time was a rather modestly operating institution, had been chosen: The two partners Moritz K. and Kurt P. were regarded to be two politically reliable players, who during the years of the Corporative State had handled the money transfer to the prohibited Austrian NSDAP through their bank. (Venus/Wenck at 112–115). Secondly, the big banks in Vienna – supposedly more suited in terms of their personnel and operations – had previously declined to undertake this task arguing that it would negatively influence international relations. It was feared that "the emigrants would withdraw their declarations after their departure as having been given under coercion and that foreign courts would assess the legal position differently than German courts" (statement by Heinrich Ga., who in April or May 1938 led negotiations regarding Operation Gildemeester with the *Länderbank*; quoted from Venus/Wenck at 131) – it is to be assumed that this is a contemporary, sober legal analysis of Operation Gildemeester. This subject is treated in a more detailed manner later in the text.

- In particular, point I of the minutes taken from memory reproduced in the findings on the extensive authority of the banking house *Krentschker & Co.* in tax-law matters shows the governmental influence on the structuring of the trust agreement. Most notable is the fact that a bank assumes the representation of its clients in tax-related matters. Such an activity does not fall under the typical activities of a bank (for example, compare with the exhaustive list of the currently authorized banking transactions in para. 1 (1) *Bankwesengesetz* ["Austrian Banking Act"]). From a current legal point of view, the legitimacy of the mentioned extensive power of representation in tax-matters is also extremely doubtful. On the basis of today's prevailing provisions on professional ethics and practice such an activity is reserved for tax advisors, auditors and lawyers and cannot – at least not professionally – be performed by a bank. It can be left open whether this would also apply to the legal situation at the time. However, the purpose of this provision is evident: Through the bank, the tax authorities secured the direct access to the respective assets of the taxpayer for the payment of the (discriminatory) tax liabilities. It could also be assumed that the banking house *Krentschker & Co.* in its role as a representative of the taxpayer would not perform its duties in an independent manner for the benefit of the clients.

Where the City of Vienna in its statement of 9 September 2005 finally alleges that Venus/Wenck do not answer the question whether Operation Gildemeester constituted a forced seizure, this is not logical in relation to two issues. Firstly, the City of Vienna uses the above-mentioned quotation of Charles Ka. as the only proof for their claim. However, this quotation is taken from the introductory chapter, in which the main task of the authors is to summarize the status of the research and to describe previous evaluations of Operation Gildemeester. It would also be more than surprising if in a book of more than 700 pages the final evaluation by the authors was to be found on page 23 and the following pages of the introductory chapter. More meaningful by far are the statements by the authors given in the summary:

genter Weise offengelegt. Der umfängliche Einfluss des NS-Staates kann insbesondere an folgenden Punkten festgemacht werden:

• Die Bestellung des Bankhauses Krentschker & Co. zum Treuhänder der Gildemeester-Aktion erfolgte durch den Staatskommissar in der Privatwirtschaft, der zugleich Leiter der Vermögensverkehrsstelle war. Den Tätigkeitsschwerpunkt dieser im Mai 1938 eingerichteten Behörde bildete auf der einen Seite die Entgegennahme und Administrierung der von den jüdischen BürgerInnen abzugebenden Vermögensanmeldungen, andererseits war sie die Genehmigungsstelle für die Veräußerung und Verpachtung von Betrieben, wenn Juden an solchen Rechtsgeschäften beteiligt waren. Die Hauptaufgabe der Vermögensverkehrsstelle lag somit in der Durchführung und Genehmigung der „Arisierungen" (vergleiche dazu Hans *Witek*, „Arisierungen" in Wien. Aspekte nationalsozialistischer Enteignungspolitik 1938–1940. In: Emmerich *Talos*, Ernst *Hanisch*, Wolfgang *Neugebauer* and Reinhard *Sieder* (Hg.), NS-Herrschaft in Österreich. Ein Handbuch, Wien 2000, S. 795ff). Von Seiten des NS-Regimes wurde eine Bank im Rahmen der Gildemeester-Aktion deswegen eingeschaltet, um die „ordnungsgemäße" Erfassung, Verwaltung und Verwertung der zu übernehmenden Vermögenswerte sicherzustellen. (*Venus/Wenck*, S. 131). Die Wahl auf das bis dahin recht bescheiden agierende Bankhaus Krentschker hatte zwei Gründe: Man sah in den beiden Gesellschaftern Moritz K. und Kurt P. zwei politisch zuverlässige Akteure, die in den Jahren des Ständestaates über ihre Bank den Geldtransfer an die verbotene österreichische NSDAP abgewickelt hatten. (*Venus/Wenck*, S. 112–115). Zum anderen hatten bereits zuvor Wiener Großbanken – von ihrem Personal- und Geschäftsapparat an sich wohl besser geeignet – die Übernahme dieser Aufgabe mit der Begründung abgelehnt, dass darunter die internationalen Beziehungen leiden könnten. Man befürchtete, „dass die Emigranten nach der Ausreise ihre Erklärungen als unter Zwang abgegeben widerrufen werden und dass ausländische Gerichte die Rechtslage anders als deutsche Gerichte beurteilen" würden (Aussage von Heinrich Ga., der im April oder Mai 1938 Verhandlungen mit der Länderbank über die Aktion Gildemeester geführt hat; zitiert nach *Venus/Wenck*, S. 131) – wohl eine zeitgenössische, nüchterne juristische Analyse der Aktion Gildemeester. Auf diese Frage wird unten noch näher eingegangen werden.

• Insbesondere Punkt I des in den Feststellungen wiedergegebenen Gedenkprotokolls über die umfassende Bevollmächtigung des Bankhauses Krentschker & Co. in steuerrechtlichen Angelegenheiten lässt die behördliche Einflussnahme auf die Ausgestaltung des Treuhandvertrages erkennen. Auffallend daran ist zunächst, dass eine Bank für ihre Kunden die Vertretung in allen steuerlichen Agenden übernimmt. Eine solche Tätigkeit fällt nicht unter die klassischen Tätigkeiten einer Bank (vergleiche etwa nur die taxative Aufzählung der aktuell zugelassenen Bankgeschäfte in § 1 Abs 1 Bankwesengesetz [BWG]); auch müssen – wieder auf die heutige Rechtslage abgestellt – erhebliche Zweifel an der Zulässigkeit einer solch umfassenden Vertretungsbefugnis in steuerlichen Angelegenheiten aufkommen. Aufgrund der geltenden berufsrechtlichen Vorschriften ist eine solche Tätigkeit den SteuerberaterInnen, WirtschaftsprüferInnen und RechtsanwältInnen vorbehalten und darf nicht – zumindest nicht gewerbsmäßig – von einer Bank ausgeübt werden. Mag hier dahingestellt bleiben, ob dieser Befund auch im Lichte der damaligen Rechtslage zutreffend ist oder nicht, so ist der mit dieser Bestimmung verfolgte Zweck evident: Die Finanzbehörden sicherten sich über die Bank den direkten Zugriff auf das jeweilige Vermögen der Steuerpflichtigen zur Tilgung der (diskriminierenden) Steuerverbindlichkeiten. Auch konnte man davon ausgehen, dass das Bankhaus Krentschker & Co. als Vertreter des Steuerpflichtigen sein Mandat nicht in unabhängiger Weise zugunsten des Vertretenen ausüben würde.

"In reality, very soon the 'trust model' turned out to be a quasi expropriation: Those persons who entrusted a trustee with their assets usually forfeited every right of disposal from the moment of entrustment, at least as long as their assets at that time were located within the borders of the Reich. Primarily, the trustee saw his function not as a lawyer for his clients but rather acted strictly on the basis of the then prevailing anti-Jewish regulations – irrespective of attempts to later justify this role." (Venus/Wenck at 528) and: "For the most part, the beneficiaries lost all their rights, even to dispose of certain parts of their assets, after having transferred their assets. Consequently, they were dependent on alms from the trustee in order to be able to pay for living expenses, for the support of their families or for the purchases and costs indispensable for the preparation of their departure." (Venus/Wenck at 531).

124 When basing this knowledge on the present case, the transfer of the assets to the Gildemeester trustee, not the sale to the Reich Treasury, is to be taken as the relevant point in time for the assessment of the seizure. With the conclusion of the contract, each individual participant lost every right of disposal concerning his former property, even if – as was the case with Dr. Dagobert R. – for the time being he remained the owner according to the land register. The concerned person also adopted the same view as shown in the explanations in his property notice of 15 December 1938 (see above margin note 41). The trustee could dispose of the assets at any time without restrictions. This was due to the obligation to issue special powers-of-attorney for the benefit of the lawyers of Operation Gildemeester under the trust agreement (see above margin notes 33 and 56). The internal relationship between the trustee and the beneficiary was not characterized by a duty of loyalty. Merely as an aside, it should be mentioned that this sort of contract would have to be considered *contra bonos mores* according to general principles of civil law. The beneficiary left his entire assets behind in order to be able to leave the country more or less securely and undisturbed. Of course, the trustee was very well aware of this motive. As Venus/Wenck have proven, Jewish citizens were pressured to conclude the trust agreement also by means of threat (Venus/Wenck at 159). However, this could not be proven in the present case.

125 Finally, in order to prevent any unauthorized sale, the trustee in coordination with the Property Transaction Office had the Gildemeester participants issue promissory notes regarding alleged loan agreements, which were then used for providing the trustee with security through a mortgage. This particular *modus operandi* is also documented in this case. This loan was granted regardless of whether it indeed was necessary. In many cases, there were sufficient funds available anyway (Venus/Wenck at 230 f. and 238). On 27 July 1938, the State Commissioner for Private Enterprises commented on this *modus operandi* in a letter to the banking house *Krentschker & Co.* as follows:

"In view of our endeavor to first of all collect the Reich Flight Tax amounts in order to be able to make them available to the Reich Flight Tax office, I approve the registration of such a mortgage loan, however, with the explicit provision that the emigrating Jew himself may under no circumstances be allowed to obtain this mortgage loan." (quoted from Venus/Wenck, at 232)

126 The fact that Dr. Dagobert R. had personally signed the purchase contract for the property subject of this application does not affect the point of time of the seizure but was solely explained by the fact that he had not yet emigrated. In order to seemingly imply that the transaction was voluntary, the owner according to the land register was allowed to sign. The findings have shown that the completed purchase contract had been presented to Dr.

Wenn die Stadt Wien in ihrer Stellungnahme vom 9. September 2005 schließlich vermeint, dass *Venus/Wenck* die Frage, ob es sich bei der Gildemeester-Aktion um eine zwangsweise Entziehung handelte, unbeantwortet lassen, so ist dies in zweifacher Hinsicht nicht nachvollziehbar. Zum einen bringt die Stadt Wien das bereits oben wiedergegebene Zitat von Charles Ka. als einzigen Beleg für ihre Behauptung. Dieses Zitat stammt jedoch aus dem Einleitungskapitel, wo es den AutorInnen im Wesentlichen darum geht, den Forschungsstand zusammenzufassen und bisherige Einschätzungen der Aktion Gildemeester wiederzugeben. Im Übrigen wäre es mehr als verwunderlich, würde sich in einem mehr als 700 Seiten starken Werk die abschließende Beurteilung der AutorInnen schon auf den Seiten 23f im Einleitungskapitel vorfinden. Ungleich aussagekräftiger sind da die Aussagen der AutorInnen in der Zusammenfassung:

„Das ‚Treuhandmodell' entpuppte sich in Wahrheit sehr bald als verkappte Enteignung: Diejenigen, die ihr Vermögen dem Treuhänder anvertrauten, begaben sich in der Regel vom Zeitpunkt der Übergabe ihres Vermögens jedweder Verfügungsgewalt, zumindest soweit sich dieses zu diesem Zeitpunkt innerhalb der Reichsgrenzen befand. Der Treuhänder sah seine Rolle, ungeachtet nachträglicher Rechtfertigungsversuche, primär nicht als Anwalt seiner Klienten, sondern agierte strikt auf der Basis der damals geltenden antijüdischen Vorschriften." [*Venus/Wenck*, S. 528] und: „Zumeist verloren die Treugeber ab dem Zeitpunkt der Übergabe jeden Anspruch, selbst über einzelne Vermögensteile verfügen zu können, und waren damit auf Almosen des Treuhänders angewiesen, um die für die Lebenshaltung, die Unterstützung von Angehörigen oder zur Vorbereitung der Ausreise unentbehrlichen Anschaffungen und Ausgaben bestreiten zu können." (*Venus/Wenck*, S. 531)

Legt man dieses Wissen dem konkreten Fall zugrunde, dann ist für die Frage der Entziehung als Beurteilungszeitpunkt nicht erst der Verkauf an den Reichsfiskus heranzuziehen, sondern bereits die Übergabe des Vermögens an den Gildemeester-Treuhänder. Mit dem Abschluss dieses Vertrages verlor der einzelne Teilnehmer jede Verfügungsmacht über sein bisheriges Eigentum, auch wenn er – wie im Fall von Dr. Dagobert R. – einstweilen noch grundbücherlicher Eigentümer geblieben ist. Das sah auch der Betroffene selbst so, wie die Ausführungen in seinem Vermögensbekenntnis vom 15. Dezember 1938 gezeigt haben (siehe oben Rz 41). Durch die mit dem Treuhandvertrag einhergehende Verpflichtung zur Ausstellung von Spezialvollmachten zugunsten der Rechtsanwälte der Gildemeester-Aktion (siehe oben Rz 33 und 56) konnte der Treuhänder im Übrigen jederzeit uneingeschränkt über das Vermögen verfügen. Eine Bindung im Innenverhältnis gab es nicht. Nur am Rande sei erwähnt, dass ein solcher Vertrag nach allgemeinen zivilrechtlichen Grundsätzen als sittenwidrig zu beurteilen wäre. Der Treugeber ließ sein gesamtes Vermögen zurück, um einigermaßen sicher und unbehelligt ausreisen zu können. Dieses Motiv war natürlich auch dem Treuhänder bestens bekannt. Wie *Venus/Wenck* nachgewiesen haben, wurden jüdische BürgerInnen auch durch Einsatz von Drohungen zum Abschluss des Treuhandvertrages verhalten (*Venus/Wenck*, S. 159). Dies konnte im konkreten Fall jedoch nicht nachgewiesen werden. 124

Um schließlich jeder eigenmächtigen Veräußerung vorzubeugen, ließ sich der Treuhänder in Abstimmung mit der Vermögensverkehrsstelle von den Gildemeester-Teilnehmern Schuldscheine über angeblich abgeschlossene Darlehensverträge ausstellen, die dann zu seiner hypothekarischen Sicherung verwendet wurden. Auch diese Vorgehensweise ist im konkreten Fall dokumentiert. Diese Darlehensvergabe geschah unabhängig davon, ob überhaupt eine Notwendigkeit dafür bestand. In vielen Fällen waren ohnehin genug liquide Mittel vorhanden. (*Venus/Wenck*, S. 230f und 238). Der Staatskommissar 125

Dagobert R. purely for the purpose of obtaining his signature (margin note 50). Hence, in this property transaction not the slightest freedom of contract is identifiable. Where the City of Vienna in its statement of 9 September 2005 points out that "Dr. R[...] himself spurred the activities as a vendor", then it must be replied that he had not become a vendor of his own free will. For whatever reasons he then appealed against the ruling, whether because he was hoping that the full amount from the property transaction would finally be provided to him at his free disposal in some form, or because he still had confidence in a procedure in conformity with the rule of the law, is completely irrelevant for this question. It shall be only mentioned as an aside that during the first and second instance restitution proceedings he was reproached for this behavior in order to argue that the contract was concluded freely (see above margin notes 77 and 81). The lodging of an appeal against the decision of an administrative body does not by itself present an adequate measure of private autonomy corresponding to the principle of freedom of contract.

127   Additionally, whenever and where necessary in his view, the trustee assumed his extensive right of disposal of the property which was handed over to him. This has been demonstrated by the case of the previously emigrated claimant, which was described for comparison in the findings.

128   In its statement of 9 September 2005, the City of Vienna points out that the Higher Administration for Settlement regarded the appointment of the banking house *Krentschker & Co.* as trustee for the property transaction R./Air-District Commando as invalid. This statement appears correct from a strictly legalistic point of view, i.e. when considered under the then prevailing law, particularly para. 17 (1) and (3) of the Ordinance on the Use of Jewish Property of 3 December 1938, *GBlÖ* ("Austrian Law Gazette") 633/1938. Nevertheless, the Higher Administration for Settlement immediately weakens its legal point of view by dealing with content-related matters regarding the property transaction R./Air-District Commando in the same letter with the banking house *Krentschker & Co.* Finally, the Higher Administration for Settlement seems to have abandoned its legal position altogether when on 21 January 1941 it wrote to the banking house *Krentschker & Co.* that upon presentation to the Air-District Commando XVII of the decision by the State Commissioner for Private Enterprises, it would receive the proceeds from the sale. This again exemplifies the intermingling of and partially also the dissolution of the distinction between public and private law, which was typical of the National Socialist state (see above margin note 123 on the role of the banking house *Krentschker & Co.* within Operation Gildemeester). If one wanted to really subject the described occurrences to a very strict juridical analysis, then generally the appointment of the banking house *Krentschker & Co.* by decision of the State Commissioner for Private Enterprises of 30 May 1938 as trustee for the property of the Gildemeester participants would be unlawful. It would not only be unlawful in relation to individual property transactions. The reason for this is that the statutory basis of this decision cannot be identified. In reality, there were no provisions which would have been able to support such a decision. What the National Socialist authorities really had in mind was encapsulated in a letter of February 1941 by the Reich Minister for Nutrition and Agriculture to the Reich Governor in Vienna (see above margin note 52): Jews should emigrate as soon as possible, while leaving their entire assets for the benefit of the National Socialist state.

129   When examining the submission by the applicants for restitution more closely, it has to be admitted that Operation Gildemeester was only – if at all – mentioned in passing and the argument was centered on the seizure by the Reich Treasury (compare with margin note 62). However, the information given by the aggrieved party himself in the property notice

für die Privatwirtschaft kommentierte diese Vorgehensweise in einem Schreiben an das Bankhaus Krentschker & Co. vom 27. Juli 1938 folgendermaßen:

„Angesichts unseres Bestrebens, die Reichsfluchtsteuerbeträge in erster Linie einzutreiben, um sie der Reichsfluchtsteuerstelle zur Verfügung stellen zu können, billige ich die Eintragung eines solchen Hypothekarkredites, jedoch mit der ausdrücklichen Maßgabe, dass der auswandernde Jude selber unter keinen Umständen in den Besitz dieses Hypothekarkredites kommen darf." (zitiert nach *Venus/Wenck*, S. 232)

Dass Dr. Dagobert R. den Kaufvertrag für die gegenständliche Liegenschaft eigenhändig unterfertigt hat, vermag am Entziehungszeitpunkt nichts zu ändern, sondern lag einzig darin begründet, dass er noch nicht emigriert war. Um den Anschein der Freiwilligkeit zu wahren, ließ man den grundbücherlichen Eigentümer unterschreiben. Die Feststellungen haben gezeigt, dass Dr. Dagobert R. der bereits fertige Kaufvertrag nur mehr zum Unterschreiben vorgelegt worden ist (Rz 50). Es ist bei dieser Liegenschaftstransaktion damit kein Mindestmaß an privatautonomer Gestaltungsmöglichkeit erkennbar. Wenn die Stadt Wien in ihrer Stellungnahme vom 9. September 2005 darauf verweist, dass „Dr. R. selbst Tätigkeiten als Verkäufer setzte", so ist dem entgegenzuhalten, dass er eben nicht aufgrund einer freien Willensäußerung zum Verkäufer geworden ist. Aus welchen Gründen er dann den Genehmigungsbescheid anfocht, sei es, dass er hoffte, der volle Betrag aus der Liegenschaftstransaktion werde ihm schließlich doch in irgendeiner Form zur Verfügung stehen oder sei es sein noch immer vorhandenes Vertrauen in ein rechtsstaatliches Verfahren, ist für diese Frage gänzlich irrelevant. Nur am Rande sei bemerkt, dass ihm dieses Verhalten bereits von der 1. und 2. Instanz im damaligen Rückstellungsverfahren als Argument für einen auf einen freien Willen beruhenden Vertragsabschluss vorgehalten wurde (siehe oben Rz 77 und 81). Allein in der Erhebung eines Rechtsmittels gegen den Bescheid einer Verwaltungsbehörde ist kein dem Prinzip der Vertragsfreiheit entsprechendes Maß an Selbstbestimmung zu sehen.

126

Wie der in den Feststellungen wiedergegebene Vergleichsfall zur bereits emigrierten Antragstellerin gezeigt hat, nahm der Treuhänder im Übrigen seine umfassende Verfügungsbefugnis über das übernommene Vermögen wahr, wenn und soweit dies ihm notwendig erschien.

127

Die Stadt Wien weist in ihrer Stellungnahme vom 9. September 2005 darauf hin, dass die Obere Siedlungsbehörde die Bestellung des Bankhauses Krentschker & Co. zum Treuhänder für die Liegenschaftstransaktion R. – Luftgaukommando als unwirksam angesehen hat. Aus formalrechtlicher Sicht ist diese Aussage nach dem damals geltenden Recht – in concreto § 17 Abs 1 und 3 der Verordnung über den Einsatz des jüdischen Vermögens vom 3. Dezember 1938, Gesetzblatt für das Land Österreich (GBlÖ) 633/1938 – korrekt. Gleichwohl schwächt die Obere Siedlungsbehörde ihre Rechtsansicht gleich selbst ab, wenn sie im selben Brief dennoch zu inhaltlichen Fragen betreffend die Liegenschaftstransaktion R. – Luftgaukommando mit dem Bankhaus Krentschker & Co. korrespondiert. Schließlich scheint sie ihre Rechtsposition überhaupt aufgegeben zu haben, da sie dem Bankhaus Krentschker & Co. am 21. Jänner 1941 schreibt, dass es bei Vorweis des Bescheides des Staatskommissars für die Privatwirtschaft beim Luftgaukommando XVII den Kaufpreis erhalten würde. Hier zeigt sich wieder die für den NS-Staat typische Vermischung von und teilweise auch Auflösung der Trennung von öffentlichem Recht und Privatrecht (siehe dazu bereits oben Rz 123 zur Rolle des Bankhauses Krentschker & Co. im Rahmen der Gildemeester-Aktion). Wollte man die beschriebenen Vorgänge wirklich einer streng juristischen Analyse unterziehen, so wäre die Bestellung des Bankhauses Krentschker & Co. durch den Bescheid des Staatskommissars in der Privatwirtschaft vom 30. Mai

128

Arbitration Panel for *In Rem* Restitution – Decision No. 24/2005

of 15 December 1938, in which he talked of having transferred all assets to the banking house *Krentschker & Co.*, contradict this argument (see above margin note 41). Dr. Dagobert R. could no longer speak for himself during the restitution proceedings. However, in the opinion of the Arbitration Panel, it would take the then claimants for restitution's obligation to substantiate too far if one would have expected them to deliver a detailed submission on and a precise assessment of Operation Gildemeester in a form which was made possible only decades later through the research of the Historical Commission. One also has to bear in mind the contemporary circumstances of the Gildemeester participants. It is notorious that during the first days and weeks after the *Anschluss*, especially wealthy Jews were affected in an exceptional way by the persecution and harassments of the National Socialist regime. With this in mind, it is understandable that one would join Operation Gildemeester in order to leave the country safely and rapidly – at least to some extent. The fact that then, after the war, during the restitution proceedings Operation Gildemeester had not – as in this case – been substantiated as would have been necessary (which will be shown in a moment) in order to successfully assert the claim before the restitution authorities, is hardly surprising. Under the impression of the experiences made after the *Anschluss* it was anyhow assumed that the property transfers had come about in an unlawful way and that the proceedings would be decided in favor of the aggrieved parties. Also, the submission by the claimants in the restitution proceedings on 11 October 1960 in which they explain that the search for a motive for the property seizure was unnecessary in any case, suggests this conclusion, as their father had in any case lost his real property during National Socialism (see above margin note 73).

130   An hypothetical treatment of the restitution proceedings based on the previously stated analysis would lead one to arrive at the following conclusion: According to the juridical practice of the Supreme Administrative Court, the complete loss of the power to dispose of one's assets and not only the subsequent act of acquiring such assets fulfill the elements of a seizure as defined in Sec. 1 (2) second case of the Third State Treaty Implementation Act, if this loss of the power of disposal was caused solely by the political persecution of the affected person (decision no. 0272/60 of the Supreme Administrative Court, 29 November 1962). The wording of this statutory definition of seizure is as follows: "Acquisitions of this kind only constitute a seizure in the meaning of the restitution laws if [...] the owner had been forced to sell solely on the basis of political persecution." The decision quoted above was issued in relation to a sales trustee appointed for the assets of a Jewish citizen. The service of the decision regarding the appointment of the sales trustee was considered as the point of seizure.

131   According to the statements made above, in the case at issue, the loss of the power to dispose of assets occurred at the time of the signing of the contract with the trustee. The crucial motive for signing the trust agreement was the religious and origin-related persecution of Dr. Dagobert R. Therefore, a seizure also exists as defined by law (Sec. 28 (1) item 1 of the GSF Law). In its ruling of 10 October 1963 regarding the restitution of the real estate subject to the proceedings, the Supreme Administrative Court did refer to the case of the sales trustee. However, it believed that through Dr. Dagobert R.'s personal signing of the purchase contract, the banking house *Krentschker & Co.* cannot be regarded as a sales trustee and therefore the application of the existing juridical practice on this specific case was denied. In doing this, the Supreme Administrative Court alleged that the vendor had a certain degree of freedom to dispose of his assets, which – as has been shown above – as a Gildemeester participant he no longer had. Hence, the restitution authorities, by applying the juridical practice of the Supreme Administrative Court on the loss of the

1938 zum Treuhänder des Vermögens der Gildemeester-TeilnehmerIn überhaupt – und nicht nur auf eine einzelne Vermögenstransaktion bezogen – unwirksam. Es ist nämlich nicht erkennbar, auf welcher gesetzlichen Grundlage dieser Bescheid ergangen ist. Tatsächlich gab es auch keine Normen, die einen solchen Bescheid hätten stützen können. Worum es den NS-Behörden wirklich ging, brachte der Reichsminister für Ernährung und Landwirtschaft in seinem Schreiben vom Februar 1941 an den Reichstatthalter in Wien auf den Punkt (siehe oben Rz 52): Juden sollten unter Zurücklassung ihres gesamten Vermögens zugunsten des NS-Staates ehest auswandern.

Unterzieht man das Vorbringen der Rückstellungswerberinnen einer genaueren Betrachtung, so ist zuzugestehen, dass die Gildemeester-Aktion – wenn überhaupt – nur am Rande Erwähnung fand und man den Schwerpunkt des Vorbringens auf die Entziehung durch den Reichsfiskus legte (vergleiche insbesondere Rz 62). Im Widerspruch zu diesem Vorbringen stehen allerdings die Angaben, die der Geschädigte selbst in seinem Vermögensbekenntnis vom 15. Dezember 1938 gemacht hat, wo er davon sprach, er habe alle Aktiven dem Bankhaus Krentschker & Co. übertragen (siehe oben Rz 41). Dr. Dagobert R. konnte im Rückstellungsverfahren nicht mehr selbst zu Wort kommen. Es würde nach Ansicht der Schiedsinstanz die Konkretisierungspflichten der damaligen Rückstellungswerberinnen jedoch bei weitem überspannen, hätte man von ihnen ein detailliertes Vorbringen zur und eine präzise Würdigung der Gildemeester-Aktion in der Form erwartet, in der das erst Jahrzehnte später durch die Forschungen der Historikerkommission ermöglicht wurde. Auch muss man sich die damaligen Umstände, in der sich die Gildemeester-TeilnehmerInnen befunden haben, entsprechend vergegenwärtigen. Es ist notorisch, dass gerade vermögende Juden in den ersten Tagen und Wochen nach dem „Anschluss" in besonderer Weise von der Verfolgung und den Schikanen des NS-Regimes betroffen waren. Vor diesem Hintergrund ist es verständlich, dass man sich einer Aktion wie der Gildemeester-Aktion anschloss, um wenigstens einigermaßen gesichert und rasch das Land verlassen zu können. Dass man dann nach dem Krieg im Rückstellungsverfahren – wie im konkreten Fall – die Gildemeester-Aktion nicht in der Weise durch entsprechendes Vorbringen substantiiert hat, wie es – was gleich zu zeigen sein wird –, nötig gewesen wäre, um vor den Rückstellungsbehörden den Anspruch erfolgreich durchsetzen zu können, vermag nicht zu verwundern. Unter dem Eindruck der nach dem „Anschluss" gemachten Erfahrungen ging man ohnehin davon aus, dass die Vermögensverschiebungen in unrechtmäßiger Weise zustande gekommen seien und man daher Recht bekommen würde. Auch das im Rückstellungsverfahren von den Antragstellerinnen erstattete Vorbringen vom 11. Oktober 1960 legt diese Schlussfolgerung nahe, wenn sie darin ausführen, dass eine Suche nach dem Motiv der Vermögensentziehung ohnehin vernachlässigbar erscheine, da ihr Vater im Nationalsozialismus seinen Grundbesitz auf jeden Fall verloren hätte (siehe oben Rz 73).

129

Legt man das bisher Gesagte in hypothetischer Weise einem Rückstellungsverfahren zugrunde, käme man zu folgendem Ergebnis: Nach der Judikatur des VwGH erfüllt bereits der gänzliche Verlust der Verfügungsmacht – und nicht erst der nachfolgende Erwerbsakt – den Entziehungstatbestand des § 1 Abs 2, 2. Fall des 3. StVDG, wenn dieser Verlust der Verfügungsmacht seine Ursache allein in der politischen Verfolgung des Betroffenen hatte (VwGH 29. November 1962 Zl. 0272/60). Dieser Entziehungstatbestand lautet im Wortlaut: „Derartige Erwerbungen stellen nur dann eine Entziehung im Sinne der Rückstellungsgesetze dar, wenn [...] der Eigentümer lediglich auf Grund politischer Verfolgung zur Veräußerung genötigt worden ist." Die oben zitierte Entscheidung erging zur Bestellung eines Verkaufstreuhänders für das Vermögen eines jüdischen Bürgers, wobei als Entziehungszeitpunkt die Zustellung der Verfügung über die Bestellung an den Verkaufstreuhänder angesehen wurde.

130

Arbitration Panel for *In Rem* Restitution – Decision No. 24/2005

power to dispose of assets freely, would have had to affirm the existence of a seizure in accordance with para. 1 (2) second case of the Third State Treaty Implementation Act.

132 The applicant has, among other things, received compensation for her father's, Dr. Dagobert R.'s, confiscated bank balance, which he held with the banking house *Krentschker & Co.* and for the Jewish capital levy paid by him. The applicant for compensation could not assert the value of the seized property before the Compensation Fund since compensation of lost real property was not provided for by law (Sec. 1 (3) of the *Abgeltungsfondsgesetz* ["Compensation Fund Law"]). Hence, the compensation payment made by the Compensation Fund referred to a different matter and cannot be qualified as a so-called previous measure according to Sec. 32 (1) of the GSF Law. Hence, the submission of 9 September 2005 by the City of Vienna regarding this matter has no legal basis.

133 Therefore, a restitution of the property parcels, which on 17 January 2001 were owned by the City of Vienna, was to be recommended.

Dr. Josef Aicher, university professor, Chairman
Dr.Dr.h.c. Erich Kussbach, LL.M., honorary professor and retired ambassador
MMag. Dr. August Reinisch, LL.M., university professor

Nach dem oben Gesagten trat der Verlust der Verfügungsmacht im konkreten Fall im 131 Zeitpunkt des Vertragsabschlusses mit dem Treuhänder ein. Das entscheidende Motiv für den Abschluss des Treuhandvertrages lag in der religiösen und abstammungsbedingten Verfolgung des Dr. Dagobert R. Damit liegt auch die Entziehung im Sinne des Gesetzes vor (§ 28 Abs 1 Z 1 EF-G). Der VwGH nahm in seinem Erkenntnis vom 10. Oktober 1963 betreffend die Rückstellung der verfahrensgegenständlichen Liegenschaft zwar auf den Fall des Verkaufstreuhänders Bezug, meinte aber, dass aufgrund des persönlichen Abschlusses des Kaufvertrages durch Dr. Dagobert R. das Bankhaus Krentschker & Co. nicht als Verkaufstreuhänder gesehen werden könne und verneinte damit die Anwendung der diesbezüglichen Entscheidungspraxis auf den konkreten Fall. Der VwGH unterstellte damit dem Verkäufer ein Maß an Dispositionsmöglichkeiten über sein Vermögen, das er – wie bereits gezeigt wurde – als Teilnehmer der Gildemeester-Aktion nicht mehr hatte. Die Rückstellungsbehörden hätten daher unter Anwendung der Judikatur des VwGH zum Verlust der Verfügungsmacht das Vorliegen des Entziehungstatbestandes nach § 1 Abs 2, 2. Fall des 3. StVDG bejahen müssen.

Die Antragstellerin erhielt durch den Abgeltungsfonds unter anderem eine Entschädigung für das konfiszierte Bankguthaben ihres Vaters Dr. Dagobert R., welches dieser beim Bankhaus Krentschker & Co. hatte, und für die von ihm gezahlte Judenvermögensabgabe. Die Entschädigungswerberin konnte den Wert der entzogenen Liegenschaft nicht vor dem Abgeltungsfonds geltend machen, da ein Ersatz für verlorenes Grundvermögen gesetzlich nicht vorgesehen war (§ 1 Abs 3 Abgeltungsfondsgesetz). Die durch den Abgeltungsfonds erbrachte Entschädigungsleistung bezog sich damit auf ein Aliud und kann nicht als so genannte frühere Maßnahme nach § 32 Abs 1 EF-G qualifiziert werden. Das diesbezügliche Vorbringen der Stadt Wien vom 9. September 2005 geht damit ins Leere. 132

Es war daher für die am 17. Jänner 2001 im Eigentum der Stadt Wien stehenden Grundstücke eine Empfehlung zur Rückgabe auszusprechen. 133

o.Univ.-Prof. Dr. Josef Aicher, Vorsitzender
Honorarprofessor Dr.Dr.h.c. Erich Kussbach LL.M., Botschafter i.R.
ao.Univ.-Prof. MMag. Dr. August Reinisch LL.M.

Press Release Decision No. 25/2005[1]

Vienna, Inzersdorf

On 15 November 2005, the Arbitration Panel for *In Rem* Restitution accepted the application for restitution of one-third of a property in Inzersdorf owned by the City of Vienna. The fact that this share of the property has never been subject of prior proceedings was significant for this decision. The remaining two-thirds, in contrast, had been decided on in prior proceedings. The Arbitration Panel rejected the applications for restitution of these two-thirds as these prior proceedings did not reveal an extreme injustice.

The property subject of the application was owned by Margarete R., Dr. Hans H. and Marianne W. in 1938. To save their lives, Dr. Hans H. and the family of the deceased Marianne W. had to leave the country and had to sell all the properties which belonged to them. The third one-third owner, Margarete R., remained in Vienna with her "Aryan" husband. She was placed under house arrest. She was also forced to sell her properties and/or donate these to her children who were considered "second grade half castes". In 1940, the "aryanized" company Gustav & Wilhelm H. acquired the 5,309 m^2 property in Inzersdorf for a purchase price of 58,000 Reichsmark. In 1943, Viktor O., a shareholder of the company Gustav & Wilhelm H., acquired the properties for himself. In 1949, the company Gustav & Wilhelm H. re-purchased the area for a total of 150,000 Schilling from Viktor O. In 1947 and 1948 the families of the two one-third owners, Dr. Hans H. and Marianne W., submitted applications for restitution of the property. The one-third owner, Margarete R., did not submit an application. The heirs of Marianne W. and Hans H. entered into settlement agreements with the company Gustav & Wilhelm H. in 1949 and 1950, in which they waived the restitution of their shares of the property.

The Arbitration Panel considered it uncontentious that the siblings, Margarete R., Dr. Hans H. and Marianne W., were considered Jews in accordance with the Nuremburg Laws of 15 September 1935 and were thus persecuted for reasons of origin and religion. In its juridical appraisal, the Arbitration Panel had to examine whether the property in Inzersdorf was sold in connection with the NS persecution of the co-owners. In the opinion of the Arbitration Panel, the fact that inheritance tax was paid by Margarete R. for her siblings does not change anything with regard to the fact that the sale of the property took place due to the persecution of the owners and as such constituted a seizure. The Arbitration Panel also had to examine whether prior proceedings regarding the restitution of the shares of the property existed which required the Arbitration Panel to distinguish between the one-third ownership of Margarete R. and the two-thirds ownership of the estate of Marianne W. and Dr. Hans H. Marianne W. and Dr. Hans H. submitted applications for restitution with respect to their shares of the property which were concluded by settlement. The Arbitration Panel did not identify an extreme injustice with respect to these settlements. The decisive factor for this assessment was the fact that the two-thirds owners intentionally waived their claims for restitution because the proceeds from the sale had been used for their benefit to pay inheritance tax. The history of the process and terms of the settlement conclusion did not indicate that the freedom of contract of the concerned parties had been restricted. Similarly, a concurrent dispute over shares of the parties to the settlement in the company Gustav & Wilhelm H. did not allow such an as-

---

[1] An application for reopening is currently being examined in conjunction with this decision.

Pressemitteilung Entscheidung Nr. 25/2005[1]

Wien, Inzersdorf

Die Schiedsinstanz für Naturalrestitution hat am 15. November 2005 den Rückstellungsanspruch auf ein Drittel einer der Stadt Wien gehörenden Liegenschaft in Inzersdorf bejaht. Ausschlaggebend dafür war, dass dieser Liegenschaftsanteil niemals Gegenstand eines früheren Verfahrens war. Demgegenüber waren Ansprüche auf die restlichen zwei Drittelanteile bereits in früheren Verfahren geregelt worden. Da hierbei keine extreme Ungerechtigkeit vorlag, lehnte die Schiedsinstanz die betreffenden Rückstellungsanträge ab.

Die beantragte Liegenschaft befand sich 1938 im Eigentum der Geschwister Margarete R., Dr. Hans H. und Marianne W. Dr. Hans H. und die Familie der verstorbenen Marianne W. mussten, um ihr Leben zu retten, das Land verlassen und hatten sämtliche ihnen gehörenden Liegenschaften zu verkaufen. Die dritte Dritteleigentümerin, Margarete R., blieb bei ihrem „arischen" Ehemann in Wien, wo sie unter Hausarrest stand. Auch sie war gezwungen, ihre Liegenschaften zu verkaufen bzw. an ihre als so genannte „Mischlinge 2. Grades" geltenden Kinder zu verschenken. Im Jahr 1940 erwarb die „arisierte" Firma Gustav & Wilhelm H. die 5.309 m^2 große Liegenschaft in Inzersdorf um einen Kaufpreis von 58.000,– Reichsmark. 1943 erwarb Viktor O., ein Gesellschafter der Firma Gustav & Wilhelm H., die Liegenschaft für sich. Im Jahr 1949 kaufte die Firma Gustav & Wilhelm H. den Grund zu einem Gesamtpreis von 150.000,– Schilling von Viktor O. wieder zurück. 1947 und 1948 hatten die Familien von zwei Drittelanteilseigentümern, Dr. Hans H. und Marianne W., Rückstellungsanträge zur Liegenschaft eingebracht. Die Dritteleigentümerin Margarete R. stellte keinen Antrag. Die Erben nach Marianne W. und Hans H. schlossen 1949 und 1950 Vergleiche mit der Firma Gustav & Wilhelm H., in denen sie auf die Rückstellung ihrer Liegenschaftsanteile verzichteten.

Für die Schiedsinstanz war unstrittig, dass die Geschwister Margarete R., Dr. Hans H. und Marianne W. gemäß den Nürnberger Gesetzen vom 15. September 1935 als Juden galten und deshalb aus Gründen der Abstammung und Religion verfolgt wurden. In ihrer rechtlichen Beurteilung hatte die Schiedsinstanz zu prüfen, ob die Liegenschaft in Inzersdorf im Zusammenhang mit der NS-Verfolgung der Miteigentümer verkauft wurde. Der Umstand, dass aus dem Verkaufserlös die von Margarete R. geleisteten Erbschaftsteuerzahlungen für ihre Geschwister abgegolten wurden, ändert nach Ansicht der Schiedsinstanz nichts daran, dass der Verkauf der Liegenschaft aufgrund der Verfolgung der Eigentümer erfolgte und damit eine Entziehung darstellte. Außerdem hatte die Schiedsinstanz zu prüfen, ob bereits ein früheres Verfahren in Bezug auf die Rückstellung der Liegenschaftsanteile vorlag. Hierbei war zwischen dem 1/3-Eigentum der Margarete R. und dem 2/3-Eigentum der Verlassenschaft nach Marianne W. und des Dr. Hans H. zu unterscheiden. Letztere brachten hinsichtlich ihrer Liegenschaftsanteile Rückstellungsanträge ein, welche durch Vergleiche beendet wurden. In Bezug auf diese Vergleichsabschlüsse konnte die Schiedsinstanz keine extreme Ungerechtigkeit feststellen. Maßgebend für diese Einschätzung war der Umstand, dass die 2/3-Eigentümer bewusst auf ihre Rückstellungsansprüche verzichteten, da der Verkaufserlös der Liegenschaftsanteile in ihrem Interesse zur Abgeltung von Erbschaftssteuerzahlungen verwendet worden war. Die Überlieferung zu den Modalitäten des Vergleichsabschlusses enthielt überdies keinen Hinweis darauf, dass die Privatautonomie der Beteiligen eingeschränkt gewesen

---

[1] Zu dieser Entscheidung wird derzeit ein Antrag auf Wiederaufnahme geprüft.

sumption. With respect to the shares of the property which had been the subject of the settlement, prior proceedings existed.

No prior proceedings could be established with respect to the one-third share of Margarete R. The Arbitration Panel therefore considered the claim of the heirs of Margarete R. to be merited. As a municipal building is located on the property today, the Arbitration Panel considers the restitution not practical and will award a comparable asset after consultation with the City of Vienna.

For use by media; not legally binding upon the Arbitration Panel for In Rem Restitution.

wäre. Auch eine zeitgleich laufende familiäre Auseinandersetzung um Anteile der Vergleichsparteien an der Firma Gustav & Wilhelm H. ließ keine diesbezügliche Annahme zu. Hinsichtlich der verglichenen Liegenschaftsanteile lag daher ein früheres Verfahren vor.

Bezüglich des 1/3-Anteiles von Margarete R. konnte kein früheres Verfahren festgestellt werden. Es wurde daher von der Schiedsinstanz der Anspruch der Erben von Margarete R. als dem Grunde nach zu Recht bestehend angesehen. Da sich auf dieser Liegenschaft heute ein Gemeindebau befindet, sieht die Schiedsinstanz eine Rückstellung als nicht zweckmäßig an und wird nach Konsultationen mit der Stadt Wien einen vergleichbaren Vermögenswert zusprechen.

Zur Verwendung durch die Medien bestimmter Text, der die Schiedsinstanz nicht bindet.

Arbitration Panel for *In Rem* Restitution

Decision number 25/2005[1]

The Arbitration Panel for *In Rem* Restitution (Chairman Dr. Josef Aicher, university professor, and Dr.Dr.h.c. Erich Kussbach LL.M., retired ambassador and honorary professor, as well as MMag. Dr. August Reinisch LL.M, university professor, as Members) decided on 15 November 2005 in the legal matter Ing. Hansjörg R., Stephen C. H., Anne H., Vivian H., Eve H., Dr. Marc H., Dr. Joan Hu., Monica W., Martin W.[2], Vivian De B. W., Philip W., Rosemarie W., all represented by the lawyer Stephen M. Harnik, regarding *in rem* restitution of the properties, register numbers ("EZ") X1–X8, cadastral district ("KG") Inzersdorf-Stadt:

> The application of Hansjörg R. for *in rem* restitution of the property EZ X9 (formerly EZ X1–X8), KG Inzersdorf-Stadt concerning the one-third share of Margarete R. is merited. The Arbitration Panel confirms the applicability of Sec. 34 of the *Entschädigungsfondsgesetz* ("General Settlement Fund Law" – GSF Law). After consultation with the City of Vienna, the Arbitration Panel will award a comparable asset.

> The applications of Stephen C. H., Anne H., Vivian H., Eve H., Dr. Marc H., Dr. Joan Hu, Monica W., Martin W., Vivian De B. W., Philip W., Rosemarie W. for *in rem* restitution of the property EZ X9 (formerly known as EZ X1–X8), KG Inzersdorf-Stadt with regard to the two one-third shares of Hans H. and Marianne R. are rejected.

Reasons:

1. Submission by the Applicants

1 In their applications, filed with the General Settlement Fund on 28 May 2003, the applicants requested the restitution of the properties EZ X1–X8, KG Inzersdorf-Stadt.

2 The applicants stated the following:

3 The exclusive ownership title to the concerned properties had been in the name of Gustav H. who had been born on 11 November 1857 and had died on 7 September 1937. His daughters Margarete R. and Marianne W. as well as his son Dr. Hans H. had each inherited one-third of the property parcels. This was clearly documented in the land register extracts.

4 After the *Anschluss* in 1938, Gustav H.'s children had been forced to "sell" their portions of the properties to the aryanized "Reg. Company Gustav and Wilhelm H[…]". In 1943, the property parcels had been transferred to Dr. Viktor O.

---

[1] An application for reopening is currently being examined in conjunction with this decision.

[2] Rectification at the time of going to press: Martin W., the son of Marianne W. and Otto W. born on 12 September 1925 is erroneously listed as an applicant in the judgment. In fact, Martin W. – as correctly stated in margin note 112 – was already deceased. The rejection of the application therefore does not apply to Martin W., but to his heirs.

Schiedsinstanz für Naturalrestitution

Entscheidungsnummer 25/2005[1]

Die Schiedsinstanz für Naturalrestitution beschließt am 15. November 2005 durch den Vorsitzenden o.Univ.-Prof. Dr. Josef Aicher und die Schiedsinstanzmitglieder Honorarprofessor Dr.Dr.h.c. Erich Kussbach LL.M., Botschafter i.R. und ao.Univ.-Prof. MMag. Dr. August Reinisch LL.M. in der Rechtssache Ing. Hansjörg R., Stephen C. H., Anne H., Vivian H., Eve H., Dr. Marc H., Dr. Joan Hu., Monica W., Martin W.[2], Vivian De B. W., Philip W., Rosemarie W., sämtliche vertreten durch Rechtsanwalt (RA) Stephen M. Harnik, wegen Naturalrestitution der Liegenschaften Einlagezahl (EZ) X1–X8, Katastralgemeinde (KG) Inzersdorf-Stadt:

Der Anspruch von Ing. Hansjörg R. auf Naturalrestitution der Liegenschaft EZ X9 (vormals EZ X1– X8), KG Inzersdorf-Stadt hinsichtlich des Drittelanteils der Margarete R. besteht dem Grunde nach zu Recht. Die Schiedsinstanz sieht einen Fall des § 34 Entschädigungsfondsgesetz (EF-G) als gegeben an. Die Schiedsinstanz wird nach Konsultationen mit der Stadt Wien einen vergleichbaren Vermögenswert zusprechen.

Die Anträge von Stephen C. H., Anne H., Vivian H., Eve H., Dr. Marc H., Dr. Joan Hu., Monica W., Martin W., Vivian De B. W., Philip W., Rosemarie W. auf Naturalrestitution der Liegenschaft EZ X9 (vormals EZ X1–X8), KG Inzersdorf-Stadt werden hinsichtlich der zwei Drittelanteile des Hans H. und der Marianne W. abgelehnt.

Begründung:

1. Vorbringen der AntragstellerInnen

Mit Anträgen an den Allgemeinen Entschädigungsfonds vom 28. Mai 2003 begehrten die AntragstellerInnen die Rückstellung der Liegenschaften EZ X1–X8, KG Inzersdorf-Stadt. 1

Folgendes wurde von den AntragstellerInnen vorgebracht: 2

Das Alleineigentumsrecht an den betreffenden Liegenschaften habe auf den Namen Gustav H., der am 11. November 1857 geboren und am 7. September 1937 gestorben sei, gelautet. Seine zwei Töchter Margarete R. und Marianne W. sowie sein Sohn Dr. Hans H. hätten die Grundstücke zu je einem Drittel geerbt. Dies sei klar in den Grundbuchsauszügen dokumentiert. 3

Nach dem „Anschluss" 1938 seien die Kinder von Gustav H. zum „Verkauf" ihrer Anteile der Grundstücke an die arisierte „prot. Firma Gustav und Wilhelm H." gezwungen worden. 1943 seien die Grundstücke an Dr. Viktor O. übertragen worden. 4

---

[1] Zu dieser Entscheidung wird derzeit ein Antrag auf Wiederaufnahme geprüft.
[2] Berichtigung zum Zeitpunkt der Drucklegung: Der am 12. September 1925 als Sohn von Marianne W. und Otto W. geborene Martin W. wurde im Spruch versehentlich als Antragsteller angeführt. Tatsächlich ist Martin W. – wie in Rz 112 richtig ausgeführt – vorverstorben. Die Ablehnung des Antrags bezieht sich daher nicht auf Martin W., sondern auf dessen ErbInnen.

5	After the war, following a settlement with Dr. O., the property parcels had been "restituted". However, they had not been returned to the original owners but were instead returned to "Reg. Company Gustav and Wilhelm H[…]". A share of 50 % had belonged to the heirs of Wilhelm H. The remaining 50 % had belonged to the heirs of Gustav H. For this reason, the heirs of Wilhelm H. had been wrongfully included in the settlement. Instead of the original one-third share, Ing. Hansjörg R., son and heir of Margarete R., and Dr. Otto W., husband and heir of Marianne R., had only received one-eighth and Hans H. only one-quarter of the property.
6	According to the enclosed purchase contract, the "Reg. Company Gustav and Wilhelm H[…]" had sold the properties to the City of Vienna.
7	In a memorandum which was also enclosed with the applications, Ing. Hansjörg R. recalls that

"the aryanization [was] carried out by mutual agreement but under pressure from external circumstances. […] Prior to the aryanization, the estate had not yet been devolved. A 12.5 % share of H[…] Company was received by my mother. This share was only transferred to her after 1945. I immediately concluded a restitution settlement with the aryanizers in 1945 under the condition that my mother's 12.5 % share would be restituted to us without any deductions. I joined the company in 1945 as an authorized signatory and became a partner in the company in 1948 through my mother's shares which she had transferred to me. […] I do not remember any details of the transactions with H[…]'s properties mentioned by Dr. F[…] Especially, I definitely did not know that they had belonged to Gustav H[…] personally before the war."

8	In a statement of 1 July 2004, the applicants, represented by the lawyer Stephen M. Harnik, submitted that:
9	A settlement between Margarete R. and Dr. Viktor O. regarding the property shares subject of the proceedings had never been reached. Due to the extreme injustice of the settlements, the heirs of Dr. Hans H. and Marianne R. were eligible to file for restitution.
10	It would be illogical and inconsistent if settlement negotiations between Margarete R. and Dr. O. regarding the Gustav & Wilhelm H. Company had been registered with the responsible authorities, but then it had not been announced to these responsible authorities that the stated settlement between the same parties had taken place. However, if such a settlement had been concluded before the enactment of the *Dritte Rückstellungsgesetz* ("Third Restitution Act"), then para. 13 (2) of this Act would have demanded the registration of such a settlement. Furthermore, on the first page of the *Anmeldung entzogener Vermögen* ("Notice of Seized Property") of Dr. O. of March 1947, two handwritten notes were to be found, which refer to private settlements from the years 1949 and 1950. Even as late as 1950, no reference to any kind of settlement regarding Margarete R's property shares had existed.
11	Hence, prior proceedings regarding Margarete R.'s property shares did not exist.
12	Regarding the shares of Marianne W. and Hans H., the prior proceedings had constituted an extreme injustice as defined by the GSF Law. The H. family members had waived their claims, as the proceeds had been used to pay the inheritance tax on the estate of Gustav H. in 1940. The "release of eight seized property parcels in Vienna" by the tax office Moabit-West would also allow the conclusion that Dr. Hans H. had never received the proceeds from the sale for his free disposal. According to these documents, 16,658.29 Reichsmark had been repaid to Margarete R. for paid inheritance taxes and the rest of the pro-

Schiedsinstanz für Naturalrestitution – Entscheidung Nr. 25/2005

Nach dem Krieg seien die Grundstücke einem Vergleich mit Dr. O. folgend „restituiert" worden. Jedoch seien sie nicht an die ursprünglichen EigentümerInnen zurückgegeben worden, sondern an die „prot. Firma Gustav und Wilhelm H.", welche zu 50 % den ErbInnen von Wilhelm H. und zu 50 % den ErbInnen von Gustav H. gehört habe. Deshalb seien die ErbInnen von Wilhelm H. fälschlicherweise in den Vergleich miteinbezogen worden. Anstatt des ursprünglichen Drittels hätten Ing. Hansjörg R., der Sohn und Erbe von Margarete R., und Dr. Otto W., Ehemann und Erbe von Marianne W., lediglich 1/8, und Hans H. lediglich 1/4 des Grundstückeigentums bekommen. 5

Entsprechend dem beigelegten Kaufvertrag habe die „prot. Firma Gustav und Wilhelm H." die Liegenschaften an die Stadt Wien verkauft. 6

In einem ebenfalls den Anträgen beigelegten Memorandum erinnert sich Ing. Hansjörg R., dass 7

„die Arisierung einvernehmlich, aber unter dem Zwang der äußeren Umstände durchgeführt worden [ist]. [...] Die Verlassenschaft war vor der Arisierung noch nicht eingeantwortet worden. Meiner Mutter kam von der Firma H[…]. ein 12,5% Anteil zu, der ihr erst nach 1945 übereignet wurde. Ich selbst schloss mit den Arisierern gleich im Jahr 1945 einen Rückstellungsvergleich und zwar mit der Bedingung, dass der 12,5% Anteil meiner Mutter uns ohne Abzüge rückgestellt wurde. Ich trat 1945 als Prokurist in die Firma ein und wurde 1948 mit den Anteilen meiner Mutter, die sie mir übertragen hatte, Gesellschafter der Firma. [...] Über die Transaktionen mit den Gründen von H[…], die Herr Dr. F[…] erwähnt hat, sind mir keine Details erinnerlich, insbesondere wusste ich sicher nicht, dass sie vor dem Krieg Gustav H[…] persönlich gehört hatten."

Mit Schriftsatz vom 1. Juli 2004 brachten die AntragstellerInnen, vertreten durch RA Stephen M. Harnik, vor: 8

Es sei niemals ein Vergleich zwischen Margarete R. und Dr. Viktor O. hinsichtlich der verfahrensgegenständlichen Liegenschaftsanteile zustande gekommen. Dr. Hans H.s und Marianne W.s ErbInnen seien aufgrund der extremen Ungerechtigkeit der Vergleiche rückstellungsberechtigt. 9

Es sei unlogisch und inkonsistent, sollten Vergleichsverhandlungen zwischen Margarete R. und Dr. O. betreffend die Firma Gustav & Wilhelm H. bei den zuständigen Behörden angemeldet worden sein, dass das Zustandekommen des behaupteten Vergleiches zwischen den gleichen Parteien nicht den zuständigen Behörden bekannt gemacht worden sei. Falls jedoch solch ein Vergleich vor der Erlassung des Dritten Rückstellungsgesetzes (RStG) abgeschlossen worden wäre, hätte § 13 Abs 2 dieses Gesetzes die Einbringung eines solchen Vergleiches verlangt. Weiters seien auf der ersten Seite der „Anmeldung entzogener Vermögen" des Dr. O. vom März 1947 zwei handgeschriebene Notizen zu finden, welche auf private Vergleiche aus dem Jahr 1949 und 1950 verweisen. Eben auch zu einem so späten Zeitpunkt wie 1950 sei kein Hinweis auf irgendeinen Vergleich hinsichtlich Margarete R.s Liegenschaftsanteile vorgelegen. 10

Es habe damit kein früheres Verfahren betreffend die Liegenschaftsanteile der Margarete R. vorgelegen. 11

Hinsichtlich der Anteile von Marianne W. und Hans H. sei bei den früheren Verfahren eine extreme Ungerechtigkeit iSd EF-G vorgelegen. In beiden Vergleichen sei durch die Mitglieder der Familie H. auf ihre Rechte verzichtet worden, da der Preis 1940 zur Begleichung der Erbschaftssteuer der Verlassenschaft nach Gustav H. verwendet worden sei. Aus der „Freigabe von acht beschlagnahmten Grundstücken in Wien" durch das Finanz- 12

ceeds had been transferred to the "frozen emigrant account no. 13652" at the *Länderbank*. Therefore, the proceeds from this sale had never reached the H. family but had been used to pay taxes and to freeze all liquid assets. Further, with the confiscation order of 10 February 1941, all of Dr. H.'s remaining assets had been confiscated by the *Gestapo* ("Secret State Police").

13 Hence, Dr. H.'s heirs were entitled to have their shares of the property restituted without taking into consideration the purchase price or its use since they had never received the proceeds from the sale. Surely, it did not make sense to conclude such a "settlement" if an alternative, for example the involvement of the Restitution Commission, would undoubtedly have produced a significantly better result. Hence, this had not been a "settlement" but rather a pretext for depriving Dr. H. of his share of the property without conducting proceedings and a hearing. This constituted an extreme injustice.

14 The same applied to the shares of Marianne W.

15 It was very doubtful whether the purchase price of 1940 corresponded with the then current market value since the price of the properties in their entirety had amounted to 58,000 Reichsmark plus 400 Reichsmark *Entjudungsauflage* ("de-jewification fee"). In comparison, Dr. O. had sold the properties to the Gustav & Wilhelm H. Company for 150,000 Schilling. When considering the exchange rate of 1:1 after the war, this would result in a factor of 2.5. However, in contrast to the years directly following the war, property values were relatively low.

16 If the properties had not increased in value between 1940 and the time of the conclusion of the settlement, then the settlement, in comparison to a restitution would have represented a loss and would therefore have been uneconomical and senseless without settlement payments. Further, in accordance with Austrian law, the essence of a settlement was to reach a compromise. In this case, the heirs of Marianne W. and Dr. H. had simply transferred the property for the original price concluded in the sale of 1940. A much better result could have been achieved if the Restitution Commission had decided the case.

17 It was generally known that the properties had been very well positioned and that the site had been designated a residential area.

18 Hence, the restitution of the one-third share of Margarete R. is requested on the basis of the absence of prior proceedings and the restitution of the two one-third shares of Hans H. and Otto W. on the basis of the existence of an extreme injustice as defined in the GSF Law.

19 By letter dated 14 January 2005, the applicants, represented by Stephan M. Harnik submitted:

20 The files, which were researched by the Arbitration Panel and then conveyed to the applicants, proved that the purchase price of 58,000 Reichsmark had been below market value. A letter dated 17 May 1941 from the *Preisüberwachungsstelle* ("Price Control Board") of the chief of police in Vienna had quoted the market value as 13 Reichsmark per m^2. This value had also formed the basis for the purchase price, which Viktor O. had paid in 1943 to the Gustav & Wilhelm H. Company. In addition, the property had been desirable and of special interest to the aryanized Gustav & Wilhelm H. Company as it bordered on the company grounds. Under normal circumstances, the company would have been an ideal purchaser and would have been prepared to pay more for the property. In regard to the utility value of the property it was to be pointed out that in 1953, the City of Vienna had not paid less than 50 Schilling per m^2 for the property in question as well as for further property parcels.

amt Moabit-West könne ebenfalls geschlossen werden, dass Dr. Hans H. niemals den Kaufpreis zur freien Verfügung erlangt habe. Entsprechend dieser Dokumente seien 16.658,29 Reichsmark als Rückzahlung für bezahlte Erbschaftssteuern an Margarete R. und der Rest des Kaufpreises auf das „Auswanderersperrkonto Nr. 13652" bei der Länderbank gezahlt worden. So hätten die Erträgnisse dieses Verkaufes niemals ihren Weg in die Hände der Familie H. gefunden, sondern seien verwendet worden, um Steuern zu zahlen und alle flüssigen Vermögenswerte einzufrieren. Weiters sei mit Beschlagnahmeverfügung vom 10. Februar 1941 Dr. H.s gesamtes verbleibendes Vermögen durch die Gestapo beschlagnahmt worden.

Daher seien Dr. H.s ErbInnen berechtigt, ihre Anteile an der Liegenschaft ohne Bedachtnahme auf den Kaufpreis oder dessen Verwendung zurückzuerhalten, da sie niemals die Früchte des Verkaufes erhalten hätten. Sicherlich mache es keinen Sinn, solch einen „Vergleich" abzuschließen, wenn eine Alternative, z.B. die Einschaltung der Rückstellungskommission, ohne Zweifel ein viel besseres Ergebnis erbracht hätte. Daher sei dies kein „Vergleich" gewesen, sondern ein Vorwand, um Dr. H. um seinen Liegenschaftsanteil ohne Prozess und ohne Verhandlung zu bringen. Dies stelle eine extreme Ungerechtigkeit dar. 13

Dasselbe gelte für die Anteile der Marianne W. 14

Es sei sehr fraglich, ob der Kaufpreis von 1940 dem Marktwert entsprochen habe, da der Preis der Liegenschaften in ihrer Gesamtheit 58.000,- Reichsmark, plus 400,- Reichsmark Entjudungsauflage ausgemacht habe. Auf der anderen Seite habe Dr. O. 1949 die Liegenschaften an die Firma Gustav & Wilhelm H. für 150.000,- Schilling verkauft. Bedenke man die Nachkriegsumrechnungsrate von 1:1, zeige dies einen Faktor von 2,5. Im Gegensatz zu den unmittelbar auf den Krieg folgenden Jahren seien die Werte von Liegenschaften jedoch relativ niedrig gewesen. 15

Wenn die Liegenschaften zwischen 1940 und dem Zeitpunkt des Vergleichsabschlusses nicht an Wert gewonnen hätten, wäre der Vergleich verglichen mit einer Rückstellung ein Verlust und ohne Vergleichszahlungen daher unökonomisch und sinnlos. Weiters sei nach österreichischem Recht die Quintessenz eines Vergleiches, einen Kompromiss zu erreichen. In diesem Fall hätten die ErbInnen der Marianne W. und Dr. H. einfach die Liegenschaft zu dem Originalpreis von 1940 übergeben. Hätte die Rückstellungskommission den Fall entschieden, hätte ein wesentlich besseres Ergebnis erzielt werden können. 16

Es sei allgemein bekannt gewesen, dass die Liegenschaften in einer sehr guten Lage, welche als Wohngebiet gewidmet gewesen sei, gelegen seien. 17

Es wird daher eine Rückstellung der Liegenschaft hinsichtlich des Drittelanteils von Margarete R. aufgrund des Fehlens eines früheren Verfahrens, hinsichtlich der zwei Drittelanteile von Hans H. und Otto W. aufgrund des Vorliegens einer extremen Ungerechtigkeit iSd EF-G beantragt. 18

Mit Schriftsatz vom 14. Januar 2005 brachten die AntragstellerInnen, vertreten durch Stephen M. Harnik, vor: 19

Die von der Schiedsinstanz recherchierten, an die AntragstellerInnen übermittelten Akten würden bestätigen, dass der Kaufpreis von 58.000,- Reichsmark unter dem Marktwert gelegen seien. Ein Schreiben der Preisüberwachungsstelle des Polizeipräsidenten in Wien vom 17. Mai 1941 habe den Verkehrswert mit 13,- Reichsmark pro m^2 angegeben, der auch als Grundlage für den von Viktor O. 1943 an die Firma Gustav & Wilhelm H. bezahlten Kaufpreis gebildet habe. Zudem sei die Liegenschaft für die arisierte Firma Gus- 20

2. Submission by the City of Vienna

21 On 24 March 2005, the City of Vienna submitted a statement:

22 The property parcels subject of these proceedings had not been solely private property but were supposed to have served the business purposes of the company.

23 The "aryanization" had not solely represented an act of external pressure, as clearly the outcome was more or less under control due to the family connections surrounding the sale.

24 After the war, settlements had been concluded and by mutual agreement, results had been reached, which obviously had been acceptable for everybody involved.

25 At the time of the land acquisition by the City of Vienna, all of these settlements had long since been concluded. Ing. Hansjörg R. and Dr. Hans H. had benefited financially as partners of the company.

26 Evidently, internal family disputes had triggered the current application.

27 In the evaluation of the requirements for an application in accordance with the GSF Law it was essentially submitted that two restitution proceedings had been pending regarding the two-third shares. These proceedings were both finally concluded with a settlement. Further, the owner of the one-third share, Margarete R., had also concluded a settlement in the course of the clarification of her claims as a partner of the Gustav & Wilhelm H. Company. Clause three of this settlement had stated "that hereby all reciprocal claims resulting from an entitlement to restitution are settled." It was to be deduced from this clause that the properties concerned had also been covered by this ruling. This explained why a separate settlement regarding this one-third evidently did not exist.

28 It was remarkable that the applicant Ing. Hansjörg R. stated that there had already been a decision regarding his claims. Their reaction to the indication made by the Arbitration Panel was to allege that no settlement had ever been concluded.

29 It was obvious that during the processing and settlement of the estate of Gustav H., inheritance taxes also had to be paid. Where the proceeds from the sale of the property to the (aryanized) Gustav & Wilhelm H. Company had served to pay these inheritance taxes, this payment was justifiable and no injustice could be recognized. The heirs of Dr. Hans H. and Dr. Otto W. had also profited from the fact that through this the relevant inheritance taxes did not have to be paid by them anymore, which had obviously been to their advantage.

30 In addition, it was doubtful whether the property parcels, seen from an economic perspective, had not already belonged to the company assets anyway. This would explain the lower purchase price which would have served to cover the costs of the inheritance taxes.

31 These properties did not represent restitutable public property as defined by Sec. 28 (1) 2 of the GSF Law, as the settlements concluded regarding the concerned properties could not be considered as being extremely unjust.

32 The public authorities had not in any way been involved in the restitution proceedings. The restitution proceedings had taken place in the course of family disputes. From an overall economic perspective, this had possibly facilitated the conclusion of settlements for the extended family. In retrospect, internal resentments – which most certainly could also be existent in the fold of families – had not been able to be conclusively resolved.

33 In any case, it was not justifiable nor did it correspond with the intentions of the GSF Law that possible human or financial shortcomings of settlement conclusions – as sug-

tav & Wilhelm H. von besonderem Interesse und wünschenswert gewesen, da sie an das Firmengelände angrenzte. Unter normalen Umständen wäre die Firma ein guter Käufer und bereit gewesen, mehr für die Liegenschaft zu bezahlen. Im Hinblick auf den Nutzwert der Liegenschaft sei darauf hinzuweisen, dass die Stadt Wien bereits 1953 nicht weniger als 50,– Schilling pro m^2 für die betreffende Liegenschaft und weitere Grundstücke bezahlt habe.

2. Vorbringen der Stadt Wien

Am 24. März 2005 brachte die Stadt Wien eine Stellungnahme ein: 21

Die verfahrensgegenständlichen Grundstücke hätten kein reines Privateigentum dargestellt, sondern hätten Betriebszwecken der Firma dienen sollen. 22

Die „Arisierung" sei kein reiner Zwangsakt von außen gewesen, da die Auswirkungen aufgrund der Verwandtschaftsverhältnisse offensichtlich einigermaßen unter Kontrolle gehalten worden seien. 23

Nach dem Krieg seien Vergleiche abgeschlossen worden und einvernehmliche, offenbar für alle akzeptable Ergebnisse erzielt worden. 24

Zum Zeitpunkt des Grunderwerbes durch die Stadt Wien seien all diese Vergleiche längst geschlossen gewesen. Ing. Hansjörg R. und Dr. Hans H. hätten als Gesellschafter der Firma finanziell profitiert. 25

Es hätten offenbar interne Familienzwistigkeiten zu der jetzigen Antragstellung geführt. 26

In der Beurteilung der Antragsvoraussetzungen nach dem EF-G wurde im Wesentlichen vorgebracht, dass hinsichtlich der 2/3-Anteile zwei Rückstellungsverfahren anhängig gewesen seien, die jeweils mit einem Vergleich endgültig beendet worden seien. Des Weiteren sei von der 1/3-Eigentümerin Margarete R. im Zuge der Abklärung ihrer Ansprüche als Gesellschafterin der Firma Gustav & Wilhelm H. ebenfalls ein Vergleich abgeschlossen worden, in dessen Punkt 3 festgelegt worden sei, „dass alle gegenseitigen Ansprüche aus dem Titel der Restitution damit ausgeglichen sind." Aus dieser Bestimmung sei abzuleiten, dass davon auch die gegenständlichen Liegenschaften umfasst seien. Dies erkläre auch, warum ein eigener Vergleich betreffend dieses Drittels offenbar nicht vorliege. 27

Bemerkenswert sei, dass der Antragsteller Ing. Hansjörg R. anführe, dass über seine Ansprüche bereits eine Entscheidung vorliege. Als Reaktion auf den Hinweis durch die Schiedsinstanz sei behauptet worden, dass es nie einen Vergleich gegeben habe. 28

Es liege auf der Hand, dass anlässlich der Verlassenschaftsabhandlung nach Gustav H. auch Erbschaftssteuern zu bezahlen gewesen seien. Wenn die Einnahmen aus dem Liegenschaftsverkauf an die (arisierte) Firma Gustav & Wilhelm H. der Abdeckung dieser Erbschaftssteuern gedient hätten, so sei das nachvollziehbar und es könne darin keine Ungerechtigkeit erblickt werden. Auch hätten die ErbInnen nach Dr. Hans H. und Dr. Otto W. insoferne profitiert, als die entsprechenden Erbschaftssteuern auf diese Weise von ihnen nicht mehr geleistet hätten werden müssen, was einen nachvollziehbaren Vorteil für sie gebracht habe. 29

Darüber hinaus sei zweifelhaft, ob die Grundstücke wirtschaftlich gesehen nicht ohnehin bereits zum Firmenvermögen gehört hätten. Damit sei ein geringerer Kaufpreis zu erklären, der zur Abdeckung der Erbschaftssteuern gedient habe. 30

Arbitration Panel for *In Rem* Restitution – Decision No. 25/2005

gested by the applicants – should in the end be the responsibility of the regional administrative body, the City of Vienna. It was only eight years after the National Socialist regime that the City of Vienna in any case had appeared as a serious and bona fide purchaser of land which had previously been subject of a family dispute.

34   Hence, *in rem* restitution had to be denied.

35   On 29 April 2005, Stephen M. Harnik replied to the statement of 24 March 2005 by the City of Vienna.

36   In the opinion of the applicants, the properties represented strictly private property and from an economic point of view had not belonged to the company. If contemporary documents had shown that the properties had belonged to the company or that the transfer to the company could not have taken place during the course of the aryanization of the company and hence a separate legal transaction had been necessary, then these were to be seen as strategic maneuvers, intended to convince the Nazis to agree to the aryanization of the properties for the company in order to prevent them being forfeited to the German Reich. However, the way the property had been dealt with before, during and after World War II demonstrated that the property had always been regarded and also treated as the property of Gustav H. and/or of his heirs. There is no circumstantial evidence that could call these facts into doubt.

37   The opinion of the City of Vienna that the aryanization of H.'s property "had not strictly represented an act of external pressure" was not correct. In spite of the familial relationship between the aryanizer Viktor O. and Hans H., the entire H. property had in any case been an object of a seizure and aryanization. Through the unavoidable emigration, the H. family had merely tried to minimize the effects of the damage. The files showed that every collusion between H. and O./V. had been punished with lies in the litigation after the war since O./V. firmly opposed all of H. family's efforts for the restitution of its property. O. had double-crossed the H.s more than once: At first, he had convinced them to transfer the company to him. Finally, he had capitalized on their trust, which had been triggered through desperation rather than positive commitment to him. After the war, O. had construed all events to his advantage in order to secure as much as possible for himself of what once he had been "entrusted" with; which, however, in reality had had to be transferred to him under pressure.

38   The purchase price of 1940 had been calculated so as to exactly cover the fees incurred for the estate. None of the heirs of Gustav H. had ever received any proceeds of the sale. The settlements concluded between Viktor O. and Hans H./Otto W. were extremely unjust as their rights had been withheld from them. Strangely enough, the properties had been sold to the Gustav & Wilhelm H. Company on 26 October 1949. The purchase price that had been paid by the Gustav & Wilhelm H. Company for the properties had been significantly higher than that which the aryanizers had paid in 1940. The settlement that had been concluded between O. and W. half a year later showed that O. had profited from a pretext and deception and that he had played the one off against the other.

39   As partners, the aggrieved lawful owners had regained possession of the properties and had profited from their sale to the City of Vienna at a higher price. However, this could not compensate for a fundamental injustice, especially since the company had bought the property from the previous aryanizer.

40   The rights of the heirs of Gustav H. had been infringed several times, for which they had not received any compensation. If the restitution proceedings had been conclusively decided then inevitably the properties would have had to be restituted to the heirs of Gustav H.

Da hinsichtlich der Rückstellung der gegenständlichen Liegenschaften Vergleiche ge- 31
schlossen worden seien, die nicht als extrem ungerecht zu beurteilen seien, stellten diese
Liegenschaften gemäß § 28 Abs 1 Z 2 EF-G kein restitutionsfähiges öffentliches Vermögen dar.

In die Rückstellungsverfahren sei die öffentliche Hand auf keine Art und Weise invol- 32
viert gewesen, sie hätten im Rahmen familiärer Auseinandersetzungen stattgefunden, was
möglicherweise im Sinne gesamtwirtschaftlicher Aspekte der Großfamilie einerseits den
Abschluss von Vergleichen erleichtert habe. Rückblickend – wie das im Schoße von Familien auch durchaus der Fall sein könne – habe man interne Ressentiments wohl nicht
endgültig bereinigen können.

Dass eine allfällige menschliche bzw. auch finanzielle Unzulänglichkeit von Ver- 33
gleichsabschlüssen aber – wie die AntragstellerInnen vermeinten – letztendlich die Gebietskörperschaft Stadt Wien treffen sollte, die überhaupt erst acht Jahre nach dem nationalsozialistischen Regime als in jeder Hinsicht seriöse und gutgläubige Käuferin vormals
familienintern umstrittener Flächen aufgetreten sei, sei jedenfalls nicht nachvollziehbar
und entspräche auch nicht jenen Intentionen, die dem EF-G zugrunde lägen.

Die Naturalrestitution müsse daher verwehrt bleiben. 34

Am 29. April 2005 replizierte Stephen M. Harnik auf die Stellungnahme der Stadt Wien 35
vom 24. März 2005.

Die AntragstellerInnen seien der Ansicht, dass die Liegenschaften einen reinen Privat- 36
besitz darstellen würden und wirtschaftlich gesehen nicht zur Firma gehört hätten. Wenn
in zeitgenössischen Dokumenten davon die Rede sei, dass die Grundstücke wirtschaftlich
zur Firma gehört hätten bzw. der Übertrag auf die Firma nicht im Zuge der Arisierung der
Firma hätte erfolgen können und daher ein eigenes Rechtsgeschäft notwendig gewesen sei,
so seien dies strategische Manöver gewesen, um die Nazis davon zu überzeugen, der Arisierung der Liegenschaften für die Firma zuzustimmen, um einen Verfall an das Deutsche
Reich zu verhindern. Der Umgang mit der Liegenschaft vor, während und nach dem
2. Weltkrieg zeige jedoch, dass die Liegenschaften immer als Eigentum von Gustav H.
bzw. dessen ErbInnen angesehen und auch so behandelt worden seien. Kein einziges Indiz
könne diesen Sachverhalt in Zweifel ziehen.

Die Ansicht der Stadt Wien, die Arisierung des H.-Vermögens sei „kein reiner Zwangs- 37
akt von außen" gewesen, sei nicht richtig. Trotz des Verwandtschaftsverhältnisses zwischen dem Ariseur Viktor O. und Hans H. sei das gesamte H.-Vermögen unter allen Umständen Gegenstand einer Entziehung und Arisierung gewesen. Die Familie H. habe
lediglich versucht, die Auswirkungen des Schadens durch die unausweichliche Emigration zu minimieren. Aus den Akten sei ersichtlich, dass jedes „abgekartete Spiel" zwischen
H. und O./V. in dem Rechtsstreit nach dem Krieg Lügen gestraft worden sei, da O./V. energisch jede Bemühung der H.s um die Rückstellung ihres Vermögens opponierten. O. habe
mit den H.s mehr als einmal ein doppeltes Spiel getrieben: Zunächst habe er sie davon
überzeugt, ihm die Firma zu übertragen. Aus deren Vertrauen, das mehr aus Verzweiflung,
denn positiver Hingabe entstanden sei, habe er schließlich Kapital geschlagen. Nach dem
Krieg habe O. alle Ereignisse zu seinen Gunsten konstruiert und damit so viel als möglich
für sich sichern wollen, was ihm einst „anvertraut" worden sei, jedoch tatsächlich unter
Zwang übergeben hätte werden müssen.

Der Kaufpreis aus dem Jahr 1940 sei gerade so niedrig berechnet worden, um die an- 38
gefallenen Verlassenschaftsgebühren abzudecken. Keiner der ErbInnen nach Gustav H.

That would have been a more favorable result than the actual non-compensation. Hence, the two settlements constituted an extreme injustice in accordance with the GSF Law.

41 It could not be derived from the files that the current applications were a result of internal resentments between the heirs of Gustav H. and the heirs of Wilhelm H.

3. Evidence

42 Evidence was obtained by reviewing the documents enclosed with the applications for *in rem* restitution.

43 The following documents were obtained by the Arbitration Panel as additional documentation:

44 Austrian State Archives, Archives of the Republic, property notice 29404, Margarete R.; Austrian State Archives, Archives of the Republic, property notice 26595, Karl R.; Austrian State Archives, Archives of the Republic, property notice 24533, Otto W.; Austrian State Archives, Archives of the Republic, property notice 64698, Gustav H.; Austrian State Archives, Archives of the Republic, property notice 8649, Emil H.; Austrian State Archives, Archives of the Republic, Property Transaction Office Lg. (property no.) 7563, Margarete R.; Austrian State Archives, Archives of the Republic, Property Transaction Office 7835 Ind., vol. I + II, Gustav & Wilhelm H; Austrian State Archives, Archives of the Republic, Compensation Fund 3237/1, Hans H.; Austrian State Archives, Archives of the Republic, Compensation Fund 5259/1, Otto W.; Austrian State Archives, Archives of the Republic, Compensation Fund 2031/1, Elisabeth H., Austrian State Archives, Archives of the Republic, Financial Directorate 16242, Hans H.;

45 Municipal Department 8 Vienna Municipal and Regional Archives, processing and settlement of the estate District Court 1 A 766/37, Gustav H.; Municipal Department 8 Vienna Municipal and Regional Archives, settlement and processing of the estate District Court 2 A 1293/38, Marianne W.; Municipal Department 8 Vienna Municipal and Regional Archives, settlement and processing of the estate District Court 1 A 291/31, Wilhelm H.; Municipal Department 8 Vienna Municipal and Regional Archives, settlement and processing of the estate District Court 8 A 763/46, Doris R.; District Court I Innere Stadt, settlement and processing of the estate District Court 9 A 449/70, Margarete R.; Municipal Department 8 Vienna Municipal and Regional Archives, Ordinance on the Notification of Seized Property 10., I-248; Municipal Department 8 Vienna Municipal and Regional Archives, Ordinance on the Notification of Seized Property 10., 262, 115; Municipal Department 8 Vienna Municipal and Regional Archives, Ordinance on the Notification of Seized Property 10., 372; Municipal Department 8 Vienna Municipal and Regional Archives, Ordinance on the Notification of Seized Property 10., 652; Municipal Department 8 Vienna Municipal and Regional Archives, Ordinance on the Notification of Seized Property 4., C 38; Municipal Department 8 Vienna Municipal and Regional Archives, Ordinance on the Notification of Seized Property 21., C 86; Municipal Department 8 Vienna Municipal and Regional Archives, Ordinance on the Notification of Seized Property 10., 259; Municipal Department 8 Vienna Municipal and Regional Archives, Ordinance on the Notification of Seized Property 6, 1283; Municipal Department 8 Vienna Municipal and Regional Archives, Ordinance on the Notification of Seized Property 10., 375; Municipal Department 8 Vienna Municipal and Regional Archives, Ordinance on the Notification of Seized Property 10., 260; Municipal Department 8 Vienna Municipal and Regional Archives, Ordinance on the Notification of Seized Property 10., C 125;

46 Austrian State Archives, State Financial Procurator's Office 2380, Hans H.; Austrian State Archives, State Financial Procurator's Office 3905, Hans H.; Austrian State Archives,

habe je den Erlös des Kaufpreises erhalten. Die abgeschlossenen Vergleiche zwischen Viktor O. und Hans H./Otto W. seien extrem ungerecht gewesen, da ihnen ihre Rechte vorenthalten worden seien. Merkwürdigerweise seien die Liegenschaften am 26. Oktober 1949 an die Firma Gustav & Wilhelm H. verkauft worden. Der Kaufpreis, den die Firma Gustav & Wilhelm H. 1949 für die Liegenschaften bezahlt habe, sei bedeutend höher gewesen als jener, den die Ariseure 1940 bezahlt hätten. Der ein halbes Jahr später abgeschlossene Vergleich zwischen O. und W. zeige, dass O. durch einen Vorwand und Täuschung profitiert und eine Seite gegen die andere ausgespielt habe.

Die geschädigten, rechtmäßigen EigentümerInnen seien zwar als GesellschafterInnen wieder in den Besitz der Liegenschaften gelangt und hätten durch den Verkauf dieser an die Stadt Wien zu einem höheren Preis profitiert, jedoch könne dies kein essentielles Unrecht aufwiegen, zumal die Firma die Liegenschaft vom früheren Ariseur gekauft habe. 39

Den ErbInnen nach Gustav H. sei mehrmals ihr Recht vorenthalten worden und sie hätten keine Entschädigung dafür erhalten. Wäre das Rückstellungsverfahren endgültig entschieden worden, hätten die Liegenschaften notwendigerweise an die Erben nach Gustav H. zurückgegeben werden müssen. Dies wäre ein günstigeres Ergebnis als die tatsächliche Nicht-Entschädigung gewesen. Daher würden die beiden Vergleiche eine extreme Ungerechtigkeit iSd EF-G darstellen. 40

Dass die jetzigen Anträge auf Naturalrestitution das Ergebnis interner Ressentiments zwischen den ErbInnen von Gustav H. und jenen von Wilhelm H. seien, sei aus den Akten nicht zu erkennen. 41

3. Beweise

Beweis wurde erhoben durch Einsichtnahme in die den Anträgen auf Naturalrestitution beigelegten Dokumente. 42

Folgende Dokumente wurden als ergänzende Dokumentation durch die Schiedsinstanz eingeholt: 43

Österreichisches Staatsarchiv (ÖStA), Archiv der Republik (AdR), Vermögensanmeldung (VA) 29404, Margarete R.; ÖStA, AdR, VA 26595, Karl R.; ÖStA, AdR, VA 24533, Otto W.; ÖStA, AdR, VA 64698, Gustav H.; ÖStA, AdR, VA 8649, Emil H.; ÖStA, AdR, Vermögensverkehrsstelle (VVSt) 7563 Lg., Margarete R.; ÖStA, AdR, VVSt 7835 Ind., Band I + II, Gustav & Wilhelm H.; ÖStA, Ageltungsfonds (AF) 3237/1, Hans H.; ÖStA, AdR, AF 5259/1, Otto W.; ÖStA, AdR, AF 2031/1, Elisabeth H., ÖStA, Finanzlandesdirektion (FLD) 16242, Hans H.; 44

Magistratsabteilung 8 Wiener Stadt- und Landesarchiv (MA 8 WStLA), Verlassenschaftsabhandlung BG 1 A 766/37, Gustav H.; MA 8 WStLA, Verlassenschaftsabhandlung BG 2 A 1293/38, Marianne W.; MA 8 WStLA, Verlassenschaftsabhandlung BG 1 A 291/31, Wilhelm H.; MA 8 WStLA, Verlassenschaftsabhandlung BG 8 A 763/46, Doris R.; BG I Innere Stadt, Verlassenschaftsabhandlung BG 9 A 449/70, Margarete R.; MA 8 WStLA, Vermögensentziehungs-Anmeldeverordnung (VEAV) 10., I-248; MA 8 WStLA, VEAV 10., 262, 115; MA 8 WStLA, VEAV 10., 372; MA 8 WStLA, VEAV 10., 652; MA 8 WStLA, VEAV 4., C 38; MA 8 WStLA, VEAV 21., C 86; MA 8 WStLA, VEAV 10., 259; MA 8 WStLA, VEAV 6., 1283; MA 8 WStLA, VEAV 10. 375; MA 8 WStLA, VEAV 10. 260; MA 8 WStLA, VEAV 10., C 125; 45

ÖStA, AdR, Finanzpokuratur (FinProk) 2380, Hans H.; ÖStA, FinProk 3905, Hans H.; ÖStA, Bundesministerium für Vermögenssicherung (BMVS) Kt. 4892, Stephan H.; ÖStA, 46

Federal Ministry for Property Control box 4892, Stephan H; Austrian State Archives, collection agencies, property index EZ X1–X8, KG Inzersdorf-Stadt; Austrian State Archives, Property Transaction Office, box 1387, reports by the German sugar industry on aryanizations and liquidations of Jewish businesses; Austrian State Archives, Financial Directorate 17605, Karl R;

47 Municipal Department 8 Vienna, Municipal and Regional Archives, excerpt from the trade register Gustav & Wilhelm H. as well as Lehmann: registered companies, 1938 and 1942;

48 District Court I Innere Stadt, trade register file no. 14026 (transcribed from trade register file no. 4136), Gustav & Wilhelm H.;

49 Municipal Department 8 Vienna, Municipal and Regional Archives trade register 7, trade register file no. 23.358, Viktor S. & Söhne;

50 District Court Favoriten, collection of documents, EZ X1–X8, KG Inzersdorf-Stadt as well as land register copies concerning the same.

51 Literature:

52 Ulrike Felber; Peter Melichar; Markus Priller; Berthold Unfried, Fritz Weber, *Ökonomie der Arisierung. Teil 1: Grundzüge, Akteure und Institutionen*. Vienna (Oldenbourg) 2004 (= Publications of the Austrian Historical Commission, vol. 10/1);

53 As above: *Ökonomie der Arisierung. Teil 2: Wirtschaftssektoren, Branchen, Falldarstellungen*. Vienna (Oldenbourg) 2004 (= Publications of the Austrian Historical Commission, vol. 10/1);

54 John Lichtblau, *Jüdische Unternehmer in Österreich nach 1945. Oral History und ihre Forschungsperspektiven für die postfaschistische jüdische Geschichte*. In: Martha Keil/ Klaus Lohrmann (eds.): Studien zur Geschichte der Juden in Österreich. Vienna/ Cologne/ Weimar 1994 (= Handbuch zur Geschichte der Juden in Österreich, series B, volume 2);

55 Hans H., *Zwischen zwei Welten. Erinnerungen, Dokumente, Prosa, Bilder*. Wels 1985.

4. Established Facts

a) Company History

56 In 1891, the brothers Gustav and Wilhelm H. founded the chocolate and sugar-products factory "Gustav and Wilhelm H[…]" (referred to in the following text as G&W H.). The company had been registered in the trade register since 26 September 1891, under the number "Ges. 37, 239" and "trade register file no. 4136" as a general commercial partnership; seated in Vienna. The factory was situated in a block of buildings which was enclosed by B.-platz, Be.-gasse, the I.-straße and G.-gasse. At the beginning of World War I, H. employed between 1,200 and 1,400 persons. In 1921 and 1924, the family's next generation entered the company. Both of Wilhelm H.'s sons, Stephan (as at 6 May 1921) and Karl H. (as at 4 January 1924), as well as Gustav H.'s son, Dr. Hans H. (as at 6 May 1921), became partners. On 8 May 1931 Gustav H.'s son-in-law and Marianne W.'s husband, Dr. Otto W., also became a partner of the company. Hans, Stephan and Karl H. each owned a 25 % share in the company; Otto W. owned a 12.5 % share. The remaining 12.5 % was held by Gustav H.

57 After Gustav H.'s death on 7 September 1937, Margarete R. was the sole heir of the one-eighth share of Gustav H. in the Gustav & Wilhelm H. Company. The processing and settlement of the estate was carried out after the *Anschluss* of Austria to the German Reich.

Sammelstelle (SSt), Liegenschaftskartei EZ X1–X8, KG Inzersdorf-Stadt; ÖStA, VVSt, Kt. 1387, Berichte der deutschen Zuckerwarenindustrie über Arisierungen und Liquidierungen jüdischer Betriebe; ÖStA, FLD 17605, Karl R.;

MA 8 WStLA, Handelregisterauszug (HRA) Gustav & Wilhelm H. sowie Lehmann: Protokollierte Firmen, 1938 und 1942; 47

Bezirksgericht (BG) I Innere Stadt, Handelsregister HRA 14026 (umgeschrieben von HRA 4136), Gustav & Wilhem H.; 48

MA 8 WStLA, Handelsregister 7 HRA 23.358, Victor S. & Söhne; 49

BG Favoriten, Urkundensammlung, EZ X1–X8, KG Inzersdorf-Stadt sowie Grundbuch-Kopien zu ebenda. 50

Literatur zu den Feststellungen: 51

Ulrike *Felber,* Peter *Melichar,* Markus *Priller,* Berthold *Unfried,* Fritz *Weber,* Ökonomie der Arisierung. Teil 1: Grundzüge, Akteure und Institutionen, Wien (Oldenbourg) 2004 (= Veröffentlichungen der Österreichischen Historikerkommission, Band 10/1). 52

Dies., Ökonomie der Arisierung. Teil 2: Wirtschaftssektoren, Branchen, Falldarstellungen, Wien (Oldenbourg) 2004 (= Veröffentlichungen der Österreichischen Historikerkommission, Band 10/2). 53

John *Lichtblau,* Jüdische Unternehmer in Österreich nach 1945. Oral History und ihre Forschungsperspektiven für die postfaschistische jüdische Geschichte. In: Martha *Keil*/ Klaus *Lohrmann* et al. (Hrsg.), Studien zur Geschichte der Juden in Österreich, Wien/ Köln/Weimar 1994 (= Handbuch zur Geschichte der Juden in Österreich, Reihe B, Band 2). 54

Hans *H.*, Zwischen zwei Welten. Erinnerungen, Dokumente, Prosa, Bilder, Wels 1985. 55

4. *Festgestellter Sachverhalt*

a) Firmengeschichte

Die Brüder Gustav und Wilhelm H. gründeten im Jahr 1891 die Schokolade- und Zuckerwarenfabrik „Gustav und Wilhelm H […]". Das Unternehmen war seit 26. September 1891 als Offene Handelsgesellschaft (OHG) im Handelsregister mit der Nummer Ges. 37, 239 bzw. HRA 4136 mit Sitz in Wien eingetragen. Die Fabrik befand sich auf einem Baublock, der vom B.-platz, der Be.-gasse, der I.-straße und der G.-gasse eingeschlossen war. Zu Beginn des Ersten Weltkrieges beschäftigte H. bereits 1200 bis 1400 Personen. 1921 bzw. 1924 trat die junge Generation der Familie in die Firma ein. Gesellschafter wurden einerseits die beiden Söhne von Wilhelm H., Stephan (seit 6. Mai 1921) und Karl H. (seit 4. Januar 1924), sowie der Sohn von Gustav H., Dr. Hans H. (seit 6. Mai 1921). Am 8. Mai 1931 wurde auch der Schwiegersohn von Gustav H. und Ehegatte von Marianne W., Dr. Otto W., Gesellschafter des Unternehmens. Hans, Stephan und Karl H. waren zu je 25 % an der Firma beteiligt, Otto W. zu 12,5 %. Die restlichen 12,5 % fielen auf Gustav H. 56

Margarete R. war nach dem Tod von Gustav H. am 7. September 1937 die Universalerbin des 1/8-Anteiles von Gustav H. an der Firma Gustav & Wilhelm H. Die Verlassenschaftsabhandlung wurde nach dem „Anschluss" Österreichs an das Deutsche Reich geführt, daher kam es nicht mehr zur Eintragung von Margarete R. als Gesellschafterin der Firma ins Handelsregister. In ihrer VA Nr. 50189 an die Vermögensverkehrsstelle (im Folgenden VVSt) ist dieser 1/8-Anteil von Margarete R. an der obigen Firma mit einem reinen Wert von 335.729,64 Reichsmark und dem Vermerk angegeben, dass diese Vermögenschaft noch nicht eingeantwortet sei. 57

Hence, Margarete R. was not registered as a partner in the company in the trade register. In her property notice no. 50189 at the *Vermögensverkehrstelle* ("Property Transaction Office"), this one-eighth share of Margarete R. of the abovementioned company is recorded as having an absolute value of 335,729.64 Reichsmark. It included a note that this property had not yet been devolved.

58   The aryanization of the company was implemented shortly after the *Anschluss*. Foreseeing political persecution under National Socialist rule, Hans H. decided to emigrate in April 1938 and taking into consideration the unavoidable forced seizure of the company he decided to find a purchaser. After several fruitless negotiations with the Swiss N.-group and after the conclusion of a conditional preliminary agreement with the German rival-company Ro., a solution within the family was able to be reached with Dr. Viktor O. O. had already worked for the company for several years, was considered an "Aryan" in accordance with the Nuremberg Laws, and was married to the sister of Hans H.'s second wife.

59   On 9 June 1938, the Gustav & Wilhelm H. Company submitted to O. a takeover offer of the company in case the contract with the Ro. Company from Reichenau in Saxony should not come to fruition. In the letter addressed to Viktor O. the following was stated:

60   "You are joining the Gustav &Wilhelm H[…] Company as a partner. All partners agree that the company is not to be dissolved if a partner resigns but that the company will continue to exist among the remaining partners. The previous partners of the general commercial partnership resign so that the company can be continued by you and one or two new partners, which you will identify. The former partners are to be dealt with in such a way that the remaining partners pay them 3,000,000 Schilling (three million Schilling) as a share of the company assets – 1,500,000 Schilling immediately and the rest in yearly installments of 375,000 Schilling. Each purchase Schilling bears 4 1/2 % interest and the interest is to be paid every three months in arrears. The price of 3,000,000 Schilling is for the company's total assets, especially for the factory land, including the bordering empty lot, the factory building […]"

as well as all machines, furnishings, fixtures, existing raw material, patents, trademarks and other rights.

61   Viktor O. was able to obtain as a new partner for the takeover a financially strong partner, his uncle Franz V., who was a personal friend of Hermann Göring. On 9 July 1938, the State Commissioner for Private Enterprises issued the temporary approval for the takeover of the G&W H. Company by Franz V. and his two nephews Herbert V. and Viktor O. Among other things, this approval was given on the condition that in taking over the company the purchasers "are to draw up a precise list of the assets and liabilities as at the day of the takeover with the provisional administrator and to submit it to the Property Transaction Office." The final approval was issued after an audit with notification of 18 November 1938 by the Property Transaction Office. A purchase price of 1.8 million Reichsmark and a de-jewification fee of 400,000 Reichsmark were fixed; the fee was paid by "Jews" and "aryanizers". Each of them paid 50 %. Through this, the previous Jewish partners Stephan, Karl and Hans H. as well as Otto W. and Gustav H., who was still recorded in the trade register but had already passed away, withdrew as partners and were followed by Franz V. and his two nephews Herbert V. and Viktor O. who took their place as new partners of the company.

62   The purchase contract which was presented to the Property Transaction Office was supplemented by an agreement, which had been settled with O. in Paris and in London, where

Die Arisierung der Firma wurde bereits kurz nach dem „Anschluss" eingeleitet. In Voraussicht auf eine politische Verfolgung unter nationalsozialistischer Herrschaft entschloss sich Hans H. bereits im April 1938 auszuwandern und in Anbetracht der unausweichlichen zwangsweisen Entziehung des Unternehmens einen Käufer zu finden. Nach einigen vergeblichen Verhandlungen mit dem schweizerischen N.-Konzern und dem Abschluss eines bedingten Vorvertrages mit der deutschen Konkurrenzfirma Ro. konnte eine „innerfamiliäre" Lösung mit Dr. Viktor O. erzielt werden. O. war bereits seit einigen Jahren in der Firma tätig, galt nach den Nürnberger Rassegesetzen als „Arier" und war mit der Schwester von Hans H.s zweiter Ehefrau verheiratet. 58

Am 9. Juni 1938 unterbreitete die Firma Gustav & Wilhelm H. Viktor O. ein Angebot zur Übernahme der Firma, sollte der Vertrag mit der Firma Ro. aus Reichenau in Sachsen nicht zustande kommen. In dem an Viktor O. adressierten Schreiben wurde festgehalten: 59

„Sie treten als Gesellschafter in die offene Handelsgesellschaft Gustav & Wilhelm H[...] ein. Sämtliche Gesellschafter vereinbaren, dass das Ausscheiden von Gesellschaftern die Gesellschaft nicht zur Auflösung bringt, sondern dass die Gesellschaft unter den übrigen Gesellschaftern fortbesteht. Die bisherigen Gesellschafter der offenen Handelsgesellschaft scheiden alsdann aus, sodass die Gesellschaft von Ihnen, zusammen mit einem oder zwei neuen Gesellschaftern, die Sie uns namhaft machen, fortbetrieben wird. Die Auseinandersetzung mit den alten Gesellschaftern erfolgt in der Weise, dass die verbleibenden Gesellschafter ihnen als Anteil am Gesellschaftsvermögen den Betrag von S 3,000.000,– (drei Millionen Schilling), und zwar S.1,500.000,– sofort und den Rest in Jahresraten von S. 375.000,– zahlen, wobei der jeweilige Kaufpreisschilling mit 4 1/2 % verzinst wird und die Zinsen vierteljährlich im nachhinein zu entrichten sind. Der Preis von S.3,000.000,– versteht sich für das gesamte Firmenvermögen, wie es liegt und steht, insbesondere für das Fabriksgrundstück einschliesslich dem angrenzenden unbebauten Terrain, das Fabriksgebäude [...]" 60

sowie sämtliche Maschinen, Mobiliar, Einrichtungsgegenstände, das vorhandene Rohmaterial, Patente, Schutzmarken und sonstige Rechte.

Viktor O. konnte für die Übernahme einen finanzkräftigen Partner, seinen Onkel Franz V., der ein persönlicher Freund Hermann Görings war, als neuen Gesellschafter gewinnen. Am 9. Juli 1938 erteilte der Staatskommissar für die Privatwirtschaft die vorläufige Genehmigung für die Übernahme der Firma Gustav & Wilhelm H. durch Franz V. und seine beiden Neffen Herbert V. und Viktor O. Diese Genehmigung war unter anderem an die Bedingung gebunden, dass die Erwerber bei Betriebsübernahme „im Verein mit dem kommissarischen Verwalter eine genaue Aufstellung der Aktiven und Passiven nach dem Stand des Tages der Betriebsführung zu machen und diese an die Vermögensverkehrsstelle abzugeben [haben]". Die endgültige Genehmigung erteilte die VVSt nach einer Wirtschaftsprüfung mit Bescheid vom 18. November 1938. Als Kaufpreis wurden 1,800.000,– Reichsmark und eine „Entjudungsauflage" von 400.000,– Reichsmark festgesetzt; diese wurde von „Juden" und „Ariseuren" gemeinsam je zur Hälfte bezahlt. Damit schieden die früheren jüdischen Gesellschafter Stephan, Karl und Hans H. sowie Otto W. und der noch im Handelsregister eingetragene, jedoch bereits verstorbene Gustav H. als Gesellschafter aus, und anstelle von diesen traten Franz V. und seine beiden Neffen Herbert V. sowie Viktor O. als neue Gesellschafter in die Firma ein. 61

Der VVSt vorgelegte Kaufvertrag wurde durch ein in Paris und London, wohin Stephan, Karl und Hans H. mittlerweile emigriert waren, abgeschlossenes Abkommen mit O. ergänzt. In diesem Abkommen wurde festgehalten, dass für die Dauer der NS-Herrschaft 62

Stephan, Karl and Hans H. had emigrated to by this time. In this agreement, it had been recorded that for the duration of National Socialist rule O. and V. were to run the company as trustees. In return, the H. brothers were to obtain the rights to distribute H. products in certain countries, including Great Britain and the USA, using their trademarks. In doing so they were entitled to be involved in the export business of the Viennese company.

63   During the aryanization proceedings, Margarete R., who was the only original partner to remain in Austria with her children, Hansjörg and Doris, throughout the entire duration of National Socialist rule, also had to sell to the new partners, Franz and Herbert V. as well as Viktor O., her 12.5 % share of the company pursuant to the purchase contract of 9 June 1938, including the supplement of 16 and 24 June 1938.

64   The company was continuously modernized from 1938 onwards and with the aid of financial means from Franz V. extensive machinery was purchased. After the war, the restitution of the company shares to the previous partners was the subject of restitution proceedings, which continued for several years.

65   On 5 May 1948, Margarete R., Dr. Viktor O., Herbert V. and Dr. Hans O., the legatee of the already deceased Franz V., signed an agreement settling the claims for restitution in accordance with the stipulations contained in para. 13 of the *Bundesgesetz über die Nichtigkeit von Vermögensentziehungen* ("Federal Law on the Annulment of Property Seizures") of 6 February 1947, *BGBl.* ("Federal Law Gazette") No. 54/1947. Initially, it was recorded in the settlement that Margarete R., contrary to Viktor O. and Franz V., was of the opinion that the provisions of the Third Restitution Act were to be applied to the company's entire assets; and not, as was the opinion of V. and O., that a distinction between two parts of the assets was to be made: namely that part of the assets which was existent on 31 July 1937 and to which the regulations of the law were to be applied and that part, which was acquired by the new partners after the takeover of the company and which according to the purchasers was not to be regarded as confiscated since it was non-existent at the time of the company purchase. In the opinion of the purchasers, a transfer of the ownership and other rights regarding this second part of the assets would only be possible through an amicable and separate legal transaction. Margarete R. did not share this opinion, she rather supported the notion that the regulations of the Third Restitution Act were to be applied to the total assets existent at the time.

66   In item II of the settlement, it was recorded that Margarete R. had inherited the one-eighth share of the company from Gustav H. after his death on 7 September 1937 and that she sold this share to Franz and Herbert V. as well as Viktor O. pursuant to the contract dated 9 June 1938, including a supplement dated 31 July 1938 and 24 June 1938, effective as at 31 July 1938. Additionally, it was recorded in this item of the settlement that the share of the company assets of Franz V., Viktor O. and Herbert V. had grown. Finally, in item III it was agreed that Dr. Viktor O. and Herbert V. were to restitute the one-eighth share of the company assets to which Margarete R. had been entitled at the point of sale in return for the cash payment of the mutually agreed sum of 80,000 Schilling. Margarete R. agreed to accept the restitution and, at the same time, entered into the general commercial partnership Gustav & Wilhelm H. as a public partner. In addition, the aryanizers issued the explicit assent that "Mrs. R[…] may at any time transfer her company shares, company rights including signing and representation authorizations to her son Hansjörg R[…]; the son then enters the company as a partner entitled to representation and as an executive."

67   On 5 May 1948, in addition to the separately mutually agreed legal transaction mentioned in this settlement, Margarete R. signed a contract with Dr. Viktor O, Herbert V. as

O. mit V. die Firma treuhänderisch leiten sollte und die Brüder H. dafür das Recht bekommen sollten, in bestimmten Ländern, u. a. in Großbritannien und den USA, H.-Produkte unter Verwendung von deren Markenrechten zu vertreiben und sich auf diese Art in das Exportgeschäft der Wiener Firma einzuschalten.

Im Zuge des Arisierungsverfahrens musste auch Margarete R., die als einzige der früheren GesellschafterInnen während der gesamten nationalsozialistischen Herrschaft gemeinsam mit ihren Kindern Hansjörg und Doris in Österreich verblieb, ihren 12,5 %igen Firmenanteil mit Kaufvertrag vom 9. Juni 1938 samt Nachtrag vom 16. bzw. 24. Juni 1938 an die neuen Gesellschafter Franz und Herbert V. sowie Viktor O. verkaufen. 63

Ab 1938 wurde die Firma fortlaufend modernisiert und mit Hilfe der finanziellen Mittel von Franz V. ein umfangreicher Maschinenpark angekauft. Nach Kriegsende war die Rückstellung der Gesellschaftsanteile an die früheren GesellschafterInnen Gegenstand eines über mehrere Jahre laufenden Rückstellungsverfahrens. 64

Am 5. Mai 1948 schloss Margarete R. gemeinsam mit Dr. Viktor O., Herbert V. sowie Dr. Hans O., dem Legatar nach dem inzwischen verstorbenen Franz V., einen Vergleich zur Bereinigung von Rückstellungsansprüchen iSd Bestimmungen des § 13 des Bundesgesetzes vom 6. Februar 1947, Bundesgesetzblatt (BGBl) 54/1947 über die Nichtigkeit von Vermögensentziehungen. Darin wurde zunächst festgehalten, dass Margarete R. im Gegensatz zu Viktor O. und Franz V. der Ansicht war, dass auf das gesamte Gesellschaftsvermögen die Bestimmungen des 3. RStG anzuwenden seien und nicht – wie nach Ansicht von O. und V. – zwischen zwei Teilen des Vermögens zu unterscheiden sei, nämlich jenem Teil, der am 31. Juli 1937 vorhanden war und auf den die Bestimmungen des Gesetzes anzuwenden wären, und jenem Teil, der nach Übernahme der Firma durch die neuen Gesellschafter erworben wurde und welcher, da zum Zeitpunkt des Firmenerwerbs nicht vorhanden, nach Ansicht der Erwerber nicht als entzogen anzusehen sei. Eine Übertragung der Eigentums- und sonstigen Rechte an diesem zweiten Teil des Vermögens sei nach Ansicht der Erwerber nur durch ein einvernehmliches, gesondertes Rechtsgeschäft möglich. Margarete R. teilte diesen Standpunkt nicht, sie war vielmehr der Ansicht, dass auf das gesamte derzeit vorhandene Vermögen die Bestimmungen des 3. RStG anzuwenden seien. 65

In Punkt II des Vergleichs wurde festgehalten, dass Margarete R. den Achtelanteil an der Gesellschaft von Gustav H. nach dessen Tod am 7. September 1937 im Erbgang erworben hatte und sie diesen mit Vertrag vom 9. Juni 1938 samt Nachtrag vom 31. Juli 1938 bzw. 24. Juni 1938 mit Stichtag 31. Juli 1938 an Franz und Herbert V. sowie Viktor O. veräußert hat. Zudem wurde in diesem Punkt des Vergleichs festgehalten, dass der Anteil des Gesellschaftsvermögens von Franz V., Viktor O. und Herbert V. zugewachsen ist. In Punkt III wurde schließlich vereinbart, dass die Herren Dr. Viktor O. und Herbert V. den Achtelanteil an dem Gesellschaftsvermögen, wie er Margarete R. im Zeitpunkt der Veräußerung zustand, an Margarete R. Zug um Zug gegen Barzahlung des einvernehmlich festgesetzten Betrages von 80.000,– Schilling zurückzustellen haben. Margarete R. erklärte sich zur Annahme der Rückstellung bereit und trat gleichzeitig als öffentliche Gesellschafterin in die Offene Handelsgesellschaft Gustav & Wilhelm H. ein. Die Ariseure erteilten zudem die ausdrückliche Zustimmung, dass „Frau R[...] jederzeit ihre Gesellschaftsanteile, Gesellschaftsrechte, samt Zeichnungs- und Vertretungsbefugnissen, an ihren Sohn Hansjörg R[...] überträgt, und dieser dann als geschäftsführender und vertretungsbefugter Gesellschafter in die Gesellschaft eintritt". 66

Am 5. Mai 1948 schloss Margarete R. mit Dr. Viktor O., Herbert V. sowie Dr. Hans O. zusätzlich zu dem in diesem Vergleich angesprochenen einvernehmlichen, gesonderten 67

well as Dr. Hans O. regarding the share of the company assets which according to Viktor O. and Hans V. they were not obliged to restitute. In the contract the following was agreed upon:

> "Dr. Viktor O[...] and Herbert V[...] transfer a one-eighth share of the part of the company assets, which in their opinion belongs to them and is not subject to compulsory restitution, as at 1 April 1948 to Mrs. Margarete R[...] By this means, as at 1 April 1948, she acquires a one-eighth share of the company's total assets, taking into consideration the company assets restituted to her in the settlement. Hence, Mrs. R[...] will be credited one-eighth of today's balance of the capital accounts of the partners in a capital account set up in her name. Effective 1 April 1948, Mrs. R[...] will also take a one-eighth share in the profits and losses of the company."

In item II of the contract, the parties agreed to appoint a court of arbitration and to instruct it with

> "the determination of the amount of the payment for the transfer of assets agreed in item I, to which the purchasers are entitled. [...] The amount payable established by arbitral award is due to be paid to the acquirers within four weeks of the award. The parties to the contract agree that the contract and the settlement, which is to be concluded at the same time, on the asserted restitution claims represent an integral whole."

In a supplementary settlement as defined in the *Vermögensentziehungs-Anmeldungsverordnung* ("Ordinance on the Notification of Seized Property") the settlement partners waived the use of such an arbitration court and agreed that "for the final settlement of all alleged claims of any kind, the parties obligated to restitution are to pay an amount of 50,000 Schilling to the parties entitled to restitution [...]."

68   After Margarete R. had concluded a settlement regarding the restitution of her share of the company on 5 May 1948 and had entered the company as a public partner, the still pending hearings of the restitution matter regarding the Gustav & Wilhelm H. Company were now also conducted against her by the applicants and former partners Hans, Stephan and Karl H. as well as Otto W. The restitution proceedings in this matter were recorded under file number 50 Rk 488/48 at the Restitution Commission established with the Regional Court for Civil Matters Vienna. In a restitution settlement of 27 April 1949, Hans, Karl and Stephen H. as well as Otto W. withdrew this claim for restitution, which was directed against Margarete R. and agreed that her son Hans be registered in the trade register as a partner. Regarding this, the settlement states:

> "Since pursuant to item VI. of the restitution settlement of 5 May 1948 between Margarete R[...] and the parties obligated to restitution Mrs. Margarete R[...] is able to transfer her company shares and company rights to her son Hansjörg R[...], Mr. Hansjörg R[...] enters into this obligation assumed by Mrs. Margarete R[...]"

69   From this point on at the latest, the interests of Hansjörg R. and his mother Margarete followed

> "more the interests of the 'aryanizers' than those of the claimants for restitution. This fact rendered visible a divide within the H[...] family; namely between those members, which clearly placed their priorities with the Viennese company and those members, which also reserved the option of a substantial transfer abroad of the company activities."

A divide within the family can be seen to have occurred earlier, which manifested itself in the arguments surrounding the appointment of a public administrator for the Gustav & Wilhelm H. Company by the Federal Ministry of Property Control.

Rechtsgeschäft einen Vertrag betreffend den von Viktor O. und Herbert V. nicht als rückstellungspflichtig angesehenen Anteil an dem Gesellschaftsvermögen. Darin wurde vereinbart:

„Die Herren Dr. Viktor O[...] und Herbert V[...] übertragen einen Achtelanteil an dem nach ihrer Auffassung ihnen gehörigen, der Restitutionspflicht nicht unterliegenden Gesellschaftsvermögen wie es am 1. April 1948 lag und stand, an Frau Margarete R [...], womit diese unter Berücksichtigung des ihr mit Vergleich restituierten Gesellschaftsvermögens einen Achtelanteil an dem Gesamtvermögen der Gesellschaft mit dem Stande 1. April 1948 erwirbt. Frau R[...] wird daher auf einem für sie zu eröffnenden Kapitalkonto ein Achtel der Summe der heute bei der Gesellschaft bestehenden Kapitalkonten der Gesellschafter gutzubringen sein. Frau R[...] wird mit Wirksamkeit vom 1. April 1948 auch mit einem Achtel an dem Gewinn und Verlust der Gesellschaft teilhaben."

In Punkt II. des Vertrags einigten sich die Parteien darauf, ein Schiedsgericht zu bestellen und damit zu beauftragen,

„die Höhe der den Erwerbern zustehenden Leistung für die in Punkt I. gemachte Vermögensübertragung festzusetzen. [...] Die durch Schiedsspruch festgesetzte Leistung wird binnen vier Wochen nach Fällung des Schiedsspruches an die Erwerber fällig. Die Vertragsteile sind darüber einig, dass dieser Vertrag und der gleichzeitig abzuschließende Vergleich über die geltendgemachten Restitutionsansprüche ein einheitliches Ganzes darstellen."

In einer ergänzenden Vergleichsanzeige iSd Vermögensentziehungs-Anmeldungsverordnung (VEAV) verzichteten die VergleichspartnerInnen auf die Konstituierung eines solchen Schiedsgerichts und einigten sich darauf, dass „zur endgültigen Endfertigung aller wie immer gearteten vermeintlichen Ansprüche der Rückstellungspflichtigen an die Rückstellungsberechtigten ein Betrag von S 50.000,– [...] zu bezahlen ist."

Nachdem sich am 5. Mai 1948 Margarete R. hinsichtlich der Rückstellung ihres Firmenanteils verglichen hatte und als öffentliche Gesellschafterin in die Firma eingetreten war, wurden die noch ausständigen Verhandlungen in der Rückstellungssache betreffend die Firma Gustav & Wilhelm H. von den Antragstellern und früheren Gesellschaftern Hans, Stephan und Karl H. sowie Otto W. gegen die Antragsgegner Viktor O., Herbert V. und dem Legatar von Franz V. nun auch gegen Margarete R. geführt. Das diesbezügliche Rückstellungsverfahren wurde bei der am Landesgericht für Zivilrechtssachen (LGfZRS) Wien eingerichteten Rückstellungskommission unter dem Aktenzeichen 50 Rk 488/48 geführt. In einem Rückstellungsvergleich vom 27. April 1949 zogen Hans, Karl und Stephan H. sowie Otto W. diesen gegen Margarete R. gerichteten Rückstellungsantrag zurück und erklärten sich damit einverstanden, dass ihr Sohn Hansjörg als Gesellschafter ins Handelsregister aufgenommen wird. Dazu heißt es im Vergleich:

68

„Da gemäß Punkt VI. des Rückstellungsvergleiches der Frau Margarete R[...] mit den Rückstellungspflichtigen vom 5. Mai 1948 vorgesehen ist, dass Frau Margarete R[...] ihre Gesellschaftsanteile und Gesellschaftsrechte an ihren Sohn Hansjörg R[...] übertragen kann, so tritt Herr Hansjörg R[...] dieser von Frau Margarete R[...] übernommenen Verpflichtung bei."

Spätestens ab diesem Zeitpunkt verliefen die Interessen von Hansjörg R. und seiner Mutter Margarete „mehr entlang jener der ‚Ariseure' denn jener der Rückstellungswerber. Darin wurde eine Bruchlinie innerhalb der Familie H[...] sichtbar und zwar zwischen

69

Arbitration Panel for *In Rem* Restitution – Decision No. 25/2005

70 In 1945, the claimant, Hansjörg R., the son of Margarete R., was – in agreement with the former partners who were still in exile – conferred the individual power of attorney and appointed temporary director of the company in order to reopen the operation and to represent the claims of the family members. With this arrangement in place, Hansjörg R. secured an early entry into the company and at the same time a strong position within the enterprise. The Federal Ministry of Property Control intended to appoint a public administrator for the Gustav & Wilhelm H. Company. In order to prevent an outsider from assuming this position, on 26 May 1945 Hansjörg R. wrote to the State Secretary in the government office responsible for National Nutrition that he had applied for the provisional management of the company

> "with the complete approval of the other partners [...] and of their representatives, to enable a smooth reversal of the aryanization in the spirit of compensation. [...] For this reason, I hardly believe that in this case there is a necessity, or that it is in the interest of the public, to appoint an outsider as provisional administrator. Therefore, I ask to refrain from this and to confirm my appointment."

R. received support from Josef Wi., the chairman of the employee committee, who had also supported Hansjörg R. on 9 July 1945.

71 In 1946 Stephan H., who at that point in time was still abroad, submitted an application to the Federal Ministry of Property Control for his own appointment as public administrator of the Gustav & Wilhelm H. Company. However, the application was not granted by the Federal Ministry of Property Control since upon the entry of Hansjörg R. into the company, a siphoning off of assets seemed not very probable and according to the Federal Ministry of Property Control sufficient evidence for such a danger could not be found. Hence, Stephan H. was appointed merely a public supervisor with limited authority. He was not entitled to act as a sole authorized signatory for the company and – for example – could not sign contracts abroad for the import of raw material.

72 In order to resume control over the Viennese production plant – especially over the machinery which had been considerably extended during the war – after the entry of Margarete R. into the company, the previous manager Stephan H. intervened once again at the Federal Ministry of Property Control for his appointment as a public administrator of the Gustav & Wilhelm H. Company. In a corresponding application of 2 April 1949 by Hans, Karl and Stephan H. to the Federal Ministry of Property Control, the claimants accused the partner Margarete R. of having made "unwarranted withdrawals" from the company profits and that hence the suspicion that assets were being siphoned off is present. Concerning this it is stated:

73 "Since 1 April 1948 – that is since the conclusion of her settlement with the aryanizers in accordance with para. 13 of the Third Restitution Act – Mrs. Margarete R[...] has received a management salary of 10,000 Schilling [...] credited to her account each month. The pay of her son Ing. Jörg R[...] is included in this amount and actually in principle there are no objections. However, she has withdrawn 241,000 Schilling. These payments which are listed as round numbers amount to almost one million. [...] As a matter of form, it is explicitly declared that Mrs. R[...] is not being compared with the aryanizers; she herself belongs to the politically aggrieved, is the sister of Dr. Hans H[...] and cousin of the Kommerzialrat Stephan H[...] and Charles H[...] and has presumably only performed the unjustified withdrawals in order to save for herself what was still to be saved."

jenen, die eindeutig prioritär auf die Wiener Firma setzten und jenen, die sich auch die Option einer hauptsächlichen Verlagerung der Firmentätigkeit ins Ausland offen hielten." Eine Bruchlinie innerhalb der Familie ist bereits zu einem früheren Zeitpunkt deutlich, die sich anhand der Auseinandersetzungen um die Einsetzung eines öffentlichen Verwalters für die Firma Gustav & Wilhelm H. durch das BMVS zeigt.

Dem Antragsteller und Sohn von Margarete R., Hansjörg R., wurde bereits 1945 im Einvernehmen mit den noch in der Emigration befindlichen früheren GesellschafterInnen von der Firma Gustav & Wilhelm H. die Einzelprokura erteilt und zum provisorischen Leiter der Firma ernannt, um den Betrieb wieder aufzunehmen und die Ansprüche der Familienangehörigen zu vertreten. Hansjörg R. sicherte sich mit dieser Regelung einen frühzeitigen Eintritt in die Firma und gleichzeitig eine starke Stellung innerhalb des Unternehmens. Das BMVS beabsichtigte, einen öffentlichen Verwalter für die Firma Gustav & Wilhelm H. einzusetzen. Um zu verhindern, dass ein Außenstehender mit dieser Funktion betraut wird, schrieb Hansjörg R. am 26. Mai 1945 an den Staatssekretär im Staatsamt für Volksernährung, dass er sich „in vollem Einverständnis mit den übrigen Gesellschaftern [...] und deren Vertretern" um die kommissarische Leitung der Firma beworben habe, 70

„um im Sinne der Wiedergutmachung eine reibungslose Rückführung der Arisierung zu ermöglichen. [...] Ich glaube daher kaum, dass in diesem Fall die Notwendigkeit besteht, noch dass es im Interesse der Allgemeinheit liegen kann, einen Außenstehenden als kommissarischen Verwalter einzusetzen, ersuche daher davon Abstand nehmen zu wollen und meine Bestellung zu bestätigen."

Unterstützung erhielt R. von Josef Wi., dem Obmann des Betriebsrates, der sich am 9. Juli 1945 ebenfalls für Hansjörg R. einsetzte.

Im Jahr 1946 brachte Stephan H., der sich zu diesem Zeitpunkt noch im Ausland befand, beim BMVS einen Antrag auf Einsetzung seiner Person als öffentlicher Verwalter der Firma Gustav & Wilhelm H. ein. Diesem Antrag wurde jedoch nicht vom BMVS stattgegeben, da der Eintritt von Hansjörg R. eine Vermögensverschleppung unwahrscheinlich erscheinen ließ bzw. keine für das BMVS ausreichenden Beweise für eine solche Gefahr vorgelegt werden konnten. Stephan H. wurde daher lediglich zur öffentlichen Aufsichtsperson bestellt, deren Befugnisse eingeschränkt waren. So war er nicht allein für die Firma zeichnungsberechtigt und konnte z. B. keine Verträge zur Einfuhr von Rohmaterial im Ausland abschließen. 71

Um den Einfluss auf die Wiener Produktionsstätte, insbesondere auf den in den Kriegsjahren erheblich erweiterten Maschinenpark wiederzuerlangen, intervenierte der frühere Geschäftsführer Stephan H. nach dem Eintritt von Margarete R. in die Gesellschaft nochmals beim BMVS für die Einsetzung seiner Person als öffentlicher Verwalter der Firma Gustav & Wilhelm H. In einem entsprechenden Antrag von Hans, Karl und Stephan H. an das BMVS vom 2. April 1949 warfen die Antragsteller der Gesellschafterin Margarete R. vor, aus den Gewinnen der Firma „ungerechtfertigte Entnahmen" vorgenommen zu haben und dass somit der Verdacht einer Verschleppung von Vermögenschaften bestehe. Dazu heißt es: 72

„Frau Margarete R[...] hat sich am 1. April 1948, also seit Abschluß ihres Vergleiches nach § 13 des 3. Rückstellungsgesetzes mit den Ariseuren, einen Unternehmerlohn von S 10.000,– pro Monat [...] gutschreiben lassen. In diesem Betrag ist das Gehalt ihres Sohnes, Ing. Jörg R[...], eingeschlossen und an sich bestünde dagegen kein Einwand. Sie hat jedoch S 241.000,– entnommen. Diese Beträge, die durchwegs mit runden Zif- 73

74	In her counterstatement Margarete R. categorically repudiates these accusations as "incorrect". The claimants intended to create a convenient position for the upcoming restitution negotiations. Stephan H. intended to "prejudice" the restitution proceedings by applying to be appointed as public administrator and to bring the machinery under the ownership of the emigrated H.'s in order to be able to use it in the production plants abroad; O.'s arguments were the same in his counterstatement.

75	After the settlements of 27 April and of 20 May 1949 between the claimants Hans, Karl and Stephan H. as well as Otto W. and the adverse parties Viktor O., Herbert V., the estate of Franz V. and Margarete R., all claimants withdrew the claim for restitution against Margarete R. In return, Margarete R. undertook to

> "admit some or all of the claimants to the G. & W. H[…] Company as public partners in accordance with a legally binding decision by the Restitution Commission or a restitution settlement and to submit to the trade register at any time all registrations necessary for the registration of the claimants as public partners of the abovementioned general commercial partnership and to make all necessary applications. Since Mrs. Margarete R[…] can transfer her company shares and her company rights to her son Hansjörg R[…] at any time pursuant to item VI of the restitution settlement of 5 May 1948 between Mrs. Margarete R[…] and the party obliged to restitute, Mr. Hansjörg R[…] joins this undertaking which has been assumed by Mrs. Margarete R[…]"

76	Also on 20 May 1949, in a partial decision by the Restitution Commission established with the Regional Court for Civil Matters Vienna regarding the restitution matter 50 Rk 588/48 the following was recorded:

77	"1. The adverse parties Dr. Viktor O[…] and Herbert V[…] are jointly and severally responsible for the restitution of 7/8th of the enterprise operated under the name Gustav & Wilhelm H[…] Company also comprising the properties belonging to the company and the company name, namely in a ratio of two-eighths for the claimants Dr. Hans H[…], Charles H[…] and Stephan H[…] and one-eighth for the claimant Otto W[…] This is to happen with immediate effect and sanctioned with enforcement upon noncompliance. In case of enforcement, the aforementioned adverse parties are further responsible without delay for making any statements which are necessary for the re-registration of the claimants in the trade register of the Commercial Court Vienna and for the deletion of the adverse parties from this register.

78	2. The authorities of the claimants regarding the enterprise which is to be restituted are limited to those of a public administrator in order to secure the counterclaims of the adverse parties.

79	3. The decision on all further mutual claims shall be reserved for the continued proceedings, which shall be reopened upon request by a party after this partial decision has become final and binding."

80	On 4 June 1949, Hansjörg R. was registered as a new partner in the trade register with his mother's company shares, which she had previously transferred to him. At the same time Margarete R. left the company.

81	On 9 June 1949, Otto W. concluded a settlement regarding the restitution matter 50 Rk 588/48. In the settlement it was agreed that Viktor O. and Herbert V. transfer to Otto W "from their shares 11.25 % of the entire business" on the condition "that according to the statement of the adverse parties of 25 April 1949 the share of Mr. Franz V[…] who on his death exited the company passes over to Viktor O[…] and Herbert V[…]." In item I of the settlement the following is explained regarding the reactivated war-damage claim: "Dr.

fern angegeben sind, erreichen fast 1 Million. [...] Ordnungshalber sei ausdrücklich erklärt, daß Frau R[...] den Ariseuren nicht gleichgestellt wird; sie gehört selbst zu den politisch Geschädigten, ist die Schwester von Dr. Hans H[...] und Cousine des Herrn Kommerzialrat Stephan H[...] und Charles H[...] und hat die ungerechtfertigten Entnahmen vermutlich nur getätigt, um für sich zu retten, was zu retten war."

In ihrer Gegenäußerung weist Margarete R. diese Vorwürfe als „unrichtig" entschieden zurück. Es ginge den Antragstellern darum, sich für die bevorstehenden Rückstellungsverhandlungen eine günstige Ausgangsposition zu schaffen. Stephan H. wolle mit dem Antrag auf Bestellung zum öffentlichen Verwalter das Rückstellungsverfahren „präjudizieren" und die emigrierten H.s in den Besitz des Maschinenparks bringen, um diesen für die im Ausland errichteten Produktionsstätten verwenden zu können; so auch die Argumentation von O. in seiner Gegenäußerung.

Nach Vergleichen vom 27. April und vom 20. Mai 1949 zwischen den Antragstellern Hans, Karl und Stephan H. sowie Otto W. und den AntragsgegnerInnen Viktor O., Herbert V., Verlassenschaft nach Franz V. und Margarete R. zogen sämtliche Antragsteller den Rückstellungsantrag gegen Margarete R. zurück. Margarete R. verpflichtete sich im Gegenzug gegenüber den Antragstellern,

„einzelne oder alle der Antragsteller nach Maßgabe eines rechtkräftigen Erkenntnisses der Rückstellungskommission oder eines Rückstellungsvergleiches in die Gesellschaft G. & W. H. als öffentliche Gesellschafter aufzunehmen und jederzeit gegenüber dem Handelsregister alle zur Eintragung der Antragsteller als offene Handelsgesellschafter der oben genannten OHG, notwendigen Eintragungen abzugeben und alle notwendigen Eingaben mitzufertigen. Da gemäß Punkt VI. des Rückstellungsvergleiches der Frau Margarete R[...] mit dem Rückstellungspflichtigen vom 5. Mai 1948 vorgesehen ist, dass Frau Margarete R[...] jederzeit ihre Gesellschaftsanteile und Gesellschaftsrechte an ihren Sohn Hansjörg R[...] übertragen kann, so tritt Herr Hansjörg R[...] dieser von Frau Margarete R[...] übernommenen Verpflichtung bei."

Ebenfalls am 20. Mai 1949 wurde in einem Teilerkenntnis der beim LGfZRS Wien eingerichteten Rückstellungskommission betreffend die Rückstellungssache 50 Rk 588/48 festgehalten:

„1. Die Antragsgegner Dr. Viktor O[...] und Herbert V[...] sind zur ungeteilten Hand schuldig, den Antragsstellern 7/8 des unter der Firma Gustav & Wilhelm H[...] betriebenen Unternehmens einschließlich der dazugehörigen Realitäten und des Firmenwortlautes zurückzustellen u.zw. im Verhältnisse von je 2/8 für die Antragsteller Dr. Hans H[...], Charles H[...] und Stephan H[...] und 1/8 für den Antragsteller Otto W[...], dies unverzüglich bei sonstiger Exekution. Die vorangenannten Antragsgegner sind weiters schuldig, sofort bei Exekution alle Erklärungen abzugeben, die zur Wiedereintragung der Antragsteller im Firmenregister des Handelsgerichtes (HG) Wien und zur Löschung der Antragsgegner aus diesem Register erforderlich sind.
2. Die Befugnisse der Antragsteller in Bezug auf das rückzustellende Unternehmen werden zur Sicherung der Gegenansprüche der Antragsgegner auf die eines öffentlichen Verwalters eingeschränkt.
3. Die Entscheidung über alle weiteren gegenseitigen Ansprüche wird dem fortgesetzten Verfahren vorbehalten, das nach Rechtskraft dieses Teilerkenntnisses über Parteienantrag aufgenommen werden wird."

Am 4. Juni 1949 wurde Hansjörg R. mit den Gesellschaftsanteilen seiner Mutter, die sie zuvor ihm übertragen hatte, als neuer Gesellschafter ins Handelsregister eingetragen. Gleichzeitig trat Margarete R. aus der Gesellschaft aus.

W[…] pays half of 12.5 %, i. e. 6.25 %, of the entire war damage amounting to 2,094,111.25 Schilling, i.e. 130,881.95 Schilling […]."

82   In a settlement dated 20 February 1950 between the claimants Hans, Stephan and Karl H. and the adverse parties Viktor O. and Herbert V., it was agreed that Viktor O. and Herbert V. transfer to the claimants "from their company shares 67.5 % of the entire business".

"This builds on the assumption that according to the statement by the adverse parties of 25 April 1949, the share of Mr. Franz V[…] who on his death exited the company passes over to Dr. Viktor O[…] and Herbert V[…] Hence, as a final result each of the Messrs H[…] shall own 22.5 % of the total assets."

In item II of the settlement, it was determined that from the profit made between 1 January 1948 and 28 August 1948 a share of only 500,000 Schilling accrues to Mr. H. According to the agreement reached in item II, the Messrs H. were liable for half of the 75 % of the reactivated war-damage claim – hence for 37.5 % – of the entire war damage. Viktor O. and Herbert and Franz V. were also liable for 37.5 %.

83   Stephan, Karl and Hans H. as well as Otto W. were recorded in the trade register as partners after all previous partners had concluded restitution settlements regarding their company shares.

84   Otto W. filed an action against Hansjörg R. at the Regional Court for Civil Matters in Vienna with matter number 40 Cg 177/49 for the surrender of his one-eighth share. However, Hansjörg R., as partner, refused to give his signature which was necessary to record Otto W. in the trade register and filed an appeal with the Commercial Court Vienna against the decision of 22 August 1950 by the Commercial Court Vienna, regarding the registration of Otto W. as a partner of the Gustav & Wilhelm H. Company. The Higher Regional Court for Civil Matters in Vienna granted the appeal. The appeal filed against it by Otto W. was rejected on 29 November 1950 by the Supreme Court. Hence, Otto W. was not registered as a public partner in the trade register.

85   In 1953 Viktor O. retired as a partner from the Gustav & Wilhelm H. Company. Herbert V. remained a partner of the company until his death in 1963.

b) History of the Property

86   Gustav H. purchased the properties EZ X1–X8, KG Inzersdorf-Stadt from countess A. pursuant to the purchase contract dated 19 June 1913. These had a total area of 1,476 square fathoms and the total purchase price amounted to 147,000 Crowns. On 20 June 1913, the ownership title to the concerned properties was recorded in the land register for Gustav H. Gustav H. died on 7 September 1937 without leaving a last will and testament. With the certificate of inheritance of 16 May 1939, each of Gustav H.'s three children, Margarete R. née H., Dr. Hans H. and Marianne W., née H., inherited one-third of the estate; including the properties EZ X1–X8. However, the devolution took place after Austria's *Anschluss* to National Socialist Germany and – since all heirs to the estate were considered Jews according to the Nuremberg Laws – in accordance with the new special legal provisions for Jews.

87   In 1940, the value of the properties amounted to 58,040 Reichsmark. With the purchase contract dated 2 July 1940 including the supplement of 28 August 1941, the aryanized Gustav & Wilhelm H. Company acquired the properties EZ X1–X8 with a total area of 5309 m^2 for 58,399 Reichsmark (11 Reichsmark/m^2) from the owners Margarete R. (represented by the lawyer Karl Bü.), the estate of Marianne W. (represented by the legal advisor

Am 9. Juni 1949 schloss Otto W. in der Rückstellungssache 50 Rk 588/48 einen Vergleich. Darin wurde vereinbart, dass Viktor O. und Herbert V. „von ihren Geschäftsanteilen 11,25% des Gesamtunternehmens" an Otto W. übertragen, wobei vorausgesetzt wurde, „dass nach der Erklärung der Rückstellungsgegner vom 25.4.1949 der Geschäftsanteil des durch Tod ausgeschiedenen Herrn Franz V[...] den Herren Viktor O[...] und Herbert V[...] zugewachsen ist." Von der reaktivierten Kriegssachschadensforderung führt der Vergleich in Punkt I aus, „trägt Herr Dr. W[...] die Hälfte von 12,5%, demnach 6,25% des gesamten Kriegssachschadens von S 2,094.111,25, demnach S 130.881,95 [...]." 81

In einem Vergleich zwischen Hans, Stephan und Karl H. auf Seiten der Antragsteller und Viktor O. und Herbert V. auf Seiten der Antragsgegner vom 20. Februar 1950 wurde vereinbart, dass Viktor O. und Herbert V. „von ihren Geschäftsanteilen 67,5 % des Gesamtunternehmens" an die Antragsteller übertragen. 82

„Dabei wird vorausgesetzt, dass nach der Erklärung der Rückstellungsgegner vom 25.IV.1949 der Geschäftsanteil des durch Tod ausgeschiedenen Herrn Franz V[...] den Herren Dr. Viktor O[...] und Herbert V[...] zugewachsen ist. Als Endergebnis muss daher jeder der Herren H[...]. 22.5% des Gesamtvermögens besitzen."

In Punkt II des Vergleichs wurde festgelegt, dass von den Gewinnen der Zeit vom 1. Januar 1948 bis 28. August 1948 den Herrn H. nur ein Gewinnanteil von 500.000,– Schilling zufalle. Von der reaktivierten Kriegssachschadensforderung trugen laut Vereinbarung in Punkt III des Vergleichs die Herren H. zusammen die Hälfte von 75 %, demnach 37,5 % des gesamten Kriegssachschadens und die Viktor O. und Herbert und Franz V. tragen ebenfalls 37,5 %.

Nachdem alle früheren GesellschafterInnen somit Rückstellungsvergleiche hinsichtlich ihrer Firmenanteile abgeschlossen hatten, wurden Stephan, Karl und Hans H. sowie Otto W. als Gesellschafter ins Handelsregister eingetragen. 83

Otto W. brachte beim LGfZRS Wien zur Geschäftszahl 40 Cg 177/49 eine Klage gegen Hansjörg R. auf Herausgabe seines Achtel-Gesellschaftsanteils ein. Hansjörg R. verweigerte als Gesellschafter jedoch seine Unterschrift, die zur Eintragung von Otto W. ins Handelsregister notwendig war, und brachte beim Handelsgericht Wien einen Rekurs gegen den Beschluss des Handelsgerichts Wien vom 22. August 1950 ein, betreffend die Eintragung von Otto W. als Gesellschafter der Firma Gustav & Wilhelm H. Dem Rekurs wurde vom Oberlandesgericht (OLG) Wien Folge gegeben, der dagegen erhobene Revisionsrekurs von Otto W. wurde vom Obersten Gerichtshof (OGH) am 29. November 1950 abgewiesen. Otto W. wurde daher nicht als öffentlicher Gesellschafter ins Handelsregister aufgenommen. 84

1953 schied Viktor O. als Gesellschafter aus der Firma Gustav & Wilhelm H. aus. Herbert V. blieb bis zu seinem Tod im Jahr 1963 Gesellschafter der Firma. 85

b) Geschichte der Liegenschaft

Mit Kaufvertrag vom 19. Juni 1913 kaufte Gustav H. die Liegenschaften EZ X1–X8, KG Inzersdorf-Stadt mit insgesamt 1476 Quadratklaftern von Gräfin A. zu einem Gesamtkaufpreis von 147.000 Kronen. Das Eigentumsrecht für die betreffenden Liegenschaften wurde am 20. Juni 1913 für Gustav H. grundbücherlich einverleibt. Gustav H. starb am 7. September 1937, ohne einen letzten Willen zu hinterlassen. Mit der Einantwortungsurkunde vom 16. Mai 1939 wurde den drei Kindern von Gustav H., Margarete R., geb. H., Dr. Hans H. und Marianne W., geb. H., der Nachlass – darunter die Liegen- 86

Michael St.) and Hans H. (represented by the lawyer Erwin L.). The purchase price was supposed to be paid immediately in cash to each of the representatives after the incorporation into the land register, each receiving one-third, i. e. 19,466.33 Reichsmark. Item VI of the contract stipulated that the property fee (transfer fee) was to be paid by the purchaser and the vendors; each paying half. The properties were not encumbered in any way. In item VII, Margarete R. approved the purchase contract under the following condition:

88 "The signatories to the contract acknowledge in a legally binding manner that Mrs. Margarete R[…] grants her approval of the present purchase contract solely under the condition that the other two vendors […] immediately after receiving the purchase price reimburse Mrs. R[…] for the fees for the processing and settlement of the estate which they are liable for and which have meanwhile been advanced by Margarete R[…] Accordingly, upon receipt of the purchase price, the estate of Marianne W[…] and Dr. Hans H[…] undertake to each immediately pay Mrs. Margarete R[…]'s representative, Dr. Karl Bü[…], 16,658.29 Reichsmark which represents each person's one third share of the fees for the processing and settlement of the estate paid by Mrs. Margarete R[…] This amounts to a total of 49,974.86 Reichsmark."

Item XII stipulated that the purchase contract subject to the approval of the Property Transaction Office is considered concluded. In item XIII it was recorded that the vendors are "non-Aryan" and the purchasers "Aryan".

89 On 8 September 1939, the purchase contract was approved by the Property Transaction Office under the following conditions:

"The purchase price was fixed at 58,000 Reichsmark […]. The purchase price can be offset such that the encumbrances which have been registered in the land register until the time of the incorporation of the ownership title of the purchaser (the purchasers) can be assumed and paid. The non-recorded and unpaid public taxes of the vendor (capital gains tax) and the interest debts mentioned in supplement 1 can also be paid by offsetting against the purchase price. The costs, expenses and commissions associated with the conclusion and implementation of the abovementioned purchase contract can – as long as they are to be covered by the purchase price according to agreement – also be disbursed. Further, upon presentation of the invoices the following payments can be paid for the benefit of the vendor directly to the eligible parties for the purpose of emigration: shipping charges for the relocation of property, expenses for the payment of train tickets, boat and airline tickets, as well as the entry visa. The balance of the purchase price […] is to be paid into an account in the name of the vendor, which is frozen in accordance with para. 59 f. of the *Devisengesetz* ("Foreign Exchange Law") and designated as "proceeds from de-jewification". This account is to be opened with a foreign exchange bank in the Ostmark and is to be accessed only with the approval of the *Devisenstelle* ("Foreign Exchange Board") Vienna, department for supervision. The use of monies, which have not been paid into the abovementioned account, is to be accounted for in detail through original receipts to the Foreign Exchange Board Vienna, department for supervision, within 14 days."

90 Further, in supplement 1 the vendor was instructed by the Property Transaction Office "to pay within four weeks from the day of receipt of this approval an amount of 400 Reichsmark […] as de-jewification fee to the postal bank account no. 6526, *Österreichische Kontrollbank für Industrie und Handel*, department C."

91 On 28 August 1941, in an addendum to the purchase contract, Margarete R. explained that she will not exercise her rights stipulated in the condition recorded in item VII

schaften EZ X1–X8 – zu je einem Drittel eingeantwortet. Die Einantwortung fand allerdings nach dem „Anschluss" Österreichs an das nationalsozialistische Deutschland und – da alle in den Nachlass eingeantworteten ErbInnen nach den Nürnberger Gesetzen als Juden galten – unter den neuen gesetzlichen Sonderbestimmungen für Juden statt.

Der Wert der Liegenschaften betrug im Jahr 1940 58.040,– Reichsmark. Mit Kaufvertrag vom 2. Juli 1940 samt Nachtrag vom 28. August 1941 erwarb die arisierte Firma Gustav & Wilhelm H. die Liegenschaften EZ X1–X8 im Ausmaß von insgesamt 5.309 m² von den EigentümerInnen Margarete R. (vertreten durch RA Karl Bü.), Verlassenschaft nach Marianne W. (vertreten durch Konsulent Michael St.) und Hans H. (vertreten durch RA Erwin L.) zu einem Preis von 58.399,– Reichsmark (11,– Reichsmark /m²). Der Kaufpreis sollte nach durchgeführter grundbücherlicher Eintragung sofort in bar zu je einem Drittel, somit 19.466,33 Reichsmark an die Vertreter zu gleichen Teilen ausbezahlt werden. In Punkt VI des Vertrages wurde festgehalten, dass die Liegenschaftsgebühr (Übertragungsgebühr) von der Käuferin und den Verkäufern je zur Hälfte getragen werden sollte. Auf den Liegenschaften hafteten keinerlei Lasten. In Punkt VII erteilte Margarete R. dem Kaufvertrag nur unter folgender Bedingung ihre Zustimmung: 87

„Die vertragsschließenden Teile nehmen rechtsverbindlich zur Kenntnis, dass Frau Margarete R[…] dem gegenständlichen Kaufvertrag nur unter der Bedingung ihre Zustimmung erteilt, dass die beiden anderen Verkäufer […] sofort nach Erhalt des Kaufpreises die auf sie entfallenen, unterdessen von Margarete R[...] für sie ausgelegten Verlassenschaftsgebühren an Frau R[…] ersetzen. Dementsprechend verpflichten sich die Verlassenschaft nach Frau Marianne W.[…] und Herr Dr. Hans H[…] an Frau Margarete R[…] sofort nach Erhalt des Kaufpreises je RM 16.658,29 […], das ist je ein Drittel der von Frau Margarete R[   ] entrichteten Verlassenschaftsgebühren per zusammen RM 49.974,86, zu Handen ihres Vertreters Dr. Karl Bü[...], zu bezahlen." 88

Unter Punkt XII wurde festgehalten, dass der Kaufvertrag vorbehaltlich der Genehmigung der VVSt als abgeschlossen gilt, und in Punkt XIII wurde festgehalten, dass die VerkäuferInnen „Nichtarier" und die Käufer „Arier" sind.

Am 8. September 1939 wurde der Kaufvertrag von der VVSt mit folgenden Bedingungen genehmigt: 89

„Der Kaufpreis wurde mit RM 58.000,– […] festgesetzt. In Anrechnung auf den Kaufpreis können die bis zum Zeitpunkt der Einverleibung des Eigentumsrechtes des Käufers (der Käufer) eingetragenen bücherlichen Lasten übernommen und bezahlt werden. Ebenso können in Anrechnung auf den Kaufpreis die nicht einverleibten rückständigen öffentlichen Abgaben des Veräußerers (Wertzuwachsabgabe) und die in der Beilage 1 angeführten Zinsrückstände bezahlt werden. Die mit Abschluss und Durchführung des oben angeführten Kaufvertrages verbundenen Kosten, Spesen und Provisionen können, soweit sie laut Vereinbarung aus dem Kaufpreis zu decken sind, gleichfalls ausbezahlt werden. Weiters können unmittelbar an die Forderungsberechtigten, zugunsten des Verkäufers, zum Zwecke der Auswanderung gegen Vorlage der Rechnungen, folgende Zahlungen geleistet werden: Speditionskosten für die Versendung des Umzugsgutes, Kosten für Bezahlung der Eisenbahnfahrkarten, Schiffs- und Flugkarten, sowie die Einreisevisa. Der Restkaufpreis ist […] auf ein den Namen des Verkäufers lautendes, gemäß § 59 ff Devisengesetz gesperrtes, mit der Bezeichnung „Entjudungserlös" versehenes Konto bei einer in der Ostmark geführten Devisenbank zu bezahlen, über welches nur mit Genehmigung der Devisenstelle Wien, Überwachungsabteilung, verfügt werden darf. Die Verwendung der nicht auf das oben angeführte Konto erlegten

"because my advanced fees for the processing and settlement of the estate amounting to 16,658.29 Reichsmark for each seem to be secured due to the release certificate of the tax office Moabit dated 21 June 1941 regarding the co-ownership of Dr. Hans H[...], and due to the ruling by the Foreign Exchange Board Vienna of 23 July 1941 also regarding the co-ownership of the estate of Marianne W[...]."

92 On 14 August 1939, the *Kreiswirtschaftsamt* ("District Trade Office") of the National Socialist Party gave its approval to the Property Transaction Office regarding the purchase of the property by the Gustav & Wilhelm H. Company and stated: "The District Trade Office has no objections to the acquisition of the parcels EZ [X1, X2, X3, X4, X5, X6, X7, X8], all KG Inzersdorf (Margarete R[...]) by the G. & W. H[...] Company, Vienna 10., B[...]-platz 3/5." On 28 May 1941 attorney-at-law L., after making an enquiry regarding this matter, received confirmation from the district administration for the 10th district that any of the property parcels situated in EZ X1–X8 were no longer to be used for agricultural purposes and that they are to be regarded as construction land.

93 On 18 June 1940 Margarete R. and her "Aryan" husband Karl Theodor R., represented by the lawyer Dr. Hö., applied to the Property Transaction Office for the approval of a donation which would allow further property shares inherited by Margarete R. from the estate of Gustav H. to be transferred to her daughter Doris and her son Hansjörg R. who in accordance with the Nuremberg Laws were considered as so called "first-degree half-castes".

94 Among other things, the one-third share of the properties EZ X1–X8, KG Inzersdorf-Stadt was also cited in the donation contract. On 3 July 1940, Hö. withdrew the application for the approval of the donation regarding these property shares after the Property Transaction Office notified the lawyer Hö. that this property "pursuant to the approval of 8 September 1939 had already been completely sold to the Aryan G. & W. H[...] Company for a purchase price of 58,000."

95 On 2 July 1940, the tax office Alsergrund issued a so-called tax clearance certificate to Margarete R., in which the following was stated:

96 "There is no concern with respect to the tax status of the Jew Margarete Sara R[...] and her Aryan husband Karl Theodor R[...] Currently, there is no obstacle to a donation by the Jew Margarete Sara R[...] to her children. A Reich Flight Tax for the mentioned Jew is not applicable at the moment as she herself has made a statement to the tax office Innere Stadt Ost that she has no intention of leaving the country."[3]

97 Regarding the recipients of the donation, Hansjörg and Doris R., the National Socialist Party regional administration in Vienna issued a notice of political harmlessness. The letter dated 29 August 1940 to the Property Transaction Office contains the following: "Politically, nothing of concern has become known about the above mentioned person."

98 On 19 October 1940, the lawyer Hö. repeated his application to the Property Transaction Office for the approval of the donation contract. The revised contract was signed by Hansjörg R. and Theodor Karl R. who was the father of Doris, who at that time was still a minor. The Property Transaction Office approved the contract on 22 October and imposed a two-year ban on the sale of the properties.

---

[3] Rectification at the time of going to press: The first two sentences of this quotation should read: "There is no concern with respect to the tax status of the Jew Margarete Sara and her Aryan husband Karl Theodor R[...]. Therefore, there is no obstacle to a donation by the Jew Margarete Sara R[...] to her children."

Gelder ist binnen 14 Tagen bei der Devisenstelle Wien, Überwachungsabteilung, im Einzelnen durch Originalbelege nachzuweisen."

In der Beilage 1 wurde dem Käufer von der VVSt weiters aufgetragen, „binnen vier Wochen vom Tage des Erhalts dieser Genehmigung, als Entjudungsauflage einen Betrag vom RM 400,– [...] auf das Postsparkassenkonto Nr. 6526, Österreichische Kontrollbank für Industrie und Handel, Abteilung C, Wien, zur Einzahlung zu bringen."

In einem Nachtrag zum Kaufvertrag erklärte Margarete R. am 28. August 1941, dass sie von der in Punkt VII festgehaltenen Bedingung Abstand nimmt,

„weil durch den Freigabeschein des Finanzamtes Moabit vom 21.6.1941 hinsichtlich des Miteigentümers Dr. Hans H[...] und durch den Bescheid der Devisenstelle Wien vom 23. Juli 1941 auch hinsichtlich der Miteigentümerin Verlassenschaft nach Marianne W[...]. meine Ansprüche für verauslagte Verlassenschaftsgebühren im Betrage von je RM 16.658.29 gesichert erscheinen."

Bereits am 14. August 1939 hatte das Kreiswirtschaftsamt der NSDAP hinsichtlich des Ankaufs der Liegenschaft durch die Firma Gustav & Wilhelm H. an die VVSt ihre Einwilligung gegeben und meinte: „Das Kreiswirtschaftsamt hat gegen die Erwerbung der Parzellen EZ [X1, X2, X3, X4, X5, X6, X7, X8], sämtl. KG Inzersdorf (Margarete R[...]) durch die Firma G. & W. H[...], Wien 10., B[...]-platz 3/5 nichts einzuwenden." Am 28. Mai 1941 erhielt RA L. auf eine entsprechende Anfrage hin die Bestätigung von der Bezirksverwaltung für den 10. Bezirk, dass die in den EZ X1–X8 liegenden Grundstücke allesamt landwirtschaftlich nicht mehr genutzt werden und als Bauplätze anzusehen sind.

Am 18. Juni 1940 hatten Margarete R. und ihr „arischer" Ehemann, Karl Theodor R., vertreten durch RA Dr. Hö., an die VVSt einen Antrag auf Genehmigung einer Schenkung gestellt. Damit sollten weitere, aus der Verlassenschaft nach Gustav H. der Margarete R. zugekommene Liegenschaftsanteile an ihre Tochter Doris und ihren Sohn Hansjörg übertragen werden, die nach den Nürnberger Rassegesetzen als so genannte „Mischlinge Ersten Grades" galten.

In dem Schenkungsvertrag war unter anderem auch der Drittelanteil an den Liegenschaften EZ X1–X8, KG Inzersdorf-Stadt aufgeführt. Nach einem Hinweis der VVSt an RA Hö., dass diese Liegenschaft „bereits mit Genehmigung vom 8.9.1939 zur Gänze an die arische Firma G. &. W. H[...] zu einem Kaufpreis von 58.000,– verkauft wurde", zog Hö. am 3. Juli 1940 den Antrag auf Genehmigung der Schenkung hinsichtlich dieser Liegenschaftsanteile zurück.

Am 2. Juli 1940 stellte das Finanzamt Alsergrund eine so genannte steuerliche Unbedenklichkeitsbescheinigung für Margarete R. aus. Darin hieß es:

„Gegen die Jüdin Margarete Sara R[...] und deren arischen Gatten Karl Theodor R[...] bestehen h.a. keine steuerl. Bedenken. Einer Schenkung der Jüdin Margarete Sara R[...] an ihre Kinder steht derzeit h.a. nichts im Wege. Eine Reichsfluchtsteuer für die genannte Jüdin ist derzt. nicht gegeben, da dieselbe im Finanzamt Innere Stadt Ost eine Erklärung abgegeben hat, daß sie nicht auszureisen gedenkt."[3]

---

[3] Berichtigung zum Zeitpunkt der Drucklegung: Die ersten beiden Sätze dieses Zitats lauten korrekt: „Gegen die Jüdin Margarete Sara und deren arischen Gatten Karl Theodor R[...] bestehen h.a. keine steuerl. Bedenken. Einer Schenkung der Jüdin Margarete Sara R[...] an ihre Kinder steht daher h.a. nichts im Wege."

99 On 3 February 1941, the entire assets of Dr. Hans H., who at that point in time had already emigrated to England, were confiscated by the Secret State Police, central office Vienna, on the basis of a confiscation order for the benefit of the German Reich. Hans H. had been arrested before his emigration because he had refused to sell the Gustav & Wilhelm H. Company. He was only released after agreeing to the sale of the company. He was also officially permitted to leave the country, however, procedures were initiated to have his citizenship withdrawn. Due to these pending procedures against Hans H., the tax office Moabit-West in Berlin was responsible for the enforcement of the seizure and later confiscation of the property of the emigrated Hans H. for the benefit of the German Reich. Since the citizenship procedures against Hans H. were initiated prior to the still pending incorporation in the land register, it had become necessary for the tax office Moabit-West to release Hans H.'s property shares. With the decision of 21 June 1941, the tax office Moabit-West approved the release of the one-third share of the concerned properties of Hans H. which had been applied for by the attorney-at-law L., who functioned as the representative of the Gustav & Wilhelm H. Company. Further, the confiscation order regarding this one-third share was repealed and it was ordered that one-third of the entire purchase price, hence 16,658.29 Reichsmark, was to be paid to Margarete R. for the advanced fees for the processing and settlement of the estate. The 2,675.04 Reichsmark which remained from the purchase price after the deduction of the fees for the processing and settlement of the estate were to be paid to the frozen emigration-account, no. 13652.

100 On 29 July 1943, Viktor O. paid the Gustav & Wilhelm H. Company 100,000 Reichsmark for the properties EZ X1–X8 (5,309 m^2) together with four further properties, which at that point in time were owned by the Gustav & Wilhelm H. Company. In item X of the contract, vendor and purchaser stated that no Jews were involved in this legal transaction.

101 After the end of the war, Viktor O. registered the properties as seized assets and stated on the registration form that this registration was being made merely for "precautionary" reasons, as the properties had not been seized. In a supplement to item 2 (prior owners) O. explained this fact as follows:

102 "The legal reason for the sale of this property parcel lay in the fact that inheritance tax was to be paid for the estate of the deceased Mr. Gustav H[…], which the co-heiress of Mr. Gustav H[…], Mrs. Margarete R[…] had paid in advance. She wanted to have the advanced cash returned. According to my knowledge, this case did not involve a seizure."

103 On 26 October 1949, Hans H. withdrew the claim for restitution of his shares of the concerned properties and concluded a settlement in return for him waiving his claim. The claim had been submitted to the Restitution Commission established with the Regional Court for Civil Matters Vienna under number 60 Rk 1019/48. As was recorded in the settlement, this took place "in consideration of the fact that inheritance tax for the deceased Gustav H[…] […] was paid from the proceeds of the sale received at the time. Dr. Hans H[…] had a one-third share of this inheritance […]".

104 On 26 October 1949, the Gustav & Wilhelm H. Company bought the properties EZ X1–X8 (5,309 m^2) back from O. for a total price of 150,000 Schilling. The partner Hansjörg R., who had in the meantime become an authorized signatory, signed the contract. At the same time, O. issued a receipt for the purchase price and declared by affidavit that "he does not belong to the persons mentioned in para. 17 (2) and (3) of the *Verbotsgesetz* ("Prohibition Law") of 1947 (National Socialist Law)." The legal transaction could be concluded by Hansjörg R. due to the fact that until then he had worked in the company as an

Hinsichtlich der GeschenknehmerInnen Hansjörg und Doris R. stellte die NSDAP- 97
Gauleitung in Wien die politische Unbedenklichkeit aus. In dem Schreiben vom 29. August 1940 an die VVSt heißt es dazu: „Gegen Obengenannte ist in politischer Hinsicht nichts Gegenteiliges bekannt geworden."

Am 19. Oktober 1940 wiederholte RA Hö. seinen Antrag auf Genehmigung des Schen- 98
kungsvertrages bei der VVSt. Der überarbeitete Vertrag wurde Theodor Karl R., dem Vater von der zu diesem Zeitpunkt noch Minderjährigen Doris und Hansjörg R. unterzeichnet. Die VVSt genehmigte den Vertrag am 22. Oktober und belegte die Liegenschaften mit einem zweijährigen Veräußerungsverbot.

Am 3. Februar 1941 wurde per Beschlagnahmeverfügung das gesamte stehende und 99
liegende Vermögen des zu diesem Zeitpunkt bereits nach England emigrierten Dr. Hans H. von der Geheimen Staatspolizei, Staatspolizeileitstelle Wien, zugunsten des Deutschen Reiches eingezogen. Vor seiner Emigration war Hans H. inhaftiert worden, weil er sich geweigert hatte, die Firma Gustav & Wilhelm H. zu verkaufen. Erst nach erfolgter Zustimmung zum Verkauf der Firma wurde er freigelassen, seine Ausreise bewilligt, jedoch ein Ausbürgerungsverfahren gegen ihn eingeleitet. Für die Durchführung der Beschlagnahme und spätere Einziehung des Vermögens des emigrierten Hans H. zugunsten des Deutschen Reiches war wegen des gegen Hans H. anhängigen Ausbürgerungsverfahrens das Finanzamt Moabit-West in Berlin zuständig. Da das Ausbürgerungsverfahren gegen Hans H. vor der noch ausständigen grundbücherlichen Eintragung eingeleitet wurde, war die Freigabe der Liegenschaftsanteile von Hans H. durch das Finanzamt Moabit-West notwendig geworden. Mit Bescheid vom 21. Juni 1941 genehmigte das Finanzamt Moabit-West die von RA L. als Vertreter der Firma Gustav & Wilhelm H. beantragte Freigabe des Drittelanteils an den betreffenden Liegenschaften von Hans H., hob die Beschlagnahmeverfügung hinsichtlich dieses Drittelanteils auf und verfügte, dass von dem Drittelanteil des Gesamtkaufpreises, und zwar 16.658,29 Reichsmark an Frau Margarete R. für verauslagte Verlassenschaftsgebühren abzuführen waren. Die nach Abzug der Verlassenschaftsgebühr aus dem Kaufpreis verbleibenden 2.675,04 Reichsmark waren auf das Auswanderungssperrkonto Nr. 13652 einzuzahlen.

Am 29. Juli 1943 kaufte Viktor O. die Liegenschaften EZ X1-X8 (5.309 m^2) gemein- 100
sam mit vier weiteren Liegenschaften, die zu diesem Zeitpunkt im Eigentum der Firma Gustav & Wilhelm H. standen, von der Firma Gustav & Wilhelm H. zu einem Gesamtkaufpreis von 100.000,– Reichsmark. Unter Punkt X des Vertrages erklärten Verkäufer und Käufer, dass an diesem Rechtsgeschäft keine Juden beteiligt seien.

Nach Kriegsende meldete Viktor O. die Liegenschaften EZ X1–X8 als entzogenes Ver- 101
mögen an und hielt auf dem Anmeldeformular fest, dass diese Anmeldung lediglich „vorsorglich" erfolge, da ein Entzug der Liegenschaften nicht vorliege. In einer Beilage zu Punkt 2 (frühere Eigentümer) begründete O. dies folgendermaßen:

„Der Rechtsgrund dieses Grundstückverkaufs war darin gelegen, dass für den Nach- 102
lass nach dem verstorbenen Herrn Gustav H[…] Erbschaftssteuern zu bezahlen waren, welche die Miterbin des Herrn Gustav H[…], Frau Margarete R[…], vorgestreckt hatte und auf diese Weise das ausgelegte Bargeld zurückbekommen wollte. Um eine Entziehung hat es sich nach meiner Kenntnis in diesem Falle nicht gehandelt."

Am 26. Oktober 1949 zog Hans H. den bei der Rückstellungskommission beim 103
LGfZRS Wien unter 60 Rk 1019/48 eingebrachten Antrag auf Rückstellung seiner Anteile an den betreffenden Liegenschaften mit einem Vergleich unter Verzicht auf seinen Anspruch zurück. Dies geschah, wie im Vergleich festgehalten wurde, „in Anbetracht dessen, dass aus dem seinerzeit empfangenen Kaufpreis Erbschaftssteuern nach dem verstorbe-

authorized signatory and had become a partner on 4 June 1949 through his mother Margarete's shares (12.5 %) and was solely authorized to sign.

105 Otto W., who had inherited the estate of the deceased Marianne W. with his two sons Thomas W. and Martin W. also submitted a claim for restitution of a one-third share of the concerned property. The claim was directed against Viktor O. and was submitted to the Restitution Commission established with the Regional Court for Civil Law Matters Vienna and was given reference number 60 Rk 432/47. On 18 April 1950, in the same way as Hans H. and with the same expected outcome, the claimants waived their claims to the property in a settlement. In a partial decision by the Restitution Commission of 24 April 1950, Viktor O.'s obligation to restitute was pronounced. On 26 April 1950, in a letter to the municipal district authorities for the 10th district, Dr. Paul Viktor Win., the attorney of Otto, Thomas and Martin W. stated:

> "The parties in dispute have now concluded an out-of-court settlement as defined in para. 13 of the Third Restitution Act, in which the claimants waive their rights to restitution of the mentioned shares in the property. The reason for this settlement was that inheritance tax for Mr. Gustav H[…], the father-in-law of Dr. Otto W[…] and grandfather of Thomas and Martin W[…] was paid from the proceeds of the sale received at the time. The deceased wife of Dr. Otto W[…] and mother of Thomas and Martin W[…], who was the daughter of Gustav H[…], was involved in this. Through this settlement, all mutual claims were declared settled. On behalf of the claimants, I convey this information in accordance with para. 13 of the Third Restitution Act and request confirmation in accordance with para. 29 of the Third Restitution Act."

106 Pursuant to the purchase contract of 20 February and 2 March 1953 the Gustav & Wilhelm H. Company sold to the City of Vienna the properties along with six further properties (EZ X10–X15, KG Inzersdorf-Stadt) for a total of 483,050 Schilling. In the 1960s, the City of Vienna built municipal residential building estates on these and bordering properties. This resulted in mergers of register numbers and property parcels in 1965. In the years 1965/66 the register numbers EZ X1–X5 as well as X7 and X8 merged with EZ X6 and joined under property parcel number Y1/150.

107 On 17 January 2001, EZ X9 (formerly X1–X8), KG Inzersdorf-Stadt, was wholly-owned by the City of Vienna.

5. Eligibility to file Applications

108 Hansjörg R. was born on 16 January 1920 as the son of Margarete R., née H., and Ing. Karl Theodor R. Doris R. was born on 26 October 1922 as the daughter of Margarete R., née H., and Ing. Karl Theodor R. Doris R. died on 10 October 1946 in Vienna. On 22 September 1947, the District Court Innere Stadt Vienna awarded half of the estate to each of her parents, Ing. Karl and Margarete R. Margarete R. died on 2 May 1970 in Vienna. On the basis of her last will and testament of 27 October 1953, Margarete R.'s estate was devolved in its entirety to her son Ing. Hansjörg R on 14 August 1970 by the District Court Innere Stadt Vienna.

109 Hans H. died on 12 July 1987 in the USA. By way of last will and testament Hans H. divided his assets between his sons Peter H. and Mark E. H.

110 Prof. Peter H. was born on 11 January 1920 as the son of Dr. John (Hans) H. and Grete H., née Ste. Eve H. was born as the daughter of Peter H. and Christine H., née Me., on

nen Gustav H[…] […] bezahlt wurden, an welchem Erbe Herr Dr. Hans H[…] zu 1/3 interessiert war […]".

Ebenfalls am 26. Oktober 1949 kaufte die Firma Gustav & Wilhelm H. die Liegenschaften EZ X1–X8 (5.309 m^2) zu einem Gesamtpreis von 150.000,– Schilling von O. wieder zurück, wobei der inzwischen zeichnungsberechtigte Gesellschafter Hansjörg R. diesen Vertrag unterzeichnete. Gleichzeitig quittierte O. den Empfang des Kaufpreises und erklärte eidesstattlich, „nicht zu den in § 17, Abs 2 und 3 des Verbotsgesetzes 1947 (Nationalsozialistengesetz) aufgezählten Personen zu gehören." Das Rechtsgeschäft konnte durch Hansjörg R. deshalb abgeschlossen werden, weil der bis dahin als Prokurist in der Firma Tätige am 4. Juni 1949 mit den Anteilen seiner Mutter Margarete (12,5 %) Gesellschafter geworden und allein zeichnungsberechtigt war.

Otto W., dem gemeinsam mit seinen beiden Söhnen Thomas und Martin W. der Nachlass der verstorbenen Marianne W. eingeantwortet worden war, brachte unter 60 Rk 432/47 bei der beim LGfZRS Wien eingerichteten Rückstellungskommission ebenfalls einen Antrag gegen Viktor O. auf Rückstellung eines Drittelanteils an der betreffenden Liegenschaft ein. So wie Hans H. verzichteten die Antragsteller unter den selben Vorzeichen in einem Vergleich am 18. April 1950 auf ihre Ansprüche an der Liegenschaft. In einem Teilerkenntnis der Rückstellungskommission vom 24. April 1950 wurde die Rückstellungsverpflichtung von Viktor O. ausgesprochen. Am 26. April 1950 richtete der RA von Otto, Thomas und Martin W., Dr. Paul Victor Win., ein Schreiben an das magistratische Bezirksamt für den zehnten Bezirk und führte aus:

„Die Streitteile haben nunmehr im Sinne des Par. 13 des 3. Rückstellungsgesetzes einen außergerichtlichen Vergleich geschlossen, in welchem die Antragsteller auf die Rückstellung der genannten Liegenschaftsteile verzichtet haben. Der Grund dieses Vergleichs ist darin gelegen, dass aus dem seinerzeit empfangenen Kaufpreis die Erbschaftssteuern nach Herrn Gustav H[…], Schwiegervater des Herrn Dr. Otto W[…] und Grossvater des Thomas und Martin W[…], bezahlt wurden, woran die verstorbene Gattin von Herrn Dr. Otto W[…] und Mutter des Thomas und Martin W[…], welche Tochter des Herrn Gustav H[…] war, beteiligt war. Durch diesen Vergleich sind sämtliche gegenseitigen Ansprüche als ausgeglichen erklärt worden. Namens der Antragsteller teile ich dies gem. Par. 13 des 3. Rückstellungsgesetzes mit und bitte um Bestätigung gem. Par. 29 3. RstG."

Mit Kaufvertrag vom 20. Februar und 2. März 1953 verkaufte die Firma Gustav & Wilhelm H. die Liegenschaften gemeinsam mit sechs weiteren Grundstücken (EZ X10–X15, KG Inzersdorf-Stadt) zu einem Gesamtkaufpreis von 483.050,– Schilling an die Stadt Wien. Diese errichtete in den 1960er-Jahren auf diesen und den umliegenden Grundstücken städtische Wohnhausanlagen, weshalb es 1965 zu Einlagezahl- und Grundstücksvereinigungen kam. In den Jahren 1965/66 wurden die EZ X1–X5 sowie X7, X8 mit der EZ X6 zusammengeführt und zum Grundstück Y1/150 vereinigt.

Am 17. Januar 2001 stand die EZ X9 (ehemals X1–X8), KG Inzersdorf-Stadt, im Alleineigentum der Stadt Wien.

5. Antragsberechtigung

Hansjörg R. wurde am 16. Jänner 1920 als Sohn von Margarete R., geb. H., und Ing. Karl Theodor R. geboren. Doris R. wurde am 26. Oktober 1922 als Tochter von Margarete R., geb. H., und Ing. Karl Theodor R. geboren. Doris R. verstarb am 10. Oktober 1946 in Wien. Ihr Nachlass wurde am 22. September 1947 ihren Eltern Ing. Karl und Margare-

Arbitration Panel for *In Rem* Restitution – Decision No. 25/2005

20 August 1961. Joan Hu., née H., was born on 27 October 1952 as the daughter of Peter and Christine H. Anne H. was born as the daughter of Peter H. and Katrina H., née Bu., on 14 September 1944. Peter H. died on 7 November 1998 in the USA. Vivian H. was born on 10 November 1954 as the daughter of Peter H. and Christine H., née Me. Stephen C. H. was born on 14 May 1960 in Northampton as the son of Peter H. and Christine H., née Me. Joan Hu. and Stephen C. H. were appointed executors of his last will and testament.

111 Dr. Marc H. was born on 12 January 1919 as the son of Dr. John (Hans) H. and Grete H., née Ste.

112 On 12 September 1925, Martin W. was born as the son of Marianne W., née H., and Dr. Otto W. Rosemarie W. married Martin W. on 26 September 1955 and is now the widow of the deceased Martin W. Vivian de B. W. was born in Buenos Aires on 19 March 1961 as the daughter of Martin W. and Rosemarie W., née P. Philip W. was born in Vienna on 21 July 1958 as the son of Martin W. and Rosemarie W., née P.

113 Thomas W. was born in Vienna on 9 October 1921 as the son of Dr. Otto W. and Marianne W., née H. Monica W. was born in San Martin on 24 January 1954 as the daughter of Thomas W. and Ella T.

6. Consideration of Evidence

114 The established facts are based upon the presented unobjectionable documents, the public land register, the reports by the Historical Commission, archive material researched by the Arbitration Panel and the submission by the applicants.

115 The findings regarding the value of the property in the year 1940 are based on an expert valuation by the government building surveyor Ing. Richard Herrmann of 29 July 1939. He estimated the market value of the properties to be 58,040 Reichsmark according to the following breakdown:

Property parcel	Y2/51	734 m^2	at 10 Reichsmark	=	7,340 Reichsmark
Property parcel	Y2/52	622 m^2	at 10 Reichsmark	=	6,220 Reichsmark
Property parcel	Y2/53	824 m^2	at 12 Reichsmark	=	9,888 Reichsmark
Property parcel	Y2/49	712 m^2	at 8 Reichsmark	=	5,696 Reichsmark
Property parcel	Y2/50	694 m^2	at 11 Reichsmark	=	7,634 Reichsmark
Property parcel	Y1/150	662 m^2	at 12 Reichsmark	=	7,944 Reichsmark
Property parcel	Y2/48	475 m^2	at 12 Reichsmark	=	5,700 Reichsmark
Property parcel	Y2/47	586 m^2	at 13 Reichsmark	=	7,618 Reichsmark
Total		5,309 m^2		=	58,040 Reichsmark

116 This expert opinion seems plausible as three years after this seizure an unobjectionable sale took place and the price per square meter of this sale differed by merely 2 Reichsmark from the original price per square meter. This increase in price is also entirely reasonable as at that point in time the properties had already been re-designated as development land.

117 The fact that the interests of Hansjörg R. and of his mother were closer to the 'aryanizers' than to those of the applicants for restitution is based on the report by the Historical Commission (see: Felber et al., volume 10/1 at 282).

118 The established facts regarding the restitution proceedings are based upon the files of the Ordinance on the Notification of Seized Property as the restitution files had been discarded and merely a few documents – for example the copies of the settlements – were to be found.

Schiedsinstanz für Naturalrestitution – Entscheidung Nr. 25/2005

te R. je zur Hälfte durch das BG Innere Stadt Wien eingeantwortet. Margarete R. verstarb am 2. Mai 1970 in Wien. Margarete R.s Nachlass wurde am 14. August 1970 aufgrund des Testamentes vom 27. Oktober 1953 ihrem Sohn Ing. Hansjörg R. durch das BG Innere Stadt Wien zur Gänze eingeantwortet.

Hans H. verstarb am 12. Juli 1987 in den USA. Hans H. verteilte sein Vermögen mittels Testament an seine Söhne Peter H. und Marc E. H. 109

Prof. Peter H. wurde am 11. Jänner 1920 als Sohn von Dr. John (Hans) H. und Grete H., geb. Ste., geboren. Eve H. wurde als Tochter von Peter H. und Christine H., geb. Me., am 20. August 1961 geboren. Joan Hu., geb. H., wurde am 27. Oktober 1952 als Tochter von Peter und Christine H. geboren. Anne H. wurde als Tochter von Peter H. und Katrina H., geb. Bu., am 14. September 1944 geboren. Peter H. verstarb am 7. November 1998 in den USA. Vivian H. wurde am 10. November 1954 als Tochter von Peter H. und Christine H., geb. Me., geboren. Stephen C. H. wurde als Sohn von Peter H. und Christine H., geb. Me., am 14. Mai 1960 in Northampton geboren. Joan Hu. und Stephen C. H. wurden als ExekutorInnen seines letzen Willen bestimmt. 110

Dr. Marc H. wurde am 12. Jänner 1919 als Sohn von Dr. John (Hans) H. und Grete H., geb. Ste., geboren. 111

Martin W. wurde am 12. September 1925 als Sohn von Marianne W., geb. H., und Dr. Otto W. geboren. Rosemarie W. heiratete Martin W. am 26. September 1955 und ist jetzt die Witwe des vorverstorbenen Martin W. Vivian de Bruno W. wurde am 19. März 1961 als Tochter von Martin W. und Rosemarie W., geb. P., in Buenos Aires geboren. Philip W. wurde am 21. Juli 1958 als Sohn von Martin W. und Rosemarie W., geb. P., in Wien geboren. 112

Thomas W. wurde als Sohn von Dr. Otto W. und Marianne W., geb. H., am 9. Oktober 1921 in Wien geboren. Monica W. wurde als Tochter von Thomas W. und Ella T. am 24. Jänner 1954 in San Martin geboren. 113

6. Beweiswürdigung

Der festgestellte Sachverhalt gründet sich auf die vorgelegten unbedenklichen Urkunden, das offene Grundbuch, die Berichte der Historikerkommission, seitens der Schiedsinstanz recherchierte Archivalien und das Vorbringen der AntragstellerInnen. 114

Die Feststellung hinsichtlich des Wertes der Liegenschaft im Jahr 1940 gründet sich auf ein Schätzgutachten von Baurat Ing. Richard Herrmann vom 29. Juli 1939. Dieser schätzte den Verkehrswert der Liegenschaften auf 58.040,– Reichsmark. Aufgeschlüsselt auf die einzelnen Grundstücke wurde darin vorgerechnet: 115

Gst.	Y2/51	734 m^2	à RM 10,–	=	RM 7.340,–
Gst.	Y2/52	622 m^2	à RM 10,–	=	RM 6.220,–
Gst.	Y2/53	824 m^2	à RM 12,–	=	RM 9.888,–
Gst.	Y2/49	712 m^2	à RM 8,–	=	RM 5.696,–
Gst.	Y2/50	694 m^2	à RM 11,–	=	RM 7.634,–
Gst.	Y1/150	662 m^2	à RM 12,–	=	RM 7.944,–
Gst.	Y2/48	475 m^2	à RM 12,–	=	RM 5.700,–
Gst.	Y2/47	586 m^2	à RM 13,–	=	RM 7.618,–
Zusammen		5.309 m^2		=	RM 58.040,–

Dieses Gutachten scheint plausibel, da drei Jahre nach diesem Entzug ein unbedenklicher Verkauf stattfand und der Quadratmeterpreis dieses Verkaufes um lediglich 2,– Reichsmark vom ursprünglichen Quadratmeterpreis abwich. Diese Preissteigerung ist 116

7. Juridical Appraisal

a) Eligibility to File Applications

119 In accordance with Sec. 27 (2) of the GSF Law, the heirs of the originally aggrieved persons are eligible to file applications applying *mutatis mutandis* the provisions of the *Allgemeines bürgerliches Gesetzbuch* ("[Austrian] General Civil Code"). The Arbitration Panel assumes that according to the previously cited provision, the proof of the right to inherit – if no conflicting evidence is presented – is sufficient for the eligibility to file applications. All applicants are descendants of the originally aggrieved persons Margarete R., Hans H. and Marianne W. Hence, they are their legal heirs. No evidence conflicting with this right to inherit has been presented. Thus, the Arbitration Panel regards the individual applicants as eligible based on the proven right to inherit.

b) Persecution

120 In accordance with Sec. 27 of the GSF Law, persons and their heirs are entitled to file applications if one of the listed grounds for persecution – namely on political grounds, grounds of origin, religion, nationality, sexual orientation, physical or mental handicap or of accusations of so-called asociality – exists and/or they left the country in order to escape such persecution. Margarete R., née H., Dr. Hans H. and Marianne W., née H., were persecuted for racial reasons and on religious grounds as they were all considered Jews in accordance with the Nuremberg Laws of 15 September 1935.

c) Publicly-owned Property

121 In accordance with Sec. 28 (1) item 3 of the GSF Law, the term "publicly-owned property" covers properties which on 17 January 2001 were exclusively and directly owned by the Federation or by a legal person under public or private law wholly-owned, directly or indirectly, by the Federation. In accordance with Sec. 38 of the GSF Law, provinces or municipalities can provide for the Arbitration Panel to examine applications for *in rem* restitution applying *mutatis mutandis* these provisions. With the decision of the municipal council of 27 June 2001, according to Sec. 38 GSF Law the City of Vienna declared the Arbitration Panel responsible for examining the applications for restitution of publicly-owned property belonging to the City of Vienna. Hence, the Arbitration Panel is to examine applications for *in rem* restitution of properties which on 17 January 2001 were exclusively and directly owned by the municipality of Vienna or by a legal person under public or private law wholly-owned, directly or indirectly, by the municipality Vienna. The property EZ X9 (comprising the former properties EZ X1–X8), KG Inzersdorf-Stadt was owned by the City of Vienna on the cut off day.

d) Seizure on the Basis of One of the Mentioned Grounds for Persecution

122 In accordance with Sec. 28 (1) item 1 of the GSF Law, the property had to have been seized between 12 March 1938 and 9 May 1945 from the previous owner on the basis of one of the abovementioned grounds. Hence, the main question is whether the sale of the properties EZ X1–X8 was connected to the persecution of Margarete R., Marianne W. and Hans H.

123 The sale of the properties EZ X1–X8 KG Inzersdorf-Stadt was linked with the escape of the other co-owners. Margarete R.'s siblings had to leave the country in order to survive. Hence, they had to sell all of the properties owned by them. Therefore, the siblings' attempt to repay Margarete R. the inheritance tax which she had advanced by selling the

auch durchaus nachvollziehbar, da zu diesem Zeitpunkt die Liegenschaften schon in Bauland umgewidmet war.

Dass die Interessen von Hansjörg R. und seiner Mutter Margarete mehr entlang jener der „Ariseure", als denn jener der Rückstellungswerber verliefen, gründet sich auf den Bericht der Historikerkommission (vgl.: *Felber* et al., Band 10/1, 282.) 117

Die Feststellungen hinsichtlich der Rückstellungsverfahren gründen sich auf die Akten der VEAV, da die Rückstellungsakten skartiert wurden und lediglich noch einzelne Dokumente, wie die Abschriften der Vergleiche, auffindbar waren. 118

7. Rechtliche Beurteilung

a) Antragsberechtigung

Gemäß § 27 Abs 2 EF-G sind ErbInnen der ursprünglich Geschädigten in sinngemäßer Anwendung der Bestimmungen des österreichischen Allgemeinen bürgerlichen Gesetzbuches (ABGB) antragsberechtigt. Die Schiedsinstanz geht davon aus, dass nach der vorzitierten Bestimmung der Nachweis des gesetzlichen Erbrechts, wenn nicht stärkere Berufungsgründe dargetan werden, für die Antragsberechtigung ausreichend ist. Sämtliche AntragstellerInnen sind DeszendentInnen der ursprünglich Geschädigten, Margarete R., Hans H. und Marianne W., somit deren gesetzliche ErbInnen. Es wurde kein diesem Erbrecht entgegenstehender Nachweis vorgelegt. Hiermit sieht die Schiedsinstanz die Antragsberechtigung der einzelnen AntragstellerInnen aufgrund des nachgewiesenen Erbrechts als gegeben an. 119

b) Verfolgung

Gemäß § 27 EF-G sind Personen und deren ErbInnen antragsberechtigt, wenn einer der aufgelisteten Verfolgungsgründe, nämlich Verfolgung aus politischen Gründen, aus Gründen der Abstammung, Religion, Nationalität, sexuellen Orientierung, aufgrund einer körperlichen oder geistigen Behinderung oder aufgrund des Vorwurfes der sogenannten Asozialität, vorliegt bzw. diese das Land verlassen haben, um einer solchen Verfolgung zu entgehen. Margarete R., geb. H., Dr. Hans H. und Marianne W., geb. H. waren sowohl aus rassischen als auch aus religiösen Gründen verfolgt, da alle gemäß den Nürnberger Gesetzen vom 15. September 1935 als Juden galten. 120

c) Öffentliches Vermögen

Gemäß § 28 Abs 1 Z 3 EF-G umfasst der Begriff „öffentliches Vermögen" Liegenschaften, welche sich am 17. Jänner 2001 ausschließlich und unmittelbar im Eigentum des Bundes oder einer unmittelbar oder mittelbar im Alleineigentum des Bundes stehenden juristischen Person des öffentlichen oder privaten Rechts befanden. Gemäß § 38 EF-G können Länder oder Gemeinden die Schiedsinstanz zur Prüfung von Anträgen auf Naturalrestitution in sinngemäßer Anwendung dieser Bestimmungen vorsehen. Die Stadt Wien machte die Schiedsinstanz mit Gemeinderatsbeschluss vom 27. Juni 2001 zur Prüfung von Anträgen auf Naturalrestitution von öffentlichem Vermögen der Stadt Wien gemäß § 38 EF-G zuständig. Die Schiedsinstanz hat daher auch Anträge auf Naturalrestitution von Liegenschaften zu prüfen, die sich zum Stichtag 17. Jänner 2001 ausschließlich und unmittelbar im Eigentum der Gemeinde Wien oder einer unmittelbar oder mittelbar im Eigentum der Gemeinde Wien stehenden juristischen Person des öffentlichen oder privaten Rechts befanden. Die Liegenschaft EZ X9 (bestehend aus den vormaligen Liegenschaften EZ X1–X8), KG Inzersdorf-Stadt standen zum Stichtag im Eigentum der Stadt Wien. 121

properties subject of this application, took place due to the National Socialist assumption of power.

124 Margarete R. gave away all of the properties which belonged to her. Although she was protected by her marriage to her "Aryan" husband, she could under no circumstances be certain that her property would also be protected, all the more so because in May 1938 her husband Karl R. was taken into preventive detention. Hence, after the sale of the properties in question she donated the remaining properties to her children. The thought behind this donation might have been that the child beneficiaries by definition of the Nuremberg Laws were so-called "half-castes" and a seemingly certain seizure could be prevented by transferring the assets to the children.

125 The argument of the City of Vienna that reasons for not transferring the properties into the ownership of the company but rather to leave them under the ownership of Gustav H. already existed before 1938, points to the fact that family H. had not planned to sell to the company. The fact that the company did not need these properties is shown by the sale of the properties to Dr. O. in 1943.

126 The fact that the inheritance tax advanced by Margarete R. had to be reimbursed from the proceeds of the sale does not prevent the existence of a seizure.

127 A further argument for the connection between the sale of the properties and the persecution of the owners lies within the purchase contract itself. With the purchase contract dated 2 July 1940 and the addendum dated 28 August 1941, the aryanized Gustav & Wilhelm H. Company acquired the properties EZ X1–X8 from the owners Margarete R., the estate of Marianne W. and Hans H., for the price of 58,399 Reichsmark. Under item XII, the purchase contract contains the clause "subject to the approval by the Property Transaction Office" as well as the explanation under item XIII, that the vendors are "non-Aryans" and that the purchasers are "Aryans". These clauses alone show a connection between the persecution and the execution of the sale of the properties. This is particularly corroborated by the fact that the entire execution of the purchase was dependent on approvals from the Property Transaction Office and the tax office Moabit and also by the fact that the proceeds to which Dr. Hans H. was entitled were transferred to a frozen emigration account after the deduction of the inheritance tax.

128 The Arbitration Panel notes that the seizure of the properties EZ X1–X8, KG Inzersdorf-Stadt occurred due to the origin and the religion of the originally aggrieved persons.

e) Prior Measures

129 A further prerequisite for filing an application in accordance with Sec. 28 of the GSF Law is that the property has never been subject of a claim previously decided by an Austrian court or administrative body, or settled by agreement. Also, neither the applicant nor a relative has received compensation or other consideration unless such a decision or settlement constituted an extreme injustice. The law considers prior proceedings to be those before an administrative body or court in which a material decision or a mutual agreement regarding the properties subject of the Arbitration Panel's proceedings has already been passed.

130 This wording establishes that the presence of either of these two negative prerequisites, i.e. "prior proceedings/settlement by agreement" or "other compensation" precludes a positive decision by the Arbitration Panel.

131 The difference between "prior proceedings/settlement by agreement" and "other compensation" is the following: It is only possible to examine cases of the first group for the

d) Entzug aus einem der aufgezählten Verfolgungsgründe

Gemäß § 28 Abs 1 Z 1 EF-G muss die Liegenschaft zwischen 12. März 1938 und 9. Mai 1945 den früheren EigentümerInnen aus oben genannten Verfolgungsgründen entzogen worden sein. Die Hauptfrage ist daher, ob der Verkauf der Liegenschaften EZ X1–X8 in Zusammenhang mit der Verfolgung von Margarete R., Marianne W. und Hans H. stand.

Die Liegenschaften EZ X1–X8, KG Inzersdorf-Stadt wurden im Zusammenhang mit der Flucht der anderen MiteigentümerInnen verkauft. Margarete R.s Geschwister mussten, um ihr Leben zu retten, das Land verlassen und hatten daher sämtliche ihnen gehörenden Liegenschaften zu verkaufen. Der Versuch der Geschwister, durch Verkauf der gegenständlichen Liegenschaften Margarete R. in den Genuss der Rückzahlung der durch sie ausgelegten Erbschaftssteuern zu bringen, ist daher aufgrund der nationalsozialistischen Machtergreifung erfolgt.

Margarete R. verschenkte sämtliche ihr gehörigen Liegenschaften, da sie zwar durch die Ehe mit ihrem „arischen" Mann geschützt war, jedoch keinesfalls sicher sein konnte, dass auch ihr Vermögen geschützt blieb, umso mehr als im Mai 1938 ihr Gatte Karl R. in Schutzhaft genommen wurde. Sie verschenkte daher sämtliche nach dem Verkauf der gegenständlichen Liegenschaften ihr verbliebenen Liegenschaften an ihre Kinder. Die Überlegung für diese Schenkung dürfte gewesen sein, dass die begünstigten Kinder nach Definition der Nürnberger Gesetze sogenannte „Mischlinge" waren und ein sicher scheinender Entzug durch Übertragung der Vermögenswerte auf die Kinder somit verhindert werden konnte.

Das Argument der Stadt Wien, dass schon vor 1938 Gründe vorlagen, diese Liegenschaften nicht in den Besitz der Firma zu übertragen, sondern im Eigentum Gustav H.s zu lassen, spricht dafür, dass die Familie H. keinen Verkauf an die Firma geplant hatte. Dass die Firma diese Liegenschaften nicht benötigte, zeigt deren Verkauf an Dr. O. 1943.

Der Umstand, dass aus dem Verkaufserlös die von Margarete R. ausgelegten Erbschaftssteuern ersetzt werden mussten, hindert das Vorliegen eines Entzuges nicht.

Ein weiteres Argument für einen Zusammenhang zwischen dem Verkauf der Liegenschaften und der Verfolgung der EigentümerInnen liegt im Kaufvertrag selbst. Mit Kaufvertrag vom 2. Juli 1940 samt Nachtrag vom 28. August 1941 erwarb die arisierte Firma Gustav & Wilhelm H. die Liegenschaften EZ X1–X8 von den EigentümerInnen Margarete R., Verlassenschaft nach Marianne W. und Hans H. zu einem Preis von 58.399,– Reichsmark. Der Kaufvertrag enthält unter Punkt XII die Klausel „vorbehaltlich der Genehmigung der VVSt" sowie die Erklärung unter Punkt XIII, dass die VerkäuferInnen „Nichtarier" und der Käufer „Arier" seien. Allein diese Klauseln zeigen einen Zusammenhang zwischen der Verfolgung und der Abwicklung des Verkaufes der Liegenschaften. Dies wird vor allem dadurch bekräftigt, dass die gesamte Kaufabwicklung von Genehmigungen der VVSt und des Finanzamtes Moabit abhängig war und der Dr. Hans H. zustehende Erlös nach Abzug der Erbschaftsteuer auf ein Auswanderungssperrkonto erlegt wurde.

Die Schiedsinstanz hält fest, dass der Entzug der Liegenschaften EZ X1–X8, KG Inzersdorf-Stadt aufgrund der Abstammung und Religionszugehörigkeit der ursprünglich Geschädigten erfolgt ist.

e) Frühere Maßnahmen

Eine weitere Anspruchsvoraussetzung gemäß § 28 EF-G ist, dass die Liegenschaft niemals Gegenstand einer Forderung war, die bereits zuvor durch österreichische Gerichte oder Verwaltungsbehörden entschieden oder einvernehmlich geregelt wurde, und für die

132 The second group – "other compensation" – requires a transfer of assets to the then claimant for restitution. To establish the existence of "other compensation" unequivocal evidence for a transfer of assets has to be presented.

133 With respect to prior proceedings a distinction has to be made between Margarete R.'s one-third ownership and the two-thirds ownership of the estate of Marianne W. and Dr. Hans H. Both the heirs of Marianne W. and Dr. Hans H. filed claims for restitution regarding their property shares. These claims for restitution were concluded by restitution settlement in 1949 and 1950. Hence, prior proceedings regarding the two-thirds of these properties are present.

134 Margarete R. did not file a claim regarding her one-third share of these properties.

135 If the City of Vienna now believes that the settlement between Margarete R. and Viktor O., Hans O. and Herbert V. regarding the Gustav & Wilhelm H. General Commercial Partnership represents a prior measure, then the Arbitration Panel is unable to agree with this. Only the company shares of Margarete R. were included in this settlement and under no circumstances a property which at the time of settlement was owned by an individual party to the settlement, namely Viktor O., and not by all parties to the settlement, namely all partners of the Gustav & Wilhelm H. General Commercial Partnership. Even if the general clause under item 3 of this settlement stipulates "that all mutual claims coming from the title of restitution are settled through this", only claims regarding the company property can be covered by this and not the private property of an individual partner. This is valid all the more as the settlement recorded at the same time that Viktor O. and Herbert V. were not yet in agreement with Margarete R. on whether this settlement also included the parts of the Gustav & Wilhelm H. Company which had been acquired after the takeover of the company. This transfer of the ownership rights in question regarding the properties which were not yet owned by the Gustav & Wilhelm H. General Commercial Partnership in 1938 was supposed to take place via a separate legal transaction. These regulations clearly show that the properties in question could not possibly have been included in the above-mentioned general clause as on the one hand, the properties were purchased only after the takeover of the company by the aryanizers. On the other hand, these properties were no longer owned by the company at the time of the settlement. The Arbitration Panel assumes that the properties in question were not included in the settlement. Hence, prior proceedings regarding Margarete R.'s one-third share did not exist.

136 It now remains to be examined whether the applicants or a relative received compensation or other consideration for these properties by another means. The existence of this sort of compensation or other consideration cannot be gathered from the facts presented here. Although there is circumstantial evidence which support the fact that Margarete and Hansjörg R. formed a syndicate with Dr. O. for the purpose of countering the claims of the family members who were trying to be re-admitted to the company, these indications are not convincing enough to be able to conclude that another consideration was received in accordance with Sec. 28 (1) item 2 of the GSF Law.

137 As a prior measure is not present, the claim for *in rem* restitution of a one-third share of the property EZ X9 (formally EZ X1–X8), KG Inzersdorf-Stadt by Ing. Hansjörg R. is merited.

weder der Antragsteller noch ein Verwandter auf eine andere Weise eine Entschädigung oder sonstige Gegenleistung erhalten hat, es sei denn, eine solche Entscheidung oder einvernehmliche Regelung habe eine extreme Ungerechtigkeit dargestellt. Als früheres Verfahren im Sinne dieses Gesetzes ist jedes Verfahren vor einer Verwaltungsbehörde oder einem Gericht zu verstehen, in welchem bereits bezüglich der in diesem Schiedsinstanzverfahren begehrten Liegenschaften eine materielle Entscheidung beziehungsweise eine einvernehmliche Regelung getroffen wurde.

Aus der Formulierung ergibt sich, dass das Vorliegen einer dieser beiden Negativvoraussetzungen, nämlich „früheres Verfahren/einvernehmliche Regelung" oder „sonstige Entschädigung", jede für sich eine positive Entscheidung der Schiedsinstanz ausschließt. 130

Es besteht zwischen „früherem Verfahren/einvernehmlicher Regelung" und einer „sonstigen Entschädigung" folgender Unterschied: Nur bei der ersten Fallgruppe besteht die Möglichkeit, solche Fälle auf eine „extreme Ungerechtigkeit" zu prüfen. (§§ 28 Abs 1 Z 2 und 32 Abs 2 Z 1 EF-G.) 131

Bei der zweiten Fallgruppe, „sonstige Entschädigungen", muss es zu einer vermögenswerten Leistung an den damaligen Rückstellungswerber gekommen sein. Bei der Feststellung, ob eine „sonstige Entschädigung" vorliegt, muss die vermögenswerte Leistung zweifelsfrei nachgewiesen werden können. 132

Hinsichtlich eines früheren Verfahrens ist zwischen dem 1/3-Eigentum der Margarete R. und dem 2/3-Eigentum der Verlassenschaft nach Marianne W. und des Dr. Hans H. zu unterscheiden. Sowohl die Erben nach Marianne W. als auch Dr. Hans H. brachten hinsichtlich ihrer Liegenschaftsanteile Rückstellungsanträge ein, welche 1949 bzw. 1950 mittels Rückstellungsvergleich beendet wurden. Hinsichtlich dieser 2/3 der Liegenschaften liegt daher ein früheres Verfahren vor. 133

Margarete R. strengte kein Rückstellungsverfahren hinsichtlich ihres Drittels an diesen Liegenschaften an. 134

Wenn nun die Stadt Wien meint, die frühere Maßnahme läge in dem Vergleich zwischen Margarete R. und Viktor O., Hans O. und Herbert V. bezüglich der Gustav & Wilhelm H. OHG, so kann die Schiedsinstanz dem nicht zustimmen. Von diesem Vergleich waren lediglich die Firmenanteile der Margarete R. umfasst und keinesfalls eine Liegenschaft, die sich zum Vergleichszeitpunkt im Eigentum eines einzelnen Vergleichspartners, nämlich Viktor O.s befand, und nicht im Eigentum aller VertragspartnerInnen, nämlich sämtlicher GesellschafterInnen der Gustav & Wilhelm H. OHG, stand. Auch wenn in einer Generalklausel in Punkt 3 dieses Vergleiches festgelegt ist, „dass alle gegenseitigen Ansprüche aus dem Titel der Restitution damit ausgeglichen sind", können davon lediglich Ansprüche hinsichtlich des Firmeneigentums umfasst sein und nicht das Privateigentum eines einzelnen Gesellschafters. Dies gilt umso mehr, als gleichzeitig in diesem Vergleich festgehalten wurde, dass sich Viktor O. und Herbert V. mit Margarete R. noch nicht einig waren, ob von diesem Vergleich auch jene Teile der Firma Gustav & Wilhelm H. umfasst seien, welche nach Übernahme der Firma erworben wurden. Es hätte jene Übertragung der fraglichen Eigentumsrechte, hinsichtlich der 1938 noch nicht im Eigentum der Firma Gustav & Wilhelm H. OHG befindlichen Liegenschaften, durch ein gesondertes Rechtsgeschäft erfolgen sollen. Diese Bestimmungen zeigen deutlich, dass die gegenständlichen Liegenschaften keinesfalls von der obigen Generalklausel umfasst sein konnten, da einerseits die Grundstücke erst nach Übernahme der Firma durch die Ariseure angekauft wurden und andererseits diese zum Vergleichszeitpunkt überhaupt nicht mehr im Firmeneigentum standen. Die Schiedsinstanz geht davon aus, dass die gegenständlichen Liegenschaften 135

f) Extreme Injustice

138   Hence, it remains to be examined whether the exception of Sec. 28 (1) item 2 in connection with Sec. 32 of the GSF Law regarding the two one-third shares of Hans H. and Marianne W. exists, i.e. whether the restitution settlements concluded by the heirs of Marianne W. and Dr. Hans H. are to be regarded as being "extremely unjust". In accordance with Sec. 28 (1) item 2 of the GSF Law, the Arbitration Panel can affirm an extreme injustice only "in exceptional circumstances" and must do so unanimously.

139   A prior decision by an Austrian court or an Austrian administrative body is regarded by the Arbitration Panel as being extremely unjust particularly where it is based upon a decision-making process which indicates that the legal basis used to decide has been applied unobjectively at the expense of the aggrieved person and that as a result the aggrieved person has been grossly disadvantaged regarding his or her restitution or compensation claims.

140   Initially it is to be examined whether the Restitution Commission would have approved the application for restitution when applying the legal provisions. In accordance with para. 2 of the Third Restitution Act, a seizure of assets as defined by para. 1 (1) is present particularly where the owner was subjected to political persecution under National Socialism and where the purchaser of the property does not demonstrate that the property transfer would have also taken place without the National Socialist assumption of power. In any case, the persons persecuted as Jews by National Socialism fell under the definition of "political persecution". As all aggrieved owners were Jews, in this specific case this means that the burden of proof lies with the aryanizer. He was to prove that the property transfer would have taken place also without the National Socialist assumption of power. In the partial report by the Historical Commission, in the chapter *Die österreichische Rückstellungsgesetzgebung. Eine juristische Analyse*, Vienna 2002[4], page 45, Georg Graf identified in the restitution jurisdiction

> "two circumstances in particular, which were presented by adverse parties in order to prove the independence of the transaction from the National Socialist assumption of power: Firstly, circumstances where a vendor had already intended to sell before 1938 and secondly, where economic difficulties of the owner would in any case have led to a sale."

Both circumstances mentioned by Graf do not apply in this case firstly as there was no intention to sell prior to 1938 and secondly not only Margarete R. who was even able to advance the inheritance tax but also her brothers had sufficient other assets at their disposal in order to pay for liabilities connected to the inheritance. Under no circumstances, can one speak of economic difficulties of the owner or an indebtedness of the properties.

141   Further, the exempting facts of para. 2 of the Third Restitution Act would be fulfilled if the "property had been sold prior to the National Socialist assumption of power under the same or similar conditions as it was after the takeover (ÖJZ 1951/170/113)." (In: Lansky/Rathkolb/Steiner (eds.), *Restitutionsgesetze. Kommentar*, para. 2 Third Restitution Act Decision 35, page 91). Without the National Socialist assumption of power the heirs of

---

[4] Supplementation at the time of going to press: From 2002 to 2003, this text could be found under http://www.historikerkommission.gv.at/deutsch-home.html and was published in 2003 as: Georg Graf, *Die österreichische Rückstellungsgesetzgebung. Eine juristische Analyse*, Vienna (Oldenbourg) 2003 (= Publications of the Austrian Historical Commission, Volume 2).

von diesem Vergleich nicht umfasst waren und daher bezüglich des Drittelanteils der Margarete R. kein früheres Verfahren vorlag.

Es bleibt nun zu prüfen, ob die AntragstellerInnen oder ein Verwandter nicht auf eine andere Weise eine Entschädigung oder sonstige Gegenleistung für diese Liegenschaften erhalten haben. Dem vorliegenden Sachverhalt lässt sich eine solche Entschädigung oder sonstige Gegenleistung nicht entnehmen. Wenngleich einige Indizien dafür sprechen, dass Margarete und Hansjörg R. mit Dr. O. eine zweckgerichtete Interessengemeinschaft gegen Ansprüche der wieder in die Firma Aufnahme suchenden Familienmitglieder bildeten, so sind diese Anhaltspunkte nicht aussagekräftig genug, um auf eine sonstige Gegenleistung iSd § 28 Abs 2 EF-G schließen zu können. 136

Da diesbezüglich keine frühere Maßnahme vorliegt, besteht der Anspruch von Ing. Hansjörg R. auf Naturalrestitution eines Drittelanteiles an der Liegenschaft EZ X9 (vormals EZ X1–X8), KG Inzersdorf-Stadt, dem Grunde nach zu Recht. 137

f) Extreme Ungerechtigkeit

Zu prüfen bleibt daher hinsichtlich der zwei Drittelanteile von Hans H. und Marianne W., ob der Ausnahmetatbestand des § 28 Abs 1 Z 2 iVm § 32 EF-G vorliegt, nämlich ob die von den Erben nach Marianne W. und von Dr. Hans H. abgeschlossenen Rückstellungsvergleiche als „extrem ungerecht" zu betrachten sind. Dass eine extreme Ungerechtigkeit vorliegt, kann die Schiedsinstanz laut § 28 Abs 1 Z 2 EF-G nur „in besonderen Ausnahmefällen" und nur einstimmig bejahen. 138

Eine frühere Entscheidung eines österreichischen Gerichts oder einer österreichischen Verwaltungsbehörde wird von der Schiedsinstanz insbesondere dann als extrem ungerecht angesehen, wenn sie auf einer Entscheidungsfindung beruht, die darauf hindeutet, dass gesetzliche Entscheidungsgrundlagen objektiv unvertretbar zu Lasten des Geschädigten angewendet worden sind und der Geschädigte dadurch im Ergebnis hinsichtlich seiner Rückstellungs- oder Entschädigungsansprüche grob benachteiligt worden ist. 139

Es ist zunächst zu prüfen, ob die Rückstellungskommission dem Rückstellungsantrag in Anwendung der Gesetzesbestimmungen stattgegeben hätte. Gemäß § 2 des 3. RStG liegt eine Vermögensentziehung im Sinne des § 1 Abs 1 insbesondere dann vor, wenn der Eigentümer politischer Verfolgung durch den Nationalsozialismus unterworfen war und der Erwerber des Vermögens nicht dartut, dass die Vermögensübertragung auch unabhängig von der Machtergreifung des Nationalsozialismus erfolgt wäre. Unter den Begriff „politische Verfolgung" fielen jedenfalls die unter dem Nationalsozialismus als Juden verfolgte Personen. Da sämtliche geschädigten EigentümerInnen jüdisch waren, bedeutet dies im konkreten Fall, dass der Ariseur die Beweislast zu tragen hatte, dass der Eigentumsübergang auch ohne die Machtergreifung der Nationalsozialisten stattgefunden hätte. Im Teilbericht der Historikerkommission von Georg *Graf*, Die österreichische Rückstellungsgesetzgebung. Eine juristische Analyse (Wien 2002)[4], Seite 45, identifizierte dieser in der Rückstellungsrechtsprechung 140

„vor allem zwei Umstände, die von den Antragsgegnern zur Begründung der Unabhängigkeit der Transaktion von der Machtergreifung des Nationalsozialismus ange-

---

[4] Ergänzung zum Zeitpunkt der Drucklegung: Dieser Text war von 2002 bis 2003 unter http://www.historikerkommission.gv.at/deutsch-home.html abrufbar und wurde 2003 veröffentlicht als: Georg *Graf*, Die österreichische Rückstellungsgesetzgebung. Eine juristische Analyse, Wien (Oldenbourg) 2003 (= Veröffentlichungen der österreichischen Historikerkommission, Band 2) entnommen.

Marianne W. and Hans H. would not have had to leave the country. Hence, their financial circumstances would have been different; especially the great need for cash for the payment of the Reich Flight Tax would not have existed. Hence, it cannot be assumed that the aggrieved owners would have sold the properties without the National Socialist assumption of power.

142 Hence, when applying the restitution case law of the time to this specific case, the restitution of the property shares by the Restitution Commission was to be expected. It is to be assumed that the claimants for restitution – especially due to their legal representation – could foresee during the proceedings that the properties would have had to be restituted.

143 Henceforth, it is to be questioned whether the content of the settlements is to be regarded as extremely unjust in the meaning of the GSF Law.

144 The fact that the applicants for restitution waived their claims in spite of their knowledge of the restitution case law shows that they regarded the property transfer of 1940 as a valid legal transaction. This is because inheritance tax was paid from the proceeds received at that time. In the view of the claimants for restitution, the decision by the Restitution Commission would have meant that the restitution would take place in return for the surrender of the proceeds from the sale. Incidentally, it is also possible that unknown, familial motives contributed to the conclusion of this settlement.

145 As the Arbitration Panel has already established in prior decisions (for example in decision number 3/2003), the notion of freedom of contract inherent in a settlement is to be considered when evaluating the presence of an extreme injustice. Regularly, during restitution proceedings a discrepancy manifests itself between the value of the property in question and the settlement sum, as during settlements an amicable new agreement of contentious or dubious entitlements takes place with mutual concessions (para. 1380 [Austrian] General Civil Code). Even if a discrepancy in value is created from the waiving of a share, this can still be supported by the principle of freedom of contract.

146 It can be derived from the exceptional nature of the regulations contained in Sec. 28 and Sec. 32 GSF Law and in the provision of Sec. 20 item 2 of the GSF Law that a discrepancy in value between the result of the settlement and a decision by the Restitution Commission alone is not sufficient for the assumption of an extreme injustice.

147 Hence, an insufficient prior compensation by itself does not represent an extreme injustice as long as the principle of the freedom of contract has been adhered to; that is if no circumstantial evidence support the fact that the claimants for restitution could not decide freely. In the case of settlement conclusions possible restrictions of freedom of contract are to be particularly considered. Such restrictions can for example be triggered by economic imbalances or where the claimants for restitution lacked information.

148 Indications of these sorts of restrictions of freedom of contract have not been presented by the parties. The Arbitration Panel could also not find any indications of this kind, even after intensive research. Since, as has been explained, a positive decision by the Restitution Commission could have been expected, it can be assumed that the risk of the claimants for restitution of losing the case was negligible. There are also no indications that the parties were economically unequal. As has already been explained, there certainly is evidence which make an alliance of convenience between Viktor O. and Margarete and Hansjörg R. seem likely. However, it is not possible to prove that any party was pressured during the proceedings regarding the concerned property. Hence, in this case it could also not be proven that the aryanizers exerted pressure by using the simultaneously pend-

führt wurden, nämlich 1. bereits vor 1938 bestehende Verkaufsabsichten des Veräußerers sowie 2. wirtschaftliche Schwierigkeiten des Eigentümers, die in jedem Fall zu einer Veräußerung geführt hätten."

Beide von Graf genannten Umstände treffen in diesem Fall nicht zu, da einerseits vor 1938 keinerlei Verkaufsabsichten bestanden und andererseits sowohl von Margarete R., welche sogar die Erbschaftssteuer vorstrecken konnte, als auch auf Seiten ihrer Brüder genügend andere Vermögenswerte zur Verfügung standen, um die Verbindlichkeiten aus dem Erbfall zu berichtigen. Keinesfalls kann von wirtschaftlichen Schwierigkeiten der EigentümerInnen oder von einer Überschuldung der Liegenschaften gesprochen werden.

Des Weiteren würde dem Befreiungstatbestand des § 2 des 3. RStG entsprochen werden, wenn die „Liegenschaft vor der nationalsozialistischen Machtergreifung unter gleichen oder ähnlichen Bedingungen veräußert worden wäre, wie danach (ÖJZ 1951/170/ 113)." (In: *Lansky/Rathkolb/Steiner* (Hg.), Restitutionsgesetze. Kommentar § 2 3. RStG E 35, Seite 91). Ohne nationalsozialistische Machtergreifung hätten die Erben nach Marianne W. und Hans H. das Land nicht verlassen müssen, und es wäre daher auch ihr Vermögensstand ein anderer gewesen; vor allem hätte nicht ein großer Bedarf an Bargeld zur Begleichung der Reichsfluchtsteuer bestanden. Es ist daher nicht anzunehmen, dass die geschädigten EigentümerInnen ohne nationalsozialistische Machtergreifung den Verkauf der Liegenschaften getätigt hätten. 141

Legt man daher die damalige Rückstellungsrechtsprechung dem konkreten Fall zugrunde, dann war eine Rückstellung der Liegenschaftsanteile durch die Rückstellungskommission zu erwarten. Es ist davon auszugehen, dass die Rückstellungswerber, insbesondere aufgrund ihrer anwaltlichen Vertretung, bereits während des Verfahrens absehen konnten, dass die Liegenschaften zurückgestellt werden hätten müssen. 142

Fraglich ist nun, ob der Inhalt der Vergleiche als extrem ungerecht iSd EF-G anzusehen ist. 143

Dass die Rückstellungswerber trotz des Wissens um die Rückstellungsrechtsprechung auf ihre Ansprüche verzichteten, zeigt, dass sie den Eigentumsübergang aus dem Jahr 1940 als gültiges Rechtsgeschäft angesehen haben. Dies deshalb, da aus dem seinerzeit empfangenen Kaufpreis Erbschaftssteuern bezahlt wurden. In den Augen der Rückstellungswerber hätte die Rückstellungskommissionsentscheidung die Rückstellung Zug um Zug gegen Herausgabe des Kaufpreis bedeutet. Im Übrigen könnten auch nicht bekannte, familieninterne Beweggründe zu diesem Vergleichsabschluss beigetragen haben. 144

Wie die Schiedsinstanz bereits in früheren Entscheidungen festgestellt hat (etwa in Entscheidung Nummer 3/2003), ist bei der Beurteilung des Vorliegens einer extremen Ungerechtigkeit auf den einem Vergleich innewohnenden Gedanken der Privatautonomie Rücksicht zu nehmen. Da bei Vergleichen unter beiderseitigem Nachgeben eine einverständliche neue Festlegung strittiger oder zweifelhafter Rechte erfolgt (§ 1380 ABGB), ist auch bei Rückstellungsvergleichen regelmäßig eine Differenz zwischen dem Wert der strittigen Liegenschaft und der Vergleichssumme vorhanden. Selbst dann, wenn das Wertmissverhältnis in einem Verzicht auf irgendeinen Anteil besteht, kann dies immer noch durch die Privatautonomie getragen sein. 145

Aus dem Ausnahmecharakter der Regelungen der §§ 28 und 32 EF-G und der Bestimmung § 20 Z 2 EF-G kann abgeleitet werden, dass ein Wertmissverhältnis zwischen dem Ergebnis des Vergleiches und einer Entscheidung der Rückstellungskommission allein nicht für die Annahme einer extremen Ungerechtigkeit ausreicht. 146

ing H. company restitution case which led to the waiving of the claims of the claimants for restitution.

149   Hence, an extreme injustice cannot be recognized in the settlements at issue here.

150   Therefore, the *in rem* restitution of the two one-third shares of the properties EZ X1–X8, KG Inzersdorf-Stadt, which belonged to the estate of Marianne W. and Dr. Hans H. was to be rejected.

Dr. Josef Aicher, university professor, Chairman
Dr.Dr.h.c. Erich Kussbach, LL.M., honorary professor and retired ambassador
MMag. Dr. August Reinisch, LL.M., university professor

Schiedsinstanz für Naturalrestitution – Entscheidung Nr. 25/2005

Eine unzureichende frühere Entschädigung stellt daher für sich alleine keinen Fall der extremen Ungerechtigkeit dar, sofern die Privatautonomie gewahrt wurde, d.h. keine Indizien dafür sprechen, dass die Rückstellungswerber nicht frei entscheiden konnten. Bei Vergleichsabschlüssen ist insbesondere auf mögliche Einschränkungen der Privatautonomie Bedacht zu nehmen. Solche Einschränkungen können sich etwa aus wirtschaftlichen Ungleichgewichtslagen oder aus Informationsdefiziten beim Rückstellungswerber ergeben. 147

Indizien für derartige Einschränkungen der Privatautonomie sind von den Parteien nicht dargetan worden. Auch die Schiedsinstanz hat trotz intensiver Nachforschungen keine diesbezüglichen Hinweise erkennen können. Da, wie dargetan, mit einer positiven Entscheidung der Rückstellungskommission zu rechnen gewesen wäre, kann von einem geringen Prozessrisiko für die Rückstellungswerber ausgegangen werden. Auch gibt es keine Hinweise darauf, dass sich wirtschaftlich ungleiche Parteien gegenüberstanden. Wie bereits ausgeführt, liegen durchaus Indizien vor, die ein Zweckbündnis zwischen Viktor O. und Margarete und Hansjörg R. wahrscheinlich scheinen lassen. Ob daraus jedoch eine Drucksituation im Verfahren um die gegenständliche Liegenschaft abgeleitet werden kann, ist nicht beweisbar. Im konkreten Fall konnte daher auch nicht nachgewiesen werden, dass mit der gleichzeitig anhängigen Rückstellungssache hinsichtlich der Firma H. von den Ariseuren Druck ausgeübt wurde, der zum Anspruchsverzicht durch die Rückstellungswerber geführt hat. 148

Es kann daher in den vorliegenden Vergleichen keine extreme Ungerechtigkeit gesehen werden. 149

Die Naturalrestitution der zwei Drittelanteile an den Liegenschaften EZ X1–X8, KG Inzersdorf-Stadt, die dem Nachlass nach Marianne W. und Dr. Hans H. gehört hatten, war daher abzulehnen. 150

o.Univ.-Prof. Dr. Josef Aicher, Vorsitzender
Honorarprofessor Dr.Dr.h.c. Erich Kussbach LL.M., Botschafter i.R.
ao.Univ.-Prof. MMag. Dr. August Reinisch LL.M.

Press Release Decision No. 26/2005

Carinthia, Villach

On 15 November 2005, the Arbitration Panel for *In Rem* Restitution rejected the restitution of three properties in Villach owned by the Austrian Federal Railways. There were no indications of any political persecution of the original owners of the property.

The property – the subdivision into three properties only took place after the Second World War – was owned by the M. spouses in March 1938. In April 1940, the German Reich Railways approached the M. spouses to negotiate the transfer of the property. By May 1941, the conditions of the transfer were agreed upon. A total of 72,307.50 Reichsmark were to be paid for the 7,445 m^2 property parcel, including all buildings located on it.

Subsequently, the M. spouses refused to sign the purchase contract which had been prepared by the German Reich Railways for the purpose of recording the sale in the land register. The German Reich Railways sued the M. couple demanding performance of the contract agreed upon in May 1941. The Regional Court Klagenfurt ruled in favour of the German Reich Railways in October 1942. On the basis of the legally binding decision, the ownership transfer was carried out in January 1943. The M. spouses, however, refused to accept the proceeds from the sale amounting to 72,307.50 Reichsmark which they had been awarded pursuant to the court's decision. They approached various political decision-making bodies during the NS era – for example Hitler's Chancellery and the Carinthian regional NS administration – with the request to annul the property transactions which according to their opinion were illegal. However, they only received negative responses.

After the end of the Second World War, the M. spouses directed essentially the same requests to political offices of the Republic of Austria – for example to the Federal President, the Federal Chancellor and to several ministries and ministers. Neither the M. spouses nor their heirs ever initiated proceedings in accordance with the restitution acts. During the 1950s, Maria M. finally received a payment of 35,000 Schilling for her former property. It was not possible to establish the details of this payment.

Both applicants – two grandchildren of the M. spouses – asserted in their applications that the Yugoslavian origin of the husband Anton M. had been causal for the seizure of the properties during the NS era. However, the applicants could not provide evidence to this effect. The Arbitration Panel could only establish that Anton M. was born in Lower Styria, district Marburg-Land, in 1872. This, however, is insufficient for the allocation to a certain nationality as the population in this district is made up of approximately 80 % Slovenians and 20 % Germans. There was no indication found anywhere that the asserted origin of Anton M. had played a role during the transaction with the German Reich Railways.

One of the necessary prerequisites for *in rem* restitution is the persecution by the NS regime on one of the grounds listed exhaustively in the GSF Law. Origin and nationality also form part of these grounds. As the claimants could not prove this point – and in general no further indications for grounds of persecution could be identified – the Arbitration Panel had to reject the application solely for this reason.

For use by media; not legally binding upon the Arbitration Panel for In Rem Restitution.

Pressemitteilung Entscheidung Nr. 26/2005

Kärnten, Villach

Die Schiedsinstanz für Naturalrestitution hat am 15. November 2005 die Rückstellung dreier Liegenschaften der Österreichischen Bundesbahnen in Villach abgelehnt. Es lagen keine Hinweise für eine politische Verfolgung der ursprünglichen Liegenschaftseigentümer vor.

Die Liegenschaft – die Aufteilung in drei Liegenschaften fand erst nach dem Zweiten Weltkrieg statt – befand sich im März 1938 im Eigentum des Ehepaares M. Im April 1940 trat die Deutsche Reichsbahn an das Ehepaar M. heran, um mit ihm über die Abtretung der Liegenschaft zu verhandeln. Bis zum Mai 1941 konnte man über die Bedingungen der Abtretung eine Einigung erzielen. Für das 7.445 m² große Grundstück mit allen darauf befindlichen Gebäuden sollte ein Gesamtkaufpreis von 72.307,50 Reichsmark gezahlt werden.

Das Ehepaar M. weigerte sich in späterer Folge jedoch, den zur grundbücherlichen Durchführung von der Deutschen Reichsbahn errichteten Kaufvertrag zu unterschreiben. Die Deutsche Reichsbahn klagte daraufhin das Ehepaar M. auf Einhaltung der im Mai 1941 getroffenen Vereinbarung und bekam vom Landgericht Klagenfurt im Oktober 1942 Recht. Aufgrund des rechtskräftigen Urteiles wurde im Jänner 1943 der Eigentümerwechsel vollzogen. Das Ehepaar M. weigerte sich allerdings, den ihm mit dem Urteil zugesprochenen Kaufpreis von 72.307,50 Reichsmark anzunehmen. Es wandte sich bereits in der NS-Zeit an verschiedene politische Entscheidungsträger – so etwa an die Kanzlei Hitlers und an die Kärntner Gauleitung – mit dem Ersuchen um Rückgängigmachung der seiner Ansicht nach unrechtmäßigen Liegenschaftstransaktion. Es bekam jedoch immer negative Antworten.

Nach dem Ende des Zweiten Weltkrieges richtete das Ehepaar M. im Wesentlichen gleichlautende Bitten an politische Stellen der Republik Österreich – etwa an den Bundespräsidenten, an den Bundeskanzler und an mehrere Ministerien bzw. Minister. Ein Verfahren nach den Rückstellungsgesetzen leiteten das Ehepaar M. oder ihre Erben niemals ein. In den 1950er Jahren erhielt Frau M. schließlich eine Zahlung von 35.000,- Schilling für ihren früheren Grundbesitz. Nähere Details zu dieser Zahlung konnten nicht festgestellt werden.

Die beiden Antragsteller – zwei Enkel des Ehepaares M. – bringen in ihren Anträgen vor, die jugoslawische Abstammung des Ehemannes Anton M. sei kausal für den Entzug der Liegenschaften in der NS-Zeit gewesen. Beweise dazu konnten die Antragsteller jedoch nicht vorlegen. Die Schiedsinstanz konnte lediglich feststellen, dass Anton M. 1872 in der Untersteiermark, im Bezirk Marburg-Land geboren worden war. Dies reicht für die Zuordnung zu einer bestimmten Nationalität allerdings nicht aus, da sich die Bevölkerung in diesem Bezirk zu etwa 80 % aus Slowenen und zu 20 % aus Deutschen zusammensetzte. Es fand sich nirgends ein Hinweis darauf, dass die behauptete Abstammung von Anton M. bei der Transaktion mit der Deutschen Reichsbahn eine Rolle gespielt hätte.

Eine der notwendigen Voraussetzungen für die Naturalrestitution ist die Verfolgung aus einem der im Entschädigungsfondsgesetz abschließend aufgezählten Gründen durch das NS-Regime. Dazu zählen auch die Abstammung bzw. Nationalität. Da dieser Nachweis von den Antragstellern nicht erbracht werden konnte – und im Übrigen auch keine sonstigen Hinweise auf Verfolgungsgründe manifest geworden sind –, musste die Schiedsinstanz schon aus diesem Grund den Antrag ablehnen.

Zur Verwendung durch die Medien bestimmter Text, der die Schiedsinstanz nicht bindet.

Arbitration Panel for *In Rem* Restitution

Decision number 26/2005

The Arbitration Panel for *In Rem* Restitution (Chairman Dr. Josef Aicher, university professor, and Dr.Dr.h.c. Erich Kussbach LL.M., retired ambassador and honorary professor, as well as MMag. Dr. August Reinisch LL.M, university professor, as Members) decided on 15 November 2005 in the legal matter of the first applicant the estate of Eduard M., deceased on 11 March 2002, and the second applicant Edith M., both represented by Dr. Herbert Hübel, lawyer in Salzburg, regarding *in rem* restitution of the properties with the register numbers ("EZ") X1, X2 and X3, cadastral district ("KG") Seebach:

1. The application of the first applicant for restitution of the properties EZ X1, X2 and X3, KG Seebach, is rejected.

2. The application of the second applicant for restitution of the properties EZ X1, X2 and X3, KG Seebach, is rejected.

Reasons:

1. Submission by the Applicants

1   With the applications filed with the General Settlement Fund on 5 August 2003, the first and second applicants sought the restitution of the property located at St. Leonhard Z, 9500 Villach, formerly EZ X4, KG Seebach. At the point of seizure, the property had consisted of the property parcels Y1, Y2/1, Y2/5 and Y2/6. The total area had amounted to approximately 7,500 m^2. Approximately 180 m^2 of this area had been developed and had consisted of a basement, two stories and a top floor with a total of seven apartments and an outbuilding. During the course of the seizure, the property had been transferred to the railway register. After it had been transferred back to the land register in the years 1961 and 1981 respectively, the area had evidently been divided into the new property parcels Y2/1, Y2/6 and Y2/7.

2   Anton M., born on 21 July 1872, and his wife Marianne (aka Maria Anna), born on 31 October 1877, had each owned half of the above-mentioned property. Anton M. was of Yugoslavian origin. In 1941, the German Reich Railways had tried to gain possession of the property. To legitimize the process from a legal point of view, the M. couple had been pressured to sign a purchase contract. In spite of massive intimidation and threats – especially in connection with Anton M.'s origins – the M. couple had firmly resisted acceptance of the contract. The purchase price offered by the Reich Railways had only represented a symbolic amount in comparison to the true value of the property.

3   Subsequently, the Reich Railways had sued for non-performance of an allegedly verbally concluded purchase contract. In view of the political pressure which was burdening the court, the decision had been in favor of the Reich Railways. However, the court – as is now generally known – could not be regarded as being impartial since the legal transaction had already been null and void due to *laesio enormis*. The former owners received 35,000 Schilling from the allegedly unlawfully fixed purchase price of 70,939.46 Reichsmark.

4   Eduard M., born on 22 June 1938 (whose rights are now evidently being asserted by the first applicant), was the grandson of the aggrieved owner. The probate proceedings concerning the estate of Eduard M. had been pending at the District Court Salzburg under file

Schiedsinstanz für Naturalrestitution

Entscheidungsnummer 26/2005

Die Schiedsinstanz für Naturalrestitution beschließt am 15. November 2005 durch den Vorsitzenden o.Univ.-Prof. Dr. Josef Aicher und die Schiedsinstanzmitglieder Honorarprofessor Dr.Dr.h.c. Erich Kussbach LL.M., Botschafter i.R. und ao.Univ.-Prof. MMag. Dr. August Reinisch LL.M. in der Rechtssache 1. Verlassenschaft nach dem am 11. März 2002 verstorbenen Eduard M. und 2. Edith M., beide vertreten durch Dr. Herbert Hübel, Rechtsanwalt (RA) in Salzburg, wegen Naturalrestitution der Liegenschaften mit den Einlagezahlen (EZ) X1, X2 und X3, Katastralgemeinde (KG) Seebach:

Der Antrag der Erstantragstellerin auf Rückgabe der Liegenschaften mit den EZ X1, X2 und X3, KG Seebach, wird abgelehnt.

Der Antrag der Zweitantragstellerin auf Rückgabe der Liegenschaften mit den EZ X1, X2 und X3, KG Seebach, wird abgelehnt.

Begründung:

1. Vorbringen der Antragstellerinnen

Die Erst- und die Zweitantragstellerin begehrten mit ihren am 5. August 2003 beim Allgemeinen Entschädigungsfonds eingelangten Anträgen die Rückstellung der Liegenschaft mit der Adresse St. Leonhard Z, 9500 Villach, frühere Grundbuchseinlage X4, KG Seebach. Diese Liegenschaft habe zum Zeitpunkt der Entziehung aus den Grundstücken Y1, Y2/1, Y2/5 und Y2/6 mit einer Gesamtfläche von ca. 7.500 m² bestanden. Davon seien ca. 180 m² verbaute Fläche gewesen, die einen Keller, zwei Vollgeschosse und ein Dachgeschoss mit insgesamt sieben Wohnungen und ein Wirtschaftsgebäude umfasst habe. Im Rahmen der Entziehung sei die Liegenschaft in das Eisenbahnbuch übertragen worden. Nach der Rückübertragung in das Grundbuch in den Jahren 1961 bzw. 1981 sei die Fläche offenbar auf die neuen Grundstücke Y2/1, Y2/6 und Y2/7 aufgeteilt worden. 1

Der am 21. Juli 1872 geborene Anton M. und seine am 31. Oktober 1877 geborene Ehefrau Marianne (auch Maria Anna) M. seien je zur Hälfte EigentümerInnen der genannten Liegenschaft gewesen. Anton M. sei jugoslawischer Abstammung gewesen. Im Jahr 1941 habe die Deutsche Reichsbahn versucht, die Liegenschaft an sich zu bringen. Um dem Ganzen einen legalen Anstrich zu geben, habe man die Eheleute M. zu einer Unterfertigung des Kaufvertrages gedrängt. Trotz massivster Einschüchterungen und Drohungen – insbesondere im Hinblick auf Anton M.s Herkunft –, hätten sich die Eheleute M. standhaft geweigert, den Vertrag anzunehmen. Der von der Reichsbahn angebotene Kaufpreis habe im Vergleich zum wahren Wert der Liegenschaft nämlich nur einen symbolischen Betrag dargestellt. 2

Daraufhin habe die Reichsbahn auf Erfüllung eines angeblich mündlich abgeschlossenen Kaufvertrages geklagt. Das Gericht habe angesichts des politischen Druckes, der auf diesem lastete, zugunsten der Reichsbahn entschieden. Das Gericht könne allerdings – wie heute allgemein bekannt sei – nicht als unabhängig betrachtet werden, da das Rechtsgeschäft bereits wegen laesio enormis nichtig gewesen sei. Von dem angeblichen, rechtswidrig zustande gekommenen Kaufpreis von 70.939,46 Reichsmark seien schließlich 35.000,– Schilling an die ehemaligen EigentümerInnen ausgezahlt worden. 3

Eduard M., geboren am 22. Juni 1938 (dessen Rechte die Erstantragstellerin nun offenbar geltend macht), sei der Enkel der geschädigten EigentümerInnen. Das Verlassen- 4

Arbitration Panel for *In Rem* Restitution – Decision No. 26/2005

number A 215/02y. However, by decision of 27 September 2002, these proceedings had been discontinued due to the initiation of bankruptcy proceedings. On account of his indebtedness, Eduard M. had no heirs.

5   The second applicant, who was born on 3 August 1947, was also a granddaughter of the aggrieved owners. Eduard M. and the second applicant were heirs to the aggrieved owners. Probate proceedings had not been carried out after Marianne M.'s death due to the lack of assets. The son, Eduard Karl M., born on 17 July 1902, would have been entitled to the inheritance. The probate proceedings regarding the estate of Eduard Karl M. had been initiated with the District Court Hallein under file number 371/85. However, due to lack of assets, there was no processing and settlement of the estate.

6   The asserted claim for *in rem* restitution had never before been decided by an Austrian court or administrative body or settled by agreement.

2. Established Facts

7   Anton. M. was born on 21 July 1872 in Lendorf, district Marburg-Land, Styria, as the son of Anton M. and Maria M., née L. Whether Anton M. had belonged to the German-speaking or to the Slovenian-speaking population cannot be established. On 18 February 1900, in St. Nicolai at Villach, Anton M. married Maria Anna S., who was born in St. Leonhard at Villach, duchy of Carinthia, on 31 October 1877. At this point in time, Anton M. was a relief engine driver in Villach.

8   On 9 June 1910, Anton and Maria M. each acquired 50 % of the property EZ X4, KG Seebach. This property consisted of the property parcels Y2/1 garden, Y2/5 lawn, Y2/6 field and Y1 developed area with the house St. Leonhard Z.

9   In December 1940, the German Reich Railways approached the M. couple via the Reich Railways Directorate Villach in order to negotiate the transfer of their property. It cannot be established why the German Reich Railways needed this real estate. On 21 December 1940, Maria M. went to see a certain Dr. St. of the Reich Railways Directorate Villach concerning this matter. In the course of this meeting, an agreement was reached between the people involved: the M. couple agreed to accept the maximum price for their property determined by the *Preisbildungsstelle* ("Pricing Authority"). However, the basis for the valuation of the buildings and the trees and bushes which were situated on the property was supposed to be formed on the basis of an estimate carried out by the experts from the railways.

10   On 9 May 1941, the Pricing Authority determined the appropriate price per m^2 at 2.50 Reichsmark. At the beginning of May, Ing. Weger inspected the buildings on the property. On this basis, he prepared a valuation opinion. On 20 May 1941, experts from the Reich Railways made an estimate regarding the trees and bushes. After the completion of this valuation, on the same day, the M. couple signed a declaration presented by the Reich Railways. According to this declaration, the M. couple agreed to the transfer of their property, taking as a basis the square meter price, which had been announced by the Pricing Authority, and the valuation. The declaration was made under the condition that, should the Pricing Authority later determine a higher price, the new price would replace the original price. However, a new assessment of the square meter price did not take place.

11   During the next months, the M. couple and their two sons, Anton and Eduard M., repeatedly turned to Dr. St. from the Reich Railways Directorate Villach. During these meetings, the primary topic of discussion was the provision of a substitute property of equal

schaftsverfahren betreffend Eduard M. sei beim Bezirksgericht (BG) Salzburg zu Geschäftszahl (GZ) A 215/02y anhängig gewesen. Mit Beschluss vom 27. September 2002 sei dieses Verfahren jedoch wegen Konkurseröffnung eingestellt worden. Aufgrund der Überschuldung habe es keine ErbInnen von Eduard M. gegeben.

Die am 3. August 1947 geborene Zweitantragstellerin sei ebenfalls Enkelin der geschädigten EigentümerInnen. Eduard M. und die Zweitantragstellerin seien ErbInnen der geschädigten EigentümerInnen. Nach dem Tod Marianne M.s sei mangels Vermögen kein Verlassenschaftsverfahren durchgeführt worden. Erbberechtigt wäre der Sohn Eduard Karl M., geboren am 17. Juli 1902, gewesen. Das Verlassenschaftsverfahren nach Eduard Karl M. sei beim BG Hallein zu GZ 371/85 eingeleitet worden. Mangels Vermögen sei die Verlassenschaft allerdings nicht abgehandelt worden.

Die geltend gemachte Forderung auf Naturalrestitution sei niemals zuvor durch österreichische Gerichte oder Verwaltungsbehörden entschieden oder einvernehmlich geregelt worden.

2. Festgestellter Sachverhalt

Anton M. wurde am 21. Juli 1872 in Lendorf, Bezirk Marburg-Land, Land Steiermark, als Sohn von Anton M. und Maria M., geborene L., geboren. Ob Anton M. der deutschsprachigen oder der slowenischsprachigen Bevölkerungsgruppe angehört hat, kann nicht festgestellt werden. Anton M. heiratete am 18. Februar 1900 in St. Nicolai zu Villach die am 31. Oktober 1877 in St. Leonhard bei Villach, Herzogtum Kärnten, geborene Maria Anna S. Anton M. übte zu dieser Zeit den Beruf eines Lokomotivführer-Substituten in Villach aus.

Am 9. Juni 1910 erwarben Anton und Maria M. je zur Hälfte die Liegenschaft mit der EZ X4, KG Seebach. Diese Liegenschaft bestand aus den Grundstücken Y2/1 Garten, Y2/5 Wiese, Y2/6 Acker und Y1 Bauarea mit dem Haus St. Leonhard Z.

Im Dezember 1940 trat die Deutsche Reichsbahn über die Reichsbahndirektion Villach an das Ehepaar M. heran, um mit ihm über die Abtretung seiner Liegenschaft zu verhandeln. Warum die Deutsche Reichsbahn diese Liegenschaft benötigte, kann nicht festgestellt werden. Am 21. Dezember 1940 sprach Maria M. in dieser Sache bei einem Dr. St. von der Reichsbahndirektion Villach vor. Dabei wurde zwischen den Beteiligten eine Einigung erzielt: Das Ehepaar M. unterwarf sich dem von der Preisbildungsstelle festzusetzenden Höchstpreis für ihr Grundstück. Die Grundlage für die Bewertung der auf der Liegenschaft befindlichen Gebäude und der Bäume und Sträucher sollte hingegen eine von den bahneigenen Sachverständigen durchzuführende Schätzung bilden.

Die Preisbildungsstelle legte am 9. Mai 1941 den angemessenen Quadratmeterpreis auf 2,50 Reichsmark fest. Anfang Mai besichtigte ein Ing. Weger die Baulichkeiten der Liegenschaft und erstellte auf dieser Grundlage ein Schätzgutachten. Am 20. Mai 1941 nahmen Sachverständige der Reichsbahn die Schätzung der Bäume und Sträucher vor. Nach Abschluss dieser Schätzung unterschrieb das Ehepaar M. am selben Tag eine von der Reichsbahn vorgelegte Erklärung. Danach stimmte das Ehepaar M. der Abtretung ihres Grundstückes unter Zugrundelegung des von der Preisbildungsstelle mitgeteilten Quadratmeterpreises und der durchgeführten Schätzgutachten zu. Die Erklärung wurde unter der Bedingung gemacht, dass dann, wenn die Preisbildungsstelle einen höheren Preis festsetzen sollte, dieser den ursprünglichen Preis ersetzen sollte. Eine Neufestsetzung des Quadratmeterpreises unterblieb jedoch.

value for the M. couple. During these discussions, Dr. St. repeatedly mentioned that the Reich Railways had the option to expropriate the property and that the Reich Railways were not obliged to provide a substitute property, but would make an effort to do so.

12   Approximately eight months after the signing of the declaration, on 20 May 1941, the German Reich Railways sent a purchase contract to the M. couple regarding the property in question. This contract, in excerpts, read as follows:

"[…] 1.) Mr. Anton and Mrs. Maria M[…] sell and transfer and the German Reich Railways purchases and takes over the property EZ [X4], recorded in the land register of tax district Seebach, for the creation of various Reich Railways constructions. It consists of the entire property parcel number [Y2/1] (garden) cadastral area of 4724 m², the entire property parcel number [Y2/5] (lawn) cadastral area of 441 m², the entire property parcel number [Y2/6] (field) cadastral area of 1789 m², the entire property parcel number BA [Y1], cadastral area of 491 m², a total of 7445 m² for the price of 2.50 Reichsmark per m², hence for the total of 18,612.50 Reichsmark, and the residential building, including outbuilding, situated on the property number BA [Y1], with all that is immovable, including the iron low-flame stoves and ovens, the water well with an electrical unit, the dry well, the ash pit and all fences, which are situated on this property, for the all-inclusive price of 50,000 Reichsmark. Thus, for the total purchase price of 68,612.50 Reichsmark […]. Further, a compensation of 3,695 Reichsmark will be paid for the trees and bushes situated on this property. […]
11.) The Reich Railways Directorate Villach confirms herewith, as defined by para. 40 of the law of 19 May 1874, *Öst. RGBl.* ("Austrian Empire Law Gazette") No. 70, as amended by para. 55 of the Administration Relief Act dated 21 July 1925, *BGBl.* ("Federal Law Gazette") No. 277, that the redeemed properties are designated for railway-operating purposes.
12.) The vendors hereby declare by affidavit, as defined by the *GBl f d L Öst* ("Law Gazette for the Territory of Austria") No. 633 and *RGBl.* ("Reich Law Gazette") No. 91 from 1938 that this is not Jewish property."

The couple refused to sign this purchase contract.

13   Then, in 1942 at the Regional Court Klagenfurt under file number 12 Cg 97/42, the German Reich Railways sued the M. couple demanding performance of the contract. On 28 October 1942, after a hearing had taken place, a decision was passed by Viktor W., the sole judge. Anton and Maria M. were found guilty and ordered to transfer the two property halves of EZ X4, KG Seebach, unencumbered, into the ownership of the German Reich Railways for a purchase price of 72,307.50 Reichsmark.

14   On an unspecified day – however before 18 November 1942 – the lawyer Dr. Karl G., representative of the M. couple during the lawsuit against the German Reich Railways, informed his clients that the decision of 28 October 1942 was due to become legally binding. Among other things, he pointed out that they were entitled to the right of appeal: "In my opinion, in view of the present evidential (witnesses) and legal position, there would be no prospect of achieving an amendment of the decision in your favor by means of an appeal at the Higher Regional Court for Civil Matters in Graz." The M. couple did not appeal this decision.

15   On 21 December 1942, the German Reich Railways applied to the Local Court Klagenfurt for the partitioning-off of the property parcels Y2/1, Y2/5, Y2/6 and Y1. After these property parcels had been merged and recorded in the railway register of the Crown-Prince-Rudolf-Train by the Local Court Vienna on 27 January 1943, EZ X4, KG Seebach, was

Schiedsinstanz für Naturalrestitution – Entscheidung Nr. 26/2005

In den nächsten Monaten wandten sich das Ehepaar M. und ihre beiden Söhne Anton und Eduard M. wiederholt an Dr. St. von der Reichsbahndirektion Villach, wobei vor allem über die Bereitstellung eines gleichwertigen Ersatzgrundstückes für das Ehepaar M. gesprochen wurde. Bei diesen Gesprächen erwähnte Dr. St. wiederholt, dass die Reichsbahn die Möglichkeit der Enteignung habe und sie zur Bereitstellung eines Ersatzgrundstückes nicht verpflichtet sei, er sich aber darum bemühen werde. 11

Etwa acht Monate nach Unterfertigung der Erklärung am 20. Mai 1941 sandte die Deutsche Reichsbahn dem Ehepaar M. einen Kaufvertrag über die gegenständliche Liegenschaft zu. Dieser Vertrag lautet auszugsweise wie folgt: 12

„[...] 1.) Herrn [sic] Anton und Frau Maria M[...] verkaufen und übergeben und die Deutsche Reichsbahn kauft und übernimmt zur Schaffung verschiedener Reichsbahnanlagen die im Grundbuch der StG Seebach eingetragene Liegenschaft GEZ [X4], bestehend aus dem ganzen Grundstück Nr [Y2/1] (Garten) im Katastralausmaß von 4724 m², dem ganzen Grundstück Nr [Y2/5] (Wiese) im Katastralausmaß von 441 m², dem ganzen Grundstück Nr [Y2/6] (Acker) im Katastralausmaß von 1789 m², dem ganzen Grundstück Nr BA [Y1] im Katastralausmaß von 491 m², zusammen 7445 m² zum Preise von 2,50 RM je m², somit zum Kaufschilling von 18. 612,50 RM und das auf dem Grundstück Nr. BA [Y1] befindliche Wohnhaus samt Nebengebäude mit allem Niet- und Nagelfesten, einschließlich der eisernen Sparherde und Öfen, dem Brunnen mit elektrischem Aggregat, der Sickergrube, der Aschengrube und sämtlicher auf dieser Liegenschaft befindlichen Zäune zum Pauschalpreis von 50. 000,– RM, somit zum Gesamtkaufpreisschilling von 68.612, 50 RM [...]. Ferner wird für die auf dieser Liegenschaft befindlichen Bäume und Sträucher eine Entschädigung von 3 695,– RM gezahlt. [...]

11.) Die Reichsbahndirektion Villach bestätigt hiermit im Sinne des § 40 des Ges vom 19.5.1874, Öst RGBl Nr 70, in der Fassung des Art 55 des VEG vom 21.7.1925, RGBl 277, daß die eingelösten Grundstücke für Eisenbahnbetriebszwecke bestimmt sind.

12.) Die Verkäufer erklären hiermit im Sinne des GBl f d L Öst Nr 633 und RGBl Nr 91 aus 1938 eidesstättig, daß es sich um keinen jüdischen Besitz handelt."

Das Ehepaar M. weigerte sich, diesen Kaufvertrag zu unterschreiben.

Daraufhin klagte die Deutsche Reichsbahn im Jahr 1942 zur Zahl 12 Cg 97/42 des Landgerichtes (LG) Klagenfurt das Ehepaar M. auf Vertragszuhaltung. Nach durchgeführter mündlicher Verhandlung erging am 28. Oktober 1942 durch den Einzelrichter Viktor W. das Urteil. Anton und Maria M. wurden schuldig gesprochen, der Deutschen Reichsbahn die beiden Liegenschaftshälften der Grundbuchseinlage X4, KG Seebach, zu einem Kaufpreis von 72.307,50 Reichsmark lastenfrei ins Eigentum zu übergeben. 13

An einem nicht näher bekannten Tag – jedenfalls aber vor dem 18. November 1942 – informierte RA Dr. Karl G., Vertreter des Ehepaares M. im Prozess gegen die Deutsche Reichsbahn, seine MandantInnen über die bald eintretende Rechtskraft des Urteiles vom 28. Oktober 1942. Er wies unter anderem darauf hin, dass ihnen das Rechtsmittel der Berufung zustehe: „Meines Erachtens würden Sie bei der vorliegenden Beweis- (Zeugen) und Rechtslage keine Aussicht haben, im Wege der Berufung an das Oberlandesgericht Graz eine Abänderung des Urteiles zu Ihren Gunsten zu erreichen." Das Ehepaar M. erhob keine Berufung gegen das Urteil. 14

Am 21. Dezember 1942 suchte die Deutsche Reichsbahn beim Amtsgericht Klagenfurt um Abschreibung der Grundstücke Y2/1, Y2/5, Y2/6 und Y1 an. Nach der Zuschreibung dieser Grundstücke zur Eisenbahneinlage des Eisenbahnbuches für die Kronprinz-Rudolf- 15

deleted on 12 February 1943 as there were no further properties registered under this particular register number.

16 During the pending lawsuit and also after the legally binding conclusion of the proceedings, the M. couple and sons sought assistance from various National Socialist departments to remedy this matter. In a letter from the M. couple dated 23 September 1942 to the *Führer* it said among other things:

> "[…] For this reason we request you profusely, honored *Führer*, to help us so that the German Reich Railways refrain from taking away our property in Villach-St. Leonhard [Z] for which we have so struggled, or that at least it only expropriate the property parcels belonging to our house for a reasonable price. Should, however, the German Reich Railways really need our property parcels as well as our house for railway purposes, then the German Reich Railways shall at least construct a house of equivalent value on a property parcel belonging to the Reich Railway and situated in the nearest vicinity. […] We have raised a lot of children and we have also raised them in line with national ideals. For instance, our son who died recently had been a member of the Nationalist Party since 1923 and foreman in the National Socialist Motor Corps. Our son Eduard joined the National Socialist Party in the year 1934 and was punished with 14 days arrest for his illegal activities during the *Systemzeit* [National Socialist term for the Austrian 'corporative State']. He was also forced to give up his thriving pastry shop for these reasons. […]"

17 These letters did not achieve any changes in the ownership status of the property in question. A new assessment of the purchase price also did not take place. The payment of the purchase price to the M. couple did not take place as they refused to accept the money.

18 After the re-establishment of the Republic of Austria, the M. couple turned to, among other places, the Federal Government, department for compensation, the Financial Directorate for Carinthia, to the Federal Chancellary, and to the Federal Chancellors Leopold Figl and Julius Raab, with the request for the restitution of their former property. In its reply to the M. couple of 15 March 1947, the Financial Directorate initially referred to the *Erste Rückstellungsgesetz* ("First Restitution Act"). According to this Act, restitutions can only be carried out under the condition that the property has been seized by the German Reich due to abrogated Reich legal provisions or through administrative acts. However, in the case in question, this requirement was not met as the property had been granted to the Reich Railways by a court order of the Regional Court Klagenfurt. Finally, the Financial Directorate informed the M. couple of the imminent enactment of the *Dritte Rückstellungsgesetz* ("Third Restitution Act") which was applicable to the case. Proceedings in accordance with the Third Restitution Act were not initiated by the M. couple or by their legal successors.

19 Anton M. died on 11 July 1952. His estate was devolved to Marianne M. on 8 August 1955.

20 On 16 December 1954, Marianne M. directed a letter to the Federal Ministry of Transport in which she – in reaction to a previous suggestion by the Ministry – presented a settlement proposal. Marianne M. claimed the amount of 350,000 Schilling as compensation for the property in question. Whether this letter was followed by settlement talks or negotiations between the persons involved cannot be established.

21 In August 1955, Marianne M. turned to the Federal Ministry of Finance. Once again she requested the restitution of the property in question or reasonable compensation, without, however, stating a concrete sum. Finally, Marianne M. informed them that she would never recognize the expropriation of that time.

Bahn durch das Amtsgericht Wien am 27. Jänner 1943 wurde die Grundbuchseinlage X4, KG Seebach, am 12. Februar 1943 mangels weiteren Gutsbestandes gelöscht.

Sowohl das Ehepaar M. als auch ihre Söhne ersuchten noch während des anhängigen Prozesses und auch nach rechtskräftigem Abschluss des Verfahrens verschiedene NSDAP-Dienststellen um Abhilfe in dieser Angelegenheit. In einem Schreiben des Ehepaares M. vom 23. September 1942 an den „Führer" hieß es unter anderem: 16

„[...] Wir bitten Sie verehrten Führer daher vielmals, uns dahin zu helfen, dass die Deutschen Reichsbahnen von der Wegnahme unseres schwer erkämpften Besitzes in Villach-St. Leonhard [Z] Abstand nimmt, oder wenigstens nur die zu unserem Hause gehörigen Grundstücke zum angemessenen Preise enteignet. Sollte aber die Deutsche Reichsbahn unbedingt unsere Grundstücke als auch unser Haus für Bahnzwecke benötigen, dann möge uns wenigstens die Deutsche Reichsbahn ein gleichwertiges Haus, auf einen [sic] ihr gehörigen, in nächster Nähe befindlichen Grundstücke errichten. [...] Wir haben eine Reihe Kinder grossgezogen und sie auch im nationalen Sinne erzogen. So war unser kürzlichst verstorbener Sohn seit dem Jahr 1923 Mitglied der NSDAP. und Rottenführer in der NSKK. Der Sohn Eduard ist im Jahre 1934 der NSDAP. beigetreten und wurde für die illegale Betätigung in der Systemzeit mit 14 Tagen Arrest bestraft und wurde er auch aus diesem Grunde gezwungen, sein gutgehendes Konditoreigeschäft aufzugeben.[...]"

Diese Schreiben bewirkten keine Änderung der Eigentumsverhältnisse an der gegenständlichen Liegenschaft. Auch eine Neufestsetzung des Kaufpreises unterblieb. Eine Auszahlung des Kaufpreises an das Ehepaar M. unterblieb, da es sich weigerte, das Geld anzunehmen. 17

Nach Wiedererrichtung der Republik Österreich wandte sich das Ehepaar M. unter anderem an die Bundesregierung, Abteilung Wiedergutmachung, an die Finanzlandesdirektion (FLD) für Kärnten, an das Bundeskanzleramt (BKA) sowie an die Bundeskanzler Leopold Figl und Julius Raab, mit dem Ersuchen um Rückstellung ihres früheren Grundbesitzes. Die FLD verwies in ihrer Antwort vom 15. März 1947 an das Ehepaar M. zunächst auf das Erste Rückstellungsgesetz (1. RStG). Nach diesem Gesetz könnten Rückstellungen nur unter der Voraussetzung erfolgen, wenn das Vermögen vom Deutschen Reich aufgrund von aufgehobenen reichsrechtlichen Vorschriften oder durch verwaltungsbehördliche Verfügung entzogen worden sei. Diese Voraussetzung treffe aber im gegenständlichen Fall nicht zu, da das Vermögen durch einen Gerichtsbeschluss des Landesgerichtes Klagenfurt der Deutschen Reichsbahn zuerkannt worden sei. Abschließend wies die FLD das Ehepaar M. auf das baldige Inkrafttreten des Dritten Rückstellungsgesetzes (3. RStG) hin, welches auf den Fall anwendbar sei. Ein Verfahren nach dem Dritten Rückstellungsgesetz wurde durch das Ehepaar M. oder ihre Rechtsnachfolger nicht eingeleitet. 18

Anton M. verstarb am 11. Juli 1952. Sein Nachlass wurde Marianne M. am 8. August 1955 eingeantwortet. 19

Am 16. Dezember 1954 richtete Marianne M. ein Schreiben an das Bundesministerium für Verkehr, in dem sie – als Reaktion auf eine bereits zuvor gemachte Anregung des Ministeriums hin – einen Vergleichsvorschlag unterbreitete. Marianne M. verlangte als Entschädigung für die gegenständliche Liegenschaft den Betrag von 350.000,– Schilling. Ob diesem Schreiben Vergleichsgespräche oder -verhandlungen zwischen den Beteiligten gefolgt sind, kann nicht festgestellt werden. 20

22 On 22 January 1956, Marianne M. addressed a letter to "your Excellency". It cannot be established for whom it was intended. This letter, in excerpts, has the following content:

"[…] However, we could not enjoy our property for long, because under the one-time Nazi-regime we were forced to sell our house to the Reich Railways. We were subjected to this pressure all the more so because my husband was Yugoslavian and for this reason, as he would not sell, he was continually threatened with grave punishments because of his nationality. We were promised 70,000 Reichsmark for the sale of our property in Villach St. Leonhard [Z]. However, so far we have only received a total of 35,000 Schilling. Hence, in my plight I turn to you, your Excellency, after so many unsuccessful attempts, in order to finally attain my rights and therefore also the still outstanding amount of the purchase price […]."

When, by whom and on what basis the amount of 35,000 Schilling was paid to Marianne M. cannot be established.

23 Marianne M. died on 15 July 1956 without leaving an inheritance. Her son Eduard Karl M. died on 1 December 1985. A processing and settlement of the estate did not take place as there was no property present. Eduard Karl M. had at least two direct descendants: Eduard Alois M., born on 22 June 1938 and the second applicant who was born on 3 August 1947.

24 Eduard Alois M. died on 11 March 2002. On 7 October 2002, bankruptcy proceedings were initiated with the Regional Court Salzburg under file number 23 S 482/02f. The bankruptcy court appointed Dr. Konrad Ferner, attorney-at-law in Salzburg, as trustee of a bankrupt estate. On 27 May 2003, Dr. Konrad Ferner authorized Dr. Herbert Hübel, attorney-at-law in Salzburg, to assert any restitution claims. The bankruptcy was closed on 21 October 2004.

3. Evidence

25 Evidence was taken by reviewing the following documents enclosed with the application for *in rem* restitution: certificate of baptism of Anton M., main rectory Kötsch; birth certificate and certificate of baptism of Maria Anna M., née S., town rectory St. Nicolai at Villach; marriage certificate of Anton M. and Maria Anna S., town rectory St. Nicolai at Villach; birth certificate and certificate of baptism of Eduard Karl M., town rectory St. Nicolai in Villach; birth certificate of Eduard Alois M., town rectory Hallein; death certificate of Eduard Alois M., registry office association Salzburg; birth certificate of Edith M., registry office Hallein; certificate of inheritance to the estate of Anton M., file number A 453/52, District Court Villach; special land-register extract concerning EZ X4, KG Seebach, District Court Villach; layout plan concerning the division into parcels of land of the property EZ X4, KG Seebach; excerpt from the digital cadastral index concerning the plots of the KG Seebach; land register extract concerning EZ X1, KG Seebach; land register extract concerning EZ X2, KG Seebach; land register extract concerning EZ X3, KG Seebach; letter from Marianne M., 22 January 1956; notification of outcome of the processing and settlement of the estate of Eduard Karl M., file number A 371/85, District Court Hallein; undated contract draft of the German Reich Railways, Reich Railways Directorate Villach, regarding property EZ X4, KG Seebach; copies of minutes of 10 September 1942 and 19 October 1942 concerning 12 Cg 97/42, Regional Court Klagenfurt; order of the Local Court Villach of 13 February 1943 on E 1207/42; letter from Eduard M. to the *Führer's* Chancellary, 21 September 1942; letter from the *Führer's* Chancellary, 5 October 1942; letter by the Reich Minister for Transport, 12 October 1942; letter by Anton and Maria M. to the *Führer*, 23 September 1942; letter by lawyer Dr. Karl G., 13 December

Im August 1955 wandte sich Marianne M. an das Bundesministerium für Finanzen. Sie 21
bat nochmals um Rückstellung der gegenständlichen Liegenschaft bzw. um eine angemessene Entschädigung, ohne jedoch eine konkrete Summe zu nennen. Abschließend wies Marianne M. darauf hin, dass sie die seinerzeitige Enteignung niemals anerkennen werde.

Am 22. Jänner 1956 richtete Marianne M. einen Brief an „Eure Exzellenz". Wer damit 22
gemeint ist, kann nicht festgestellt werden. Dieser Brief hat auszugsweise folgenden Inhalt:

„[...] Wir sollten uns jedoch nicht lange unseres Besitzes erfreuen, den [sic] unter den [sic] verflossenen Nazi-Regime wurden wir gezwungen, unser Haus an die Reichsbahn zu veräußern. Diesem Drucke waren wir um so mehr ausgesetzt, als mein Mann Jugoslawe war und man Ihm deswegen immer wegen seiner Nationalität schwere Strafen für den Fall des nicht-Verkaufes [sic] androhte. Als Erlös für den Verkauf unserer Liegenschaft in Villach St. Leonhart [Z] wurden uns 70.000,– RM zugesagt. Bis heute haben wir jedoch nur insgesamt 35.000 Schilling erhalten. Ich wende mich daher in meiner Not an Eure Exzellenz nach so vielen erfolglosen Versuchen, endlich zu meinem Rechte und damit auch zu der noch ausstehenden Kaufpreissumme zu gelangen [...]."

Wann, von wem und auf welcher Grundlage der Betrag von 35.000,– Schilling an Marianne M. gezahlt wurde, kann nicht festgestellt werden.

Marianne M. verstarb am 15. Juli 1956 ohne Hinterlassung eines Nachlasses. Ihr Sohn 23
Eduard Karl M. verstarb am 1. Dezember 1985. Da kein Vermögen vorhanden war, unterblieb die Verlassenschaftsabhandlung. Eduard Karl M. hat zumindest zwei direkte Nachkommen, den am 22. Juni 1938 geborenen Eduard Alois M. und die am 3. August 1947 geborene Zweitantragstellerin.

Eduard Alois M. verstarb am 11. März 2002. Über die Verlassenschaft nach Eduard 24
Alois M. wurde am 7. Oktober 2002 durch das Landesgericht Salzburg zur Zahl 23 S 482/02f der Konkurs eröffnet. Zum Masseverwalter bestellte das Konkursgericht Dr. Konrad Ferner, RA in Salzburg. Dr. Konrad Ferner bevollmächtigte am 27. Mai 2003 Dr. Herbert Hübel, RA in Salzburg, zur Geltendmachung von Rückstellungsansprüchen. Der Konkurs wurde am 21. Oktober 2004 aufgehoben.

3. Beweise

Beweis wurde erhoben durch Einsichtnahme in folgende dem Antrag auf Naturalresti- 25
tution beigelegten Dokumente: Taufschein von Anton M., Hauptpfarramt Kötsch; Geburts- und Taufschein von Maria Anna M., geb. S., Stadtpfarramt St. Nicolai zu Villach; Trauungsschein von Anton M. und Maria Anna S., Stadtpfarramt St. Nicolai zu Villach; Geburts- und Taufschein von Eduard Karl M., Stadtpfarramt St. Nicolai in Villach; Geburtsurkunde von Eduard Alois M., Stadtpfarramt Hallein; Sterbeurkunde von Eduard Alois M., Standesamtsverband Salzburg; Geburtsurkunde von Edith M., Standesamt Hallein; Einantwortungsurkunde zur Verlassenschaft nach Anton M., GZ A 453/52, BG Villach; Besonderer Grundbuchsauszug zur EZ X4, KG Seebach, BG Villach; Lageplan zur Parzellierung der Liegenschaft EZ X4, KG Seebach; Auszug aus der Digitalen Katastralmappe zu Parzellen der KG Seebach; Grundbuchsauszug zur EZ X1, KG Seebach; Grundbuchsauszug zur EZ X2, KG Seebach; Grundbuchsauszug zur EZ X3, KG Seebach; Brief von Marianne M., 22. Jänner 1956; Mitteilung des Abhandlungsergebnisses zur Verlassenschaft nach Eduard Karl M., GZ A 371/85, BG Hallein; Undatierter Vertragsentwurf der Deutschen Reichsbahn, Reichsbahndirektion Villach, zur Liegenschaft EZ X4, KG

1942 (based on the content, the letter probably dates from 13 November 1942); letter from Anton and Maria M. to the head of the regional administration Dr. R., 21 May 1943; letter from the NS-regional administration Carinthia to Eduard M., 23 June 1943; letter from Eduard M. to the head of the regional administration Dr. R., 12 July 1943; letter from the *Führer's* Chancellary to Anton M., 20 July 1944; letter from the NS-regional administration Carinthia to Anton M., 31 July 1944; letter from Anton and Maria M. to the Federal Government, department for compensation, 10 August 1946; letter from Anton and Maria M. to the Financial Directorate in Klagenfurt, 10 March 1947; letter from the Financial Directorate for Carinthia to Anton and Anna [sic] M., 15 March 1947; letter from Anton and Maria M. to the Federal Chancellary, 13 October 1948; letter from Anton and Marianne M. to the Federal Chancellor Dr. Figl, 3 September 1951; letter from the Federal Chancellary to Anton and Marianne M., 20 September 1951; administrative certificate from the District Court Villach, 15 November 1951; letter from Maria M. to Federal Chancellor Dr. Raab, 17 November 1953; letter from Marianne M. to the Federal Ministry for Transport, 16 December 1954; letter from Marianne M. to the Federal Ministry of Finance, August 1955; death record regarding Marianne M., file number A 197/56, District Court Hallein.

26 The following documents were viewed by the Arbitration Panel: Railway register of the Crown-Prince-Rudolf-Train, District Court Vienna-Stadt; decision by the District Court Klagenfurt of 28 October 1942 on 12 Cg 97/42 (copy), document collection on the Crown-Prince-Rudolf-Train daily file no. 24/43, District Court Innere Stadt – Vienna.

4. Consideration of Evidence

27 The following is to be noted concerning the inability to establish the origin of Anton M.: The submitted bilingual certificate of baptism is completed in German. However, this does not permit the conclusion that Anton M. belonged to the German-speaking population. The reason for this could also be that the parish priest who completed the form only spoke or preferred the German language. Historical documents can also not provide clarity. In 1910, the population in the Marburg-District was composed of approximately 80 % Slovenes and 20 % Germans (according to the nationality map of the Austro-Hungarian monarchy in Adam Wandruszka and Peter Urbanitsch (Eds.), *Die Habsburgermonarchie 1848–1918* vol. III, 2nd fascicle, map case, Vienna 1980).

28 The findings concerning the negotiations on the transfer of the property and the associated agreements reached largely follow the decision by the District Court Klagenfurt dated 28 October 1942. The Arbitration Panel sees no reason to doubt the findings reached in this decision. The explanations given by the M. couple in the extensive correspondence with various administrative bodies and with departments of the National Socialist State as well as of the Republic of Austria do not change anything in this regard. Also, the repeated references after 1945 to alleged Nazi-methods applied by the Reich Railways are not supported by the documents. Finally, there is also a lack of evidence of any kind confirming the massive threats and intimidation claimed by the applicants.

29 The finding that Anton and Maria M. refused to accept the purchase price results, among other things, from their letter of 13 October 1948 to the Federal Chancellary and to the Federal Chancellor Leopold Figl. Obviously, the M. couple wanted to avoid any kind of "recognition" of the sale of the property.

30 The finding that Anton and Maria M. and/or their legal successors did not initiate restitution proceedings results from the railway register of the Crown-Prince-Rudolf-Train. Pursuant to para. 24 (1) of the Third Restitution Act, the Restitution Commission is re-

Seebach; Protokollsabschriften vom 10. September 1942 und 19. Oktober 1942 zu 12 Cg 97/42, LG Klagenfurt; Beschluss des Amtsgerichtes Villach vom 13. Februar 1943 zu E 1207/42; Schreiben von Eduard M. an die Kanzlei des Führers, 21. September 1942; Schreiben der Kanzlei des Führers, 5. Oktober 1942; Schreiben des Reichsverkehrsministers, 12. Oktober 1942; Schreiben von Anton und Maria M. an den Führer, 23. September 1942; Schreiben von RA Dr. Karl G., 13. Dezember 1942 (aufgrund des Inhaltes wohl vom 13. November 1942); Schreiben von Anton und Maria M. an Gauleiter Dr. R., 21. Mai 1943; Schreiben der Gauleitung Kärnten an Eduard M., 23. Juni 1943; Schreiben von Eduard M. an Gauleiter Dr. R., 12. Juli 1943; Schreiben der Kanzlei des Führers an Anton M., 20. Juli 1944; Schreiben der Gauleitung Kärnten an Anton M., 31. Juli 1944; Schreiben von Anton und Maria M. an die Bundesregierung, Abteilung Wiedergutmachung, 10. August 1946; Schreiben von Anton und Maria M. an die FLD in Klagenfurt, 10. März 1947; Schreiben der FLD für Kärnten an Anton und Anna [sic] M., 15. März 1947; Schreiben von Anton und Maria M. an das BKA, 13. Oktober 1948; Schreiben von Anton und Marianne M. an Bundeskanzler Dr. Figl, 3. September 1951; Schreiben des BKA an Anton und Marianne M., 20. September 1951; Amtsbestätigung des BG Villach, 15. November 1951; Schreiben von Maria M. an Bundeskanzler Dr. Raab, 17. November 1953; Schreiben von Marianne M. an das Bundesministerium für Verkehr, 16. Dezember 1954; Schreiben von Marianne M. an das Bundesministerium für Finanzen, August 1955; Todfallsaufnahme zu Marianne M., GZ A 197/56, BG Hallein.

Folgende Dokumente wurden durch die Schiedsinstanz eingesehen: Eisenbahnbuch zur Kronprinz-Rudolf-Bahn, BG Innere Stadt-Wien; Urteil des LG Klagenfurt vom 28. Oktober 1942 zu 12 Cg 97/42 (Abschrift), Urkundensammlung zur Kronprinz-Rudolf-Bahn TZ 24/43, BG Innere Stadt – Wien. 26

4. Beweiswürdigung

Zur fehlenden Feststellbarkeit der Herkunft von Anton M. ist Folgendes anzumerken: 27
Der vorgelegte zweisprachige Taufschein ist zwar auf deutsch ausgefüllt, dies lässt jedoch nicht per se den Schluss zu, dass Anton M. der deutschsprachigen Bevölkerungsgruppe angehört hat. Dies könnte seinen Grund auch darin haben, dass der ausfüllende Pfarrer nur deutsch gesprochen oder die deutsche Sprache bevorzugt hat. Auch historische Unterlagen können hier keine Klarheit verschaffen. Die Bevölkerung im Bezirk Marburg–Land setzte sich 1910 aus ca. 80 % Slowenen und 20 % Deutschen zusammen (dies nach der Nationalitätenkarte der österreichisch-ungarischen Monarchie in Adam *Wandruszka* und Peter *Urbanitsch* (Hrsg.), Die Habsburgermonarchie 1848–1918, Bd. III, 2. Teilband (Kartentasche) Wien 1980).

Die Feststellungen zu den Verhandlungen über die Abtretung des Grundstückes und die 28
dazu getroffenen Vereinbarungen folgen weitgehend dem Urteil des LG Klagenfurt vom 28. Oktober 1942. Die Schiedsinstanz sieht keinen Grund, an den darin getroffenen Feststellungen zu zweifeln. Daran vermögen auch die Ausführungen des Ehepaars M. in seiner umfangreichen Korrespondenz an verschiedene Behörden und Dienststellen, sowohl des NS-Staates als auch der Republik Österreich, nichts zu ändern. Auch der nach 1945 wiederholt vorgebrachte Hinweis auf von der Reichsbahn angeblich angewendeten Nazi-Methoden findet keine Stütze in den Dokumenten. Schließlich fehlt auch jeder Beleg, für die von den Antragstellerinnen behaupteten, massivsten Drohungen und Einschüchterungen.

Die Feststellung, dass sich Anton und Maria M. weigerten, den Kaufpreis anzunehmen, 29
ergibt sich unter anderem aus ihrem Schreiben an das BKA vom 13. Oktober 1948 und an

quired to arrange for the recording of the restitution proceedings in the land register. However, no such note is to be found in the railway register of the Crown-Prince-Rudolf-Train. This is also confirmed by the correspondence of the M. couple after World War II. In their letters there are numerous indications which show that according to the information they had received the restitution laws were not applicable and since German property is concerned the matter did not fall under the jurisdiction of the Austrian authorities.

5. Juridical Appraisal

31   Concerning the eligibility of the first applicant to file an application, it is to be explained that according to the notification of 15 September 2005 by her representative, the probate proceedings for Eduard Alois M. had been discontinued on 27 September 2002 due to the initiation of bankruptcy proceedings. On account of the indebtedness there had been no heirs. Where a processing and settlement of the estate had not taken place due to the lack of property, the estate retains the capacity of being a party in a lawsuit (see Welser in Rummel para. 547 (Austrian) General Civil Code [3rd edition] margin note 6 and Schubert in Fasching II [2nd edition] ante para 1 Code of Civil Procedure margin note 66). The first applicant continues to be duly represented. The Arbitration Panel does not have any information which would show that the power of attorney which was issued on 27 May 2003 to Dr. Herbert Hübel by the trustee of a bankrupt estate Dr. Konrad Ferner, the legal representative of the first applicant, had been revoked or terminated. The termination of bankruptcy proceedings, which took place in the meantime, does not change that. Due to the lack of regulations to the contrary, legal acts which were performed by the bodies administering the bankruptcy in principle remain effective also after the termination of bankruptcy (see Jelinek/Nunner-Krautgasser in Konecny/Schubert [eds.], commentary on insolvency laws para. 59 of the Bankruptcy Act margin note 33; Supreme Court 22 November 1977, 4 Ob 400/77).

32   The second applicant and Eduard Alois. M., whose rights are being asserted by the first applicant, are direct descendants of the former property owners Anton and Maria. M., however, they are not the universal successors to Maria M. as universal succession has not taken place as the devolution to Maria M. and her son Eduard M. had not occured. However, they belong to the circle of statutory heirs. According to the Arbitration Panel, this is sufficient for the eligibility to file applications as defined by Sec. 27 (2) of the *Entschädigungsfondsgesetz* ("General Settlement Fund Law", GSF Law).

33   At first, the applicants submitted that the Yugoslav origins of Anton M. had been causal in the seizure of the property. On 4 July 2005, the Arbitration Panel, with reference to the relevant regulations in its Rules of Procedure, requested that the applicants specify this assertion and present supporting evidence. The applicants pointed out in their reply of 15 September 2005 that there were no documents concerning the Yugoslav citizenship and that also other written evidence of discrimination was not present.

34   The procedure of taking evidence merely showed that Anton M. was born in lower Styria. However, it is not certain whether he belonged to the German-speaking or to the Slovenian-speaking population. In the evidence, there are no indications that Anton M.'s claimed Yugoslav origins were of importance during the property transaction. This is only mentioned in Marianne M.'s letter of 22 January 1956 (refer to margin note 22) without a more detailed explanation of the circumstances of the predicament which was claimed in this letter. Finally, the non-initiation of restitution proceedings can also be regarded as a substantial indication that Anton M.'s claimed origins did not have any influence on the sale

Bundeskanzler Leopold Figl vom 3. September 1951. Das Ehepaar M. wollte dadurch offenbar jeden Anschein einer „Anerkennung" des Liegenschaftsverkaufes vermeiden.

Die Feststellung, dass Anton und Maria M. bzw. ihre RechtsnachfolgerInnen kein Rückstellungsverfahren eingeleitet haben, ergibt sich aus dem Eisenbahnbuch zur Kronprinz-Rudolf-Bahn. Gemäß § 24 Abs 1 3. RStG hat die Rückstellungskommission zwingend die Anmerkung der Einleitung des Rückstellungsverfahrens im Grundbuch zu veranlassen. Eine solche Anmerkung findet sich im Eisenbahnbuch zur Kronprinz-Rudolf-Bahn jedoch nicht. Dies wird auch durch die vom Ehepaar M. nach Ende des Zweiten Weltkrieges geführte Korrespondenz bestätigt. In seinen Schreiben findet sich mehrmals der Hinweis, dass nach ihnen erteilten Auskünften die Rückstellungsgesetze nicht anwendbar seien, bzw. da es sich um Deutsches Eigentum handle, die Sache nicht in die Zuständigkeit der österreichischen Behörden falle.

5. Rechtliche Beurteilung

Zur Antragslegitimation der Erstantragstellerin ist auszuführen, dass laut Mitteilung ihres Vertreters vom 15. September 2005 das Verlassenschaftsverfahren nach Eduard Alois M. am 27. September 2002 wegen Konkurseröffnung eingestellt worden sei. Aufgrund der Überschuldung habe es keine ErbInnen gegeben. Hat mangels Vermögen keine Verlassenschaftsabhandlung stattgefunden, bleibt der Nachlass parteifähig (vgl. *Welser* in *Rummel*[3] § 547 ABGB Rz 6 und *Schubert* in *Fasching* II[2] Vor § 1 ZPO Rz 66). Die Erstantragstellerin ist auch weiterhin ordnungsgemäß vertreten. Es liegen der Schiedsinstanz keine Informationen vor, dass die am 27. Mai 2003 vom Masseverwalter Dr. Konrad Ferner als gesetzlicher Vertreter der Erstantragstellerin an Dr. Herbert Hübel erteilte Vollmacht widerrufen oder gekündigt worden wäre. Daran vermag auch die zwischenzeitig erfolgte Konkursaufhebung nichts zu ändern. Mangels entgegenstehender Regelung bleiben Rechtshandlungen, die die Konkursorgane gesetzt haben, grundsätzlich auch nach Konkursaufhebung wirksam (vgl. *Jelinek, Nunner-Krautgasser* in *Konecny, Schubert* (Hg.), Kommentar zu den Insolvenzgesetzen § 59 KO Rz 33; Oberster Gerichtshof (OGH) 22. November 1977, 4 Ob 400/77).

Die Zweitantragstellerin und Eduard Alois M., dessen Rechte die Erstantragstellerin geltend macht, sind direkte Nachkommen der ehemaligen LiegenschaftseigentümerInnen Anton und Maria M. Die genannten Personen sind zwar keine Gesamtrechtsnachfolger nach Maria M., da mangels Einantwortung nach Maria M. und nach ihrem Sohn Eduard M. keine Gesamtrechtsnachfolge eingetreten ist, sie gehören aber zum Kreis der gesetzlichen ErbInnen. Dies ist nach Ansicht der Schiedsinstanz für die Antragslegitimation nach § 27 Abs 2 Entschädigungsfondsgesetz (EF-G) ausreichend.

Die Antragstellerinnen haben zunächst vorgebracht, dass die jugoslawische Abstammung von Anton M. kausal für den Entzug der Liegenschaft gewesen sei. Am 4. Juli 2005 hat die Schiedsinstanz die Antragstellerinnen mit Hinweis auf die einschlägigen Bestimmungen in ihrer Geschäfts- und Verfahrensordnung aufgefordert, dieses Vorbringen zu präzisieren und entsprechende Beweise vorzulegen. Die Antragstellerinnen wiesen in ihrer Antwort vom 15. September 2005 darauf hin, dass es keine Dokumente über die jugoslawische Staatsangehörigkeit gebe und auch andere schriftliche Beweise für eine Diskriminierung nicht vorliegen würden.

Das Beweisverfahren hat bloß gezeigt, dass Anton M. in der Untersteiermark geboren worden war, wobei nicht feststeht, ob er der deutsch- oder slowenischsprachigen Bevölkerungsgruppe angehört hatte. In den Beweismitteln finden sich keine Hinweise darauf,

Arbitration Panel for *In Rem* Restitution – Decision No. 26/2005

of the property. It can be assumed that the M. couple would have had opportunities to conduct proceedings of this kind when keeping in mind their other efforts to regain their property. The numerous petitions made to the various, especially political, decision-makers, clearly illustrate this. Obviously it must have been clear for the M. couple, that due to the lack of political persecution or other predicaments motivated by National Socialism, the requirements for a property confiscation as defined by para. 2 (1) or (2) of the Third Restitution Act were not met.

35 Hence, origin as a ground for persecution, which was asserted by the applicants, did not exist. The presence of other grounds for persecution was not asserted by the applicants. However, it should be remarked that no indications for this were found within the evidence. However, Sec. 27 (1) of the GSF Law requires as a prerequisite for the restitution of a property that one of the grounds for persecution mentioned in the law is present. The applications were to be rejected solely for this reason, since this requirement is not fulfilled. The further legal requirements for an *in rem* restitution no longer needed to be examined.

36 Whether the applicants can duly assert their claim before the general courts of law does not have to be assessed by the Arbitration Panel. The relevant decisions are merely referred to: Constitutional Court/Constitutional Court Decision Collection 8980, 8981 and 8982 Supreme Court 5 Ob231/98a.

Dr. Josef Aicher, university professor, Chairman
Dr. Dr. h. c. Erich Kussbach, LL. M., honorary professor and retired ambassador
MMag. Dr. August Reinisch, LL. M., university professor

dass bei der Liegenschaftstransaktion die behauptete jugoslawische Abstammung von Anton M. eine Rolle gespielt hätte. Lediglich im Schreiben Marianne M.s vom 22. Jänner 1956 wird dies erwähnt (siehe oben Rz 22), ohne dass nähere Umstände der darin behaupteten Zwangslage dargelegt werden. Schließlich kann auch das nicht eingeleitete Rückstellungsverfahren als gewichtiges Indiz gesehen werden, dass die behauptete Herkunft von Anton M. beim Verkauf der Liegenschaft keine Rolle gespielt hat. Es kann angenommen werden, dass das Ehepaar M. Möglichkeiten gehabt hätte, ein solches Verfahren zu führen, wenn man sich seine sonstigen Bemühungen um Wiedererlangung seiner Liegenschaft vor Augen führt. Die zahlreichen Eingaben an verschiedene, vor allem politische Entscheidungsträger zeigen dies deutlich. Es dürfte dem Ehepaar M. offenbar klar gewesen sein, dass mangels politischer Verfolgung oder sonstiger nationalsozialistisch motivierter Zwangslage der Tatbestand der Vermögensentziehung nach § 2 Abs 1 oder 2 3. RStG nicht vorlag.

Der von den Antragstellerinnen behauptete Verfolgungsgrund der Abstammung liegt somit nicht vor. Das Vorliegen anderer Verfolgungsgründe haben die Antragstellerinnen nicht behauptet; es sei jedoch angemerkt, dass sich in den Beweismitteln diesbezüglich auch keine Hinweise finden lassen. § 27 Abs 1 EF-G verlangt jedoch als Voraussetzung für die Rückgabe einer Liegenschaft, dass einer der dort genannten Verfolgungsgründe vorliegt. Da es bereits an der Erfüllung dieses Tatbestandsmerkmales fehlt, waren die Anträge schon aus diesem Grund abzulehnen. Die weiteren gesetzlichen Voraussetzungen für eine Naturalrestitution waren nicht mehr zu prüfen. 35

Ob die Antragstellerinnen ihren Anspruch im ordentlichen Rechtsweg durchsetzen können, muss die Schiedsinstanz nicht beurteilen. Auf die einschlägigen Entscheidungen des Verfassungsgerichtshofes (VfGH) Erkenntnisse und Beschlüsse des Verfassungsgerichtshofes (VfSlg) 8980, 8981 und 8982 und OGH 5 Ob 231/98a wird lediglich verwiesen. 36

o.Univ.-Prof. Dr. Josef Aicher, Vorsitzender
Honorarprofessor Dr.Dr.h.c. Erich Kussbach LL.M., Botschafter i.R.
ao.Univ.-Prof. MMag. Dr. August Reinisch LL.M.

Press Release Decision No. 27/2005[1]

Vienna, Josefstadt

On 15 November 2005, the Arbitration Panel for *In Rem* Restitution recommended to the competent Federal Minister the restitution of a property owned by the Republic of Austria in Vienna, Josefstadt because the settlement between the Republic of Austria and the collection agencies dating from 1966 was extremely unjust.

The subject of the application is a former sanatorium in the eighth municipal district of Vienna. In 1925, Dr. Lothar F. took over the building from his father. It had been erected as sanatorium before the turn of the century. He continued the operation of the renowned sanatorium. In April 1938, Dr. Lothar F. and his wife – both from Jewish families – were victims of anti-Semitic behaviour by the National Socialists. Dr. Lothar F. was released from his duties as operating manager. A NSDAP member acted as "provisional manager". On 3 April 1938 the spouses committed suicide.

All possible relatives entitled to the inheritance of the childless couple were considered Jews in accordance with the National Socialists laws. Their assets were subjected to discriminatory actions and were successively seized. Some members of the family managed to flee abroad, others were deported and died.

The trustee of the estate, who had been appointed due to the absence of heirs, sold the property to the German Armed Forces in March 1939. Since May 1938 the property had been used by the Army Recruitment Inspectorate. The purchase amount of 310,000 Reichsmark served predominately to cover all debts of the estate.

After the end of the war, the building was confiscated by the American occupying authorities. The ownership to the property was transferred to the Republic of Austria pursuant to the *Staatsvertrag* ("State Treaty") of 1955. From this point in time until today, the premises have been rented to US-American institutions. The restitution of the building was initially requested by a legatee of Dr. Lothar F. The Supreme Restitution Commission ruled against his eligibility to file an application due to the restricted number of eligible heirs stipulated in the restitution acts.

In 1960, the collection agencies, which – in the course of the transformation of the State Treaty – had been created in 1957 as receiving organizations for heirless property, submitted an application for restitution of the property. The value of the property was 6 million Schilling according to expert opinions of the time. After long proceedings, the Republic of Austria and the collection agencies agreed in December 1965 to a lump sum payment for the property in the amount of 700,000 Schilling. This settlement took place within the framework of a general settlement totalling 22.7 million Schilling with respect to claims of the collection agencies against the Federation for the restitution of property which had remained heirless and had belonged to people who had been persecuted by the National Socialist regime. The settlement between the Republic of Austria and the collection agencies was legally sanctioned by the enactment of the Collection Agencies Settlement Act of 7 July 1966.

In the current proceedings, the Arbitration Panel confirmed the existence of a seizure despite existing debts of the deceased because the eligible legal heirs of the deceased were all Jews and had no opportunity to accept the inheritance and thus acquire the property. The Ar-

---

[1] See also decision no. 27a/2006, 27b/2007, 27c/2008 and decision no. 371/2007 in conjunction with this decision.

Pressemitteilung Entscheidung Nr. 27/2005[1]

Wien, Josefstadt

Die Schiedsinstanz für Naturalrestitution hat am 15. November 2005 die Rückstellung einer im Eigentum der Republik Österreich stehenden Liegenschaft in Wien, Josefstadt dem zuständigen Bundesminister empfohlen. Denn der Vergleich zwischen der Republik und den Sammelstellen im Jahre 1966 war extrem ungerecht.

Gegenstand des Verfahrens ist ein ehemaliges Sanatorium im achten Wiener Gemeindebezirk. Dr. Lothar F. übernahm das vor der Jahrhundertwende als Heilanstalt errichtete Gebäude von seinem Vater im Jahr 1925 und führte den prominenten Sanatoriumsbetrieb weiter. Im April des Jahres 1938 fielen Dr. Lothar F. ebenso wie seine Frau – beide aus jüdischen Familien stammend – antisemitischen Aktionen der Nationalsozialisten zum Opfer. Die Betriebsführung wurde Dr. Lothar F. aus der Hand genommen und von einem NSDAP-Mitglied als "kommissarischer Leiter" ausgeübt. Am 3. April 1938 nahmen sich die Eheleute das Leben.

Alle in Frage kommenden erbberechtigten Verwandten des kinderlosen Ehepaares galten nach den nationalsozialistischen Gesetzen als Juden. Ihr Vermögen unterlag diskriminierenden Maßnahmen und wurde sukzessive entzogen. Einigen Familienmitgliedern gelang die Flucht ins Ausland, andere wurden deportiert und kamen ums Leben.

Der mangels Erben eingesetzte Verlassenschaftskurator verkaufte die Liegenschaft, die schon seit Mai 1938 von der Wehrersatzinspektion genutzt worden war, im März 1939 an die Deutsche Wehrmacht. Die Kaufsumme von 310.000,– Reichsmark diente vor allem der Deckung von Schulden des Nachlasses.

Nach Kriegsende wurde das Gebäude von den amerikanischen Besatzungsbehörden beschlagnahmt. Das Eigentum daran ging mit dem Staatsvertrag 1955 auf die Republik Österreich über. US-amerikanische Institutionen sind bis heute eingemietet. Die Rückstellung des Gebäudes wurde 1946 zunächst von einem Vermächtnisnehmer nach Dr. Lothar F. begehrt. Die Oberste Rückstellungskommission verneinte 1952 aufgrund des enggefassten Erbenkreises der Rückstellungsgesetze dessen Antragsberechtigung.

1960 brachten die Sammelstellen, die in Umsetzung des Staatsvertrages als Auffangorganisation für erbloses Vermögen im Jahr 1957 geschaffen worden waren, einen Antrag auf Rückstellung der Liegenschaft ein. Deren Wert betrug laut damaligem Sachverständigengutachten über sechs Millionen Schilling. Nach längerem Verfahren einigten sich die Republik Österreich und die Sammelstellen im Dezember 1965 auf eine Abfindung für die Liegenschaft in Höhe von 700.000,– Schilling. Dieser Vergleich erfolgte im Rahmen eines Generalvergleichs von insgesamt 22,700.000,– Schilling über die Ansprüche der Sammelstellen gegen den Bund auf Rückstellung von erblos gebliebenen Vermögen, die durch den Nationalsozialismus verfolgten Personen gehört hatten. Der Vergleich zwischen der Republik Österreich und den Sammelstellen wurde durch Erlassung des Sammelstellen-Abgeltungsgesetzes vom 7. Juli 1966 auch gesetzlich verankert.

Im gegenständlichen Verfahren bejahte die Schiedsinstanz den Entzug trotz vorhandener Schulden des Verstorbenen, da die berechtigten gesetzlichen Erben des Verstorbenen alle als Juden verfolgt waren und keine Möglichkeit hatten, die Erbschaft anzutreten und damit die Liegenschaft zu erwerben.

---

[1] Siehe zu dieser Entscheidung auch die Entscheidungen Nr. 27a/2006, 27b/2007, 27c/2008 und Entscheidung Nr. 371/2007.

bitration Panel further decided that the restitution proceedings initiated by the collection agencies qualified as "prior measures" in the meaning of the *Entschädigungsfondsgesetz* (General Settlement Fund Law – GSF Law), which prevented a recommendation for restitution by the Arbitration Panel.

However, the Arbitration Panel considered the lump sum settlement contained in the Collection Agencies Settlement Act as an exception of a prior measure. In the course of the general resolution of the claims of the collection agencies against the Republic, consideration was given to the conclusion of the settlement of the property in Josefstadt and to the organization of its content which had no connection to the claim for restitution and which would not have been relevant for an applicant for restitution intent on his or her own interests. Priority during the negotiations was given to a quick dissolution of the collection agencies whose claims against the Republic were to be reconciled without "protracted and costly proceedings". After the general resolution was delayed, the claim for the property at issue was no longer given the necessary impetus by the collection agencies. The Arbitration Panel therefore identified a deficiency in the collection agencies settlement regarding the claim for the former sanatorium and considered this to be an indication for the existence of an "extreme injustice".

A further indication was the difference between the value of the property of more than 6 million Schilling and the settlement amount of 700,000 Schilling. In the view of the Arbitration Panel, this discrepancy in value alone does not constitute a case of extreme injustice but it can be considered as an indication of such injustice. Prerequisite for this would be that the restitution authority would have had to affirm the restitution claim to the property in question in correct application of the law.

The Arbitration Panel assumed that the Financial Directorate for Vienna, Lower Austria and Burgenland as the restitution authority would have had to pronounce the restitution of the property in accordance with the case law of the time as the contentious core issue of the proceedings, i.e. whether a seizure of the property as defined by the restitution acts existed, would have had to be affirmed by the Financial Directorate due to the persecution of the heirs of Dr. Lothar F. The Financial Directorate, however assessed the claim for restitution of the property to be unmerited. Since this impending negative decision by the Financial Directorate substantially influenced the conclusion of the settlement to the detriment of the former claimant, the Collection Agency, an objectively unacceptable interpretation of the restitution acts became the basis of the settlement.

The Arbitration Panel therefore ruled that the striking discrepancy in value between a correct hypothetical restitution decision and the settlement sum reached, along with the markedly divergent interests of the Collection Agency in comparison to those interests which were to be assumed by a restitution claimant, amounted to an "extreme injustice" of the settlement at issue.

For use by media; not legally binding upon the Arbitration Panel for In Rem Restitution.

Weiters entschied die Schiedsinstanz, dass die von den Sammelstellen geführten Rückstellungsverfahren „frühere Maßnahmen" im Sinne des Entschädigungsfondsgesetzes darstellen, die an sich eine Empfehlung der Rückstellung durch die Schiedsinstanz ausschließen.

Sie betrachtete den im Sammelstellen-Abgeltungsgesetz enthaltenen Pauschalvergleich jedoch als einen Ausnahmefall einer früheren Maßnahme. In Folge der Generalbereinigung der Ansprüche der Sammelstelle gegen die Republik seien nämlich zum Abschluss des Vergleichs über die Liegenschaft in der Josefstadt und zu dessen inhaltlicher Ausgestaltung Überlegungen eingeflossen, die in keinem Zusammenhang mit dem Rückstellungsanspruch gestanden hatten und bei einem auf seine Interessen bedachten Rückstellungswerber nicht zum Tragen gekommen wären. So stand im Vordergrund der Verhandlungen die zügige Auflösung der Sammelstellen, deren Ansprüche gegen die Republik ohne „langwierige und kostspielige Verfahren" abgefunden werden sollten. Nachdem die Generalbereinigung in Aussicht gestellt worden war, wurde die Forderung für die gegenständliche Liegenschaft von den Sammelstellen nicht mehr mit dem notwendigen Nachdruck betrieben. Die Schiedsinstanz erblickte daher im Sammelstellen-Vergleich hinsichtlich des Anspruchs auf das ehemalige Sanatorium eine Unzulänglichkeit und sah dies als einen Anhaltspunkt für das Vorliegen einer „extremen Ungerechtigkeit".

Ein weiterer Anhaltspunkt war die Differenz zwischen dem Wert der Liegenschaft von über 6 Millionen Schilling und der Vergleichssumme von 700.000,– Schilling. Nach Ansicht der Schiedsinstanz begründet diese Wertdifferenz für sich genommen zwar nicht das Vorliegen einer extremen Ungerechtigkeit, kann aber als ein Indiz für eine solche gewertet werden. Dafür sei jedoch Voraussetzung, dass die Rückstellungsbehörde den Rückstellungsanspruch auf die gegenständliche Liegenschaft bei korrekter Gesetzesanwendung bejahen hätte müssen.

Die Schiedsinstanz geht davon aus, dass die Finanzlandesdirektion für Wien, Niederösterreich und Burgenland (FLD) als Rückstellungsbehörde nach der damaligen Judikatur die Rückstellung der Liegenschaft hätte aussprechen müssen, da die strittige Kernfrage des Verfahrens, ob eine Entziehung der Liegenschaft im Sinne der Rückstellungsgesetze vorlag, aufgrund der Verfolgung der Erben des Dr. Lothar F. von der FLD zu bejahen gewesen wäre. Tatsächlich aber schätzte die FLD den Rückstellungsanspruch auf die gegenständliche Liegenschaft negativ ein. Da diese drohende Ablehnung durch die FLD wesentlich den Abschluss des Vergleiches zum Nachteil der damaligen Antragstellerin, der Sammelstelle, beeinflusste, geriet eine objektiv unvertretbare Auslegung der Rückstellungsgesetze zur Grundlage des Vergleiches.

Die Schiedsinstanz sprach daher aus, dass die eklatante Wertdifferenz zwischen einer korrekten hypothetischen Rückstellungsentscheidung und der erzielten Vergleichssumme im Zusammenspiel mit der markant abweichenden Interessenlage der Sammelstelle gemessen an den Interessen eines Rückstellungswerbers für das Vorliegen einer extremen Ungerechtigkeit des gegenständlichen Vergleichs spreche.

Zur Verwendung durch die Medien bestimmter Text, der die Schiedsinstanz nicht bindet.

Arbitration Panel for *In Rem* Restitution

Decision number 27/2005[1]

The Arbitration Panel for *In Rem* Restitution (Chairman Dr. Josef Aicher, university professor, and Dr. Dr. h. c. Erich Kussbach LL.M., retired ambassador and honorary professor, as well as MMag. Dr. August Reinisch LL.M, university professor, as Members) decided on 15 November 2005 in the legal matter of Stephan G. and Marion R.-G., both represented by Dr. Helmut Scheubrein, notary in Vienna as well as by Lansky, Ganzger & Partner, attorneys (limited liability partnership) in Vienna, and Dr. Marc R., attorney in Zurich, as well as Robert Re., Doris A. and Alfred S., all represented by both Dr. Helmut Scheubrein and by Lansky, Ganzger & Partner, and Marietta P. and Andrew G., both represented by Dr. Helmut Scheubrein, and Christopher An. and Richard An., regarding *in rem* restitution of the property S.-gasse 14, register number ("EZ") X1, cadastral district ("KG") Josefstadt:

The application for *in rem* restitution of the property S.-gasse 14, EZ X1, KG Josefstadt, is granted, and a recommendation for the restitution of the property in question is made to the competent Federal Minister.

Reasons:

Case History

1 The applicants Robert Re., Richard An. and Christopher An. applied for the restitution of the property in question with their applications filed on 24 April 2002. The Arbitration Panel requested that the applicants supply the necessary evidence of their eligibility to file an application as heirs of the original property owner pursuant to Sec. 27 (2) of the *Entschädigungsfondsgesetz* ("General Settlement Fund Law" – GSF Law).

2 On 10 September 2002, the Arbitration Panel requested the Federal Government to submit a statement in accordance with Sec. 30 of the GSF Law. This statement was submitted on 2 December 2002 by the State Financial Procurator's Office as representative of the Republic of Austria. In the statement, the State Financial Procurator's Office suggested that the application for *in rem* restitution not be granted due to the absence of the statutory requirements. It presented a series of arguments which were explained more precisely later in the proceedings (see point 2.).

3 On 10 February 2003, the applicants withdrew their applications.

1. Submission by the Applicants

1.1 Applications of Richard An. and Christopher An.

4 On 13 January 2004 and 27 January 2004 respectively, Richard An. and Christopher An. resubmitted to the Arbitration Panel their applications for *in rem* restitution regarding S.-gasse 14, land register ("GB") 01005, EZ X1, KG Josefstadt.

---

[1] See also supplementary decision nos. 27a/2006, 27b/2007, 27c/2008 and decision number 371/2007 in conjunction with this decision.

Schiedsinstanz für Naturalrestitution

Entscheidungsnummer 27/2005[1]

Die Schiedsinstanz für Naturalrestitution beschließt am 15. November 2005 durch den Vorsitzenden o.Univ.-Prof. Dr. Josef Aicher und die Schiedsinstanzmitglieder Honorarprofessor Dr.Dr.h.c. Erich Kussbach LL.M., Botschafter i.R. und ao.Univ.-Prof. MMag. Dr. August Reinisch LL.M. in der Rechtssache Stephan G., Marion R.-G., beide vertreten sowohl durch Dr. Helmut Scheubrein, Notar in Wien, als auch durch Lansky, Ganzger & Partner, Rechtsanwälte GmbH in Wien, und Dr. Marc R., Rechtsanwalt (RA) in Zürich, sowie Robert Re., Doris A. und Alfred S., sämtliche vertreten sowohl durch Dr. Helmut Scheubrein als auch durch Lansky, Ganzger & Partner, sowie Marietta P. und Andrew G., beide vertreten durch Dr. Helmut Scheubrein, und Christopher An. und Richard An. wegen Naturalrestitution der Liegenschaft S.-gasse 14, Einlagezahl (EZ) X1, Katastralgemeinde (KG) Josefstadt:

> **Dem Antrag auf Naturalrestitution der Liegenschaft S.-gasse 14, EZ X1, KG Josefstadt, wird stattgegeben und dem zuständigen Bundesminister die Rückstellung der antragsgegenständlichen Liegenschaft empfohlen.**

Begründung:

Vorgeschichte

Mit Antrag vom 24. April 2002 begehrten die Antragsteller Robert Re., Richard An. und Christopher An. die Rückstellung der gegenständlichen Liegenschaft. Die Schiedsinstanz ersuchte die Antragsteller um Nachreichung der erforderlichen Nachweise ihrer Antragsberechtigung als Erben des ursprünglichen Liegenschaftseigentümers im Sinne von § 27 Abs 2 Entschädigungsfondsgesetz (EF-G). 1

Am 10. September 2002 wurde seitens der Schiedsinstanz die Bundesregierung um Abgabe einer Stellungnahme iSd § 30 EF-G ersucht. Diese Stellungnahme wurde durch die Finanzprokuratur als Vertreterin der Republik Österreich am 2. Dezember 2002 eingebracht. Die Finanzprokuratur regte darin an, dem Antrag auf Naturalrestitution mangels Vorliegen der gesetzlichen Voraussetzungen nicht Folge zu geben. Dabei brachte sie eine Reihe von Argumenten vor, die im späteren Verfahren ausführlicher dargelegt wurden (siehe Punkt 2.). 2

Die Antragsteller zogen ihre Anträge am 10. Februar 2003 zurück. 3

1. Vorbringen der AntragstellerInnen

1.1 Anträge von Richard An. und Christopher An.

Richard An. und Christopher An. brachten am 13. Jänner 2004 bzw. am 27. Jänner 2004 erneut bei der Schiedsinstanz Naturalrestitutionsanträge hinsichtlich S.-gasse 14, Grundbuch (GB) 01005, EZ X1, KG Josefstadt ein. 4

---

[1] Siehe zu dieser Entscheidung auch die Zusatzentscheidungen Nr. 27a/2006, 27b/2007, 27c/2008 sowie Entscheidung Nr. 371/2007.

1.2 Applications of Andrew G., Stefan G., Marion R.-G., Robert Re., (Eva Pe.), Doris A., Alfred S. and Marietta P.

5   Marion R.-G. submitted an application for *in rem* restitution of the property S.-gasse 12-14, B.-gasse 11, Vienna 8, GB 01005, EZ X1, KG Josefstadt on 10 April 2003, through Lansky, Ganzger & Partner, attorneys (limited liability partnership).

6   On 25 February 2003, the applicants Andrew G., Stephan G., Marion R.-G., Robert Re., Eva Pe., Doris A. and Alfred S. submitted a "safeguarding application" to the Arbitration Panel through the notary Dr. Helmut Scheubrein, with which they applied for *in rem* restitution of the property S.-gasse 12-14, B.-gasse 11, Vienna 8, GB 01005, EZ X1, KG Josefstadt.

7   It was asserted that the applicants had been legal successors of the original owner of the property, Dr. Lothar F. All applicants had in fact been descendants of the grandparents of Dr. Lothar F., Carl Ro. and Caroline Ro.

8   In the application it was explained regarding the property S.-gasse 14 that the building which had occupied this site in 1886 had been purchased by Dr. Albin E. He had ordered the erection of a new building which was intended as a sanatorium. In 1892 it had been extended onto the plot B.-gasse 11. The sanatorium had been purchased by Dr. Julius F. in 1895 who had, however, gotten into financial difficulties. In 1939, the German Reich (Reich Treasury) had bought the property. Since 1958, it has been owned by the Republic of Austria (Federal Construction Office), who leased it to the Embassy of the United States.

9   Since 18 July 1925, Dr. Lothar F. had been the sole owner of the property on the basis of a certificate of inheritance from the District Court Josefstadt 1 A 181/23–24.

10   F.'s last will and testament dated 10 October 1937 had been for the benefit of his wife Suse. The alternate heirs were his parents-in-law, *in eventu* subsequent alternate heirs

> "[…] and I expressly determine that my sister Hertha L[…]and any of her possible descendants are to be excluded from succession so that the testamentary succession has to occur in the way of a statutory succession, which would be applicable had my sister Hertha L[…] and any of her possible descendants not existed."

11   On 2 April 1938, in a later addition to the will, Dr. F. had appointed Mr. John Henry D., district VIII, L.-gasse 19 as executor of his last will and testament and had bequeathed to him all of his weaponry and jewelry. According to a report on the assets and liabilities by the trustee of the estate, these had been handed over to John Henry D. on an unknown date.

12   On 3 April 1938, the decedent and his wife had committed simultaneous suicide.

13   On 14 April 1938, the parents-in-law appointed by Dr. Lothar F. in his will had submitted a conditional declaration of acceptance of the inheritance in the probate proceedings of their daughter and renounced the right to the inheritance of the estate of Lothar F., initially conducted under number 1 A 251/38 at the District Court Josefstadt and then under number 14 A 107/40 at the District Court Innere Stadt – Vienna.

14   The estate had appeared heirless. On 28 April 1938, Dr. Alfred St., attorney in Vienna 6, G.-straße 15 had been appointed trustee of the estate.

15   John Henry D. had not accepted his appointment as executor of the estate conferred to him in the will. The edict for the summoning of unknown heirs had been issued.

1.2 Anträge von Andrew G., Stephan G., Marion R.-G., Robert Re., (Eva Pe.), Doris A., Alfred S. und Marietta P.

Marion R.-G. brachte am 10. April 2003 durch Lansky, Ganzger & Partner, Rechtsanwälte GmbH, einen Antrag auf Naturalrestitution der Liegenschaft S.-gasse 12–14, B.-gasse 11, Wien 8, GB 01005, EZ X1, KG Josefstadt, ein.

Die AntragstellerInnen Andrew G., Stephan G., Marion R.-G., Robert Re., Eva Pe., Doris A. und Alfred S. stellten am 25. Februar 2003 durch Notar Dr. Helmut Scheubrein einen „Wahrungsantrag" an die Schiedsinstanz, mit dem sie die Naturalrestitution der Liegenschaft S.-gasse 12–14, B.-gasse 11, Wien 8, GB 01005, EZ X1, KG Josefstadt, begehrten.

Geltend gemacht wurde, dass die AntragstellerInnen RechtsnachfolgerInnen des ursprünglichen Eigentümers der Liegenschaft, Dr. Lothar F., seien. Sämtliche AntragstellerInnen seien nämlich Nachkommen des Großelternpaares von Dr. Lothar F., Carl Ro. und Caroline Ro.

Im Antrag wurde zur Liegenschaft S.-gasse 14 ausgeführt, dass der Vorgängerbau 1886 von Dr. Albin E. gekauft worden sei. Dieser habe einen zum Sanatorium bestimmten Neubau errichten lassen. 1892 sei eine Erweiterung auf die Parzelle B.-gasse 11 erfolgt. Das Sanatorium sei von Dr. Julius F. 1895 angekauft worden, der jedoch in finanzielle Schwierigkeiten geraten sei. 1939 habe das Deutsche Reich (Reichsfiskus) das Objekt gekauft. Seit 1958 befinde es sich im Eigentum der Republik Österreich (Bundesbaudirektion), die es an die Botschaft der Vereinigten Staaten vermiete.

Seit 18. Juli 1925 sei Dr. Lothar F. aufgrund der Einantwortungsurkunde des Bezirksgerichts (BG) Josefstadt 1 A 181/23–24 Alleineigentümer der Liegenschaft.

Das Testament F.s vom 10. Oktober 1937 sei zugunsten seiner Gattin Suse gewesen, die ErsatzerbInnenen die Schwiegereltern, in eventu die ErsatzerbInnen

„[...] und bestimme ausdrücklich, dass meine Schwester Hertha L[...] und deren etwaige Deszendenten von der Erbfolge auszuschließen ist, so dass als testamentarische Erbfolge die gesetzliche Erbfolge in der Weise einzutreten hat, die Geltung hätte, wenn meine Schwester Hertha L[...] und deren etwaige Deszendenz nicht vorhanden wären."

In einem Nachtrag zum Testament vom 2. April 1938 habe Dr. F. als Testamentsvollstrecker Herrn John Henry D., VIII, L.-gasse 19, eingesetzt und diesem auch seine gesamten Waffen und den Schmuck vermacht. Diese seien laut Bericht des Verlassenschaftskurators zu den Aktiven und Passiven auch John Henry D. zu unbekannter Zeit ausgehändigt worden.

Am 3. April 1938 sei der Tod des Erblassers und seiner Gattin durch Selbsttötung zum gleichen Zeitpunkt erfolgt.

Am 14. April 1938 hätten die testamentarisch eingesetzten Schwiegereltern von Dr. Lothar F. im Verlassenschaftsverfahren ihrer Tochter eine bedingte Erbserklärung abgegeben und sich des Erbrechts in der Verlassenschaft nach Lothar F., vorerst zu 1 A 251/38 BG Josefstadt geführt, danach zu 14 A 107/40 BG Innere Stadt Wien, entschlagen.

Die Verlassenschaft sei als erbenlos erschienen. Am 28. April 1938 sei Dr. Alfred St., RA in Wien 6, G.-straße 15, zum Verlassenschaftskurator bestellt worden.

John Henry D. habe das ihm letztwillig übertragene Amt als Testamentsvollstrecker nicht angenommen. Das Edikt zur Einberufung unbekannter ErbInnen sei erlassen worden.

16 The *Wehrmacht* ("German Armed Forces") had requisitioned the building on 1 May 1938. The trustee of the estate had not been able to oppose this requisition, as an irrevocable requisition right had existed for the purposes of the Armed Forces.

17 On 18 June 1938, John Henry D. had asserted his claims to the estate.

18 On 25 August, the Army Recruitment Inspectorate had moved into the building. For this reason, the valuation had only been calculated regarding the land (75,225 Reichsmark) and building value (205,560 Reichsmark), as the continued operation of the sanatorium had been out of the question. Hence, the valuation was 295,357 Reichsmark.

19 On 6 May 1939, pursuant to a purchase contract between the estate of Dr. Lothar F., represented by the trustee of the estate Dr. Alfred St., and the German Reich, Reich Treasury (Army) had become the owner of the property. The purchase price of 310,000 Reichsmark had included a brokerage fee of 9,000 Reichsmark for the sale of the property parcel.

20 According to a letter from the *NSDAP* ("National Socialist German Workers Party"), regional administration Vienna dated 5 October 1939, the liquidation of the sanatorium company and the consequent dismissal of the employees of the company had been necessary as a result of the takeover of the sanatorium "F[…]" by the Army Recruitment Inspectorate.

21 Sometime around May 1942, a reversion of the estate had taken place.

22 On 13 December 1946, John Henry D., as legatee, had requested the return of the estate.

23 An official certificate dated 1 January 1947, issued by the District Court Innere Stadt Vienna after consultation with the State Financial Procurator's Office, demonstrated that John Henry D., a businessman in London, 56 W. Square SW1 was to be considered legatee and as statutory heirs had not come forward, then pursuant to para. 726 of the *Allgemeine Bürgerliche Gesetzbuch* ("[Austrian] General Civil Code") John Henry D. appeared solely entitled to the inheritance.

24 The Supreme Restitution Commission at the Supreme Court had denied the return of the decedent's property to D. on 5 July 1952, as he did not belong to the group of heirs designated in the will and only these heirs were entitled to claim according to para. 14 of the *Dritte Rückstellungsgesetz* ("Third Restitution Act").

25 In the restitution proceedings 7 R-V-20591/57, and/or VR-V 21,850-6/57 a claim dating prior to 1938 for the amount of 20,000 Gold Dollar had been asserted. The restitution had, however, been prevented from being successful as due to the receipt of cancellation, the claim was considered to have been expired.

26 On 4 January 1958, the property had passed into the ownership of the Republic of Austria on the basis of Article 22 of the Austrian *Staatsvertrag* ("State Treaty") of 15 May 1955, *BGBl.* ("Federal Law Gazette") No. 152/55 in connection with para. 11 of the *Erste Staatsvertragsdurchführungsgesetz* ("First State Treaty Implementation Act") Federal Law Gazette No. 165 of 25 July 1956. The ownership titles for the Republic of Austria had been incorporated into the land register on 4 January 1958.

27 On 26 February 1970, following an order from the Federal Ministry of Finance of 26 February 1970, no. 53.076-16/1970 the Financial Directorate Vienna had handed over the property to the Federal Ministry for Building Affairs and Technology.

28 On request of the Arbitration Panel of 25 February 2003 to submit documents as proof of the applicants' right to inherit in accordance with the GSF Law as well as to compile a

Schiedsinstanz für Naturalrestitution – Entscheidung Nr. 27/2005

Die Deutsche Wehrmacht habe am 1. Mai 1938 das Gebäude in Anspruch genommen. 16
Gegen diese Inanspruchnahme habe sich der Verlassenschaftskurator nicht zur Wehr setzen können, da für die Zwecke der Wehrmacht ein nicht zu beseitigendes Anforderungsrecht bestanden habe.

John Henry D. habe am 18. Juni 1938 Ansprüche an die Verlassenschaft gestellt. 17

Am 25. August sei das Gebäude von der Wehrersatz-Inspektion Wien bezogen worden. 18
Daher sei die Schätzung nur nach Grund (75.225,- Reichsmark) und Bauwert (205.560,- Reichsmark) berechnet worden, da auch die Weiterführung des Sanatoriums nicht in Frage gekommen sei. Die Schätzung habe somit in Summe 295.357,- Reichsmark betragen.

Am 6. Mai 1939 sei aufgrund des Kaufvertrages zwischen der Verlassenschaft nach Dr. 19
Lothar F., vertreten durch den Verlassenschaftskurator Dr. Alfred St., das Deutsche Reich Reichsfiskus (Heer) Eigentümer der Liegenschaft geworden. Der Kaufpreis von 310.000,- Reichsmark habe das Vermittlungshonorar für den Grundstücksverkauf von 9.000,- Reichsmark inkludiert.

Laut Schreiben der NSDAP, Gauleitung Wien, vom 5. Oktober 1939 sei durch die Übernahme des Sanatoriums „F[…]" seitens der Wehrersatzinspektion Wien die Auflösung des Sanatoriumsbetriebes und dadurch bedingt die Entlassung der Angestellten des Betriebes erforderlich gewesen. 20

Etwa im Mai 1942 sei es zum Heimfall des Nachlasses gekommen. 21

Am 13. Dezember 1946 habe John Henry D. als Legatar die Verlassenschaft gefordert. 22

Eine Amtsbestätigung des Bezirksgerichtes Innere Stadt Wien nach Rücksprache mit 23
der Finanzprokuratur vom 1. Jänner 1947 zeige, dass John Henry D., Kaufmann in London, 56 W. Square SW1 als Legatar anzusehen sei und, da sich gesetzliche ErbInnen nicht gemeldet haben, gemäß § 726 Allgemeines bürgerliches Gesetzbuch (ABGB) einzig und allein John Henry D. zur Erbschaft berufen erscheine.

Die Oberste Rückstellungskommission beim Obersten Gerichtshof (OGH) habe die 24
Rückgabe der erblasserischen Liegenschaft an D. am 5. Juli 1952 abgelehnt, da er nicht zum Kreis der im Testament bedachten ErbInnen gehöre und nur diesen ein Anspruch nach § 14 des Dritten Rückstellungsgesetzes (3. RStG) zustehe.

Im Rückstellungsverfahren 7 R-V-20591/57 bzw. VR-V 21.850-6/57 sei eine Forde- 25
rung in der Höhe von 20.000,- Golddollar aus der Zeit vor 1938 geltend gemacht worden. Der Rückstellung sei aber der Erfolg verwehrt geblieben, da aufgrund der Löschungsquittung die Forderung als erloschen angesehen worden sei.

Am 4. Jänner 1958 sei aufgrund des Artikels 22 des österreichischen Staatsvertrages 26
(StV) vom 15. Mai 1955, Bundesgesetzblatt (BGBl) 152/55, in Verbindung mit § 11 des Ersten Staatsvertragsdurchführungsgesetzes (1. StVDG) vom 25. Juli 1956, BGBl 165, die Liegenschaft in das Eigentum der Republik Österreich übergegangen. Die Eigentumsrechte für die Republik seien am 4. Jänner 1958 grundbücherlich einverleibt worden.

Am 26. Februar 1970 sei mit Erlass des Bundesministeriums für Finanzen (BMF) vom 27
26. Februar 1970, Zl. 53.076-16/1970, die Liegenschaft von der Finanzlandesdirektion (FLD) Wien an das Bundesministerium für Bauten und Technik übergeben worden.

Nach Aufforderung der Schiedsinstanz vom 25. Februar 2003, Dokumente zum Beleg 28
des Erbrechts der AntragstellerInnen im Sinne des E-FG vorzulegen sowie zu dem Sammelstellenverfahren betreffend S.-gasse 14 Vorbringen zu erstatten, brachte Dr. Scheubrein am 28. Mai 2003 für alle sieben AntragstellerInnen Anträge ein und legte ein Kon-

Arbitration Panel for *In Rem* Restitution – Decision No. 27/2005

submission on the collection agencies' proceedings regarding S.-gasse 14, Dr. Scheubrein filed applications for all seven applicants and enclosed a collection of documents relevant to the inheritance rights as well as the applicants' powers of attorney.

29   With a supplementary letter dated 4 and 5 August 2003, on behalf of the applicants, Dr. Scheubrein commented on the restitution proceedings by the collection agencies, which ended in 1966 with the *Sammelstellenabgeltungsgesetz* ("Collection Agencies Settlement Act").

30   In this regard, the applicants referred to Graf's comments on the Collection Agencies Settlement Act (Georg Graf, *Die österreichische Rückstellungsgesetzgebung. Eine juristische Analyse*, Vienna 2002, at 233–234)[2]. He considered the collection agencies' settlement of 1966, which was intended to be a statutory "kind of settlement solution" for unresolved claims of the collection agencies against the Federation, as problematic, as among other things the extent to which the collection agencies had actually been entitled to claims to assets and whether the settled assets had really been heirless remained unresolved (ibid 233).

31   Regarding this matter, the author writes: "in the case that there had been people who would possibly have been aggrieved owners or heirs of the aggrieved owners, the solution must certainly be considered problematic" (ibid. 234).

32   Furthermore, the applicants referred to the following passage in the partial report by the Historical Commission by Margot Werner and Michael Wladika (*Die Tätigkeit der Sammelstellen*, Vienna 2002, at 56)[3]: "The collection agencies represented the claims of a legatee to Dr. Lothar F. for restitution of the property in restitution proceedings against the Republic of Austria."

33   It would have to be assumed that the collection agencies would have represented the interests of John Henry D., who died on 3 August 1960 "without knowledge of the concluded settlement". In the statement it was furthermore addressed that the Supreme Restitution Commission had denied the restitution of the property initiated by D. with the explanation that that he did not belong to the circle of heirs restricted by para. 14 of the Third Restitution Act (59 Rk 146/50). As in 1960, the legatee had already passed away, it was now questionable "in whose name and on whose behalf and based on which circumstances the settlement was concluded." As the legatee had only been eligible to the claim in the case of the absence of testamentary or statutory heirs according to para. 726 of the (Austrian) General Civil Code, the *Sammelstellengesetz* ("Collection Agencies Act") of 1966 had disadvantaged these very heirs of Dr. Lothar F. The conclusion of the settlement in the amount of 700,000 Schilling by the Collection Agency on behalf of the legatee had taken place without the latter having proven his right to inherit.

---

[2]   Supplementation at time of going to press: From 2002 to 2003, this text could be found under http://www.historikerkommission.gv.at/deutsch_home.html and was published in 2003 as: Georg Graf, *Die österreichische Rückstellungsgesetzgebung. Eine juristische Analyse*, Vienna (Oldenbourg) 2003 (= Publications of the Austrian Historical Commission, vol. 2).

[3]   Supplementation at time of going to press: From 2002 to 2003, this text could be found under http://www.historikerkommission.gv.at/deutsch_home.html and was published in 2004 as: Margot Werner and Michael Wladika, *Die Tätigkeit der Sammelstellen*, Vienna (Oldenbourg) 2004 (= Publications of the Austrian Historical Commission, vol. 28).

volut an erbrechtlich relevanten Dokumenten sowie Vollmachten der AntragstellerInnen bei.

Mit ergänzenden Schreiben vom 4. und 5. August 2003 nahm Dr. Scheubrein im Namen der AntragstellerInnen Stellung zum Rückstellungsverfahren durch die Sammelstellen (SSt), das mit dem Sammelstellenabgeltungsgesetz 1966 endete. 29

Die AntragstellerInnen verwiesen in diesem Zusammenhang auf die Ausführungen Grafs zum Sammelstellenabgeltungsgesetz (Georg *Graf,* Die österreichische Rückstellungsgesetzgebung. Eine juristische Analyse, Wien 2002, 233–234)[2]. Dieser betrachtet den Sammelstellenvergleich 1966, der per Gesetz „eine Art Vergleichslösung" für offene Ansprüche der Sammelstelle gegenüber dem Bund vorsah, als problematisch, da u. a. offen bleibe, inwieweit die Ansprüche der Sammelstelle auf die Vermögenswerte tatsächlich berechtigt waren und ob es sich bei den verglichenen Vermögenswerten tatsächlich um erbloses Vermögen gehandelt habe (ebenda 233). 30

Der Autor meint dazu: „Falls doch Personen vorhanden gewesen wären, die als geschädigte Eigentümer oder Erben der geschädigten Eigentümer in Frage gekommen wären, so müsste die Lösung durchaus als problematisch angesehen werden" (ebenda 234). 31

Weiters verwiesen die AntragstellerInnen auf folgende Stelle im Teilbericht der Historikerkommission von Margot *Werner* und Michael *Wladika* (Die Tätigkeit der Sammelstellen, Wien 2002, 56)[3]: „Die Sammelstellen vertraten die Ansprüche eines Legatars nach Dr. Lothar F. auf Rückstellung der Liegenschaft im Rückstellungsverfahren gegen die Republik Österreich." 32

„In Unkenntnis des geschlossenen Vergleichs" müsse man davon ausgehen, dass die Sammelstellen die Interessen von John Henry D. vertreten hätten, der am 3. August 1960 verstorben sei. Im Vorbringen wurde weiters darauf eingegangen, dass die Oberste Rückstellungskommission die von D. angestrengte Rückstellung der Liegenschaft mit der Begründung verwehrt habe, dieser falle nicht unter den durch § 14 des 3. RStG begrenzten Erbenkreis (59 Rk 146/50). Nun sei fraglich, da der Legatar bereits 1960 verstorben sei, „in welchem Namen und Auftrag und aufgrund welcher Umstände der Vergleich geschlossen wurde". Da der Legatar nur im Falle des Fehlens testamentarischer oder gesetzlicher ErbInnen nach § 726 ABGB anspruchsberechtigt gewesen sei, habe das Sammelstellenabgeltungsgesetz von 1966 ebendiese ErbInnen nach Dr. Lothar F. benachteiligt. Der Abschluss des Vergleiches von 700.000,– Schilling durch die Sammelstelle im Namen des Legatars sei erfolgt, ohne dass Letzterer sein Erbrecht nachgewiesen habe. 33

Die für eine Empfehlung der Schiedsinstanz erforderliche „extreme Ungerechtigkeit" sei also in der historischen Gesetzgebung gelegen, die 34

---

[2] Ergänzung zum Zeitpunkt der Drucklegung: Dieser Text war von 2002 bis 2003 unter http://www.historikerkommission.gv.at/deutsch_home.html abrufbar und wurde 2003 veröffentlicht als: Georg *Graf,* Die österreichische Rückstellungsgesetzgebung. Eine juristische Analyse, Wien (Oldenbourg) 2003 (= Veröffentlichungen der Österreichischen Historikerkommission, Band 2).

[3] Ergänzung zum Zeitpunkt der Drucklegung: Dieser Text war von 2002 bis 2003 unter http://www.historikerkommission.gv.at/deutsch_home.html abrufbar und wurde 2004 veröffentlicht als: Margot *Werner* und Michael *Wladika,* Die Tätigkeit der Sammelstellen, Wien (Oldenbourg) 2004 (= Veröffentlichungen der Österreichischen Historikerkommission, Band 28).

Arbitration Panel for *In Rem* Restitution – Decision No. 27/2005

34 The "extreme injustice" required for a recommendation by the Arbitration Panel had also been apparent in the historical legislation, which

"[…] on the one hand in 1966 and prior made the claims to the property of the heirs according to the (Austrian) General Civil Code impossible and on the other hand made the claims of the legatee according to para. 726 of the (Austrian) General Civil Code possible through *ad hoc* legislation […]".

35 In a letter dated 22 July 2005 enclosing the inheritance documents, notary Dr. Scheubrein informed that the applicant Eva Pe. had died on 9 December 2003 and that her testamentary heirs were her daughters Marietta P. and Doris A., each inheriting one half.

2. Statement of the State Financial Procurator's Office

36 In a letter dated 27 October 2003, the State Financial Procurator's Office, as representative of the Republic of Austria, submitted a statement on the present application. In the statement, the State Financial Procurator's Office took the view that the prerequisites of the GSF Law for a recommendation for the restitution of the property in question were not fulfilled and suggested that the application in question not be granted.

37 The property in question had been sold from the estate of Dr. F. to the German Reich for a seemingly adequate purchase price of 310,000 Reichsmark in order to pay the estate's liabilities. The proceeds from the sale had passed undiminished to the estate as a legal person.

38 After the liquidation of the remaining assets and paying off the estate's liabilities and the processing and settlement costs through partial payment, the net remaining estate of 15,434.62 Reichsmark had been handed over to the German Reich in 1942 as revertible.

39 The assertion of claims to the remaining net estate would not have been made pursuant to the restitution acts but pursuant to the *HfD JGS* ("High Decree Law Gazette") – High Decree of 12 October 1835, Collection of Laws no. 90) 1835/90, and had been possible within the statute of limitations.

40 The object of the restitution application according to the General Settlement Fund Law could not, however, be the claim under inheritance law to the remaining estate but only the property, which had been sold from the estate.

41 Hence, the sale of the property by the trustee of the estate in the course of the probate proceedings did not present a process which could be regarded as a seizure of property in the meaning of the General Settlement Fund Law: The estate would have been in no position to cover its debts without the sale of the property.

42 Even if one were to consider the sale of the property a confiscation in the meaning of the General Settlement Fund Law it was to be taken into consideration that the property had been the object of a settlement between the Republic of Austria and the collection agencies. It could clearly be gathered from the GSF Law and the Washington Agreement that in cases of this kind, a reopening of claims that have already been dealt with was only possible in exceptional cases. Sec. 28 (1) item 2 of the GSF Law required that the **property** [emphasis in the statement] must not have been the object of a settled claim and the **applicant** [emphasis in the statement] must not have otherwise received compensation or a consideration. This provision therefore contained two prerequisites which must be cumulatively fulfilled. The first prerequisite was object-related and did not differentiate between settlements with the aggrieved owner and/or or his/her legal successors and those with the collection agencies. Only the second prerequisite of Sec. 28 (1) item 2 was subject-relat-

"[...] auf der einen Seite im Jahr 1966 und vorher den Erben nach dem ABGB die Ansprüche auf die Liegenschaft verunmöglichte und auf der anderen Seite durch Anlassgesetzgebung dem Legatar nach § 726 ABGB Ansprüche ermöglichte [...]."

Mit Schreiben vom 22. Juli 2005 teilte Notar Dr. Scheubrein unter Beilegung der Erbdokumente mit, dass die Antragstellerin Eva Pe. am 9. Dezember 2003 verstorben sei und dass deren testamentarische Erbinnen je zur Hälfte deren Töchter Marietta P. und Doris A. seien.

2. Stellungnahme der Finanzprokuratur

Die Finanzprokuratur gab als Vertreterin der Republik Österreich mit Schreiben vom 27. Oktober 2003 eine Stellungnahme zum vorliegenden Antrag ab. Darin vertrat die Finanzprokuratur die Ansicht, dass die Voraussetzungen des Entschädigungsfondsgesetzes für eine Empfehlung zur Herausgabe der gegenständlichen Liegenschaft nicht vorliegen und regte an, dem gegenständlichen Antrag nicht Folge zu geben.

Die gegenständliche Liegenschaft sei von der Verlassenschaft nach Dr. F. zur Bezahlung der Nachlassverbindlichkeiten zu einem offenbar angemessenen Kaufpreis von 310.000,– Reichsmark an das Deutsche Reich veräußert worden. Der Kaufpreis sei der Verlassenschaft als juristischer Person ungeschmälert zugeflossen.

Der nach Liquidierung der sonstigen Aktiven und Tilgung der Nachlassverbindlichkeiten und der Abhandlungskosten durch teilweise Bezahlung verbliebene reine Nachlass von 15.434,62 Reichsmark sei dem Deutschen Reich im Jahre 1942 als heimfällig übergeben worden.

Die Geltendmachung von Ansprüchen auf den verbliebenen reinen Nachlass habe sich nicht nach den Rückstellungsgesetzen gerichtet, sondern nach dem HfD JGS 1835/90 (Hofdekret vom 12. Oktober 1835, Justizgesetzsammlung Nr. 90), und sei innerhalb der Verjährungsfrist möglich gewesen.

Gegenstand des Restitutionsantrages nach dem Entschädigungsfondsgesetz könne jedoch nicht der erbrechtliche Anspruch auf den verbliebenen Nachlass, sondern nur die von der Verlassenschaft veräußerte Liegenschaft sein.

Der Verkauf der Liegenschaft durch den Verlassenschaftskurator im Zuge des Verlassenschaftsverfahrens stelle daher aus der Sicht des Entschädigungsfondsgesetzes keinen Vorgang dar, der als Vermögensentziehung angesehen werden könne: Ohne den Liegenschaftsverkauf wäre die Verlassenschaft keinesfalls in der Lage gewesen, ihre Schulden abzudecken.

Selbst wenn man den Verkauf der Liegenschaft als Vermögensentziehung im Sinne des Entschädigungsfondsgesetzes ansehen würde, sei zu berücksichtigen, dass die Liegenschaft Gegenstand eines Vergleiches zwischen der Republik Österreich und den Sammelstellen gewesen sei. Dem EF-G und dem Washingtoner Abkommen könne klar entnommen werden, dass in derartigen Fällen ein Aufrollen bereits erledigter Ansprüche nur in Ausnahmefällen möglich sei. § 28 Abs 1 Z 2 EF-G setze voraus, dass die **Liegenschaft** [Hervorhebung in der Stellungnahme] nicht Gegenstand einer verglichenen Forderung gewesen sein dürfe und der **Antragsteller** [Hervorhebung in der Stellungnahme] nicht auf andere Weise eine Entschädigung oder Gegenleistung erhalten habe dürfen. Diese Bestimmung enthalte sohin zwei Voraussetzungen, die kumulativ erfüllt sein müssen. Die erste Voraussetzung sei objektbezogen und unterscheide nicht zwischen Vergleichen mit dem geschädigten Eigentümer bzw. dessen RechtsnachfolgerInnen und solchen mit den

ed and was geared towards the applicant according to the GSF Law and/or his/her legal predecessor. The Washington Agreement and the GSF Law had by no means intended to subject the collection agencies' system to a general revision and to reopen all cases that had been handled by the collection agencies at the time. It must be particularly emphasized here that both the Agreement and the GSF Law are geared towards particular exceptional cases ("except in exceptional circumstances" see Annex A, letter g ii of item 3).

43   The restrictions which limit the eligibility to file an application to closer relatives provided for in the restitution acts and the related establishment of the collection agencies had been carried out on the express wishes of the victims' organizations and would not form the basis for the exceptional circumstances in the meaning of the General Settlement Fund Law. The reasoning behind these restrictions according to the explanatory remarks on the government bill of the First and Third Restitution Acts was to "preclude from the right to the inheritance distant relatives, who under normal circumstances would have never come into consideration and had had no contact with the decedent". In order to prevent that heirless property would be reverted to the state and that the state would profit from mass murder and genocide of whole families, the utilization of these assets for the benefit of persecuted victims by a receiving organization, the subsequently established collections agencies, had been planned.

44   The settlements concluded by the collection agencies were therefore not to be considered "exceptional circumstances" in the meaning of the GSF Law.

45   Incidentally, the entirely adequate purchase price had passed undiminished to the dormant estate, so the previous owner had received an appropriate consideration in the meaning of Sec. 28 (1) item 2 of the GSF Law. As a legal person, the dormant estate was not a "relative" of the applicants, however, the term "relative" was inevitably to be broadly interpreted. On the one hand, it could be inferred from the purpose of the provision that non-related testamentary heirs were also to be subsumed under this term, on the other hand it was inevitably to be understood that it also comprised the dormant estate, as Sec. 27 of the GSF Law also had to be interpreted so that in the case of a confiscation of property from a dormant estate, the heirs of the decedent were to be eligible to file an application. A focus on the dormant estate, which as a legal person itself had no heirs, would result in the heirs under no circumstances being entitled to file an application according to Sec. 27 of the GSF Law if a seizure of property had actually taken place to the detriment of the dormant estate.

a) Rejoinder by the Applicants

46   With a letter dated 4 December 2003, Dr. Scheubrein submitted a rejoinder to the statement of the State Financial Procurator's Office:

47   The Sanatorium F. had been purchased in 1895 by Dr. med. Julius F., born on 3 December 1859 in Schüttenhofen and deceased on 1 May 1923 in Vienna. Together with his son, Dr. Lothar F., born on 3 February 1897 and deceased on 3 April 1938, they had transformed it into an important private medical establishment for the Jewish bourgeoisie. It had been a treatment center, a maternity clinic and old age people's home of "best and Jewish reputation". The asset losses of the Jewish middle classes due to the world economic crisis at the end of the 1920s had also led to the collapse of businesses in the field of private medical services.

48   This had led to a composition settlement in 1933, which Dr. Lothar F. had raised through foreign capital, namely through investors and family members. The later monetary claims

Sammelstellen. Lediglich die zweite Voraussetzung des § 28 Abs 1 Z 2 sei subjektbezogen und stelle auf den Antragsteller nach dem EF-G bzw. dessen Rechtsvorgänger ab. Es sei durch das Washingtoner Abkommen und das Entschädigungsfondsgesetz keinesfalls beabsichtig gewesen, das System der Sammelstellen einer generellen Revision zu unterziehen und alle Fälle, die seinerzeit über die Sammelstellen abgewickelt worden seien, wieder aufzurollen. Hier sei besonders zu betonen, dass sowohl im Abkommen als auch im Entschädigungsfondsgesetz auf besondere Ausnahmefälle („except in exceptional circumstances", vgl. Annex A, Z 3 lit. g ii) abgestellt werde.

Die in den Rückstellungsgesetzen vorgenommenen Beschränkungen der Antragslegitimation auf nähere Angehörige und damit zusammenhängend die Einrichtung der Sammelstellen sei über ausdrücklichen Wunsch von Opferorganisationen vorgenommen worden und würden keine Ausnahmefälle im Sinne des Entschädigungsfondsgesetzes bilden. Die Ratio dieser Einschränkung habe laut Erläuternden Bemerkungen zur Regierungsvorlage des Ersten Rückstellungsgesetzes (1. RStG) und 3. RStG darin bestanden, „weitschichtige Verwandte, die unter normalen Umständen nie zum Zuge gekommen wären und keinen Kontakt mit dem Erblasser gehabt hätten, vom Erbrechte auszuschließen". Um auszuschließen, dass erbloses Vermögen dem Staat anheimfallen und dieser durch die Massenmorde und Ausrottung ganzer Familien profitieren würde, sei die Verwertung dieser Vermögenswerte zugunsten verfolgter Opfer durch eine Auffangorganisation, die späteren Sammelstellen, geplant gewesen. 43

Die von den Sammelstellen abgeschlossenen Vergleiche seien somit nicht als „besondere Ausnahmefälle" iSd EF-G anzusehen. 44

Im Übrigen sei der durchaus angemessene Kaufpreis dem ruhenden Nachlass ungeschmälert zugeflossen, sodass der frühere Eigentümer eine angemessene Gegenleistung iSd § 28 Abs 1 Z 2 EF-G erhalten habe. Der ruhende Nachlass sei als juristische Person zwar kein „Verwandter" der AntragstellerInnen, doch sei der Begriff „Verwandter" hier zwangsläufig weit auszulegen. Einerseits ergebe sich aus dem Telos der Bestimmung, dass hierunter auch nicht verwandte TestamentserbInnen zu subsumieren seien, andererseits sei er zwangsläufig so zu verstehen, dass er auch den ruhenden Nachlass mitumfasse, da auch § 27 EF-G so ausgelegt werden müsse, dass im Falle einer Vermögensentziehung gegen einen ruhenden Nachlass die ErbInnen des Erblassers antragsberechtigt seien. Ein Abstellen auf den ruhenden Nachlass, der als juristische Person selbst keine ErbInnen habe, würde dazu führen, dass den ErbInnen nach § 27 EF-G auch dann keinesfalls eine Antragslegitimation zukommen könnte, wenn tatsächlich eine Vermögensentziehung zu Lasten des ruhenden Nachlasses stattgefunden hätte. 45

a) Entgegnung der AntragstellerInnen

Notar Dr. Scheubrein brachte mit Schreiben vom 4. Dezember 2003 eine Entgegnung zur Stellungnahme der Finanzprokuratur ein: 46

Das Sanatorium F. sei 1895 durch Dr. med. Julius F., geboren am 3. Dezember 1859 in Schüttenhofen und verstorben am 1. Mai 1923 in Wien, gekauft worden. Dieser habe es gemeinsam mit seinem Sohn Dr. Lothar F., geboren am 3. Februar 1897 und verstorben am 3. April 1938, zu einer für das jüdische Bürgertum wichtigen privaten medizinischen Einrichtung ausgebaut. Es sei Behandlungsstätte, Gebärklinik und Altenbetreuungseinrichtung von „bestem und jüdischem Ruf" gewesen. Die Vermögensverluste des jüdischen Bürgertums aufgrund der Weltwährungskrise Ende der 20er Jahre hätten auch im Geschäftsfeld der privaten medizinischen Dienstleistung zu Geschäftseinbrüchen geführt. 47

of the siblings of Julius F. (B. and Dr. E. F.) had been mentioned by name. Neither the company nor the property had had to be sold.

49 The creditors had acted passively. The passive behavior of the creditors before the occupation could be clearly ascertained from the fact that the note in the land register on the initiation of the auction procedure regarding the Gold Dollar claims of Ernst Si., Benedikt W. and Luis Si. had been removed before the occupation.

50 On 4 March 1938, the "Sanatorium Dr. F[…] Operating Company Ltd." had been founded by Dr. Fritz Er., Dr. Josef Gü., Dr. Sigmund Sin., Dr. Ernst Sp. and Dr. Stefan K. The company's business revolved around the renting of the property belonging to Dr. Lothar F., EZ X1, GB Josefstadt, S.-gasse 14 and the leasehold operation of the Sanatorium run by Dr. Lothar F., which had been accommodated in this house. This company had been dissolved by the general meeting of 8 April 1938 (see file from the Commercial Court Vienna HSG C 25–86).

51 On 12 March 1938, the *Anschluss* of Austria to the German Reich had taken place. Dr. Scheubrein referred at this point to the homepage of the *Documentation Center of Austrian Resistance* (www.doew.at). The depiction of events in Austria around the time of the *Anschluss* under the title "suicide as the last resort" was quoted from:

52 During the night hours leading up to 12 March 1938, the first violent attacks against Austria's Jewish population had already taken place. Windows and shop displays had been smashed, Jews had been arrested, attacked, humiliated and forced to clean pavements etc. by Storm Division men, Hitler Youth members and men with National Socialist insignia. Dr Scheubrein quoted verbatim:

> "The Jews of Austria were effectively outlawed during the first weeks after the *Anschluss*. Hatred, Aryan arrogance, jealousy and decades of socially accepted anti-Semitism erupted in the form of sadism, brutality and a seemingly medieval 'Jew hunt'." Further on in the quotation it said: "In view of the brutal mistreatments, cruel humiliations and extensive robbing, for many Austrian Jews suicide seemed the only way out. In 1938, the number of suicides among the Jewish population of Austria rose to almost 500."

53 It could be inferred from the letter dated 12 March 1990 from Eva Pe., a cousin of Dr. Lothar F. and co-applicant, to Cynthia Miller, Deputy Director of the Office of European Affairs, which was enclosed with the application in question that Dr. Lothar F. had been forced to wash the street. As the owner of a private sanatorium for well-to-do Jewish citizens, he had been a "primary target of the seemingly medieval 'Jew hunt'".

54 Out of desperation over these personal humiliations and the wild aryanizations in the days directly following the *Anschluss*, Dr. Lothar F. had seen no other solution than to kill his wife and himself. A key motive had certainly also been that F. had been unable to bear the barbaric behavior of the mob towards his Jewish clientele and had been unable to do anything to protect his patients from it.

55 Regarding the suicide of the spouses Dr. Lothar and Susanne F., Dr. Scheubrein cited further from the police report contained in Dr. Lothar F.'s probate file: "The numerous farewell notes indicate the suicidal intention – presumably due to the prevailing circumstances, as the deceased are of Jewish race".

56 In the rejoinder, it was further cited from the police report that the keys to Dr. Lothar F.'s private office had been "handed over to the porter of the sanatorium, Adolf J[…], in order that they be passed on to the provisional manager of the sanatorium party comrade M[…]."

Schiedsinstanz für Naturalrestitution – Entscheidung Nr. 27/2005

Dies habe 1933 zu einem Ausgleich geführt, den Dr. Lothar F. durch Aufnahme von 48
Fremdkapital, nämlich durch Investoren und Familienmitglieder, erzielt habe. Namentlich
erwähnt seien spätere Geldforderungen der Geschwister von Julius F. (B. und Dr. E. F.).
Man habe weder Betrieb noch Liegenschaft veräußern müssen.

Die Gläubiger hätten sich passiv verhalten. Das passive Verhalten der Gläubiger vor 49
der Okkupation ergebe sich eindeutig daraus, dass im Grundbuch die Anmerkung der Einleitung des Versteigerungsverfahrens aufgrund der Golddollar-Forderungen von Ernst Si.,
Benedikt W. und Luis Si. noch vor der Okkupation gelöscht worden sei.

Mit Datum vom 4. März 1938 sei von Dr. Fritz Er., Dr. Josef Gü., Dr. Sigmund Sin., Dr. 50
Ernst Sp. und Dr. Stefan K. die „Sanatorium Dr. F[…] Betriebsgesellschaft m.b.H." errichtet worden. Gegenstand des Unternehmens sei die Miete der Dr. Lothar F. eigentümlich gehörigen Liegenschaft EZ X1, GB Josefstadt, S.-gasse 14, und der pachtweise Betrieb des in diesem Hause untergebrachten von Dr. Lothar F. betriebenen Sanatoriums
gewesen. Diese Gesellschaft sei mit Generalversammlung vom 8. April 1938 aufgelöst
worden (siehe Akt des Handelsgerichts [HG] Wien HSG C 25–86).

Am 12. März 1938 sei es zum „Anschluss" Österreichs an das Deutsche Reich ge- 51
kommen. Dr. Scheubrein verwies an dieser Stelle auf die Homepage des „Dokumentationsarchivs des österreichischen Widerstandes" (DÖW) (www.doew.at). Zitiert wurde die
Schilderung der Ereignisse um den „Anschluss" in Österreich unter dem Titel „Selbstmord
als letzter Ausweg":

Bereits während der Nachtstunden zum 12. März 1938 sei es zu den ersten Ausschrei- 52
tungen gegen die jüdische Bevölkerung Österreichs gekommen. Fenster und Geschäftsauslagen seien eingeschlagen worden, Juden von SA-Leuten, HJ-Angehörigen und von
Männern mit nationalsozialistischen Abzeichen verhaftet, geschlagen, gedemütigt und gezwungen worden, Gehsteige etc. zu reiben. Wörtlich zitierte Dr. Scheubrein:

„Die Juden Österreichs waren während der ersten Wochen nach dem ‚Anschluss'
gleichsam vogelfrei. Hass, Herrenmenschendünkel, Neid und jahrzehntelanger ‚salonfähiger' Antisemitismus brachen in Form von Sadismus, Brutalität und einer mittelalterlich anmutenden ‚Judenhatz' aus." Im Zitat lautete es weiter unten: „Angesichts der
brutalen Misshandlungen, grausamen Demütigungen und umfassenden Beraubung erschien vielen österreichischen Juden Selbstmord als einziger Ausweg. Die Zahl der
Selbstmorde innerhalb der jüdischen Bevölkerung Österreichs stieg 1938 auf nahezu
500 Personen an."

Dem in der Anlage zum gegenständlichen Antrag beigelegten Schreiben vom 12. März 53
1990 von Eva Pe., einer Cousine von Dr. Lothar F. und nunmehrige Mitantragstellerin, an
Cynthia Miller, Deputy Director des Office of European Affairs, sei zu entnehmen, dass
Dr. Lothar F. zum Waschen der Straße genötigt worden sei. Er sei als Inhaber eines Privatsanatoriums für wohlhabende jüdische Bürger „primäres Ziel der mittelalterlich anmutenden ‚Judenhatz'" gewesen.

Aus Verzweiflung über diese persönlichen Demütigungen und die wilde Arisierung in 54
den unmittelbaren Tagen nach dem „Anschluss" habe Dr. Lothar F. keinen anderen Ausweg gesehen, als sich und seine Frau selbst zu töten. Ein wesentliches Motiv sei sicher
auch darin gelegen, dass F. den barbarischen Umgang des Mobs mit der ihm anvertrauten
jüdischen Klientel nicht ertragen habe können und andererseits keine Möglichkeit gehabt
habe, seine PatientInnen davor zu bewahren.

Hinsichtlich des Selbstmordes des Ehepaares Dr. Lothar und Susanne F. zitierte Dr. 55
Scheubrein weiters aus dem im Verlassenschaftsakt nach Dr. Lothar F. enthaltenen Poli-

57 In order to explain the position of a provisional manager, Dr. Scheubrein referred to the explanations in the partial report of the Historical Commission by Felber et al, *Eigentumsänderungen in der österreichischen Industrie 1938–1945, Part I Branchen- und Falldarstellungen*, chapter 3.4., *Die wilden Arisierungen und das Kommissar(un)wesen*. The cited text relates particularly that "wild aryanizations" had taken place after the *Anschluss*, which had predominantly affected small businesses of which around 7,000 had been looted, destroyed and shut down. This "wrath of the people" had been exploited for strategic aims. The new National Socialist ruling powers would have called for a return to order as soon as they were in danger of losing control over events. The new "order" had been very fragile until it had become established. A first attempt at channeling the "spontaneous" "aryanization movement" had taken place through the *Gesetz über die Bestellung von kommissarischen Verwaltern und kommissarischen Überwachungspersonen* ("Law on the Appointment of Provisional Administrators and Provisional Supervisors") of 13 April 1938. The State Commissioner for Private Enterprises, Walter Ra., had been entrusted with the implementation of the resulting measures, who according to the Historical Commission had on the whole concentrated on legalizing the existing state of affairs. Among other things, Dr. Scheubrein quoted the following word for word:

> "In reality, aiding this 'decent State' in its injustice was not easy. Despite all of the urgent requests from the Reich Ministry of Economy being received soon after the *Anschluss* and the measures against the 'wild' commissars implemented at the end of March in the wake of the Commissar's Law, passed on 13 April 1938, lootings and 'wild' seizures of Jewish property continued throughout the entire months of March and April".

58 Furthermore, the rejoinder quoted the following passage from the mentioned Historical Commission report (at 145):

> "The Reich Commissar had legalized the commissar system as a 'necessary evil' in order to prevent destruction on the occasion of the assumption of power, as was then to happen in November 1938. The ordinances on the registration of 'Jewish' property, the appointment of provisional administrators of 'Jewish' companies and the establishment of the *Vermögensverkehrsstelle* ["Property Transaction Office"] in 1938 were also attempts to get the movement towards aryanizations 'from below' (the 'wild aryanizations') and the commissar system under control, by passing laws and founding organizations. Bürckel took a hard line with the self-appointed commissars and the commissar system, which stood in the way of systematic 'aryanization', was essentially liquidated in July and August 1938."

59 In the rejoinder, it was subsequently argued that the probate proceedings regarding Dr. Lothar F.'s estate were not comparable with probate proceedings conducted in conformity with the rule of law:

60 According to a report by the trustee of the estate, Dr. Alfred St., the German Armed Forces had already laid claim to the building S.-gasse 14 in Vienna 8 on 1 May 1938 and had occupied parts of it to allow for the Army Recruitment Inspectorate Vienna to be newly established.

61 The Army Recruitment Inspectorate Vienna had moved into the Sanatorium F. on 25 August 1938 at the time of the property valuation and at this time alteration work had already been carried out. As the Sanatorium had no longer been operating on the cut off day, i.e. Dr. Lothar F.'s day of death, 3 April 1938, it could be seen from the bases of the valuation that the valuation according to the capitalized earnings had not been carried out.

zeibericht: „Aus mehreren Abschiedsschreiben geht die Selbstmordabsicht – vermutlich wegen der herrschenden Verhältnisse, da die Toten jüdischer Rasse sind – hervor."

Weiters wurde in der Entgegnung aus diesem Polizeibericht zitiert, dass die Schlüssel zum Privatbüro von Dr. Lothar F. „dem Portier des Sanatoriums Adolf J[…] zwecks Übergabe an den dzt. Kommissarischen Leiter des Sanatoriums Pg. M[…] eingehändigt" worden seien. 56

Zur Erläuterung der Position eines kommissarischen Leiters verwies Dr. Scheubrein auf die Ausführungen des Teilberichts der Historikerkommission von *Felber* et al., Eigentumsänderungen in der österreichischen Industrie 1938–1945, Teil I, Branchen- und Falldarstellungen, Kapitel 3.4., Die wilden Arisierungen und das Kommissar(un)wesen. Im zitierten Text wird insbesondere geschildert, dass es nach dem „Anschluss" zu „wilden Arisierungen" gekommen sei, die vor allem kleine Geschäfte betroffen habe, von denen rund 7.000 geplündert, zerstört und geschlossen worden seien. Diese „Volkswut" sei für strategische Ziele instrumentalisiert worden. Die neuen nationalsozialistischen Machthaber hätten, sobald Gefahr drohte, die Kontrolle über das Geschehen zu verlieren, wieder zur Ordnung gerufen. Die neue „Ordnung" sei aber bis zur ihrer Etablierung noch sehr fragil gewesen. Ein erster Versuch der Kanalisierung der „spontanen" „Arisierungsbewegung" sei durch das Gesetz über die Bestellung von kommissarischen Verwaltern und kommissarischen Überwachungspersonen vom 13. April 1938 erfolgt. Mit der Durchführung der sich daraus ergebenden Maßnahmen sei der Staatskommissar in der Privatwirtschaft, Walter Ra., betraut worden, der sich laut Historikerkommissionsbericht im Großen und Ganzen darauf beschränkt habe, den hergestellten Zustand zu legalisieren. Wörtlich zitierte Dr. Scheubrein unter anderem Folgendes: 57

„Diesem ‚anständigen Staat' zu seinem Unrecht zu verhelfen, war in der Tat nicht einfach. Trotz aller bald nach dem ‚Anschluss' einlangenden Urgenzen aus dem RWM und der Ende März einsetzenden Maßnahmen gegen die ‚wilden' Kommissare im Gefolge des am 13. April 1938 erlassenen Kommissars-Gesetzes dauerten Plünderungen und ‚wilde' Beschlagnahmen jüdischen Vermögens den ganzen März und April hindurch an."

Weiters gab die Entgegnung folgende Passage des genannten Historikerkommissionsberichts wieder (Seite 145): 58

„Der Reichskommissar hatte das Kommissarsystem als ‚notwendiges Übel' legalisiert, um Zerstörungen, wie sie dann im November 1938 vorkommen sollten, anlässlich der Machtübernahme zu verhindern. Die Verordnungen zur Erfassung der ‚jüdischen' Vermögen, über die Bestellung von kommissarischen Verwaltern ‚jüdischer' Betriebe und die Errichtung der Vermögensverkehrsstelle im April 1938 waren auch Versuche, die Bewegung zur ‚Arisierung' ‚von unten' (die ‚wilden Arisierungen') und das Kommissarsystem durch Normensetzung und Organisationsgründung in den Griff zu bekommen. Die selbst eingesetzten Kommissare wurden im Sommer 1938 von Bürckel an die Kandare genommen und das Kommissarsystem, das der systematischen ‚Arisierung' im Wege stand, im wesentlichen im Juli und August 1938 liquidiert."

In der Entgegnung wurde in der Folge argumentiert, dass das nach Dr. Lothar F. geführte Verlassenschaftsverfahren nicht mit einem in einem Rechtsstaat abgewickelten Verlassenschaftsverfahren vergleichbar sei: 59

Laut Bericht des Verlassenschaftskurators Dr. Alfred St. habe schon am 1. Mai 1938 die Deutsche Wehrmacht das Gebäude S.-gasse 14 in Wien 8 in Anspruch genommen und es teilweise für die in Wien neu zu errichtende Wehrersatzinspektion Wien belegt. 60

62 Under normal circumstances, the value of the company would, however, have been decisive in proving that the property would **not** [emphasis in the statement] have had to be sold to cover the claims.

63 In this regard, the rejoinder referred to p. 127 f. of the above-mentioned report from the Historical Commission by Felber et. al., in which the report deals with the calculation of the value of a company. Accordingly, the value of a company is calculated on the basis of the average net earnings of a company over a lengthy period of time and these net earnings are then capitalized. The entire company value, according to the quoted explanations, also includes the immaterial goods, i.e. beyond the net real value, for instance the quality of the company's management, industrial secrets, bank accounts, attractive location, business reputation etc.

64 Further, the tenancy agreement with the "Sanatorium Dr. F[…] Operating Company Ltd." and the leasehold operation of the sanatorium, located in S.-gasse 14 and until then run by Dr. Lothar F., had not had "any effects on the proceedings", although this tenancy agreement was on record. Thus it was stated in the report of the court commissioner Dr. N. of 11 April 1938, that "the sanatorium of the decedent in Vienna VIII, S[…]gasse 14 is under provisional management and according to the parents-in-law, the decedent, Dr. Lothar F[…], concluded a contract a few weeks before his death, regarding the leasing of this sanatorium."

65 The sale of the property to the German Reich, Reich Treasury (Army) had occurred pursuant to the purchase contract dated 20 March 1939. The option of a sale on the open market had not been available to the trustee of the estate. Rent for the period of use of the building had not been paid by the German Reich.

66 Therefore, the acquisition of the property by the German Reich, Reich Treasury (Army) had not taken place in good faith, as one of numerous prerequisites for the affirmation of good faith is that the vendor had freely selected the purchaser. In this regard, the rejoinder referred to Georg Graf *Die österreichische Rückstellungsgesetzgebung. Eine juristische Analyse,* Vienna 2002.

67 The purchase price for the property had been influenced or prescribed by the National Socialist administration with the aim of passing as much liquidity to the estate as possible in order to satisfy the non-Jewish creditors. This had been documented in a memo from 6 September 1938 in the "list of Jewish assets as at 27 April 1938 with regards to the estate of Dr. Lothar F[…]". In part 5 of this file "P.G. Dipl B[…]: 'heirs none, Reich Treasury purchases property for Army Recruitment Inspectorate, money to cover debts'" had been noted in red ink.

68 The mortgage debts of Ernst Si., Benedikt W. and Luis Si. had amounted to 45,000 Gold Dollars, plus outstanding interest and taxes. This had been equivalent to 157,453.07 Reichsmark. By way of comparison, 115,002.67 Reichsmark (or around 41 % of the total debts of the estate of 282,989.19 Reichsmark) had been paid to the German Reich into a frozen account as *Reichsfluchtsteuer* ("Reich Flight Tax") for the three mentioned creditors. This process therefore complied with the classic model of a seizure of Jewish property.

69 The part of the proceeds from the sale of the property which exceeded the monetary claims of the Aryan creditors, according to the final report of the trustee of the estate by Dkfm. Franz Sta., had been paid back to the German Reich by means of the Reich Flight Tax.

Das Sanatorium F. sei am 25. August 1938, dem Zeitpunkt der Schätzung der Liegen- 61
schaft, von der Wehrersatzinspektion Wien bezogen worden und es seien zu diesem Zeitpunkt bereits Adaptierungsarbeiten vorgenommen gewesen. Da das Sanatorium zum Stichtag, nämlich dem Todestag des Dr. Lothar F. am 3. April 1938, außer Betrieb gewesen sei, sei aus den Bewertungsgrundlagen zu sehen, dass die Bewertung nach dem Ertrag nicht durchgeführt worden sei.

Jedoch wäre der Wert des Betriebes unter normalen Umständen ausschlaggebend dafür 62
gewesen, dass die Liegenschaft **nicht** [Hervorhebung im Schriftsatz] zur Deckung der Forderungen hätte veräußert werden müssen.

In diesem Zusammenhang verwies die Entgegnung auf Seite 127 f. des oben genann- 63
ten Berichts der Historikerkommission von *Felber* et al., in der sich der Bericht mit der Errechnung des Wertes eines Unternehmens befasst. Demzufolge wird der Unternehmenswert anhand des durchschnittlichen Reinertrages des Unternehmens einer längeren Periode errechnet und dieser Reinertrag dann kapitalisiert. Der gesamte Unternehmenswert beinhaltet laut den zitierten Ausführungen auch die immateriellen Güter, also über den reinen Sachwert hinaus auch etwa die Qualität der Leitung eines Betriebes, Fabrikationsgeheimnisse, Bankverbindungen, günstige Lage, geschäftlicher Ruf usw.

Des Weiteren habe der Pachtvertrag mit der „Sanatorium Dr. F[…] Betriebsgesellschaft 64
m. b. H." und der pachtweise Betrieb des in der S.-gasse 14 untergebrachten, bisher von Dr. F. betriebenen Sanatoriums keinen „wie auch immer gearteten Niederschlag im Verfahren" gehabt, obwohl dieser Pachtvertrag aktenbekannt war. So habe es im Bericht des Gerichtskommissärs Dr. N. vom 11. April 1938 gelautet: „Das Sanatorium des Erblassers in Wien VIII., S[…]gasse 14 steht unter kommissarischer Leitung und hat der Erblasser Dr. Lothar F[…] wenige Wochen vor seinem Ableben laut Angabe der erbl. Schwiegereltern einen Vertrag punkto Verpachtung dieses Sanatoriums geschlossen."

Der Verkauf der Liegenschaft an das Deutsche Reich/Reichsfiskus Heer sei mit Kauf- 65
vertrag vom 20. März 1939 erfolgt. Die Variante des freihändigen Verkaufes der Liegenschaft sei dem Verlassenschaftskurator nicht zur Verfügung gestanden. Miete sei für die Zeit der Nutzung vom Deutschen Reich nicht beglichen worden.

Somit sei die Liegenschaft vom Deutschen Reich/Reichsfiskus Heer nicht redlich er- 66
worben worden, da eine von mehreren Voraussetzungen für die Bejahung der Redlichkeit darin bestehe, dass sich der Verkäufer den Käufer frei ausgesucht habe. Hiezu verwies die Entgegnung auf Georg *Graf*, Die österreichische Rückstellungsgesetzgebung. Eine juristische Analyse, Wien 2002.

Die Höhe des Kaufpreises der Liegenschaft sei von Seiten der NS-Administration be- 67
einflusst bzw. vorgeschrieben worden mit dem Ziel, der Verlassenschaft nach Möglichkeit soviel an Liquidität zukommen zu lassen, um die nichtjüdischen Gläubiger zu befriedigen. Dies sei in einer Notiz vom 6. September 1938 im „Verzeichnis über das Vermögen von Juden nach dem Stand vom 27. April 1938 betreffend Verlassenschaft nach Dr. Lothar F[…]" dokumentiert. Dort sei in Aktenteil Nr. 5 in roter Schrift vermerkt: „P.G. Dipl B[...]: ‚Erben keine, Reichsfiskus kauft LS für Wehrersatzinspektion, Geld zur Deckung der Schulden.'"

Die Hypothekarschulden von Ernst Si., Benedikt W. und Luis Si. hätten in Summe 68
45.000,– Golddollar plus rückständiger Zinsen und Steuern betragen. Dies seien umgerechnet 157.453,07 Reichsmark gewesen. Im Vergleichswege seien dafür 115.002,67 Reichsmark (oder ca. 41 % der Gesamtschulden der Verlassenschaft von 282.989,19 Reichsmark) als Reichsfluchtsteuer für die genannten drei Gläubiger auf Sperrkonten an

70 Patients' fees had not been claimed. Parts of the inventory had been sold on the open market by the trustee of the estate for around 50 % of their estimated value. According to supplement A of Dkfm. Sta.'s final report, the sanatorium had entirely ceased to operate on 30 September 1938 and the books had been closed by the sanatorium's employees. Considerable parts of the claims of the non-Jewish creditors had resulted from this forced closure.

71 Furthermore, the following was to be quoted from the examination of the final report on page 6: "B. F[...] and Dr. E. F[...], who are relatives of Dr. Lothar F[...], Dr. Erd[...] Siegfried and Dr. Sin[...] have not yet registered their claims, as is also the case with Ge[...] R., who remained altogether unknown." The people referred to are Dr. Bernhard F., born on 3 June 1857, died on 20 December 1936 as well as Dr. Ernst Jakob F., born on 8 April 1865 and died on 4 January 1943, whose descendants now, among other people, requested the *in rem* restitution of the property in question.

72 Subsequently, Dr. Scheubrein argued that during probate proceedings, in which the usual principles of the rule of law are adhered to and the then valid para. 131 of the *Außerstreitgesetz* ("Non-Contentious Proceedings Act") was to be applied, in any case these persons or their legal successors would have had to have been granted the opportunity to participate in the proceedings or that representatives *in absentia* for the statutory heirs mentioned in the last will and testament should have been appointed. As these persons were known to be Jews, however, all due care had been ignored and they had no opportunity to intervene in the proceedings.

73 On 5 September 1941, the Chief Finance President Vienna had laid claim to the estate of Dr. Lothar F. as heirless property and had applied to have the estate declared revertible for the benefit of the German Reich.

74 Dr. Scheubrein further asserted the reference of the State Financial Procurator's Office that the reverted amount should have been claimed from the Republic in accordance with High Decree Law Gazette 1835/90 within the statutory deadline was not logical. Besides the potentially low sum, a claim from the Federation under civil law would have failed due to the circumstance that the Republic of Austria had not been the legal successor to the German Reich.

75 The current statement of the State Financial Procurator's Office maintained, without modification, its historical position in the period after 1945 which was explained in the above mentioned report of the Historical Commission by Felber et al. Regarding this, the rejoinder cites p. 203 ff of the mentioned report, which essentially contained the following:

76 In the settlement proceedings concerning heirless or unclaimed property or discriminatory taxes or similar levies, the interests of Austria had in a way led the Austrian negotiation position to resemble that of the aryanizers as the Austrian representatives had been interested in paying as little as possible. They had therefore taken a stance which tended to minimize Jewish material losses. The basis of the Austrian position had been that due to the lack of legal continuity with the National Socialist state, the Republic could not be held responsible for compensating the property seizure that had taken place during National Socialist rule. At that time, Austria had not yet emerged as a State and legal person and had not been able to undertake to compensate the damages caused but had merely to restitute the seized properties insofar as they had still been available in Austria.

das Deutsche Reich ergangen. Dieser Vorgang entspreche somit dem klassischen Bild der Entziehung von jüdischem Eigentum.

Derjenige Teil der Erlöse für die Liegenschaft, welcher die Geldforderungen der arischen Gläubiger überstieg, sei laut Überprüfung des Endberichtes des Verlassenschaftskurator durch Dkfm. Franz Sta. über die Reichsfluchtsteuer wieder an das Deutsche Reich zurückerstattet worden. 69

Patientenhonorare seien nicht gefordert worden. Teile des Inventars seien vom Verlassenschaftskurator um ungefähr 50 % des Schätzwertes freihändig verkauft worden. Laut Beilage A zu Dkfm. Sta.s Endbericht sei der Sanatoriumsbetrieb mit 30. September 1938 zur Gänze geschlossen und durch die Angestellten des Sanatoriums die Bücher abgeschlossen worden. Wesentliche Teile der Forderungen der nichtjüdischen Gläubiger seien aus dieser zwangsweisen Schließung resultiert. 70

Des Weiteren sei der Überprüfung des Endberichts auf Seite 6 Folgendes zu entnehmen: „B. F[…] und Dr. E. F[…], die Verwandte von Dr. Lothar F[…] sind, Dr. Erd[…] Siegfried und Dr. Sin[…] haben ihre Forderungen nicht angemeldet, ebenso Ge[…] R., der überhaupt unbekannt blieb." Hierbei handle es sich um Bernhard F., geboren am 3. Juni 1857 und gestorben am 20. Dezember 1936, sowie um Dr. Ernst Jakob F., geboren am 8. April 1865 und gestorben am 4. Jänner 1943, deren Nachkommen nunmehr neben anderen Personen die Naturalrestitution der gegenständlichen Liegenschaft begehrten. 71

In Folge argumentierte Dr. Scheubrein, dass bei einem Verlassenschaftsverfahren unter Einhaltung üblicher rechtsstaatlicher Grundsätze und unter Anwendung des damals gültigen § 131 Außerstreitgesetz (AußStG) jedenfalls diesen Personen bzw. deren Rechtsnachfolgern die Möglichkeit der Verfahrensbeteiligung eingeräumt hätte werden müssen oder dass Abwesenheitskuratoren für die testamentarisch erwähnten gesetzlichen ErbInnen bestellt werden hätten müssen. Da diese aber als Juden bekannt gewesen seien, sei jegliche Obsorge vernachlässigt worden und hätten diese keine Möglichkeit gehabt, im Verfahren einzuschreiten. 72

Mit Datum 5. September 1941 habe der Oberfinanzpräsident (OFP) Wien den Nachlass nach Dr. Lothar F. als erblos in Anspruch genommen und beantragt, den Nachlass zugunsten des Deutschen Reiches für heimfällig zu erklären. 73

Dr. Scheubrein machte weiters geltend, der Verweis der Finanzprokuratur, dass der Heimfallsbetrag von der Republik entsprechend HfD JGS 1835/90 innerhalb der gesetzlichen Fristen zu fordern gewesen wäre, sei nicht nachvollziehbar. Abgesehen von dem potentiell geringen Erlös wäre eine zivilrechtliche Forderung an den Bund bereits an dem Umstand gescheitert, dass die Republik Österreich nicht Rechtsnachfolgerin nach dem Deutschen Reich gewesen sei. 74

Die aktuelle Stellungnahme der Finanzprokuratur führe deren historische Position in der Zeit nach 1945, welche von der Historikerkommission in ihrem oben erwähnten Bericht von *Felber* et al. erläutert werde, unmodifiziert weiter. Hiezu zitierte die Entgegnung Seite 203 ff aus dem genannten Bericht, der im Wesentlichen Folgendes beinhalte: 75

In den Entschädigungsverfahren bei erblosen bzw. nichtbeanspruchten Vermögen oder wegen diskriminierenden Abgaben und Ähnlichem sei die österreichische Verhandlungsposition in gewisser Hinsicht interessensmäßig an die Seite der Ariseure geraten, da die österreichischen Vertreter Interesse gehabt hätten, möglichst wenig zu zahlen. Sie hätten daher eine Position vertreten, welche die jüdischen materiellen Verluste tendenziell minimiert habe. Grundlage der österreichischen Position sei gewesen, dass die Republik man- 76

77 Dr. Scheubrein further explained that pursuant to Sec. 28 of the GSF Law, the Arbitration Panel was to examine applications for *in rem* restitution which fulfill two prerequisites: they may never have been the subject of a previously decided claim **and** [emphasis in the statement] no compensation may have been paid to the applicant or a relative unless such a previous decision or ruling had constituted an extreme injustice.

78 Both prerequisites were directly connected. One prerequisite was not plausible without the other, with the result that an application only did not fall within the competence of the Arbitration Panel if the applicant or his/her ancestors according to the law of succession had already been affected by a decision of Austrian courts or administrative bodies, with the exception that such a decision/settlement by agreement had constituted an extreme injustice.

79 In the rejoinder, the applicants' representative again summarized the arguments as follows:

80 Had National Socialist persecution not taken place in the years 1938 to 1945, the property of Dr. Lothar F. would firstly not have reverted to the State, secondly would also not have been over-indebted and thirdly the sale of the property in order to cover the debts would not have been necessary.

81 To expatiate on this, Scheubrein explained that a reversion to the State would not have taken place without National Socialism, as statutory and testamentary heirs had always been on record. However, these legal successors had only been racially persecuted persons as they all would have been considered Jews in accordance with the Nuremberg Laws of 15 September 1935, and due to their flight to enemy territories of the German Reich had been located abroad or in the case of Rosa G., née Ro., had been murdered in Theresienstadt.

82 Without National Socialist persecution, the sale of the property in order to cover the outstanding accounts, which were minimal in relation to the actual value of the estate, would not have been necessary, as the majority of the outstanding accounts had resulted from the wild aryanization and subsequent closure of the company. Additionally, the German Armed Forces had requisitioned the building for its own uses.

83 The Republic had *de facto* received a property in a primary location without paying any relevant consideration. A claim for the return of the reverted estate of Dr. Lothar F. would have been unsuccessful, as Austria had not been the legal successor to the German Reich. In the case of the improbable success of a civil action for the surrender of the estate, the proceeds would only have amounted to a fraction of the actual value of the seized property which was the result of incorrect probate proceedings, and which the Republic of Austria had actually possessed since the ownership title had been recorded on the basis of Article 22 of the Austrian State Treaty of 15 May 1955 (Federal Law Gazette No. 152/1955) in conjunction with para. 11 of the First State Treaty Implementation Act of 25 July 1956 (Federal Law Gazette No. 165/1956).

84 The payment of 700,000 Schilling to the collection agencies within the scope of the Collection Agencies Settlement Act of 7 July 1966 (Federal Law Gazette No. 150/1966) had occurred without a logical basis and represented in any case an extreme injustice for the statutory heirs of Dr. Lothar F.

85 However, none of the statutory heirs of the third *parentela* would have had a claim to restitution of the property. This was only made possible by the GSF Law.

gels Rechtskontinuität mit dem NS-Staat nicht zu einer Wiedergutmachung der Vermögensentziehung während der NS-Herrschaft verhalten werden könne. Österreich, das als Staat und Rechtsperson in jener Zeit nicht in Erscheinung getreten sei, habe sich auch nicht zur Wiedergutmachung der angerichteten Schäden verpflichten können, sondern lediglich zur Rückstellung der entzogenen Vermögenschaften, soweit sie noch in Österreich vorhanden gewesen seien.

Dr. Scheubrein führte weiters aus, dass gemäß § 28 EF-G die Schiedsinstanz Anträge auf Naturalrestitution von Liegenschaften zu prüfen habe, die zwei Bedingungen erfüllen: Sie dürfen niemals Gegenstand einer entschiedenen Forderung gewesen sein **und** [Hervorhebung im Schriftsatz] es dürfe keine Entschädigung für den Antragsteller oder einen Verwandten geleistet worden sein, oder eine solche Entscheidung bzw. Regelung müsse eine extreme Ungerechtigkeit darstellen. 77

Die beiden Bedingungen stünden im unmittelbaren Zusammenhang. Es sei eine Bedingung nicht ohne die andere denkbar, sodass sich eine Unzuständigkeit der Schiedsinstanz nur dann ergebe, wenn der Antragsteller selbst oder dessen erbrechtlich relevanten Vorfahren von einer Entscheidung durch österreichische Gerichte oder Verwaltungsbehörden betroffen gewesen seien, außer eine solche Entscheidung/einvernehmliche Regelung habe eine extreme Ungerechtigkeit dargestellt. 78

In der Entgegnung fasste der Vertreter der AntragstellerInnen die Argumente nochmals wie folgt zusammen: 79

Ohne nationalsozialistische Verfolgung in den Jahren 1938 bis 1945 sei erstens das Vermögen von Dr. Lothar F. weder dem Staat anheim gefallen noch zweitens überschuldet gewesen, noch sei drittens der Verkauf der Liegenschaft notwendig gewesen, um die Schulden abzudecken. 80

Dies ausführend erläuterte Scheubrein, dass es ohne Nationalsozialismus zu keinem Heimfall an den Staat gekommen wäre, da gesetzliche und testamentarische ErbInnen immer aktenbekannt gewesen seien. Jedoch seien ausschließlich rassisch verfolgte Personen zur Erbfolge berufen gewesen, da alle gemäß den Nürnberger Gesetzen vom 15. September 1935 als Juden gegolten hätten, welche sich aufgrund der Flucht im für das Deutsche Reich feindlichen Ausland befunden hätten oder auch im Falle von Rosa G. geb. Ro. in Theresienstadt ermordet worden seien. 81

Ohne nationalsozialistische Verfolgung wäre der Verkauf der Liegenschaft zur Deckung der in Relation zum tatsächlichen Wert der Erbmasse geringen Außenstände nicht notwendig gewesen. Denn die Außenstände seien mehrheitlich aus der wilden Arisierung und somit zwangsweisen Schließung des Betriebes resultiert. Zudem habe die Deutsche Wehrmacht die Liegenschaft für sich angefordert. 82

Die Republik habe de facto ohne relevante Gegenleistung eine Liegenschaft in bester Lage erhalten. Ein Herausgabeantrag betreffend den heimfälligen Nachlass Dr. Lothar F.s wäre ins Leere gegangen, da Österreich nicht Rechtsnachfolger des Deutschen Reiches gewesen sei. Für den Fall eines unwahrscheinlichen Erfolges einer Zivilklage auf Herausgabe des Nachlasses hätte der Erlös nur einen Bruchteil des tatsächlichen Wertes der durch ein unkorrektes Verlassenschaftsverfahren entzogenen Liegenschaft ergeben, über welche die Republik Österreich tatsächlich seit der Einverleibung der Eigentumsrechte aufgrund des Art. 22 des österreichischen Staatsvertrages vom 15. Mai 1955 (BGBl 152/1955, StV 1955) iVm § 11 des 1. StVDG vom 25. Juli 1956 (BGBl 165/1956, 1. StVDG) verfügt habe. 83

Die Zahlung von 700.000,– Schilling an die Sammelstellen im Rahmen des Sammelstellenabgeltungsgesetzes vom 7. Juli 1966 (BGBl 150/1966) sei ohne nachvollziehbaren 84

Arbitration Panel for *In Rem* Restitution – Decision No. 27/2005

86   In the place of the deceased aggrieved owner, all previous restitution acts had only considered spouses, direct ancestors and descendants of the aggrieved person and further statutory heirs as eligible for restitution in the case that they had lived with the aggrieved owner.

87   The Arbitration Panel was therefore requested to recommend to the competent Federal Minister the *in rem* restitution of the property subject of this application in favor of the applicants represented by the Notary Dr. Scheubrein.

b) Supplementary Statements by the Applicants

88   As a supplement to these statements, the law firm Lansky Ganzger & Partner and attorney-at-law Dr. Marc R. R., as legal representatives of the applicants Marion R.-G., Stephan G. and Robert Re., submitted a further statement on 29 April 2005.

89   In the statement, the legal representatives began with the history of the building in S.-gasse and explained that the sanatorium managed by Dr. F. had been the biggest private sanatorium in Vienna for births, general medicine and geriatric care. It had been used by wealthy families and numerous celebrities. The world's best doctors and the famous "Billroth-nurses" had worked in the clinic.

90   The sanatorium had always been fully booked although the international monetary crisis in 1933 had led to a composition settlement. Investors and family members had provided funds to avert the sale of the company and the property. The notice of the initiation of the auction procedure for claims of the mortgagees Ernst and Benedikt W. and Luis Si. had been deleted from the land register in 1935. This contradicted the assertions of the State Financial Procurator's Office, according to which pressure from the creditors would have been expected before the *Anschluss* and the sale of the property would have been necessary to satisfy the creditors.

91   Furthermore it is submitted that since the *Anschluss*, the sanatorium had been occupied by the National Socialists and among other things, Dr. Lothar F. had been forced to clean the staircase with a toothbrush. F. had been demoted to the role of a "janitor" in his own company, while a provisional manager appointed by the National Socialists had been entrusted with the management of the sanatorium. Due to the then prevailing circumstances, Dr. Lothar F. and his wife had seen suicide as the only way out.

92   Several points made in the explanations by the State Financial Procurator's Office were contested in the statement:

93   The estate had not been so over-indebted that the sale of the sanatorium would have been required. In 1936, when one of the applicants had been born in the Sanatorium F., the private clinic had been in its prime and had had many patients. Neither the expert valuation of 1938 nor the final report by the trustee of the estate had been suitable justification for the sale of the property.

94   The total sum of the liens of 5,972.83 Reichsmark (less than 2 % of the proceeds from the sale) encumbering the property was not at all equivalent to the proceeds of 310,000 Reichsmark achieved by the sale at the time or to the actual value of the property. The sale of the property in order to release the liens had not been necessary.

95   With regards to the valuation report by building officer Ing. Herrmann, it was submitted that from an economic perspective, the value of the constituent parts and of the building did not have any implications for the value of the company. In the case at hand, only an assessment of the net asset value of the company (real value, current market value of

Grund erfolgt und stelle jedenfalls für die gesetzlichen ErbInnen des Dr. Lothar F. eine extreme Ungerechtigkeit dar.

Jedoch hätte keiner der gesetzlichen ErbInnen der dritten Parentel Restitutionsansprüche auf die Liegenschaft gehabt, diese Möglichkeit eröffne erst das EF-G. 85

Alle vorangegangenen Rückstellungsgesetze hätten anstelle des verstorbenen geschädigten Eigentümers lediglich Ehegatten, unmittelbare Vor- und Nachfahren des Geschädigten sowie weitere gesetzliche ErbInnen nur für den Fall als rückstellungsberechtigt angesehen, dass sie in Hausgemeinschaft mit dem Geschädigten gelebt hätten. 86

Die Schiedsinstanz werde somit gebeten, eine Empfehlung zur Naturalrestitution der gegenständlichen Liegenschaft zugunsten der vom Notar Scheubrein vertretenen AntragstellerInnen an den zuständigen Bundesminister abzugeben. 87

b) Ergänzende Ausführungen der AntragstellerInnen

In Ergänzung zu diesen Ausführungen brachte die Kanzlei Lansky, Ganzger & Partner und RA Dr. Marc R. R. als Rechtsvertreter der AntragstellerInnen Marion R.-G., Stephan G. und Robert Re. am 29. April 2005 einen weiteren Schriftsatz ein. 88

Darin gingen die Rechtsvertreter vorweg auf die Geschichte des Gebäudes in der S.-gasse ein und führten aus, das von Dr. F. geleitete Sanatorium sei das größte private Sanatorium Wiens für Geburten, allgemeine Medizin und Altenpflege gewesen. Es sei von wohlhabenden Familien und zahlreichen Prominenten frequentiert worden. Es seien die weltbesten Ärzte und die berühmten „Billroth-Krankenschwestern" in der Klinik beschäftigt gewesen. 89

Der Sanatoriumsbetrieb sei immer ausgebucht gewesen, wobei die Umsatzeinbußen durch die Weltwährungskrise 1933 zu einem Ausgleich geführt hätten. Investoren und Familienangehörige hätten durch ihre Gelder eine Veräußerung des Betriebes und der Liegenschaft abgewendet. Die Anmerkung der Einleitung des Versteigerungsverfahrens für Forderungen der Hypothekargläubiger Ernst und Benedikt W. und Luis Si. sei 1935 im Grundbuch wieder gelöscht worden. Dies stünde den Behauptungen der Finanzprokuratur entgegen, wonach vor dem „Anschluss" ein Druck seitens der Gläubiger zu erwarten und der Liegenschaftsverkauf zur Gläubigerbefriedigung notwendig gewesen sei. 90

Weiters wird vorgebracht vor, dass ab dem „Anschluss" die Nationalsozialisten das Sanatorium okkupiert hätten und Lothar F. unter anderem gezwungen worden sei, das Stiegenhaus mit einer Zahnbürste zu reinigen. F. sei zum „Hausmeister" in seinem eigenem Unternehmen degradiert worden, während ein von den Nationalsozialisten beauftragter kommissarischer Leiter mit der Führung des Sanatoriums betraut worden sei. Dr. Lothar F. und seine Gattin hätten aufgrund der herrschenden Umstände keinen anderen Ausweg als den Selbstmord gesehen. 91

Die Ausführungen der Finanzprokuratur wurden im Schriftsatz hinsichtlich mehrerer Punkte bestritten: 92

Der Nachlass sei nicht dermaßen überschuldet gewesen, dass ein Verkauf des Sanatoriums vonnöten gewesen sei. 1936, als eine der Antragstellerinnen im Sanatorium F. zur Welt gekommen sei, sei die Privatklinik in ihrer Blütezeit gestanden und stark frequentiert gewesen. Weder das Schätzgutachten von 1938 noch der Endbericht des Verlassenschaftskurators seien zur Rechtfertigung des Liegenschaftsverkaufs geeignet. 93

Der Gesamtbetrag der auf der Liegenschaft lastenden Pfandrechte von 5.972,83 Reichsmark (unter 2 % des Verkaufserlöses) sei in keiner Relation zum damals erzielten 94

the assets) had been undertaken. However, if proceedings had been conducted correctly, an assessment according to the capitalized income value should have taken place. The value of a company as a whole was far higher than the sum of its constituent parts. The immaterial assets of a company included, for example, the quality of the company management, the working environment, the skills of the employees, production secrets, bank accounts, an attractive location, expansion possibilities, good will etc. A correct valuation would have resulted in far higher proceeds from the sale, and for these reasons the sale of the building had had no relation to the covering of the estate's debts.

96 Furthermore, the information contained in the valuation report that the sanatorium had no longer been operating on the cut off day of 3 April 1938 was incorrect. Also according to the final report by the trustee of the estate, the sanatorium had still been in operation during the commissioning of the building by the German Armed Forces.

97 Additionally, the "Sanatorium Dr. F[...] Operating Company Ltd.", founded on 4 March 1938 and dissolved on 8 April 1938, a business which revolved around the renting of the property and the leasehold operation of the sanatorium had not been reflected in the documents of the probate proceedings. The trustee of the estate would have been able to draw on the proceeds from the renting/leasing to cover the debts of the estate, which would have prevented the sale of the sanatorium.

98 The sale of the sanatorium to cover the debts of the estate had been fictitiously alleged to be an "emergency sale" in order to make the sale seem legitimate. However, it presented a typical case of wild aryanization, as the building at least half a year before the sale had been unlawfully taken into the possession of its later purchaser and alteration work had also been undertaken by the purchaser. The Army Recruitment Inspectorate had moved into the building without any form of institutional consultation having taken place.

99 Pursuant to para. 417 of the (Austrian) General Civil Code, the user and/or site manager in bad faith was to pay the landowner a fee for the use of the property. Furthermore, the owner of the land had the right to have the property restored to its former condition. The trustee of the estate had not only permitted the Army Recruitment Inspectorate to move into the building and begin alteration work, but had also neglected to charge for its use. This should have been paid to the estate.

100 The following was gathered from the invoice book of the trustee of the estate: The German Armed Forces had already partially requisitioned the building by 1 May 1938 and had partially occupied it for the soon to be established Army Recruitment Inspectorate in Vienna. The trustee of the estate had been unable to oppose this move, as an irrevocable right of requisition had existed for the purposes of the German Armed Forces. The requisitioning of rooms of the sanatorium had disrupted the operation of the sanatorium, although there had only been a few patients in the sanatorium at the time. The reason for this was that the sanatorium had mainly been frequented by foreigners and Jews.

101 A clear discrepancy between the invoice book and the valuation report was evident, above all in the latter it was explained that the company had already ceased to operate on 3 April 1938.

102 Regarding the adequacy of the purchase price of 310,000 Reichsmark for the property, it was explained in the statement that the German Armed Forces had already taken over the sanatorium almost in its entirety by 1 July 1938. It had been agreed by the trustee of the estate and the military district administration that from the time of the requisitioning of the building, the German Reich had to pay rent, which would, however, not be charged in the case that they purchased the building. According to the invoice book of the trustee

Verkaufserlös von 310.000,– Reichsmark bzw. zum eigentlichen Liegenschaftswert gestanden. Der Verkauf der Liegenschaft sei zur Bereinigung der Pfandrechte nicht notwendig gewesen.

Zum Schätzgutachten durch Baurat Ing. Herrmann wurde vorgebracht, dass aus betriebswirtschaftlicher Sicht der Wert der Einzelteile und des Gebäudes nichts über die Bewertung des Unternehmens aussage. Im gegenständlichen Fall sei lediglich eine Bewertung nach dem Substanzwert des Unternehmens (Sachwert, gegenwärtiger Verkehrswert der Aktiven) vorgenommen worden. Richtigerweise hätte jedoch eine Bewertung nach dem Ertragswert stattfinden müssen. Der Wert eines Unternehmens als Ganzes sei weitaus höher als die Summe der Einzelteile. Zu den immateriellen Werten eines Unternehmens zählten beispielsweise die Qualität der Betriebsleitung, das Betriebsklima, die Geschicklichkeit der ArbeiterInnen, Fabrikationsgeheimnisse, Bankverbindung, günstige Lage, Expansionsmöglichkeiten, good will etc. Bei richtiger Bewertung hätte sich ein weitaus höherer Verkaufserlös ergeben, und daher sei der Gebäudeverkauf in keiner Relation zur Deckung der Nachlassschulden gestanden. 95

Darüber hinaus sei die im Schätzungsgutachten enthaltene Information unrichtig, dass das Sanatorium zum Stichtag des 3. April 1938 außer Betrieb gestanden sei. Auch laut Endbericht des Verlassenschaftskurators sei der Sanatoriumsbetrieb sogar noch während der Inbetriebnahme durch die Deutsche Wehrmacht aufrecht gewesen. 96

Zudem habe die am 4. März 1938 gegründete und am 8. April 1938 aufgelöste „Sanatorium Dr. F[…] Betriebsgesellschaft m.b.H.", welche die Miete der Liegenschaft sowie den pachtweisen Betrieb des Sanatoriums zum Gegenstand hatte, keinen Niederschlag in den Unterlagen des Verlassenschaftsverfahrens gefunden. Der Verlassenschaftskurator hätte die Erlöse aus der Vermietung/Verpachtung zur Deckung der Nachlassschulden heranziehen können, wodurch der Sanatoriumsverkauf zu verhindern gewesen wäre. 97

Der angebliche „Notverkauf" des Sanatoriums zur Deckung der Nachlassschulden sei eine Fiktion gewesen, um den Verkauf als rechtmäßig erscheinen zu lassen. Es läge aber ein typischer Fall wilder Arisierung vor, da das Gebäude zumindest ein halbes Jahr vor dem Verkauf durch den späteren Käufer unrechtmäßig in Besitz genommen worden sei und von diesem auch Adaptierungsarbeiten vorgenommen worden seien. Der Bezug des Gebäudes durch die Wehrersatzinspektion sei ohne jegliche institutionelle Rückbindung erfolgt. 98

In Anwendung des § 417 ABGB habe der unredliche Benützer bzw. Bauführer dem Grundeigentümer ein Benützungsentgelt zu bezahlen. Weiters habe der Grundeigentümer einen Anspruch auf Wiederherstellung des früheren Zustandes. Der Verlassenschaftskurator habe nicht nur den Bezug des Gebäudes durch die Wehrersatzinspektion und die durch diese begonnenen Adaptierungsarbeiten zugelassen, sondern habe es auch verabsäumt, ein Benützungsentgelt zu verlangen. Dieses hätte dem Nachlass zufließen müssen. 99

Aus dem Verrechnungsbuch des Verlassenschaftskurators gehe Folgendes hervor: Die Deutsche Wehrmacht habe das Gebäude bereits teilweise am 1. Mai 1938 in Anspruch genommen und es teilweise für die in Wien neu zu errichtende Wehrmachtsinspektion belegt. Dagegen habe sich der Verlassenschaftskurator nicht zur Wehr setzen können, da für die Zwecke der Wehrmacht ein nicht zu beseitigendes Anforderungsrecht bestanden habe. Durch die Inanspruchnahme von Räumen des Sanatoriums sei eine Störung im Sanatoriumsbetrieb eingetreten, obwohl um diese Zeit nur wenige Patienten im Sanatorium gewesen seien. Der Grund habe darin gelegen, dass das Sanatorium zumeist von Ausländern und Juden besucht worden sei. 100

of the estate, an amount of 85,000 Reichsmark had been deducted from the purchase price so that the actual purchase price had then only amounted to 225,000 Reichsmark. This advance payment of 85,000 Reichsmark had not been used as a payment for the use of the building but to satisfy the claims of the employees. It resulted from a letter from the trustee of the estate to the court that the German Reich had not wanted to pay the brokerage fee of 9,000 Reichsmark, so that this amount had also been deducted from the purchase price. Thus, the proceeds had only amounted to 216,000 Reichsmark.

103   The purchase price had also not been paid to the estate, as it was determined in the purchase contract that the proceeds were to be paid into a frozen account with the designation "de-jewification proceeds", which could only have been disposed of with the approval of the *Devisenstelle* ("Foreign Exchange Board") Vienna. The payment of the proceeds from the sale to the estate had never been intended, the purchase price which had seemingly been paid for the property had therefore returned to the German Reich, which constituted a typical act of aryanization.

104   The supposed payment to the mortgages had also been a pretext to disguise the actual use of the proceeds from the sale. The mortgage claims of the Jewish creditors amounting to 157,453.07 Reichsmark had never been paid off. In order to cancel the mortgages, a settlement of 115,002.67 Reichsmark had been reached. This amount should have been paid to the estate, however, this did not occur. Part of the amount (46,666 Reichsmark) had been withheld as Reich Flight Tax, which complied with the classic model of a seizure of Jewish property. Another portion (35,002 Reichsmark for Benedikt W. and 23,334 Reichsmark for Louis Si.) had been paid into frozen accounts of the German Reich. A further 10,000 Reichsmark had been withheld for legal fees. Thus the settlement sum, which still had constituted 41 % of the estate's total debts, had never been paid to the estate.

105   It resulted from all contentions that the supposed emergency sale of the sanatorium to cover the estate's debts had only served to disguise what had actually taken place, that is to say the aryanization of the sanatorium.

106   Regarding the reversion of the remaining net estate, para. 760 of the (Austrian) General Civil Code was referred to, according to which the estate reverted to the state as heirless property if no eligible successors existed or no-one acquired the inheritance. During the release of the inheritance, the provisions of paras. 128 to 130 of the Non-Contentious Proceedings Act, which were also in force at the time, were to be applied. Accordingly, if the heirs were unknown or had not wished to make use of their right, the court was to appoint a trustee of the estate and to summon the unknown heirs by means of an edict. The trustee of the estate had been obliged to at least attempt to find the heirs. However, there had been no attempts made whatsoever to seek out the heirs although the details of the relatives Bernard and Dr. Ernst Jakob F. were both recorded in the files. Had the trustee of the estate fulfilled his obligation to seek out the heirs, he would at least have come across Dr. Ernst F., who had still been alive at the time, or his descendents and he would have received the information regarding the death of Bernard F. in 1936. The reversion of the estate had therefore occurred unlawfully as the procedural rules of paras. 128 to 131 of the Non-Contentious Proceedings Act had not been complied with and it was under no circumstances a matter of an heirless estate. In view of the fact that the relatives of Dr. Lothar F. had been Jews, the probate court had not considered it necessary to seek out the heirs particularly as the practice at the time was one of seizing property from Jews and not supplying property to them.

107   Hence, the heirs of Lothar F. had clearly been disregarded and the estate had been unlawfully reverted to the German Reich in 1942.

Schiedsinstanz für Naturalrestitution – Entscheidung Nr. 27/2005

Es zeige sich ein klarer Widerspruch zwischen dem Verrechnungsbuch des Verlassenschaftskurators und dem Schätzgutachten, zumal in Letzterem ausgeführt werde, der Betrieb sei bereits am 3. April 1938 stillgestanden. 101

Hinsichtlich der Angemessenheit des Kaufpreises für die Liegenschaft von 310.000,– Reichsmark wurde im Schriftsatz ausgeführt, dass die Wehrmacht das Sanatorium bereits ab 1. Juli 1938 nahezu vollständig in Betrieb genommen habe. Es sei zwischen dem Verlassenschaftskurator und der Wehrkreisverwaltung vereinbart worden, dass das Deutsche Reich ab Inanspruchnahme des Gebäudes einen Zins zu zahlen habe, dieser aber im Falle des Ankaufes des Gebäudes nicht in Anrechnung gebracht werden solle. Laut Verrechnungsbuch des Verlassenschaftskurators sei auf den Kaufpreis der Betrag von 85.000,– Reichsmark angerechnet worden, so dass der eigentliche Kaufpreis nur noch 225.000,– Reichsmark betragen habe. Dieser Vorschuss von 85.000,– Reichsmark sei nicht als Benützungsentgelt für die Inanspruchnahme des Gebäudes, sondern zur Befriedigung der Ansprüche der Bediensteten verwendet worden. Aus einem Schreiben des Verlassenschaftskurators ans Gericht gehe hervor, dass das Deutsche Reich die Vermittlungsgebühr von 9.000,– Reichsmark nicht bezahlen wollte, so dass auch diese auf den Verkaufserlös in Anrechnung gebracht worden sei. Somit habe der Erlös nur 216.000,– Reichsmark betragen. 102

Der Kaufpreis sei auch der Verlassenschaft nicht zugeflossen, da im Kaufvertrag festgelegt worden sei, der Erlös sei auf ein Sperrkonto mit der Bezeichnung „Entjudungserlös" zu bezahlen, über welches nur mit der Genehmigung der Devisenstelle Wien verfügt werden dürfe. Die Zuführung des Verkaufserlöses an den Nachlass sei nie beabsichtigt gewesen, der scheinbar für die Liegenschaft bezahlte Kaufpreis sei somit wieder an das Deutsche Reich zurückgeflossen, was einen typischen Akt der Arisierung darstelle. 103

Auch sei die angebliche Befriedigung der Hypothekargläubiger ein Vorwand gewesen, um die tatsächliche Verwendung des Verkaufserlöses zu verschleiern. Die Hypothekarforderungen der jüdischen Gläubiger in Höhe von 157.453,07 Reichsmark seien nie befriedigt worden. Zur Löschung der Hypotheken sei ein Vergleich von 115.002,67 Reichsmark geschlossen worden. Dieser Betrag hätte dem Nachlass zufließen müssen, was jedoch nicht der Fall gewesen sei. Ein Teil des Betrages (46.666,– Reichsmark) sei als Reichsfluchtsteuer einbehalten worden, was dem klassischen Bilde der Entziehung von jüdischem Eigentum entspreche. Ein anderer Teil (35.002,– Reichsmark für Benedikt W. und 23.334,– Reichsmark für Louis Si.) sei auf Sperrkonten des Deutschen Reiches gegangen. Weitere 10.000,– Reichsmark seien für Rechtsanwaltskosten einbehalten worden. Somit sei die Vergleichssumme, welche immerhin 41 % der Gesamtschulden der Verlassenschaft ausgemacht habe, niemals dem Nachlass zugeflossen. 104

Aus allem bisher Vorgebrachten gehe hervor, dass der angebliche Notverkauf des Sanatoriums zur Deckung der Nachlassschulden allein der Verschleierung des Tatsächlichen diente, nämlich der Arisierung des Sanatoriums. 105

Hinsichtlich des Heimfalls des verbliebenen reinen Nachlasses wurde auf § 760 ABGB verwiesen, wonach die Verlassenschaft als erbloses Gut dem Staat anheim falle, wenn kein zur Erbfolge Berechtigter vorhanden sei oder wenn niemand die Erbschaft erwerbe. Bei der Überlassung der Erbschaft seien die Bestimmungen §§ 128 bis 130 AußStrG, welche auch damals in Geltung standen, anzuwenden. Demzufolge habe das Gericht, falls die ErbInnen unbekannt seien oder diese von ihrem Recht keinen Gebrauch machen wollten, einen Verlassenschaftskurator zu bestellen und die unbekannten ErbInnen durch Edikt zu laden. Der Verlassenschaftskurator sei verpflichtet, die Ausforschung der ErbInnen zumindest zu versuchen. Es habe jedoch überhaupt keine Ausforschung vorhandener ErbIn- 106

108 With regard to the argument of the State Financial Procurator's Office that the heirs would have been able to sue for their claims to the reverted estate, the following was explained:

109 It defies all logic to assume that people who had been able to escape death by a hair's breadth by emigrating and who had had to rebuild their entire lives would have sued for the assertion of their right to inherit. Furthermore, the heirs had not known of the probate proceedings and had probably also not known of the contents of the last will and testament.

110 It was to be noted with regard to the restitution proceedings that the circle of claimants had been very limited in the earlier restitution acts. Only spouses and direct ancestors and descendants of the aggrieved person had been eligible to claim and further statutory heirs had only been eligible if they had lived with the aggrieved person. A claim for restitution by the current applicants would have been unsuccessful due to their lacking eligibility to file an application.

111 Proceedings for the recovery of the reverted property would also have been in vain, as it was generally known that the Republic of Austria took the legal position that it was not the legal successor to the German Reich.

112 Concerning the settlement reached with the Collection Agency A, it was particularly explained that:

113 Pursuant to Sec. 32 of the GSF Law, the Arbitration Panel did not decide on applications which were already previously decided by Austrian courts or administrative bodies or settled by agreement. Neither the applicant nor a relative may have otherwise received compensation or other consideration for the properties at issue. It followed from this that the applicant or other relative of the deceased must have been beneficiary of a settlement. The settlement with the Collection Agency addressed here by the State Financial Procurator's Office, however, did not affect the applicants in the least, particularly as the settlement had not been reached with their participation. The parties to the settlement had been the Republic of Austria and the Collection Agency A.

114 Of the settlement amount, only 700,000 Schilling had been used to settle possible claims to the property in question by the Collection Agency, which had been far from the true value of the property. Even the State Financial Procurator's Office had explained that according to master builder DI Weidisch, the value of the property had been estimated at 6.2 million Schilling in 1963.

115 As the primary subject matter of the provisions of the Collection Agencies Settlement Act had been the question of property which had remained heirless, it was not logical that the restitution claim of the collection agencies had been settled. The legislator would have been obliged to seek out the actual, still living heirs. Had the legislator/the Republic undertaken this endeavor, then it would have been obvious that the claims of the collection agencies to restitution of the property would under no circumstances have been subsumable under the Collection Agencies Settlement Act, particularly as in the case of the estate of Lothar F., it did not involve heirless property.

116 On the basis of these statements concerning the facts of the case, the following was explained regarding the individual prerequisites according to Sec. 28 of the GSF Law:

117 The requisitioning of the sanatorium by the National Socialists while Dr. Lothar F. was still alive and the occupation of the building in its entirety by the German Armed Forces after F.'s suicide constituted a property seizure in the meaning of Sec. 28 of the GSF Law.

nen stattgefunden, obwohl die Verwandten Bernard und Dr. Ernst Jakob F. aktenkundig gewesen seien. Wäre der Verlassenschaftskurator seiner Pflicht zur Erbenausforschung nachgekommen, so wäre er zumindest auf den damals noch lebenden Dr. Ernst F. bzw. dessen Nachkommen gestoßen und hätte die Information vom Ableben Bernard F.s im Jahre 1936 erhalten. Der Heimfall des Nachlasses sei daher zu Unrecht erfolgt, da die Verfahrensvorschriften §§ 128 bis 131 AußStrG nicht eingehalten worden seien und es sich keineswegs um einen erbenlosen Nachlass gehandelt habe. Angesichts der Tatsachte, dass es sich bei den Verwandten Lothar F.s um Juden gehandelt habe, habe das Verlassenschaftsgericht die Ausforschung für nicht notwendig erachtet, zumal die damalige Praxis jene des Vermögensentzuges von Juden und nicht Vermögenszuführung an sie war.

Somit seien die ErbInnen von Lothar F. klar übergangen und der Nachlass 1942 dem Deutschen Reich rechtswidrig als heimfällig übergeben worden. 107

Zum Argument der Finanzprokuratur, die ErbInnen hätten ihre Ansprüche auf den heimgefallenen Nachlass einklagen können, wurde ausgeführt: 108

Es entbehre jeder Logik anzunehmen, dass Menschen, die dem Tod durch Flucht ins Ausland um ein Haar entkommen konnten und ihre gesamte Existenz neu aufbauen mussten, eine Erbrechtsklage zur Geltendmachung ihres Erbrechts anstrengten. Darüber hinaus seien die ErbInnen in Unkenntnis des durchgeführten Verlassenschaftsverfahrens und wahrscheinlich auch in Unkenntnis des Testamentsinhaltes gewesen. 109

Zur Einleitung eines Rückstellungsverfahrens sei zu sagen, dass der Kreis der AntragstellerInnen in den früheren Rückstellungsgesetzen sehr eng gefasst gewesen sei. Antragsberechtigt seien ausschließlich Ehegatten sowie unmittelbare Vor- und Nachfahren des Geschädigten gewesen, weitere gesetzliche ErbInnen nur dann, wenn sie in Hausgemeinschaft mit dem Geschädigten gelebt hätten. Ein Rückstellungsantrag der nunmehrigen AntragstellerInnen wäre angesichts der fehlenden Antragsberechtigung ins Leere gegangen. 110

Ebenso wäre eine Heimfallsklage [sic!] vergebens gewesen, da allgemein bekannt sei, dass die Republik Österreich die Rechtsposition vertrete, nicht Rechtsnachfolger nach dem Deutschen Reich zu sein. 111

Hinsichtlich des mit der Sammelstelle A geschlossenen Vergleichs wurde insbesondere ausgeführt: 112

Gemäß § 32 EF-G entscheide die Schiedsinstanz nicht über Forderungen, die bereits zuvor von österreichischen Gerichten oder Verwaltungsbehörden entschieden oder einvernehmlich geregelt wurden. Weder der Antragsteller noch ein Verwandter dürfe auf andere Weise eine Entschädigung oder eine sonstige Gegenleistung für die in Frage stehenden Vermögenswerte erhalten haben. Daraus gehe hervor, dass der Antragsteller oder ein sonstiger Verwandter des Verstorbenen Nutznießer eines Vergleiches sein müsse. Der von der Finanzprokuratur hier angesprochene Vergleich mit den Sammelstellen tangiere hingegen die Antragsteller in keinster Weise, zumal der Vergleich ja nicht mit ihnen zustande gekommen sei. Vergleichsparteien seien die Republik Österreich und die Sammelstelle A gewesen. 113

Vom Vergleichsbetrag seien lediglich 700.000,- Schilling auf die Abgeltung allfälliger Ansprüche der Sammelstelle auf die gegenständliche Liegenschaft entfallen, was bei weitem nicht dem wahren Liegenschaftswert entsprochen habe. Selbst die Finanzprokuratur habe ausgeführt, dass gemäß Baumeister DI Weidisch die Liegenschaft 1963 auf 6,200.000,- Schilling geschätzt wurde. 114

Arbitration Panel for *In Rem* Restitution – Decision No. 27/2005

118 After the death of F., no proper probate proceedings had taken place and the provisions of paras. 128 to 131 of the Non-Contentious Proceedings Act had not been adhered to. As already explained, the sale of the property had had no relation to the estate's debts and had not been necessary to cover these debts. Additionally, the proceeds from the sale had been too low, as only the value of the building had been taken into account in the valuation report and not the considerably higher capitalized income value of a flourishing company. The proceeds from the sale had, however, not been paid undiminished to the estate but had instead been paid into a frozen account designated "de-jewification proceeds", which could only be accessed with the consent of the German Reich. The proceeds from the sale had also not been used to pay off the creditors or mortgagees but the sum resulting from the settlement reached with them had been used to pay their Reich Flight Tax or had been paid into frozen accounts. From these facts it could be derived that the sale of the property to the German Reich should be considered a property seizure in the meaning of Sec. 28 of the GSF Law.

119 It clearly resulted from Sec. 28 (1) item 2 of the GSF Law that the two cited prerequisites must both be fulfilled as they are directly connected to one another. Either an applicant or relative must have been the beneficiary of a previous decision or settlement by agreement. In this case, this requirement was not fulfilled.

120 The settlement between the Republic of Austria and the collection agencies had taken place without the heirs having first been sought out and informed. The settlement amount had neither been paid to one of the present applicants nor to any other relative of Lothar F.

121 With regard to the opinion of the State Financial Procurator's Office that an adequate purchase price had been paid undiminished to the dormant estate and therefore the previous owner had received an adequate consideration in the meaning of para. 28 (1) item 2 of the GSF Law, it was argued that the estate had been dormant and therefore, due to a lack of a legal transfer of the inheritance, it had had no owners who would have been able to receive the purchase price as an adequate consideration. The assumption of the State Financial Procurator's Office that the dormant estate is also to be seen as a relative of the applicants is erroneous and incomprehensible.

122 The opinion of the State Financial Procurator's Office that the settlement with the collection agencies did not constitute an extreme injustice was countered by the fact that the claim for restitution of the property had not been subsumable under the Non-Contentious Proceedings Act, particularly as it had not involved heirless property. As, however, no endeavors had been made to seek out the heirs, the property had become subject of the settlement, concluded in 1965.

123 As the legal prerequisites were fulfilled, the Arbitration Panel was therefore requested to recommend the restitution of the property in question to the competent Federal Minister in favor of the applicants.

4. Statement by the State Financial Procurator's Office

124 In a letter dated 14 June 2005, the State Financial Procurator's Office supplemented its statement concerning the present application and confirmed its view that the prerequisites stipulated by the GSF Law for a restitution recommendation have not been met, and maintained the entire contents of its statement of October 2003:

125 Initially the State Financial Procurator's Office focused on the status of the assets of Dr. F.'s estate. The question of the necessity of the property sale could not be answered on

Da primärer Regelungsgegenstand des Sammelstellen-Abgeltungsgesetzes die Frage von erblos gebliebenem Vermögen gewesen sei, sei es nicht nachvollziehbar, weshalb der Rückstellungsanspruch der Sammelstellen verglichen worden sei. Der Gesetzgeber wäre dazu verpflichtet gewesen, die tatsächlichen und noch am Leben befindlichen ErbInnen auszuforschen. Hätte der Gesetzgeber/die Republik diese Anstrengungen unternommen, so wäre klar gewesen, dass die Ansprüche der Sammelstellen auf Rückstellung der Liegenschaft keinesfalls unter das Sammelstellen-Abgeltungsgesetz subsumierbar gewesen wären, zumal es sich beim Nachlass Lothar F.s nicht um erbenloses Vermögen handelte. 115

Basierend auf diesen Darlegungen zum Sachverhalt wurde zu den einzelnen Voraussetzungen nach § 28 EF-G ausgeführt: 116

Die Inbesitznahme des Sanatoriums durch die Nationalsozialisten bereits zu Lebzeiten Dr. Lothar F.s und die Vereinnahmung des Gebäudes zur Gänze durch die Deutsche Wehrmacht nach F.s Selbstmord stelle bereits einen Vorgang der Vermögensentziehung iSd § 28 EF-G dar. 117

Es habe nach Ableben F.s kein ordentliches Verlassenschaftsverfahren stattgefunden bzw. seien die Bestimmungen §§ 128 bis 131 AußerStrG nicht eingehalten worden. Wie bereits ausgeführt, habe der Liegenschaftsverkauf in keiner Relation zu den Nachlassschulden gestanden und sei nicht zur Deckung der Schulden notwendig gewesen. Zudem sei der Verkaufserlös zu niedrig gewesen, da nur der Wert des Gebäudes im Schätzgutachten herangezogen wurde und nicht der weitaus höhere Ertragswert eines florierenden Unternehmens. Der Verkaufserlös sei jedoch nicht ungeschmälert dem Nachlass zugeflossen, sondern wurde auf ein Sperrkonto mit der Bezeichnung „Entjudungserlös" einbezahlt, auf welches lediglich mit Zustimmung des Deutschen Reiches zugegriffen werden durfte. Der Verkaufserlös sei auch nicht zur Befriedigung der Geld- bzw. Hypothekargläubiger verwendet worden, sondern sei die aus dem Vergleich mit diesen resultierende Summe zur Begleichung von deren Reichsfluchtsteuer verwendet bzw. auf Sperrkonten erlegt worden. Aus all dem lasse sich ableiten, dass der Verkauf der Liegenschaft an das Deutsche Reich als Vermögensentziehung iSd § 28 EF-G zu werten sei. 118

Aus § 28 Abs. 1 Z 2 EF-G gehe klar hervor, dass die darin genannten zwei Voraussetzungen gemeinsam vorliegen müssten, da sie in einem unmittelbaren Zusammenhang stünden. Es müsse entweder ein Antragsteller oder ein Verwandter Nutznießer einer früheren Entscheidung oder einvernehmlichen Regelung gewesen sein. Diese Voraussetzung sei hier nicht gegeben. 119

Der Vergleich zwischen der Republik Österreich und den Sammelstellen sei ohne vorherige Ausforschung und Verständigung der ErbInnen erfolgt. Die Vergleichssumme sei weder an einen der hier auftretenden AntragstellerInnen noch an einen sonstigen Verwandten Lothar F.s gegangen. 120

Hinsichtlich der Ansicht der Finanzprokuratur, der angemessene Kaufpreis sei dem ruhenden Nachlass ungeschmälert zugeflossen und hätte daher der frühere Eigentümer eine angemessene Gegenleistung iSd § 28 Abs 1 Z 2 EF-G erhalten, wurde argumentiert, dass der Nachlass ein ruhender gewesen sei, und daher habe es mangels Einantwortung keinen Eigentümer gegeben, der den Kaufpreis als angemessene Gegenleistung erhalten hätte können. Die Annahme der Finanzprokuratur, dass auch der ruhende Nachlass als Verwandter der AntragstellerInnen anzusehen ist, sei verfehlt und unverständlich. 121

Der Meinung der Finanzprokuratur, der Vergleich mit den Sammelstellen stelle keine extreme Ungerechtigkeit dar, wurde entgegnet, dass der Antrag auf Rückstellung der Liegenschaft an die Sammelstellen nicht unter das Sammelstellen-Abgeltungsgesetz zu sub- 122

the basis of the property valuation itself, but only on the basis of a comparison of the estate's liabilities with the assets. Only if the other assets had sufficed to cover the estate's liabilities would the probate proceedings have been concluded without a sale. According to the final report of the trustee of the estate, the estate had been 54,277.01 Reichsmark in debt as per the inventory. 201,422.92 Reichsmark had been paid to the estate's creditors as a "settlement amount". Furthermore, expenses of 81,566.27 Reichsmark had accumulated during the course of the probate proceedings. The proceeds from the assets had amounted to 337,264.54 Reichsmark of which 310,892.78 had come from the sanatorium including furniture and household items. Thus, it had not been possible to pay off the estate's creditors and to cover the processing and settlement costs with the proceeds from the remaining assets. The question regarding the inclusion of the capitalized income value of the property in the valuation from that time could therefore be laid to rest.

126 Both the circumstances surrounding the establishment of the Sanatorium Dr. F. Operating Company Ltd., the partners of which also appeared as creditors of the estate and the operation of which had supposedly already ceased in July 1938 and whether and in what form the property had actually been used until its sale were unclear.

127 Insofar as the applicants refer to a part of the purchase price of the property as not being paid to the estate but only having been used for the settlement of liabilities, it was to be noted that the claims of the sanatorium employees had also had to be paid from the estate. The submission that the settlement amount in connection with the cancellation of the mortgages should have been paid to the estate is also to be answered by the fact that it concerned a liability of the estate, so that this amount could not have formed part of the estate. The applicants were correct in that the utilization of the settlement amount complied with the classic model of the seizure of Jewish property, however, this seizure did not concern the estate as debtor but those Jewish estate creditors whose claims had been entirely or partially withheld from them or who had not asserted a claim from the outset.

128 Thus it does not result from the submissions by the applicants and the new documents that it would have been possible to wind up the estate without the sale of the property in question.

129 Regarding the reversion of the estate, the State Financial Procurator's Office explained the following: It was to be remembered that not the property but the remaining estate (around 15,500 Reichsmark) had been affected. The relevant judicial practice was referred to. Hence, in its decision of 26 May 1948, 3 Ob 147, the Supreme Court had dismissed the petition for the invalidation of probate proceedings including the devolution of the inheritance in favor of the German Reich on the basis that where new claims to the inheritance arose after the legally binding devolution, these claims were to be asserted by means of an inheritance recovery action in accordance with para. 823 of the (Austrian) General Civil Code (compare Heller/Rauscher, *Die Rechtsprechung der Rückstellungskommission,* Vienna (Manz) 1949, E 184). It was to be added that the statutory period of limitation for this was 40 years. Furthermore, the Supreme Restitution Commission had decided in the case subject of this application that even if the declaration of reversion of the estate had been a property seizure, it would only have concerned the reverted property and not the properties which had earlier been excluded from the estate (Supreme Restitution Commission 5 July 1952, Rkv 143/52 on the claim of John Henry D.).

130 For the sake of completeness, the State Financial Procurator's Office also commented on the settlement with the Collection Agency as follows: The applicants had themselves explained in their letter dated 28 April 2005 that they would not have had any claim to restitution under the restitution acts as they had not shown the necessary kinship to the dece-

sumieren gewesen sei, zumal es sich hierbei nicht um erbenloses Vermögen gehandelt habe. Da jedoch sämtliche Anstrengungen zur Ausforschung der ErbInnen unterblieben seien, sei die Liegenschaft Gegenstand des 1965 geschlossenen Vergleichs geworden.

Da die gesetzlichen Voraussetzungen erfüllt seien, werde die Schiedsinstanz somit gebeten, eine Empfehlung zur Naturalrestitution der gegenständlichen Liegenschaft zugunsten der AntragstellerInnen an den zuständigen Bundesminister abzugeben.

4. Stellungnahme der Finanzprokuratur

Die Finanzprokuratur ergänzte mit Schreiben vom 14. Juni 2005 ihre Stellungnahme zum vorliegenden Antrag und bekräftigte ihre Ansicht, dass die Voraussetzungen des EF-G für eine Rückstellungsempfehlung nicht vorliegen und hielt ihre Stellungnahme von Oktober 2003 vollinhaltlich aufrecht:

Zunächst thematisierte die Finanzprokuratur die Vermögenssituation des Nachlasses nach Dr. F. Die Frage der Notwendigkeit des Liegenschaftsverkaufes könne nicht anhand der Bewertung der Liegenschaft selbst, sondern nur auf Basis einer Gegenüberstellung der Nachlassverbindlichkeiten und der Aktiva beantwortet werden. Nur wenn das sonstige Vermögen zur Abdeckung der Verbindlichkeiten des Nachlasses ausgereicht hätte, wäre die Verlassenschaft auch ohne Verkauf der Liegenschaft zu beenden gewesen. Nach dem Schlussbericht des Verlassenschaftskurators sei der Nachlass laut Inventar mit 54.277,01 Reichsmark überschuldet gewesen. An die Verlassenschaftsgläubiger seien 201.422,92 Reichsmark als „Ausgleichsquote" gezahlt worden. Weiters seien während des Verlassenschaftsverfahrens Auslagen von 81.566,27 Reichsmark entstanden. Die Erlöse aus den Aktiven hätten 337.264,54 Reichsmark betragen, wovon 310.892,78 Reichsmark auf das Sanatorium inklusive Hauseinrichtung entfallen seien. Mit den Erlösen aus dem sonstigen Vermögen wäre somit eine Befriedigung der Verlassenschaftsgläubiger und eine Bedeckung der Abhandlungskosten nicht möglich gewesen. Die Frage nach der Einbeziehung des Ertragswertes der Liegenschaft in die seinerzeitige Schätzung könne daher auf sich beruhen.

Unklar seien sowohl die Umstände der Gründung der Sanatorium Dr. F. Betriebsgesellschaft m.b.H., deren Gesellschafter auch als Geldgläubiger der Verlassenschaft aufscheinen und deren Betrieb vermutlich bereits Juli 1938 eingestellt worden sei, als auch, ob und in welcher Form die Liegenschaft bis zu ihrem Verkauf tatsächlich genutzt worden sei.

Insoweit die AntragstellerInnen darauf hinwiesen, dass ein Teil des Kaufpreises der Liegenschaft nicht der Verlassenschaft zugeflossen, sondern zur Tilgung von Verbindlichkeiten verwendet worden sei, sei darauf hinzuweisen, dass unter anderem auch die Ansprüche der Bediensteten des Sanatoriums von der Verlassenschaft zu bedienen gewesen seien. Auch dem Vorbringen, der Vergleichsbetrag im Zusammenhang mit der Löschung der Hypotheken hätte dem Nachlass zufließen müssen, sei zu erwidern, dass es sich dabei um eine Verbindlichkeit des Nachlasses handle, so dass ein Geldfluss in den Nachlass nicht stattfinden habe können. Es sei den AntragstellerInnen zwar darin beizupflichten, dass die Verwendung des Vergleichsbetrages dem klassischen Bilde der Entziehung jüdischen Vermögens entspreche, doch treffe diese Entziehung nicht den Nachlass als Schuldner, sondern jene jüdischen Nachlassgläubiger, denen ihre Forderungen ganz oder teilweise vorenthalten worden seien oder die von vornherein keine Forderung geltend gemacht hätten.

Aus dem Vorbringen der AntragstellerInnen und den neuen Unterlagen ergebe sich sohin nicht, dass es möglich gewesen wäre, den Nachlass ohne Veräußerung der gegenständlichen Liegenschaft abzuwickeln.

dent required by these acts. In its original statement, the Federal Government had already referred to the legal-political background of the restriction on the right to inherit. If the restitution legislation had purposely defined the circle of those entitled to claim more narrowly than the statutory provisions on succession and had created the collection agencies for properties which the descendants of the aggrieved owner had not been able to claim due to this restriction, then this cannot be qualified as a particular exception and therefore not as an "extreme injustice" in the meaning of the GSF Law, which would justify a recommendation for restitution.

131   Regarding the content of the settlement with the collection agencies it was only to be noted that not only the value of the property but also the valuation of each of the chances of winning the case had been relevant for the assessment of the settlement amount. With the backdrop of the sale of the property during the course of the probate proceedings, the settlement was to be evaluated as favorable. Both sides had accepted a significant risk of losing the case and also the amount of 600,000 Schilling for the property had been considered acceptable by the Collection Agency in June 1965.

132   For the sake of completeness, it was to be mentioned that the Collection Agencies Settlement Act, although its primary aim had been to deal with property which had remained heirless, other unresolved specific restitution cases – for example the former Sanatorium F. – had also been included following the initiative of the collection agencies. The Sanatorium F. had not been dealt with as heirless property in the meaning of the Collection Agencies Settlement Act.

133   In summary, the Federal Government considered the prerequisites for a recommendation of restitution of the property in question by the Arbitration Panel not to have been fulfilled.

5. Evidence

134   Evidence was taken by reviewing the following documents which were enclosed with the application for *in rem* restitution:

135   Family trees drawn up by the applicants of the families F. and Ro.; extracts from the probate file of Lothar F. 1 A 251/38 District Court Josefstadt and 14 A 107/40 District Court Innere Stadt Vienna; historical portrayal of the Sanatorium F. in S.-gasse 12-14/B.-gasse 11 from 1886 to 1970 (changes in ownership and restitution proceedings) written by the applicants; marriage certificate of Rudolf G. and Rosa Ro. (marriage on 28 September 1890) issued in Vienna, I., Seitenstettengasse 4, registry office of the Jewish Community Vienna on 3 April 1996; Letter from DI Jaroslav Klenovský from Brno dated 22 April 1996 regarding the inscription on the grave of Rosa G. (year of death 1942 in Theresienstadt); birth certificate of Andreas G. (German translation) issued on 7 March 2002 by the municipal office for Prague 1; birth certificate of Herbert G. (German translation) issued on 7 March 2002 by the municipal office for Prague 1; certified copy from the death register regarding Herbert G. (date of death 19 September 1968) issued by the British General Consulate in Milan on 25 July 2002; certified copy from the death register regarding Amalia G. (date of death 19 December 1999), County of East Sussex, Eastbourne, issued on 20 December 1999; birth certificate of Stefan G. (German translation) issued on 7 March 2002 by the municipal office for Prague 1; birth certificate of Georg G. (German translation) issued on 7 March 2002 by the municipal office for Prague 1; death certificate of George G. (date of death 4 February 1973) New York State Department of Health, Bureau of Vital Records, issued on 5 February 1973; marriage certificate of Georg G. and Gerta

Zum Heimfall des Nachlasses führte die Finanzprokuratur Folgendes aus: Es sei daran zu erinnern, dass nicht die Liegenschaft, sondern der verbliebene Nachlass (rund 15.500,– Reichsmark) davon betroffen gewesen sei. Es sei auf die diesbezügliche Judikatur verwiesen. So habe der OGH in seinem Erkenntnis vom 26. Mai 1948, 3 Ob 147, den Antrag, ein Verlassenschaftsverfahren samt der zugunsten des Großdeutschen Reiches ergangenen Einantwortung für nichtig zu erklären, zurückgewiesen, da bei Hervorkommen neuer Erbansprüche nach rechtskräftiger Einantwortung diese Ansprüche durch Erbschaftsklage nach § 823 ABGB geltend zu machen seien (vgl. *Heller/Rauscher,* Die Rechtsprechung der Rückstellungskommission, Wien (Manz) 1949, E 184). Es sei hinzuzufügen, dass die Verjährung hiefür 40 Jahre betrage. Weiters habe die Oberste Rückstellungskommission im vorliegenden Fall ausgesprochen, dass selbst dann, wenn die Kadukerklärung des Nachlasses eine Vermögensentziehung wäre, diese nur das heimgefallene Vermögen und nicht die schon früher aus dem Nachlass ausgeschiedenen Liegenschaften betroffen hätte (ORK 5. Juli 1952, Aktenkürzel zu Verfahren vor der Obersten Rückstellungskommission (Rkv) 143/52, zum Antrag John Henry D.). 129

Der Vollständigkeit halber nahm die Finanzprokuratur auch hinsichtlich des Vergleiches mit der Sammelstelle wie folgt Stellung: Die AntragstellerInnen hätten in ihrem Schriftsatz vom 28. April 2005 selbst ausgeführt, dass sie nach den Rückstellungsgesetzen keinen Rückstellungsanspruch gehabt hätten, da sie zum Erblasser nicht das dort geforderte nahe Verwandtschaftsverhältnis aufgewiesen hätten. Die Bundesregierung habe bereits in ihrer ursprünglichen Stellungnahme auf den rechtspolitischen Hintergrund dieser Einschränkung des Erbrechts hingewiesen. Wenn die Rückstellungsgesetzgebung den Kreis der Anspruchsberechtigten bewusst enger als das gesetzliche Erbrecht gefasst habe und für das Vermögen, das aufgrund dieser Einschränkung nicht von Nachkommen des geschädigten Eigentümers in Anspruch habe genommen werden können, die Sammelstellen geschaffen habe, so könne das nicht als besonderer Ausnahmefall und daher auch nicht als „extreme Ungerechtigkeit" iSd EF-G qualifiziert werden, die eine Empfehlung auf Restitution rechtfertige. 130

Inhaltlich sei zum Vergleich mit der Sammelstelle lediglich darauf hinzuweisen, dass für die Bemessung des Vergleichsbetrages nicht nur der Wert der Liegenschaft, sondern auch die jeweilige Bewertung der eigenen Prozesschancen relevant gewesen seien. Vor dem Hintergrund des Liegenschaftsverkaufes im Zuge des Verlassenschaftsverfahrens sei der Vergleich als günstig zu bewerten. Beide Seiten hätten ein nicht unerhebliches Prozessrisiko angenommen und seitens der Sammelstelle sei im Juni 1965 auch der Betrag von 600.000,– Schilling für die Liegenschaft als akzeptabel erachtet worden. 131

Der Vollständigkeit halber sei zu erwähnen, dass das Sammelstellen-Abgeltungsgesetz zwar in erster Linie die Regelung des erblos gebliebenen Vermögens zum Ziel gehabt habe, dass aber über Betreiben der Sammelstelle auch andere offene konkrete Rückstellungsfälle – wie die des ehemaligen Sanatoriums F. – einbezogen worden seien. Das Sanatorium F. sei nicht als erbloses Vermögen iSd Sammelstellen-Abgeltungsgesetzes behandelt worden. 132

Zusammenfassend erachte die Bundesregierung daher die Voraussetzungen für eine Empfehlung der Schiedsinstanz auf Rückgabe der gegenständlichen Liegenschaft als nicht gegeben. 133

5. Beweise

Beweis wurde erhoben durch Einsichtnahme in folgende, den Anträgen auf Naturalrestitution beigelegte Dokumente: 134

W. (marriage on 26 February 1933) issued by the Jewish Community Vienna on 5 February 2002; birth certificate of Marion Elisabeth G. issued by the Jewish Community Vienna on 5 February 2002; marriage certificate of Jacques R. and Marion Elisabeth G. of 8 September 1957, State of New York, City of Larchmont, Rabbi Leonard Sc.; extract from the marriage register regarding Bernhard F. and Cäcilie Kl. (marriage on 6 March 1892) issued by the Jewish Community Vienna on 22 January 2002; death certificate of Bernhard F. issued by the Jewish Community Vienna on 19 February 2002; birth certificate of Cäcilie Kl. issued by the Jewish Community Vienna on 18 March 2003; letter from Ernst F. dated 29 January1942 from Angers, France, to Eva Pe. (certified copy); birth certificate of Paul F. issued by the Jewish Community Vienna on 3 December 2001; death certificate of Paul F. (date of death 8 February 1967) New York State Department of Health, issued on 17 August 2001; marriage certificate of Paul F. and Margarethe Elisabeth Wei. issued by the evangelical rectory A.B. Vienna-Innere Stadt on 3 January 2002; death certificate of Margarethe F. (date of death 30 November 1990) City of New York, Department of Health, Bureau of Vital Records, issued on 15 August 2001; excerpt from the probate file of Margarethe F., State of New York Surrogate's Court, County of New York, file no. 2335/1991 containing a written affidavit by Lena La. regarding the kinship of Margarethe F. dated 23 July 1991, the will of Margarethe F. of 19 September 1988, application for the issue of a probate to Alfred S. of 4 June 1991; birth certificate of Marie F. issued by the Jewish Community Vienna on 3 December 2001; death certificate of Marie Re. (date of death 24 April 1965) issued by the registry office Vienna-Alsergrund now Vienna-Innere Stadt on 9 November 2001; certificate of inheritance of the estate of Marie Re. to Anton Re. of 9 March 1966 from probate file 9 A 371/65 District Court Innere Stadt Vienna; excerpt from the marriage register regarding Anton Re. and Maria F. (marriage on 5 June 1920) issued by the rectory St. Karl Borromäus on 12 November 2001; death certificate of Anton Re. (date of death 16 March 1968) issued by the Jewish Community Vienna on 8 November 2001; certificate of inheritance of the estate of Anton Re. to Elizabeth An. and Robert Re. of 1 August 1968 from the probate file of Anton Re. 9 A 281/68 District Court Innere Stadt Vienna; excerpt from the baptismal register regarding Robert Re. issued by the rectory St. Karl Borromäus on 12 November 2001; birth and baptism certificate of Robert Bernhard Ferdinand Hermann Anton Re. issued by the rectory St. Karl Borromäus on 11 July 1921; excerpt from the baptismal register regarding Elisabeth Re. issued by the rectory St. Karl Borromäus am 12 November 2001; death certificate of Elizabeth An. (date of death 13 April 1971) County of Santa Clara, San Jose, California issued on 20 July 2001; birth certificate of Richard Anthony An. City of New York, Department of Health, issued on 17 July 2001; birth certificate of Christopher Clinton An., State of Vermont, Department of Health, issued on 28 August 2001; birth certificate of Jakob Ernst F. (German translation) issued on 13 December 2001 by the municipal office for Prague 1; birth certificate of Georg G. (German translation) issued on 7 March 2002 by the municipal office for Prague 1; excerpt from the probate file of Dr. Ernst Jakob F. 5 A 663/46 District Court Döbling containing a letter from the office of the mayor of the 14th District of the city of Paris of 24 February 1943 and the certificate of inheritance of the estate of Dr. Ernst F. to Eva Pe. and Margarethe S. of 28 June 1949; excerpt from the register of births regarding Eva F. issued by the Jewish Community Vienna on 22 January 2002; marriage certificate of Georg Pe. and Eva F. issued by the Jewish Community Vienna on 3 December 2001; marriage certificate of Charles David A. and Doris Maria Pe. issued on 14 November 1959, State of New York, County of Westchester, Eastchester, Minister Theodore Br. including the associated marriage license of Charles David A. and Doris Maria Pe. issued by New York State Department of Health on 13 November 1959; birth certificate of Margarethe F.

Schiedsinstanz für Naturalrestitution – Entscheidung Nr. 27/2005

Von Antragstellerseite erstellte Stammbäume der Familien F. und Ro.; Auszüge aus 135
dem Verlassenschaftsakt nach Lothar F. 1 A 251/38 BG Josefstadt bzw. 14 A 107/40 BG
Innere Stadt Wien; von Antragstellerseite verfasste historische Darstellung zum Sanatorium F. in der S.-gasse 12–14/B.-gasse 11 von 1886 bis 1970 (Eigentümerwechsel und Rückstellungsverfahren); Heiratsurkunde Rudolf G. und Rosa Ro. (Eheschließung am 28. September 1890) ausgestellt in Wien, I., Seitenstettengasse 4, Matrikelamt der Israelitischen
Kultusgemeinde Wien (IKG) am 3. April 1996; Schreiben von DI Jaroslav Klenovský aus
Brünn vom 22. April 1996 über Grabinschrift Rosa G.s (Sterbejahr 1942 in Theresienstadt); Geburtsurkunde Andreas G. (deutsche Übersetzung) ausgestellt am 7. März 2002
vom Stadtamt für Prag 1; Geburtsurkunde Herbert G. (deutsche Übersetzung) ausgestellt
am 7. März 2002 vom Stadtamt für Prag 1; beglaubigte Abschrift aus dem Sterbebuch zu
Herbert G. (Sterbedatum 19. September 1968) ausgestellt vom Britischen Generalkonsulat in Mailand am 25. Juli 2002; beglaubigte Abschrift aus dem Sterbebuch zu Amalia G.
(Sterbedatum 19. Dezember 1999), County of East Sussex, Eastbourne, ausgestellt am
20. Dezember 1999; Geburtsurkunde Stefan G. (deutsche Übersetzung) ausgestellt am
7. März 2002 vom Stadtamt für Prag 1; Geburtsurkunde Georg G. (deutsche Übersetzung)
ausgestellt am 7. März 2002 vom Stadtamt für Prag 1; Sterbeurkunde George G. (Sterbedatum 4. Februar 1973), New York State Department of Health, Bureau of Vital Records,
ausgestellt am 5. Februar 1973; Heiratsurkunde Georg G. und Gerta W. (Eheschließung
am 26. Februar 1933) ausgestellt von der IKG Wien am 5. Februar 2002; Geburtsurkunde
Marion Elisabeth G. ausgestellt von der IKG Wien am 5. Februar 2002; Trauungszeugnis
Jacques R. und Marion Elisabeth G. vom 8. September 1957, State of New York, City of
Larchmont, Rabbi Leonard Sc.; Auszug aus dem Trauungsbuch zu Bernhard F. und Cäcilie Kl. (Eheschließung am 6. März 1892) ausgestellt von der IKG Wien am 22. Jänner 2002;
Sterbeurkunde Bernhard F. ausgestellt von der IKG Wien am 19. Februar 2002; Geburtsurkunde Cäcilie Kl. ausgestellt von der IKG Wien am 18. März 2003; Schreiben Ernst F.s
vom 29. Jänner 1942 aus Angers, Frankreich, an Eva Pe. (beglaubigte Kopie); Geburtsurkunde Paul F. ausgestellt von der IKG Wien am 3. Dezember 2001; Sterbeurkunde Paul F.
(Sterbedatum 8. Februar 1967) New York State Department of Health, ausgestellt am
17. August 2001; Heiratsurkunde Paul F. und Margarethe Elisabeth Wei. ausgestellt vom
Evangelischen Pfarramt A.B. Wien-Innere Stadt am 3. Jänner 2002; Sterbeurkunde Margarethe F. (Sterbedatum 30. November 1990) City of New York, Department of Health,
Bureau of Vital Records, ausgestellt am 15. August 2001; Auszug aus dem Verlassenschaftsakt von Margarethe F., State of New York Surrogate's Court, County of New York,
Geschäftszahl 2335/1991 beinhaltend eine schriftliche beeidigte Erklärung von Lena La.
zu den Verwandtschaftsverhältnissen Margarethe F.s vom 23. Juli 1991, das Testament
Margarethe F.s vom 19. September 1988, Antrag auf Erteilung eines Probate an Alfred S.
vom 4. Juni 1991; Geburtsurkunde Marie F. ausgestellt von der IKG Wien am 3. Dezember 2001; Sterbeurkunde Marie Re. (Sterbedatum 24. April 1965) ausgestellt vom
Standesamt Wien-Alsergrund jetzt Wien-Innere Stadt am 9. November 2001; Einantwortungsurkunde des Nachlasses nach Marie Re. an Anton Re. vom 9. März 1966 aus Verlassenschaftsakt 9 A 371/65 BG Innere Stadt Wien; Auszug aus dem Trauungsbuch zu Anton
Re. und Maria F. (Eheschließung am 5. Juni 1920) ausgestellt vom Pfarramt St. Karl Borromäus am 12. November 2001; Sterbeurkunde Anton Re. (Sterbedatum 16. März 1968)
ausgestellt von der IKG Wien am 8. November 2001; Einantwortungsurkunde des Nachlasses nach Anton Re. an Elizabeth An. und Robert Re. vom 1. August 1968 aus Verlassenschaftsakt nach Anton Re. 9 A 281/68 BG Innere Stadt Wien; Auszug aus dem Taufbuch zu Robert Re. ausgestellt vom Pfarramt St. Karl Borromäus am 12. November 2001;
Geburts- und Taufschein Robert Bernhard Ferdinand Hermann Anton Re. ausgestellt vom

Arbitration Panel for *In Rem* Restitution – Decision No. 27/2005

(German translation) issued on 13 December 2001 by the municipal office for Prague 1; death certificate of Margaret S. (date of death 30 August 1977) issued on 31 August 1977 by New York State Department of Health; excerpt from the probate file of Margaret S., Surrogate's Court, County of Westchester, matter no. 1977 2754 containing the application for the issue of a probate to Alfred S. of 31 August 1977 and last will and testament of Margaret S. of 17 May 1974; marriage certificate of Paul S. and Margarethe F. issued on 5 February 2002, municipal department 61, Vienna; official certificate concerning the ownership of KG Josefstadt EZ X1 as at 12 March 1938 und 17 January 2001 issued by District Court Josefstadt in 1082 Vienna on 25 February 2003; excerpt from the probate file of Lothar F. 1 A 251/38 District Court Josefstadt and 14 A 107/40 District Court Innere Stadt Vienna containing the valuation report of Sanatorium F. of 25 August 1938 and letter from the National Socialist Party, German Labor Front to Alfred St. dated 5 October 1939; registry disclosures of 25 August 2000 from the Vienna Municipal and Regional Archives, municipal department 8, 1082 Vienna, regarding Lothar and Susanne F.; birth certificate of Lothar F. issued by the Jewish Community Vienna on 3 December 2001; death certificate of Lothar F. issued by the evangelical rectory A.B. Vienna-Innere Stadt on 30 January 2002; marriage certificate of Dr. Lothar F. and Susa F. issued by the evangelical rectory A.B. Vienna-Innere Stadt on 30 January 2002; death certificate of Susanna F. (date of death 3 April 1938) issued by the evangelical rectory A.B. Vienna-Innere Stadt on 30 January 2002; excerpt from the marriage register regarding Dr. Julius F. and Albertine Ro. issued by the Jewish Community Vienna on 22 January 2002; birth certificate of Albertine Ro. issued by the Jewish Community Vienna on 5 February 2002; marriage certificate of Carl Ro. and Caroline Gu. issued by the Jewish Community Vienna on 5 February 2002; birth certificate of Rosa Ro. issued by the Jewish Community Vienna on 5 February 2002; marriage certificate Rudolf G. and Rosa Ro. issued by the Jewish Community Vienna on 5 February 2002; excerpts from the probate file of Elizabeth C. An., Superior Court of the State of California in and for the County of Santa Clara matter no. P20131 containing the decision to issue a probate to the Crocker-Citizens National Bank of 12 May 1971, Sixth and Final Account and Report of Administration by the Crocker-Citizens National Bank and application of the Crocker-Citizens National Bank for the final settlement on the testament (Sixth and Final Account and Report of Administration by Trustee of Testament Trust and Petition for Settlement), decision on the acceptance of the final account of the Crocker National Bank und dissolution of the trust upon the allocation of the remaining balance to be shared equally between Christopher und Richard An. on 7 October 1977; excerpts from the probate file of Anton Re. 9 A 281/68 District Court Innere Stadt Vienna containing a statement by Robert Re. and Elizabeth An. (submission of last will and testament, declaration of inheritance) of 15 May 1968 together with the death certificate of Anton Re. of 18 March 1968, announcement of the last declaration of intention of Anton Re. on 17 May 1968, approval of a deadline extension of 28 June 1968, certificate of inheritance of Anton Re. to Robert Re. and Elizabeth Re., each receiving one half, of 1 August 1968; request from the Office for Geneology Nemec/Gruber to the District Court Innere Stadt Vienna to view the probate files of Marie und Anton Re. on behalf of the *Hoerner Bank* of 27 February 2001 together with "power-of-attorney to investigate" of the *Hoerner Bank*; request from the Office for Geneology Nemec/Gruber to the District Court Innere Stadt Vienna of 31 October 2001 regarding copies of the certificates of inheritance of Marie und Anton Re., together with the power-of-attorney for the Office for Geneology Nemec/Gruber granted by Notary Dr. Scheubrein (himself given power-of-attorney by Robert Re., Richard An., Eva Pe., Alfred A. S., Erna Ne. De V.); excerpts from the probate file of Marie Re. 9 A 371/65 District Court Innere Stadt Vienna: announcement of the last declaration of intention of Marie Re. on 17 May

Pfarramt St. Karl Borromäus am 11. Juli 1921; Auszug aus dem Taufbuch zu Elisabeth Re. ausgestellt vom Pfarramt St. Karl Borromäus am 12. November 2001; Sterbeurkunde Elizabeth An. (Sterbedatum 13. April 1971) County of Santa Clara, San Jose, California ausgestellt am 20. Juli 2001; Geburtsurkunde Richard Anthony An. City of New York, Department of Health, ausgestellt am 17. Juli 2001; Geburtsurkunde Christopher Clinton An., State of Vermont, Department of Health, ausgestellt am 28. August 2001; Geburtsurkunde Jakob Ernst F. (deutsche Übersetzung) ausgestellt am 13. Dezember 2001 vom Stadtamt für Prag 1; Geburtsurkunde Georg G. (deutsche Übersetzung) ausgestellt am 7. März 2002 vom Stadtamt für Prag 1; Auszug aus dem Verlassenschaftsakt nach Dr. Ernst Jakob F. 5 A 663/46 BG Döbling beinhaltend ein Schreiben des Bürgermeisteramtes für den 14. Bezirk der Stadt Paris vom 24. Februar 1943 sowie die Einantwortungsurkunde des Nachlasses nach Dr. Ernst F. an Eva Pe. und Margarethe S. vom 28.6.1949; Auszug aus dem Geburtsbuch zu Eva F. ausgestellt von der IKG Wien am 22. Jänner 2002; Heiratsurkunde Georg Pe. und Eva F. ausgestellt von der IKG Wien am 3. Dezember 2001; Heiratsurkunde Charles David A. und Doris Maria Pe. ausgestellt vom 14. November 1959, State of New York, County of Westchester, Eastchester, Minister Theodore Br. samt dazugehöriger Heiratslizenz Charles David A. und Doris Maria Pe. ausgestellt vom New York State Department of Health am 13. November 1959; Geburtsurkunde Margarethe F. (deutsche Übersetzung) ausgestellt am 13. Dezember 2001 vom Stadtamt für Prag 1; Sterbeurkunde Margaret S. (Sterbedatum 30. August 1977) ausgestellt am 31. August 1977 vom New York State Department of Health; Auszug aus Verlassenschaftsakt nach Margaret S., Surrogate's Court, County of Westchester, Geschäftszahl 1977 2754 beinhaltend Antrag auf Erteilung eines Probate an Alfred S. vom 31. August 1977 und Testament von Margaret S. vom 17. Mai 1974; Heiratsurkunde Paul S. und Margarethe F. ausgestellt am 5. Februar 2002, Magistratsabteilung (MA) 61, Wien; Amtsbestätigung betreffend Eigentum an KG Josefstadt EZ X1 zum 12. März 1938 und 17. Jänner 2001 ausgestellt vom BG Josefstadt in 1082 Wien am 25.2.2003; Auszug aus dem Verlassenschaftsakt nach Lothar F. 1 A 251/38 BG Josefstadt bzw. 14 A 107/40 BG Innere Stadt Wien beinhaltend Schätzgutachten zum Sanatorium F. vom 25. August 1938 und Schreiben der NSDAP, Deutsche Arbeitsfront an Alfred St. vom 5. Oktober 1939; Meldeauskünfte vom 25. August 2000 des Wiener Stadt- und Landesarchivs (WStLA), MA 8, 1082 Wien, zu Lothar und Susanne F.; Geburtsurkunde Lothar F. ausgestellt von der IKG Wien am 3. Dezember 2001; Sterbeurkunde Lothar F. ausgestellt vom Evangelischen Pfarramt A.B. Wien-Innere Stadt am 30. Jänner 2002; Heiratsurkunde Dr. Lothar F. und Susa F. ausgestellt vom Evangelischen Pfarramt A.B. Wien-Innere Stadt am 30. Jänner 2002; Sterbeurkunde Susanna F. (Sterbedatum 3. April 1938) ausgestellt vom Evangelischen Pfarramt A.B. Wien-Innere Stadt am 30. Jänner 2002; Auszug aus dem Trauungsbuch zu Dr. Julius F. und Albertine Ro. ausgestellt von der IKG Wien am 22. Jänner 2002; Geburtsurkunde Albertine Ro. ausgestellt von der IKG Wien am 5. Februar 2002; Heiratsurkunde Carl Ro. und Caroline Gu. ausgestellt von der IKG Wien am 5. Februar 2002; Geburtsurkunde Rosa Ro. ausgestellt von der IKG Wien am 5. Februar 2002; Heiratsurkunde Rudolf G. und Rosa Ro. ausgestellt von der IKG Wien am 5. Februar 2002; Auszüge aus dem Verlassenschaftsakt nach Elizabeth C. An., Superior Court of the State of California in and for the County of Santa Clara Geschäftszahl P20131 beinhaltend den Beschluss zur Erteilung eines Probate an die Crocker-Citizens National Bank vom 12. Mai 1971, Sechste und letzte Rechnungslegung und Verwaltungsbericht der Crocker National Bank sowie Antrag der Crocker National Bank auf endgültige Regelung des testamentarisch eingesetzten Trusts (Sixth and Final Account and Report of Administration by Trustee of Testament Trust and Petition for Settlement), Beschluss über Annahme der Schlussrechnung der Crocker National Bank und Auflösung des

Arbitration Panel for *In Rem* Restitution – Decision No. 27/2005

1968 consisting of a mutual last will and testament of 29 September 1960 and a codicil of the same date, informative letter from attorney-at-law Dr. Ri. to Elisabeth An. and Robert Re. dated 22 February 1966 regarding the content of the last will and testament of Marie Re., notice to the District Court Innere Stadt Vienna of 24 February 1966 regarding the fulfillment of the last will and testament and codicil by Anton Re., cost account of 16 August 1966. Letter from Dr. Scheubrein dated 20 July 2005 regarding the death of Eva Pe. and announcement of her daughters as heirs, each inheriting a half; death certificate of Eva Pe. (date of death 9 December 2003) issued by Registry of Vital Records and Statistics, Massachusetts, on 11 December 2003; last will and testament of Eva Pe. of 7 November 1984, declaration of assignment of Gerda E. Bl. to her daughter Marion R.-G. of 21 November 2005; property notice no. 27449, Lothar F.

136   Copies of files and secondary sources submitted by the Office for Geneology Nemec/Gruber regarding the Sanatorium S.-gasse: Vienna Municipal and Regional Archives, Commercial Court file Sanatorium Dr. F. Operating Company Ltd. in Liquidation HSG C 25/86; excerpts from the probate file of Lothar F. 1A 251/38 District Court Josefstadt and 14 A 107/40 District Court Innere Stadt Vienna; excerpts from various reports by the Historical Commission.

137   The following documents were produced by the Historical Commission as case documentation:

138   Case documentation of the Historical Commission regarding S.-gasse 14, EZ X1, KG Josefstadt (= Edith Leisch-Prost, Verena Pawlowsky, Harald Wendelin, *Project IN REM-Documentation of all properties owned by the Republic of Austria on 17 January 2001*, Vienna 2002, documentation regarding the property S.-gasse 14, KG Josefstadt, EZ X1); memorandum from the Federal Ministry for Foreign Affairs to the Historical Commission dated 30 January 2001: Compilation of relevant facts regarding the property S.-gasse 14; excerpt from the ÖJZ 1953/evidence gazette no. 87 on para. 14 (2) of the Third Restitution Act (right of the legatee); summary of the particular right to inherit of the legatee according to para. 726 of the (Austrian) General Civil Code; Collection Agencies Settlement Act (Federal Law Gazette No. 150/1966) with government bill and explanatory remarks; excerpts from the probate file of Lothar F. 1 A 251/38 District Court Josefstadt and 14 A 107/40 District Court Innere Stadt Vienna, excerpts from the reopened probate file of Lothar F. 1 A 251/38 District Court Josefstadt and 7 A 693/52 and 14 A 107/40 District Court Innere Stadt Vienna; files of the Property Transaction Office: Marie Re., property notice no. 50210, Anton Re., property notice no. 50211 including the confiscation order from the *Gestapo* ("Secret State Police") 26 September 1941 of the assets of Anton and Marie Re. and their children Elisabeth and Robert and Reich Flight Tax decision, Margarethe F., property notice no. 20728, Dr. Ernst F., property notice no. 1027, estate of Bernard F., property notice no. 20727 und supplementary property notice of 25 July 1938.

139   The following documents were obtained by the Arbitration Panel as supplementary documentation:

140   Files from the Austrian State Archives, department Archives of the Republic, record group 06 finances: Files of the Property Transaction Office: Lg. 7906 (Margarethe F.), Lg. 6444 (Lothar F.); Cecilie F., property notice no. 11588, Margarethe F., property notice no. 21138; files of the State Financial Procurator's Office dept. 6: VI-27470 (Lothar F.), VI-30254 (Ida De.), VI-26483 vol. I and vol. II; collection agencies file 393 und 393a; Federal Ministry for Property Control and Economic Planning, dept. 9, no.124.595 (Hertha F.,

Trusts unter Zuwendung des verbleibenden Guthabens zu gleichen Teilen an Christopher und Richard An. am 7. Oktober 1977; Auszüge aus dem Verlassenschaftsakt nach Anton Re. 9 A 281/68 BG Innere Stadt Wien beinhaltend Schriftsatz von Robert Re. und Elizabeth An. (Testamentsvorlage, Erbserklärung) vom 15. Mai 1968 mitsamt Sterbeurkunde Anton Re. vom 18. März 1968, Kundmachung der letzten Willensenserklärung des Anton Re. am 17. Mai 1968, Fristerstreckungsbewilligung vom 28. Juni 1968, Einantwortungsurkunde nach Anton Re. an Robert Re. und Elizabeth Re. je zur Hälfte vom 1. August 1968; Ersuchen Büro für Genealogie Nemec/Gruber an BG Innere Stadt Wien um Akteneinsicht in Verlassenschaftsakten Marie und Anton Re. im Auftrag der Hoerner Bank vom 27. Februar 2001 mitsamt „Ermittlungsvollmacht" der Hoerner Bank; Bitte des Büros für Genealogie Nemec/Gruber an das BG Innere Stadt Wien vom 31. Oktober 2001 über Kopien der Einantwortungsurkunden nach Marie und Anton Re., mitsamt Vollmacht an das Büro für Genealogie Nemec/Gruber erteilt von Notar Dr. Scheubrein (dieser Bevollmächtigter von Robert Re., Richard An., Eva Pe., Alfred A. S., Erna Ne. De V.). Auszüge aus dem Verlassenschaftsakt nach Marie Re. 9 A 371/65 BG Innere Stadt Wien: Kundmachung der letzten Willenserklärung der Marie Re. am 17. Mai 1968 bestehend aus wechselseitigem Testament von 29. September 1960 sowie einem Kodizill gleichen Datums, Verständigungsschreiben des RA Dr. Rinesch an Elisabeth An. und Robert Re. vom 22. Februar 1966 über den Inhalt des letzten Willen von Marie Re., Meldung an BG Innere Stadt Wien vom 24. Februar 1966 über die Erfüllung des Testaments und Kodizills durch Anton Re., Kostenrechnung vom 16. August 1966. Schreiben Dr. Scheubreins vom 20. Juli 2005 über das Ableben Eva Pe.s und Bekanntgabe ihrer Töchter als Erbinnen je zur Hälfte; Sterbeurkunde Eva Pe. (Sterbedatum 9. Dezember 2003) ausgestellt vom Registry of Vital Recors and Statistics, Massachusetts, am 11. Dezember 2003; Testament Eva Pe.s vom 7. November 1984, Abtretungserklärung von Gerda E. Bl. an ihre Tochter Marion R.-G. vom 21. November 2005; Vermögensanmeldung (VA) Nr. 27449, Lothar F.

Kopien von Akten und Sekundärquellen, eingebracht durch das Büro für Genealogie Nemec/Gruber zum Sanatorium S.-gasse: WStLA, Handelsgerichtakt Sanatorium Dr. F. Betriebsgesellschaft m.b.H. in Liquidation HSG C 25/86; Auszüge aus dem Verlassenschaftsakt nach Lothar F. 1 A 251/38 BG Josefstadt bzw. 14 A 107/40 BG Innere Stadt Wien; Auszüge aus diversen Berichten der Historikerkommission. 136

Folgende Dokumente wurden als Falldokumentation durch die Historikerkommission beigebracht: 137

Falldokumentation der Historikerkommission zur S.-gasse 14, EZ X1, KG Josefstadt (= Edith Leisch-Prost, Verena Pawlowsky, Harald Wendelin, Projekt IN REM-Dokumentation aller am 17. Jänner 2001 im Eigentum der Republik Österreich befindlichen Liegenschaften, Wien 2002, Dokumentation zur Liegenschaft S.-gasse 14, KG Josefstadt, EZ X1); Memo des Bundesministeriums für auswärtige Angelegenheiten an die Historikerkommission vom 30. Jänner 2001: Zusammenfassung relevanter Fakten betreffend Liegenschaft S.-gasse 14; Auszug aus Österreichische Juristenzeitung (ÖJZ) 1953/EvBl. Nr. 87 zu § 14 Abs 2 (Drittes RückstG, Recht des Legatars); Abriss über das außerordentliche Erbrecht des Legatars nach § 726 ABGB; Sammelstellen-Abgeltungsgesetz (BGBl Nr. 150/1966) mit Regierungsvorlage und Erläuternden Bemerkungen; Auszüge aus dem Verlassenschaftsakt Lothar F. 1 A 251/38 BG Josefstadt bzw. 14 A 107/40 BG Innere Stadt Wien, Auszüge aus dem wiederaufgenommenen Verlassenschaftsakt Lothar F. 1 A 251/38 BG Josefstadt bzw. 7 A 693/52 bzw. 14 A 107/40 BG Innere Stadt Wien; Akten der Vermögensverkehrsstelle (VVSt): Marie Re., VA Nr. 50210, Anton Re., VA Nr. 50211 samt Beschlagnahmeverfügung durch Gestapo 26. September 1941 des Vermögens von Anton 138

NY); Austrian State Archives, depot room 3/6, collection agencies' suspension files: minutes of the collection agencies' board of trustees sessions: 22nd session (25 November 1963), 23rd session (25 March 1964), 24th session (9 June 1964), 25th session (23. November 1964), 26th session (13 May 1965), 27th session (9 November 1965), 28th session (6 December 1965), 29th session (25 May 1966), 30th session (3 November 1966), 31st session (11 May 1967), collection agencies' suspension file C1 "Fund A – circulars", collection agencies' suspension file B2 "Financial Directorate from 1 January 1965", collection agencies' suspension file D1/1 "A-Ministry of Finance general from 1 January 1966", collection agencies' suspension file D2 "Financial Directorate until the end of 1964", collection agencies' suspension file D1/1, D1/3 "Ministry of Finance general until the end of 1965", collection agencies' suspension file C1a "circulars to members of the board of trustees from 1 January 1966", collection agencies' suspension file C8 "correspondence Reg. Rat Kr.", collection agencies' suspension file C8a "Reg. Rat Kr." as of 1 January 1963); Federal Ministry of Finance no. 275.679-34/61 (collection agencies: investigation costs); Austrian State Archives, depot room 3/5: property index EZ X1, various copies from the index volume of dept. 16, Federal Ministry of Finance, case related, 2nd row on the left, right hand side, file "Weidisch", fee note, 2nd row on the left, right hand side, file Collection Agency A, 2, drafts regarding the report of the board of trustees 300–; minutes of the Council of Ministers Klaus II, box 244, minutes of the decision 7; Federal Ministry of Finance, no. 60.415-16b/66 (presentation to the Council of Ministers); Federal Ministry of Finance, no. 70.253-17b/66 (box 5427); Federal Ministry of Finance, estate Klein, box 20 (excerpts); index of names of provisional administrators, Property Transaction Office room of the Austrian State Archives, Archives of the Republic 06, duplicate: "M[…] Josef, provisional director of the Sanatorium F[…], Vienna, VIII., B[…]str. 17, […] appointed provisional administrator on 30 April 1938."; Austrian State Archives, depot room 3/5, mobile shelves on the left side, Bene file "Collection Agency A. Sessions of the board of trustees", copy of the insertion to the 22nd session of the board of trustees; Federal Ministry of Finance, Immovable German Property, Vienna, box 1, documents regarding EZ X1/KG Josefstadt; Federal Ministry for Property Control and Economic Planning, no. 109.300-4/46; Archives of the Republic/portfolio of the Lazarett files – Lazarett index, excerpt p. 23 (undated).

141 Files from the Vienna Municipal and Regional Archives: Registration queries regarding Robert Re., Lothar F., Dr. Julius F., John Henry D., Paul F.; notification pursuant to the Ordinance on the Notification of Seized Property no. 1167/8 concerning Dr. Lothar F./S.-gasse 14; Commercial Court file C 25/86 Sanatorium F.; probate file of Bernhard F. A 4 306, District Court Margareten (1 A 233/65).

142 Court records of the District Court Innere Stadt Vienna: excerpts from the probate file of Lothar F. 1 A 251/38 District Court Josefstadt and 7 A 693/52 District Court Innere Stadt Vienna as supplements to the findings of the Historical Commission.

143 Civil status queries of the municipal department 61, City of Vienna: Family Adolf Wei. and Hedwig Emilie Wei., Margarethe, Elsa, Katharina; Familie Bernard F. and Cäcilie, Paul, Maria; Dr. Julius F. and children, Hertha, Lothar, Dr.Lothar F. and parents, Dr. Julius and Albertine F.

144 Copies of files of the municipal department 37, building inspection, City of Vienna: Documents regarding EZ X1/KG Josefstadt (together with a letter dated 10 June 1952).

145 Copies from the historical land register: EZ X2 und EZ X3, KG Josefstadt.

146 Copies from the 1938 Viennese address book "Lehmann": Entries under the name F. and under S.-gasse 14 in Vienna.

und Marie Re. sowie deren Kinder Elisabeth und Robert und Reichsfluchtsteuerbescheid, Margarethe F., VA Nr. 20728, Dr. Ernst F., VA Nr.1027, Verlassenschaft nach Bernard F., VA Nr. 20727 und Ergänzungs-VA vom 25. Juli 1938.

Folgende Dokumente wurden als ergänzende Dokumentation durch die Schiedsinstanz eingeholt: 139

Akten aus dem Österreichischen Staatsarchiv (ÖStA), Abteilung Archiv der Republik (AdR), Bestandsgruppe 06 Finanzen: Akten der VVSt: Lg. 7906 (Margarethe F.), Lg. 6444 (Lothar F.); Cecilie F., VA Nr. 11588, Margarethe F., VA Nr. 21138; Akten der Finanzprokuratur Abt. 6: VI-27470 (Lothar F.), VI-30254 (Ida De.), VI-26483 Bd. I und Bd. II; Sammelstellenstellenakt 393 und 393a; Bundesministerium für Vermögenssicherung und Wirtschaftsplanung (BMVS), Abt. 9, Zl.124.595 (Hertha F., NY); ÖStA, Depot-Raum 3/6, Sammelstellen-Hängeordner: Niederschriften der Sammelsstellen-Kuratoriumssitzungen: 22. Sitzung (25. November 1963), 23. Sitzung (25. März 1964), 24. Sitzung (9. Juni 1964), 25. Sitzung (23. November 1964), 26. Sitzung (13. Mai 1965), 27. Sitzung (9. November 1965), 28. Sitzung (6. Dezember 1965), 29. Sitzung (25. Mai 1966), 30. Sitzung (3. November 1966), 31. Sitzung (11. Mai 1967), Sammelstellen-Hängeordner C1 „Fonds A – Zirkulare", Sammelstellen-Hängeordner B2 „Finanzlandesdirektion ab 1.1.1965", Sammelstellen-Hängeordner D1/1 „A-Finanzministerium allgemein ab 1.1.66", Sammelstellen-Hängeordner D2 „Finanzlandesdirektion bis Ende 1964", Sammelstellen-Hängeordner D1/1, D1/3 „Finanzministerium allgemeines bis Ende 1965", Sammelstellen-Hängeordner C1a „Zirkulare an Kuratoriumsmitglieder ab 1.1.66", Sammelstellen-Hängeordner C8 „Korrespondenz Reg. Rat Kr.", Sammelstellen-Hängeordner C8a „Reg. Rat Kr. ab 1.1. 1963); BMF Zl. 275.679-34/61 (Sammelstellen: Ausforschungskosten), ÖStA, Depot-Raum 3/5: Immobilienkartei EZ X1, Div. Kopien aus Indexband der Abt. 16, BMF, sachlich, 2. Gang links, rechte Seite, Ordner „Weidisch", Honorarnote, 2. Gang links, rechte Seite, Ordner Sammelstelle A, 2, Entwürfe zu Kuratoriumsbericht 300–; Ministerratsprotokolle Klaus II, Kt. 244, Beschlussprotokoll 7; BMF, Zl. 60.415-16b/66 (Vortrag an den Ministerrat); BMF, Zl 70.253-17b/66, (ex. Kt. 5427); BMF, Nachlass Klein, Karton 20 (Auszüge); Namenskartei der kommissarischen Verwalter, VVSt-Raum des ÖStA, AdR 06, Abschrift: „M[…] Josef, Kommiss. Leiter des Sanatorium F.[…], Wien, VIII., B[…]str. 17, [...] bestellt zum komm. Verwalter am 30.4. 1938."; ÖStA, Depot-Raum 3/5, Rollregale linke Seite, Bene Ordner „Sammelstelle A. Kuratorium Sitzungen", Kopie der Einlage zur 22. Kuratoriumssitzung; BMF, Unbewegliches deutsches Eigentum, Wien, Karton 1, Unterlagen zur EZ X1/KG Josefstadt; BMVS, Zl. 109.300-4/46; AdR/Bestand Lazarettakten – Lazarettverzeichnis, Auszug S. 23 (undatiert). 140

Akten aus dem WStLA: Meldeabfragen von Robert Re., Lothar F., Dr. Julius F., John Henry D., Paul F.; Anmeldung gemäß Vermögensentziehungs-Anmeldeverordnung (VEAV) Nr. 1167/8 betreffend Dr. Lothar F./S.-gasse 14; Handelsgerichtsakt C 25/86 Sanatorium F.; Verlassenschaftsakt Bernhard F. A 4 306, BG Margareten (1 A 233/65). 141

Gerichtsakten BG Innere Stadt Wien: Auszüge aus dem Verlassenschaftsakt Lothar F. 1 A 251/38 BG Josefstadt bzw. 7 A 693/52 BG Innere Stadt Wien in Ergänzung zum Befund der Historikerkommission. 142

Personenstandsabfragen der MA 61, Stadt Wien: Familie Adolf Wei. und Hedwig Emilie Wei., Margarethe, Elsa, Katharina; Familie Bernard F. und Cäcilie, Paul, Maria; Dr. Julius F. und Kinder, Hertha, Lothar, Dr. Lothar F. und Eltern, Dr. Julius und Albertine F. 143

Kopien von Akten der MA 37, Baupolizei, Stadt Wien: Unterlagen zur EZ X1/KG Josefstadt (samt Schreiben vom 10. Juni 1952). 144

147 Information from the registry office of the Jewish Community Vienna: Confirmation from the manager of the registry office of the Jewish Community Vienna that the parents of Bernhard and Julius F. were called Daniel and Marie F., née Ka.; Confirmation from the manager of the registry office of the Jewish Community Vienna that Bernhard F. married Cäcilie Kl. and Julius F. married Albertine Ro.

148 Copy of an index card from the holdings of the Federal Ministry of Finance, section I-presidential section: Index card concerning Dr. Lothar and Susanne F. regarding the restitution of S.-gasse 14.

149 Copies of the office directory concerning foreign representation authorities in Austria.

150 Excerpts from the database of the project "Collection of Names of the Austrian Holocaust Victims" by the Documentation Centre of Austrian Resistance Vienna regarding Ida Be.

151 Various letters: Letter from the *Bundesimmobiliengesellschaft* ("Federal Real Estate Corporation") dated 9 January 2004, minutes of a transfer of 15 October 1970, Financial Directorate file GA XV-2/503-1077/70 (transferred from the Federal Real Estate Corporation), letter from the Arbitration Panel to the US Embassy dated 11 April 2005, reply from the US Embassy dated 18 April 2005.

152 Literature

Bruno Simma and Hans-Peter Folz, *Restitution und Entschädigung im Völkerrecht. Die Verpflichtungen der Republik Österreich nach 1945 im Lichte ihrer außenpolitischen Praxis* (= Publications of the Austrian Historical Commission. Online version) Vienna 2002[4]; Othmar Tuider, *Die Wehrkreise XVII und XVIII. 1938–1945*, Vienna 1975; Rudolf Absolon, *Wehrgesetz und Wehrdienst 1935–1945. Das Personalwesen in der Wehrmacht*, Boppard am Rhein 1960; Institut Theresienstädter Initiative und Dokumentationsarchiv des Österreichischen Widerstandes (Ed.), *Theresienstädter Gedenkbuch. Österreichische Jüdinnen und Juden in Theresienstadt 1942–1945*, Prague 2005.

6. Established Facts

153 Dr. Lothar F., born on 3 February 1897 had been the owner of the property S.-gasse 14 and B.-gasse 11, EZ X1, tax district Josefstadt since 1925. Dr. F. was a doctor and operated a sanatorium in the buildings belonging to the property S.-gasse 14 as the sole proprietor.

154 On 11 October 1933 the opening of the judicial composition proceedings concerning the property of Dr. Lothar F. was recorded in the land register and on 9 December of the same year this notice was deleted. On 21 March 1935, the initiation of the auction procedure for the property was recorded in the land register, this notice was, however, deleted on 18 November of the same year.

155 On 4 March 1938, Dr. Fritz Er., Dr. Josef Gü., Dr. Siegmund Sin. and Ernst Sp. signed a contract at the substitute notary, Dr. Friedrich H.'s office for the establishment of a limited company based in Vienna with the name "Sanatorium Dr. F[…] Operating Company Ltd."

---

[4] Supplementation at time of going to press: From 2002 to 2003, this text could be found under http://www.historikerkommission.gv.at/deutsch_home.html and was published in 2004 as: Bruno Simma and Hans-Peter Folz, *Restitution und Entschädigung im Völkerrecht. Die Verpflichtungen der Republik Österreich nach 1945 im Lichte ihrer außenpolitischen Praxis*, Vienna (Oldenbourg) 2004 (= Publications of the Austrian Historical Commission, vol. 6).

Kopien aus dem historischen GB: EZ X2 und EZ X3, KG Josefstadt. 145

Kopien aus dem Adressbuch Wien 1938 „Lehmann": Eintragungen unter dem Namen 146
F. und unter S.-gasse 14 in Wien.

Auskünfte des Matrikenamtes der IKG Wien: Bestätigung der Matrikenführerin der 147
IKG, dass die Eltern von Bernhard und Julius F. Daniel und Marie F., née Ka. hießen; Bestätigung von Matrikenführerin der IKG, dass Bernhard F. Cäcilie Kl. und Julius F. Albertine Ro. geheiratet hat.

Kopie einer Karteikarte aus dem Bestand des Finanzministeriums, Sektion I-Präsidial- 148
sektion: Karteikarte betreffend Dr. Lothar und Susanne F. hinsichtlich Rückstellung S.-gasse 14.

Kopien des Amtskalenders betreffend auswärtige Vertretungsbehörden in Österreich. 149

Auszüge aus der Datenbank zum Projekt „Namentliche Erfassung der österreichischen 150
Opfer des Holocaust" des DÖW Wien zu Ida Be.

Diverse Schreiben: Schreiben der Bundesimmobiliengesellschaft (BIG) vom 9. Jänner 151
2004, Übergabeprotokoll vom 15. Oktober 1970, FLD Akt GA XV-2/503-1077/70 (übergeben durch BIG), Schreiben der Schiedsinstanz an die US Botschaft vom 11. April 2005, Antwortschreiben der US Botschaft vom 18. April 2005.

Literatur zu den Feststellungen 152

Bruno *Simma* und Hans-Peter *Folz*, Restitution und Entschädigung im Völkerrecht. Die Verpflichtungen der Republik Österreich nach 1945 im Lichte ihrer außenpolitischen Praxis (= Bericht der Österreichischen Historikerkommission, Onlineversion) Wien 2002[4]; Othmar *Tuider*, Die Wehrkreise XVII und XVIII. 1938–1945, Wien 1975; Rudolf *Absolon*, Wehrgesetz und Wehrdienst 1935–1945. Das Personalwesen in der Wehrmacht, Boppard am Rhein 1960; *Institut Theresienstädter Initiative und Dokumentationsarchiv des Österreichischen Widerstandes* (Hg.), Theresienstädter Gedenkbuch. Österreichische Jüdinnen und Juden in Theresienstadt 1942–1945, Prag 2005.

6. *Festgestellter Sachverhalt*

Dr. Lothar F., geboren am 3. Februar 1897, war seit 1925 Eigentümer der Liegenschaft 153
S.-gasse 14 und B.-gasse 11, EZ X1, Steuergemeinde Josefstadt. Dr. F. war Arzt und führte in dem zur Liegenschaft S.-gasse 14 gehörigen Gebäude als Einzelunternehmer einen Sanatoriumsbetrieb.

Am 11. Oktober 1933 wurde im Grundbuch die Eröffnung des Ausgleichsverfahrens 154
über das Vermögen des Dr. Lothar F. angemerkt und am 9. Dezember desselben Jahres wieder gelöscht. Am 21. März 1935 wurde die Einleitung des Versteigerungsverfahrens der Liegenschaft angemerkt, diese Anmerkung jedoch am 18. November desselben Jahres wieder gelöscht.

Am 4. März 1938 schlossen Dr. Fritz Er., Dr. Josef Gü., Dr. Siegmund Sin. und Ernst 155
Sp. bei Notarssubstitut Dr. Friedrich H. einen Vertrag zur Errichtung einer Gesellschaft mit

---

[4] Ergänzung zum Zeitpunkt der Drucklegung: Dieser Text war von 2002 bis 2003 unter http://www.historikerkommission.gv.at/deutsch_home.html abrufbar und wurde 2004 veröffentlicht als: Bruno *Simma* und Hans-Peter *Folz*, Restitution und Entschädigung im Völkerrecht. Die Verpflichtungen der Republik Österreich nach 1945 im Lichte ihrer außenpolitischen Praxis, Wien (Oldenbourg) 2004 (= Veröffentlichungen der Österreichischen Historikerkommission, Band 6).

The purpose of the company was to be the renting of the property S.-gasse 14 and the leasehold operation of the sanatorium. From the share capital of 50,000 Schilling, 20,000 Schilling were to be made available when the contract was prepared, i.e. before it had been recorded by the Commercial Court and the rest "should be made available as required upon the request of the manager". The first fiscal year was to begin on the day of the company's entry in the trade register of the Commercial Court Vienna and to end on 31 December 1938 and the following years were to last from 1 January to 31 December.

156 In point 8 of the contract, attorney-at-law Dr. Stefan K. was authorized, if necessary, to amend the contents of the contract pursuant to the binding legal provisions or instructions of the authorities.

157 On 26 April 1938, it was entered into the trade register that this company had been dissolved with the decision of the shareholders' meeting of 8 April 1938 as "the unresolved circumstances which arose" as a consequence of the death of Dr. Lothar F. made "the operation of the sanatorium company by the limited partnership, only registered on 26 March 1938, impossible". The company went into liquidation. The liquidator was Dr. Julius Mo. in Vienna 1., J.-straße 6.

158 It cannot be established whether Dr. Lothar F. concluded a contract with the "Sanatorium Dr. F[…] Operating Company Ltd." with regards to the leasing of the sanatorium.

159 The company was deleted on 7 January 1940.

160 **PROBATE PROCEEDINGS**

161 On 2 or 3 April 1938, Dr. Lothar F. and his wife Susanne F. were forced to wash the pavement in front of the "Sanatorium F[…]" in S.-gasse 14.

162 On 3 April 1938, the childless couple Dr. Lothar F. and Susanne F., born on 28 April 1904 committed suicide in their apartment at Vienna 8, B.-gasse 11, which was connected to the sanatorium. The probate proceedings were conducted at the District Court Josefstadt under no. 1 A 251/38 and 1 A 252/38 and later at the Local Court Vienna under no. 14 A 107/40. In the death record dated 5 April 1938, it was noted regarding the next of kin that the parents Dr. Julius and Albertine F. had already passed away and the sister of Lothar F., Hertha L., was resident in America. Dr. Ernst F., General Manager of the So. Corporation was recorded as brother of the father of the decedent. In both cases it was declared that more specific details were not known.

163 In a police report to the District Court Josefstadt dated 4 April 1938, it was assumed that the reason for the double suicide was as follows: "The suicidal intention – presumably due to the prevailing circumstances, as the deceased are of the Jewish race – is evident from numerous suicide notes."

164 On 8 April 1938, Dr. F.'s last declaration of intent, consisting of his last will and testament of 10 October 1937 and two codicils dated 2 April 1938, was opened by notary Dr. Hermann N. as court commissioner in the presence of Dr. Ernst Kat. and Emil Be. Dr. Ernst Kat., as an attorney, represented the parents of the deceased Susanne F., Emil Be., born on 6 May 1868 and Ida Be., born on 20 March 1880.

165 F.'s last will and testament designated his wife, Susanne F., as his universal successor and his parents-in-law, Ida and Emil Be., as alternate heirs. Should these heirs also not accept the inheritance, F. instructed in his last will and testament that the statutory right of succession come into effect with the express exclusion of his sister Hertha L. and her descendants.

beschränkter Haftung mit dem Namen: „Sanatorium Dr. F[…] Betriebsgesellschaft m.b.H." mit Sitz in Wien. Gegenstand des Unternehmens sollte die Miete der Liegenschaft S.-gasse 14 und der pachtweise Betrieb des Sanatoriums sein. Von dem Stammkapital von 50.000,– Schilling sollten 20.000,– Schilling mit Vertragserrichtung, also noch vor handelsgerichtlicher Protokollierung, der Rest „über Aufforderung der Geschäftsführer nach Bedarf zur Verfügung gestellt werden". Das erste Geschäftsjahr sollte mit dem Tag der Eintragung in das Firmenregister des Handelsgerichtes Wien beginnen und mit 31. Dezember 1938 enden, die folgenden von 1. Jänner bis 31. Dezember dauern.

In Punkt 8 des Vertrages wurde RA Dr. Stefan K. ermächtigt, den Vertragsinhalt gegebenenfalls gemäß den zwingenden Rechtsvorschriften oder Vorgaben von Behörden abzuändern. 156

Im Handelsregister wurde am 26. April 1938 eingetragen, dass sich diese Gesellschaft mit Beschluss der Generalversammlung vom 8. April 1938 aufgelöst hatte, da die infolge des Todes von Dr. Lothar F. „eingetretenen ungeklärten Verhältnisse die Aufnahme des Sanatoriumsbetriebes durch die erst am 26.3.1938 registrierte Gesellschaft m.b.H. unmöglich" machten. Die Gesellschaft trat in Liquidation. Liquidator war Dr. Julius Mo., in Wien 1., J.-straße 6. 157

Nicht festgestellt werden kann, ob Dr. Lothar F. mit der „Sanatorium Dr. F[…] Betriebsgesellschaft m.b.H." einen Vertrag über die Verpachtung des Sanatoriums abgeschlossen hat. 158

Die Gesellschaft wurde am 7. Jänner 1940 gelöscht. 159

VERLASSENSCHAFTSVERFAHREN 160

Am 2. oder 3. April 1938 wurden Dr. Lothar F. und seine Frau Susanne F. gezwungen, den Gehsteig vor dem „Sanatorium F[…]" in der S.-gasse 14 zu waschen. 161

Am 3. April 1938 beging das kinderlose Ehepaar Dr. Lothar F. und Susanne F., geboren am 28. April 1904, in ihrer an das Sanatorium anschließenden Wohnung in Wien 8, B.-gasse 11, Selbstmord. Das Verlassenschaftsverfahren wurde am BG Josefstadt zu 1 A 251/38 bzw. 1 A 252/38, später am Amtsgericht Wien zu 14 A 107/40, geführt. In der Todfallsaufnahme vom 5. April 1938 wurde hinsichtlich der nächsten Verwandten vermerkt, dass die Eltern Dr. Julius und Albertine F. vorverstorben seien und sich die Schwester Lothar F.s Hertha L. in Amerika befände. Als Bruder des erblichen Vaters wurde Dr. Ernst F., Generaldirektor der So. AG, verzeichnet. In beiden Fällen wurde angegeben, dass nähere Daten unbekannt seien. 162

Im Polizeibericht an das BG Josefstadt vom 4. April 1938 wurde als Grund für den Doppelselbstmord Folgendes angenommen: „Aus mehreren Abschiedsschreiben geht die Selbstmordabsicht – vermutlich wegen der herrschenden Verhältnisse, da die Toten jüdischer Rasse sind – hervor." 163

Am 8. April 1938 wurde die letzte Willenserklärung Lothar F.s, bestehend aus dessen Testament vom 10. Oktober 1937 und zwei Kodizillen, datiert mit 2. April 1938, durch Notar Dr. Hermann N. als Gerichtskommissär gegenüber Dr. Ernst Kat. und gegenüber Emil Be. eröffnet. Dr. Ernst Kat. vertrat als Anwalt die Eltern der verstorbenen Susanne F., Emil Be., geboren am 6. Mai 1868, und Ida Be., geboren am 20. März 1880. 164

F.s Testament sah seine Frau Susanne F. als Universalerbin und seine Schwiegereltern Ida und Emil Be. als ErsatzerbInnen vor. Sollten auch diese das Erbe nicht antreten, ordnete F. in seinem letzten Willen das Eintreten des gesetzlichen Erbrechtes unter ausdrücklichem Ausschluss seiner Schwester Hertha L. und deren Nachkommen an. 165

166   In one of the two codicils created on 2 April 1938, Lothar F. designated John Henry D. as executor and bequeathed him weaponry and jewelry. In the second codicil of the same date, Lothar F. left instructions for his and his wife's burials.

167   On 5 April 1938, John Henry D. informed notary Dr. N. he would not accept the appointment as executor conferred to him in the codicil.

168   On 14 April 1938, Dr. Kat. announced the conditional declaration of acceptance of the inheritance of Susanne F. by Emil and Ida Be. and their waiving of the inheritance of Dr. Lothar F. (The estate of Susanne F. consisted of assets amounting to 1,548.67 Reichsmark and furniture amounting to 1,542.25 Reichsmark. The estate of Susanne F. was devolved to her parents with the certificate of inheritance of 21 August 1940.)

169   With the decision of 28 April 1938 by the District Court Josefstadt, the edict was issued for the summoning of unknown heirs of Dr. Lothar F. and notary N. was entrusted with the compilation of inventories in both processing and settlement proceedings of the spouses F. On the same day, the District Court Josefstadt appointed attorney-at-law Dr. Alfred St. as trustee of the estate in the probate proceedings regarding Dr. Lothar F.

170   On 12 May 1938, on the request of the District Court Josefstadt, the official gazette of the *Wiener Zeitung* newspaper published a notice to inform the unknown heirs of Dr. Lothar F. as he had not "left a testamentary disposition". In the edict it was announced that people wanting to make a claim to the estate were to inform the court and provide proof of their right to the inheritance within six months. After the expiry of the deadline, insofar as the claims had been proved, the estate would be handed over; if this had not been the case it would be seized for the benefit of the state.

171   In a letter addressed to the trustee of the estate Dr. St. dated 18 July 1938, John Henry D. requested an explanation of why Dr. St. had explained to him in a previous letter that no testamentary disposition had been made in his [D.'s] favor in the last will and testament of Dr. F. D. explained that he was familiar with the documents, according to which he had indeed been remembered in the form of a testamentary disposition from Dr. Lothar F. as had his daughter Peggy Jane D. by Susanne F.

172   At a later, unknown point in time, Dr. St. handed over the bequeathed objects.

173   **SALE OF THE PROPERTY**

174   Prior to the suicide of the spouses F., the sanatorium had already no longer been run, or at least not been run alone by Dr. Lothar F. The police report of 4 April 1938 established that the keys to the apartment, which had been sealed after the suicide and to the office "were handed over to the current provisional manager of the sanatorium, party comrade M[...]". M. was eventually appointed as "provisional administrator" of the sanatorium on 30 April 1938.

175   On the basis of the *Kundmachung der Verordnung über die Anmeldung des Vermögens von Juden* ("Announcement of the Ordinance on the Registration of Jewish Property") of 26 April 1938, *GBl f d LÖ*. ("Austrian Law Gazette"), the trustee of the estate submitted a property notice for the deceased Dr. Lothar F. On a sheet enclosed with the registration it was noted: "Heirs: none. Reich Treasury purchases for the Army Recruitment Inspectorate. Money to cover debts".

176   During the course of the probate proceedings an expert opinion on the value of the property S.-gasse 14 was obtained. In the expert valuation by Baurat Ing. Richard Herrmann

In einem der beiden am 2. April 1938 verfassten Kodizille bestimmte Lothar F. John 166
Henry D. zum Testamentsvollstrecker und vermachte ihm Waffen und Schmuck. Im zweiten Kodizill desselben Datums traf Lothar F. Regelungen für seine Bestattung und die seiner Frau.

Am 5. April 1938 gab John Henry D. bei Notar Dr. N. bekannt, das ihm durch das Kodizill übertragene Amt eines Testamentsvollstreckers nicht anzunehmen. 167

Am 14. April 1938 gab Dr. Kat. dem BG Josefstadt die bedingte Erbserklärung von 168
Emil und Ida Be. nach Susanne F. sowie deren Ausschlagung der Erbschaft nach Dr. Lothar F. bekannt. (Der Nachlass von Susanne F. bestand aus Wertgegenständen im Wert von 1.548,67 Reichsmark und Wohnungseinrichtung im Wert von 1.542,25 Reichsmark. Mit Einantwortungsurkunde vom 21. August 1940 wurde die Verlassenschaft Susanne F.s Eltern eingeantwortet.)

Mit Beschluss des BG Josefstadt vom 28. April 1938 wurde das Edikt zur Einberufung 169
der unbekannten ErbInnen nach Dr. Lothar F. erlassen und Notar N. mit der Errichtung der Inventare in beiden Abhandlungsverfahren nach dem Ehepaar F. beauftragt. Am selben Tag bestellte das BG Josefstadt RA Dr. Alfred St. zum Verlassenschaftskurator im Verlassenschaftsverfahren nach Dr. Lothar F.

Am 12. Mai 1938 veröffentlichte das Amtsblatt zur Wiener Zeitung im Auftrag des BG 170
Josefstadt eine Einschaltung zur Verständigung der unbekannten ErbInnen nach Dr. Lothar F., da dieser „eine letztwillige Verfügung nicht hinterlassen" habe. Im Edikt wurde verlautbart, dass Personen, die Anspruch auf die Verlassenschaft erheben wollten, dies binnen sechs Monaten dem Gericht mitzuteilen und ihr Erbrecht nachzuweisen hätten. Nach Ablauf der Frist werde die Verlassenschaft, soweit die Ansprüche nachgewiesen sein würden, herausgegeben, soweit dies nicht geschehen sei, zugunsten des Staates eingezogen werden.

Mit Schreiben vom 18. Juli 1938 wandte sich John Henry D. an den Verlassenschaftskurator Dr. St. mit dem Ersuchen um Aufklärung, aus welchem Grund Dr. St. ihm in einem vorangegangenen Schreiben erklärt habe, dass in Dr. F.s Testament keine Verfügung zu seinen Gunsten getroffen worden sei. D. führte aus, dass ihm die Dokumente bekannt seien, wonach er von Dr. Lothar F. und seine Tochter Peggy Jane D. von Susanne F., wenn auch nicht im Testament, doch sehr wohl in Form einer letztwilligen Verfügung bedacht worden seien. 171

Zu einem späteren, unbekannten Zeitpunkt händigte Dr. St. die vermachten Gegenstände aus. 172

LIEGENSCHAFTSVERKAUF 173

Bereits vor dem Selbstmord des Ehepaars F. wurde das Sanatorium nicht mehr bzw. 174
nicht allein von Dr. Lothar F. geführt. Der Polizeibericht vom 4. April 1938 hielt fest, dass die Schlüssel der nach dem Selbstmord versiegelten Wohnung und des Büros dem „dzt. kommissarischen Leiter des Sanatoriums Pg. [Parteigenosse] M[…] eingehändigt" wurden. Dieser wurde schließlich am 30. April 1938 als „kommissarischer Verwalter" des Sanatoriums eingesetzt.

Der Verlassenschaftskurator brachte am 16. Juli 1938 gemäß der „Kundmachung der 175
Verordnung über die Anmeldung des Vermögens von Juden vom 26. April 1938", Gesetzblatt für das Land Österreich (GBl.f.d.L.Ö). 1938/102, eine VA für den verstorbenen Dr. Lothar F. ein. Auf dem dazugehörigen Einlageblatt war vermerkt: „Erben keine. Reichsfiskus kauft für die Wehrersatzinspektion. Geld zur Deckung der Schulden."

Im Zuge des Nachlassverfahrens wurde ein Gutachten über den Wert der Liegenschaft 176
S.-gasse 14 eingeholt. In diesem Schätzgutachten von Baurat Ing. Richard Herrmann vom

of 25 August 1938, on the cut off day of 3 April 1938, the property was valued at 295,000 Reichsmark.

177 Pursuant to the purchase contract of 20 and 27 March 1939, the German Reich, Reich Treasury (Army), represented by the Military District Administration 18 in Vienna, it in turn represented by Karl Wi., acquired from the estate of Dr. Lothar F., represented by the trustee of the estate Dr. Alfred St., the property S.-gasse 14 and B.-gasse 11, EZ X1, KG Josefstadt "inclusive of all rights and appliances as are entitled to the current owner."

178 The agreed purchase price amounted to 310,000 Reichsmark. At the time of the purchase contract, 85,000 Reichsmark had already been deposited and a "separate arrangement had been made" regarding the remaining amount of 225,000 Reichsmark. The purchase price, which had initially been fixed at 300,000 Reichsmark had been raised by 9,000 Reichsmark on the part of the vendor for the payment of the brokerage fee. It cannot be established, why the final purchase price was raised by a further 1,000 Reichsmark to 310,000 Reichsmark.

179 Para. 12 of the purchase contract, which was included in the draft, recorded that: "Dr. Alfred St[…] as trustee of the estate declares that the deceased, Dr. Lothar F[…], was a Jew". This did not, however, appear in the text of the final contract.

180 The contract determined that the cut off day for the settlement of the encumbrances and benefits as well as the transfer of risk to be 1 July 1938, as according to the contract, from this day the army site administration had begun to use the building. The vendor undertook to hand over the property free from registered encumbrances, liens and other debts.

181 According to the final report of the trustee of the estate, the Army Recruitment Inspectorate had, however, already requisitioned the building by 1 May 1938.

182 The purchase contract was approved by the Probate Court (Local Court Josefstadt) on 21 April 1939.

183 On 28 April 1939 the approval from the Property Transaction Office was granted, which ordered, on the basis of para. 15 of the Announcement of 3 December 1938, Austrian Law Gazette No. 633/38,

"the purchase price to be paid into an account in the name of the vendor designated "de-jewification proceeds" pursuant to para. 59 ff. of the *Devisengesetz* ("Foreign Exchange Law") at a Foreign Exchange Bank operating in the Ostmark, which may only be disposed of with the approval of the Foreign Exchange Board, surveillance department."

184 On 9 May 1939, on the basis of the purchase contract of 20/27 March 1939 and the power-of-attorney of 25 March 1939, the ownership title was recorded for the German Reich, Reich Treasury (Army).

185 The entire proceeds of the sale went to the estate.

186 **COLLECTION PROCEEDINGS**

187 During the probate proceedings, collection proceedings were repeatedly conducted against the estate:

188 On 7 April 1938, attorney-at-law Dr. Emil Fa. was appointed by the Enforcement Court in the proceedings under no. 27 E 2512/38 22 as the temporary representative of the estate of Dr. Lothar F. The collection proceedings, initiated while Dr. F. was still alive, concerned a claim of 7,000 Schilling, with Mrs Sári Sz. as the instigating party.

25. August 1938 wurde das „Sanatorium F." zum Stichtag 3. April 1938 mit 295.000,–
Reichsmark bewertet.

Mit Kaufvertrag vom 20. bzw. 27. März 1939 erwarb das Deutsche Reich, Reichsfiskus 176
(Heer), vertreten durch die Wehrkreisverwaltung 18 in Wien, diese vertreten durch Karl Wi.,
von der Verlassenschaft nach Dr. Lothar F., vertreten durch den Verlassenschaftskurator Dr.
Alfred St., die Liegenschaft S.-gasse 14 und B.-gasse 11, EZ X1, KG Josefstadt „samt allen
Rechten und Zubehör, wie sie der derzeitigen Eigentümerin zustehen."

Der vereinbarte Kaufpreis betrug 310.000,– Reichsmark, wobei ein Betrag von 177
85.000,– Reichsmark bereits zum Zeitpunkt des Kaufvertrages erlegt und über den Restbetrag von 225.000,– Reichsmark eine „separate Regelung getroffen" worden war. Die
Kaufpreissumme, die zuvor mit 300.000,– Reichsmark fixiert worden war, hatte sich um
die Übernahme von 9.000,– Reichsmark seitens der Verkäuferin für die Zahlung der Vermittlungsprovision erhöht. Nicht festgestellt werden kann, warum der endgültige Kaufpreis um weitere 1.000,– Reichsmark auf 310.000,– Reichsmark erhöht wurde.

Der noch im Entwurf vorgesehene § 12 des Kaufvertrages, in dem festgehalten war: 178
„Herr Dr. Alfred St[…] als Verlassenschaftskurator gibt an, dass der verstorbene Dr. Lothar F[…] Jude war", scheint im endgültigen Vertragstext nicht mehr auf.

Der Vertrag bestimmte als Stichtag für die Verrechnung von Lasten und Nutzen sowie 179
den Gefahrenübergang den 1. Juli 1938, da ab diesem Tag laut Vertrag die Heeresstandortverwaltung das Gebäude in Benutzung genommen hatte. Die Verkäuferin verpflichtete
sich, die Liegenschaft frei von bücherlichen Lasten und Pfandrechten und sonstigen Schulden zu übergeben.

Laut Endbericht des Verlassenschaftskurators hatte die Wehrersatzinspektion das Ge- 180
bäude S.-gasse 14 jedoch bereits ab 1. Mai 1938 in Anspruch genommen.

Der Kaufvertrag wurde am 21. April 1939 durch das Verlassenschaftsgericht (Amts- 181
gericht Josefstadt) genehmigt.

Am 28. April 1939 erfolgte die Genehmigung durch die Vermögensverkehrsstelle, wobei 182
diese anordnete, aufgrund § 15 der Kundmachung vom 3. Dezember 1938, GBl.f.d.L.Ö Nr.
633/38,

„den Kaufpreis auf ein auf den Namen des Verkäufers lautendes gemäss § 59 ff Devi- 183
sengesetz gesperrtes mit der Bezeichnung ‚Entjudungserlös' versehenes Konto bei einer
in der Ostmark geführten Devisenbank zu bezahlen, über welches nur mit Genehmigung
der Devisenstelle Wien, Überwachungsabteilung, verfügt werden darf."

Am 9. Mai 1939 wurde aufgrund des Kaufvertrages vom 20./27. März 1939 und der 184
Vollmacht vom 27. März 1939 das Eigentumsrecht für das Deutsche Reich, Reichsfiskus
(Heer), einverleibt.

Der gesamte Kaufpreis floss der Verlassenschaft zu. 185

EXEKUTIONSVERFAHREN 186

Während des Verlassenschaftsverfahrens wurde wiederholt gegen den Nachlass Exe- 187
kution geführt:

Vom Exekutionsgericht Wien wurde am 7. April 1938 RA Dr. Emil Fa. im Verfahren 188
unter der Zahl 27 E 2512/38/22 zum einstweiligen Vertreter des Nachlasses nach Dr. Lothar F. bestellt. In diesem noch zu Lebzeiten Dr. F.s eingeleiteten Exekutionsverfahren ging
es um die Forderung von 7.000,– Schilling von Frau Sári Sz. als betreibende Partei.

189   Dr. Fa. requested the District Court Josefstadt for the consent of the processing and settlement authorities to file an application for postponement with the Enforcement Court Vienna. In this request for approval, received by the District Court Josefstadt on 28 April 1938, he informed that auctioning of the seized "apartment furniture etc. etc." of the decedent was to take place on 3 June 1938, in order to satisfy the claim of Mrs Sári Sz. He relied on para. 2 of the law of 25 April 1938, *GBlÖ*. ("Austrian Law Gazette") No. 88, according to which no postponement of auction procedures and no sale of chattels on the open market would take place if the liable person was a Jew. He explained that although the decedent was a Jew, it could be expected that a reversion would take place, as the testamentary heirs had renounced their inheritance rights and according to obtained information, remaining heirs of the decedent had either been paid off or their place of residence was unknown. Thus, according to Dr. Fa. the postponement of the implementation of the collection proceedings could be expected as the property would then possibly "no longer be Jewish". For this reason, the Probate Court was to approve his application for postponement and forward the enclosed application for postponement to the Enforcement Court Vienna.

190   In this application for postponement to the Enforcement Court Vienna, Dr. Fa. gave the same reasons as in his request to the District Court Josefstadt and he additionally explained:

"It concerns exquisite apartment furniture of a cultivated and wealthy man, which with the appropriate auctioning and restructuring of the art market in Vienna will without doubt result in a higher value and therefore will create a greater possibility of paying off the creditors."

Dr. Fa. argued further that the month of June is unfavorable due to the beginning of the holidays and the "reorganization of the companies, who are the only ones likely to attend the auction".

191   On 28 April 1938, the District Court Josefstadt informed the Enforcement Court Vienna that by a decision of the same day, Dr. Albert St. was appointed trustee of the estate and the forwarded application for the postponement of the collection proceedings was approved by the processing and settlement authorities and was endorsed as being in the interest of the estate.

192   The application for postponement was dismissed by the Enforcement Court Vienna on 12 May 1938 for the reason that none of the exhaustive reasons for postponement stated in para. 42 of the *Exekutionsordnung* ("Enforcement Act") were present, and the prerequisites of the law of 25 April 1938, Austrian Law Gazette No. 88 were absent. The objects seized for Sári Sz. were transferred to the Enforcement Court for auction at the end of May 1938. Simultaneously, the Enforcement Court relieved Dr. Fa. of his post as temporary representative of the estate.

193   Furthermore, chattels from the estate were handed over to the parents-in-law of Dr. F. as the heirs of Susanne F. and to John Henry D. as the legatee.

194   In the probate proceedings, a series of creditors (for goods, money and mortgages) registered their claims. On 8 July 1938 under no. 51 E 414/38-1, the Regional Court for Civil Matters Vienna approved the forced creation of a lien through the incorporation into the land register against the property S.-gasse 14 for the benefit of the instigating party, the Workers Medical Insurance Company Vienna for claims of 4,209.80 Reichsmark and 1,018.64 Reichsmark. On 31 July 1938 the Regional Court for Civil Matters Vienna further approved, under no. 51 E 619/38-1, the forced creation of a lien against the property S.-gasse 14 through the incorporation into the land register for the benefit of the instigating party Municipal Department 11 Vienna, for claims amounting to 523.88 Reichsmark.

Dr. Fa. ersuchte das BG Josefstadt um die abhandlungsbehördliche Zustimmung zur 189
Stellung eines Aufschiebungsantrages beim Exekutionsgericht Wien. In diesem Genehmigungsgesuch, das am 28. April 1938 beim BG Josefstadt einlangte, teilte er mit, dass die Versteigerung der gepfändeten „Wohnungseinrichtung und etc. etc." des Erblassers zur Hereinbringung der Forderung von Frau Sz. am 3. Juni 1938 stattfinden solle. Er stütze sich auf § 2 des Gesetzes vom 25. April 1938, GBlÖ Nr. 88, wonach keine Aufschiebung anhängiger Versteigerungsverfahren und keine Durchführung von Fahrnisverkäufen stattfände, wenn der Verpflichtete Jude sei. Er führte aus, dass zwar der Erblasser Jude sei, da jedoch die TestamentserbInnen einen Erbverzicht geleistet hätten und da laut eingeholter Erkundigungen die übrigen ErbInnen des Erblassers entweder ausbezahlt worden bzw. unbekannten Aufenthaltes seien, mit dem Eintritt des Heimfallsrechtes zu rechnen sei. Somit sei laut Dr. Fa. mit der Aufschiebung der Exekutionsdurchführung zu rechnen, da die Verlassenschaft dann möglicherweise „nicht mehr jüdisch" sei. Aus diesem Grunde solle das Verlassenschaftsgericht seinen Aufschiebungsantrag genehmigen und den beigelegten Antrag auf Aufschiebung an das Exekutionsgericht Wien weiterleiten.

Diesen an das Exekutionsgericht Wien gerichteten Aufschiebungsantrag begründete 190
Dr. Fa. in gleicher Weise wie sein Gesuch an das BG Josefstadt und führte zudem aus:
„Es handelt sich um eine erlesene Wohnungseinrichtung eines kultivierten und vermögenden Mannes, welche bei sachgemäßer Versteigerung und neuer Gestaltung des Kunstmarktes in Wien ohne Zweifel einen höheren Wert ergeben und damit eine erhöhte Befriedigungsmöglichkeit für die Gläubiger schaffen wird."

Weiters argumentierte Dr. Fa., dass der Monat Juni wegen des bevorstehenden Ferienbeginns und der „Neugliederung der als Auktionsbesucher allein in Betracht kommenden Firmen ungünstig" sei.

Das Bezirksgericht Josefstadt verständigte am 28. April 1938 das Exekutionsgericht 191
Wien, dass mit Beschluss desselben Tages RA Dr. Alfred St. zum Verlassenschaftskurator bestellt und der weitergeleitete Exekutionsaufschiebungsantrag abhandlungsbehördlich genehmigt und als im Interesse des Nachlasses liegend befürwortet werde.

Der Aufschiebungsantrag wurde durch das Exekutionsgericht Wien am 12. Mai 1938 192
mit der Begründung abgewiesen, dass keine der in § 42 der Exekutionsordnung taxativ angeführten Aufschiebungsgründe vorlägen und auch die Voraussetzungen des Gesetzes vom 25. April 1938, GBlÖ Nr. 88, fehlten. Die für Sári Sz. gepfändeten Gegenstände wurden Ende Mai 1938 an das Exekutionsgericht zur Auktion überstellt. Gleichzeitig enthob das Exekutionsgericht Dr. Fa. seines Amtes als einstweiliger Vertreter des Nachlasses.

Weiters wurden Fahrnisse aus der Verlassenschaft an die Schwiegereltern Dr. F.s als Er- 193
bInnen von Susanne F. und an John Henry D. als Legatar ausgefolgt.

Im Verlassenschaftsverfahren meldeten eine Reihe von Waren-, Geld- und Hypothe- 194
karglaäubigern ihre Forderungen an. Zu 51 E 414/38-1 bewilligte das Landesgericht für Zivilrechtssachen (LGfZRS) Wien am 8. Juli 1938 die zwangsweise Pfandrechtsbegründung durch bücherliche Einverleibung auf der Liegenschaft S.-gasse 14 zugunsten der betreibenden Partei Arbeiter-Krankenversicherungskasse Wien wegen Forderungen von 4.209,80 Reichsmark und 1.018,64 Reichsmark. Weiters bewilligte das LGfZRS Wien zu 51 E 619/38-1 am 31. Juli 1938 die zwangsweise Pfandrechtsbegründung durch bücherliche Einverleibung auf der Liegenschaft S.-gasse 14 zugunsten der betreibenden Partei MA 11 Wien wegen Forderungen von 523,88 Reichsmark.

RA Dr. St. traf Vereinbarungen mit den Gläubigern, wonach den Warengläubigern eine 195
Quote von 30 %, den Geldgläubigern eine Quote von 50 % und den Hypothekargläubigern je nach Rang eine Quote zwischen 50 % und 80 % bezahlt wurde.

Arbitration Panel for *In Rem* Restitution – Decision No. 27/2005

195 Attorney-at-law Dr. St. reached agreements with the creditors, according to which the goods creditors were paid 30 % of the money owing, the money creditors 50 % and the mortgage creditors between 50 % and 80 % according their ranking.

196 During the examination of the final report of the trustee of the estate Dr. St., dated 13 May 1942, by accounts expert Diplomkaufmann Franz Sta., he confirmed the findings of the final report and established that:

197 The sum of the assets estimated in the inventory amounted to 339,281.61 Reichsmark, which contrasted with the sum of liabilities of 393,558.62 Reichsmark. This resulted in an over-indebtedness of 54,277.01 Reichsmark.

198 The sum of the actual proceeds amounted to 331,264.04 Reichsmark, which was opposed to the composition quotas of 201,422.92 Reichsmark. This resulted in a surplus of 129,841.12 Reichsmark.

199 The assets increased by interest on bank accounts and securities as well as settlements of the operation of the sanatorium so that the total proceeds of the estate amounted to 331,623.81 Reichsmark.

200 Expenses of the estate were also to be added to the composition quotas, namely: 10,845.51 Reichsmark for a loan for the operation of the sanatorium, 4,000 Reichsmark in wages to the "provisional administrator", 2,253.68 Reichsmark for the ongoing payment of wages and salaries, 499,81 Reichsmark for social security contributions, 313.33 Reichsmark for the Invalid Fund, 1,912.42 Reichsmark for court and notary costs, 13,975 Reichsmark for property transfer taxes, 8,000 Reichsmark for the court commission fee for Notary N., 9,000 Reichsmark brokerage fee for the sale of the house, 1,980 Reichsmark for experts' opinions, 27,089.55 Reichsmark for redundancy payments to employees, 210.68 Reichsmark for lawyers' fees, 136.02 Reichsmark for various expenses and 1,450.27 Reichsmark burial costs.

201 This resulted in total expenses of 282,989.19 Reichsmark.

202 The resulting total surplus of 48,634.62 Reichsmark was reduced by the nominal amount of 200 Reichsmark for German Reich bonds which fell to the German Reich, so that the final assets of the estate amounted to 48,434.62 Reichsmark.

203 In particular the following results from the explanations of Dkfm. Sta. regarding individual items of the assets of the final report:

204 A series of items concerning valuables, furniture, clothes and linen had been excluded from the estate, either due to their surrender as property of Susanne F. to her parents or by transfer to the legatee Henry D. or due to a pending seizure for the auctioneers. The remaining items were sold on the open market for about 50 % of their estimated value.

205 Regarding the individual items of the liabilities, particularly the following can be derived from Dkfm. Sta.'s explanations:

206 A settlement amounting to 115,002.67 Reichsmark (approx. 73 % of the claim) was concluded with the representative of the Jewish mortgage creditors Ernst Si., Benedikt W. and Louis Si., whose claims were calculated to total 157,453 Reichsmark in the final report. (From this amount, 46,666.67 Reichsmark was used to pay the Reich Flight Tax of the creditors, 58,336 Reichsmark was paid into the frozen accounts of Benedikt W. and Louis Si. at the *Länderbank* and 10,000 Reichsmark was used for legal costs, according to the final report.)

207 The composition quotas of the other mortgage creditors amounted to an average of 66.3 % of the claims.

In Überprüfung des vom Verlassenschaftskurator Dr. St. erstellten Endberichtes vom 13. Mai 1942 durch den Buchsachverständigen Diplomkaufmann Franz Sta. bestätigte dieser die Ergebnisse des Endberichtes und stellte fest: 196

Die Summe der im Inventar geschätzten Aktiven betrug 339.281,61 Reichsmark, denen die Summe der errechneten Passiven von 393.558,62 Reichsmark gegenüberstanden. Daraus ergab sich eine Überschuldung in Höhe von 54.277,01 Reichsmark. 197

Die Summe der tatsächlichen Erlöse betrug 331.264,04 Reichsmark, denen die Summe der Ausgleichsquoten von 201.422,92 Reichsmark gegenüberstand. Daraus erfolgte ein Überschuss von 129.841,12 Reichsmark. 198

Die Aktiven erhöhten sich um Zinsen auf Einlagebücher und Wertpapiere sowie Verrechnungen des Sanatoriumsbetriebes, sodass die Gesamteinnahmen der Verlassenschaft 331.623,81 Reichsmark betrugen. 199

Den Ausgleichquoten waren Spesen nach der Verlassenschaft hinzuzurechnen, nämlich: 10.845,51 Reichsmark für Zuschuss zum Sanatoriumsbetrieb, 4.000,– Reichsmark für Entlohnung des „kommissarischen Verwalters", 2.253,68 Reichsmark für laufende Löhne und Gehälter, 499,81 Reichsmark für Soziale Abgaben, 313,33 Reichsmark für Invalidenfonds, 1.912,42 Reichsmark für Gerichts- und Notargebühren, 13.975,– Reichsmark für Verkehrssteuern, 8.000,– Reichsmark für Gerichtskommissionsgebühr Notar N., 9.000,– Reichsmark Vermittlungsgebühr für Hausverkauf, 1.980,– Reichsmark für Sachverständigengutachten, 27.089,55 Reichsmark Abfertigungen für Angestellte, 210,68 Reichsmark für Rechtsanwaltskosten, 136,02 Reichsmark für verschiedene Spesen und 1.450,27 Reichsmark für Beerdigungskosten. 200

Dies ergab eine Summe der Gesamtausgaben von 282.989,19 Reichsmark. 201

Der sich daraus ergebende Gesamtüberschuss von 48.634,62 Reichsmark wurde durch die an das Deutsche Reich fallende Nominale für Deutsche Reichsanleihen von 200,– Reichsmark verringert, sodass das Endvermögen des Nachlasses 48.434,62 Reichsmark ausmachte. 202

Aus Dkfm. Sta.s Ausführungen zu einzelnen Posten der Aktiva des Endberichtes geht insbesondere Folgendes hervor: 203

Eine Reihe von Gegenständen betreffend Wertgegenstände, Wohnungseinrichtung, Kleidung und Wäsche war aus dem Nachlass ausgeschieden worden. Entweder durch Ausfolgung als Eigentum von Susanne F. an deren Eltern oder durch Übergabe an den Legatar D. oder wegen einer anhängigen Pfändung an die Auktionshalle. Die restlichen Gegenstände wurden um ca. 50 % des Schätzwertes freihändig verkauft. 204

Hinsichtlich der einzelnen Posten der Passiva erschließt sich aus Dkfm. Sta.s Ausführungen des Endberichtes insbesondere Folgendes: 205

Mit dem Vertreter der jüdischen Hypothekargläubiger Ernst Si., Benedikt W. und Louis Si., deren Forderungen im Endbericht mit einer Summe von 157.453,– Reichsmark errechnet wurden, wurde ein Vergleich in Höhe von 115.002,67 Reichsmark (entspricht ca. 73 % der Forderung) geschlossen. (Von dieser Summe entfiel laut Bericht 46.666,67 Reichsmark auf die „Reichsfluchtsteuer" der Gläubiger, 58.336,– Reichsmark auf die Sperrkonten von Benedikt W. und Louis Si. bei der Länderbank und 10.000,– Reichsmark auf Rechtsanwaltskosten.) 206

Die Ausgleichquoten der anderen Hypothekargläubiger betrugen durchschnittlich 66,3 % der Forderung. 207

208   With regard to debts totaling 47,905.77 Reichsmark for money creditors, loan claims of "B. F[…]", "E. F[…]", and "R. Ge[…]" were not registered. Claims from the investments of "Dr. Er[…] Siegfried" and "Dr. Sin[…] R." were also not registered. The total sum of these unregistered claims was 29,765.77 Reichsmark (in each case the entire amount of the debt).

209   Dkfm. Sta. further explained that:

"the debts which were designated as deposits in the books were not able to be determined, as deposits were not available at all and the employees were also unable to give any information on this matter. The bailors stated in supplement 4 are partially unknown to the employees and are partially escaped Jews or former Jewish patients. None of these persons registered a claim."

The sum of the debts designated as "deposits" was, according to the report, 27,822.15 Reichsmark.

210   Regarding the 3,803.11 Reichsmark for claims for outstanding wages, Dkfm. Sta. made a note of the fact that all affected creditors had waived the payment of these claims "of predominately Jewish doctors".

211   After the deduction of costs of 600 Reichsmark for the examination of the accounts by Dkfm. Sta. as well as the costs of the trustee of the estate, designated at 33,000 Reichsmark, an amount of 14,834.62 Reichsmark remained. Dr. St. transferred this cash amount to the Higher Finance Pay Office Vienna, Lower Danube to the Reichsbank – bank account no. 10/111.

212   **USE OF THE SANATORIUM**

213   The Army Recruitment Inspectorate had requisitioned the building S.-gasse 14 – at least partially – from 1 May 1938. From 1 July 1938, the building was occupied almost in its entirety by the Army Recruitment Inspectorate. This date (1 July 1938) was also designated in the purchase contract as the cut off day for the retroactive settlement of encumbrances and profits and for the transfer of the risk.

214   At the point of the suicide of Dr. Lothar F., the sanatorium was still in operation. It was, however, interrupted by the increased usage of the building by the German Armed Forces (Army Recruitment Inspectorate). Employees of the sanatorium were given notice from June 1938. Also, additional costs arose through the takeover of the building by the German Armed Forces, as operating theaters were to be cleared and business premises had to be rented for the storage of the cleared medical equipment. These costs were settled through the sale of parts of the inventory of the sanatorium which were left to the trustee of the estate by the Army Recruitment Inspectorate.

215   It was agreed between St. and the military district administration that in the case that the military district administration did not follow through with the intended purchase of the house the German Reich was to pay rent from the time of the use of the house.

216   The Army Recruitment Inspectorate had the task of recruiting conscripts for the Armed Forces. In addition to personnel, the Army Recruitment Organizations were also responsible for material supplements and replacement of material.

217   From 21 September 1943, the property was used as reserve military hospital XXII.

218   On 1 August 1945, the building was confiscated by the American occupying powers and subsequently used by "Service Building Head-Quarter U.S.F.A." (United States

Betreffend Schulden von insgesamt 47.905,77 Reichsmark für GeldgläubigerInnen 208
wurden Darlehensforderungen von „B. F[...]", „E. F[...]" und „R. Ge[...]" nicht angemeldet. Ebenso wurden Forderung aus Einlagen von „Dr. Er[...] Siegfried" und „Dr.
Sin[...]R." nicht angemeldet. Der Gesamtbetrag dieser nicht angemeldeten Forderungen
war 29.765,77 Reichsmark (jeweils voller Schuldbetrag).

Dkfm. Sta. führte weiters aus: 209

„Die in den Büchern als Depots bezeichneten Schulden waren nicht feststellbar, weil
Depots überhaupt nicht vorhanden waren und auch die Angestellten darüber keine Auskunft geben konnten. Die in Beilage 4 angeführten Hinterleger sind den Angestellten
teils überhaupt unbekannt, teils sind es geflüchtete Juden oder ehemalige jüdische Patienten. Eine Forderung wurde von keinem angemeldet."

Die Summe der als „Depots" bezeichneten Schulden habe laut Bericht RM 27.822,15
betragen.

Hinsichtlich 3.803,11 Reichsmark für rückständige Honoraransprüche vermerkte 210
Dkfm. Sta., dass auf die Bezahlung dieser Forderungen „hauptsächlich jüdischer Ärzte"
sämtliche betroffenen Gläubiger verzichtet hätten.

Nach Abzug der Kosten für die Rechnungsprüfung durch Dkfm. Sta. von 600,– Reichs- 211
mark sowie der Kosten des Verlassenschaftskurators, die mit 33.000,– Reichsmark bestimmt wurden, verblieb eine Summe von 14.834,62 Reichsmark. Diesen Barbetrag überwies Dr. St. am 5. August 1942 an die Oberfinanzkasse Wien, Nieder-Donau auf das
Reichsbank-Girokonto Nr. 10/111.

SANATORIUMSNUTZUNG 212

Die Wehrersatzinspektion hatte das Gebäude S.-gasse 14 bereits ab 1. Mai 1938 – zu- 213
mindest zum Teil – in Anspruch genommen. Ab 1. Juli 1938 war das Gebäude beinahe zur
Gänze von der Wehrersatzinspektion eingenommen. Dieses Datum (1. Juli 1938) wurde
auch im Kaufvertrag als Stichtag für die rückwirkende Verrechnung von Lasten und Nutzen sowie für den Gefahrenübergang bestimmt.

Zum Zeitpunkt des Selbstmordes von Dr. Lothar F. war der Sanatoriumsbetrieb auf- 214
recht. Dieser wurde jedoch durch die zunehmende Nutzung des Gebäudes durch die Deutsche Wehrmacht (Wehrersatzinspektion) gestört. MitarbeiterInnen des Sanatoriums wurden ab Juni 1938 gekündigt. Zusätzlich entstanden durch die Inanspruchnahme des
Gebäudes durch die Wehrmacht Mehraufwendungen, da Operationssäle zu räumen waren
und für die Unterbringung der geräumten medizinischen Einrichtungen ein Geschäftslo-
kal angemietet werden musste. Diese Kosten wurden durch den Abverkauf von Inventar-
teilen des Sanatoriums, die dem Verlassenschaftskurator von der Wehrersatzinspektion
überlassen wurden, beglichen.

Zwischen St. und der Wehrkreisverwaltung wurde für den Fall, dass der vorgesehene 215
Ankauf des Hauses durch Letztere nicht stattfinden würde, angedacht, dass das Deutsche
Reich ab Inanspruchnahme einen Zins zu zahlen habe.

Die Wehrersatzinspektion hatte zur Aufgabe, Wehrpflichtige für die Wehrmacht zu re- 216
krutieren. Den Wehrersatzorganisationen oblagen aber neben den personellen auch die materiellen Ergänzungs- und Ersatzaufgaben.

Ab dem 21. September 1943 stand die Liegenschaft als Reservelazarett XXII in Ver- 217
wendung.

Forces Austria). America internally, the USCOA (United States High Commissioner Office Austria) was responsible for the American establishments at S.-gasse 14. From 1953 onwards, the information and culture departments of the American Embassy were also accommodated in the building. This establishment is still situated in the building today.

219 On 4 January 1958, on the basis of Article 22 of the State Treaty of Vienna 1955 and para. 11 (2) of the First State Treaty Implementation Act of 25 July 1956, Federal Law Gazette 165/1956, the ownership title to the property at S.-gasse 14, EZ X1, KG Josefstadt was incorporated into the land register for the Republic of Austria.

220 Pursuant to the lease agreement of 9 June 1958 the Republic of Austria, represented by the Ministry of Finance, itself represented by the Financial Directorate for Vienna, Lower Austria and Burgenland, department for property control and restitution matters rented the property S.-gasse 14 to the State Department of the USA for use as diplomatic and/or consular representation in Vienna for the monthly rental of 20,000 Schilling. The agreement determined that the lease agreement "shall annul all agreements previously reached by the named partners which in any way concern the property". It was agreed that the lease agreement should be retroactively effective from 1 July 1957 for an indefinite period.

221 If and to what extent rent was paid by the American Embassy from 1 August 1945 to 1 July 1957 could not be established.

222 Due to the order from the Federal Ministry of Finance of 26 February 1970, no. 53,076-16/1970, the Financial Directorate Vienna, Lower Austria and Burgenland, department XV (property control and restitution matters) transferred the property subject of this application to the Ministry for Building Affairs and Technology (Building Administration).

223 On 17 January 2001, the property was entirely owned by the Republic of Austria (Federal Building Administration).

224 Since 10 December 2002 (official certificate), the building has been owned by the Federal Real Estate Corporation Ltd., N.-gasse 29, 1030 Vienna whose only shareholder is the Republic of Austria.

225 REQUEST FOR RESTITUTION OF HERTHA L.

226 On 3 January 1946, Hertha L., the sister of Lothar F. turned to the U.S. Reparations, Deliveries and Restitution Division of the U.S. Allied Commission for Austria in New York and by means of an affidavit, claimed the ownership title to the Sanatorium F. as sole living relative. In her letter she named a U.S. institution as the occupiers of the building. On 30 January 1946, the New York lawyer of Hertha L., Harold Fe., repeated this request and informed the U.S. Reparations, Deliveries and Restitution Division that he would give Mr. John Henry D. in London power-of-attorney to represent Hertha L. in this restitution claim. In May 1947, the claim for restitution, via the Headquarters of the USA in Vienna, duly reached department 9 of the Federal Ministry for Property Control and Economic Planning which was responsible for matters of properties which had been seized through private legal transactions. On 17 June 1947, this department sent "leaflets (A-B)" to Hertha L. The claim for restitution was filed on the same day with the comment that the filing period had lapsed. The file was closed. It cannot be established if this claim to restitution was further pursued.

Am 1. August 1945 wurde das Gebäude von den amerikanischen Besatzungsbehörden 218
beschlagnahmt und in der Folge vom „Service Building Head-Quarter U.S.F.A" (United
States Forces Austria) genutzt. Inneramerikanisch war das USCOA (United States High
Commissioner Office Austria) für die amerikanischen Einrichtungen in der S.-gasse 14 zuständig. Ab 1953 war auch die Informations- und Kulturabteilung der amerikanischen Botschaft im Gebäude untergebracht. Diese Einrichtung hat bis heute in diesem Gebäude ihren
Sitz.

Am 4. Jänner 1958 wurde aufgrund des Art. 22 des Staatsvertrages von Wien 1955 und 219
§ 11 Abs 2 des 1. StVDG vom 25. Juli 1956, BGBl 165/1956, das Eigentumsrecht an der
Liegenschaft in der S.-gasse 14, EZ X1, KG Josefstadt, für die Republik Österreich einverleibt.

Die Liegenschaft S.-gasse 14 wurde mit Mietvertrag vom 9. Juni 1958 von der Repu- 220
blik Österreich, vertreten durch das Finanzministerium, dieses vertreten durch die FLD für
Wien, Niederösterreich und Burgenland, Dienststelle für Vermögenssicherungs- und
Rückstellungsangelegenheiten, an das Außenministerium der USA zur Verwendung als diplomatische und/oder Konsularvertretung in Wien um den monatlichen Mietzins von
20.000,– Schilling vermietet. Im Vertrag war festgehalten, dass der Mietvertrag „alle bisher von den genannten Partnern eingegangenen Vereinbarungen, welche in irgendeiner
Form die Liegenschaften betreffen, außer Kraft setzt". Vereinbart wurde, dass der Mietvertrag rückwirkend vom 1. Juli 1957 auf unbestimmte Zeit wirksam sein sollte.

Ob und in welcher Höhe von der amerikanischen Botschaft von 1. August 1945 bis 221
1. Juli 1957 Mietzins gezahlt wurde, konnte nicht festgestellt werden.

Aufgrund des Erlasses des BMF vom 26. Februar 1970, Zl. 53.076-16/1970, übergab 222
die FLD für Wien, Niederösterreich und Burgenland, Geschäftsabteilung XV (Vermögenssicherungs- und Rückstellungsangelegenheiten), die gegenständliche Liegenschaft
am 15. Oktober 1970 an das Ministerium für Bauten und Technik (Gebäudeverwaltung).

Am 17. Jänner 2001 stand die Liegenschaft zur Gänze im Eigentum der Republik Öster- 223
reich (Bundesgebäudeverwaltung).

Die Liegenschaft ist seit 10. Dezember 2002 (Amtsbestätigung) im Eigentum der Bun- 224
desimmobiliengesellschaft m.b.H., N.-gasse 29, 1030 Wien, deren einziger Gesellschafter die Republik Österreich ist.

RÜCKSTELLUNGSBEGEHREN HERTHA L. 225

Am 3. Jänner 1946 wandte sich Hertha L., die Schwester Lothar F.s, an die U.S. Repa- 226
rations, Deliveries & Restitution Division der U.S. Allied Commission for Austria in New
York und beantragte in Form einer eidesstattlichen Erklärung als einzig lebende Verwandte das Eigentumsrecht am Sanatorium F. Als Nutzer der Liegenschaft nannte sie in ihrem
Schreiben eine U.S.-Institution. Am 30. Jänner 1946 wiederholte der New Yorker Anwalt
Hertha L.s, Harold Fe., diese Anfrage und teilte der U.S. Reparations, Deliveries & Restitution Division mit, dass er Herrn John Henry D. in London bevollmächtigen werde, Hertha L. in diesem Rückstellungsbegehren zu vertreten. Im Mai 1947 gelangte das Rückstellungsbegehren über die Headquarters der USA in Wien ordnungsgemäß an die Abteilung 9
des BMVS, die für Angelegenheiten der durch Privatrechtsgeschäfte entzogenen Vermögenschaften zuständig war. Diese Abteilung versandte am 17. Juni 1947 „Merkblätter (A–
B)" an Hertha L. Der Restitutionsantrag wurde mit dem Vermerk, die Eingabe sei durch
Zeitablauf überholt, am selben Tag eingelegt und der Akt abgeschlossen. Eine weitere Verfolgung dieses Rückstellungsbegehrens konnte nicht festgestellt werden.

Arbitration Panel for *In Rem* Restitution – Decision No. 27/2005

227 **RESTITUTION PROCEEDINGS D.**

228 On 11 November 1946, the Ministry for Property Control and Economic Planning registered the property EZ X1, KG Josefstadt as seized property in accordance with the *Vermögensentziehungs-Anmeldungsverordnung* ("Ordinance on the Registration of Seized Property") of 15 September 1946, Federal Law Gazette No. 166/46.

229 John Henry D. obtained an official certificate from the District Court Innere Stadt on 1 April 1947, which showed that D., as legatee, would be solely entitled to the inheritance in the absence of statutory heirs and that he had not been requested to declare his acceptance of the inheritance during the course of the probate proceedings, whereupon the estate had reverted to the German Reich as heirless property.

230 In 1950, John Henry D. claimed the restitution of the property and the surrender of its earnings at the Restitution Commission at the Regional Court for Civil Matters Vienna pursuant to the Third Restitution Act. He asserted that the purchase contract concluded between the estate of Dr. Lothar F. as vendor and the German Reich (Reich Treasury Army) regarding the property EZ X1, KG Josefstadt had been invalid in accordance with paras. 1 and 2 of the Third Restitution Act, as the decedent had been considered a Jew. He based his eligibility to file a claim on para. 726 of the (Austrian) General Civil Code, according to which he, as legatee, was to be considered as heir after the lapse of all testamentary and statutory heirs.

231 On 23 December 1950, as a result of the decision of the Restitution Commission at the Regional Court for Civil Matters Vienna of 13 December 1950, 59 RK 146/50-3, the initiation of the restitution proceedings was noted in the land register.

232 The claim was rejected with the decision of the Restitution Commission of 12 December 1951 for the reason that the claimant D., despite knowledge of the last will and testament, had not submitted a declaration of the acceptance of the inheritance and therefore the estate had reverted to the Treasury. D. would have had to assert and enforce his claims through an inheritance recovery action in line with para. 823 a [sic!] of the (Austrian) General Civil Code.

233 Simultaneously, D. applied for the initiation of a supplementary processing and settlement of the estate of Dr. Lothar F. at the District Court Innere Stadt Vienna on 19 February 1952 due to newly created assets, namely the restitution claim to the property S.-gasse 14. At the same time, he submitted a conditional declaration of the acceptance of the inheritance. In his application, D. explained that he had only just been informed that neither testamentary appointed heirs nor the statutory heirs had submitted a declaration of the acceptance of the inheritance and therefore, in accordance with para. 726 of the (Austrian) General Civil Code, he was entitled to the inheritance as legatee. The application was granted with the decision of 24 September 1952 under no. 7 A 693/52.

234 D. lodged an appeal against the decision of the Restitution Commission at the Regional Court for Civil Matters Vienna with the Higher Restitution Commission. The Higher Restitution Commission, however, upheld the decision of the first instance and moreover explained that D. had not been informed by the Probate Court in charge of the processing and settlement that no statutory heir had been in contact. D. had also not been requested to submit a declaration of the acceptance of the inheritance. The Higher Restitution Commission concluded from this that the reversion of the estate had been in no way connected to political persecution but that the claims of the legatee, D., had been overlooked in the processing and settlement proceedings.

RÜCKSTELLUNGSVERFAHREN D.

Am 11. November 1946 meldete das BMVS die Liegenschaft EZ X1, KG Josefstadt laut der VEAV vom 15. September 1946, BGBl 166/46, als entzogenes Vermögen an.

John Henry D. erwirkte beim BG Innere Stadt Wien mit 1. April 1947 eine Amtsbestätigung, die auswies, dass D. als Legatar mangels gesetzlicher ErbInnen allein zur Erbschaft berufen wäre und im Zuge des Verlassenschaftsverfahrens nicht zur Erbserklärung aufgefordert worden sei, worauf die Verlassenschaft als erbloses Gut dem Deutschen Reich anheimgefallen sei.

1950 beantragte John Henry D. bei der Rückstellungskommission beim LGfZRS Wien gemäß dem 3. RStG die Rückstellung der Liegenschaft S.-gasse 14 sowie die Ausfolgung der Erträgnisse. Er machte geltend, dass der zwischen der Verlassenschaft nach Dr. Lothar F. als Verkäuferin und dem Deutschen Reich (Reichsfiskus Heer) geschlossene Kaufvertrag über die Liegenschaft EZ X1, KG Josefstadt nichtig im Sinne der §§ 1 und 2 des 3. RStG gewesen sei, da der Erblasser als Jude gegolten habe. Seine Antragslegitimation begründete er mit § 726 ABGB, wonach er als Legatar nach Wegfall sämtlicher testamentarischen und gesetzlichen ErbInnen als Erbe zu betrachten sei.

Am 23. Dezember 1950 wurde zufolge des Beschlusses der Rückstellungskommission beim LGfZRS Wien vom 13. Dezember 1950, 59 RK 146/50-3, die Einleitung des Rückstellungsverfahrens im Grundbuch angemerkt.

Der Antrag wurde mit Erkenntnis von 12. Dezember 1951 von der Rückstellungskommission mit der Begründung abgewiesen, dass der Antragsteller D. trotz Kenntnis des Testamentes keine Erbserklärung abgegeben habe und daher der Nachlass dem Fiskus anheimgefallen sei. D. müsse seine Ansprüche im Wege der Erbschaftsklage nach § 823 a [sic!] ABGB geltend machen und durchsetzen.

Parallel dazu beantragte D. beim BG Innere Stadt Wien am 19. Februar 1952 die Einleitung einer Nachtragsabhandlung nach Dr. Lothar F. aufgrund des neu hervorgekommenen Vermögens, nämlich des Rückstellungsanspruches auf die Liegenschaft S.-gasse 14. Gleichzeitig gab er eine bedingte Erbserklärung ab. In seinem Antrag führte D. aus, dass er erst jetzt darüber informiert worden sei, dass weder testamentarisch berufene noch die gesetzlichen ErbInnen eine Erbserklärung abgegeben hatten und daher er gemäß § 726 ABGB als Legatar zur Erbschaft berufen sei. Dem Antrag wurde mit Beschluss vom 24. September 1952 zu 7 A 693/52 entsprochen.

Gegen das Erkenntnis der Rückstellungskommission beim LGfZRS Wien legte D. Rechtsmittel bei der Rückstellungsoberkommission ein. Diese bestätigte jedoch die Entscheidung der ersten Instanz und führte zudem aus, D. sei vom Abhandlungsgericht nicht darüber verständigt worden, dass sich keine gesetzlichen ErbInnen gemeldet haben. D. sei auch nicht zur Abgabe einer Erbserklärung aufgefordert worden. Daraus schloss die Rückstellungsoberkommission, dass der Heimfall des Nachlasses in keiner Verbindung mit einer politischen Verfolgung gestanden sei, sondern dass die Ansprüche des Legatars D. im Abhandlungsverfahren übersehen worden seien.

Dagegen führte D. Beschwerde bei der Obersten Rückstellungskommission und argumentierte, dass er aufgrund politischer Verfolgung auch im Falle einer Aufforderung zur Erbserklärung nicht in der Lage gewesen wäre, eine Erbserklärung abzugeben. Er sei infolge Entziehung seines Erbrechts befugt, den Rückstellungsanspruch ohne Klage nach § 823 ABGB geltend zu machen.

Arbitration Panel for *In Rem* Restitution – Decision No. 27/2005

235 D. lodged a complaint against this decision with the Supreme Restitution Commission and argued that even in the case that he had been requested to give a declaration of the acceptance of the inheritance, he would not have been in a position to submit such a declaration due to political persecution. As a result of the denial of his right to the inheritance, he was entitled to assert the restitution claim without an action in accordance with para. 823 of the (Austrian) General Civil Code.

236 The Supreme Restitution Commission did not grant the complaint of the claimant D. In its decision of 5 July 1952 under no. Rkv 143/52 it explained: Only the sale of the property by the trustee of the estate could be considered as a seizure of property. However, the claimant lacked the eligibility to file a claim to the property as he did not belong to the circle of heirs named in para. 14 of the Third Restitution Act. He had not been appointed heir by the decedent and it could only be derived from the codicil that the decedent had intended to leave him weaponry and jewelry but not the whole estate. A legatee was only ever eligible to claim for the restitution of bequests which had been seized from him. For this reason it would have been of no advantage to the claimant had he submitted the declaration of acceptance of the inheritance in accordance with para. 726 of the (Austrian) General Civil Code. For this reason, the question of why he had neglected to submit a declaration can be laid to rest. Even if the declaration of reversion regarding the estate was a property seizure, it had no longer concerned the property, which had been previously excluded from the estate. Furthermore, the declaration of reversion had borne no relation to the restitution claim as the claimant had been denied the eligibility to file for a claim pursuant to para. 14 of the Third Restitution Act.

237 Having been informed of the negative decision of the Supreme Restitution Commission, the supplementary processing and settlement of the estate of Dr. Lothar F., upon request of John Henry D., was declared closed with the decision of the District Court Innere Stadt Vienna on 10 October 1952 for lack of supplements to the estate.

238 **RESTITUTION PROCEEDINGS OF THE COLLECTION AGENCY**

239 **Application for Restitution**

240 On 19 October 1960, Collection Agency A submitted an application for the restitution of the property S.-gasse 14 with the Financial Directorate for Vienna, Lower Austria and Burgenland, in accordance with the *Zweite Rückstellungsgesetz* ("Second Restitution Act").

241 Collection Agency A cited the Federal Law of 13 March 1957 on the Creation of Receiving Organizations pursuant to Article 26 para. 2[5] of the State Treaty, Federal Law Gazette No. 73/1957 as amended by the Federal Laws nos. 285/1958, 62/1959 and 306/1959, according to which all properties, legal rights and interests named in Article 26 para. 2 of the State Treaty to which people who were members of the Jewish Religious Community on 31 December 1937 were entitled, were transferred to the Collection Agency A.

242 The Collection Agency asserted that the acquisition of the property EZ X1, KG Josefstadt by the German Reich, Reich Treasury (Army) had represented a seizure in the meaning of the restitution acts, pursuant to para. 1 (1) of the *Dritte Staatsvertragsdurchführungsgesetz* ("Third State Treaty Implementation Act"). Dr. F. had been considered a Jew in accordance with the Nuremberg Laws and the purchase contract concerning the property in question had been approved by the Property Transaction Office on 28 April 1939. It can be further derived from the approval that the purchase price of 310,000 Reichsmark was

---

[5] Footnote no. 5 applies only to the German text.

Die Oberste Rückstellungskommission gab der Beschwerde des Antragstellers D. nicht 236
Folge. In ihrer Entscheidung vom 5. Juli 1952 zu Rkv 143/52 führte sie aus: Als Vermögensentziehung komme nur der Verkauf der Liegenschaft durch den Verlassenschaftskurator in Frage. Dem Antragsteller fehle aber für einen auf die Liegenschaft gerichteten Rückstellungsanspruch die Antragslegitimation, da er nicht in den Erbenkreis des § 14 des 3. RStG falle. Er sei vom Erblasser nicht zum Erben eingesetzt worden und aus dem Kodizill könne nur der Wille des Erblassers ersehen werden, ihm Waffen und Schmuck, nicht aber den ganzen Nachlass zuzuwenden. Ein Legatar sei immer nur legitimiert, die Rückstellung eines ihm entzogenen Vermächtnisses zu begehren. Aus diesem Grunde wäre für den Antragsteller nichts gewonnen, hätte er die Erbserklärung nach § 726 ABGB abgegeben. Darum könne die Frage, warum er sie unterlassen hat, auf sich beruhen. Auch wenn die Heimfallserklärung des Nachlasses eine Vermögensentziehung war, habe sie nicht mehr die vorher aus dem Nachlass ausgeschiedene Liegenschaft betroffen. Darüber hinaus stünde die Heimfallserklärung nicht im Zusammenhang mit dem Rückstellungsanspruch, da dem Antragsteller aus genannten Gründen gemäß § 14 des 3. RStG die Legitimation abzusprechen sei.

Nach Kenntnis der ablehnenden Entscheidung durch die Oberste Rückstellungskommission wurde auf Antrag von John Henry D. die Nachtragsabhandlung nach Dr. Lothar 237
F. mit Beschluss des BG Innere Stadt Wien am 10. Oktober 1952 mangels Nachtragsnachlasses für beendet erklärt.

RÜCKSTELLUNGSVERFAHREN DER SAMMELSTELLE 238
Rückstellungsantrag 239

Am 19. Oktober 1960 brachte die Sammelstelle A einen Antrag auf Rückstellung der 240
Liegenschaft S.-gasse 14 nach dem Zweiten Rückstellungsgesetz (2. RStG) bei der FLD für Wien, Niederösterreich und Burgenland ein.

Die Sammelstelle A berief sich auf das Bundesgesetz vom 13. März 1957 über die 241
Schaffung von Auffangorganisationen gemäß Artikel 26 § 2[5] des Staatsvertrags, BGBl 73/1957 in der Fassung der Bundesgesetze Nummern 285/1958, 62/1959 und 306/1959, wonach der Sammelstelle A alle in Artikel 26 § 2 des Staatsvertrages genannten Vermögenschaften, gesetzlichen Rechte und Interessen übertragen wurden, die Personen zustanden, die am 31. Dezember 1937 der israelitischen Religionsgemeinschaft angehört haben.

Die Sammelstelle machte geltend, dass der Erwerb der Liegenschaft EZ X1, KG Josefstadt, durch das Deutsche Reich, Reichsfiskus (Heer) eine Entziehung im Sinne der 242
Rückstellungsgesetze gemäß § 1 Abs 1 des Dritten Staatsvertragsdurchführungsgesetzes (3. StVDG) darstelle. Dr. F. sei Jude im Sinne der Nürnberger Gesetze gewesen, und der Kaufvertrag über die gegenständliche Liegenschaft sei durch die Vermögensverkehrsstelle am 28. April 1939 genehmigt worden. Aus der Genehmigung gehe weiters hervor, dass der Kaufpreis von 310.000,– Reichsmark gemäß § 59 ff Devisengesetz (Gesetz über die Devisenbewirtschaftung vom 12. Dezember 1938, RGBl I S. 1733) auf ein gesperrtes Konto mit der Bezeichnung „Entjudungserlös" zu bezahlen war, über welches nur mit Genehmigung der Vermögensverkehrsstelle verfügt werden durfte.

Abschließend verwies die Sammelstelle A darauf, dass eine Anmeldung gemäß Artikel 26 § 2 des Staatsvertrages nicht vorlag. 243

---
[5] Die Bezeichnungen „Artikel 26 § 2" und „Artikel 26 Abs 2" betreffend den Staatsvertrag von 1955 werden synonym verwendet.

243 Finally, the Collection Agency A referred to the fact that there was no registration pursuant to Article 26 para. 2 of the State Treaty.

to be paid into a frozen account designated "de-jewification proceeds" which could only be disposed of with the approval of the Property Transaction Office, pursuant to para. 59 ff. of the Foreign Exchange Law (*Gesetz über die Devisenbewirtschaftung* – Foreign Exchange Control Law of 12 December 1938, *RGBl.* ("Reich Law Gazette") I p. 1733).

243 Finally, the Collection Agency A referred to the fact that there was no registration pursuant to Article 26 para. 2 of the State Treaty.

244 The Collection Agency B approved the conduct of the restitution proceedings in accordance with para. 2 (3) of the *Auffangorganisationengesetz* ("Receiving Organizations Act").

245 Statement by the State Financial Procurator's Office of 7 March 1961

246 In its statement of 7 March 1961, the State Financial Procurator's Office contested the restitution claim and cited the provisions of the Third State Treaty Implementation Act (Federal Law of 17 July 1957, with which further provisions for the implementation of part IV of the State Treaty of 15 May 1955, Federal Law Gazette no. 152 were enacted, Federal Law Gazette No. 176/1957). Third State Treaty Implementation Act dealt with acquisitions by the German Reich during the occupation of Austria for the purposes of the Armed Forces or the defense of the Reich on the basis of legal transactions or other legal acts.

247 The State Financial Procurator's Office particularly submitted that the property of Dr. Lothar F. had already been likely to be subject to insolvency proceedings before the National Socialist assumption of power. According to the State Financial Procurator's Office, the property in question would have to have definitely been sold at that time as the constant lack of means had rendered the payment of the debts and the continued operation of the company untenable. The property had been "completely encumbered" with liens and under pressure from creditors. As early as 1933 judicial composition proceedings had been conducted.

248 Further, the State Financial Procurator's Office explained that due to lack of a declaration of acceptance of the inheritance from the appointed heirs, a trustee of the estate had to be appointed in accordance with the provisions of the Non-Contentious Proceedings Act. In this regard, the Procurator's Office commented on the heirs that "[…] there are also no grounds for the assumption that they are to be considered racially persecuted". The summoning of the unknown heirs and the entire probate and sale proceedings had taken place in accordance with the law.

249 The State Financial Procurator's Office further submitted that the estate had not been subject to political persecution and that no pressure had been exerted on the said estate in the necessary sale of the property. The estate had been able to select the purchaser of its own free will. The estate had also received an adequate consideration for its disposal and had only thus been able to pay off its creditors in an out-of-court settlement for which the sale of the property had been imperative and completely independent of the National Socialist assumption of power. Hence, the requirements for a seizure were not met, particularly those under Article 1 para. 1 (2) of the Third State Treaty Implementation Act.

250 The State Financial Procurator's Office based this on the probate file, particularly on the examination of the final report of the trustee of the estate. The Procurator's Office referred to the estimated valued of the property of 295,000 Reichsmark resulting from the examination and to the fact that the property had also been sold for this amount. On the day of death, an over-indebtedness of at least 54,277.01 Reichsmark had existed. The total of the paid composition quotas of 201,422.92 Reichsmark had only turned out to be so low

Die Sammelstelle B stimmte im Sinne des § 2 Abs 3 des Auffangorganisationengesetzes der Durchführung des Rückstellungsverfahrens durch die Sammelstelle A zu. 244

Äußerung der Finanzprokuratur vom 7. März 1961 245

Die Finanzprokuratur bestritt in ihrer Äußerung vom 7. März 1961 den Rückstellungsanspruch und berief sich auf die Bestimmungen des 3. StVDG (Bundesgesetz vom 17. Juli 1957, womit weitere Bestimmungen zur Durchführung des IV. Teiles des Staatsvertrages vom 15. Mai 1955, BGBl Nr. 152, erlassen werden, BGBl 176/1957), welches Erwerbungen durch das Deutsche Reich während der deutschen Besetzung Österreichs für Zwecke der Wehrmacht oder der Reichsverteidigung aufgrund von Rechtsgeschäften oder sonstigen Rechtshandlungen zum Gegenstand hatte. 246

Im Einzelnen brachte die Finanzprokuratur vor, dass Dr. Lothar F.s Vermögen bereits vor der NS-Machtergreifung insolvenzreif gewesen sei. Laut Finanzprokuratur hätte die gegenständliche Liegenschaft um diese Zeit auf alle Fälle veräußert werden müssen, der dauernde Mangel an Geldmitteln habe die Bezahlung der Schulden und die Weiterführung des Betriebes unmöglich gemacht. Die Liegenschaft sei mit Pfandrechten „ausgelastet" gewesen und GläubigerInnen hätten gedrängt. Schon 1933 sei ein Ausgleichsverfahren abgewickelt worden. 247

Weiters führte die Finanzprokuratur aus, dass mangels Erbserklärung der eingesetzten ErbInnen, gemäß den Bestimmungen des Außerstreitgesetzes ein Verlassenschaftskurator bestellt werden musste. Die Prokuratur äußerte sich in diesem Zusammenhang zu den ErbInnen, dass „[...] im übrigen keinerlei Handhaben für die Annahme vorhanden sind, daß sie als rassisch verfolgt anzusehen sind." Die Einberufung der unbekannten ErbInnen sowie das gesamte Verlassenschafts- und Veräußerungsverfahren sei rechtmäßig erfolgt. 248

Die Finanzprokuratur brachte des Weiteren vor, dass die Verlassenschaft nicht politischer Verfolgung ausgesetzt gewesen sei und dass auf diese bei der notwendigen Veräußerung der Liegenschaft kein Druck ausgeübt worden sei. Die Verlassenschaft habe den Käufer frei wählen können. Die Verlassenschaft habe eine angemessene Gegenleistung zu ihrer Verfügung erhalten und habe nur so ihre GläubigerInnen in einem außergerichtlichen Ausgleich abfinden können, wozu die Veräußerung der Liegenschaft unerlässlich und von der nationalsozialistischen Machtergreifung völlig unabhängig gewesen sei. Somit fehle es am Tatbestand einer Entziehung, insbesondere im Sinne des Artikel I § 1 Abs 2 des 3. StVDG. 249

Die Finanzprokuratur stützte sich hierzu auf den Verlassenschaftsakt, insbesondere auf die Überprüfung des Endberichts des Verlassenschaftskurators. Sie verwies auf den aus der Überprüfung hervorgehenden Schätzwert der Liegenschaft von 295.000,- Reichsmark und dass die Liegenschaft auch um diesen Preis veräußert wurde. Es habe zum Todestag eine Überschuldung von mindestens 54.277,01 Reichsmark bestanden. Die Summe der gezahlten Ausgleichsquoten von 201.422,92 Reichsmark sei nur deshalb so niedrig ausgefallen, weil viele GläubigerInnen, insbesondere PfandgläubigerInnen, Juden waren. Laut Ansicht der Finanzprokuratur wäre auch ohne NS-Machtergreifung auf alle Fälle ein Ausgleich ohne Veräußerung der Liegenschaft unmöglich gewesen. Daher scheide eine Veräußerung lediglich auf Grund politischer Verfolgung völlig aus. 250

Für den Fall, dass die FLD zu einer anderen Rechtsbeurteilung gelangen sollte, wandte die Finanzprokuratur als Forderung den seinerzeitigen Kaufpreis sowie sämtliche Ansprüche des redlichen Erwerbers gemäß § 5 des 3. RStG ein, insbesondere Ansprüche in noch unbekannter Höhe aus Behebung der Schäden an der Liegenschaft. 251

because many creditors, particularly lienors, were Jews. In the opinion of the State Financial Procurator's Office, without the National Socialist assumption of power a composition settlement without the sale of the property would at all events have been impossible. Therefore, a sale solely on the ground of political persecution was entirely precluded.

251   In the case that the Financial Directorate should reach a different legal assessment, the State Financial Procurator's Office asserted a claim for the purchase price paid earlier and all claims to which an acquirer in good faith is entitled to pursuant to para. 5 of the Third Restitution Act, particularly claims of still unknown amounts for the repair of the damages to the property.

252 Statement by the Collection Agency of 18 September 1961

253   In its statement of 18 September 1961 regarding the explanations of the State Financial Procurator's Office, the Collection Agency expressed the opinion that the sale of the property would never have taken place without Hitler's assumption of power in Austria. It referred to the decision of the Supreme Restitution Commission of 25 December 1948, Rkv 158/48. Pursuant to this decision, over-indebtedness only justified the assumption of a property transfer which also would have taken place without the National Socialist assumption of power where under the given circumstances the financial difficulties were insurmountable. It was further stated in the cited decision that: "The absence of this requirement can also be concluded from the passive behavior of the creditors before the occupation".

254   The Collection Agency saw the passive behavior of the creditors in the present case as due to the fact that the recording of the initiation of the auction procedure for the lienors had been deleted in 1935 before the National Socialist assumption of power.

255   The Collection Agency further submitted that according to the probate file for Dr. Lothar F., the surplus amount after the sale had amounted to 15,434.62 Reichsmark and it was therefore clear that overcoming Dr. F.'s financial difficulties had not been a hopeless endeavor. In this regard, it referred to the decision Rkv 206/48. The low composition quota, which was due to the fact that many of the creditors were Jews, did not change anything. The property sale had occurred solely due to political persecution. Without this persecution, Dr. F. and his wife would not have committed suicide.

256   Further to this, the Collection Agency asserted political persecution of the heirs and referred to the fact that both the testamentary heirs, the parents of Susanne F. and the subsidiary appointed statutory heirs, the relatives of Dr. F., were Jews and hence racially persecuted. It was incorrect to conclude from the fact that the testamentary heirs had not advised that they had not been interested in accepting the inheritance due to the over-indebtedness of the estate. The Collection Agency further explained in this regard that it had been known that the emigration of Jews could only take place on the condition of a tax clearance certificate. This certificate was only obtainable upon the payment of all taxes, also including the Reich Flight Tax. Therefore, under the then prevailing circumstances it had been better to tacitly forego an inheritance to retain the possibility of a speedy emigration. The non-submission of the declaration of acceptance of the inheritance was therefore only caused by political persecution of the heirs.

257   In summary, the Collection Agency submitted that the prerequisites for the restitution according to the provisions of Article 1 para. 1 (2) of the Third State Treaty Implementation Act had been met.

Stellungnahme der Sammelstelle vom 18. September 1961 252

Die Sammelstelle vertrat in ihrer Stellungnahme zur Äußerung der Finanzprokuratur 253
vom 18. September 1961 die Ansicht, dass die Veräußerung der Liegenschaft ohne die
Machtergreifung Hitlers in Österreich niemals stattgefunden hätte. Sie berief sich auf die
Entscheidung der Obersten Rückstellungskommission vom 25. September 1948, Rkv
158/48. Gemäß dieser Entscheidung begründe Überschuldung die Annahme einer auch
ohne die Machtergreifung des Nationalsozialismus erfolgten Vermögensübertragung nur
im Falle der Aussichtslosigkeit, unter den gegebenen Verhältnissen die finanziellen Schwierigkeiten
zu überwinden. In der genannten Entscheidung heiße es weiter: „Aus dem passiven
Verhalten der Gläubiger vor der Okkupation folgt das Fehlen dieser Voraussetzung."

Die Sammelstelle sah das passive Verhalten der Gläubiger im gegenständlichen Fall 254
damit gegeben, dass die Anmerkung der Einleitung des Versteigerungsverfahrens für die
Pfandrechtsgläubiger im Jahre 1935 vor der nationalsozialistischen Machtübernahme wieder
gelöscht worden war.

Die Sammelstelle brachte weiters vor, dass laut Verlassenschaftsakt nach Dr. Lothar 255
F. die Hyperocha 15.434,62 Reichsmark betragen habe und daraus eindeutig zu schließen
sei, dass die Überwindung von Dr. F.s finanziellen Schwierigkeiten nicht aussichtslos
gewesen sei. Hierzu verwies sie auf die Entscheidung Rkv 206/48. Auch die niedrige
Ausgleichquote, die ihren Grund darin hatte, dass viele GläubigerInnen Juden waren, ändere
daran nichts. Die Liegenschaftsveräußerung sei lediglich auf Grund politischer Verfolgung
erfolgt. Ohne diese hätten sich Dr. F. und seine Gattin nicht das Leben genommen.

Des Weiteren machte die Sammelstelle die politische Verfolgung der ErbInnen geltend 256
und wies darauf hin, dass sowohl die testamentarischen ErbInnen, die Eltern von Susanne
F., als auch die subsidiär berufenen gesetzlichen ErbInnen, die Verwandten von Dr. F.,
Juden und damit rassisch Verfolgte waren. Es sei unrichtig, aus der Tatsache, dass die testamentarisch
berufenen ErbInnen sich nicht gemeldet hätten, zu schließen, dass sie am Antritt
des Erbes wegen der Überschuldung der Verlassenschaft nicht interessiert gewesen
seien. Die Sammelstelle führte dazu weiters aus, es sei bekannt, dass die Auswanderung
von Juden nur unter der Voraussetzung einer Steuerunbedenklichkeitserklärung erfolgen
konnte. Diese sei nur bei Bezahlung aller Steuern, darunter auch der Reichsfluchtsteuer,
zu erhalten gewesen. Daher sei es unter den damaligen Verhältnissen besser gewesen, stillschweigend
auf ein Erbe zu verzichten und dadurch die Möglichkeit einer schnellen Auswanderung
zu behalten. Die Nichtabgabe der Erbserklärung habe daher nur in der politischen
Verfolgung der ErbInnen ihre Ursache.

Die Sammelstelle brachte zusammenfassend vor, dass somit die Voraussetzungen für 257
die Rückstellung auch nach den Bestimmungen des Artikel I § 1 Abs 2 des 3. StVDG vorliegen
würden.

Anregung der Finanzprokuratur ans Bundesministerium für Finanzen wegen Vergleichsverhandlungen 258

In einem Schreiben von Dr. Ba. von der Finanzprokuratur vom 5. Oktober 1961 an das 259
BMF ersuchte dieser um die Genehmigung, der Sammelstelle A ein Vergleichsangebot unterbreiten
zu dürfen. In dem Schreiben wurde die Ansicht vertreten, dass nicht auszuschließen
sei, dass wegen der strengen Auffassung des Verwaltungsgerichtshofes (VwGH)

258 **Suggestion of the State Financial Procurator's Office to the Federal Ministry of Finance regarding settlement negotiations**

259 In a letter from Dr. Ba. of the State Financial Procurator's Office to the Federal Ministry of Finance dated 5 October 1961, he requested the approval to be able to submit a settlement offer to the Collection Agency A. In this letter, the opinion was expressed that due to the Supreme Administrative Court's strict interpretation of the exempting facts stipulated in para. 2 (1) of the Third Restitution Act it could not be ruled out that the restitution could be successful despite the applicability of the Third State Treaty Implementation Act. He further pointed out that the property in question may well be of high value and the completion of the proceedings by way of a settlement would therefore be beneficial. In connection with the request for the disclosure of the maximum amount of the settlement deemed by the Federal Ministry it was stated: "The merits of the case for both parties must be approximately equal." Dr. Ba. recommended that if the Federal Ministry should adopt the settlement suggestion, then a reasonably low settlement offer was to be made in November or December 1961.

260 In the responding letter of the Federal Ministry of Finance by Dr. Wit. dated 17 October 1961, he rejected the necessity of a settlement proposal with reference to the decision of the Supreme Restitution Commission in the restitution proceedings of John Henry D. Dr. Wit. interpreted the opinion of the court to the effect that even if the declaration of the reversion of the estate of Dr. F. was to be construed as a seizure, the declaration could only concern the reverted assets and not the previously sold property.

261 **Second Statement by the State Financial Procurator's Office of 30 October 1961**

262 In the proceedings the State Financial Procurator's Office, in its second statement of 30 October 1961, contested the submissions of the Collection Agency and referred to its first statement. It was still to be established whether Susanne F. was a Jew. Had Dr. F. still remained alive, he would still not have been able to retain the property, even without the National Socialist assumption of power. This could be gathered from the over-indebtedness and the previous settlement. There had been pressure from creditors, as can be deduced from the land register. Collection procedures had also already been conducted by the creditor Sári Sz.

263 At the beginning of November 1961 a further request was made by Dr. Ba. to the Federal Ministry of Finance to be authorized to enter into settlement negotiations with the Collection Agency. Dr. Ba. referred to the fact that in the proceedings of the legatee John Henry D., the Supreme Restitution Commission had only denied his eligibility to file an application. It had, however, taken into consideration that the sale of the property could constitute a seizure.

264 Dr. Wit. again conveyed to the State Financial Procurator's Office on 20 January 1962 that on the part of the Federal Ministry of Finance, no resolution of the restitution case by way of settlement would be taken into consideration but instead the Financial Directorate should be called upon to make a decision by means of an order.

265 With regard to the request from the Collection Agency to the Financial Directorate for Vienna, Lower Austria and Burgenland to defer the decision, as settlement negotiations were to be started with the Republic of Austria, Dr. Ba. informed Dr. Fi. from Collection Agency A by telephone on 22 January 1963 that as a result of instructions from the Federal Ministry of Finance, he could not automatically consent to a deferral. Dr. Ba. explained that in the case that an offer was not received by the Collection Agency by 15 February

hinsichtlich des Befreiungstatbestandes des § 2 Abs 1 des 3. RStG der Sammelstelle letztlich die Rückstellung trotz des Greifens des 3. StVDG gelingen könnte. Er gab weiters zu bedenken, dass es sich bei dem gegenständlichen Gebäude wohl um ein solches von großem Wert handeln dürfte und eine vergleichsweise Verfahrenserledigung daher günstig wäre. Im Zusammenhang mit der Bitte um Mitteilung des vom Bundesministerium erachteten Vergleichshöchstbetrages hieß es: „Die Verfahrenschancen müssen wohl als ungefähr gleich groß angesehen werden." Dr. Ba. empfahl, falls das Bundesministerium die Vergleichsanregung aufgreifen sollte, ein nicht allzu hoch gehaltenes Vergleichsangebot im November oder Dezember 1961 zu stellen.

Im Antwortschreiben des BMF durch Dr. Wit. vom 17. Oktober 1961 verneinte dieser die Notwendigkeit eines Vergleichsvorschlages mit Verweis auf die Entscheidung der Obersten Rückstellungskommission im Rückstellungsverfahren von John Henry D. Dr. Wit. legte die Meinung des Gerichts dahingehend aus, dass, selbst wenn in der Heimfallserklärung des Nachlasses nach Dr. F. eine Entziehung zu erblicken wäre, diese nur das heimgefallene Vermögen und nicht die früher verkaufte Liegenschaft betreffen könnte.

260

Zweite Äußerung der Finanzprokuratur vom 30. Oktober 1961

261

Die Finanzprokuratur bestritt im Verfahren in ihrer zweiten Äußerung vom 30. Oktober 1961 das Vorbringen der Sammelstelle und verwies auf ihre erste Äußerung. Es sei noch zu erheben, ob Susanne F. Jüdin war. Wäre Dr. F. am Leben geblieben, hätte er auch ohne nationalsozialistische Machtergreifung die gegenständliche Liegenschaft nicht behalten können. Dies sei aus der Überschuldung und dem seinerzeitigen Ausgleich zu folgern. Andrängende GläubigerInnen seien vorhanden gewesen, wie aus dem Grundbuch hervorgehe. Auch sei längst von der Gläubigerin Sári Sz. Exekution geführt worden.

262

Anfang November 1961 erfolgte ein weiteres Ersuchen Dr. Ba.s an das BMF, mit der Sammelstelle in Vergleichsverhandlungen treten zu dürfen. Dr. Ba. wies darauf hin, dass die Oberste Rückstellungskommission im Rückstellungsverfahren des Legatars D. lediglich dessen Antragslegitimation verneint habe. Sie habe jedoch in Betracht gezogen, dass der Verkauf der Liegenschaft eine Entziehung darstellen könnte.

263

Dr. Wit. teilte der Finanzprokuratur am 30. Jänner 1962 erneut mit, dass seitens des BMF keine vergleichsweise Regelung des Rückstellungsfalles in Erwägung gezogen werde, sondern die FLD zur bescheidmäßigen Entscheidung aufgefordert werden solle.

264

Im Hinblick auf das Ersuchen der Sammelstelle an die FLD für Wien, Niederösterreich und Burgenland, mit der Entscheidung zu warten, da Vergleichsverhandlungen mit der Republik Österreich aufgenommen werden sollten, verständigte Dr. Ba. am 22. Jänner 1963 Dr. Fi. von der Sammelstelle A telefonisch davon, dass er infolge Weisung des BMF nicht ohne weiteres einem Zuwarten zustimmen könne. Dr. Ba. erklärte, er würde die FLD um Entscheidung ersuchen, falls nicht bis zum 15. Februar 1963 ein Anbot der Sammelstelle einlange. Dr. Ba. wies darauf hin, dass der Fall nicht eindeutig sei, dass er jedoch vielleicht die Möglichkeit biete,

265

„auch eine Bereinigung jener Fälle herbeizuführen, in denen die Sammelstelle infolge formeller Fehler (Fristversäumnis) trotz eindeutigem Entziehungstatbestand etwa geringfügige Miteigentumsanteile (an ihnen sonst zur Gänze zugekommenen Liegenschaften) verloren hat."

Arbitration Panel for *In Rem* Restitution – Decision No. 27/2005

1963, he would ask the Financial Directorate for a decision. Dr. Ba. referred to the fact that the case was not clear, but that it possibly, however, offers the opportunity

> "to resolve those cases in which the Collection Agency, as a result of procedural errors (missing of deadlines) – despite clearly meeting the requirements of a seizure – lost for example small shares of co-ownership (to a property which it would otherwise have received in their entirety)".

266 Settlement Proposals

267 On the occasion of negotiations before the Financial Directorate on 21 February 1963, Dr. Fi. from Collection Agency A announced to Dr. Ba. a settlement offer concerning the former Sanatorium F. Accordingly, the settlement amount of 250,000 Schilling would be proposed by the Collection Agency A. According to an expert opinion, the estimated value of the property was 6 million Schilling.

268 On 22 February 1963, the director of Collection Agency A, Dr. Georg Weis submitted a settlement offer of 300,000 Schilling to the State Financial Procurator's Office regarding the restitution claim for the property S.-gasse 14. The Collection Agency had commissioned a valuation of the property, the written result of which had not yet been available. The expert had, however, conveyed by telephone that the property had an estimated value of 7 million Schilling. Dr. Weis concluded by referring to the fact that the approval for the conclusion of the settlement offer by the board of trustees of Collection Agency A was not yet available.

269 On 5 March 1963, Dr. Ba. informed the Federal Ministry of Finance of the written settlement offer of Collection Agency A and expressed the view that the amount could be reduced to between 250,000 and 275,000 Schilling. Furthermore, Dr. Ba. noted that the State Financial Procurator's Office

> "particularly due to the status of the proceedings, considered such a settlement appropriate if the property had also only been worth around 3 million Schilling (the expert opinion of the Collection Agency will assert 7 million Schilling) and if possible earnings of 250,000 Schilling should presently exist".

Regarding the status of the proceedings, Dr. Ba. explained that although Article I para. 1 (2) of the Third State Treaty Implementation Act could be applied because the Reich Treasury – Army had appeared as purchaser and a lack of financial means existed,

> "however, it cannot be denied that the owner Dr. Lothar F[…] committed suicide on 3 April 1938 – this suicide could far more be attributed to the National Socialist assumption of power than to the indebtedness which had existed for years. This case therefore seems prejudicial, particularly as it could give rise to a discussion (presumably before the Constitutional Court) whether the Third State Treaty Implementation Act complies with Article 26 of the State Treaty. It seems that it cannot be ruled out that it will develop into an international case, particularly as it concerns an apparently advantageous case for the Collection Agency which it could particularly exploit if its low settlement offer is not accepted".

270 In a letter dated 3 April 1963, the Federal Ministry of Finance declared itself principally in agreement with the conclusion of the restitution proceedings by means of a settlement, however, it emphasized that this was not due to considerations "which are to be attributed to a prejudicial legal situation […]". At the same time it was requested that the settlement amount be reduced to 250,000 Schilling.

Vergleichsvorschläge 266

Dr. Fi. von der Sammelstelle A kündigte anlässlich einer Verhandlung vor der FLD am 21. Februar 1963 gegenüber Dr. Ba. ein Vergleichsangebot betreffend das ehemalige Sanatorium F. an. Demnach werde die Sammelstelle A die Vergleichssumme von 250.000,– Schilling vorschlagen. Der Schätzwert der Liegenschaft betrage laut Sachverständigengutachten 6,000.000,– Schilling. 267

Am 22. Februar 1963 richtete der Geschäftsführer der Sammelstelle A, Dr. Georg Weis, an die Finanzprokuratur ein Vergleichsangebot über den Rückstellungsanspruch betreffend die Liegenschaft S.-gasse 14 in der Höhe von 300.000,– Schilling. Die Sammelstelle habe eine Schätzung der Liegenschaft in Auftrag gegeben, deren schriftliches Ergebnis ihm noch nicht vorliege. Jedoch habe der Gutachter telefonisch mitgeteilt, dass der Schätzwert ungefähr 7,000.000,– Schilling betrage. Dr. Weis wies abschließend daraufhin, dass die Genehmigung zum Abschluss des Vergleichsanbotes durch das Kuratorium der Sammelstelle A noch nicht vorliege. 268

Am 5. März 1963 berichtete Dr. Ba. dem BMF vom schriftlichen Vergleichsangebot der Sammelstelle A und äußerte die Ansicht, dass sich der Betrag auf 250.000,– Schilling bis 275.000,– Schilling ermäßigen ließe. Dr. Ba. bemerkte darüber hinaus, dass die Finanzprokuratur 269

„einen solchen Vergleich aufgrund der Verfahrenslage insbesondere dann für angezeigt hielte, wenn die Liegenschaft auch nur rund S 3.000.000,– wert wäre (das Gutachten der Sammelstelle wird S 7 Mill. behaupten) und etwa Erträgnisse in der Höhe von S 250.000,– gegenwärtig vorhanden sein sollten."

Zur Verfahrenssituation führte Dr. Ba. aus, dass zwar Artikel I § 1 Abs 2 des 3. StVDG eingreifen könnte, weil der Reichsfiskus – Heer als Erwerber aufgetreten sei und ein Mangel an Geldmitteln vorlag.

„Jedoch kann andererseits nicht geleugnet werden, dass der Eigentümer Dr. Lothar F[...] am 3. 4.1938 Selbstmord begangen hat, wobei dieser Selbstmord weitaus eher auf die Machtergreifung durch die Nationalsozialisten zurückzuführen sein dürfte, als auf die seit Jahren bestehende Verschuldung. Deshalb erscheint dieser Fall ungünstig gelagert, zumal er zu einer Diskussion (vermutlich vor dem Verfassungsgerichtshof) Anlaß sein könnte, ob das 3. StVDG dem Art. 26 des Staatsvertrages gerecht wird. Es scheint nicht ausgeschlossen, daß er sich zu einem internationalen ausweitet, zumal es sich um einen für die Sammelstelle optisch günstigen Fall handelt, den sie insbesondere dann auswerten könnte, wenn auf ihr an sich nicht hohes Vergleichsanbot nicht eingegangen wird."

Mit Schreiben vom 3. April 1963 erklärte sich das BMF mit einer vergleichsweisen Beendigung des Rückstellungsverfahrens grundsätzlich einverstanden, unterstrich jedoch, dass sie das nicht aus Erwägungen tue, „die auf eine ungünstige Beurteilung der Rechtslage zurückzuführen sind [...]". Gleichzeitig wird ersucht, den Vergleichsbetrag auf 250.000,– Schilling zu reduzieren. 270

Die Finanzprokuratur verständigte daraufhin die Sammelstelle A über ihre Ermächtigung zum maximalen Vergleichsbetrag in Höhe von 250.000,– Schilling. 271

Mit Bericht an die Kuratoriumsmitglieder der Sammelstelle vom 30. Mai 1963 beantragte Dr. Georg Weis, den von der Finanzprokuratur vorgeschlagenen Vergleich über 250.000,– Schilling abzuschließen. Er begründete dies damit, dass es in den vorangegangenen Verfahren der Sammelstelle, die nach den Bestimmungen des 3. StVDG zu beur- 272

271	As a result, the State Financial Procurator's Office informed the Collection Agency A of its authorization of the maximum settlement amount of 250,000 Schilling.

272	In a report dated 30 May 1963 to the board of trustees of the Collection Agency A, Dr. Georg Weis moved to conclude the settlement proposed by the State Financial Procurator's Office of 250,000 Schilling. He justified this by stating that the previous Collection Agency proceedings, which were to be assessed in line with the provisions of the Third State Treaty Implementation Act, had resulted in rejections in both instances. The Collection Agency had turned to the Supreme Administrative Court in all of these cases. To date, there had only been one decision, no. 2311/61, in which the complaint of the Collection Agency A had been rejected as without merit. Hence, the risk of losing the case in the proceedings in question, in which the Third State Treaty Implementation Act was also applicable, was assessed to be very high.

273	Dr. Weis explained in his proposal that it could not be established why the State Financial Procurator's Office had suggested a settlement. The results of the examination of whether the settlement proposal had come about through the intervention of the American Embassy, which had used the building in S.-gasse 14 for a part of its embassy, showed that the embassy had no knowledge whatsoever of the restitution proceedings.

274	The proposal of Dr. Weis did not receive the necessary consent from the member of the board of trustees Hi. [sic, meant is AR Anton Hy., according to the official directory 1961, he was the vice president of Group IV of the Post and Telephone Directorate for Vienna, Lower Austria and Burgenland], as he preferred the risk of restitution proceedings to the proposed settlement sum and accordingly expressed this to the Collection Agency on 11 June 1963. The objection was then noted in the Collection Agency's documents.

275	The expert opinion of the sworn court expert DI Hans Weidisch of 30 September 1963 commissioned by the Collection Agency valued the property at 6.2 million Schilling.

276	The Collection Agency conveyed this expert opinion to the State Financial Procurator's Office on 22 October 1963. In an accompanying letter, Dr. Fi. expressed the continued willingness of the Collection Agency to settle, but he was of the opinion that the valuation of 6.2 million Schilling must be taken as a starting point and that the Third State Treaty Implementation Act would not be applied in the present restitution proceedings. The Collection Agency supported this argument with the repeated rulings of the Supreme Administrative Court in its decisions (no. 2311/61 from 23 March 1963, no. 353/62 of 30 May 1963) according to which the wording and meaning of the mentioned law allowed only acquisitions of the German Reich for military purposes to be covered by this law in contrast to other property transfers in connection with the National Socialist assumption of power. The location of the property and its proximity to training areas and airbases or other military objects were decisive. The property in question is not, however, located near any such area. Finally, Dr. Fi. requested a substantial increase of the settlement amount as otherwise the Collection Agency would request the Financial Directorate to call a hearing.

277 Hearing on 10 June 1964

278	Both parties declared in the hearing on 10 June 1964 that the conclusion of a settlement was now out of the question.

279	To demonstrate the existence of a seizure in the meaning of the restitution acts, the Collection Agency argued that the sale of the property in question had been carried out by the trustee of the estate of a politically persecuted person.

teilen gewesen seien, zu Abweisung in beiden Instanzen gekommen sei. In allen Fällen habe die Sammelstelle sich an den VwGH gewandt. Bislang läge eine Entscheidung vor, Zl. 2311/61, in der die Beschwerde der Sammelstelle A als unbegründet abgewiesen worden wäre. Daher sei das Prozessrisiko in dem gegenständlichen Verfahren, in dem ebenfalls das 3. StVDG zur Anwendung komme, als sehr hoch einzuschätzen.

Dr. Weis führte in seinem Antrag aus, dass nicht festgestellt werden konnte, aus welchem Grund die Finanzprokuratur einen Vergleich vorgeschlagen habe. Die Überprüfung, ob der Vergleichsvorschlag über Intervention seitens der Amerikanischen Botschaft zustande gekommen war, die das Gebäude in der S.-gasse 14 für einen Teil der Botschaft benützte, ergab, dass diese von dem Rückstellungsverfahren überhaupt keine Kenntnis habe. 273

Der Antrag von Dr. Weis fand nicht die notwendige Zustimmung des Kuratoriumsmitgliedes Hi. [sic, gemeint ist AR Anton Hy., laut Amtskalender 1961 war er Vizepräsident der Gruppe IV der Post- und Telegraphendirektion für Wien, Niederösterreich und Burgenland], da dieser das Risiko eines Rückstellungsverfahrens gegenüber der vorgeschlagenen Abfindungssumme vorzog und der Sammelstelle am 11. Juni 1963 entsprechend Mitteilung machte. In den Unterlagen der Sammelstellen wurde daraufhin die Beeinspruchung vermerkt. 274

Das von der Sammelstelle in Auftrag gegebene Gutachten des beeideten Sachverständigen DI Hans Weidisch vom 30. September 1963 bewertete die Liegenschaft von 6,200.000,– Schilling. 275

Die Sammelstelle übermittelte dieses Gutachten an die Finanzprokuratur am 22. Oktober 1963. Im Begleitschreiben dazu erklärte Dr. Fi. nach wie vor die Vergleichsbereitschaft der Sammelstelle, meinte jedoch, dass man von der vorliegenden Schätzung von 6,200.000,– Schilling ausgehen müsse und dass im gegenständlichen Rückstellungsverfahren das 3. StVDG nicht zur Anwendung komme. Sie argumentierte dies damit, dass der VwGH wiederholt in seinen Entscheidungen (Zl. 2311/61 vom 23. März 1963, Zl. 353/62 vom 30. Mai 1963) ausgesprochen habe, dass nach dem Wortlaut und dem Sinn des genannten Gesetzes nur Erwerbungen des Deutschen Reiches für militärische Zwecke anders als die sonstigen Vermögensübertragungen im Zusammenhang mit der nationalsozialistischen Machtübernahme behandelt würden. Hierbei sei die örtliche Lage des Grundstückes und der räumliche Zusammenhang des Grundstückes mit Übungs- oder Flugplätzen oder sonstigen militärischen Objekten ausschlaggebend. Die gegenständliche Liegenschaft stehe aber in keinem solchen örtlichen oder räumlichen Zusammenhang. Abschließend ersuchte Dr. Fi. um wesentliche Erhöhung des Vergleichsbetrages, anderenfalls die Sammelstelle die FLD um Anberaumung einer Verhandlung ersuchen würde. 276

Verhandlung am 10. Juni 1964 277

Beide Parteien erklärten in der mündlichen Verhandlung am 10. Juni 1964, dass ein Vergleichabschluss nicht mehr in Frage komme. 278

Die Sammelstelle argumentierte das Vorliegen einer Entziehung im Sinne der Rückstellungsgesetze damit, dass der Verkauf der gegenständlichen Liegenschaft vom Nachlasskurator einer politisch verfolgten Person durchgeführt worden sei. 279

Sie bestritt unter Heranziehung der relevanten Entscheidungen der Obersten Rückstellungskommission (Rkv 158/48, 161/48, 206/48, 278/49, 338/49) das Vorliegen des Befreiungstatbestandes des § 2 Abs 1 des 3. RStG, wonach keine Entziehung vorliege, wenn es auch ohne nationalsozialistische Machtübernahme zur Veräußerung der Liegenschaft gekommen wäre. Nach Ansicht der Sammelstelle lag der Befreiungstatbestand im gegen- 280

Arbitration Panel for *In Rem* Restitution – Decision No. 27/2005

280   With reference to the relevant decisions of the Supreme Restitution Commission (Rkv 158/48, 161/48, 206/48, 278/49, 338/49), the Collection Agency disputed the existence of the exempting facts of para. 2 (1) of the Third Restitution Act, according to which a seizure did not exist if the property would have also been sold without the National Socialist assumption of power. In the opinion of the Collection Agency, a case of exempting facts did not exist as no desperate financial situation which could only have been resolved through the sale of the property existed.

281   Furthermore, with reference to the relevant judicial practice of the Supreme Administrative Court (particularly no. 2633/59 of 20 December 1962), the Collection Agency disputed the applicability of the Third State Treaty Implementation Act pointing to the lack of connection between the location and existing military objects.

282   The State Financial Procurator's Office disputed the submissions of the Collection Agency and referred to its previous explanations and submissions. Moreover, it was of the opinion that the sale of the property had been handled by the trustee of the estate during lawful probate proceedings and referred to the decision of the Supreme Restitution Commission of 22 March 1962, Rkv 13/61.

283   **Statement by the Collection Agency of 22 July 1964**

284   In its statement of 22 July 1964, the Collection Agency submitted that the decision Rkv 13/61, cited by the State Financial Procurator's Office in the hearing, was founded on fundamentally different facts of the case than those in the proceedings at hand.

285   In the cited case, the cause of death was of natural causes in contrast to the suicide of Dr. F., which was closely connected to his Jewish origin.

286   The Collection Agency cited another difference that the element of force during the sale had been missing in the case cited by the State Financial Procurator's Office, however, it had been present in the case of Dr. F. Neither he nor his wife would have taken their lives without the National Socialist assumption of power. Further, the estate of Dr. F. would not have remained heirless, as under normal circumstances the Jewish parents-in-law would have accepted the inheritance. The Collection Agency further pointed out that the other subsidiary heirs were also "racially" persecuted persons.

287   As in its earlier explanations, the Collection Agency submitted that the heirs were not interested in accepting the inheritance under the then prevailing circumstances and that doing so would have even prevented their emigration. In summary, it put forward that in contrast to the cited decision, in which it could not even be confirmed that a persecuted heir had been appointed as heir, "in the present case it has been indisputably proven that solely politically persecuted persons had been appointed as heirs."

288   In this context, the Collection Agency referred to the decision of the Supreme Restitution Commission of 22 May 1964, no. Rkv 5/64

"in which it is ruled that even the sale of an estate belonging to a non-persecuted person prior to its devolution to a persecuted person constituted a null and void seizure of property if an act of racial persecution had occurred, as in the proceedings Rkv 5/64 through the approval of the purchase contract by the district administrator in accordance with the Ordinance on the Use of Jewish Property, the reduction of the purchase price to the detriment of the estate and the prescription of a de-jewification fee."

289   The Collection Agency argued that concerning the estate of Dr. Lothar F., an act of racial persecution had been effected in the meaning of the decision Rkv 5/64

ständlichen Fall nicht vor, da keine aussichtslose finanzielle Situation bestanden habe, die nur durch den Verkauf der Liegenschaft hätte saniert werden können.

Weiters bestritt sie unter Berufung auf die einschlägige Judikatur des VwGH (insbes. Zl. 2633/59 vom 20. Dezember 1962) die Anwendbarkeit des 3. StVDG unter Hinweis auf den fehlenden örtlichen Zusammenhang mit bestehenden militärischen Objekten. 281

Die Finanzprokuratur bestritt das Vorbringen der Sammelstelle und verwies auf ihre bisherigen Äußerungen und Anträge. Darüber hinaus vertrat sie die Ansicht, dass der Verkauf der Liegenschaft durch den Verlassenschaftskurator im Rahmen eines gesetzmäßigen Verlassenschaftsverfahrens abgewickelt worden sei und berief sich auf die Entscheidung der Obersten Rückstellungskommission vom 22. März 1962, Rkv 13/61. 282

Schriftsatz der Sammelstelle vom 22. Juli 1964 283

Die Sammelstelle brachte in ihrem Schriftsatz vom 22. Juli 1964 vor, dass die von der Finanzprokuratur in der mündlichen Verhandlung angeführte Entscheidung Rkv 13/61 auf einem wesentlich anderen Sachverhalt beruhe, als der, der im gegenständlichen Verfahren vorliege. 284

So sei die Todesursache beim zitierten Fall eine natürliche im Gegensatz zum Selbstmord Dr. F.s, der in engem Zusammenhang mit seiner jüdischen Abstammung stehe. 285

Als einen weiteren Unterschied nannte die Sammelstelle, dass es in der von der Finanzprokuratur genannten Entscheidung am Zwangselement bei der Veräußerung gemangelt habe, nicht jedoch im Falle Dr. F. Sowohl er als auch seine Frau hätten sich ohne NS-Machtergreifung nicht das Leben genommen. Des Weiteren wäre der Nachlass nach Dr. F. nicht erblos geblieben, da die jüdischen Schwiegereltern unter normalen Verhältnissen das Erbe angetreten hätten. Die Sammelstelle wies weiters darauf hin, dass auch die weiteren subsidiären ErbInnen „rassisch" verfolgte Personen waren. 286

Wie in ihren früheren Ausführungen brachte die Sammelstelle vor, dass die ErbInnen unter den damaligen Verhältnissen nicht am Antritt der Erbschaft interessiert waren und dass sie eine solche sogar an der Auswanderung gehindert hätte. Sie führte zusammenfassend ins Treffen, es sei, im Gegensatz zur zitierten Entscheidung, in der nicht einmal bescheinigt werden konnte, dass ein verfolgter Erbe zur Erbfolge berufen war, „im gegenständliche Falle eindeutig bewiesen, dass zur Erbfolge lediglich politisch verfolgte Personen berufen waren." 287

Die Sammelstelle verwies in diesem Zusammenhang auf die Entscheidung der Obersten Rückstellungskommission vom 22. Mai 1964, Zl. Rkv 5/64, 288

"in welcher ausgesprochen wird, dass selbst der Verkauf eines einer nicht verfolgten Person gehörigen Nachlasses vor dessen Einantwortung an eine verfolgte Person als nichtige Vermögensentziehung gilt, wenn beim Verkauf des Nachlasses eine rassische Verfolgungshandlung gesetzt wurde, wie im Verfahren Rkv 5/64 durch Genehmigung des Kaufvertrages durch den Landrat nach der Einsatzverordnung, Herabsetzung des Kaufpreises zum Nachteil der Verlassenschaft und Vorschreibung einer Entjudungsauflage."

Die Sammelstelle argumentierte, dass bezüglich des Nachlasses nach Dr. Lothar F. eine „rassische" Verfolgungshandlung im Sinne der Entscheidung Rkv 5/64 gesetzt wurde, 289

„da der Kaufvertrag durch die Vermögensverkehrsstelle zur Zl. 6805/39 genehmigt werden musste und da in dieser Genehmigung verfügt wurde, dass der Kaufpreis von RM 310.000,– auf ein auf den Namen des Verkäufers, also auf den Namen des Dr. Lo-

"since the purchase contract had to be approved by the Property Transaction Office under no. 6805/39 and since it was ordered in this approval that the purchase price of 310,000 Reichsmark was to be deposited in an account in the name of the vendor, i.e. in the name of Dr. Lothar F[…] designated 'de-jewification proceeds', pursuant to para. 59 ff. of the Foreign Exchange Law."

290 **Comments of the State Financial Procurator's Office of 12 August 1964**

291 In its comments of 12 August 1964, the State Financial Procurator's Office agreed that the applicability of para. 2 (1) of the Third Restitution Act concerning a dormant estate does not refer to the political persecution of the decedent but of the heir.

292 However, the State Financial Procurator's Office raised the objection that because the appointed heirs, the parents-in-law of Dr. F., had not submitted a declaration of the acceptance of the inheritance, the estate had remained heirless. Therefore, political persecution of the heirless estate could not be assumed.

293 Furthermore, the State Financial Procurator's Office disputed that Ida and Emil Be. had not submitted a declaration of the acceptance of the inheritance in order not to hinder their planned emigration. The State Financial Procurator's Office was of the opinion that the spouses Be. had refrained from submitting a declaration of the acceptance of the inheritance in view of the desperate financial state of the estate. This could also be deduced from the fact that the spouses Be. did accept the inheritance of their daughter Susanne F.

294 Regarding the decision of the Supreme Restitution Commission of 22 May 1964, Rkv 5/64 cited by the Collection Agency, the State Financial Procurator's Office asserted that it could be of no benefit for the case at hand as the decision was founded on different facts and circumstances, i.e. an actual act of seizure.

295 For the rest, the State Financial Procurator's Office referred to its previous comments and requested that the restitution application be rejected.

296 **Further Negotiations**

297 On 30 September 1964, Dr. Ilse Fi. from the Collection Agency approached John Henry D. in London by letter and inquired whether he knew, as the legatee of Dr. Lothar F., if Dr. F. had had any living relatives at the time of his death and where they were to be found. However, John Henry D. had already passed away on 3 August 1960.

298 On the request of Dr. Fi., an appointment was made for 15 December 1964 with the State Financial Procurator's Office to discuss a possible conclusion of a settlement, in which Dr. Fi. for Collection Agency A and Dr. Sch. and Dr. Spi. for the State Financial Procurator's Office participated. In this discussion, Dr. Fi. expressed that in her opinion, the settlement amount should constitute around 4 million Schilling.

299 On 29 January 1965, a discussion took place between representatives of Collection Agency A (Dr. Weis and Dr. Fi.) and representatives of the State Financial Procurator's Office (Dr. Sch. and Dr. Spi.) to examine the requirements for a possible settlement in the restitution matter Dr. F. Following the discussion, the representatives of the Financial Directorate directed a query to Mr. Ma., the director of the Office for Property Control and Restitution Matters at the Financial Directorate for Vienna, Lower Austria and Burgenland. Mr. Ma. was asked therein to establish how the Sanatorium was used after the death of Dr. F. and further to inform them of the earnings of the property as well as the expenses.

300 On 12 February 1965, Mr. Ma. conveyed the report of inquiry of the field service concerning the property S.-gasse 14 to the State Financial Procurator's Office. He informed

thar F[...] zu lautendes, gemäß § 59 ff Devisengesetz gesperrtes mit der Bezeichnung „Entjudungserlös" versehenes Konto zu erlegen sei."

Äußerung der Finanzprokuratur vom 12. August 1964

In ihrer Äußerung vom 12. August 1964 stimmte die Finanzprokuratur zu, dass sich die Anwendbarkeit des § 2 Abs 1 des 3. RStG bei einem ruhenden Nachlass nicht nach der politischen Verfolgung des Erblassers, sondern nach der des Erben richte.

Die Prokuratur wandte jedoch ein, dass deshalb, weil die berufenen ErbInnen, die Schwiegereltern von Dr. F., keine Erbserklärung abgegeben haben, der Nachlass erblos geblieben sei. Daher könne eine politische Verfolgung des erblosen Nachlasses nicht angenommen werden.

Weiters bestritt die Finanzprokuratur, dass Ida und Emil Be. keine Erbserklärung abgegeben hatten, um ihre geplante Auswanderung nicht durch den Antritt der Erbschaft zu verhindern. Die Finanzprokuratur vertrat die Ansicht, das Ehepaar Be. habe von einer Erbserklärung im Hinblick auf die aussichtslose finanzielle Lage des Nachlasses abgesehen. Das sei auch daraus zu entnehmen, dass die Ehegatten Be. sehr wohl das Erbe ihrer Tochter Susanne F. angetreten haben.

Hinsichtlich des von der Sammelstelle angeführten Beschlusses der Obersten Rückstellungskommission vom 22. Mai 1964, Rkv 5/64, meinte die Finanzprokuratur, dass für den gegenständlichen Fall nichts gewonnen werden könnte, da der Entscheidung ein anderer Sachverhalt, nämlich eine konkrete Entziehungshandlung, zugrunde liege.

Im Übrigen verwies die Finanzprokuratur auf ihre bisherigen Ausführungen und beantragte die Abweisung der Rückstellungsantrages.

Weitere Verhandlungen

Am 30. September 1964 wandte sich Dr. Ilse Fi. von der Sammelstelle per Brief an John Henry D. in London mit der Frage, ob er als Legatar nach Dr. Lothar F. wüsste, welche lebenden Verwandten Dr. F. zum Zeitpunkt seines Todes hatte und wo diese sich befunden hatten. John Henry D. war aber bereits am 3. August 1960 verstorben.

Auf Dr. Fi.s Ersuchen wurde ein Termin zu einer Besprechung eines allfälligen Vergleichsabschlusses mit der Finanzprokuratur für den 15. Dezember 1964 vereinbart, an der neben Dr. Fi. für die Sammelstelle A auch Dr. Sch. und Dr. Spi. für die Finanzprokuratur teilnahmen. In dieser Besprechung brachte Dr. Fi. zum Ausdruck, dass der Vergleichsbetrag ihrer Ansicht nach etwa 4,000.000,– Schilling betragen müsste.

Am 29. Jänner 1965 fand eine Besprechung zwischen Vertretern der Sammelstelle A (Dr. Weis und Dr. Fi.) und Vertretern der Finanzprokuratur (Dr. Sch. und Dr. Spi.) zur Prüfung der Voraussetzungen für einen allfälligen Vergleich in der Rückstellungssache Dr. F. statt. Im Anschluss an die Besprechung richteten die Vertreter der FLD eine Anfrage an Herrn Ma., den Leiter der Dienststelle für Vermögenssicherungs- und Rückstellungsangelegenheiten bei der FLD für Wien, Niederösterreich und Burgenland. Darin wurde Herr Ma. ersucht, zu ermitteln, in welcher Weise das Sanatorium nach dem Tod Dr. F.s verwendet wurde und weiters, die Erträgnisse der Liegenschaft sowie die Aufwendungen für diese bekannt zu geben.

Am 12. Februar 1965 übermittelte Herr Ma. der Finanzprokuratur den Erhebungsbericht des Außendienstes betreffend die Liegenschaft S.-gasse 14. Dabei teilte er mit, dass für die Liegenschaft seit 1. April 1948 insgesamt 1,194.237,39 Schilling für Erhaltungs-

them that since 1 April 1948 a total of 1,194,237.39 Schilling had been spent on maintenance work for the property and that currently earnings of 138,508.92 Schilling were available. The monthly rental was 20,000 Schilling, from which the landlord had to pay the general running costs (with the exception of electricity, gas, water and heating costs). Pursuant to the lease agreement, the lessee had to pay the landlord any running costs in excess of 22,114.25 Schilling annually.

301 Further negotiations by the Collection Agency at a ministerial level were led by department 16b of the Ministry of Finance, which was responsible for restitution matters and supervision concerning the restitution and property matters processed by the Financial Directorate. These negotiations were led by MR Josef Mi.

302 In a letter dated 14 April 1965, Dr. Georg Weis suggested to MR Josef Mi. at the Federal Ministry of Finance with regard to their prior discussion and after consultations with the board of trustees of the Collection Agency that

"they are prepared to negotiate a lump sum settlement for all [underlined] unresolved claims of both Collection Agencies against the Republic of Austria. The claims concerned were a) pursuant to the draft of the 5th amendment to the Receiving Organizations Act; b) against the Dy[…] Corporation […] amounting to around 60 million Schilling; c) concerning 8,066,619 Schilling which were transferred to the account no. 10551 of the Carinthian Regional Government […]; d) concerning Sanatorium F[...], the file of which was pending under VR-V 40037–37/64 at the Financial Directorate Vienna. Without doubt, it would be practical to settle all [underlined] of these claims together. The duties of the collection agencies could then be swiftly concluded, whereas otherwise the collection agencies would still have to remain active for years until the settlement of all claims had become legally binding. I believe, subject to the consent of the board of trustees, that 60 million Schilling would be an appropriate settlement amount for all of these claims. The settlement amount could be paid in yearly installments of 12 million Schilling. It may not be forgotten that even should the 5th amendment not become law, the tax exemption provided for in the amendment would have to be embodied in law."

Dr. Weis further informed that delegates of the collection agencies were available for a discussion with the Federal Minister of Finance.

303 In the 26th meeting of the board of trustees on 13 May 1965 the proceedings Dy. Corporation, Carinthian accounts [J.], Schl. Company and Sanatorium F. were mentioned as unresolved important restitution proceedings and it was determined that the proceedings concerning Sanatorium F. constituted proceedings in accordance with the State Treaty Implementation Act. The sum in dispute was calculated to be "around 6 million Schilling". It was noted that "all of these proceedings were legally exceptionally complicated" and settlements were desirable. It was further explained that the 5th amendment to the Receiving Organizations Act was to be seen as having been quasi accepted by Parliament although the Federal Ministry of Finance had informed in a discussion that the Minister of Finance wished to resolve the claims of the collection agencies with a monetary payment. Dr. Weis further asserted that he would inform the Federal Ministry of Finance that the collection agencies were in principle prepared to negotiate regarding the settlement of their claims, however he demanded that, with the exception of the Schl. case, all cases cited in the enclosure would also be simultaneously dealt with.

304 On 26 May 1965, a meeting regarding the contents of this letter took place at the Federal Ministry of Finance in the presence of representatives of various offices of the Ministry, the Financial Directorate and the State Financial Procurator's Office. Specifically,

arbeiten aufgewendet worden seien und dass derzeit Erträgnisse von 138.508,92 Schilling zur Verfügung stünden. Der monatliche Mietzins belaufe sich auf 20.000,– Schilling, wovon der Vermieter die allgemeinen Betriebskosten (mit Ausnahme der Kosten für Strom, Gas, Wasser und Heizung) zu tragen habe. Laut Mietvertrag habe jedoch der Mieter dem Vermieter etwaige über jährlich 22.114,25 Schilling liegende Betriebskosten zu ersetzen.

Die weiteren Verhandlungen der Sammelstelle auf Ministeriumsebene wurden von Abteilung 16b des Finanzministeriums, die für Rückstellungsangelegenheiten sowie Aufsicht bezüglich der von der FLD bearbeiteten Rückstellungs- und Vermögensangelegenheiten zuständig war und unter Leitung von MR Josef Mi. stand, geführt. 301

Am 14. April 1965 richtete Dr. Georg Weis in einem Schreiben an MR Josef Mi. im BMF den Vorschlag, dass Bezug nehmend auf eine zuvorgegangene Unterredung mit selbigem und nach Rücksprache mit den Kuratoren der Sammelstellen 302

„diese bereit sind, über die Pauschalabfindung aller [unterstrichen] noch offenen Ansprüche der beiden Sammelstellen gegen die Republik Österreich zu verhandeln. Es handelt sich um die Ansprüche a) nach dem Entwurf der 5. Novelle Auffangorganisationengesetz; b) gegen die Dy[…] AG […] im Werte von ungefähr 60 Millionen Schilling; c) wegen S 8,066.619.-, welche auf das Konto Nr. 10551 der Kärntner Landesregierung übertragen wurden […]; d) wegen des Sanatoriums F[…], welcher Akt unter VR-V 40037–37/64 bei der Finanzlandesdirektion Wien anhängig ist. Es wäre zweifellos zweckmäßig, alle [unterstrichen] diese Ansprüche gemeinsam zu vergleichen. Die Tätigkeit der Sammelstellen könnte dann rasch beendet werden, während die Sammelstellen sonst bis zur rechtskräftigen Erledigung aller Ansprüche noch durch Jahre tätig bleiben müßten. Vorbehaltlich der Zustimmung der Kuratorien glaube ich, daß 60 Millionen Schilling ein angemessener Vergleichsbetrag für alle diese Ansprüche wären. Der Vergleichsbetrag könnte in fünf Jahresraten von je 12 Millionen Schilling bezahlt werden. Nicht vergessen darf werden, daß, auch wenn die 5. Novelle nicht Gesetz werden sollte, die in der Novelle vorgesehene Steuerbefreiung gesetzlich verankert werden müsste."

Weiter kündigte Dr. Weis an, dass Delegierte der Sammelstellen für eine Besprechung mit dem Bundesminister für Finanzen zur Verfügung stünden.

In der 26. Kuratoriumssitzung am 13. Mai 1965 wurden als noch offene wichtige Rückstellungsverfahren der Sammelstelle die Verfahren Dy. AG, Kärntner Konten [J.], Firma Schl. und Sanatorium F. erwähnt und festgehalten, dass es sich beim Verfahren wegen des Sanatoriums F. um ein Verfahren nach dem StVDG handle. Der Wert des Streitgegenstandes wurde mit „ungefähr 6 Millionen Schilling" bemessen. Es wurde dabei angemerkt, dass „alle diese Verfahren rechtlich ausserordentlich kompliziert" liegen und Vergleiche erstebenswert seien. Weiter wurde ausgeführt, dass die 5. Novelle zum Auffangorganisationengesetz als quasi vom Parlament angenommen zugesagt worden war, das BMF jedoch nun in einer Unterredung informiert habe, dass der Finanzminister wünsche, die Ansprüche der Sammelstellen durch eine Geldzahlung abzulösen. Dr. Weis meinte weiter, dass er dem BMF mitteilen werde, dass die Sammelstellen grundsätzlich bereit seien, wegen der Abfindung ihrer Ansprüche zu verhandeln, jedoch verlange, dass auch die in der Beilage angeführten Fälle mit Ausnahme des Falles Schl. gleichzeitig mitverhandelt würden. 303

Am 26. Mai 1965 fand im BMF zum Inhalt dieses Schreibens eine Sitzung unter Beisein von Vertretern verschiedener Dienststellen des Ministeriums sowie der FLD und der Finanzprokuratur statt. Konkret war der von Dr. Weis angebotene Betrag von 60 Millionen Schilling für eine Generalbereinigung mit den Sammelstellen unter Inkludierung des 304

the subject of debate was the amount of 60 million Schilling proposed by Dr. Weis for a general settlement with the collection agencies, including the Sanatorium F. The participants of the collection agencies considered a general settlement as practical. With regard to the Sanatorium F., it was conveyed by the State Financial Procurator's Office that "settlement negotiations with the Collection Agency would take place on the basis of 300,000 Schilling, based on the value of the Sanatorium F[…] of 3 million Schilling. Should it become evident that the value of the property was higher, a correspondingly higher settlement amount would be justifiable." At the same time, it was decided by the participants to demand a breakdown of the amount of 60 million Schilling from Dr. Weis.

305 On 18 June 1965, Dr. Weis informed a member of the board of trustees, Regierungsrat Wilhelm Kr., by letter of the protracted and intense discussions with representatives of the Ministry of Finance regarding the settlement of the Collection Agency's claims pursuant to the planned 5th amendment to the Receiving Organizations Act. In respect to the Sanatorium F., Dr. Weis wrote: "for the F[…]claim, for which I requested 1 million Schilling, 600,000 Schilling have been offered. This is also acceptable. Maybe a further 200,000 Schilling can be accepted. If, however, a general settlement was to be reached, I would not negotiate further for such an amount."

306 On 21 October 1965, the department 16b of the Federal Ministry of Finance compiled an internal report directed at the Federal Minister on the subject of the general settlement with the Collection Agencies. Main focus of the report was the manner in which to proceed and the amount of the individual claims. With regard to the Sanatorium F. the amount of 600,000 Schilling was emphasized and it was stressed that "the matter was to be dealt with *urgently* [sic] as otherwise it was possible that new claims could be asserted by the 'collection agencies'". It was further noted that the Sanatorium F. constituted a valuable property, which was rented out by the Republic of Austria for an attractive rental and that the Financial Directorate Vienna denied the existence of a restitution claim. It was expressly stated: "Upon further inquiry, the Financial Directorate Vienna, which is to decide on this claim, denied the existence of a restitution claim." The State Financial Procurator's Office had been interested in a settlement for a long time but had not been able to achieve this due to resistance from the department 16a of the Federal Ministry of Finance. Originally, the collection agencies had asked for 1 million Schilling but had later reduced this amount to 800,000 Schilling. The settlement amount was justified by the collection agencies in that the property had a value of at least 7 million Schilling. In the report it was further speculated that the "claim evidently seemed to be aimed at settling on an amount of 700,000 Schilling." This was deduced from the previous intention to only demand 600,000 Schilling because the value of the property was previously denoted as 6 million Schilling. It was further stated in the report that concerning the resolution of the so-called heirless property, the collection agencies – subject to a settlement conclusion – had waived all claims to earnings from the property.

307 In the 27th meeting of the board of trustees on 9 November 1965, Dr. Georg Weis informed the members of the board of trustees that talks with the Federal Minister of Finance should take place in the second half of November. It appeared that the government was prepared to pay 16 to 17 million Schilling in order to settle the claims pursuant to the planned 5th amendment to the Receiving Organizations Act and regarding the Sanatorium F.

308 On 17 November 1965, a further meeting concerning the settlement with the collection agencies took place at the Federal Ministry of Finance in the presence of MR Mi. and representatives of departments 16, 16b and 17b and the State Financial Procurator's Office.

Sanatoriums F. Gegenstand der Debatte. Die Teilnehmer der Sitzung betrachteten eine Generalbereinigung dabei als zweckmäßig. Bezüglich des Sanatoriums F. wurde seitens der Finanzprokuratur mitgeteilt, dass „mit der Sammelstelle Vergleichsverhandlungen auf der Basis von S 300.000,–– unter Zugrundelegung eines Wertes des Sanatoriums F[…] von 3. Mill. S laufen würden. Sollte sich herausstellen, daß der Wert des Sanatoriums höher sei, so wäre auch eine entsprechende Erhöhung des Vergleichsbetrages vertretbar." Gleichzeitig wurde von den TeilnehmerInnen beschlossen, von Dr. Weis eine Aufschlüsselung des Betrages von 60 Millionen Schilling einzufordern.

Am 18. Juni 1965 berichtete Dr. Weis dem Kuratoriumsmitglied Regierungsrat Wilhelm Kr. in einem Schreiben über langwierige und heftige Diskussionen mit VertreterInnen des Finanzministeriums zur Abfindung von Ansprüchen der Sammelstelle nach der geplanten 5. Novelle zum Auffangorganisationengesetz. Hinsichtlich des Sanatoriums F. schrieb Dr. Weis: „Für den Anspruch F[...], für den ich 1 Million gefordert hatte, werden S. 600.000,- geboten. Auch das ist akzeptabel. Vielleicht kann man weitere S. 200.000,- durchsetzen. Wenn es aber zu einer Gesamtbereinigung kommt, würde ich wegen eines solchen Betrages nicht mehr viel hin und her handeln." 305

Am 21. Oktober 1965 verfasste die Abteilung 16b des Bundesministeriums für Finanzen einen hausinternen, an den Bundesminister gerichteten Bericht zum Thema des Generalvergleiches mit den Sammelstellen. Darin wurden vor allem Vorgangsweise und Höhe der Einzelforderungen thematisiert. Betreffend das Sanatorium F. wurde der Betrag von 600.000,- Schilling unterstrichen und betont, dass „die Angelegenheit *dringlich* [sic] behandelt werden soll, weil ansonsten allenfalls noch neue Forderungen von den ‚Sammelstellen' erhoben werden könnten." Vermerkt wurde weiter, dass das Sanatorium F. ein wertvolles Objekt darstelle, welches von der Republik zu einem günstigen Mietzins vermietet sei, sowie dass die FLD Wien das Bestehen eines Rückstellungsanspruches verneine. Ausdrücklich wurde festgehalten: „Die FLD Wien, die über diesen Antrag zu entscheiden hat, verneint auf Rückfrage das Bestehen eines Rückstellungsanspruches." Die Finanzprokuratur sei seit langem an einem Vergleich interessiert, hätte diesen wegen des Widerstandes der Abt. 16a des Bundesministeriums für Finanzen aber bislang nicht verwirklichen können. Die Sammelstellen hätten ursprünglich 1 Million Schilling gefordert, hätten diesen Betrag später auf 800.000,- Schilling reduziert. Die Höhe des Vergleichsbetrages würde von den Sammelstellen damit begründet, dass das Objekt mindestens einen Wert von 7 Millionen Schilling habe. Im Bericht wird weiter spekuliert, dass das „Begehren offenbar darauf abgestellt zu sein scheint, auf einen Vergleichsbetrag von 700.000,- Schilling herabzugehen." Dies ginge aus der seinerzeitigen Absicht hervor, nur 600.000,- Schilling zu verlangen, weil der Wert des Objektes früher mit 6 Millionen Schilling angegeben wurde. Weiter wurde in dem Bericht angeführt, dass betreffend die Ablöse des so genannten erblosen Vermögens die Sammelstellen – vorbehaltlich eines Vergleichsabschlusses – auf irgendwelche Erträgnisse aus diesen Liegenschaften verzichtet haben. 306

In der 27. Kuratoriumssitzung am 9. November 1965 informierte Dr. Georg Weis die Kuratoriumsmitglieder, dass eine Unterredung der Sammelstellen mit dem Bundesminister für Finanzen in der zweiten Novemberhälfte stattfinden sollte. Es habe den Anschein, dass die Regierung bereit sei, zur Abfindung der Ansprüche auf Grund der geplanten 5. Novelle zum Auffangorganisationengesetz und in Sachen Sanatorium F. 16 bis 17 Millionen Schilling zu zahlen. 307

Am 17. November 1965 fand im BMF im Beisein von MR Mi. sowie von Vertretern der Abteilungen 16, 16b und 17b und der Finanzprokuratur eine weitere Sitzung wegen 308

Arbitration Panel for *In Rem* Restitution – Decision No. 27/2005

Concerning the debate on the Dy. Corporation, the representatives of department 16b asserted that

> "in line with the intentions of the Federal Minister Dr. Schmitz, considerations of domestic and foreign policy call for a generous settlement and in the case that the differences with the collection agencies regarding the reparation are to be conclusively settled and the latter could thus discontinue their activities, this circumstance alone would justify an increase in the intended amounts."

With regard to the Sanatorium F., it was noted by the State Financial Procurator's Office that "a settlement payment of 600,000 Schilling, which could possibly be a little higher, can be deemed acceptable".

309 On 26 November 1965, a further meeting with the same people took place, in which Dr. Georg Weis and Dr. Fi. also participated. In the minutes of the State Financial Procurator's Office, it was noted that the discussion on the contentious matters, "of which there were underlying legal problems only in the cases of the Dy[…] Corporation and Sanatorium F[…]", was futile as "due to a lack of availability of lawyers who were familiar with the legal problems on the part of the collection agencies, details" could not be explored. It was proposed by the Ministry of Finance that instead of further discussion, all (financial) differences could be split 50:50.

310 In the 28th meeting of the board of trustees on 6 December 1965, Regierungsrat Kr. reported on Georg Weis' settlement negotiations with the Ministry of Finance on 26 November 1965. In these negotiations at the Ministry of Finance, 800,000 Schilling was requested by the Collection Agency for the Sanatorium F.; 700,000 Schilling was offered by the Republic of Austria. Concerning the general settlement, the other claims of the Collection Agency consisted of 16,175,079 Schilling for the settlement of the claims pursuant to the 5th amendment to the Receiving Organizations Act; 2,000,000 Schilling for J. and 10,000,000 Schilling for the Dy. Corporation. The Republic of Austria offered 14,000,000 Schilling for the former, 1,250,000 Schilling for J. and 6,500,000 for Dy. Corporation. In total this amounted to 22,450,000 Schilling. This amount was accepted and passed as the results of the negotiations by the Collection Agency in the 28th meeting of the board of trustees. Subsequently, among other things the resolution was passed "to declare that the Collection Agency A upon payment […] to the collective assets of both collection agencies, shall assert no further claims of whatever nature against the Republic of Austria."

311 On 13 December 1965, Dr. Weis and Dr. Fi. concluded a general settlement with the Federal Ministry of Finance. The settlement amount in the end totaled 22,700,000 Schilling, of which 700,000 Schilling fell to the Sanatorium F.

312 The value of the property at this time was at least 6.2 million Schilling.

313 On 14 December 1965, Dr. Georg Weis informed the members of the board of trustees of the Collection Agency A that he had concluded the settlement with the government the previous day on the basis of his authorization by the board of trustees after he had succeeded "in raising the payment from the Republic of Austria to the collection agencies by 250,000 Schilling." Only the wording and certain conditions would have to be agreed. As before, it was necessary to wait for the law to be passed according to which the settlement was to be carried out.

314 On 28 February 1966, Dr. Georg Weis sent a letter to MR Mi. in the Federal Ministry of Finance in which he explained with reference to further negotiation talks of 23 Feb-

des Vergleichs mit den Sammelstellen statt. Von Vertretern der Abt. 16b wurde in der Debatte um die Dy. AG geltend gemacht, dass

„wie dies auch den Intentionen des Bundesministers Dr. Schmitz entspreche, innen- und außenpolitische Erwägungen eine großzügige Bereinigung gebieten, bzw. dass für den Fall, dass die Wiedergutmachungsdifferenzen mit den Sammelstellen endgültig bereinigt werden und letztere ihre Tätigkeit sohin einstellen könnten, schon dieser Umstand eine Erhöhung der vorgesehenen Beträge rechtfertigen würde."

Betreffend das Sanatorium F. wurde von der Finanzprokuratur angemerkt, „eine Vergleichszahlung von S 600.000,–, die unter Umständen auch etwas höher sein könnte, als vertretbar bezeichnen zu können."

Am 26. November 1965 fand eine weitere Sitzung desselben Personenkreises statt, an der auch Dr. Georg Weis und Dr. Fi. teilnahmen. Im Sitzungsprotokoll der Finanzprokuratur wurde vermerkt, dass die Diskussion über die Streitpunkte, „denen eigentlich nur in den Fällen Dy[…] AG und Sanatorium F[…] juristische Probleme zugrunde lagen", fruchtlos verliefen, da „mangels Vorhandenseins von mit den Rechtsproblemen vertrauten Juristen seitens der Sammelstellen nicht in Details" eingegangen werden konnte. Es wurde seitens des Finanzministeriums vorgeschlagen, statt einer weiteren Diskussion sämtliche (finanziellen) Differenzen im Verhältnis 50 : 50 zu teilen. 309

In der 28. Kuratoriumssitzung am 6. Dezember 1965 berichtete Regierungsrat Kr. über die Vergleichsverhandlung von Dr. Georg Weis mit dem Finanzministerium vom 26. November 1965. In dieser Verhandlung im Finanzministerium war für das Sanatorium F. von der Sammelstelle 800.000,– Schilling gefordert worden, seitens der Republik Österreich wurden dafür 700.000,– Schilling geboten. Den Gesamtvergleich betreffend bestanden die weiteren Forderungen der Sammelstelle in 16.175.059,– Schilling für die Abgeltung der Ansprüche nach der 5. Novelle zum Auffangorganisationengesetz, 2,000.000,– Schilling für die J. und 10,000.000,– Schilling für die Dy. AG. Seitens der Republik würden für ersteres 14,000.000,– Schilling geboten, für die J. 1.250.000,– Schilling und für Dy. AG 6,500.000,– Schilling. Im Gesamten ergab das einen Betrag von 22,450.000,– Schilling. Dieser Betrag wurde als Verhandlungsergebnis seitens der Sammelstelle in der 28. Kuratoriumssitzung akzeptiert und beschlossen. Daraufhin wurde unter anderem der Beschluss gefasst „zu erklären, dass die Sammelstelle A nach Zahlung […] an das gemeinsame Vermögen der beiden Sammelstellen keine weiteren Ansprüche welcher Art immer an die Republik Österreich stellen wird." 310

Am 13. Dezember 1965 schlossen Dr. Weis und Dr. Fi. mit dem BMF den Gesamtvergleich ab. Die Vergleichssumme betrug schließlich 22,700.000,– Schilling, wovon 700.000,– Schilling auf das Sanatorium F. entfielen. 311

Der Wert der Liegenschaft betrug zu diesem Zeitpunkt zumindest 6, 2 Millionen Schilling. 312

Am 14. Dezember 1965 informierte Dr. Georg Weis alle Kuratoriumsmitglieder der Sammelstelle A davon, dass er den Vergleich mit der Regierung aufgrund seiner Ermächtigung durch das Kuratorium am Vortag abgeschlossen habe, nachdem es ihm gelungen war, „die Zahlung der Republik Österreich an die Sammelstellen noch um S. 250.000,– zu erhöhen." Es seien jetzt nur noch die Formulierungen und gewisse Vorbehalte zu vereinbaren. Nach wie vor müsse natürlich das Gesetz abgewartet werden, durch welches der Vergleich durchgeführt werden solle. 313

ruary 1966 as the authorized representative of the board of trustees of the Collection Agency A:

> "In the case that the Collection Agency B was to receive the amount of 22,700,000 Schilling from the Republic of Austria on behalf of the Collection Agency A, a) the Collection Agency A declares […] all claims arising from Article 26 of the State Treaty […] to be settled. b) This declaration particularly refers to all claims of whatever nature resulting from the entitlement to restitution of the 'Sanatorium F[…]', 'J[…]', 'Dy[…] Corporation'."

315 In May 1966, the draft of the Collection Agencies Settlement Act reached the Council of Ministers. In the corresponding address before the Council of Ministers is was stressed that in this law, the obligations undertaken in Article 26 para. 2 State Treaty would be complied with and that several cases which had been disputed for years could be resolved by means of a settlement without protracted proceedings. Further, the collection agencies could end their activities early and the restitution legislation could be concluded. The settlement amount was provided for under the title "Other payments under the State Treaty" in the Federal budget estimate.

316 On 4 July 1966, Dr. Georg Weis informed the members of the board of trustees of Collection Agency A, among other things, that the government bill regarding the lump sum settlement with the collection agencies had been approved by the Finance Committee.

317 **COLLECTION AGENCIES SETTLEMENT ACT**

318 The settlement between the Republic of Austria and the Collection Agency A was embodied in law through the passing of the Collection Agencies Settlement Act of 7 July 1966, Federal Law Gazette No. 150/1966. In this law, the claims of the collection agencies against the Federation for the restitution of property which had remained heirless and had belonged to people who had been persecuted by the National Socialist regime as well as other claims, also including "for the restitution of the property EZ [X1], KG Josefstadt, (Sanatorium F[…])" were settled with a total of 22,700,000 Schilling. The portion of the total amount concerning the property S.-gasse was 700,000 Schilling. In the explanatory remarks to the government bill of the Collection Agencies Settlement Act it was noted that the collection agencies had, in principle, agreed to accept a financial settlement, however, only on the condition that other unresolved claims against the Federation, including the restitution of the Sanatorium F., would be taken care of with a settlement.

319 For the distribution of this amount between the Collection Agencies A and B, the Collection Agencies Settlement Act referred to the provision of para. 2 (3) of the *Bundesgesetz für die Aufteilung der Mittel der „Sammelstellen"* ("Federal Law for the Distribution of Funds of the 'Collection Agencies'", Federal Law Gazette No. 108/1961), according to which the Collection Agency A was to receive 80 percent and the Collection Agency B 20 percent. This was valid irrespective of paras. 7 and 8 of the *Vierte Rückstellungsanspruchsgesetz* ("Fourth Restitution Claims Act"). According to para. 7 of the mentioned act, the aggrieved owner could claim from the collection agencies the transfer of the properties which had been restituted to the agencies or the transfer of assets that the collection agencies had received by means of a settlement or other agreement in exchange for the seized property. If a notification had taken place in accordance with Article 26 para. 2 of the State Treaty, the Collection Agency was obliged to carry out the transfer, otherwise it was to be decided by the Collection Agency whether it transferred the assets which it had received to the aggrieved owner.

Am 28. Februar 1966 richtete Dr. Georg Weis ein Schreiben an MR Mi. im BMF, in welchem er bezugnehmend auf eine weitere Verhandlungsunterredung vom 23. Februar 1966 als Bevollmächtigter des Kuratoriums der Sammelstelle A erklärte: „Für den Fall, dass die Sammelstelle B z.Hd. der Sammelstelle A von der Republik Österreich den Betrag von S 22,700.000,– erhalten, a) erklären die Sammelstelle A [...] ihre sämtliche Ansprüche aus dem Artikel 26 des Staatsvertrages [...] befriedet. b) Diese Erklärung bezieht sich insbesondere auch auf alle Ansprüche welcher Art immer aus dem Titel ‚Sanatorium F[...]‘, ‚J[...]‘, Dy[...] AG‘."

Im Mai 1966 gelangte der Entwurf zum Sammelstellen-Abgeltungsgesetz vor den Ministerrat. Im entsprechenden Vortrag vor dem Ministerrat wurde betont, dass mit dem Gesetz der in Artikel 26 § 2 des Staatsvertrages übernommenen Verpflichtung nachgekommen würde und dass einige bereits seit Jahren umstrittene Fälle im Vergleichwege ohne langwierige Verfahren bereinigt werden könnten. Weiter könnten die Sammelstellen ihre Tätigkeit frühzeitig beenden und die Rückstellungsgesetzgebung abgeschlossen werden. Der Ablösebetrag wurde beim Titel „Sonstige Zahlungen aus dem Staatsvertrag" im Bundesvoranschlag 1966 vorgesehen.

Am 4. Juli 1966 teilte Dr. Georg Weis den Mitgliedern des Kuratoriums der Sammelstelle A unter anderem mit, dass der Entwurf des Gesetzes über den Pauschalvergleich mit den Sammelstellen vom Finanzausschuss genehmigt worden war.

SAMMELSTELLEN-ABGELTUNGSGESETZ

Der Vergleich zwischen der Republik Österreich und der Sammelstelle A wurde durch Erlassung des Sammelstellen-Abgeltungsgesetzes vom 7. Juli 1966, BGBl 150/1966, gesetzlich verankert. In diesem Gesetz wurden die Ansprüche der Sammelstellen gegen den Bund auf Rückstellung von erblos gebliebenen Vermögen, die durch den Nationalsozialismus verfolgten Personen gehört hatten, sowie andere Ansprüche, darunter auch „auf Rückstellung der Liegenschaft EZ [X1], KG Josefstadt (Sanatorium F[...])" mit insgesamt 22,700.000,– Schilling abgegolten. Der die Liegenschaft S.-gasse betreffende Anteil an der Gesamtsumme betrug 700.000,– Schilling. In den Erläuternden Bemerkungen zur Regierungsvorlage zum Sammelstellen-Abgeltungsgesetz wurde darauf verwiesen, dass sich die Sammelstellen grundsätzlich für eine Geldablöse bereit erklärt hätten, jedoch nur unter der Bedingung, dass auch andere noch offen gebliebene Ansprüche gegenüber dem Bund, unter anderem Rückstellung der Liegenschaft Sanatorium F., durch Vergleich geregelt würden.

Für die Aufteilung dieses Betrages auf die Sammelstellen A und B verwies das Sammelstellen-Abgeltungsgesetz auf die Bestimmung § 2 Abs 3 des Bundesgesetzes für die Aufteilung der Mittel der „Sammelstellen" (BGBl 108/1961), wonach auf die Sammelstelle A 80 Prozent und auf die Sammelstelle B 20 Prozent zu entfallen hatten. Dies galt unbeschadet der §§ 7 und 8 des 4. Rückstellungsanspruchsgesetzes. Zufolge § 7 des genannten Gesetzes konnte der geschädigte Eigentümer bei der Sammelstelle die Ausfolgung des an diese rückgestellten Vermögens beanspruchen bzw. die Ausfolgung von Vermögen, das der Sammelstelle aufgrund eines Vergleiches oder sonstigen Vertrages an Stelle des entzogenen Vermögens zugekommen war. War eine Anmeldung nach Artikel 26 § 2 des Staatsvertrages erfolgt, war die Sammelstelle zur Ausfolgung verpflichtet, andernfalls stand es der Sammelstelle frei, ob sie das ihr zugekommene Vermögen an die geschädigten EigentümerInnen ausfolgte.

So wurden die von der Sammelstelle erhaltenen Vergleichssummen für die Fälle „Dy[...] AG" und „J[...]" an die Billigkeitswerber (nach Abzug einer Mühewaltungsgebühr) übermittelt.

Arbitration Panel for *In Rem* Restitution – Decision No. 27/2005

320   Hence, the settlement amounts received for the cases "Dy[…] Corporation" and "J[…]" were conveyed to the applicants for equitable relief (upon deduction of a fee for trouble taken).

321   However, such a transfer of the settlement sum for the property EZ X1, S.-gasse 14 did not occur. Neither a notification concerning the Sanatorium F. in accordance with Article 26 para. 2 of the State Treaty had taken place, nor were there any applicants for equitable relief for the property.

322   Dr. Georg Weis informed MR Mi. on 4 August 1966 that the funds from the lump sum settlement, less the amounts for the two applicants for equitable relief, were intended for individual allocations to the oldest age groups of formerly persecuted persons living in Austria.

323   On 30 September 1966, Dr. Georg Weis noted regarding the file EZ X1, KG Josefstadt, Sanatorium F. that the file had been concluded and completed. The Collection Agencies Settlement Act was cited as the reason for this.

324   On 12 October 1966, Dr. Georg Weis informed the members of the board of trustees of the Collection Agency A, among other things,

"that the payment of 22,700,000 Schilling to be made on the basis of the law no. 150/66 has been received. Of this amount, 14 million Schilling are to settle the claims for heirless property, while 700,000 Schilling of the remaining amount are allocated to the claim for Sanatorium F[…] and the remaining amount is allocated to the equity-based cases Dy[…] Corporation and J[…]."

325   In the 30th meeting of the board of trustees of the Collection Agency A on 3 November 1966, 14.7 million Schilling of the total of 22.7 million Schilling was declared as capital and reserves and 8 million Schilling was declared as administrative and third party money in the balance sheet of the Collection Agency A.

326   On 14 November 1966, the Collection Agency A withdrew its claim for the restitution of the property EZ X1, KG Josefstadt.

327   Pursuant to the order of the District Court Innere Stadt of 24 November 1966, the notice in the land register regarding the initiation of restitution proceedings in accordance with the Second Restitution Act was deleted upon request of the Financial Directorate for Vienna, Lower Austria and Burgenland of 21 November 1966, VR-V 40.085-44/66.

328   **Persons entitled to the inheritance of Lothar F.**

329   Lothar F. opted out of the Jewish Religious Community on 15 June 1917 and his wife Susanne F. opted out on 17 April 1923. They were considered Jews in accordance with the Nuremberg Laws for reasons of origin. For this reason the operation of the Sanatorium F. was subsequently put under provisional administration and Dr. F. and his wife were forced to wash the pavement in front of the sanatorium. After the death of Dr. F., his estate was initially considered "Jewish property" and a list of assets was submitted for the estate in compliance with the "Announcement of the Ordinance on the Registration of Jewish Property of 26 April 1938", Austrian Law Gazette 1938/10. The sale of the property S.-gasse 14 could only be carried out after receiving the approval of the Property Transaction Office.

330   Dr. Lothar F. died on 3 April 1938. In his last will and testament dated 10 October 1937, his wife Susanne F., née Be. (first marriage Str.) was appointed as his heir. However, she died at the same time as him.

Eine solche Ausfolgung der Abgeltungssumme für die Liegenschaft EZ X1, S.-gasse 321
14, fand jedoch nicht statt. Eine Anmeldung nach Artikel 26 § 2 des Staatsvertrages war
betreffend das Sanatorium F. nicht erfolgt, noch gab es BilligkeitswerberInnen hinsichtlich der Liegenschaft.

Dr. Georg Weis informierte MR Mi. am 4. August 1966, dass die Geldmittel aus dem 322
Pauschalvergleich abzüglich der Summen für die beiden BilligkeitswerberInnen für individuelle Zuwendungen an die ältesten Jahrgänge in Österreich wohnhafter ehemals verfolgter Personen vorgesehen waren.

Am 30. September 1966 wurde zum Akt EZ X1 KG Josefstadt, Sanatorium F., von Dr. 323
Georg Weis vermerkt, dass der vorliegende Akt abgeschlossen werde und erledigt sei. Als
Begründung wurde das Sammelstellen-Abgeltungsgesetz genannt.

Am 12. Oktober 1966 teilte Dr. Georg Weis den Mitgliedern des Kuratoriums der Sam- 324
melstelle A unter anderem mit

„dass der aufgrund des Gesetzes Nr. 150/66 zu zahlende Betrag von S. 22,700.000,–
eingegangen ist. Von diesem Betrag sind 14 Millionen Sch. die Abgeltung der Ansprüche auf erbloses Eigentum, während vom Restbetrag S. 700.000,– auf den Anspruch
Sanatorium F[...] entfallen und der sodann verbleibende Betrag auf die Billigkeitsfälle
Dy[...] AG und J[...]."

In der 30. Kuratoriumssitzung der Sammelstelle A am 3. November 1966 wurden in der 325
Bilanz der Sammelstelle A von den 22,7 Millionen Schilling 14,700.000,– Schilling als Eigenvermögen und 8,000.000,– Schilling als Verwaltungs- und fremde Gelder deklariert.

Am 14. November 1966 zog die Sammelstelle A ihren Antrag auf Rückstellung der Lie- 326
genschaft EZ X1, KG Josefstadt zurück.

Mit Beschluss des BG Innere Stadt Wien vom 24. November 1966 wurde die grund- 327
bücherliche Anmerkung der Einleitung des Rückstellungsverfahrens nach dem 2. RStG
aufgrund des Antrages der FLD für Wien, Niederösterreich und Burgenland vom 21. November 1966, VR-V 40.085-44/66, gelöscht.

Lothar F.s Erbberechtigte 328

Dr. Lothar F. trat am 15. Juni 1917, Susanne F. am 17. April 1923 aus der Israelitischen 329
Religionsgemeinschaft aus. Sie galten aus Abstammungsgründen gemäß den Nürnberger
Gesetzen als Juden. Aus diesem Grund wurde in der Folge der Betrieb des Sanatoriums F.
unter kommissarische Verwaltung gestellt und wurden Dr. F. und seine Frau gezwungen,
den Gehsteig vor dem Sanatorium zu waschen. Nach dem Tod Dr. F.s wurde sein Nachlass zunächst als „jüdisches Vermögen" betrachtet und ein Vermögensverzeichnis gemäß
der „Kundmachung der Verordnung über die Anmeldung des Vermögens von Juden vom
26. April 1938", GBl f.d.L.Ö. 1938/10, für den Nachlass abgegeben. Auch konnte der Verkauf der Liegenschaft S.-gasse 14 erst nach Genehmigung durch die Vermögensverkehrsstelle durchgeführt werden.

Dr. Lothar F. starb am 3. April 1938. In seinem Testament vom 10. Oktober 1937 war 330
seine Ehefrau Susanne F., geborene Be. (in erster Ehe Str.), als Erbin eingesetzt. Diese starb
jedoch gleichzeitig mit ihm.

Die vorgesehenen ErsatzerbInnen, die Schwiegereltern Dr. Lothar F.s, Emil und Ida 331
Be., traten 1927 bzw. 1938 aus der Israelitischen Religionsgemeinschaft aus. Sie galten jedoch nach den Nürnberger Gesetzen von 1935 als Juden. Sie verzichteten 1938 auf ihr Erb-

Arbitration Panel for *In Rem* Restitution – Decision No. 27/2005

331 The intended alternate heirs, Dr. Lothar F.'s parents-in-law, Emil and Ida Be. opted out of the Jewish Religious Community in 1927 and 1938. However, they were considered Jews pursuant to the Nuremberg Laws of 1935. In 1938 they renounced their right to the inheritance of Lothar F., however they accepted the inheritance of their daughter Susanne F. Emil Be. died in Vienna in 1941. In 1942, Ida Be. was deported to Maly Trostinec near Minsk and murdered.

332 Hence, in accordance with Lothar F.'s testamentary disposition, the statutory succession was to come into effect, with the exclusion of his sister Hertha L., born on 23 May 1895 and her descendants. At the time of her brother's death, Hertha L. was in the USA.

333 As Dr. Lothar F.'s parents, Dr. Julius F. and Albertine F. had already died and other than Hertha L., Dr. Lothar F. had no further siblings, in line with statutory succession the descendants of both sets of deceased grandparents of Lothar F., Carl and Karoline Ro. and Daniel and Marie F. were entitled to the inheritance: Rosa G., Ernst F., Cäcilie F., Marie Re. and Paul F.

334 They were all considered Jews in the meaning of National Socialist legislation on the basis of their origin or religious affiliation and were all subjected to acts of discrimination and persecution directed against Jews:

ROSA G.

335 Rosa G., born on 28 August 1868 was Lothar F.'s maternal aunt. She was the daughter of Carl and Karoline Ro. They had another child: Albertine Ro., married F., born on 19 August 1872, died on 27 November 1904, mother of Dr. Lothar F. Rosa G. belonged to the Jewish Religious Community, at least until her marriage on 28 September 1890 to Rudolf G., born on 26 June 1863. She died on 25 January 1943 in Theresienstadt.

CÄCILIE F., MARIE RE., PAUL F.

336 Cäcilie F., née Kl., born on 27 August 1871 was the widow of Bernard F., who had passed away on 20 December 1936. He was one of Dr. Lothar F.'s two paternal uncles. As prescribed for Jews, Cäcilie F. submitted the list of assets on 30 June 1938. The list of assets for the estate of Bernhard F. was submitted on the same day. In the Reich Flight Tax decision of 20 September 1938, the value of the assets of Cäcilie F. and her children was estimated to be 180,133 Reichsmark. Cäcilie F. died in early 1942 in Angers, located in a part of France which had been occupied by National Socialist Germany since 1940. She had two children with Bernhard F.: Marie Re. and Paul F.

337 In the last will and testament of Bernhard F., dated 6 October 1933, made public by the District Court Innere Stadt Vienna on 22 December 1936, Marie Re. (90 %) and Paul F. (10 %) were appointed as heirs. In March 1938, the probate proceedings had not yet been concluded. On 30 June 1938 as prescribed for Jews, the list of assets had been submitted for the estate. In the notice of amendment regarding the list of assets for the estate of Bernhard F., one of the items recorded was the deposit of the inheritance fee and the transfer of the remaining amount to the heirs. After the submission of an unconditional declaration of the acceptance of the inheritance, the estate was devolved to the heirs Marie Re. and Paul F. in accordance with the testamentary ratios. The date of the devolution cannot be established.

338 Marie Re., née F., born on 3 February 1895 was married to Anton Re., born on 14 June 1890. She left the Jewish Community Vienna on 2 April 1920. In April 1938 she and her husband and children left their residence in Vienna. Marie and Anton declared their assets

Schiedsinstanz für Naturalrestitution – Entscheidung Nr. 27/2005

recht nach Lothar F., traten jedoch die Erbschaft nach ihrer Tochter Susanne F. an. Emil Be. starb 1941 in Wien, 1942 wurde Ida Be. nach Maly Trostinec bei Minsk deportiert und ermordet.

Somit hatte nach testamentarischer Verfügung Dr. Lothar F.s die gesetzliche Erbfolge unter Ausschluss seiner Schwester Hertha L., geboren am 23. Mai 1895, und deren Nachkommen einzutreten. Hertha L. befand sich zum Zeitpunkt des Todes ihres Bruders in den USA. 332

Da Dr. Lothar F.s Eltern, Dr. Julius F. und Albertine F., bereits verstorben waren und es neben Hertha L. keine weiteren Geschwister Dr. Lothar F.s gab, waren gemäß gesetzlicher Erbfolge die Nachkommen der beiden verstorbenen Großelternpaare Lothar F.s, Carl und Karoline Ro. und Daniel und Marie F., erbberechtigt: Rosa G., Ernst F., Cäcilie F., Marie Re. und Paul F. 333

Sie alle galten aufgrund ihrer Abstammung oder aufgrund ihrer Religionszugehörigkeit als Juden im Sinne der nationalsozialistischen Gesetzgebung und unterlagen den gegen Juden gerichteten Diskriminierungen und Verfolgungshandlungen: 334

ROSA G.

Rosa G., geboren am 28. August 1868, war Lothar F.s Tante mütterlicherseits. Sie war Tochter von Carl und Karoline Ro. Diese hatten ein weiteres Kind: Albertine Ro., verheiratete F., geboren am 19. August 1872, verstorben am 27. November 1904, Mutter Dr. Lothar F.s. Rosa G. gehörte zumindest bis zu ihrer Heirat am 28. September 1890 mit Rudolf G., geboren am 26. Juni 1863, der Israelitischen Religionsgemeinschaft an. Sie starb am 25. Jänner 1943 in Theresienstadt. 335

CÄCILIE F., MARIE RE., PAUL F.

Cäcilie F., geborene Kl., geboren am 27. August 1871, war Witwe des am 20. Dezember 1936 verstorbenen Bernard F. Dieser war einer der beiden Onkeln Dr. Lothar F.s väterlicherseits. Cäcilie F. gab am 30. Juni 1938 das für Juden vorgeschriebene Vermögensverzeichnis ab. Am selben Tag wurde auch das Vermögensverzeichnis für die Verlassenschaft nach Bernhard F. eingereicht. Im Reichsfluchtsteuerbescheid vom 20. September 1938 wurde das Vermögen von Cäcilie F. und deren Kindern mit 180.133,– Reichsmark veranschlagt. Cäcilie F. starb Anfang 1942 in Angers, gelegen im seit 1940 vom nationalsozialistischen Deutschland besetzten Teil Frankreichs. Sie hatte mit Bernhard F. zwei Kinder: Marie Re. und Paul F. 336

Im Testament Bernhard F.s vom 6. Oktober 1933, kundgemacht vom BG Innere Stadt Wien am 22. Dezember 1936, wurden Marie Re. zu 90 % und Paul F. zu 10 % als ErbInnen eingesetzt. Im März 1938 war das Verlassenschaftsverfahren noch nicht beendet, es wurde am 30. Juni 1938 für die Verlassenschaft das für Juden vorgeschriebene Vermögensverzeichnis abgegeben. In der Änderungsanzeige zum Vermögensverzeichnis des Nachlasses nach Bernhard F. wurde als einer der Posten die Erlegung der Erbgebühr und andererseits die Ausfolgung des verbleibenden Betrages an die ErbInnen verzeichnet. Den ErbInnen Marie Re. und Paul F. wurde nach Abgabe einer unbedingten Erbserklärung der Nachlass entsprechend der testamentarisch verfügten Erbquoten eingeantwortet. Der Zeitpunkt der Einantwortung kann nicht festgestellt werden. 337

Marie Re., geborene F., geboren am 3. Februar 1895, war verheiratet mit Anton Re., geboren am 14. Juni 1890. Sie trat am 2. April 1920 aus der IKG Wien aus. Im April 1938 verließ sie mit ihrem Ehemann und ihren Kindern ihren Wiener Wohnsitz. Marie und Anton 338

on 26 September 1938 from Zurich by means of a list of assets. Marie submitted assets amounting to 15,471 Reichsmark and a 90 % share of the estate of her father Bernhard F., which had been valued at 1,580,018 Reichsmark according to his list of assets. Anton Re. declared assets of 480,000 Reichsmark. In the Reich Flight Tax decision of 25 August 1939, the value of the assets of Marie and Anton Re. was estimated at 1 million Reichsmark. Pursuant to the order of the Secret State Police of 26 September 1941, the assets of Anton and Marie Re. and their children Elisabeth, born on 22 June 1925 and Robert Re., born on 20 May 1921, were confiscated.

339 Paul F., born on 9 May 1893 left the Jewish Religious Community on 30 October 1922. He was also considered a Jew according to the Nuremberg Laws. He was the deputy director of the So.-factory and took part in the "Emigration Operation Gildemeester" with his wife Margarethe F. in order to be able to quickly emigrate and to be able to pay the taxes prescribed by the National Socialist regime (Reich Flight Tax, Jewish capital levy) through the liquidation of their assets. The aim of Operation Gildemeester was to organize, finance and accelerate the emigration of needy persons who were not members of the Jewish Religious Community but who were, however, considered Jews in accordance with the Nuremberg Laws. For this purpose, wealthy Jews were to transfer their entire assets to the trustee appointed by the State Commissioner for Private Enterprises on 30 May 1938, the banking house *Krentschker & Co.* for administration and utilization, whereby a certain percentage of these assets was to be set aside to finance the emigration operation. On 19 May 1938, Paul F. transferred his assets to the banking house *Krentschker & Co.* in trust. On 16 June 1938, Paul and Margarethe F. emigrated to Paris. On 9 January 1939, the banking house *Krentschker & Co.* assessed the assets of Paul and Margarethe F. to be worth 320,257.41 Reichsmark as at 27 April 1938.

ERNST F.

340 Dr. Ernst Jakob F., born on 8 April 1865 was the paternal uncle of Lothar F. He had two siblings: Bernhard F. (see above) and Julius F., born on 3 December 1859, died on 1 May 1923, father of Dr. Lothar F. Ernst F. had been the General Director and majority shareholder of the So. Cooperation. He emigrated to France on 17 March 1939 as a Czech national and therefore "member of the protectorate". Ernst F., his wife Ella F. and his sister-in-law Cäcilie F. were located in occupied France (Angers) in 1942. Dr. Ernst F.'s assets were declared reverted to the German Reich. Property assets and securities, insurance policies and further assets totaling at least 200,000 Reichsmark also belonged to him as a retired businessman of the So. Corporation. Dr. Ernst F. died on 4 January 1943 in Paris.

THE LEGATEE JOHN HENRY D.

341 John Henry D., who had been remembered by Dr. Lothar F. with a legacy of weaponry and jewelry, was born on 27 December 1898 in Olton, England. He was Roman Catholic, lived in Vienna, L.-gasse 19 and was married to Else, née Wei. She was the sister-in-law of Paul F. D. left Vienna on 4 September 1939 and emigrated to England.

Re. deklarierten ihr Vermögen am 26. September 1938 mittels Vermögensverzeichnisses von Zürich aus. Marie Re. gab ein Vermögen im Wert von 15.471,– Reichsmark sowie eine 90%ige Beteiligung am Nachlass nach ihrem Vater Bernhard F. an, welcher laut dessen Vermögensverzeichnis mit 1,580.018,– Reichsmark bewertet wurde. Anton Re. deklarierte ein Vermögen von 480.000,– Reichsmark. Im Reichsfluchtsteuerbescheid vom 25. August 1939 wurde das Vermögen von Marie und Anton Re. mit 1,000.000,– Reichsmark veranschlagt. Mit Verfügung der Gestapo vom 26. September 1941 wurde das Vermögen von Anton und Marie Re. sowie deren Kinder Elisabeth, geboren am 22. Juni 1925, und Robert Re., geboren am 20. Mai 1921, beschlagnahmt.

Paul F., geboren am 9. Mai 1893, trat am 30. Oktober 1922 aus der IKG Wien aus. Auch er galt jedoch nach den Nürnberger Gesetzen als Jude. Er war als Direktor-Stellvertreter in der So.-fabrik tätig und nahm mit seiner Frau Margarethe F. an der so genannten „Auswanderungsaktion Gildemeester" teil, um rasch auswandern und die vom nationalsozialistischen Regime vorgeschriebenen Steuern (Reichsfluchtsteuer, Judenvermögensabgabe) durch Liquidierung ihres Vermögens bezahlen zu können. Die Aktion Gildemeester hatte den Zweck, die Auswanderung von bedürftigen Personen, die nicht Mitglieder der IKG waren, nach den Nürnberger Gesetzen aber als Juden galten, zu organisieren, zu finanzieren und zu beschleunigen. Dazu sollten wohlhabende Juden ihr gesamtes Vermögen dem durch den Staatskommissar in der Privatwirtschaft am 30. Mai 1938 für diese Aktion bestellten Treuhänder, das Bankhaus Krentschker & Co., zur Verwaltung und Verwertung übergeben, wobei ein bestimmter Prozentsatz dieses Vermögens zur Finanzierung der Auswanderungsaktion bereitzustellen war. Am 19. Mai 1938 übergab Paul F. dem Bankhaus Krentschker & Co. treuhänderisch sein Vermögen. Am 16. Juni 1938 emigrierten Paul und Margarethe F. nach Paris. Das Bankhaus Krentschker & Co. bemaß am 9. Jänner 1939 das Vermögen von Paul und Margarethe F. zum Stand von 27. April 1938 mit 320.257,41 Reichsmark. 339

ERNST F.

Dr. Ernst Jakob F., geboren am 8. April 1865, war Onkel Dr. Lothar F.s väterlicherseits. Er hatte zwei Geschwister: Bernhard F. (siehe oben) und Julius F., geboren am 3. Dezember 1859, verstorben am 1. Mai 1923, Vater von Dr. Lothar F. Ernst F. war Generaldirektor und Hauptaktionär der So. AG gewesen. Er wanderte als tschechischer Staatsangehöriger und damit „Protektoratsangehöriger" am 17. März 1939 nach Frankreich aus. Ernst F., seine Frau Ella F. und seine Schwägerin Cäcilie F. befanden sich 1942 im vom Deutschen Reich besetzten Frankreich (Angers). Dr. Ernst F.s Vermögen wurde als dem Deutschen Reich verfallen erklärt. Zu seinem Vermögen als pensionierter Unternehmer der So. AG gehörten Liegenschaftswerte und Wertpapiere, Versicherungspolizzen und weitere Vermögenschaften in Gesamthöhe von mindestens 200.000,– Reichsmark. Dr. Ernst F. starb am 4. Jänner 1943 in Paris. 340

DER LEGATAR JOHN HENRY D.

Der von Dr. Lothar F. mit einem Vermächtnis über Waffen und Schmuck bedachte John Henry D. wurde am 27. Dezember 1898 in Olton, England, geboren. Er war römisch-katholisch, wohnte in Wien, L.-gasse 19 und war mit Else, geborene Wei., verheiratet. Diese war mit Paul F. verschwägert. D. verließ Wien am 4. September 1939 und emigrierte nach England. 341

Arbitration Panel for *In Rem* Restitution – Decision No. 27/2005

342 **The Applicants**

DESCENDANTS OF ROSA G.

343 Rosa G. passed away on 25 January 1943, leaving two sons: Herbert G. and Georg G.

344 Herbert G. was born on 25 December 1891. He married Amalia Gy., born on 20 January 1900 or 25 January 1899. Herbert G. died on 19 September 1968, his wife on 19 December 1999. Their children are Andrew (Andreas) G., born on 8 November 1925 and Stephan (Stefan) G., born on 4 November 1928.

345 Georg G., born on 2 April 1896, died on 4 February 1973 in New York State, was married to Gerta G., née W., born on 23 May 1912. Their daughter Marion R.-G. was born on 29 November 1936 in Vienna. She is married to Jacques R. Gerda E. Bl., widowed G., assigned all of her claims during the present proceedings regarding the Sanatorium F. to her daughter Marion R.-G.

346 The applicants Andrew G., Stephan G. and Marion R.-G. are therefore descendants of Rosa G.

DESCENDANTS OF MARIE RE. and PAUL F.

347 Marie Re. died on 24 April 1965 in Vienna. Her estate was devolved in its entirety to her widower Anton Re. by a certificate of inheritance dated 9 March 1966 (9 A 371/65-16). After his death on 16 March 1968, his estate was devolved in equal halves to his children Elizabeth An., née Re. and Robert B. Re. with a certificate of inheritance dated 1 August 1968 (9 A 281/68-20). Robert Re. was born on 20 May 1921 in Vienna, S.-gasse 14. His sister Elisabeth Re., born on 22 June 1925 in Vienna, S.-gasse 14, married Elizabeth An., died on 13 April 1971 in Palo Alto, California. She was divorced and left behind two sons, Richard An., born on 22 December 1952 in New York City and Christopher An. born on 13 August 1956 in Vermont. The trust established in accordance with the last will and testament of Elizabeth An. (administrated by the Crocker National Bank) was dissolved on 7 October 1977 and the balance was shared equally between Christopher and Richard An.

348 The applicants Robert Re., Richard An. and Christopher An. are therefore descendants of Marie Re.

349 Paul F. died on 8 February 1967. His wife Margarethe F., née Wei., born on 26 May 1898 died on 30 November 1990 in New York. The marriage remained childless. In her last will and testament, Margarethe F. appointed Doris A. and Alfred S. (both children of the cousin of her deceased husband, see below) as her universal legal successors.

DESCENDANTS OF ERNST F.

350 With a certificate of inheritance dated 28 June 1949 (5 A 663/46-26, District Court Döbling), Dr. Ernst F.'s estate was devolved to his daughters Eva Pe., née F., born on 29 March 1907 in Vienna, S.-gasse 14 and Margarethe S., née F., born on 13 January 1899, each receiving half.

351 Eva Pe. died on 9 December 2003. The heirs appointed in her last will and testament are her daughters Marietta P. and Doris A., each receiving half. Doris A. – also the heir of Margarethe F. (see above) – was born in Budapest on 2 April 1932 as the daughter of Eva and Georg Pe.

Schiedsinstanz für Naturalrestitution – Entscheidung Nr. 27/2005

Die AntragstellerInnen 342

NACHKOMMEN NACH ROSA G.

Rosa G. verstarb am 25. Jänner 1943 und hinterließ zwei Söhne: Herbert G. und Georg 343 G.

Herbert G. wurde am 25. Dezember 1891 geboren. Er heiratete Amalia Gy., geboren 344 am 20. Jänner 1900 oder am 25. Jänner 1899. Herbert G. verstarb am 19. September 1968, seine Frau am 19. Dezember 1999. Deren gemeinsame Kinder sind Andrew (Andreas) G., geboren am 8. November 1925, und Stephan (Stefan) G., geboren am 4. November 1928.

Georg G., geboren am 2. April 1896, verstorben am 4. Februar 1973 in New York State, 345 war verheiratet mit Gerta G., geborene W., geboren am 23. Mai 1912. Die gemeinsame Tochter Marion R.-G. wurde am 29. November 1936 in Wien geboren. Sie ist mit Jacques R. verheiratet. Gerda E. Bl., verwitwete G., trat im Rahmen des gegenständlichen Verfahrens sämtliche Ansprüche in Sachen Sanatorium F. an ihre Tochter Marion R.-G. ab.

Die AntragstellerInnen Andrew G., Stephan G. und Marion R.-G. sind somit Deszen- 346 dentInnen von Rosa G.

NACHKOMMEN NACH MARIE RE. und PAUL F.

Marie Re. starb am 24. April 1965 in Wien. Ihr Nachlass wurde mit Einantwortungs- 347 urkunde vom 9. März 1966 (9 A 371/65-16) ihrem Witwer Anton Re. zur Gänze eingeantwortet. Nach dessen Ableben am 16. März 1968 wurde sein Nachlass mit Einantwortungsurkunde vom 1. August 1968 (9 A 281/68-20) seinen Kindern Elizabeth An., geborene Re., und Robert B. Re. je zur Hälfte eingeantwortet. Robert Re. wurde am 20. Mai 1921 in Wien, S.-gasse 14, geboren. Seine Schwester Elisabeth Re., geboren am 22. Juni 1925 in Wien, S.-gasse 14, verheiratete Elizabeth An., verstarb am 13. April 1971 in Palo Alto, California. Sie war geschieden und hinterließ ihre beiden Söhne Richard An., geboren am 22. Dezember 1952 in New York City und Christopher An., geboren am 13. August 1956 in Vermont. Der gemäß dem Testament Elizabeth An.s errichtete „Trust" (verwaltet durch die Crocker National Bank) wurde am 7. Oktober 1977 aufgelöst und das Guthaben zu gleichen Teilen Christopher und Richard An. zugewiesen.

Die Antragsteller Robert Re., Richard An. und Christopher An. sind somit Deszenden- 348 ten von Marie Re.

Paul F. starb am 8. Februar 1967. Seine Frau Margarethe F., geborene Wei., geboren am 349 26. Mai 1898, starb am 30. November 1990 in New York. Die Ehe blieb kinderlos. In ihrem Testament setzte Margarethe F. zu gleichen Teilen Doris A. und Alfred S. (beides Kinder der Cousinen ihres verstorbenen Gatten, siehe unten) als ihre GesamtrechtsnachfolgerInnen ein.

NACHKOMMEN NACH ERNST F.

Dr. Ernst F.s Nachlass wurde mit Einantwortungsurkunde vom 28. Juni 1949 (5 A 350 663/46-26, BG Döbling) je zur Hälfte seinen Töchtern Eva Pe., geborene F., geboren am 29. März 1907 in Wien, S.-gasse 14, und Margarethe S., geborene F., geboren am 13. Jänner 1899, eingeantwortet.

Eva Pe. starb am 9. Dezember 2003. Ihre testamentarisch eingesetzten Erbinnen sind 351 je zur Hälfte deren Töchter Marietta P. und Doris A. Doris A. – auch Erbin nach Margarethe F. (s. o.) – wurde am 2. April 1932 in Budapest als Tochter von Eva und Georg Pe. geboren.

352   Margarethe S. died on 30 August 1977 in New York State. In her last will and testament of 17 May 1974, she nominated her son Alfred as executor and sole beneficiary of her estate. Alfred S. was born on 21 January 1927 as the son of Margarethe and Paul S.

353   The applicants Marietta P., Doris A. and Alfred S. are therefore descendants of Dr. Ernst F.

7. Consideration of Evidence

354   The established facts are based on the documents submitted by the applicants, the public land register, the reports of the Historical Commission and the archival objects researched by the Arbitration Panel.

355   In 1976, the file of the authority leading the proceedings, the Financial Directorate for Vienna, Lower Austria and Burgenland could no longer be found. A letter from the Federal Ministry of Finance to the State Financial Procurator's Office (no. 73.345/9-I/8/76) dated 26 November 1976 was enclosed with the State Financial Procurator's Office file VI-30254 (Ida De.), from which it can be inferred that it had not been possible for the Federal Ministry of Finance to obtain the restitution files of the Financial Directorate Vienna, as they were not available in the corresponding archive "VR" [= *Vermögensrestitution* "property restitution"]. The Arbitration Panel was also unable, despite intensive research, to locate the file.

356   The findings regarding the incident that on 2 or 3 April 1938, Dr. Lothar F. and his wife Susanne F. were forced by the Nazi henchmen to wash the pavement in front of the "Sanatorium F[…]" in S.-gasse 14 is founded on the logical and believable memories of Eva Pe., who had described them to Cynthia Miller, Deputy Director of the Office of European Affairs in a letter dated 12 March 1990.

357   The findings that the Sanatorium had been operating until the building had been requisitioned by the German Armed Forces results, among other things, from the letter from the head of the regional division of the "German Workers' Front" (National Socialist Party) to the trustee of the estate Dr. St. dated 5 October 1939 contained in the probate file of Lothar F., in which the head of the regional division Fö. stated: "As a result of the takeover of the Sanatorium F[...] by the Army Recruitment Inspectorate Vienna, the dissolution of the sanatorium and thus the dismissal of the company's employees was necessary."

358   The increased use of the building by the Army Recruitment Inspectorate and the settlement of additional expenses incurred by this by means of the sale of parts of the sanatorium's inventory are determined from the invoice book of the trustee of the estate, enclosure M "report on the assets – entry post no. 27".

359   The finding that the operation of the sanatorium had already been run by a provisional administrator (by the National Socialist party member M.) at the time of Dr. F.'s death and after arises, among other things, from the report of the notary N. to the District Court Josefstadt (stamp of receipt of 11 April 1938) in which he expressly wrote: "The sanatorium of the decedent in Vienna VIII., S[…]gasse 14 is under provisional management […]." In the police report of 4 April 1938 it was recorded that the keys to the apartment and office, which had been sealed after the suicide were "handed over to the current provisional manager of the sanatorium, party comrade M[…]". The listing of the provisional administrators available in the Austrian State Archives illustrates that Josef M. was finally appointed as "provisional administrator" of the sanatorium on 30 April 1938.

Margarethe S. starb am 30. August 1977 in New York State. Sie bestimmte ihren Sohn 352
Alfred S. mit Testament vom 17. Mai 1974 zum "Executor" und Alleinbegünstigten ihres
Nachlasses. Alfred S. wurde am 21. Jänner 1927 als Sohn von Margarethe und Paul S. geboren.

Die AntragstellerInnen Marietta P., Doris A. und Alfred S. sind somit DeszendentInnen 353
nach Dr. Ernst F.

7. Beweiswürdigung

Der festgestellte Sachverhalt gründet sich auf die von den AntragstellerInnen vorge- 354
legten Dokumente, das offene Grundbuch, die Berichte der Historikerkommission und die
seitens der Schiedsinstanz recherchierten Archivalien.

Der Akt der verfahrensführenden Behörde, der FLD für Wien, Niederösterreich und 355
Burgenland, galt bereits 1976 als in Verstoß geraten. Dem Akt der Finanzprokuratur VI-
30254 (Ida De.) liegt ein Schreiben des Bundesministeriums für Finanzen an die Finanzprokuratur (Zl. 73.345/9-I/8/76) vom 26. November 1976 bei, aus dem hervorgeht, dass
es dem BMF nicht möglich gewesen sei, die Rückstellungsakten der FLD in Wien zu erhalten, da sie im betreffenden Archivbestand „VR" (Vermögensrestitution) nicht vorhanden waren. Auch der Schiedsinstanz war es trotz intensiver Nachforschungen nicht möglich, den Akt ausfindig zu machen.

Die Feststellung hinsichtlich des Umstandes, dass am 2. oder 3. April 1938 Dr. Lothar 356
F. und seine Frau Susanne F. von NS-Schergen gezwungen wurden, den Gehsteig vor dem
„Sanatorium F[...]" in der S.-gasse 14 zu waschen, beruht auf den diesbezüglichen nach-
vollziehbaren und glaubwürdigen Erinnerungen von Eva Pe., die jene in einem Brief an
Cynthia Miller, Deputy Director des Office of European Affairs, datiert 12. März 1990,
ausgeführt hat.

Die Feststellung, dass das Sanatorium bis zur Inanspruchnahme des Gebäudes durch 357
die Wehrmacht in Betrieb war, ergibt sich unter anderem aus dem im Verlassenschaftsakt
nach Lothar F. befindlichen Schreiben des Gaufachabteilungsleiters der „Deutschen Arbeitsfront" (NSDAP) an den Verlassenschaftskurator Dr. St. vom 5. Oktober 1939, in dem
der Gaufachabteilungsleiter Fö. darlegte: „Durch die Übernahme des Sanatoriums ‚F[...]'
seitens der Wehrersatzinspektion Wien war die Auflösung des Sanatoriumsbetriebes erforderlich und dadurch bedingt die Entlassung der Angestellten des Betriebes."

Die zunehmende Nutzung des Gebäudes durch die Wehrersatzinspektion sowie das Be- 358
gleichen der dadurch verursachten Mehraufwendungen durch den Abverkauf von Inven-
tarteilen des Sanatoriums ergibt sich aus dem Verrechnungsbuch des Verlassenschaftskurators Beilage M „Bericht zu den Aktiven – Eingang Postzahl 27".

Die Feststellung, dass der Sanatoriumsbetrieb bereits zur Zeit des Ablebens von Dr. F. 359
und danach durch einen kommissarischen Leiter (durch das NSDAP-Mitglied M.) geführt
wurde, ergibt sich unter anderem aus dem Bericht des Notars N. an das BG Josefstadt (Eingangsstempel vom 11. April 1938), in dem dieser ausdrücklich schrieb: „Das Sanatorium
des Erblassers in Wien VIII., S[...]gasse 14 steht unter kommissarischer Leitung [...]." Bereits im Polizeibericht vom 4. April 1938 wurde festgehalten, dass die Schlüssel der nach
dem Selbstmord versiegelten Wohnung und des Büros dem „dzt. kommissarischen Leiter
des Sanatoriums Pg. [Parteigenosse] M[...] eingehändigt" wurden. Dass Josef M. schließlich am 30. April 1938 als „kommissarischer Verwalter" des Sanatoriums eingesetzt wurde,
geht aus der im ÖStA aufliegenden Namenskartei der kommissarischen Verwalter hervor.

360 The utilization of the property S.-gasse 14 as a reserve military hospital XXII can be gathered from the inquiry report of the Financial Directorate Vienna dated 5 February 1965 located in the file of the State Financial Procurator's Office VI 27470, which refers to a file memo by the valuation board of the tax office for the 8th district dated 21 September 1943 concerning this matter.

361 The use of the building after 1945 can be gathered from, among other things, the records of the Federal Ministry for Property Control and Economic Planning of November 1946 (no. 109.300-4/46), from the administrative files of the Ministry of Finance concerning immovable German Property (provincial state Vienna), from the documents of the municipal department 37 (building inspection) regarding the building S.-gasse 14 of 10 June 1952 and from the Austrian official directory of 1953 and following years.

362 The finding that the proceeds from the sale passed undiminished to the estate results from the final report of the trustee of the estate and the examination of this report by Dkfm. Franz Sta., according to which the proceeds for the assets "property" and "contents (sanatorium)" totaled 310,892.78 Reichsmark.

363 The transfer of items from F.'s estate is substantiated by the list in the enclosure B "settlement of the assets according to the account book, entry post no. 3 and 20" (probate file F. 14 A 107/40).

364 The finding regarding the value of the property follows from the conclusive expert opinion dated 30 September 1963 by the sworn court expert, DI Hans Weidisch, commissioned by the Collection Agency. This value was accepted by the Collection Agency as a guide in the settlement negotiations. Although the State Financial Procurator's Office did not determine a specific amount, the findings show, however, that the State Financial Procurator's Office found a settlement amount reasonable, if this amount was approx. 1:10 of the value of the property (see margin note 303). The final settlement amount for the Sanatorium F. of 700,000 Schilling therefore suggests that the value of the property assumed by the State Financial Procurator's Office was not below the value of the expert valuation.

365 The fact that the settlement amount of 700,000 Schilling for the Sanatorium F. had already been agreed before the creation of the Collection Agencies Settlement Act can be established from the following indications:

366 The chronology of the Collection Agencies Settlement Act is determined from the following: Presentation to the Council of Ministers May 1966 (the sum of 700,000 Schilling was mentioned as well as a reference to the agreement reached with the Collection Agency A at the end of 1965; reference to the fulfillment of the obligation in accordance with Article 26 para. 2 of the State Treaty through the planned compensation), government bill and explanatory remarks dated 10 June 1966, 86 BlgNR 11th legislative period, report of the Finance Committee of 30 June 1966, law passed on 7 July 1966, announced on 9 August 1966.

367 An annotation signed by Dr. Fi. in the collection agencies file read as follows: "This case is settled pursuant to the Collection Agencies Settlement Act (see Federal Law 150/66), 700,000 Schilling were paid". An annotation by Dr. Weis on 30 September 1966 concerning S.-gasse 14, also contained in the collection agencies' file stated: "This present file is closed and settled. Reason: Collection Agencies Settlement Act, Federal Law Gazette No. 150/66". The file number under which the Sanatorium F. proceedings were conducted at the Collection Agency (file no. 393) is stated in a list of cases which were settled by the Collection Agencies Settlement Act 1966. In a list dated 20 December 1965 of Collection Agency A and B's open cases to which the 5th amendment and/or the Second

Die Verwendung der Liegenschaft S.-gasse 14 als Reservelazarett XXII ergibt sich aus 360
dem im Akt der Finanzprokuratur VI 27470 einliegenden Erhebungsbericht der FLD vom
5. Februar 1965, der auf einen diesbezüglichen Aktenvermerk vom 21. September 1943
der Bewertungsstelle des Finanzamtes für den 8. Bezirk verweist.

Die Nutzung des Gebäudes ab 1945 ergibt sich unter anderem aus den Aufzeichnungen 361
des BMVS vom November 1946 (Zl. 109.300-4/46), den Verwaltungsakten des Finanzministeriums betreffend das unbewegliche Deutsche Eigentum (Bundesland Wien), den
Unterlagen der MA 37 (Baupolizei) zum Haus S.-gasse 14 vom 10. Juni 1952 und dem
österreichischen Amtskalender aus den Jahren 1953 ff.

Die Feststellung, dass der Erlös aus dem Verkauf dem Nachlass ungeschmälert zuge- 362
flossen ist, ergibt sich aus dem Endbericht des Verlassenschaftskurators und der Überprüfung dieses Berichts durch Dkfm. Franz Sta., wonach für die Aktiva „Liegenschaft" und
„Hauseinrichtung (Sanatorium)" der Erlös von insgesamt 310.892,78 Reichsmark verzeichnet ist.

Die Ausfolgung von Gegenständen aus dem Nachlass F.s wird insbesondere belegt 363
durch die Aufstellung in der Beilage B, „Verrechnung zu den Aktiven laut Abrechnungsbuch Eingang Postzahl 3 und 20" (Verlassenschaftsakt F. 14 A 107/40).

Die Feststellung zum Wert der Liegenschaft folgt dem von der Sammelstelle in Auf- 364
trag gegebenen schlüssigen Gutachten des beeideten Sachverständigen DI Hans Weidisch
vom 30. September 1963. Dieser Wert wurde von der Sammelstelle als Richtwert in den
Vergleichsverhandlungen akzeptiert. Seitens der Finanzprokuratur gab es zwar keine Festlegung des Schätzwertes auf einen bestimmten Betrag. Jedoch zeigen die Feststellungen,
dass die Finanzprokuratur eine Vergleichshöhe dann als vernünftig befand, wenn diese in
einer Relation von ca. 1:10 zum Wert der Liegenschaft stand (siehe Rz 303). Die endgültige Vergleichssumme über das Sanatorium F. in der Höhe von 700.000,– Schilling legt
daher nahe, dass der Wert der Liegenschaft seitens der Finanzprokuratur nicht unter dem
Wert des Sachverständigengutachtens geschätzt wurde.

Dass die Vergleichshöhe von 700.000,– Schilling für das Sanatorium F. bereits vor Ent- 365
stehung des Sammelstellen-Abgeltungsgesetzes vereinbart worden war, ergibt sich aus
folgenden Indizien:

Die Chronologie des Sammelstellen-Abgeltungsgesetzes ergibt sich aus Folgendem: 366
Ministerratsvortrag Mai 1966 (Summe 700.000,– genannt, sowie Hinweis auf mit Sammelstelle A getroffene Vereinbarung Ende 1965; Hinweis auf Erfüllung der Verpflichtung
nach Art. 26 Abs 2 StV durch die geplante Abgeltung), Regierungsvorlage und Erläuternde Bemerkungen 10. Juni 1966, 86 BlgNR 11. GP, Bericht des Finanzausschusses 30. Juni
1966, Gesetz beschlossen am 7. Juli 1966, kundgemacht am 9. August 1966.

Ein im Sammelstellenakt von Dr. Fi. unterzeichneter Vermerk lautet: „Dieser Fall 367
ist durch das Sammelstellen-Abgeltungsgesetz erledigt (siehe BG. 150/66) es wurden
S 700.000.– gezahlt". Ein ebenfalls im Sammelstellenakt enthaltener Aktenvermerk
von Dr. Weis vom 30. September 1966 betreffend S.-gasse 14 hält fest: „Der vorliegende Akt wird abgeschlossen und ist erledigt. Begründung: Sammelstellen-Abgeltungsgesetz BGBl. 150/66". In einer Liste der Fälle, die durch das Sammelstellen-Abgeltungsgesetz 1966 erledigt wurden, findet sich auch die Geschäftszahl, unter der das Verfahren
Sanatorium F. bei der Sammelstelle gelaufen ist (GZ 393). In einer Auflistung von Fällen der Sammelstellen A und B betreffend die unter die 5. Novelle fallenden bzw. nach
dem 2. RStG noch offenen Fälle mit Datum 20. Dezember 1965 findet sich ebenfalls die

Restitution Act were applicable, the matter no. 393, Sanatorium F., is also found, with the annotation: "settled separately with the Republic of Austria, 700,000 Schilling".

368   It cannot be established whether Dr. Lothar F. had concluded a lease agreement with the "Sanatorium Dr. F[…] Operating Company Ltd." This is due to the fact that documents relating to such an agreement could be found neither in the file of the Commercial Court nor in any other locations. The only evidence of this is in the report of the notary N. to the District Court Josefstadt (stamp of receipt 11 April 1938) where it was quoted: "[…] and according to the parents-in-law of the decedent, the decedent Dr. Lothar F[…] had concluded an agreement concerning the leasing of this sanatorium a few weeks prior to his death. Further details are unknown today."

369   The finding that Dr. F. and his heirs were persecuted on grounds of origin and religion is established from the unobjectionable documents and written witness statements produced by the applicants as well as from the documents gathered by the Arbitration Panel, particularly the birth and marriage certificates and the mandatory property notices pursuant to the "Announcement of the Ordinance on the Registration of Jewish Property of 26 April 1938", Austrian Law Gazette 1938/102.

370   It cannot be determined on what date the estate of Bernard F. was devolved to his children Marie Re. and Paul F. because the probate file of Bernard F. is only available in fragments. The corresponding decision of devolution only exists in the form of an undated draft to be executed by the court office. As the draft is in the file and is not crossed out or in any other way marked as invalid, it can be assumed that the devolution took place according to the draft. A further indication for this is the circumstance that in the notice of amendment to the list of assets of Bernhard F.'s estate, the deposit of the inheritance fee is recorded as one of the items and in another place the transfer of the balance to the heirs is recorded.

8. Juridical Appraisal

1. Eligibility to file an application

371   Pursuant to Sec. 27 of the GSF Law, persons who were persecuted by the National Socialist regime on political grounds, on grounds of origin, religion, nationality, sexual orientation or of physical or mental handicap or of accusations of so-called asociality or who left the country to escape such persecution are eligible to file an application.

372   Pursuant to Sec. 27 (2) of the GSF Law, heirs of such persons are also eligible to file applications applying *mutatis mutandis* the provisions of the (Austrian) General Civil Code. The Arbitration Panel assumes that proof of the statutory right to the inheritance in accordance with the cited provisions is sufficient for the eligibility to file an application, as long as no stronger grounds for appeal are presented.

373   Lothar F. and his appointed testamentary heirs, Ida and Emil Be. and the subsidiary heirs Rosa G., Ernst F., Cäcilie F., Marie Re. and Paul F. were also persecuted on grounds of origin as all were considered Jews in accordance with the Nuremberg Laws of 15 September 1935.

374   All applicants are descendants of the grandparents of the original aggrieved owner. Hence, they are statutory heirs of the third *parentela* according to para. 738 of the (Austrian) General Civil Code. Heirs from the first and second *parentela* do not exist. Lothar F. died childless. The heirs appointed by Lothar F. in his last will and testament did not accept the inheritance: His wife Susanne F. died at the same time as him, the parents-in-law

GZ 393, Sanatorium F., mit dem Vermerk: „gesondert mit Rep. Osterr. verglichen, S. 700.000,–".

Dass nicht festgestellt werden kann, ob Dr. Lothar F. mit der „Sanatorium Dr. F[…] Betriebsgesellschaft m.b.H." einen Vertrag über die Verpachtung des Sanatoriums abgeschlossen hat, liegt darin begründet, dass eine solche Vertragsurkunde weder im Akt des Handelsgerichtes noch in anderen Beständen gefunden werden konnte. Lediglich im Bericht des Notars N. an das BG Josefstadt (Eingangsstempel vom 11. April 1938) wird wiedergegeben: „[...] und hat der Erblasser Dr. Lothar F[…] wenige Wochen vor seinem Ableben laut Angabe der erbl. Schwiegereltern einen Vertrag punkto Verpachtung dieses Sanatoriums abgeschlossen. Näheres ist heute nicht bekannt." 368

Die Feststellung, dass Lothar F. sowie dessen ErbInnen aus Gründen der Abstammung und der Religion verfolgt waren, ergibt sich aus den von den AntragstellerInnen beigebrachten unbedenklichen Urkunden und schriftlichen Zeugenaussagen sowie aus den von der Schiedsinstanz erhobenen Dokumenten, insbesondere den Geburts- und Heiratsurkunden sowie der gemäß „Kundmachung der Verordnung über die Anmeldung des Vermögens von Juden vom 26. April 1938", GBl f.d.L.Ö. 1938/102, obligatorisch abzugebenden VA. 369

Dass nicht festgestellt werden kann, zu welchem Zeitpunkt der Nachlass nach Bernhard F. seinen Kindern Marie Re. und Paul F. eingeantwortet wurde, liegt daran, dass der Verlassenschaftsakt nach Bernhard F. nur fragmentarisch vorhanden ist. Der entsprechende Einantwortungsbeschluss liegt nur in Form eines für die Gerichtskanzlei auszufertigenden Entwurfs ohne Datierung vor. Da der Entwurf im Akt einliegt und nicht durchgestrichen oder in sonst einer Weise als ungültig gekennzeichnet ist, kann davon ausgegangen werden, dass es zur Einantwortung im Sinne dieses Entwurfes gekommen ist. Dafür spricht darüber hinaus auch der Umstand, dass in der Änderungsanzeige zum Vermögensverzeichnis des Nachlasses nach Bernhard F. als einer der Posten die Erlegung der Erbgebühr und an anderer Stelle die Ausfolgung des verbleibenden Betrages an die ErbInnen verzeichnet sind. 370

8. Rechtliche Beurteilung

1. Antragsberechtigung

Antragsberechtigt sind gemäß § 27 EF-G Personen, die vom nationalsozialistischen Regime aus politischen Gründen, aus Gründen der Abstammung, Religion, Nationalität, sexuellen Orientierung, aufgrund einer körperlichen oder geistigen Behinderung oder aufgrund des Vorwurfes der so genannten Asozialität verfolgt wurden oder das Land verlassen haben, um einer solchen Verfolgung zu entgehen. 371

Gemäß § 27 Abs 2 EF-G sind ErbInnen solcher Personen in sinngemäßer Anwendung der Bestimmungen des österreichischen ABGB antragsberechtigt. Die Schiedsinstanz geht davon aus, dass nach der vorzitierten Bestimmung der Nachweis des gesetzlichen Erbrechts, wenn nicht stärkere Berufungsgründe dargetan werden, für die Antragsberechtigung ausreichend ist. 372

Lothar F. sowie dessen testamentarisch eingesetzten ErbInnen Ida und Emil Be. sowie die subsidiär Erbberechtigten Rosa G., Ernst F., Cäcilie F., Marie Re. und Paul F. waren sowohl aus Gründen der Abstammung verfolgt, da alle gemäß den Nürnberger Gesetzen vom 15. September 1935 als Juden galten. 373

appointed as alternate heirs renounced their right to the inheritance. Otherwise, there are no other heirs of the second *parentela*, as Lothar F. had ordered the statutory succession with the exclusion of his sister Hertha L. and her descendants in the case that none of the intended heirs accepted the inheritance.

375 As the reversionary right of the state pursuant to para. 760 of the (Austrian) General Civil Code is not considered as a right to inherit, but as a right to acquire the net excess of an heirless estate (Welser in Rummel, *Kommentar zum Allgemeinen Bürgerlichen Gesetzbuch³*, § 760 margin note 2), the reversion of the estate of Lothar F. of around 15,000 Reichsmark does not preclude the eligibility to file an application.

376 No evidence which disproves the applicants' right to inherit was presented. The Arbitration Panel therefore views the eligibility requirement of the applicants to file an application as fulfilled on the basis of the proven right to inherit.

2. Eligibility to File a Claim

a) Seizure of the Property

377 Pursuant to Sec. 28 (1) item 1 of the GSF Law, the property must have been seized from the previous owners between 12 March 1938 and 9 May 1945 for the above named reasons in connection with the events on the territory of the present day Republic of Austria during the National Socialist period.

378 In the case at issue, the wild aryanization asserted by the applicants of the Sanatorium F. by the "provisional manager", and later the appointment of Josef M. as "provisional administrator" do not constitute such a seizure. This assumption of control of the management of the sanatorium does constitute an encroachment on the assets of Lothar F., however, this concerns the financial operation but not the authority of disposition over the property itself. Pursuant to the Law on the Appointment of Provisional Administrators and Provisional Supervisors, Austrian Law Gazette 1938/80, which entered into force on 13 April 1938, the Reich Governor, according to para. 1 leg. cit., could appoint "provisional administrators or provisional supervisors in order to safeguard important public interest for companies which have their headquarters in Austria". According to para. 2 leg. cit., the provisional administrator was authorized to carry out all legal acts for the company. During the period of administration, "the authority of the company owner is suspended". According to para. 3 of the law, the "provisional supervisor" was to ensure that the business was operated in a "manner which complies with the public interest". Their orders and instructions were to be followed within the company. The authorities of the provisional administrator therefore did not exceed the decisions concerning the sanatorium company.

379 Regarding the question of provisional administration, the Supreme Administrative Court repeatedly decided that the mere confiscation or threat of a provisional administration constituted neither a seizure nor an acquisition in the meaning of the Austrian restitution laws (see judgments Supreme Administrative Court 29 November 1962, 272/60; Supreme Administrative Court 6 June 1963 577/62).

380 The seizure did not however occur only at the time of the sale of the property in March 1939 but during the course of the settlement of the probate proceedings. At the time of the sale, the "previous owner" Lothar F. had no longer been alive. His dormant estate, represented by the trustee of the estate Dr. St., was the owner of the property.

Sämtliche AntragstellerInnen sind DeszendentInnen der Großeltern des ursprünglich Geschädigten. Sie sind damit gesetzliche ErbInnen der dritten Parentel nach § 738 ABGB. ErbInnen aus der ersten und zweiten Parentel sind nicht vorhanden. Lothar F. verstarb kinderlos. Die von Lothar F. in seinem Testament eingesetzten ErbInnen traten das Erbe nicht an: Seine Frau Susanne F. verstarb gleichzeitig mit ihm, die als ErsatzerbInnen bedachten Schwiegereltern verzichteten auf ihr Erbrecht. Es gibt auch sonst keine Berechtigten der zweiten Parentel, da Lothar F. für den Fall, dass keiner der Bedachten das Erbe antritt, das Eintreten der gesetzlichen Erbfolge unter Ausschluss seiner Schwester Hertha L. und deren Nachkommen angeordnet hat. 374

Da das Heimfallsrecht des Staates gemäß § 760 ABGB nicht als Erbrecht gilt, sondern als Recht auf Aneignung des reinen Überschusses eines erblosen Nachlasses (*Welser* in *Rummel*, Kommentar zum Allgemeinen Bürgerlichen Gesetzbuch³, § 760 Rz 2), steht auch der Heimfall des Nachlasses nach Lothar F. von rund 15.000,– Reichsmark einer Antragsberechtigung nicht entgegen. 375

Es wurde kein dem Erbrecht der AntragstellerInnen entgegenstehender Nachweis vorgelegt. Hiermit sieht die Schiedsinstanz die Antragsberechtigung der einzelnen AntragstellerInnen aufgrund des nachgewiesenen Erbrechts als gegeben an. 376

2. Anspruchsberechtigung

a) Entzug der Liegenschaft

Gemäß § 28 Abs 1 Z 1 EF-G muss die Liegenschaft zwischen 12. März 1938 und 9. Mai 1945 dem früheren Eigentümer aus oben genannten Verfolgungsgründen im Zusammenhang mit Ereignissen auf dem Gebiet der heutigen Republik Österreich während der Zeit des Nationalsozialismus entzogen worden sein. 377

Im vorliegenden Fall besteht ein solcher Entzug nicht in der von den AntragstellerInnen geltend gemachten so genannten wilden Arisierung des Sanatoriums F. durch den „kommissarischen Leiter" und später zum „kommissarischen Verwalter" bestellten Josef M. Diese Übernahme der Geschäftsführung des Sanatoriums stellt zwar einen Eingriff in das Vermögen Lothar F.s dar. Dieser bezieht sich jedoch auf den wirtschaftlichen Betrieb und nicht auf die Verfügungsbefugnis über die Liegenschaft selbst. Gemäß dem am 13. April 1938 in Kraft getretenen „Gesetz über die Bestellung von kommissarischen Verwaltern und kommissarischen Überwachungspersonen", GBlÖ 1938/80, konnte der Reichsstatthalter laut § 1 leg. cit. in „Wahrung wichtiger öffentlicher Interessen für Unternehmungen, die ihren Sitz im Lande Österreich haben, kommissarische Verwalter oder kommissarische Aufsichtspersonen" bestellen. Nach § 2 leg. cit. war der kommissarische Verwalter zu allen Rechtshandlungen für die Unternehmung befugt. Während der Dauer der Verwaltung „ruhte die Befugnis des Inhabers der Unternehmung". Die „kommissarische Aufsichtsperson" hatte nach § 3 des Gesetzes dafür Sorge zu tragen, dass der Geschäftsbetrieb in einer den „öffentlichen Interessen entsprechenden Weise geführt" wurde. Ihren Anordnungen und Weisungen war im Bereich der Unternehmung Folge zu leisten. Die Befugnisse des kommissarischen Verwalters reichten demnach nicht über Entscheidungen betreffend das Sanatoriumsunternehmen hinaus. 378

Zur Frage der kommissarischen Verwaltung entschied der VwGH wiederholt, dass die bloße Beschlagnahme oder die Androhung der kommissarischen Verwaltung weder eine Entziehung noch ein Erwerb im Sinne der österreichischen Rückstellungsgesetze sei (vgl. Erkenntnisse VwGH 29. November 1962, 272/60; VwGH 6. Juni 1963 577/62). 379

Arbitration Panel for *In Rem* Restitution – Decision No. 27/2005

381   According to the prevailing legal opinion, in the case of an inheritance and prior to the devolution, the estate is viewed as a legal person. In principle, as far as the characteristics of physical persons are concerned, those of the decedent are relevant (Welser in Rummel, *Kommentar zum Allgemeinen Bürgerlichen Gesetzbuch*[3], § 547 margin note 3). The "characteristic" as a Jew which had been assigned to the decedent in accordance with National Socialist legislation was also partially assigned to the dormant estate: Thus, the trustee of the estate submitted a property notice, mandatory for Jews, for the estate of Lothar F. The sale of the property in question, which constituted the majority of the estate's assets, took place within the parameters of what was considered an aryanization, i.e. the approval of the Property Transaction Office was obtained and the proceeds from the sale were initially paid into a frozen account designated "de-jewification proceeds". However, the proceeds were finally paid to the estate and no discriminatory taxes were paid.

382   The treatment of the estate as a "Jewish estate" was particularly evident in the conclusion from the probate proceedings that the estate was heirless. According to paras. 128 to 130 of the Non-Contentious Proceedings Act, if the heirs are entirely unknown or if known heirs do not assert their right, the court is to appoint a trustee of the estate and summon the unknown heirs by means of an edict, with the instruction to come forward within six months, otherwise the property which remained heirless would be seized by the state. The appointment of the attorney-at-law Dr. Alfred St. as trustee of the estate and the issue of the edict summoning the unknown heirs of Dr. Lothar F. was in fact decided by the District Court Josefstadt on 28 April 1938. Additionally, a notification for the unknown heirs of Lothar F. was placed in the official gazette of the *Wiener Zeitung* on 12 May 1938. Pursuant to para.132 (1) of the Non-Contentious Proceedings Act, the edict must be announced three times in the "newspapers designated for public announcements" and it is to be published "if possible also in newspapers abroad". Subsection (3) of the same provision limits this obligation, however, to the following case: "Should the advertising fees be out of proportion to the value of the estate or the share of the inheritance or the advertisement is not expected to be successful, then it can be ordered that the publication in the newspaper is only to take place once or not at all". Only one publication is evident from the probate file of Dr. F.

383   Whether the prerequisites in accordance with para. 132 (2) of the Non-Contentious Proceedings Act were met in the probate proceedings in question can, however, remain unanswered as further, pursuant to para. 129 of the Non-Contentious Proceedings Act, the trustee of the estate was also to use all remaining means to trace the heirs and their whereabouts regardless of the edict which was issued and to report to the court. However, it cannot be determined from the files that (further) efforts to trace the heirs were made by Dr. St., although in the proceedings in question a number of those entitled to the inheritance (Dr. Ernst F.) and also people who were in a position to give information (the parents-in-law of the decedent and the legatee John Henry D.) were known to the Probate Court and particularly to the trustee of the estate with their address, or at least by name.

384   Para. 131 of the Non-Contentious Proceedings Act should particularly have been applied with regard to Dr. Ernst F., who was already named in the death record. Subsection (1) of this provision provides that:

> "If the identity of an heir is known to the court, but his/her whereabouts are unknown, then a trustee shall be appointed for the same person. The trustee shall be given an appropriate deadline to trace the absent heir and inform him/her of the inheritance case, if such task has a prospect of being successful."

In the case that the attempts to seek the absent heir are hopeless or unsuccessful, the court shall, upon the instructions of the trustee, inform the absent heir by edict in accor-

Die Entziehung erfolgte jedoch nicht erst mit dem Verkauf der gegenständlichen Liegenschaft im März 1939, sondern bereits im Zuge der Abwicklung des Verlassenschaftsverfahrens. Zum Zeitpunkt des Verkaufes war der „frühere Eigentümer" Lothar F. nicht mehr am Leben. Sein ruhender Nachlass, vertreten durch den Verlassenschaftskurator Dr. St., war Eigentümer der Liegenschaft. 380

Laut herrschender Meinung wird der Nachlass nach dem Erbfall und vor der Einantwortung als eine juristische Person angesehen. Grundsätzlich sind, soweit es auf die Eigenschaften physischer Personen ankommt, jene des Erblassers maßgebend (*Welser* in *Rummel*, Kommentar zum Allgemeinen Bürgerlichen Gesetzbuch³, § 547 Rz 3). Die dem Erblasser zugeschriebene „Eigenschaft" als Jude im Sinne der nationalsozialistischen Gesetzgebung wurde in Teilaspekten auch dem ruhenden Nachlass zugeschrieben: So gab der Verlassenschaftskurator für den Nachlass nach Dr. Lothar F. eine für Juden verpflichtende Vermögensanmeldung ab. Der Verkauf der gegenständlichen Liegenschaft, die den größten Teil der Aktiva der Verlassenschaft darstellte, erfolgte im Rahmen der für Arisierungen geltenden Parameter, d. h. die Genehmigung der Vermögensverkehrsstelle wurde eingeholt und der Verkaufserlös floss zunächst auf ein Sperrkonto mit Namen „Entjudungserlös". Jedoch floss der Erlös schließlich dem Nachlass zu und es wurden keine diskriminierenden Abgaben entrichtet. 381

Die Behandlung als „jüdische Verlassenschaft" wurde insbesondere in der Abwicklung des Verlassenschaftsverfahrens als erbloser Nachlass schlagend. Nach §§ 128 bis 130 AußStrG hat das Gericht, wenn die ErbInnen gänzlich unbekannt sind oder bekannte Erben von ihrem Recht keinen Gebrauch machen, einen Verlassenschaftskurator zu bestellen und die unbekannten Erben durch Edikt mit der Aufforderung vorzuladen, sich binnen sechs Monaten zu melden, widrigenfalls die erblos gebliebene Verlassenschaft vom Staate eingezogen werde. Die Einsetzung des Rechtsanwaltes Dr. Alfred St. zum Verlassenschaftskurator sowie die Erlassung des Ediktes zur Einberufung der unbekannten ErbInnen nach Dr. Lothar F. wurde auch tatsächlich vom BG Josefstadt am 28. April 1938 beschlossen. Weiters wurde im Amtsblatt zur Wiener Zeitung am 12. Mai 1938 eine Verständigung der unbekannten ErbInnen nach Dr. Lothar F. geschaltet. Gemäß § 132 Abs 1 AußStrG bedarf es einer dreimaligen Kundmachung dieses Edikts in den „zu öffentlichen Kundmachungen bestimmten Zeitungsblättern" und ist das Edikt „nach Umständen aber auch im Auslande durch die Zeitungsblätter bekanntzumachen". Durch Abs 3 derselben Bestimmung wird jedoch diese Verpflichtung für folgenden Fall eingeschränkt: „Stehen die Einrückungsgebühren zum Werte des Nachlasses oder des Erbteiles im Missverhältnisse oder ist von der Einschaltung ein Erfolg nicht zu erwarten, so kann angeordnet werden, daß die Veröffentlichung durch die Zeitung nur einmal zu geschehen oder ganz zu unterbleiben habe." Aus dem Verlassenschaftsakt nach Dr. F. ist lediglich eine einmalige Schaltung ersichtlich. 382

Ob jedoch die Voraussetzungen nach § 132 Abs 2 AußStrG im gegenständlichen Verlassenschaftsverfahren vorlagen, kann dahingestellt bleiben, da zusätzlich gemäß § 129 AußStrG der Verlassenschaftskurator ungeachtet des ausgefertigten Ediktes auch alle übrigen zur Ausforschung der ErbInnen und ihres Aufenthaltes dienlichen Mittel anzuwenden und dem Gericht anzuzeigen hat. Aus den Akten gehen jedoch keine Bemühungen zur (weiteren) ErbInnenausforschung durch Dr. St. hervor, obwohl im gegenständlichen Verfahren einige der Erbberechtigten (Dr. Ernst F.) und auch Auskunftspersonen (die Schwiegereltern des Erblassers und der Legatar John Henry D.) dem Verlassenschaftsgericht und insbesondere dem Verlassenschaftskurator mit Adresse oder zumindest namentlich bekannt waren. 383

dance with subsection (2) leg. cit. that in the case that the person entitled to the inheritance does not come forward, then the inheritance will be accepted by the trustee in his/her name, the processing and settlement will be taken care of and the net estate owing to him/her would be kept for safekeeping at the court until the proof of his/her death and/or the death declaration. In the probate proceedings for Dr. Lothar F., no trustee was appointed for Dr. Ernst F. pursuant to para. 131 of the Non-Contentious Proceedings Act.

385   John Henry D. was also not requested to submit an acceptance of the inheritance, contrary to para. 116 of the Non-Contentious Proceedings Act in connection with para. 726 of the (Austrian) General Civil Code.

386   Neither the court nor the trustee of the estate safeguarded the interests of the statutory Jewish heirs. But even if these statutory requirements had been complied with, the probate proceedings would have at best taken place correctly from a procedural point of view. The majority of those entitled to the inheritance who were considered Jews had left the country in order to escape further persecution. Their assets had already been subject to the National Socialist process of aryanization as can be deduced from the findings in the facts regarding Cäcilie F., the estate of Bernard F., Dr. Ernst F., Paul and Margarethe F. and Marie and Anton Re. It would be illogical and would also contradict the then practice of aryanization if those same people whose current property was seized had been able to freely dispose over property which they had obtained by means of inheritance.

387   The State Financial Procurator's Office asserted in its statement of 14 June 2005 that due to the over-indebtedness of the estate, a seizure in the meaning of the GSF Law had not existed. In this regard, the following is to be explained:

388   The case law of the Restitution Commissions assumed that an over-indebtedness only justified the assumption that a seizure would also have taken place without the National Socialist assumption of power, if overcoming the financial difficulties was impossible under the given circumstances. This prerequisite would then not be met if the creditors had acted passively prior to the *Anschluss* (Rkv 158/48). Before the suicide of Lothar F. and the *Anschluss*, no creditors were exerting pressure with the exception of the collection proceedings initiated while Dr. F. was still alive (27 E 2512/38) which concerned Mrs. Sári Sz.'s claim for 7,000 Schilling.

389   Furthermore, para. 67 of the Bankruptcy Act is to be referred to when assessing the over-indebtedness of an estate, as according to para. 74 of the Non-Contentious Proceedings Act, the Bankruptcy Act determines in which cases the opening of bankruptcy proceedings was to be initiated due to encumbrances which exceeded the estate. Pursuant to para. 67 of the Bankruptcy Act, the opening of bankruptcy proceedings regarding estates also takes place in the case of over-indebtedness provided that no specific laws prescribe other measures. The provisions of the Bankruptcy Act that relate to insolvency, therefore also apply *mutatis mutandis* to over-indebtedness. According to juridical practice, over-indebtedness in the meaning of para. 67 exists if the assets exceed the liabilities and in addition a negative outlook for the estate's continued existence exists.[6] The State Financial Procurator's Office only asserted one of the statutory prerequisites constituting over-indebtedness, i.e. the excess of liabilities. It was not asserted and not stated that the second prerequisite of over-indebtedness had been fulfilled. The prognosis for its continued existence must be based on a realistic assessment of the future earnings and expenditure. The

---

[6] Rectification of this sentence at time of going to press: According to juridical practice, over-indebtedness in the meaning of para. 67 exists if the liabilities exceed the assets and in addition a negative outlook for the estate's continued existence exists.

Insbesondere hinsichtlich Dr. Ernst F., der bereits in der Todfallsaufnahme genannt wurde, hätte § 131 AußStrG zur Anwendung kommen sollen. Abs 1 dieser Bestimmung sieht vor: 384

„Ist dem Gerichte die Person eines Erben zwar bekannt, der Aufenthalt desselben aber unbekannt, so ist ein Kurator für denselben zu bestellen, welchem zwar, wenn Aussicht vorhanden ist, den Abwesenden ausforschen und ihn von dem Erbfalle verständigen zu können, eine angemessene Frist hiezu bestimmt werden kann."

Im Falle der Aussichtslosigkeit oder Erfolglosigkeit der Ausforschung des Abwesenden hat das Gericht nach Abs 2 leg. cit. auf Antrag des Kurators die Abwesenden per Edikt darüber zu verständigen, dass im Falle des Nichtmeldens des Erbberechtigten, die Erbschaft vom Kurator in seinem Namen angetreten, die Abhandlung gepflogen und der ihm gebührende reine Nachlass bis zum Beweis seines Todes bzw. der Todeserklärung für ihn bei Gericht aufbewahrt werden würde. Im Verlassenschaftsverfahren nach Dr. Lothar F. wurde für Dr. Ernst F. kein Kurator iSd § 131 AußStrG bestellt.

Auch wurde John Henry D. entgegen den Bestimmungen § 116 AußStrG iVm § 726 ABGB nicht zur Abgabe einer Erbserklärung aufgefordert. 385

Weder das Gericht noch der Verlassenschaftskurator nahmen die Interessen der gesetzlichen, jüdischen ErbInnen wahr. Doch selbst wenn diese gesetzlichen Regeln eingehalten worden wären, wäre das Verlassenschaftsverfahren bestenfalls formell korrekt abgelaufen. Die meisten der als Juden geltenden Erbberechtigten hatten das Land verlassen, um einer weiteren Verfolgung zu entgehen. Deren Vermögen war bereits zu diesem Zeitpunkt den nationalsozialistischen Arisierungsprozessen unterworfen, wie den Sachverhaltsfeststellungen zu Cäcilie F., zur Verlassenschaft nach Bernard F., zu Dr. Ernst F., Paul und Margarethe F., Marie und Anton Re. zu entnehmen ist. Es wäre widersinnig und widerspräche auch der seinerzeitigen Arisierungspraxis, dass die gleichen Personen, deren aktuelles Vermögen entzogen wurde, frei über ihr durch Erbrecht erlangtes Vermögen hätten verfügen können. 386

Die Finanzprokuratur machte in ihrer Stellungnahme vom 14. Juni 2005 geltend, dass aufgrund der Überschuldung des Nachlasses keine Entziehung iSd EF-G vorgelegen habe. Dazu ist Folgendes auszuführen: 387

Die Rechtsprechung der Rückstellungskommissionen ging davon aus, dass eine Überschuldung nur dann die Annahme begründete, dass es auch ohne Machtergreifung des Nationalsozialismus zu einer Vermögensübertragung gekommen wäre, wenn unter den gegebenen Verhältnissen die Überwindung der finanziellen Schwierigkeiten aussichtslos war. Diese Voraussetzung würde dann fehlen, wenn sich vor dem „Anschluss" die GläubigerInnen passiv verhalten hätten (Rkv 158/48). Vor dem Selbstmord Lothar F.s bzw. dem „Anschluss" drängten keine Gläubiger an. Eine Ausnahme bildet das noch zu Lebzeiten Dr. F.s eingeleitete Exekutionsverfahren (27 E 2512/38), in dem es um die Forderung von 7.000,– Schilling von Frau Sári Sz. ging. 388

Zudem ist bei der Beurteilung der Überschuldung eines Nachlasses auf § 67 Konkursordnung (KO) zu verweisen, da laut § 74 AußStrG die Konkursordnung bestimmt, in welchen Fällen wegen einer den Nachlass übersteigenden Schuldenlast Einleitungen zur Konkurseröffnung zu treffen seien. Gemäß § 67 KO findet die Eröffnung des Konkurses über Verlassenschaften, soweit besondere Gesetze nichts anderes bestimmen, auch bei Überschuldung statt. Dabei gelten die Vorschriften der Konkursordnung, die sich auf die Zahlungsunfähigkeit beziehen, sinngemäß auch für die Überschuldung. Nach Rechtsprechung 389

sanatorium company constituted a fundamental part of the estate. In what way this company would have achieved earnings taking a dynamic approach could not be established. As the findings in the established facts demonstrate, nearly all those persons entitled to the inheritance were wealthy family members and several had management positions in companies. It seems entirely plausible that those entitled to the inheritance would have continued the operation of the sanatorium had they not been subjected to persecution by the National Socialist regime. This particularly applies to Dr. Ernst F., due to his management experience as the former general director and main shareholder of the So. Corporation and to Paul F., vice general director of the So. Corporation. As is demonstrated in the facts, Dr. Ernst F. also provided funds for Lothar F.'s sanatorium company. It can be assumed that he had some insight into the economics of the sanatorium company.

390   It is in any case to be noted that no bankruptcy proceedings were opened for the estate of Lothar F. but that the trustee of the estate had come to an out-of-court settlement with the creditors.

391   In summary it is to be noted that the shortcomings in the settlement of the probate proceedings and the fact that the estate was treated as "Jewish" and the persecution of the statutory heirs after the National Socialist assumption of power resulted in the seizure of the estate and thus the property in question from those entitled to the inheritance in the meaning of the GSF Law on grounds of origin and religion.

b) Federal Ownership on the Cut Off Day

392   Pursuant to Sec. 28 (1) item 3 of the GSF Law, the notion "publicly-owned property" covers properties which on 17 January 2001 were exclusively and directly owned by the Federation or any legal person under public or private law wholly owned, directly or indirectly by the Federation. According to the findings, the Republic of Austria was the owner of the property subject of this application on the cut off day. Therefore, the property is publicly-owned in the meaning of the law.

c) Prior Proceedings in the sense of Sec. 32 GSF Law

393   A further prerequisite for filing a claim pursuant to Sec. 28 (1) item 2 of the GSF Law is that the requested property was never the subject of a claim that was previously decided by an Austrian court or administrative body, or settled by agreement, and for which the applicant or a relative has never otherwise received compensation or other consideration except if such a decision or settlement by agreement constituted an extreme injustice.

394   These prerequisites of Sec. 28 of the GSF Law are also repeated in Sec. 32 (1) of the GSF Law:

"As a matter of principle, the Arbitration Panel shall not have the authority to reopen or reconsider cases that were previously decided by Austrian courts or administrative bodies, or settled by agreement. Neither the applicant nor a relative must have otherwise received compensation or any other consideration for the property in question."

Exceptional cases in this regard are regulated by Sec. 32 (2) of the GSF Law, that is where the existence of a prior settlement or decision constitutes an extreme injustice or, in the case of a prior denial of the claim, where evidence has in the meantime become accessible to the applicant.

395   It can be established from the wording that the presence of one of these two negative prerequisites, i.e. "prior proceedings/settlement by agreement" or "other compensation", each by themselves precludes a substantive decision.

liegt eine Überschuldung iSd § 67 vor, wenn die Aktiva die Passiva übersteigen und zusätzlich eine negative Fortbestehensprognose besteht.[6] Von der Finanzprokuratur wird nur ein Tatbestand der Überschuldung, nämlich das Überwiegen der Passiva vorgebracht. Nicht behauptet und nicht dargelegt wurde, dass die zweite Tatbestandsvoraussetzung erfüllt gewesen sei. Der Fortbestehensprognose ist eine realistische Einschätzung der künftigen Erträge und Aufwendungen zugrunde zu legen. Einen wesentlichen Teil des Nachlasses stellte der Sanatoriumsbetrieb dar. Inwiefern nach einer dynamischen Betrachtungsweise dieses Unternehmen Erträgnisse erwirtschaftet hätte, konnte nicht festgestellt werden. Wie die Sachverhaltsfeststellungen zeigen, waren fast alle Erbberechtigten wohlhabende Familienmitglieder und einige in führender Position eines Betriebes tätig. Es erscheint durchaus plausibel, dass die Erbberechtigten, wären sie nicht vom nationalsozialistischen Regime verfolgt worden, den Sanatoriumsbetrieb weitergeführt hätten. Insbesondere trifft dies auf Dr. Ernst F. aufgrund seiner unternehmerischen Erfahrung als ehemaliger Generaldirektor und Hauptaktionär der So. Z. AG, sowie auf Paul F., Vize-Generaldirektor der So. Z. AG, zu. Wie aus dem Sachverhalt hervorgeht, stellte Dr. Ernst F. auch Gelder für Lothar F.s Sanatoriumsbetrieb zur Verfügung. Es kann davon ausgegangen werden, dass er einen gewissen wirtschaftlichen Einblick in den Sanatoriumsbetrieb hatte.

Festzuhalten ist jedenfalls, dass über den Nachlass nach Lothar F. kein Konkurs eröffnet wurde, sondern sich der Verlassenschaftskurator mit den GläubigerInnen außergerichtlich einigte.

Zusammenfassend ist anzumerken, dass die Mängel in der Abwicklung des Verlassenschaftsverfahrens sowie die Behandlung des Nachlasses als „jüdisch" und die Verfolgung der gesetzlichen ErbInnen nach der nationalsozialistischen Machtergreifung bewirkten, dass der Nachlass und damit auch die gegenständliche Liegenschaft den Erbberechtigten iSd EF-G aus Gründen der Abstammung und Religion entzogen wurde.

b) Bundeseigentum zum Stichtag

Gemäß § 28 Abs 1 Z 3 EF-G umfasst der Begriff „öffentliches Vermögen" Liegenschaften, welche sich am 17. Jänner 2001 ausschließlich und unmittelbar im Eigentum des Bundes oder einer unmittelbar oder mittelbar im Alleineigentum des Bundes stehenden juristischen Person des öffentlichen oder privaten Rechts befanden. Nach den Feststellungen war die Republik Österreich am Stichtag Eigentümerin der antragsgegenständlichen Liegenschaft. Es liegt daher öffentliches Vermögen im Sinne des Gesetzes vor.

c) Früheres Verfahren iSd § 32 EF-G

Eine weitere Anspruchsvoraussetzung gemäß § 28 Abs 1 Z 2 EF-G ist, dass die beantragte Liegenschaft niemals Gegenstand einer Forderung war, die bereits zuvor durch österreichische Gerichte oder Verwaltungsbehörden entschieden oder einvernehmlich geregelt wurde, und für die weder der Antragsteller noch ein Verwandter auf eine andere Weise eine Entschädigung oder sonstige Gegenleistung erhalten hat, es sei denn, eine solche Entscheidung oder einvernehmliche Regelung habe eine extreme Ungerechtigkeit dargestellt.

Diese Voraussetzungen des § 28 EF-G werden auch in § 32 Abs 1 EF-G wiederholt:

---

[6] Berichtigung dieses Satzes zum Zeitpunkt der Drucklegung: Nach Rechtsprechung liegt eine Überschuldung iSd § 67 vor, wenn die Passiva die Aktiva übersteigen und zusätzlich eine negative Fortbestehensprognose besteht.

396	Such an interpretation of the law is also confirmed by the text of the agreement which was negotiated between the Republic of Austria and the United States of America (Washington Agreement on 17 January 2001). In Annex A of this agreement the following is regulated in letter g of item 3:

> "For the purposes of restitution *in rem*, the notion of 'publicly-owned property' covers exclusively real estate/immovable property/buildings which: […] was never subject of a claim that was previously decided by an Austrian court or administrative body under prior restitution legislation or a settlement by agreement, or where claimant or relative has never otherwise received compensation or other consideration of the property in question, except in exceptional circumstances where the Panel unanimously determines that prior settlement constitutes an extreme injustice; […]."

397	The regulation contained in letter m of item 3 of the Washington Agreement which corresponds to Sec. 32 of the GSF Law reads: "The Panel legislation will provide that individual claimants (former owners or their heirs, as defined *supra* in paragraph 2(e)) are eligible to receive *in rem* restitution […] provided that the following criteria are satisfied:

> i. property is currently publicly-owned as defined in *supra* in paragraph 3 (g); **and**
> ii. […]
> iii. claim was never previously decided or settled under prior restitution legislation or claimants [sic!] or relative has never otherwise received compensation or other consideration for the property in question except in the exceptional circumstances where the Panel unanimously determines that prior settlement constituted extreme injustice; […]."

398	Any claim that has been dealt with in proceedings before an administrative body or a court in which a substantive decision or a settlement by agreement has been made concerning the property requested in the proceedings before the Arbitration Panel is to be understood as a claim in the meaning of the negative requirement "prior proceedings/settlement by agreement". In this regard, pursuant to the wording of the above-cited clauses of the agreement, only proceedings within the scope of the restitution legislation are intended. Accordingly, this negative prerequisite covers all restitution proceedings which were concluded positively or negatively for the claimant or with a settlement. A settlement by agreement covers any form of settlement which was preceded by the examination of the eligibility to file an application during the process of formal proceedings before a court or authority.

399	Sec. 32 of the GSF Law stipulates a form of *res iudicata* here which is geared towards "claims" which have already been decided without explicitly determining who must have filed the claim in the prior proceedings. It must therefore be clarified whether this means the effect of a decision the contents of which has become legally binding from a person-related view on the parties and their legal successors and from a substantive point of view only covers the object of the judgment (i.e. the ruling and facts upon which it is based) or whether Sec. 32 of the GSF Law is intended to have a broader scope.

400	The second sentence of Sec. 32 (1) of the GSF Law is to be taken into consideration in the interpretation of this prerequisite. This second sentence is based on a person-related criterion. Pursuant to the second sentence of Sec 32 (1) of the GSF Law, a positive decision by the Arbitration Panel is precluded if the applicant or another relative received compensation by another means. Hence, where such measures were taken there must have been a positive payment to the then restitution claimants/concerned parties and here the focus is on the identity and the relation to the current applicant.

"Grundsätzlich hat die Schiedsinstanz nicht über Forderungen zu entscheiden, die bereits zuvor von österreichischen Gerichten oder Verwaltungsbehörden entschieden oder einvernehmlich geregelt wurden. Weder ein Antragsteller noch ein Verwandter darf auf andere Weise eine Entschädigung oder sonstige Gegenleistung für die in Frage stehenden Vermögenswerte erhalten haben."

Ausnahmefälle hiezu regelt § 32 Abs 2 EF-G, nämlich das Vorliegen einer damaligen extrem ungerechten Regelung/Entscheidung oder, im Falle einer früheren Ablehnung, dem Antragsteller in der Zwischenzeit zugänglich gewordene Beweismittel.

Aus der Formulierung ergibt sich, dass das Vorliegen einer dieser beiden Negativvoraussetzungen, nämlich „früheres Verfahren/einvernehmliche Regelung" oder „sonstige Entschädigung", jede für sich eine materielle Entscheidung der Schiedsinstanz ausschließt.

Eine solche Auslegung des Gesetzes wird auch vom Text des Abkommens, welches am 17. Jänner 2001 zwischen den Regierungen der Republik Österreich und der Vereinigten Staaten von Amerika ausgehandelt wurde (Washingtoner Abkommen), bestätigt. In Annex A dieses Abkommens wird unter Punkt 3 lit. g. ii Folgendes geregelt:

„For the purposes of restitution *in rem*, the notion of 'publicly-owned property' covers exclusively real estate/immovable property/buildings which: [...] was never subject of a claim that was previously decided by an Austrian court or administrative body under prior restitution legislation or a settlement by agreement, or where claimant or relative has never otherwise received compensation or other consideration of the property in question, except in exceptional circumstances where the Panel unanimously determines that prior settlement constitutes an extreme injustice; [...]."

Die mit § 32 EF-G korrespondierende Bestimmung im Washingtoner Abkommen 3.m. lautet: "The Panel legislation will provide that individual claimants (former owners or their heirs, as defined *supra* in paragraph 2(e)) are eligible to receive *in rem* restitution [...] provided that the following criteria are satisfied:

i. property is currently publicly-owned as defined in *supra* in paragraph 3 (g); **and**
ii. [...]
iii. claim was never previously decided or settled under prior restitution legislation or claimants [sic!] or relative has never otherwise received compensation or other consideration for the property in question except in the exceptional circumstances where the Panel unanimously determines that prior settlement constituted extreme injustice; [...]."

Als Forderung im Sinne der Negativvoraussetzung „früheres Verfahren/einvernehmliche Regelung" ist jedes Verfahren vor einer Verwaltungsbehörde oder einem Gericht zu verstehen, in welchem bereits bezüglich der in diesem Schiedsinstanzverfahren begehrten Vermögen eine materielle Entscheidung beziehungsweise eine einvernehmliche Regelung getroffen wurde. Hierbei sind gemäß dem Wortlaut der oben zitierten Klauseln des Abkommens nur Verfahren im Rahmen der Rückstellungsgesetzgebung gemeint. Demzufolge umfasst diese Negativvoraussetzung sämtliche Rückstellungsverfahren, die für den damaligen Rückstellungswerber positiv oder negativ oder mit einem Vergleich geendet haben. Unter einvernehmlicher Regelung ist somit jede Form des Vergleiches zu verstehen, in der vorgängig im Rahmen eines formellen Verfahrens bei Gericht oder Behörde die Antragsberechtigung geprüft worden ist.

§ 32 EF-G formuliert hier eine Form von *res iudicata*, die auf bereits entschiedene „Forderungen" abstellt, ohne explizit festzulegen, wer die Forderung in einem früheren Ver-

401   The GSF Law differentiates between the proceedings before the authorities and other compensation or consideration in that only in the case of the latter can the applicant and (his/her) relations be explicitly named as the then beneficiary. This can be explained by the fact that during the conduct of proceedings by an authority, the eligibility to file an application is to be officially examined. In this regard, it is sufficient that the first alternative of Sec. 28 (1) item 2 is only intended for properties which have never been subject of a claim which was previously decided by an Austrian court or administrative body or was settled by agreement. However, the question of eligibility for restitution where a private settlement agreement had been reached is at the discretion and risk of the contracting parties. A recommendation by the Arbitration Panel shall accordingly not be precluded if "the wrong person" was granted a payment or other consideration without the involvement of an authority. It shall, however, only be precluded if the payment went to the applicant or a relative.

402   The Arbitration Panel therefore reaches the following conclusion:

403   Claims for the property in the proceedings before the Arbitration Panel which were filed within the framework of the restitution legislation and regarding which a substantive decision or settlement by agreement was reached constitute already decided or settled claims in the meaning of Sec. 32 of the GSF Law. "Prior proceedings" in the meaning of Sec. 32 of the GSF Law can under no circumstances be considered those in which solely the eligibility to file an application was decided and not the case itself. It should not be to the detriment of a current applicant if previously another non-eligible person was correctly rejected due to the absent right to claim.

404   The presence of the prerequisite of another settlement payment to relatives can already be rejected at this point, as in the case at hand, no compensation was paid to any of the applicants or their relatives. It therefore must be examined, whether the first of the negative prerequisites is fulfilled.

405   In 1950, John Henry D. claimed at the Restitution Commission at the Regional Court for Civil Matters Vienna the restitution of the property S.-gasse 14 and the transfer of the earnings pursuant to the Third Restitution Act. These proceedings were concluded with the decision of the Supreme Restitution Commission of 5 July 1952 (Rkv 143/52). These restitution proceedings could constitute "prior proceedings" as they concerned the same property, were conducted before a court and were concluded by means of a settlement. However, in its decision the Supreme Restitution Commission rejected the claim of the legatee D., for the reason that he was not eligible to file an application as he did not belong to the circle of heirs determined in para. 14 of the Third Restitution Act. For this reason, the restitution proceedings initiated by John Henry D. in 1950 do not fall under the category "prior proceedings", as only his eligibility to file an application was judged.

406   On 19 October 1960, the Collection Agency A submitted a claim at the Financial Directorate for Vienna, Lower Austria and Burgenland for the restitution of the property S.-gasse 14 in accordance with the Second Restitution Act. These proceedings were concluded with a settlement of 700,000 Schilling. This agreement between the collection agencies and the Republic of Austria was legally sanctioned by the enactment of the Collection Agencies Settlement Act of 7 July 1966, Federal Law Gazette No. 150/1966.

407   It is questionable whether the proceedings initiated by the collection agencies are to be qualified as "prior proceedings" in the meaning of Sec. 32 of the GSF Law. To answer this question, the institution of the collection agencies within the framework of the restitution legislation must be more closely examined.

fahren gestellt haben muss. Zu klären ist daher, ob damit die Wirkung der materiellen Rechtskraft gemeint ist, die in persönlicher Hinsicht die Parteien und deren Rechtsnachfolger bindet und in sachlicher Hinsicht nur den Urteilsgegenstand (Spruch und der ihm zugrunde liegende Sachverhalt) umfasst oder ob bewusst § 32 EF-G weiter gefasst ist.

Bei der Interpretation dieser Voraussetzung ist der zweite Satz des § 32 Abs 1 EF-G mitzubedenken. Dieser stellt auf ein personenbezogenes Kriterium ab. Gemäß § 32 Abs 1 2. Satz EF-G ist eine positive Entscheidung der Schiedsinstanz dann ausgeschlossen, wenn der Antragsteller oder sonst ein Verwandter eine Entschädigung auf eine andere Weise erhalten hat. Bei solchen Maßnahmen muss es demnach zu einer positiven Leistung an den damaligen Rückstellungswerber/Interessenten gekommen sein und es wird hier auf die Identität bzw. Verwandtschaft mit dem jetzigen Antragsteller abgestellt. 400

Das EF-G unterscheidet zwischen behördlichem Verfahren und sonstiger Entschädigung oder Gegenleistung in der Weise, dass nur bei letzterer explizit der Antragsteller und (seine) Verwandtschaft als damals Begünstigte genannt werden. Das lässt sich damit erklären, dass bei Durchführung eines Verfahrens durch eine Behörde die Frage der Antragslegitimation von Amts wegen zu prüfen ist. Insofern genügt es auch, dass § 28 Abs 1 Z 2, 1. Alternative nur darauf abstellt, dass die Liegenschaft niemals Gegenstand einer Forderung war, die bereits zuvor durch österreichische Gerichte oder Verwaltungsbehörden entschieden oder einvernehmlich geregelt wurde. Hingegen liegt die Frage der Rückstellungsberechtigung bei privater Entschädigungsvereinbarung im eigenen Ermessen und Risiko der Vertragsparteien. Eine Empfehlung durch die Schiedsinstanz soll demnach nicht ausgeschlossen sein, wenn „dem Falschen" außerbehördlich eine Zahlung oder eine sonstige Leistung zuteil wurde, sondern nur, wenn die Leistung an den Antragsteller oder einen Verwandten erging. 401

Die Schiedsinstanz gelangt daher zu folgender Ansicht: 402

Als bereits entschiedene bzw. verglichene Forderungen iSd § 32 EF-G gelten Ansprüche, die im Rahmen der Rückstellungsgesetzgebung auf das im Schiedsinstanzverfahren gegenständliche Vermögen erhoben wurden und über die eine materielle Entscheidung oder eine einvernehmliche Regelung getroffen wurde. Es kann als „früheres Verfahren" im Sinne des § 32 EF-G keinesfalls ein solches gelten, in welchem ausschließlich über die Antragsberechtigung und nicht in der Sache selbst abgesprochen wurde. Einem jetzigen Antragsteller soll es nicht zum Schaden gereichen, wenn bereits zuvor eine andere nicht berechtigte Person mangels Aktivlegitimation zu Recht abgewiesen wurde. 403

Das Vorliegen der Voraussetzung einer sonstigen Entschädigungsleistung an Verwandte kann an dieser Stelle bereits verneint werden, denn im gegenständlichen Fall ist an keine/n der AntragstellerInnen oder einen ihrer Verwandten eine Entschädigung erfolgt. Es ist daher zu untersuchen, ob die erste der beiden Negativvoraussetzungen erfüllt ist. 404

1950 beantragte John Henry D. bei der Rückstellungskommission beim LGfZRS Wien gemäß dem 3. RStG die Rückstellung der Liegenschaft S.-gasse 14 sowie die Ausfolgung der Erträgnisse. Dieses Verfahren endete mit Entscheidung der Obersten Rückstellungskommission vom 5. Juli 1952 (Rkv 143/52). Dieses Rückstellungsverfahren könnte als „früheres Verfahren" gelten, da es die identische Liegenschaft betraf, vor Gericht geführt und mittels Entscheidung beendet wurde. Doch die Oberste Rückstellungskommission wies in ihrer Entscheidung das Begehren des Legatars D. mit der Begründung ab, dem Antragsteller fehle die Antragslegitimation, da er nicht in den Erbenkreis des § 14 des 3. RStG falle. Aus diesem Grund fällt das von John Henry D. 1950 angestrengte Rückstellungsverfahren nicht in diese Kategorie „früheres Verfahren", da lediglich über dessen Aktivlegitimation abgesprochen wurde. 405

Arbitration Panel for *In Rem* Restitution – Decision No. 27/2005

408   In the examination of the legal position of the collection agencies within the scope of Sec. 32 of the GSF Law, it is also to be considered that this provision is to be applied in the light of Sec. 42 of the GSF Law. Accordingly, international agreements which deal with the consequences of the National Socialist period or the Second World War, particularly the State Treaty 1955 are not affected by the GSF Law.

409   Equally, in letter c of item 3 of Annex A of the Joint Statement between the Government of the United States and the Government of the Republic of Austria of 17 January 2001, the corresponding agreement is to be found: "The implementation of *in rem* restitution of publicly-owned property will have to be in conformity with Austrian constitutional law and Austria's international obligations."

410   It must also be noted that in the Exchange of Notes between the Austrian Federal Government and the Government of the United States of America of 23 January 2001 it is determined that the Austrian Federal Government and the Government of the United States are in agreement that this Exchange of Notes and the establishment of the General Settlement Fund shall not affect unilateral decisions and bilateral or multilateral agreements which deal with the consequences of the National Socialist era and the Second World War.

411   Hence the following is recorded in para. 9 of the Austrian opening note and in the replying note of the United States:

412   "The Austrian Federal Government / The United States agree/s that this Exchange of Notes and the establishment of the GSF shall not affect unilateral decisions or bilateral or multilateral agreements that dealt with the consequences of the National Socialist era or World War II."

413   In these terms, the institution and function of the collection agencies is to be examined in greater detail.

414   Under Article 26 para. 2 of the State Treaty of 15 May 1955 for the Re-establishment of an Independent and Democratic Austria, Federal Law Gazette No. 152/1955, Austria was required to set up organizations to which heirless and unclaimed property was to be transferred. The provision reads:

> "Austria agrees to take under its control all property, legal rights and interests in Austria of persons, organizations or communities which, individually or as members of groups, were the object of racial, religious or other Nazi measures of persecution where, in the case of persons, such property, rights and interests remain heirless or unclaimed for six months after the coming into force of the present Treaty, or where in the case of organizations and communities such organizations or communities have ceased to exist. Austria shall transfer such property, rights and interests to appropriate agencies or organizations [...] to be used for the relief and rehabilitation of victims or persecution by the Axis Powers [...]. Such transfers shall be effected within eighteen months from the coming into force of the present Treaty and shall include property, rights and interests required to be restored under paragraph 1 of this Artice."

415   The implementation of this obligation occurred with the Federal Law of 13 March 1957 on the Creation of Receiving Organizations, Federal Law Gazette No. 73/1957 (Receiving Organizations Act). In para. 2 (1) of the Receiving Organizations Act, all properties, legal rights and interests named in Article 26 para. 2 of the State Treaty to which persons who had been members of the Jewish Religious Community on 31 December 1937 were entitled, were transferred to Collection Agency A. Pursuant to para. 2 (2) of the Receiving Organizations Act, all those claims to properties, rights and interests that belonged to peo-

Am 19. Oktober 1960 brachte die Sammelstelle A einen Rückstellungsantrag hinsicht- 406
lich der Liegenschaft S.-gasse 14 nach dem 2. RStG bei der FLD für Wien, Niederösterreich und Burgenland ein. Dieses Verfahren wurde mit einem Vergleich über 700.000,–
Schilling beendet. Dieses Übereinkommen zwischen den Sammelstellen und der Republik
Österreich wurde durch Erlassung des Sammelstellen-Abgeltungsgesetzes vom 7. Juli
1966, BGBl 150/1966, gesetzlich sanktioniert.

Fraglich ist, ob dieses von der Sammelstelle geführte Verfahren als „früheres Verfah- 407
ren" im Sinne des § 32 EF-G zu qualifizieren ist. Dazu ist die Institution der Sammelstellen im Rahmen der Rückstellungsgesetzgebung näher zu untersuchen.

Bei der Prüfung der Rechtsstellung der Sammelstellen im Rahmen des § 32 EF-G ist 408
zusätzlich bedenken, dass diese Norm im Lichte der Bestimmung § 42 EF-G auszulegen
ist. Demzufolge werden völkerrechtliche Verträge, die sich mit den Folgen der Zeit des
Nationalsozialismus oder des Zweiten Weltkrieges befassen, insbesondere der StV 1955,
durch das EF-G nicht berührt.

Ebenso findet sich im Annex A der gemeinsamen Erklärung zwischen der Regierung 409
der Vereinigten Staaten und der Regierung der Republik Österreich vom 17. Jänner 2001
unter Z 3 lit. c die korrespondierende Vereinbarung: „The implementation of *in rem* restitution of publicly-owned property will have to be in conformity with Austrian constitutional law and Austria's international obligations." Demnach hat die Durchführung der In
Rem-Restitution in Übereinstimmung mit österreichischem Verfassungsrecht und den internationalen Verpflichtungen Österreichs zu erfolgen.

Weiters ist zu beachten, dass im Notenwechsel zwischen der österreichischen Bundes- 410
regierung und der Regierung der Vereinigten Staaten von Amerika vom 23. Jänner 2001
festgehalten wird, dass die österreichische Bundesregierung und die Regierung der Vereinigten Staaten übereinkommen, dass sich dieser Notenwechsel und die Errichtung des
Allgemeinen Entschädigungsfonds nicht auf einseitige Entscheidungen und bilaterale
oder multilaterale Vereinbarungen, die sich mit den Konsequenzen der Zeit des Nationalsozialismus und des Zweiten Weltkrieges beschäftigen, auswirken soll.

So wird in der Österreichischen Eröffnungsnote bzw. in der Antwortnote der Vereinig- 411
ten Staaten in Absatz 9 Folgendes festgehalten:

"The Austrian Federal Government / The United States agree/s that this Exchange of 412
Notes and the establishment of the GSF shall not affect unilateral decisions or bilateral
or multilateral agreements that dealt with the consequences of the National Socialist
era or World War II."

Unter diesem Gesichtspunkt ist die Einrichtung und Funktion der Sammelstellen näher 413
zu beleuchten.

Artikel 26 Abs 2 des Staatsvertrages vom 15. Mai 1955 betreffend die Wiederherstel- 414
lung eines unabhängigen und demokratischen Österreich, BGBl 152/1955 (StV 1955), verpflichtete Österreich zur Einrichtung von Organisationen, denen erbloses und nicht bean-
spruchtes Vermögen übertragen werden sollte. Die Bestimmung lautet:

„Österreich stimmt zu, alle Vermögenschaften, gesetzlichen Rechte und Interessen in
Österreich, die Personen, Organisationen oder Gemeinschaften gehören, die einzeln
oder als Mitglieder von Gruppen rassischen, religiösen oder anderen Naziverfol-
gungsmaßnahmen unterworfen worden sind, unter seine Kontrolle zu nehmen, wenn,
falls es sich um Personen handelt, diese Vermögenschaften, Rechte und Interessen ohne
Erben bleiben oder durch sechs Monate nach Inkrafttreten des vorliegenden Vertrages

ple other than those named in para. 2 (2)[7] of the Receiving Organizations Act were transferred to Collection Agency B.

416 The manner of assertion and the scope of the claims of the legal persons established by this law, i.e. "Collection Agency A and B", were subject to a later Federal statutory regulation, pursuant to para. 3 of the Receiving Organizations Act. These claims were granted with the amendment to the Receiving Organizations Act and with the Fourth Restitution Claims Act, on the basis of which the collection agencies could file claims in accordance with the individual restitution acts and receive obviously seized property through official channels. With the first amendment to the Receiving Organizations Act, Federal Law Gazette No. 285/1958, para. 3 of the Receiving Organizations Act was amended to the effect that the collection agencies could particularly raise claims which could be raised on the basis of para. 1 (1) of the First, Second and Third Restitution Acts, and had, however, not been asserted within the stipulated deadline or which could not be asserted due to the restrictions on the circle of eligible persons as set out in para. 2 (2) of the First and Second Restitution Acts and para. 14 of the Third Restitution Act or due to another reason for ineligibility to file an application.

417 In the report of the Historical Commission concerning restitution and compensation in international law (Bruno Simma and Hans-Peter Folz, *Restitution und Entschädigung im Völkerrecht. Die Verpflichtungen der Republik Österreich nach 1945 im Lichte ihrer außenpolitischen Praxis.* Vienna 2002) on pages 315 ff the authors examine the implementation of the obligations of the Republic under Article 26 para. 2 of the State Treaty 1955. In doing so the authors essentially reach the conclusion that the establishment of the collection agencies through the Receiving Organizations Act constituted a measure for the implementation of the provisions concerning deadline and procedure of Article 26 para. 2 of the State Treaty 1955, which conformed to the Treaty. The fulfillment of the substantive restitution obligations had, however, remained dependant on the later regulations governing eligibility of the collection agencies to sue. Deficiencies in the fulfillment of the Treaty had existed because the Austrian legislator had not granted the collection agencies any claims according to the *Sechste Rückstellungsgesetz* ("Sixth Restitution Act"). Additionally, in infringement of the provision of Article 26 para. 2 of the State Treaty 1955, pursuant to the judgment of the Supreme Court of 24 April 1962, the collection agencies were not permitted to raise claims in accordance with the Fifth and Seventh Restitution Acts (at 336).

418 The establishment of the collection agencies consequently took place – subject to the possible deficiencies regarding the Fifth to Seventh Restitution Acts – in fulfillment of an international law obligation of Austria stipulated in the State Treaty 1955 which conformed with the Agreement. The Receiving Organizations Act was issued in the course of the implementation of Article 26 para. 2 of the State Treaty 1955. Thus, the basis of the collection agencies is the State Treaty 1955, which constitutes one of the "bilateral or multilateral agreements" cited in the Washington Agreement (Exchange of Notes) which deal with the consequences of the National Socialist era and the Second World War and shall not be affected by the Agreement.

419 The possible deficiencies in the 5th, 6th and 7th Restitution Acts can be disregarded in this context, as only the first three restitution acts are to be taken into consideration within the scope of Arbitration Panel proceedings.

---

[7] Rectification at time of going to press: Meant is para. 2 (1) of the Receiving Organizations Act.

nicht beansprucht werden oder wenn, falls es sich um Organisationen und Gemeinschaften handelt, diese Organisationen und Gemeinschaften aufgehört haben zu bestehen. Österreich soll diese Vermögenschaften, Rechte und Interessen geeigneten [...] Dienststellen oder Organisationen übertragen, damit sie für Hilfe und Unterstützung von Opfern der Verfolgung durch die Achsenmächte und für Wiedergutmachung an solche verwendet werden; [...]. Diese Übertragung wird innerhalb von achtzehn Monaten nach Inkrafttreten des vorliegenden Vertrages durchgeführt werden und Vermögenschaften, Rechte und Interessen, deren Wiederherstellung in Paragraph 1 dieses Artikels verlangt wird, einschließen."

Die Umsetzung dieser Verpflichtung erfolgte mit dem Bundesgesetz vom 13. März 1957 über die Schaffung von Auffangorganisationen, BGBl 73/1957 (Auffangorganisationengesetz). Mit § 2 Abs 1 Auffangorganisationengesetz wurden der Sammelstelle A alle in Artikel 26 § 2 des Staatsvertrages genannten Vermögenschaften, gesetzlichen Rechte und Interessen übertragen, die Personen zustanden, die am 31. Dezember 1937 der israelitischen Religionsgemeinschaft angehört haben. Gemäß § 2 Abs 2 Auffangorganisationengesetz kamen der Sammelstelle B all jene Ansprüche auf Vermögenschaften, Rechte und Interessen zu, die anderen als in § 2 Abs 2[7] Auffangorganisationengesetz genannten Personen zustanden.

415

Die Art der Geltendmachung und der Umfang der Ansprüche der durch dieses Gesetz eingerichteten juristischen Personen „Sammelstelle A und B" waren gemäß § 3 Auffangorganisationengesetz einer späteren bundesgesetzlichen Regelung vorbehalten. Diese Einräumung von Ansprüchen erfolgte mit den Novellen zum Auffangorganisationengesetz und mit dem Vierten Rückstellungsanspruchsgesetz, aufgrund deren die Sammelstellen Ansprüche nach den einzelnen Rückstellungsgesetzen erheben konnten und offensichtlich entzogenes Vermögen vom Amts wegen erhielten. Mit der ersten Novelle zum Auffangorganisationengesetz, BGBl 285/1958, wurde § 3 Auffangorganisationengesetz dahin lautend geändert, dass die Sammelstellen insbesondere Ansprüchen erheben können, die aufgrund des § 1 Abs 1 des 1., 2. und 3. RStG erhoben werden können, innerhalb der vorgesehenen Frist jedoch nicht geltend gemacht worden sind oder wegen der Beschränkung des Kreises der Anspruchsberechtigten durch § 2 Abs 2 des 1. und 2. sowie § 14 des 3. RStG oder wegen eines sonstigen Mangels der Antragsberechtigung nicht durchgesetzt werden konnten.

416

Im Bericht der Historikerkommission betreffend Restitution und Entschädigung im Völkerrecht (Bruno *Simma* und Hans-Peter *Folz*, Restitution und Entschädigung im Völkerrecht. Die Verpflichtungen der Republik Österreich nach 1945 im Lichte ihrer außenpolitischen Praxis, Wien 2002) untersuchen die Autoren auf Seite 315ff die Umsetzung der Verpflichtungen der Republik aus Art. 26 § 2 StV 1955. Dabei gelangen die Verfasser grundsätzlich zum Ergebnis, dass die Errichtung der Sammelstellen durch das Auffangorganisationengesetz eine vertragskonforme Maßnahme zur Umsetzung der Frist- und Verfahrensbestimmungen des Art. 26 § 2 StV 1955 darstelle. Die Erfüllung der materiellen Restitutionsverpflichtungen seien jedoch von der späteren Regelung der Aktivlegitimation der Sammelstellen abhängig geblieben. Lücken in der Vertragserfüllung hätten darin bestanden, dass der österreichische Gesetzgeber den Sammelstellen keine Ansprüche nach dem 6. RStG eingeräumt habe. Zudem sei in Verletzung der Bestimmung Art. 26 § 2 StV 1955 den Sammelstellen nach dem Urteil des OGH vom 24. April 1962 die Erhebung von Ansprüchen nach dem 5. und 7. RStG verwehrt geblieben (S. 336).

417

---

[7] Berichtigung zum Zeitpunkt der Drucklegung: Gemeint ist hier § 2 Abs 1 Auffangorganisationengesetz.

420 Therefore, the Arbitration Panel considers the collection agencies proceedings conducted pursuant to the first three Restitution Acts under the same conditions as "prior proceedings" in the meaning of Sec. 32 of the GSF Law as the restitution proceedings of other claimants for restitution. This view is also reinforced by the fact that the collection agencies were authorized to file restitution claims as legal parties to the same extent that other restitution claimants were able to do on the basis of the first three Restitution Acts.

421 Furthermore as mentioned above, the collection agencies were also able to enforce claims pursuant to para. 3 of the Receiving Organizations Act, which had not been asserted within the filing period provided or had not been able to be enforced due to the restrictions on the circle of eligible persons or due to other reasons for ineligibility to file a claim.

422 This could be beneficial to restitution claimants for whom restitution remained denied for the mentioned reasons. As according to para. 7 of the Fourth Restitution Act, the aggrieved owner, as a so-called "applicant for equitable relief" could inform the collection agencies within a period of one year after the coming into effect of the act that he/she claimed the transfer of the property which had been seized from him/her and restituted to the collection agencies or for which the collection agencies had received proceeds by means of a settlement or other agreement in exchange for the property.

423 Pursuant to para. 8 (1) of the Fourth Restitution Claims Act, in those cases where a notification was made within the filing period in accordance with Article 26 para. 2 of the State Treaty, the collection agencies were obliged to transfer the property. In all other cases it was at the discretion of the collection agencies. According to para. 8 (3) the collection agencies could claim compensation for trouble taken of up to 25 % of the market value or the proceeds of the property. According to para. 10 of the act, they could assign the claim which they themselves had filed.

424 According to para. 10 of the Fourth Restitution Claims Act, an aggrieved owner could also demand the assignment of the collection agencies' claim. In this case, the aggrieved owner would enter the proceedings instead of the Collection Agency through joint declaration by the collection agency and the aggrieved owner to the body appointed to decide on the restitution claim.

425 However, none of the applicants for equitable relief made use of these possibilities under paras. 7, 8 and 10 of the Fourth Restitution Act with regard to the restitution proceedings for the property S.-gasse 14.

d) Extreme Injustice

426 As prior proceedings had already taken place regarding the property in question and the conclusion of such proceedings would preclude the restitution of the property by the Arbitration Panel in accordance with Sec. 28 (1) in connection with Sec. 32 (1) of the GSF Law, it is to be examined whether the exceptional circumstance of Sec. 28 (1) item 2 in connection with Sec. 32 of the GSF Law is present, i.e. if the outcome of the proceedings is to be considered "extremely unjust". The Arbitration Panel can confirm the existence of an extreme injustice according to Sec. 28 (1) item 2 only in "exceptional circumstances" and only unanimously. The presence of an extreme injustice of a settlement by agreement or decision is therefore to be examined on a case-by-case basis. It is, however, not the task of the Arbitration Panel to examine the general legal status and prevailing case law.

427 The case in question concerns "exceptional circumstances" in as much as not only was a settlement reached between the Collection Agency A and the Republic of Austria but this ruling was also was made part of a law, the Collection Agencies Settlement Act of 7 July

Die Einrichtung der Sammelstellen erfolgte demzufolge – vorbehaltlich der möglichen Mängel hinsichtlich des 5. bis 7. RStG – in vertragskonformer Erfüllung einer im StV 1955 normierten völkerrechtlichen Verpflichtung Österreichs. Das Auffangorganisationengesetz erfolgte in Umsetzung des Artikels 26 Abs 2 des StV 1955. Somit ist die Grundlage der Sammelstellen der StV 1955, der eines jener im Washingtoner Abkommen (Notenwechsel) genannten „bilateral or multilateral agreements" darstellt, die sich mit den Konsequenzen der Zeit des Nationalsozialismus und des Zweiten Weltkrieges beschäftigen und durch das Abkommen nicht berührt werden sollen. 418

Die etwaigen Mängel im 5., 6., und 7. RStG können in diesem Zusammenhang jedoch außer Acht gelassen werden, da regelmäßig nur die ersten drei Rückstellungsgesetze im Rahmen des Schiedsinstanzverfahrens zu berücksichtigen sind. 419

Die Schiedsinstanz betrachtet daher die nach den ersten drei Rückstellungsgesetzen geführten Verfahren der Sammelstellen unter den gleichen Bedingungen als „frühere Verfahren" iSd § 32 EF-G wie die Rückstellungsverfahren anderer RückstellungswerberInnen. Diese Ansicht wird auch dadurch bekräftigt, dass die Sammelstellen als Legalparteien ermächtigt waren, in dem Ausmaß Rückstellungsansprüche zu stellen, wie es anderen RückstellungswerberInnen aufgrund der ersten drei Rückstellungsgesetze möglich war. 420

Darüber hinaus war es den Sammelstellen, wie oben erwähnt, gemäß § 3 Auffangorganisationengesetz auch möglich, Ansprüche durchzusetzen, die nicht innerhalb der vorgesehenen Frist geltend gemacht worden waren oder wegen der Beschränkung des Kreises der Anspruchsberechtigten oder wegen eines sonstigen Mangels der Antragsberechtigung nicht durchgesetzt werden konnten. 421

Dies konnte RückstellungswerberInnen zugute kommen, denen aus den genannten Gründen die Rückstellung verwehrt blieb. Denn nach § 7 des 4. Rückstellungsanspruchsgesetzes konnte der geschädigte Eigentümer als sogenannter „Billigkeitswerber" innerhalb einer Frist von einem Jahr nach In-Kraft-Treten des Gesetzes den Sammelstellen mitteilen, dass er die Ausfolgung des ihm entzogenen, den Sammelstellen rückgestellten Vermögens bzw. den der Sammelstellen aufgrund eines Vergleiches oder sonstigen Vertrages an Stelle des Vermögens zukommenden Erlöses beanspruchte. 422

Gemäß § 8 Abs 1 des Vierten Rückstellungsanspruchsgesetzes waren die Sammelstellen in jenen Fällen, in denen eine rechtzeitige Anmeldung im Sinne des Artikels 26 Abs 2 des Staatsvertrages vorlag, zur Ausfolgung des Vermögens verpflichtet. In allen anderen Fällen stand ihnen dies frei. Nach § 8 Abs 3 konnten die Sammelstellen eine Entschädigung für ihre Mühewaltung bis zu 25 % des Verkehrswertes bzw. des Erlöses beanspruchen, nach § 10 des Gesetzes konnten sie den Anspruch, den sie selbst geltend gemacht hatten, abtreten. 423

Nach § 10 des Vierten Rückstellungsanspruchsgesetzes konnte ein geschädigter Eigentümer auch die Abtretung des Rückstellungsantrages der Sammelstelle begehren. In diesem Fall trat durch gemeinsame Anzeige der Sammelstelle und des geschädigten Eigentümers an die zur Entscheidung über den Rückstellungsantrag berufene Stelle der geschädigte Eigentümer statt der Sammelstelle in das Verfahren ein. 424

Diese Möglichkeiten nach §§ 7, 8 und 10 des 4. Rückstellungsanspruchsgesetzes wurde jedoch hinsichtlich des Rückstellungsverfahrens zur Liegenschaft S.-gasse 14 von keinem Billigkeitswerber genutzt. 425

d) Extreme Ungerechtigkeit

Da hinsichtlich der gegenständlichen Liegenschaft bereits ein früheres Verfahren stattgefunden hat und der Abschluss eines solchen die Rückstellung der Liegenschaft durch die 426

Arbitration Panel for *In Rem* Restitution – Decision No. 27/2005

1966, Federal Law Gazette No. 150/1966. The Arbitration Panel is to examine the settlement, which is based on the law, for the existence of extreme injustice.

428 If, as stated above, the settlements concluded by the collection agencies are in principle to be counted among the prior measures in the meaning of the GSF Law, it is to be considered in the present settlement that its content was in the end essentially characterized by the position of the collection agency as a temporary establishment and by its character as a receiving organization. The problems surrounding the claim regarding the property S.-gasse 14, covered by the lump sum settlement, is therefore different on the one hand to the settlements concluded by the collection agencies in previous individual proceedings and on the other hand to the agreements concluded by "private" restitution claimants. This circumstance is to be taken into consideration by the Arbitration Panel when applying the criteria for the examination of "extreme injustice" in the meaning of the GSF Law.

429 With regard to the Collection Agencies Settlement Act, Simma/Folz observe:

"The Republic has provided for numerous provisions on the settlement of collection agencies' claims within the scope of the application of Article 26 para. 2 of the State Treaty. The lump sum settlement of claims of Collection Agencies A and B by means of one-sided statutory regulation seems to be particularly problematic" (at 331).

430 Furthermore, these authors state:

"The one-sided settlement of restitution claims in accordance with the Collection Agencies Settlement Act of 7 July 1966 and pursuant to para. 8 of the *Kunst- und Kulturgutbereinigungsgesetz* ("Artistic and Cultural Assets Settlement Act") of 27 June 1969 also seem questionable under international law. One can only assume a contractual fulfillment of the obligation under Article 26 para. 2 of the State Treaty here, if the settlement by law was actually founded on a preceding settlement agreement between the Republic of Austria and the collection agencies or if the settlement amount in fact comprised the value of the settled claims."

431 Such doubts regarding a "one-sided legal regulation" through the Collection Agencies Settlement Act are not applicable to the facts of this case, as the provision contained in this act for the property S.-gasse 14 can be traced back to a preceding settlement after years of negotiations. Although there is no physical copy of the settlement due to the absence of the restitution file, it is, however, evident from the documentation concerning the settlement negotiations found in other holdings that the settlement amount named in the Collection Agencies Settlement Act for the Sanatorium F. was based on the prior agreement made between the collection agencies and the Republic of Austria. The concerned entity – the law is addressed to the Collection Agency – had contributed to the content of the settlement for the Sanatorium F. in the "settlement in the form of a law". The withdrawal of the claim by Collection Agency A in the end took place as a result of an agreement with the Republic of Austria which included the unresolved claims of the Collection Agency against the Federation.

432 However it is to be examined whether this agreement was concluded under the Collection Agency's autonomy to freely arrange its affairs and whether the agreement would have also been concluded with such contents by a restitution claimant intent on his/her own interests.

433 As expressly stated in the explanatory remarks of the government bill for the Collection Agencies Settlement Act, the overall settlement of all collection agencies' claims was sought:

"With this government bill, not only the obligation arising from Article 26 para. 2 of the State Treaty regarding heirless property of persons subject to persecution by Na-

Schiedsinstanz nach § 28 Abs 1 iVm § 32 Abs 1 EF-G ausschließen würde, ist zu prüfen, ob der Ausnahmetatbestand iSd § 28 Abs 1 Z 2 iVm § 32 EF-G vorliegt, nämlich ob das Verfahrensergebnis als „extrem ungerecht" zu betrachten ist. Dass eine extreme Ungerechtigkeit vorliegt, kann die Schiedsinstanz laut § 28 Abs 1 Z 2 nur „in besonderen Ausnahmefällen" und nur einstimmig bejahen. Das Vorliegen einer extremen Ungerechtigkeit bei einer einvernehmlichen Regelung oder Entscheidung ist daher jedenfalls im Einzelfall zu untersuchen. Nicht aber ist es Aufgabe der Schiedsinstanz, die allgemeine Gesetzeslage und die gefestigte Rechtsprechung zu prüfen.

Im gegenständlichen Verfahren handelt es sich insofern um einen „Ausnahmefall", als zwischen der Sammelstelle A und der Republik Österreich nicht nur ein Vergleich vereinbart wurde, sondern diese Regelung auch Inhalt eines Gesetzes, des Sammelstellen-Abgeltungsgesetzes vom 7. Juli 1966, BGBl 150/1966, wurde. Die Schiedsinstanz hat hier den Vergleich, der dem Gesetz zugrunde liegt, auf eine etwaige extreme Ungerechtigkeit zu prüfen. 427

Wenn auch, wie oben ausgeführt, die von den Sammelstellen geschlossenen Vergleiche grundsätzlich zu den früheren Maßnahmen iSd EF-G zu zählen sind, ist bei der vorliegenden Vergleichsregelung zu bedenken, dass deren Inhalt letztlich wesentlich von der Position der Sammelstelle als temporärer Einrichtung und von ihrem Charakter als Auffangorganisation geprägt war. Die Problematik des vom Pauschalvergleich umfassten Anspruches über die Liegenschaft S.-gasse 14 ist daher anders gelagert als die einerseits von den Sammelstellen in früheren einzelnen Verfahren abgeschlossenen Vergleiche und andererseits als die von „privaten" RückstellungswerberInnen geschlossenen Vereinbarungen. Diesen Umstand hat die Schiedsinstanz bei Anwendung des Maßstabes zur Prüfung der „extremen Ungerechtigkeit" iSd EF-G zu beachten. 428

Hinsichtlich des Sammelstellen-Abgeltungsgesetzes bemerken *Simma/Folz*: 429

„Die Republik hat mehrere gesetzliche Regelungen zu [sic!] Abgeltung von Ansprüchen der Sammelstellen im Anwendungsbereich von Art. 26 Abs 2 StV getroffen. Besonders problematisch erscheint dabei die pauschale Ablöse von Ansprüchen der Sammelstellen A und B durch einseitige gesetzliche Regelung" (S. 331).

Weiters meinen diese Autoren: 430

„Völkerrechtlich bedenklich erscheint auch die einseitige Ablöse von Rückstellungsansprüchen nach dem Sammelstellen-Abgeltungsgesetz vom 7. Juli 1966 und nach dem § 8 des Kunst- und Kulturgutbereinigungsgesetzes vom 27. Juni 1969. Hier kann nur dann von einer vertragsgemäßen Erfüllung der Verpflichtung aus Art. 26 Abs 2 StV ausgegangen werden, wenn die Ablöse durch Gesetz tatsächlich aus einer vorgeschalteten Vergleichsvereinbarung der Republik Österreich mit den Sammelstellen beruhte oder wenn die Ablösesumme tatsächlich dem Wert der abgegoltenen Ansprüche entsprach."

Solche Bedenken gegenüber einer „einseitigen gesetzlichen Regelung" durch das Sammelstellen-Abgeltungsgesetz treffen in dieser Weise auf den gegenständlichen Sachverhalt nicht zu. Denn die in diesem Gesetz enthaltene Regelung der Abgeltung für die Liegenschaft S.-gasse 14 geht auf einen vorgeschalteten Vergleich nach jahrelangen Verhandlungen zurück. Zwar liegt mangels Rückstellungsakt keine physische Ausfertigung des Vergleichs vor. Jedoch sind die Vergleichsverhandlungen in anderen Aktenbeständen dokumentiert und daraus ist ersichtlich, dass die Höhe der im Sammelstellen-Abgeltungsgesetz für das Sanatorium F. genannten Vergleichssumme auf der vorangegangenen Vereinbarung zwischen den Sammelstellen und der Republik Österreich beruhte. Die Betroffene – Gesetzesadressat ist die Sammelstelle – hat am „Vergleich in Gesetzesform" 431

Arbitration Panel for *In Rem* Restitution – Decision No. 27/2005

tional Socialism shall be fulfilled, furthermore, a few cases which have been contentious through the years will be resolved by means of a settlement. Moreover, protracted and costly proceedings are spared, a threatened legal uncertainty will be overcome and the activities of the collection agencies can be concluded early after this act has come into effect. Finally, this act constitutes the finalization of the restitution legislation." (86 BlgNR 11th legislative period p. 3)

434 In line with the intentions of the legislator, the activities of the collection agencies should therefore have been terminated in the near future: "After the payment of the settlement amount, the collection agencies can enter administrative liquidation in mid 1967." (86 BlgNR 11th legislative period p. 3)

435 In view of this objective of the Collection Agencies Settlement Act, the Arbitration Panel shares the thoughts of the Historical Commission authors insofar as the interests pursued by the collection agencies differed from those of a restitution claimant intent on his/her own interests. This is relevant where the interests of the restitution claimant differ so widely that the conduct of the claim was not given the necessary impetus. Such a settlement could not be held against a current applicant.

436 The aim of the collection agencies was to achieve a total resolution of all open claims. The focus of the settlement negotiations was the creation of a package deal for numerous contentious claims. A further aim was to rapidly conclude the activities of the Collection Agencies A and B and to dissolve the institutions. Thus, considerations contributed to the willingness to conclude the settlement regarding the Sanatorium F. and to the organization of its content which had no objective connection to the claim to the property S.-gasse 14. A restitution claimant intent on his or her own interests would not have acted in this way as considerations of this kind would not have played a role.

437 The fact that the interests of the Collection Agency did not correspond to those of a restitution claimant intent on his/her own interests results from the following:

438 As the findings demonstrated, the Collection Agency first took one stance in the restitution proceedings concerning the property S.-gasse 14, until the possibility of a lump sum settlement was raised, after which it took a different stance. Shortly before the first negotiations for a lump sum settlement in April 1945, a to-be-requested settlement amount of up to 4 million Schilling was still being considered (see margin note 298). Later, this individual claim was not of any particular importance to the Collection Agency and was no longer strenuously pursued. The president of the Collection Agency A, Georg Weis, stated on 18 June 1965 with regard to the discussions with representatives of the Ministry of Finance for the settlement of the Collection Agency's open claims: "For the F[...] claim, for which I requested 1 million Schilling, 600,000 Schilling are offered. This is also acceptable. Maybe a further 200,000 Schilling can be accepted. If, however, a general settlement was to be reached, I would not negotiate further for such an amount" (see margin note 305). In the settlement negotiations held at this time, the Collection Agency did not act in the same way as an individual who was taking care of his/her own interests would have.

439 The Arbitration Panel identifies in the Collection Agencies Settlement Act regarding the Sanatorium F. claim a deficiency in the prior restitution legislation as defined in letter d of item 2 of Annex A to the Agreement between the Austrian Federal Government and the Government of the United States of America which deals with questions of compensation and restitution for victims of National Socialism, Federal Law Gazette III Nr. 121/2001. The deficiency does not arise from the law itself. As this law, however, as

über die Abgeltung für das Sanatorium F. inhaltlich mitgewirkt. Die Antragsrückziehung durch die Sammelstelle A erfolgte schließlich aufgrund einer Einigung mit der Republik Österreich, die offene Ansprüche der Sammelstelle gegen den Bund umfasste.

Jedoch ist zu untersuchen, ob diese Vereinbarung seitens der Sammelstelle in voller Gestaltungsfreiheit abgeschlossen wurde bzw. ob sie mit diesem Inhalt auch von einem auf seine Interessen bedachten Rückstellungswerber geschlossen worden wäre. 432

Wie ausdrücklich in den Erläuternden Bemerkungen der Regierungsvorlage zum Sammelstellen-Abgeltungsgesetz formuliert ist, wurde eine Gesamtregelung aller den Sammelstellen zukommenden Ansprüche angestrebt: 433

„Mit dem vorliegenden Gesetzesentwurf soll nicht nur der in Artikel 26 § 2 des Staatsvertrages bezüglich des erblos gebliebenen Vermögens der durch den Nationalsozialismus verfolgten Personen übernommenen Verpflichtung nachgekommen werden, es werden darüber hinaus auch noch einige durch Jahre hindurch strittige Fälle im Vergleichswege bereinigt, es erübrigt sich weiters die Durchführung von langwierigen und kostspieligen Verfahren, es wird auch eine drohende Rechtsunsicherheit beseitigt und die Tätigkeit der ‚Sammelstellen' kann nach Gesetzwerdung vorzeitig [sic!] beendet werden. Schließlich stellt dieses Gesetz den Schlusspunkt unter die Rückstellungsgesetzgebung dar." (86 BlgNR 11. GP S. 3)

Nach den Vorstellungen des Gesetzgebers sollte die Tätigkeit der Sammelstellen damit in Kürze beendet sein: „Nach Auszahlung des Vergleichsbetrages können die ‚Sammelstellen' Mitte 1967 in administrative Liquidation treten." (86 BlgNR 11. GP S. 3) 434

Angesichts dieser Zielsetzung des Sammelstellen-Abgeltungsgesetzes teilt die Schiedsinstanz die Bedenken der AutorInnen der Historikerkommission, sofern sich die von der Sammelstelle verfolgten Interessen von denen eines auf seine Interessen bedachten Rückstellungswerbers unterscheiden. Relevant ist dies, wenn diese vom Rückstellungswerber unterschiedliche Interessenslage so weit führte, dass die Durchsetzung des Anspruches nicht mit dem notwendigen Nachdruck betrieben wurde. Ein solcher Vergleich könnte einem nunmehrigen Antragsteller nicht entgegengehalten werden. 435

Ziel der Sammelstelle war es, eine Gesamtbereinigung aller offenen Ansprüche zu erreichen. Im Vordergrund der Vergleichsverhandlungen stand die Junktimierung einer Vielzahl strittiger Forderungen. Des Weiteren galt es, die Tätigkeit der Sammelstellen A und B zügig abzuschließen und die Einrichtungen aufzulösen. Somit flossen in die Bereitschaft zum Abschluss des Vergleichs über das ehemalige Sanatorium F. und zu dessen inhaltlicher Ausgestaltung Überlegungen ein, die zum Rückstellungsanspruch auf die Liegenschaft S.-gasse 14 keinen sachlichen Bezug hatten. Ein auf seine Interessen bedachter Rückstellungswerber hätte nicht so agiert, da solche Überlegungen keine Rolle gespielt hätten. 436

Dass die Interessenslage der Sammelstelle tatsächlich nicht der eines auf seine Interessen bedachten Rückstellungswerbers entsprach, ergibt sich aus Folgendem: 437

Wie die Feststellungen gezeigt haben, vertrat die Sammelstelle im Rückstellungsverfahren zur Liegenschaft S.-gasse 14 bis zum Zeitpunkt der In-Aussicht-Stellung einer Pauschalabgeltung eine andere Position als danach. Als zu fordernder Vergleichsbetrag stand kurz vor den ersten Verhandlungen zum Pauschalvergleich im April 1965 noch ein Betrag bis zu 4 Millionen Schilling im Raum (siehe Rz 298). Später spielte dieser einzelne Anspruch für die Sammelstelle keine besondere Rolle und wurde von der Sammelstelle nicht mehr mit Nachdruck verfolgt. So meinte der Vorsitzende der Sammelstelle A Dr. Georg 438

demonstrated, merely reproduces a legal transaction under private law – namely the lump sum settlement between the collection agencies and the Republic of Austria – a possible deficiency was to be sought in this legal transaction.

440 Furthermore, it is to be examined whether other indications for the establishment of an extreme injustice of the settlement in the meaning of GSF Law are present.

441 Such an indication could be found in the examination of the contents of the settlement in question in the form of a difference in value between the settlement amount and the value of the property at that time. If one were to consider the value of the property S.-gasse 14, as valued by expert DI Hans Weidisch in 1963 at 6.2 million Schilling, and compare it to the settlement amount of 700,000 Schilling, then a great discrepancy in value can be established.

442 As the Arbitration Panel has already established in previous decisions (e.g. decision no. 3/2003), in judging the possible existence of an extreme injustice, the notion of freedom of contract inherent in a settlement is to be taken into consideration. As in a settlement an amicable new determination of contentious or dubious entitlements takes place with mutual concessions (para. 1380 of the [Austrian] General Civil Code), in which – in contrast to other legal transactions – *laesio enormis* is ruled out by law as a reason to appeal (para. 1386 of the [Austrian] General Civil Code) there is regularly a discrepancy between the value of the contentious property and the settlement sum in restitution settlements.

443 It can be derived from the exceptional character of the regulations of Sec. 28 and 32 of the GSF Law and the provision in Sec. 20 item 2 of the GSF Law in which an equitable payment from the Claims Committee for inadequate compensation is provided for, that a discrepancy in value between the true value of the property and the settlement sum alone does not suffice to justify the existence of an extreme injustice. If the amount of a previous compensation was inadequate, this alone does not constitute a case of extreme injustice.

444 A decision that was inadequate as to the amount may, however, indicate an extreme injustice, if the amount of the compensation indicates that the statutory basis was interpreted and applied unobjectively to the detriment of the aggrieved party and that the aggrieved party was subsequently grossly disadvantaged in the outcome of his/her restitution or compensation claims. The same applies to settlements by agreement, in so far as they do not comply with the fundamental bases of the objectively applied statutory basis and accordingly it is to be assumed that a decision-making body, applying the statutory provisions, would have arrived at a substantially more beneficial decision for the aggrieved party.

445 In this case it means that the above named discrepancy in value would in any case be considered as an indication of an extreme injustice if the Financial Directorate, as the restitution authority, would have had to affirm the restitution claim to the property S.-gasse 14 in correct application of the law.

446 The affirmation of the restitution claim to the property S.-gasse 14 relied on the question whether the Financial Directorate was obliged to affirm a seizure of property in accordance with the Third Restitution Act and in accordance with the Third State Treaty Implementation Act. Three factors were decisive: Did the seizure of the right to inherit from the potential heirs constitute a seizure of the property in the meaning of the restitution acts? Does the over-indebtedness of the estate asserted by the State Financial Procurator's Office preclude a seizure? Does the applicability of the Third State Treaty Implementation

Weis am 18. Juni 1965 hinsichtlich der Diskussionen mit Vertretern des Finanzministeriums zur Abfindung der offenen Ansprüche der Sammelstelle: „Für den Anspruch F[...], für den ich 1 Million gefordert hatte, werden S. 600.000,– geboten. Auch das ist akzeptabel. Vielleicht kann man weitere S. 200.000,– durchsetzen. Wenn es aber zu einer Gesamtbereinigung kommt, würde ich wegen eines solchen Betrages nicht mehr viel hin und her handeln" (siehe Rz 305). Die Sammelstelle handelte in den zu diesem Zeitpunkt geführten Vergleichsverhandlungen nicht so, wie ein einzelner, auf seine Interessen bedachter Rückstellungswerber agiert hätte.

Die Schiedsinstanz erblickt im Sammelstellen-Abgeltungsgesetz hinsichtlich des Anspruchs Sanatorium F. eine Unzulänglichkeit in der früheren Rückstellungsgesetzgebung iSd Z 2 lit. d Anhang A zum Abkommen zwischen der Österreichischen Bundesregierung und der Regierung der Vereinigten Staaten von Amerika zur Regelung von Fragen der Entschädigung und Restitution für Opfer des Nationalsozialismus, BGBl III Nr. 121/2001. Die Unzulänglichkeit ergibt sich zwar nicht aus dem Gesetz selbst. Da dieses Gesetz jedoch, wie gezeigt, bloß ein privatrechtliches Rechtsgeschäft – nämlich den Pauschalvergleich zwischen den Sammelstellen und der Republik Österreich – wiedergibt, war eine allfällige Unzulänglichkeit in diesem Rechtsgeschäft zu suchen. 439

Darüber hinaus ist noch zu prüfen, ob noch andere Anhaltspunkte für die Feststellung eines extrem ungerechten Vergleiches iSd EF-G vorliegen. 440

Ein derartiger Anhaltspunkt könnte bei der inhaltlichen Prüfung des gegenständlichen Vergleiches in einer Wertdifferenz zwischen dem Vergleichsbetrag und dem damaligen Wert der Liegenschaft gesehen werden. Betrachtet man also den damaligen Wert der Liegenschaft S.-gasse 14, der vom Sachverständigen DI Hans Weidisch 1963 auf 6,200.000,– Schilling geschätzt wurde, und vergleicht diesen mit dem Vergleichsbetrag von 700.000,– Schilling, ist eine große Wertdifferenz festzustellen. 441

Wie die Schiedsinstanz bereits in früheren Entscheidungen festgestellt hat (etwa in Entscheidung Nummer 3/2003), ist jedoch bei der Beurteilung des Vorliegens einer etwaigen extremen Ungerechtigkeit auf den einem Vergleich innewohnenden Gedanken der Privatautonomie Rücksicht zu nehmen. Da bei Vergleichen unter beiderseitigem Nachgeben eine einverständliche neue Festlegung strittiger oder zweifelhafter Rechte erfolgt (§ 1380 ABGB), bei der im Gegensatz zu anderen Rechtsgeschäften die Anfechtung wegen laesio enormis (Verkürzung über die Hälfte) gesetzlich ausgeschlossen ist (§ 1386 ABGB), ist bei Rückstellungsvergleichen regelmäßig eine Diskrepanz zwischen dem Wert der strittigen Liegenschaft und der Vergleichssumme verbunden. 442

Aus dem Ausnahmecharakter der Regelungen der §§ 28 und 32 EF-G und der Bestimmung § 20 Z 2 EF-G, in welcher explizit eine Billigkeitszahlung des Antragskomitees für unzureichende Entschädigungen vorgesehen ist, kann abgeleitet werden, dass ein Wertmissverhältnis zwischen dem wahren Wert der Liegenschaft und der Vergleichssumme allein nicht zur Begründung des Vorliegens eines extrem ungerechten Vergleiches ausreicht. Eine der Höhe nach unzureichende frühere Entschädigung stellt daher für sich alleine keinen Fall der extremen Ungerechtigkeit dar. 443

Eine Entscheidung, die der Höhe nach unzureichend war, kann jedoch eine extreme Ungerechtigkeit indizieren, wenn die Höhe der Entschädigung darauf hindeutet, dass gesetzliche Grundlagen objektiv unvertretbar zu Lasten des Geschädigten ausgelegt und angewendet worden sind und der Geschädigte dadurch im Ergebnis hinsichtlich seiner Rückstellungs- oder Entschädigensansprüche grob benachteiligt wurde. Selbiges gilt für einvernehmliche Regelungen, soweit diese nicht mit den wesentlichen Grundsätzen der 444

Act have to be assumed and, if yes, does its exception "sale solely due to political persecution" apply?

447 Seizure of the Right to Inherit

448 The decision of the Supreme Restitution Commission at the Supreme Court of 22 March 1962, Rkv 13/61 is important in connection with the seizure of the right to inherit as the subject of a restitution claim regarding the property. In these proceedings, the Collection Agency claimed the restitution of a property which had been sold from the estate of a Jewish woman with the approval of the Probate Court in charge of the processing and settlement and the Property Transaction Office. According to the decision of the Supreme Restitution Commission, there were no "physical heirs". The place of residence of a supposed testamentary heir in Poland was unable to be found by the Probate Court in charge of the processing and settlement. The remaining estate was claimed by the Chief Finance President Vienna-Lower Danube as heirless and declared revertible for the benefit of the German Reich.

449 The Supreme Restitution Commission ruled in its decision regarding the sale of the property by a dormant estate that the applicability of para. 2 (1) of the Third Restitution Act (presence of a property seizure) depends on the political persecution of the heir and not the political persecution of the decedent. A seizure as defined by para. 1 (1) of the Third Restitution Act could not be recognized in the sale of assets from an heirless estate merely because the decedent had been subject to political persecution by the National Socialists. For the transfer of property to have the characteristics of a seizure, an element of force, "an involuntariness, caused as a consequence of the circumstances resulting from the National Socialist assumption of power" was important. In property transfers effected by a politically persecuted owner, such force or pressure or involuntariness was to be assumed. An assumption of this kind does however not exist where the politically persecuted person was dead and the dormant estate takes his/her place. "Regardless of the theoretical construction of para. 547 of the (Austrian) General Civil Code, in answering the question whether political persecution of the estate is to be assumed, not the decedent but the heirs, to whom the property would have fallen without the transfer of property, is relevant."

450 The Supreme Restitution Commission denied the existence of a property seizure in the mentioned proceedings for the following reasons: "If, as in the present case, no politically persecuted heirs were present, then accordingly, the assumption of a property seizure through the sale of parts of the dormant estate cannot be founded on para.2 (1) of the Third Restitution Act."

451 On 10 June 1964, during the restitution proceedings for S.-gasse 14, the State Financial Procurator's Office referred to this negative decision Rkv 13/61 of the Supreme Restitution Commission and put forward the opinion that the sale of the property by the trustee of the estate had been handled within the scope of probate proceedings conducted in accordance with the law.

452 In contrast, the Collection Agency argued that the decision Rkv 13/61 was based on fundamentally different facts to those in the S.-gasse 14 proceedings. To summarize, it put forward that contrary to the cited decision, in which it could not even be confirmed that a persecuted heir had been appointed to the succession, it was "indisputably proven that only politically persecuted persons had been entitled to the inheritance."

453 The Arbitration Panel shares the view that the decision Rkv 13/61 was based on a different set of facts, as in the cited case the existence of politically persecuted heirs was not

sachlich anwendbaren Gesetzesgrundlagen übereinstimmen und dementsprechend davon auszugehen ist, dass ein Entscheidungsorgan in Anwendung der Gesetzesbestimmungen zu einer für den Geschädigten wesentlich günstigeren Entscheidung gelangt wäre.

In diesem Fall bedeutet dies, dass die oben genannte Wertdifferenz jedenfalls dann als 445 Indiz für eine extreme Ungerechtigkeit zu werten wäre, wenn die FLD als Rückstellungsbehörde den Rückstellungsanspruch auf die Liegenschaft S.-gasse 14 bei korrekter Gesetzesanwendung bejahen hätte müssen.

Die Bejahung des Rückstellungsanspruches auf die Liegenschaft S.-gasse 14 hing von 446 der Frage ab, ob die FLD eine Vermögensentziehung nach dem 3. RStG und nach dem 3. StVDG zu bejahen hatte. Dafür waren drei Fragen ausschlaggebend: Stellte die Entziehung des Erbrechts der potentiellen ErbInnen einen Entzug der Liegenschaft iSd Rückstellungsgesetze dar? Stand die von der Finanzprokuratur argumentierte Überschuldung des Nachlasses einer Entziehung entgegen? Muss von der Anwendbarkeit des 3. StVDG ausgegangen werden und, wenn ja, liegt dessen Ausnahmetatbestand „Veräußerung lediglich aus politischer Verfolgung" vor?

Entzug des Erbrechts 447

Im Zusammenhang mit der Entziehung des Erbrechts als Rückstellungsanspruch auf 448 die Liegenschaft ist die Entscheidung der Obersten Rückstellungskommission beim OGH vom 22. März 1962, Rkv 13/61, von Bedeutung. In diesem Verfahren beanspruchte die Sammelstelle die Rückstellung einer Liegenschaft, die aus dem Nachlass einer Jüdin mit Genehmigung des Abhandlungsgerichtes und der Vermögensverkehrsstelle verkauft worden war. Laut Entscheidung der Obersten Rückstellungskommission gab es keine „Leibeserben". Der Aufenthaltsort eines behaupteten Testamentserben in Polen konnte vom Abhandlungsgericht nicht ausfindig gemacht werden. Der verbliebene Nachlass wurde vom OFP Wien-Niederdonau als erblos in Anspruch genommen und zugunsten des Deutschen Reiches für heimfällig erklärt.

Die Oberste Rückstellungskommission sprach in dieser Entscheidung hinsichtlich der 449 Vermögensveräußerung durch einen ruhenden Nachlass aus, dass sich die Anwendbarkeit von § 2 Abs 1 des 3. RStG (Vorliegen einer Vermögensentziehung) nach der politischen Verfolgung des Erben und nicht nach der politischen Verfolgung des Erblassers richte. In der Veräußerung von Vermögen aus einem erblosen Nachlass könne nicht bereits deshalb eine Entziehung im Sinne des § 1 Abs 1 des 3. RStG gesehen werden, weil der Erblasser politischer Verfolgung durch den Nationalsozialismus unterworfen war. Es sei für den Entziehungscharakter einer Vermögensübertragung ein Element des Zwanges, „einer durch die infolge der nationalsozialistischen Machtergreifung bestehenden Verhältnissen bedingten Unfreiwilligkeit" wesentlich. Bei Vermögensübertragungen durch einen politisch verfolgten Eigentümer sei ein solcher Zwang oder Druck oder eine solche Unfreiwilligkeit zu vermuten. Eine solche Vermutung bestehe aber nicht, wenn die politisch Verfolgte verstorben und der ruhende Nachlass an seine Stelle getreten sei. „Ungeachtet der theoretischen Konstruktion des § 547 ABGB kommt es dann bei der Frage, ob politische Verfolgung des Nachlasses anzunehmen ist, nicht auf die Person des Erblassers, sondern auf die Person des Erben an, dem ohne die Vermögensübertragung das Vermögen zugefallen wäre."

Die Oberste Rückstellungskommission verneinte im genannten Verfahren das Vorlie- 450 gen einer Vermögensentziehung mit folgender Begründung: „Waren, wie im vorliegenden Fall, keine politisch verfolgten Erben vorhanden, kann bei der Veräußerung von Teilen des

proven. The findings in the case at issue demonstrate, however, that all heirs of Lothar F. were persecuted by the National Socialist regime and their properties were seized.

454 This also applies to the renunciation of the inheritance by the appointed testamentary heirs, the parents-in-law of Dr. F., Ida and Emil Be., even if they conditionally accepted the inheritance of their daughter. The voluntary nature of the renunciation of inheritance rights to the estate of Lothar F. cannot be assumed. As the Collection Agency submitted in its statement, had the spouses Be. accepted the inheritance, it would have prevented or considerably delayed their departure from the country in order to escape the persecution, due to the specific tax obligations for emigrating Jews (Reich Flight Tax). In contrast to the small estate of their daughter amounting to around 3,000 Reichsmark, which also only consisted of movable objects, the estate of Dr. F. consisted of an estate containing numerous assets and liabilities and above all was combined with a property and a sanatorium operation. As the fates of Emil and Ida Be. show, it was not possible for them to escape the National Socialist persecution, despite having renounced the inheritance.

455 The Arbitration Panel therefore reaches the opinion that the Financial Directorate Vienna when properly considering the judgment of the Supreme Restitution Commission would have had to qualify the seizure of the right to inherit as a property seizure as defined in the Third Restitution Act.

456 Over-indebtedness

457 The "over-indebtedness" of the estate and/or the property asserted by the State Financial Procurator's Office would not have made any difference. As stated above regarding the question of a seizure according to the GSF Law, debts did prevent the requirements of a seizure according to restitution case law being met, as long as there was still hope of these debts being settled. According to the decision of the Supreme Restitution Commission of 3 September 1949 (Rkv 278/49) it was even the duty of the acquirer, in that specific case,

> "to prove that there was absolutely no hope of overcoming the financial difficulties and that a continuous, not just temporary lack of financial means existed which rendered the payment of debts and the continuation of the company impossible, so that a sale would have been necessary under all circumstances [...]."

458 In this regard, the above statements on the question of seizure in the meaning of the GSF Law are to be referred to, where the applicable provisions of the Bankruptcy Act only permit an opening of bankruptcy proceedings for assets of an estate in the case of excessive debts and a negative outlook for its continued existence. As stated above, the State Financial Procurator's Office did neither allege nor state that the second prerequisite for the element of the case had been fulfilled. Further to this, in fact no bankruptcy proceedings were opened for the estate; instead the creditors were satisfied with composition quotas.

459 Regarding the matter of over-indebtedness, the Financial Directorate would have also had to draw on the decision of the Supreme Restitution Commission of 2 October 1948, Rkv 161/48 for its decision on the restitution claim in the F. case. The objects of these restitution proceedings were properties on which a sanatorium had been operated and which had been subject to a forced sale in 1940. The Supreme Restitution Commission ruled in this case that the claimants' debts determined by the Restitution Commission do not force

ruhenden Nachlasses die Annahme einer Vermögensentziehung demnach nicht auf § 2 Abs 1 des 3. Rückstellungsgesetzes allein gegründet werden."

Im Rahmen des Rückstellungsverfahrens zur S.-gasse 14 berief sich die Finanzprokuratur am 10. Juni 1964 auf diese ablehnende Entscheidung Rkv 13/61 der Obersten Rückstellungskommission und vertrat die Ansicht, dass der Verkauf der Liegenschaft durch den Verlassenschaftskurator im Rahmen eines gesetzmäßigen Verlassenschaftsverfahrens abgewickelt worden sei. 451

Die Sammelstelle hielt dem entgegen, dass die Entscheidung Rkv 13/61 auf einem wesentlich anderen Sacherverhalt beruhe als jenem im Verfahren S.-gasse 14. Sie führte zusammenfassend ins Treffen, es sei, im Gegensatz zur zitierten Entscheidung, in der nicht einmal bescheinigt werden konnte, dass ein verfolgter Erbe zur Erbfolge berufen war, „im gegenständlichen Falle eindeutig bewiesen, dass zur Erbfolge lediglich politisch verfolgte Personen berufen waren." 452

Die Schiedsinstanz teilt die Ansicht, dass die Entscheidung Rkv 13/61 einen anderen Sachverhalt zur Grundlage hatte, da im zitierten Fall das Vorhandensein von politisch verfolgten Erbberechtigten nicht belegt war. Die Feststellungen im gegenständlichen Verfahren zeigen hingegen, dass sämtliche zur Erbfolge nach Dr. Lothar F. berufenen Personen vom nationalsozialistischen Regime verfolgt wurden und deren Vermögen entzogen wurden. 453

Dies trifft auch auf den Erbverzicht der testamentarisch als ErbInnen eingesetzten Schwiegereltern Dr. F.s, Ida und Emil Be., zu, auch wenn diese das Erbe ihrer Tochter bedingt angenommen haben. Der Charakter der Freiwilligkeit des Erbverzichts auf den Nachlass nach Dr. F. kann nicht angenommen werden. Wie die Sammelstelle in ihren Ausführungen vorbrachte, hätte ein Antritt dieser Erbschaft das Ehepaar Be. aufgrund der spezifischen Steuerverpflichtung für auswandernde Juden („Reichsfluchtsteuer") am Verlassen des Landes, um der Verfolgung zu entkommen, gehindert bzw. beträchtlich verzögert. Im Gegensatz zum geringen Nachlass nach ihrer Tochter in Höhe von rund 3.000,- Reichsmark, das zudem lediglich aus beweglichen Gegenständen bestand, handelte es sich bei Dr. F.s Nachlass um eine Verlassenschaft, die umfangreiche Aktiva und Passiva enthielt und vor allem mit einer Liegenschaft und einem Sanatoriumsbetrieb verbunden war. Wie das weitere Schicksal von Emil und Ida Be. zeigt, gelang ihnen auch trotz ihres Erbverzichts nicht, der Verfolgung durch den Nationalsozialismus zu entkommen. 454

Die Schiedsinstanz gelangt daher zu der Ansicht, dass die FLD unter gebührender Würdigung des Erkenntnisses der Obersten Rückstellungskommission in der Entziehung des Erbrechts eine Vermögensentziehung nach dem 3. RStG sehen hätte müssen. 455

Überschuldung 456

Daran hätte auch die von der Finanzprokuratur geltend gemachte „Überschuldung" des Nachlasses bzw. der Liegenschaft nichts ändern dürfen. Wie oben zur Frage der Entziehung nach dem EF-G ausgeführt, standen Schulden laut Rückstellungsjudikatur dem Entziehungstatbestand nicht entgegen, solange deren Begleichung nicht aussichtslos war. Nach der Entscheidung der Obersten Rückstellungskommission vom 3. September 1949 (Rkv 278/49) oblag es sogar dem Erwerber, im konkreten Falle zu 457

> „beweisen, daß keinerlei Aussicht bestand, die bestehenden finanziellen Schwierigkeiten zu überwinden, und dass ein dauernder, nicht bloß vorübergehender Mangel an Geldmitteln vorlag, der die Bezahlung der Schulden und die Weiterführung des Betriebes unmöglich machte, so dass es unter allen Umständen zu einer Veräußerung hätte kommen müssen [...]."

the assumption to be made that a sale of the property would have also taken place without the National Socialist assumption of power.

> "The forced sale was only initiated after the National Socialist assumption of power and was probably attributed to the fact that, as Jews, the claimants left Austria and had to cease the operation of their company. Had the company's operation been maintained, then it could be assumed that the creditors, who were pushing for their payments, could have been satisfied from the earnings of the company. The financial situation of the claimants prior to the assumption of power could therefore not have been described as hopeless. The adverse party had particularly not asserted that the claimant would have undertaken steps to sell the property before the assumption of power. Therefore, it did not in any way produce any of the evidence which was incumbent upon it according to para. 2 (2) of the Third Restitution Act."

460 On the basis of the cited decision Rkv 161/48, the State Financial Procurator's Office would not have been successful in producing exonerating evidence in accordance with para. 2 (2) of the Third Restitution Act in the proceedings S.-gasse 14. As the findings demonstrate, nearly all persons entitled to the inheritance were wealthy family members and a few held leading positions in a company. It seems entirely plausible that those entitled to the inheritance, had they not been subject to National Socialist persecution, would have continued to operate the sanatorium. This is particularly applicable to Dr. Ernst F. on the basis of his experience as the former general director and main shareholder of the So. Corporation as well as to Paul F., the vice general director of the So. Corporation. As can be gathered from the facts, Dr. Ernst F. also made funds available to Dr. Lothar F.'s sanatorium company. It can be assumed that he had some economic insight into the operation of the sanatorium.

461 The Arbitration Panel therefore concludes that the Financial Directorate should not have been able to use the over-indebtedness argued by the State Financial Procurator's Office as reason for precluding the existence of a property seizure.

462 **Third State Treaty Implementation Act**

463 The question remains open whether the Financial Directorate was to have applied the Third State Treaty Implementation Act in its decision and whether the prerequisites for a seizure provided for therein were fulfilled.

464 According to Article I para. 1 (1) of the Third State Treaty Implementation Act (Federal Law of 10 July 1957, with which further provisions for the implementation of part IV of the State Treaty of 15 May 1955, Federal Law Gazette No. 152 were enacted) this law was to be applied to "assets, which had been acquired during the German occupation of Austria for the purposes of the German Armed Forces or the Reich defense on the basis of legal transactions or other legal acts by the German Reich".

465 As established in the facts, the German Reich, Reich Treasury (Army) acquired the property S.-gasse 14 pursuant to the purchase contract of 20 and 27 March 1939 from the estate of Dr. Lothar F.

466 The building was used by the Army Recruitment Inspectorate, which was a recruitment office for conscripts and which was also in charge of supplements and replacements of material for the German Armed Forces. From 1943, the former sanatorium served as a reserve military hospital.

In diesem Zusammenhang ist auf das zur Frage der Entziehung iSd EF-G oben Ausgeführte zu verweisen, wonach die anzuwendenden Bestimmungen der Konkursordnung eine Konkurseröffnung über das Vermögen eines Nachlasses nur bei übersteigender Schuldenlast und negativer Fortbestehensprognose zulassen. Wie oben ausgeführt, wurde von der Finanzprokuratur weder behauptet noch dargelegt, dass die zweite Tatbestandsvoraussetzung erfüllt gewesen sei. Des Weiteren wurde auch tatsächlich kein Nachlasskonkurs eröffnet, sondern die GläubigerInnen mit Ausgleichquoten befriedigt. 458

Hinsichtlich der Frage der Überschuldung hätte die FLD für ihre Entscheidung des Rückstellungsbegehrens im Falle F. auch die Entscheidung der Obersten Rückstellungskommission vom 2. Oktober 1948, Rkv 161/48, heranziehen müssen. Gegenstand dieses Rückstellungsverfahrens waren Liegenschaften, auf denen ein Sanatorium betrieben wurde und die 1940 zwangsversteigert wurden. Die Oberste Rückstellungskommission sprach hier aus, dass die von der Rückstellungskommission festgestellte Verschuldung der Antragsteller nicht zur Annahme zwinge, dass es zu einer Veräußerung der Liegenschaft auch unabhängig von der Machtergreifung durch den Nationalsozialismus gekommen wäre. 459

„Die Zwangsversteigerung wurde erst nach der Machtergreifung durch den Nationalsozialismus eingeleitet und war wohl darauf zurückzuführen, dass die Antragsteller als Juden Österreich verlassen und den Betrieb ihres Unternehmens einstellen mussten. Wäre der Betrieb aufrecht geblieben, dann konnte mit der Möglichkeit gerechnet werden, dass Gläubiger, die auf Zahlung drängten, aus den Erträgnissen des Unternehmens befriedigt werden können. Die finanzielle Lage der Antragsteller vor der Zeit der Machtübernahme konnte daher nicht als hoffnungslos bezeichnet werden. Die Antragsgegnerin hatte insbesondere nicht behauptet, dass die Antragstellerin vor der Machtergreifung Schritte unternommen hätte, um die Liegenschaft zu veräußern. Sie hat somit den ihr nach § 2 Abs 2 des 3. Rückstellungsgesetzes obliegenden Beweis keineswegs erbracht."

Unter Zugrundelegung der zitierten Entscheidung Rkv 161/48 wäre der Finanzprokuratur im Verfahren S.-gasse 14 der Entlastungsbeweis nach § 2 Abs 2 des 3. RStG nicht gelungen. Wie die Sachverhaltsfeststellungen zeigen, waren fast alle Erbberechtigten wohlhabende Familienmitglieder und einige in führender Position eines Betriebes tätig. Es erscheint durchaus plausibel, dass die Erbberechtigten, wären sie nicht vom nationalsozialistischen Regime verfolgt worden, den Sanatoriumsbetrieb weitergeführt hätten. Insbesondere trifft dies auf Dr. Ernst F. aufgrund seiner unternehmerischen Erfahrung als ehemaliger Generaldirektor und Hauptaktionär der So. AG, sowie auf Paul F., Vize-Generaldirektor der So. AG, zu. Wie aus dem Sachverhalt hervorgeht, stellte Dr. Ernst F. auch Gelder für Dr. Lothar F.s Sanatoriumsbetrieb zur Verfügung. Es kann davon ausgegangen werden, dass er einen gewissen wirtschaftlichen Einblick in den Sanatoriumsbetrieb hatte. 460

Die Schiedsinstanz geht daher davon aus, dass die FLD die von der Finanzprokuratur argumentierte Überschuldung nicht als der Vermögensentziehung entgegenstehend qualifizieren hätte dürfen. 461

Drittes Staatsvertragsdurchführungsgesetz 462

Offen bleibt die Frage, ob die FLD in ihrer Entscheidung das 3. StVDG anzuwenden hatte und ob die darin bestimmten Tatbestandsvoraussetzungen der Entziehung gegeben waren. 463

Laut Art. I § 1 Abs 1 des 3. StVDG (Bundesgesetz vom 10. Juli 1957, womit weitere Bestimmungen zur Durchführung des IV. Teiles des Staatsvertrages vom 15. Mai 1955, 464

467   Hence, the factual elements required by the provision of Article I para. 1 (1) of the Third State Treaty Implementation Act regarding the acquisition of a property for military purposes during the German occupation were fulfilled. The application of the Third State Treaty Implementation Act was therefore merited.

468   When applying the Third State Treaty Implementation Act, the restrictions for the elements of a seizure according to Article I para. 1 (2) of the law apply:

> "Acquisitions of this kind only constitute a seizure in the meaning of the restitution legislation if the then prevailing laws had been applied unlawfully in an individual case or if the owner had been forced to sell solely on the grounds of political persecution."

469   As stated above regarding the decision of the Supreme Restitution Commission, Rkv 13/61, in the case of a property sale by a dormant estate, with regard to the question of a property seizure in the meaning of the restitution legislation, the focus is to be the political persecution of the heirs. The seizure of the property subject of this application is due to the fact that the potential heirs to Dr. F. did not have the opportunity to take possession of the estate (according to their share in the inheritance) as they themselves were persecuted by the National Socialist regime.

470   As established in the facts, the attorney-at-law Dr. Fa., appointed as provisional representative of Dr. Lothar F.'s estate by the Enforcement Court, stated on 28 April 1938 that there were no heirs and that the law of reversion would probably come into effect. It was also noted in the property notice for the deceased Dr. Lothar F. of 16 July 1938: "Heirs none. Reich Treasury purchases for the Army Recruitment Inspectorate. Money to cover the debts." The sale of the property to the German Reich took place on the part of those responsible for the estate, on the premise that there were no heirs.

471   Pursuant to para. 797 of the (Austrian) General Civil Code, with devolution, an heir assumes the position of the decedent and becomes his universal legal successor. With devolution, the heirs would have become universal successors of the decedent Dr. Lothar F. and would have taken on his positions under the law of property and therefore also the position of an owner of the property S.-gasse 14. Thus, the sale of the property in question to the German Reich was not decisive for the seizure, as the property S.-gasse 14 had been seized simultaneously with the seizure of the right to the inheritance.

472   Therefore, it is demonstrated that the correct decision of the Financial Directorate should have been the restitution of the property S.-gasse 14. The findings have, however, illustrated that the Financial Directorate internally rejected the restitution claim of the Collection Agency. In fact, the department 16b of the Federal Ministry of Finance, concerned with the collection agencies' general settlement, informed the Minister of Finance on 21 October 1965 that the Financial Directorate, after inquiring, denied the restitution claim (see margin note 306).

473   Therefore, the only issue which remains to be examined is to what extent this objectively unacceptable interpretation of the law by the Financial Directorate influenced the conclusion of the settlement.

474   It is evident from the available documents that the settlement sum widely fluctuated in the course of the settlement negotiations of 1961 to 1965. The settlement sought by the Collection Agency varied between 250,000 Schilling and 4 million Schilling. It is not apparent whether rental earnings or expenses were calculated into each proposed sum. The amount of the settlement reflected far more the risk with which the Collection Agency and the adverse party assessed the outcome of the proceedings. For the Ministry of Finance,

BGBl Nr. 152, erlassen werden) war dieses Gesetz auf „Vermögenswerte, die während der deutschen Besetzung Österreichs für Zwecke der Wehrmacht oder der Reichsverteidigung auf Grund von Rechtsgeschäften oder sonstigen Rechtshandlungen durch das Deutsche Reich erworben worden sind", anzuwenden.

Wie im Sachverhalt festgestellt, erwarb das Deutsche Reich, Reichsfiskus (Heer), die Liegenschaft S.-gasse 14 mit Kaufvertrag vom 20. bzw. 27. März 1939 von der Verlassenschaft nach Dr. Lothar F. 465

Verwendet wurde das Gebäude durch die Wehrersatzinspektion, die eine Rekrutierungsstelle für Wehrpflichtige war und auch materielle Ergänzungs- und Ersatzaufgaben für die Wehrmacht wahrnahm. Ab 1943 diente das ehemalige Sanatorium als Reservelazarett. 466

Somit waren die Tatbestandselemente der Bestimmung Art. I § 1 Abs 1 des 3. StVDG hinsichtlich Erwerbes einer Liegenschaft für militärische Zwecke unter der deutschen Besatzung erfüllt. Die Anwendung des 3. StVDG war daher gegeben. 467

Unter Anwendung des 3. StVDG gilt der beschränkte Entziehungstatbestand nach Art. I § 1 Abs 2 des Gesetzes: 468

„Derartige Erwerbungen stellen nur dann eine Entziehung im Sinne der Rückstellungsgesetze dar, wenn im Einzelfall die damals geltenden Gesetze missbräuchlich angewendet worden sind oder der Eigentümer lediglich auf Grund politischer Verfolgung zur Veräußerung genötigt worden ist."

Wie oben zur Entscheidung der Obersten Rückstellungskommission, Rkv 13/61, ausgeführt, ist bei der Vermögensveräußerung durch einen ruhenden Nachlass hinsichtlich der Frage der Vermögensentziehung iSd Rückstellungsgesetze auf die politische Verfolgung der Erben abzustellen. Die Entziehung der antragsgegenständlichen Liegenschaft liegt darin, dass die potentiellen ErbInnen nach Dr. Lothar F. nicht die Möglichkeit hatten, den Nachlass (entsprechend ihrer Erbquote) in Besitz zu nehmen, da sie selbst durch das nationalsozialistische Regime verfolgt wurden. 469

Wie im Sachverhalt festgestellt, meinte der vom Exekutionsgericht zum einstweiligen Vertreter des Nachlasses nach Dr. Lothar F. bestellte RA Dr. Fa. schon am 28. April 1938, dass es keine ErbInnen gäbe und mit dem Eintritt des Heimfallsrechtes zu rechnen sei. Auch bereits in der VA für den verstorbenen Dr. Lothar F. vom 16. Juli 1938 war vermerkt: „Erben keine. Reichsfiskus kauft für die Wehrersatzinspektion. Geld zur Deckung der Schulden." Der Verkauf der Liegenschaft an das Deutsche Reich erfolgte seitens der für die Verlassenschaft Zuständigen unter der Prämisse, dass es keine ErbInnen gäbe. 470

Gemäß § 797 ABGB tritt ein Erbe mit Einantwortung in die Position des Erblassers ein und wird dessen Gesamtrechtsnachfolger. Mit Einantwortung wären die ErbInnen UniversalsukzessorInnen nach dem Erblasser Dr. Lothar F. geworden und wären in dessen vermögensrechtliche Positionen eingetreten, damit auch in die Stellung eines Eigentümers der Liegenschaft S.-gasse 14. Daher ist der Verkauf der antragsgegenständlichen Liegenschaft an das Deutsche Reich für den Entzug nicht ausschlaggebend, da den ErbInnen bereits davor mit dem Entzug ihres Erbrechts gleichzeitig auch die Liegenschaft S.-gasse 14 entzogen wurde. 471

Damit ist dargelegt, dass die korrekte Entscheidung der FLD auf Rückstellung der Liegenschaft S.-gasse 14 hätte lauten müssen. Die Sachverhaltsfeststellungen haben jedoch gezeigt, dass die FLD intern den Rückstellungsanspruch der Sammelstelle verneinte. In der Tat setzte die mit dem Sammelstellen-Generalvergleich befasste Abteilung 16b des 472

the question dominated whether, based on the over-indebtedness, a seizure in the meaning of the restitution legislation was present and therefore an obligation to restitute existed. In the arguments of the Collection Agency, although the seizure was undeniably certain, the chance of a restitution of the property was ultimately, however, estimated to be very low when applying the Third State Treaty Implementation Act.

475 As stated above, the Financial Directorate, after an enquiry, had denied the claim for restitution. For this reason, the State Financial Procurator's Office could expect the rejection of the restitution claim by the Financial Directorate in 1965. It can therefore be assumed that the Collection Agency had correctly assessed the risk of losing the case. The Collection Agency also based the settlement on this judgment.

476 As the State Financial Procurator's Office had known of the planned rejection of the claim and the Collection Agency A had correctly assessed the risk of losing the case, both fundamental for the conclusion and content of the settlement, an objectively unacceptable interpretation of the law to the gross disadvantage of the claimant therefore turned out to be the basis of the settlement.

477 The striking discrepancy in value between a correct hypothetical restitution decision and the settlement sum reached, along with the markedly divergent interests of the Collection Agency in comparison to those interests which were to be assumed by a restitution claimant, speak in favor of the settlement at issue being extremely unjust.

478 As the requirement of an extreme injustice as defined in Sec. 28 (1) item 2 in connection with Sec. 32 of the GSF Law is fulfilled, it need not be examined whether additionally, in the matter of the consideration of the rental earnings and the expenses, the bases of the restitution legislation and case law were deviated from in determining the settlement amount.

479 The Arbitration Panel therefore reaches the unanimous decision that the settlement between the then claimant and the Republic of Austria was extremely unjust. Therefore, the *in rem* restitution of the property S.-gasse 14, EZ X1, KG Josefstadt was to be recommended.

Dr. Josef Aicher, university professor, Chairman
Dr. Dr. h. c. Erich Kussbach, LL. M., honorary professor and retired ambassador
MMag. Dr. August Reinisch, LL. M., university professor

Bundesministeriums für Finanzen den Finanzminister am 21. Oktober 1965 davon in Kenntnis, dass die FLD nach Rückfrage den Rückstellungsanspruch verneine (siehe Rz 306).

Zu prüfen ist daher nun, inwiefern diese objektiv unvertretbare Gesetzesauslegung durch die FLD den Abschluss des Vergleiches beeinflusst hat. 473

Aus den vorhandenen Dokumenten ergibt sich, dass sich die Vergleichssumme im Zuge der Vergleichsverhandlungen von 1961 bis 1965 innerhalb einer großen Bandbreite bewegte. Die von der Sammelstelle geforderte Abgeltung schwankte zwischen 250.000,– und 4,000.000,– Schilling. Nicht erkennbar ist, ob in die jeweils vorgeschlagenen Summen Mieterträgnisse oder Aufwendungen einberechnet wurden. Die Höhe der Summe reflektierte vielmehr das Risiko, mit dem die Sammelstelle und die Rückstellungsgegnerin den Verfahrensausgang einschätzten. Es dominierte seitens des Finanzministeriums die Frage, ob aufgrund der Überschuldung der Liegenschaft überhaupt ein Entzug iSd Rückstellungsgesetze vorlag und damit eine Rückstellungsverpflichtung bestand. In der Argumentation der Sammelstelle stand der Entzug zwar unstrittig fest, doch wurde die Chance einer Rückstellung der Liegenschaft bei Anwendung des 3. StVDG letztlich als sehr gering eingeschätzt. 474

Wie oben ausgeführt, hatte die FLD nach Rückfrage den Rückstellungsanspruch verneint. Aus diesem Grund konnte die Finanzprokuratur 1965 mit einer Abweisung des Rückstellungsanspruches durch die FLD rechnen. Es kann daher davon ausgegangen werden, dass die Sammelstelle das Prozessrisiko richtig eingeschätzt hat. Sie legte diese Einschätzung auch dem Vergleich zugrunde. 475

Da seitens der Finanzprokuratur das Wissen um die geplante Antragsablehnung und seitens der Sammelstelle Λ das richtig vermutete hohe Prozessrisiko wesentlich für den Abschluss und Inhalt des Vergleiches waren, geriet eine objektiv unvertretbare Gesetzesauslegung zu Lasten der AntragstellerInnen damit zur Grundlage des Vergleiches. 476

Die eklatante Wertdifferenz zwischen einer korrekten hypothetischen Rückstellungsentscheidung und der erzielten Vergleichssumme spricht im Zusammenspiel mit der markant abweichenden Interessenlage der Sammelstelle im Vergleich zu den einem Rückstellungswerber zu unterstellenden Interessen für das Vorliegen einer extremen Ungerechtigkeit des gegenständlichen Vergleichs. 477

Da damit bereits das Vorliegen eines extrem ungerechten Vergleiches iSd § 28 Abs 1 Z 2 iVm § 32 EF-G erfüllt ist, kann dahin gestellt bleiben, ob zudem bei der Frage der Berücksichtigung der Mieterträgnisse und der Aufwendungen bei der Bestimmung der Vergleichssumme von den Grundlagen der Rückstellungsgesetzgebung und Judikatur abgewichen wurde. 478

Die Schiedsinstanz gelangt daher einstimmig zu der Ansicht, dass der Vergleich zwischen der damaligen Rückstellungswerberin und der Republik Österreich extrem ungerecht war. Die Naturalrestitution der Liegenschaft S.-gasse 14, EZ X1, KG Josefstadt, war daher zu empfehlen. 479

o.Univ.-Prof. Dr. Josef Aicher, Vorsitzender
Honorarprofessor Dr.Dr.h.c. Erich Kussbach LL.M., Botschafter i.R.
ao.Univ.-Prof. MMag. Dr. August Reinisch LL.M.

Press Release Decision No. 28/2005

Vienna, Hohe Warte

On 15 November 2005, the Arbitration Panel for *In Rem* Restitution rejected an application for restitution of a property in Vienna, Hohe Warte. The property had been the subject of previous proceedings. The Arbitration Panel concluded that the restitution of the property in the condition it had been in at the time of the filing of the application in 1948 did not constitute an "extreme injustice".

The property subject of the application was owned by the G. spouses in 1938 without any encumbrances. After their flight to England in 1939 – both were considered Jews according to the Nuremberg Laws – their entire assets were confiscated by the Gestapo in February 1941. The reversion to the German Reich occurred upon the enactment of the *Elfte Verordnung zum Reichsbürgergesetz* ("Eleventh Decree to the Reich Citizenship Law") of 25 November 1941.

In April 1948, Alfred G. and the estate of his then deceased wife submitted an application to the Financial Directorate Vienna, Lower Austria and Burgenland for the restitution of the property in question and the cancellation of liens for discriminatory taxes in the land register. In addition, the restitution claimants waived "expressly and irrevocably the settlement of accounts regarding the earnings" regarding the property in question. This waiver was repeated again in the restitution application of December 1949. This second restitution application, the contents of which were identical to the first, was necessary as the probate proceedings had not been concluded at the time the first application was filed. As such, the certificate of inheritance was not available. On 30 June 1950, the property in question, which had been damaged by the effects of the war, was restituted to Alfred G. and his daughter and heir of his wife, Liselotte W., in line with the application. With regard to the cancellation of the lien, the restitution claimants were advised to file a claim directly with the Land Register Court. In 1951, Alfred G. and Liselotte W. sold the property to Dr. Kurt Gr. for 145,000 Schilling. Pursuant to the concluded purchase contract, the property was transferred free of encumbrances. Kurt Gr. sold the renovated property to the Republic of Austria for 9 million Schilling in 1965.

In its juridical appraisal, the Arbitration Panel had to examine whether the former restitution of the property subject of the application in the condition it had been in at that time without a financial compensation constituted an extreme injustice. The Arbitration Panel ruled against the existence of such injustice as the restitution authority had decided in line with the application and had correctly applied the First Restitution Act. As the restitution claimants had expressly waived the settlement of accounts regarding the earnings, they had not been included in the decision. An examination of those legal provisions on which the former restitution decision had been based, does not fall within the scope of competence of the Arbitration Panel as defined by the GSF Law.

For use by media; not legally binding upon the Arbitration Panel for In Rem Restitution.

Pressemitteilung Entscheidung Nr. 28/2005

Wien, Hohe Warte

Die Schiedsinstanz für Naturalrestitution lehnte am 15. November 2005 einen Antrag auf Restitution einer Liegenschaft in Wien, Hohe Warte ab. Die Liegenschaft war bereits Gegenstand eines früheren Verfahrens gewesen. Die Schiedsinstanz gelangte zu der Ansicht, dass die Rückstellung der Liegenschaft in jenem Zustand, in dem sie sich zum Zeitpunkt der Antragstellung 1948 befunden hatte, keine extreme Ungerechtigkeit darstellt.

Die beantragte Liegenschaft befand sich 1938 lastenfrei im Eigentum des Ehepaares G. Nach ihrer Flucht 1939 nach England – beide galten nach den Nürnberger Gesetzen als Juden – wurde ihr gesamtes Vermögen im Februar 1941 durch die Gestapo beschlagnahmt. Der Verfall an das Deutsche Reich erfolgte mit dem In-Kraft-Treten der Elften Verordnung zum Reichsbürgergesetz vom 25. November 1941.

Im April 1948 beantragten Alfred G. und die Verlassenschaft nach seiner zwischenzeitlich verstorbenen Ehefrau bei der Finanzlandesdirektion für Wien, Niederösterreich und das Burgenland einerseits die Rückstellung der gegenständlichen Liegenschaft und andererseits die Löschung von Pfandrechten für diskriminierende Steuern im Grundbuch. Außerdem verzichteten die RückstellungswerberInnen „ausdrücklich und unwiderruflich auf die Abrechnung der Erträgnisse" hinsichtlich der gegenständlichen Liegenschaft. Dieser Verzicht wurde nochmals im Rückstellungsantrag vom Dezember 1949 wiederholt. Dieser zweite Rückstellungsantrag, der inhaltlich dem ersten glich, war notwendig, da zum Zeitpunkt des ersten Einbringens das Verlassenschaftsverfahren noch nicht abgehandelt war und somit die Einantwortungsurkunde gefehlt hatte. Am 30. Juni 1950 wurde die gegenständliche Liegenschaft, die durch die Kriegseinwirkungen stark beschädigt war, antragsgemäß Alfred G. und seiner Tochter und Erbin nach seiner Ehefrau, Liselotte W., zurückgestellt. Hinsichtlich der Pfandrechtslöschung wurden die RückstellungswerberInnen auf die Geltendmachung direkt beim Grundbuchgericht verwiesen. 1951 verkauften Alfred G. und Liselotte W. die Liegenschaft um 145.000,– Schilling an Dr. Kurt Gr. Entsprechend dem abgeschlossenen Kaufvertrag wurde die Liegenschaft lastenfrei übergeben. Kurt Gr. verkaufte die renovierte Liegenschaft 1965 um neun Mio. Schilling an die Republik Österreich weiter.

In ihrer rechtlichen Beurteilung hatte die Schiedsinstanz zu prüfen, ob die seinerzeitige Rückstellung der beantragten Liegenschaft in dem Zustand, in dem sie sich zu jenem Zeitpunkt befunden hatte, ohne dass eine weitere monetäre Entschädigung erfolgt war, eine extreme Ungerechtigkeit darstellt. Das Vorliegen einer solchen wurde von der Schiedsinstanz verneint, da die Rückstellungsbehörde antragsgemäß und in korrekter Anwendung des Ersten Rückstellungsgesetzes auf Rückstellung der Liegenschaft erkannt hatte. Da die RückstellungswerberInnen ausdrücklich auf Abrechnung der Mieterträgnisse verzichtet hatten, waren sie auch nicht Gegenstand der Entscheidung. Eine Überprüfung jener rechtlichen Normen, auf deren Grundlage eine frühere Rückstellungsentscheidung gefällt worden ist, fällt nicht in den vom Entschädigungsfondsgesetz festgelegten Kompetenzbereich der Schiedsinstanz.

Zur Verwendung durch die Medien bestimmter Text, der die Schiedsinstanz nicht bindet.

Arbitration Panel for *In Rem* Restitution

Decision number 28/2005

The Arbitration Panel for *In Rem* Restitution (Chairman Dr. Josef Aicher, university professor, and Dr.Dr.h.c. Erich Kussbach LL.M., retired ambassador and honorary professor, as well as MMag. Dr. August Reinisch LL.M, university professor, as Members) decided on 15 November 2005 in the legal matter Ian Thomas E. and Kathryn Joan D. regarding *in rem* restitution of the property Hohe Warte Z, register number ("EZ") X, cadastral district ("KG") Heiligenstadt:

The application for *in rem* restitution of the property Hohe Warte Z, EZ X, KG Heiligenstadt is rejected.

Reasons:

1. Submission by the Applicants

1. In an application received by the Arbitration Panel on 9 April 2003, the applicants requested the restitution of the property Hohe Warte Z, EZ X, KG Heiligenstadt and submitted the following:

2. The property Vienna XIX, Hohe Warte Z, a single family home with an area of approximately 400 m^2 and a garden with an area of approximately 10,000 m^2 had been owned by Alfred G. and his wife Ella G., who had each owned a 50 % share of the property.

3. The property had been confiscated by the *Gestapo* ("Secret State Police") without any kind of compensation having been paid. The claim subject of this application had been conclusively decided by the Austrian administrative bodies, however, the decision had constituted an extreme injustice.

4. From 9 December 1946 to June 1950, Alfred and Ella G., the grandparents of the applicants, later also Liselotte W. née G. (who had inherited the half share of Ella G.) had sought the restitution of the property. In June 1950, as a result of a decision by the Financial Directorate for Vienna, the property had been restituted to Alfred G. and Liselotte W.

5. The decision by the Financial Directorate for Vienna had, however, been extremely unjust, as it did not contain any financial elements. In June 1950, when the property had been restituted, Alfred G. was 73 years old and had no longer been able to raise any objections to the decision. He had had no choice but to sell the property as quickly as possible in the poor condition in which he had received it.

6. Alfred G. had been a well-known, successful and wealthy factory owner. With the help of numerous employees, he and his wife Ella kept the house and garden in very good condition. On 31 December 1938, Alfred G. had had net assets of more than 10 million Schilling (6.6 million Reichsmark).

7. Had the National Socialists not robbed Alfred G. of his assets, his income and his life savings, he would have had the financial means necessary for maintaining his house and the lifestyle to which he had been accustomed.

8. However, in 1938, Alfred G.'s company, the Ga.-werke and the property on which it had been located had been aryanized. His entire remaining assets had been seized and the cash had been confiscated for the payment of the *Reichsfluchtsteuer* ("Reich Flight Tax")

Schiedsinstanz für Naturalrestitution

Entscheidungsnummer 28/2005

Die Schiedsinstanz für Naturalrestitution beschließt am 15. November 2005 durch den Vorsitzenden o.Univ.-Prof. Dr. Josef Aicher und die Schiedsinstanzmitglieder Honorarprofessor Dr.Dr.h.c. Erich Kussbach LL.M., Botschafter i.R. und ao.Univ.-Prof. MMag. Dr. August Reinisch LL.M. in der Rechtssache Ian Thomas E. und Kathryn Joan D. wegen Naturalrestitution der Liegenschaft Hohe Warte Z, Einlagezahl (EZ) X, Katastralgemeinde (KG) Heiligenstadt:

Der Antrag auf Naturalrestitution der Liegenschaft Hohe Warte Z, EZ X, KG Heiligenstadt wird abgelehnt.

Begründung:

1. Vorbringen der AntragstellerInnen

Mit Antrag vom 9. April 2003 begehrten die AntragstellerInnen die Rückstellung der Liegenschaft Hohe Warte Z, EZ X, KG Heiligenstadt und brachten wie folgt vor: 1

Die Liegenschaft Wien XIX, Hohe Warte Z, ein Einfamilienhaus von ungefähr 400 m^2 mit ca. 10.000 m^2 Garten, sei je zur Hälfte im Eigentum von Alfred G. und seiner Ehefrau Ella G. gestanden. 2

Die Liegenschaft sei 1941 von der Gestapo entschädigungslos beschlagnahmt worden. Die gegenständliche Forderung sei durch die österreichischen Verwaltungsbehörden endgültig entschieden worden, wobei die Entscheidung eine extreme Ungerechtigkeit dargestellt habe. 3

Vom 9. Dezember 1946 an bis Juni 1950 hätten die Großeltern der AntragstellerInnen, Alfred und Ella G., später auch Liselotte W. geborene G. (die den Hälfteanteil nach Ella G. geerbt habe), die Rückstellung der Liegenschaft begehrt. Im Juni 1950 sei die Liegenschaft aufgrund einer Entscheidung der Finanzlandesdirektion (FLD) für Wien an Alfred G. und Liselotte W. zurückgestellt worden. 4

Die Entscheidung der FLD für Wien sei jedoch extrem ungerecht gewesen, da die Entscheidung keine finanzielle Komponente enthalten habe. Im Alter von 73 Jahren, als im Juni 1950 die Liegenschaft zurückgestellt worden sei, sei Alfred G. nicht mehr in der Lage gewesen, Einwände gegen die Entscheidung zu erheben. Es sei ihm kein anderer Ausweg geblieben, als die Liegenschaft in dem schlechten Zustand, in dem er sie erhalten habe, so schnell wie möglich zu verkaufen. 5

Alfred G. sei ein prominenter, erfolgreicher und vermögender Fabrikant in Wien gewesen. Sowohl er als auch seine Ehefrau Ella hätten das Haus samt Garten mit Hilfe zahlreicher Angestellter in einem sehr guten Zustand gehalten. Am 31. Dezember 1938 habe Alfred G. an Nettovermögen mehr als 10 Millionen Schilling (6,6 Millionen Reichsmark) besessen. 6

Hätten die Nationalsozialisten Alfred G. nicht sein Kapital, sein Einkommen und seine Lebensersparnisse geraubt, wären ihm die monetären Mittel zur Verfügung gestanden, um sein Haus behalten und seinen gewohnten Lebensstil aufrechterhalten zu können. 7

and the *Judenvermögensabgabe* ("Jewish capital levy"). The same happened to his wife Ella. Hence, by 1941 they had not only been dispossessed of their house but both of them had also been robbed of their assets, their income and their life savings.

9   However, in the decision on the restitution of Alfred G.'s house, the government had neglected to take into consideration the circumstances of Alfred G.'s life in 1950 and the fact that it had been the fault of the National Socialists that these circumstances had arisen. The fact that Alfred G. had not been compensated for the confiscated money had also not been taken into consideration. It had also not been taken into consideration that due to the lack of funds, which had been seized by the National Socialist government, he had not been able to return the estate to its original condition, as it had been at the time of confiscation. In reality, the entire estate had been in a poor condition and at the time of restitution it had been mould-ridden. Financial compensation, which would have rendered possible the repair of the damages which had occurred during the time when the property had been administered by the authorities, had never been paid.

10 The government had not offered any compensation for rental losses for the nine years during which the property had been confiscated and had been under its official administration. On the contrary, the property had only been restituted to Alfred G. under the condition that he waived the right to any compensation for rental losses.

11 Due to the fact that Alfred G. had not received any financial compensation for the losses suffered, it had also been impossible for him to keep the property. This lack of freedom of choice had been a direct consequence of the Austrian government not taking into consideration the property seizures by the National Socialist regime through aryanization and confiscation.

12 Had the government taken the presented arguments into consideration, it would have had to recognize the extreme injustice of the decision.

13 Subsequently, Alfred G. had sold the house on 26 June 1951 for 145,000 Schilling to Dr. Kurt Gr., the lawyer and adviser of the *Creditanstalt-Bankverein*. Only 14 years later, Dr. Kurt Gr. had sold it to the Republic of Austria for 9 million Schilling.

14 On 26 April 2005 and on 6 September 2005, the applicants submitted written statements. In these statements the foregoing statement was essentially repeated and it was emphasized that Dr. P., the tenant of the property in question, had reached an agreement with Mr. and Mrs. G. to move into the property in May 1939. The only proof of this "tenancy" was an unsigned memorandum that had been drafted by Dr. P. himself. The rental conditions had clearly been advantageous to him. The annual rent had amounted to 2,400 Reichsmark. The expenses, which are usually to be paid by the tenant, had to be paid by Mr. and Mrs. G. although they had no longer been resident in the country at the time.

15 The property had been seized by the Secret State Police on 19 February 1941 and had been under the administration of the Austrian authorities until 1950. Dr. Stephan L. of the Secret State Police had been responsible for the administration of Mr. and Mrs. G.'s assets. On 22 June 1941, he had concluded a new lease agreement with Dr. P.; this agreement prescribed the same annual rent of 2,400 Reichsmark. However, in addition to this it had been agreed that Dr. P. himself was to cover the usual costs connected to the property. Also, an additional amount for the use of the garden had been agreed upon. In 1941, Dr. L. had appointed Mr. S. as the property manager. His task had been to collect and transfer the rental to a Secret State Police account held with the *Creditanstalt*.

1938 sei jedoch Alfred G.s Unternehmen, die Ga.-werke, sowie das Grundstück, auf dem sich dieses befunden habe, arisiert, sein gesamtes restliches Vermögen eingezogen und das Bargeld für die Reichsfluchtsteuer und die Judenvermögensabgabe (JUVA) konfisziert worden. Seiner Ehefrau Ella sei es genauso ergangen. Bis zum Jahr 1941 sei somit nicht nur ihr Haus enteignet, sondern beiden ihr Kapital, ihr Einkommen und ihre Lebensersparnisse geraubt worden. 8

In der Entscheidung, Alfred G. sein Haus zurückzustellen, habe es die Regierung jedoch unterlassen, die Lebensumstände von Alfred G. 1950 und die Schuld der Nationalsozialisten, die erst zu diesen Umständen geführt hätten, zu berücksichtigen. Es sei ebenfalls nicht berücksichtigt worden, dass Alfred G. nicht für das konfiszierte Geld entschädigt worden sei. Auch sei nicht berücksichtigt worden, dass er mangels Vermögens, welches von der NS-Regierung entzogen worden sei, nicht mehr in der Lage gewesen sei, das Anwesen in den Zustand zurückzuführen, in welchem es sich im Zeitpunkt seiner Konfiskation befunden habe. Tatsächlich habe sich das gesamte Anwesen in einem schlechten Zustand befunden und sei zum Zeitpunkt der Rückstellung mit Schimmelpilz befallen gewesen. Auch sei keine finanzielle Entschädigung, die eine Behebung jener Schäden ermöglicht hätte, die in der Zeit entstanden seien, als sich die Liegenschaft unter der Verwaltung der Behörden befunden habe, erfolgt. 9

Auch habe die Regierung für die neun Jahre, in denen die Liegenschaft konfisziert gewesen sei und sich offiziell unter ihrer Verwaltung befunden habe, keine Mietentschädigung angeboten. Ganz im Gegenteil, Alfred G. habe die Liegenschaft nur unter der Bedingung zurückerhalten, dass er auf die Mietentschädigung verzichte. 10

Aufgrund der Tatsache, dass Alfred G. keine finanzielle Abgeltung seiner erlittenen Schäden erhalten habe, sei es ihm auch nicht mehr möglich gewesen, die Liegenschaft zu behalten. Dieses Fehlen der Wahlmöglichkeit sei eine direkte Folge der mangelnden Berücksichtigung des Vermögensentzugs durch Arisierung und Konfiszierung seitens des nationalsozialistischen Regimes durch die österreichische Regierung gewesen. 11

Hätte die Regierung die dargelegten Argumente mitberücksichtigt, so hätte sie die extreme Ungerechtigkeit der gefällten Entscheidung erkennen müssen. 12

Als Folge dessen habe Alfred G. am 26. Juni 1951 das Haus an den Rechtsanwalt (RA) und Berater der Creditanstalt-Bankverein Dr. Kurt Gr. um 145.000,– Schilling verkauft. Nur 14 Jahre später habe Dr. Kurt Gr. dieses an die Republik Österreich um 9,000.000,– Schilling verkauft. 13

Von den AntragstellerInnen wurden am 26. April 2005 und am 6. September 2005 Schriftsätze eingebracht. Darin wurde im Wesentlichen das bisherige Vorbringen wiederholt und betont, dass der Mieter der gegenständlichen Liegenschaft Dr. P. mit dem Ehepaar G. eine Vereinbarung getroffen habe, die Liegenschaft ab Mai 1939 zu beziehen. Der einzige Beweis für die Existenz dieses „Mietverhältnisses" sei ein nicht unterzeichnetes Memorandum gewesen, das Dr. P. selbst aufgesetzt habe. Die Mietbedingungen seien eindeutig sehr vorteilhaft für ihn gewesen. Die jährliche Miete habe 2.400,– Reichsmark betragen. Die Ausgaben, die für gewöhnlich der Mieter zu zahlen hätte, hätten vom Ehepaar G. bezahlt werden müssen, obwohl sie sich zu dem Zeitpunkt nicht mehr im Land befunden hätten. 14

Die Liegenschaft sei von der Gestapo am 19. Februar 1941 entzogen worden und bis 1950 unter der Verwaltung der österreichischen Behörden gestanden. Dr. Stephan L. von der Gestapo sei für die Verwaltung des Vermögens des Ehepaares G. verantwortlich gewesen. Am 22. Juni 1941 habe er mit Dr. P. einen neuen Mietvertrag abgeschlossen, der die gleiche Jahresmiete in der Höhe von 2.400,– Reichsmark vorgesehen habe. Zusätzlich 15

Arbitration Panel for *In Rem* Restitution – Decision No. 28/2005

16 In January 1947, Dr. P. had written Alfred G. a letter, in which he had requested the extension of the lease agreement. On 23 January 1948, after Alfred G. had applied for the extension, Dr. P. was supposed to vacate and hand over the property. What had happened to the property between 1948 and 1950 is not clear, but from a legal point of view it had always remained under the administration of the Austrian authorities.

17 Through the determination of the annual rent amounting to 2,400 Reichsmark in the years 1941 until 1945, the Chief Finance President should have received proceeds of approximately 9,600 Reichsmark and should have transferred them to a Secret State Police bank account until the end of the war. In the period between 1945 and January 1948, the Financial Directorate for Vienna, Lower Austria and Burgenland was supposed to have collected approximately 6,800 Reichsmark in rental earnings, so that the total sum of the rental earnings should have amounted to at least 16,400 Reichsmark.

18 Whether the house had been rented out between January 1948 and 1950 was unclear. In any case, the Austrian authorities had been responsible for renting out the property and for collecting the rental. If the ineffectiveness of the administration or corruption had been the cause of the loss of the collection of the rental earnings then this is to be attributed to the Financial Directorate as it had been responsible for the property.

19 On 20 January 1947, the first application for restitution was filed which included, in addition to the property Hohe Warte Z, further properties seized from Mr. and Mrs. G. This application had not contained a waiver. All rental earnings which had been received in the meantime had been expressly claimed. On 15 April 1948, the second application for restitution had been filed. In this application only the restitution of the property subject of this application had been requested. In the view of the applicants, two factors had been decisive for the two separate assertions for the property Hohe Warte Z. On the one hand, the necessary land register extract, which had to be presented during the filing of the application, had not been available. On the other hand, the inheritance proceedings for Ella G., who had died on 21 June 1946, had not yet been concluded at that time. It was only in this second application for restitution that the settlement of the earnings had been waived. However, this had merely been a general waiver, with which only the actually accumulated and not the entire rental earnings had been waived. On 15 December 1949, the third application for restitution was filed. The certificate of inheritance for Ella G. had been enclosed with this application. The waiver contained in this application had now elaborated the general waiver of the second application for restitution. Thus, the settlement of the earnings from the property had been waived before the Financial Directorate. The proceeds from the period of administration by the Secret State Police and by the Chief Finance President had been unaffected by this waiver. It seemed very clear that the sole beneficiary of this waiver had been the Financial Directorate. The applicants conclude from the fact that the rental earnings had only been waived before the Financial Directorate that negotiations with this authority had taken place. Today, it remained unclear why the Financial Directorate insisted on the waiver.

20 The applicants further indicated that the remaining properties which had formed part of the application for restitution of 20 January 1947 had been restituted with the decision of 10 April 1948, initially without the proceeds. In a separate decision of 15 March 1950 the rental earnings had been decided on, and a portion of these earnings had been restituted. It was important to consider that actions, with which rental or earnings had been claimed, had been settled separately from the property restitutions. This therefore showed that the assessment of the rental income had not led to a delay of the property restitutions.

Schiedsinstanz für Naturalrestitution – Entscheidung Nr. 28/2005

sei jedoch vereinbart worden, dass Dr. P. die üblichen Ausgaben, die im Zusammenhang mit der Liegenschaft standen, selber zu bestreiten habe. Auch sei ein zusätzlicher Betrag für die Benützung des Gartens vereinbart worden. 1941 habe Dr. L. einen Herrn S. zum Hausverwalter ernannt, dessen Aufgabe die Einziehung und Überweisung der Miete an die Gestapo auf ein Konto bei der Creditanstalt gewesen sei.

Im Jänner 1947 habe sich Dr. P. schriftlich an Alfred G. mit der Bitte um Verlängerung des Mietvertrages gewandt. Am 23. Jänner 1948, nachdem Alfred G. diesbezüglich einen Antrag gestellt habe, habe Dr. P. die Liegenschaft räumen und übergeben sollen. Was in der Zeit zwischen 1948 und 1950 mit der Liegenschaft passiert sei, sei unklar, jedoch sei sie rechtlich immer noch unter der Verwaltung der österreichischen Behörden gestanden. 16

Durch die Festsetzung einer Jahresmiete in der Höhe von 2.400,– Reichsmark in den Jahren 1941 bis 1945 hätten vom Oberfinanzpräsidenten (OFP) Einnahmen in der Höhe von cirka 9.600,– Reichsmark lukriert werden und bis Kriegsende auf ein Bankkonto der Gestapo überwiesen werden sollen. In der Zeit zwischen 1945 und Jänner 1948 hätte die FLD für Wien, Niederösterreich und das Burgenland ungefähr 6.800,– Reichsmark an Mieterträgnissen einnehmen sollen, so dass sich die Gesamtsumme der Mieterträgnisse auf mindestens 16.400,– Reichsmark belaufen hätte sollen. 17

Ob das Haus in den Jahren zwischen Jänner 1948 und 1950 vermietet gewesen sei, sei unklar. Jedenfalls seien die österreichischen Behörden für die Vermietung der Liegenschaft und die Entgegennahme des Mietzinses verantwortlich gewesen. Sollte die Ineffektivität der Verwaltungsführung oder Korruption zu dem Ausfall der Einnahmen der Mieterträgnisse geführt haben, so sei dies der FLD zuzurechnen, da diese für die Liegenschaft zuständig gewesen sei. 18

Am 20. Jänner 1947 sei der erste Rückstellungsantrag gestellt worden, wobei neben der Liegenschaft Hohe Warte Z auch noch weitere dem Ehepaar G. entzogene Liegenschaften beantragt worden seien. Dieser Antrag habe keinen Verzicht beinhaltet. Es seien ausdrücklich alle Mieterträgnisse, die in der Zwischenzeit erzielt worden seien, beantragt worden. Am 15. April 1948 sei der zweite Rückstellungsantrag gestellt worden. In diesem sei nur die Rückstellung der gegenständlichen Liegenschaft beantragt worden. Nach Ansicht der AntragstellerInnen seien zwei Gründe für die getrennte Geltendmachung der Liegenschaft Hohe Warte Z ausschlaggebend gewesen. Einerseits sei der erforderliche Grundbuchsauszug, der bei der Antragstellung vorgelegt werden musste, nicht zugänglich gewesen, und andererseits sei zu dieser Zeit das Erbschaftsverfahren nach Ella G., die am 21. Juni 1946 verstorben sei, noch nicht abgeschlossen gewesen. Erst in diesem zweiten Rückstellungsantrag sei auf die Abrechung der Erträgnisse verzichtet worden. Dieser Verzicht sei jedoch nur ein genereller gewesen, mit dem nur auf die tatsächlich aufgelaufenen und nicht auf die gesamten Mieteinnahmen verzichtet worden sei. Am 15. Dezember 1949 sei der dritte Rückstellungsantrag gestellt worden. Diesem sei bereits die Einantwortungsurkunde nach Ella G. beigelegt worden. Der in diesem Antrag enthaltene Verzicht habe nun den allgemeinen Verzicht des zweiten Rückstellungsantrages konkretisiert. Es sei damit auf die Abrechnung der Liegenschaftserträgnisse gegenüber der FLD verzichtet worden. Nicht berührt von diesem Verzicht seien die Erträgnisse aus der Zeit der Gestapo- bzw. der OFP-Verwaltung gewesen. Es erscheine ganz eindeutig, dass der einzige Nutznießer des Verzichts die FLD gewesen sei. Aus der Tatsache, dass auf die Mieterträgnisse nur gegenüber der FLD verzichtet worden sei, schließen die AntragstellerInnen, dass Verhandlungen mit dieser stattgefunden haben. Aus welchen Gründen die FLD auf den Verzicht bestanden haben soll, erscheine aus der heutigen Sicht unklar. 19

Allgemeiner Entschädigungsfonds 357

21 The extreme injustice of the decision also resulted from the fact that it had not been based on the principles of "natural justice". This term refers to the right to a legally competent judge and to a fair hearing, which had not been complied with during the decision making process of the Financial Directorate. The overlapping of functions held by the Financial Directorate, namely property administration, restitution processing, as well as decision-making regarding restitutions, contradicted the principle mentioned above. Furthermore, the responsible expert had made mistakes during the establishment of the facts as well as during the juridical appraisal.

22 Before the *Anschluss*, the property had not been encumbered. Regarding the personal tax debt, which on 29 March 1938 had supposedly amounted to 29,575.98 Schilling, it had been stated that it had not been paid within the deadline provided and for this reason it had been guaranteed in the land register. The payment of the outstanding taxes had been essential in order to be granted an emigration permit. By the time of the G. family's departure in May 1939, this tax debt had been covered by money which had originated from the forced sale of the Ga.-werke. Consequently, Alfred and Ella had both later owned a balance of approximately 21,720 Reichsmark. Hence, in February 1941 the G. personal tax account showed a balance of 11,000 Reichsmark. This balance had then been offset with the Reich Flight Tax and other debts. Even though the tax debts had been paid, the entry in the land register had not been cancelled. During the war, nobody in Austria had been interested in applying for its cancellation, and the claimants had had no access to the relevant files after the war. In 1941, the tax authorities had already noted that the personal tax had been paid. Despite this, after the restitution of the property in 1950, the restitution claimants had to pay the personal tax debt again. In the agreement with Dr. Gr., it had been agreed that Alfred G.'s and Liselotte W.'s "debts", recorded in the land register, were to be paid from the proceeds of the sale. The cancellation had taken place on 23 August 1951, making it clear that the amount of 29,579.98 Schilling had been paid a second time. Since the Financial Directorate had administered the property during the years 1945 to 1950, it had been responsible for making the relevant amendment to the land register.

2. *Submission by the Federal Government*

23 On 10 June 2005, the Republic of Austria submitted a statement.

24 On 12 March 1938, the property at issue had been owned by Ing. Alfred G. and his wife Ella G., who had each owned half of the property. Presumably, the owners of the property had had to emigrate in May 1939. Pursuant to the confiscation order of 19 February 1941 by the Secret State Police, their entire assets had been confiscated for the German Reich with the aim of later reverting them to the state. With the *Elfte Verordnung zum Reichsbürgergesetz* ("Eleventh Decree to the Reich Citizenship Law") of 25 November 1942, the assets of Mr. and Mrs. G. had been declared as reverted. This decree had provided for an automatic reversion of the property so that only a declaratory amendment of the land register had occurred with regards to the property. A further sale of the property by the German Reich did not take place.

25 On 3 November 1938, Mr. and Mrs. G. had concluded a rental agreement with Dr. P. This agreement assured the latter the lease as well as the unrestricted use of the garden and its produce from 15 May 1939 for the duration of five years in return for an annual rental fee. At the same time, the landlords had undertaken to duly maintain the condition of the building, to pay the taxes and duties for the house as well as to pay the fire and third party insurance. Conflicts had arisen between the Secret State Police and Dr. P. regarding the ad-

Die AntragstellerInnen wiesen weiters darauf hin, dass die übrigen Liegenschaften, die 20
im Rückstellungsantrag vom 20. Jänner 1947 beantragt worden seien, mit der Entscheidung vom 10. April 1948 zunächst ohne Erträgnisse zurückgestellt worden seien. In einer eigenen Entscheidung vom 15. März 1950 sei über die Mieterträgnisse entschieden worden, und ein Teil dieser Erträgnisse sei zurückerstattet worden. Es sei wichtig zu berücksichtigen, dass Klagen, mit denen der Mietzins bzw. die Erträgnisse eingeklagt worden seien, getrennt von den Liegenschaftsrückstellungen abgewickelt worden seien. Es zeige sich somit, dass die Bewertung der Mieteinnahmen nicht zu einer Verzögerung der Liegenschaftsrückstellungen geführt habe.

Die extreme Ungerechtigkeit der Entscheidung resultiere auch daraus, dass diese nicht 21
auf der Basis der Prinzipien der „natural justice" ergangen sei. Gemeint sei mit diesem Begriff das Recht auf den gesetzlichen Richter und auf das rechtliche Gehör, das bei dem Entscheidungsfindungsprozess von der FLD nicht gewahrt worden sei. Die Kumulation der Funktionen, die die FLD innehatte, nämlich Liegenschaftsverwaltung, Rückstellungsabwicklung als auch Entscheidungsfällung über die Rückstellung, widerspreche dem oben erwähnten Prinzip. Auch habe der zuständige Sachbearbeiter Fehler sowohl bei der Tatsachenfeststellung als auch bei der rechtlichen Beurteilung begangen.

Die Liegenschaft sei vor dem „Anschluss" unbelastet gewesen. Im Bezug auf die Perso- 22
nalsteuerschuld, die am 29. März 1938 29.575,98 Schilling betragen haben soll, sei angeführt worden, dass diese zunächst nicht in der dafür vorgesehenen Zeit gezahlt und deshalb im Grundbuch sichergestellt worden sei. Das Bezahlen der ausständigen Steuern sei essenziell für die Erteilung der Ausreisegenehmigung gewesen. Bis zur Ausreise der Familie G. im Mai 1939 sei diese Steuerschuld von dem Geld, das aus dem Zwangsverkauf der Ga.-werke hervorgegangen sei, bezahlt worden. Sowohl Alfred als auch Ella hätten dadurch später ein Guthaben von ungefähr 21.720,– Reichsmark besessen, so dass das Personalsteuerkonto der G.s mit Februar 1941 einen Saldo von 11.000,– Reichsmark aufgewiesen habe. Dieses Guthaben sei dann mit der Reichsfluchtsteuer und anderen Schulden aufgerechnet worden. Trotz Bezahlung der Steuerschulden sei die Eintragung im Grundbuch nicht gelöscht worden. In Österreich habe während des Krieges niemand Interesse gehabt, dies zu beantragen, und die AntragstellerInnen hätten nach dem Krieg keinen Zugang zu relevanten Akten gehabt. Die Steuerbehörden hätten bereits 1941 zur Kenntnis genommen, dass die Personalsteuer bezahlt worden sei, und trotzdem hätten die RückstellungswerberInnen nach Rückstellung der Liegenschaft 1950 die Personalsteuerschuld nochmals zahlen müssen. Im Vertrag mit Dr. Gr. sei vereinbart gewesen, dass die im Grundbuch eingetragenen „Schulden" von Alfred G. und Liselotte W. aus dem Kaufpreis zu bezahlen seien. Die Löschung sei am 23. August 1951 erfolgt, somit sei klar, dass der Betrag von 29.579,98 Schilling ein zweites Mal bezahlt worden sei. Da die FLD in den Jahren 1945–1950 die Liegenschaft verwaltet habe, sei sie für die bezügliche Richtigstellung im Grundbuch verantwortlich gewesen.

2. Vorbringen der Bundesregierung

Am 10. Juni 2005 brachte die Republik Österreich eine Stellungnahme ein. 23

Die gegenständliche Liegenschaft sei am 12. März 1938 je zur Hälfte im Eigentum von 24
Ing. Alfred G. und seiner Gattin Ella G. gestanden. Die LiegenschaftseigentümerInnen hätten vermutlich im Mai 1939 emigrieren müssen. Mit der Beschlagnahmeverfügung der Geheimen Staatspolizei vom 19. Februar 1941 sei deren gesamtes Vermögen mit dem Ziel des späteren Verfalls für das Deutsche Reich beschlagnahmt worden. Mit der „Elften Verordnung zum Reichsbürgergesetz vom 25. November 1942" sei das Vermögen der Ehegatten G. für verfallen erklärt worden. Diese Verordnung habe einen automatischen Ver-

equacy of the terms of the rental agreement. Dr. P. had paid the necessary maintenance expenses for the house. He had been working in proprietary matters for Mr. and Mrs. G. since 1938. Dr. P. had issued a fee of approximately 30,000 Reichsmark for these activities and had secured it with a lien on the property. Upon the intervention of Dr. L., the property administrator appointed by the Secret State Police for Mr. and Mrs. G., the amount had been reduced to 15,000 Reichsmark. On 2 January 1947, Dr. P. reported extensively to Ing. Alfred G. on the fact that after the end of the war he had commissioned absolutely necessary maintenance work.

26 On 21 April 1948, Ing. Alfred G. and the estate of his wife Ella G., who had died in Geneva on 21 January 1946, both represented by the attorney Dr. Se., had filed an application for restitution with the Financial Directorate for Vienna, Lower Austria and Burgenland based on the *Erste Rückstellungsgesetz* ("First Restitution Act"), concerning the property subject of this application. The application for restitution had contained the following statement: "I hereby expressly and irrevocably waive the settlement of accounts regarding the earnings of the property, the villa in Vienna XIX, Hohe Warte Z."

27 In a letter dated 22 April 1948, with reference to para. 2 (2) of the First Restitution Act, the Financial Directorate had called on Ing. Alfred G. to submit the certificate of inheritance for Ella G.

28 Pursuant to the certificate of inheritance no. 5 A 407/47, dated 18 October 1948, issued by the District Court Döbling, the estate of Ella G. had been devolved to their daughter Liselotte W. née G.

29 On 15 December 1949, Ing. Alfred G. and Mrs. Liselotte W., both represented by the attorney Dr. Se., had submitted a further application for restitution based on the First Restitution Act with regard to the property in question. In addition to the restitution of the property, the cancellation of various liens (Reich Flight Tax) had also been requested. Further, the application for restitution had also contained the following statement: "With a renewed express and irrevocable waiver of the settlement of the earnings before the Financial Directorate for Vienna, Lower Austria and Burgenland we request [...] that the following decision be issued"; the requested decision contained the restitution of the property and the cancellation of the lien for the Reich Flight Tax.

30 Pursuant to the decision by the Financial Directorate of 1 June 1950, the application for restitution had been granted in its entirety. Regarding the cancellation of the liabilities connected to the Reich Flight Tax, it had been pointed out that applications of this kind were to be made directly with the Land Register Court. Pursuant to para. 1 (2) of the First Restitution Act, the property was to be restituted in its current condition. Possible compensation for damages had not been provided for by the law. With regard to the liens, in accordance with para. 12 (2) of the First Restitution Act (sic!), the Financial Directorate had only been appointed to declare liens of third parties which had been acquired after the confiscation as ineffective provided the requirements precisely specified in the law had been met. In accordance with para. 1 (5) leg. cit., mortgages for securing outstanding amounts of the Reich Flight Tax and the Jewish capital levy were to be cancelled *ex officio* or upon application. In a memorandum dated 14 March 1950, earnings and expenses had each been designated as zero.

31 Pursuant to the purchase contract of 30 May 1951, Ing. G. and his daughter had sold the property to Dr. Kurt Gr. for 145,000 Schilling. It is recorded in the purchase contract that the property had been badly bomb-damaged during World War II. Furthermore, the existence of dry rot had been noted.

fall des Vermögens vorgesehen, so dass im Bezug auf Liegenschaftsvermögen nur eine deklaratorische Richtigstellung des Grundbuches erfolgt sei. Eine Weiterveräußerung der Liegenschaft durch das Deutsche Reich habe nicht stattgefunden.

Das Ehepaar G. habe am 3. November 1938 mit Dr. P. einen Mietvertrag abgeschlossen, der diesem die Miete sowie die uneingeschränkte Benützung und Fruchtnießung des Gartens vom 15. Mai 1939 für die Dauer von fünf Jahren gegen einen jährlichen Mietzins gesichert habe. Zugleich hätten sich die VermieterInnen zur ordnungsgemäßen Erhaltung des Bauzustandes, der Tragung sämtlicher Steuern und Abgaben des Hauses sowie der Bezahlung der Feuer- und Haftpflichtversicherung verpflichtet. Hinsichtlich der Angemessenheit der Konditionen des Mietvertrages sei es zu Auseinandersetzungen zwischen der Geheimen Staatspolizei und Dr. P. gekommen. Dieser habe die notwendigen Aufwendungen für den Erhalt des Hauses getätigt. Ab 1938 sei er in Vermögensangelegenheiten für die Ehegatten G. tätig gewesen. Für diese Tätigkeiten habe Dr. P. einen Honoraranspruch von ca. 30.000,- Reichsmark tituliert und pfandrechtlich auf der gegenständlichen Liegenschaft sichergestellt. Über Intervention von Dr. L., dem von der Gestapo bestellten Vermögensverwalter für das Ehepaar G., sei der Betrag auf 15.000,- Reichsmark reduziert worden. Am 2. Jänner 1947 habe Dr. P. einen umfangreichen Bericht an Ing. Alfred G. erstattet, in dem er ausgeführt habe, dass er nach Kriegsende unbedingt notwendige Erhaltungsarbeiten durchführen habe lassen. 25

Am 21. April 1948 hätten Ing. Alfred G. und die Verlassenschaft nach seiner am 21. Jänner 1946 in Genf verstorbenen Frau Ella G., beide vertreten durch RA Dr. Se., einen auf das Erste Rückstellungsgesetz (1. RStG) gestützten Rückstellungsantrag betreffend die gegenständliche Liegenschaft bei der FLD für Wien, Niederösterreich und Burgenland gestellt. Der Rückstellungsantrag habe folgende Erklärung enthalten: „Ich verzichte hiemit ausdrücklich und unwiderruflich auf die Abrechnung der Erträgnisse hinsichtlich der Liegenschaft Villa Wien XIX, Hohe Warte [Z]." 26

Mit Schreiben vom 22. April 1948 habe die FLD Ing. Alfred G. mit Hinweis auf § 2 Abs 2 1. RStG aufgefordert, die Einantwortungsurkunde nach Ella G. vorzulegen. 27

Der Nachlass nach Ella G. sei mit Einantwortungsurkunde des Bezirksgerichtes (BG) Döbling vom 18. Oktober 1948, 5 A 407/47, deren Tochter Liselotte W. geborene G. eingeantwortet worden. 28

Am 15. Dezember 1949 hätten Ing. Alfred G. und Frau Liselotte W., beide vertreten durch RA Dr. Se., bezüglich der gegenständlichen Liegenschaft neuerlich einen auf das 1. RStG gestützten Rückstellungsantrag eingebracht. Neben der Rückstellung der Liegenschaft sei auch die Löschung diverser Pfandrechte (Reichsfluchtsteuer) beantragt worden. Der Rückstellungsantrag habe weiters folgende Erklärung enthalten: „Unter nochmaligem ausdrücklichem und unwiderruflichem Verzicht auf Abrechnung der Erträgnisse gegenüber der Finanzlandesdirektion für Wien, Niederösterreich und Burgenland stellen wir [...] den Antrag auf Erlassung nachfolgenden Bescheides"; der beantragte Bescheid habe die Rückstellung der Liegenschaft und Löschung des Pfandrechtes für die Reichsfluchtsteuer zum Inhalt gehabt. 29

Mit Bescheid der FLD vom 1. Juni 1950 sei dem Rückstellungsantrag zur Gänze Folge gegeben worden. Bezüglich der Löschung der Verbindlichkeiten im Zusammenhang mit der Reichsfluchtsteuer sei darauf hingewiesen worden, dass derartige Anträge unmittelbar beim Grundbuchsgericht einzubringen seien. Gemäß § 1 Abs 2 1. RStG sei die Liegenschaft in jenem Zustand zurückzustellen, in dem sie sich befinde; allfällige Schadenersatzverpflichtungen habe das Gesetz nicht vorgesehen. Im Bezug auf Pfandrechte sei die 30

32 Pursuant to the purchase contract of 13 July 1965, Dr. Gr. had sold the property to the Republic of Austria for a purchase price of 9 million Schilling. On 17 January 2001, the Republic of Austria had still remained the owner of the property.

33 Regarding the provisions of the General Settlement Fund Law ("GSF Law"), the State Financial Procurator's Office submitted that the reopening of already settled claims is only provided for under exceptional circumstances. However, the restitution process established in the restitution laws did not, however, represent exceptional circumstances. A decision that had actually led to a restitution of the asset in question, as defined in the application at that time, could not constitute an extreme injustice.

34 The property in question was only acquired by the Republic of Austria in 1965. The contractual partner had not been the then aggrieved owners or their heirs, but a third party, to whom they had sold the property in the meantime.

35 Thus, the Republic of Austria deems that the prerequisites of the GSF Law for a recommendation for the return of the property are not fulfilled and requests the Arbitration Panel to reject the application.

3. Evidence

36 Evidence was taken by reviewing the documents enclosed with the application for *in rem* restitution.

37 The following documents were obtained by the Arbitration Panel as supplementary documentation:

38 Case documentation of the Historical Commission on Hohe Warte Z, EZ X, KG Heiligenstadt. (= Edith Leisch-Prost, Verena Pawlowsky, Harald Wendelin, *IN REM-Dokumentation. Dokumentation aller am 17. Jänner 2001 im Eigentum der Republik Österreich befindlichen Liegenschaften*, Vienna 2002.)

39 Excerpt from the electronic land register regarding EZ X, KG Heiligenstadt.

40 Files from the District Court Döbling: historical land register EZ X, KG Heiligenstadt; land register deed no. 3389/65 EZ X, KG Heiligenstadt.

41 Files from the Austrian State Archives, Archives of the Republic, department 06: property notice no. 41592 Alfred G.; property notice no. 35750 Ella G.; file from the Financial Directorate for Vienna no. 17289 Alfred and Paul G., volumes 1–5; Property Transaction Office statistics no. 7954 Garvens-werke; Compensation Fund no. 11.243 Liselotte E.; Compensation Fund no. 3052 Liselotte W.

42 Files from the Vienna Municipal and Regional Archives: District Court Döbling, representation *in absentia* no. 1 P 389/40 Alfred and Ella G.; Ordinance on the Notification of Seized Property no. 19/26 C 69 Alfred G. and Liselotte W.; Ordinance on the Notification of Seized Property no. 2/20 1532 Ga.-werke; District Court Döbling, property file 5 A 408/47 Ella G.; District Court Döbling, land register certificates 1343/19, 1793/51, 1299/38, 3461/39, 1159/41, 1347/41 and 1793/51 EZ X, KG Heiligenstadt; register information Dr. Arthur P.; Vienna address book "Lehmann" 1938, 1940, 1942.

43 Austrian Castle and Fortress Authority: file from the Federal Buildings Administration I Vienna, XIX., Döbling, property number W 0417 Hohe Warte Z.

44 File from the Municipal Authorities Department for Building, Fire and Trade Inspection on the EZ X, KG Heiligenstadt, Hohe Warte Z.

FLD gemäß § 12 Abs 2 1. RStG (sic!) nur berufen gewesen, nach der Entziehung erworbene Pfandrechte Dritter unter den im Gesetz näher bezeichneten Voraussetzungen für wirkungslos zu erklären; Hypotheken zur Besicherung von Rückständen an Reichsfluchtsteuer und JUVA seien gemäß § 1 Abs 5 leg. cit. von Amts wegen oder auf Antrag zu löschen gewesen. In einem Vermerk vom 14. März 1950 seien Erträgnisse und Aufwendungen jeweils mit null beziffert gewesen.

Mit Kaufvertrag vom 30. Mai 1951 hätten Ing. G. und seine Tochter die Liegenschaft für einen Kaufpreis von 145.000,– Schilling an Dr. Kurt Gr. verkauft. Aus dem Kaufvertrag ergebe sich, dass das Objekt durch Bombentreffer während des Zweiten Weltkrieges stark beschädigt worden sei. Weiters sei auf das Auftreten von Hausschwamm hingewiesen worden. 31

Mit Kaufvertrag vom 13. Juli 1965 habe Dr. Gr. die Liegenschaft gegen einen Kaufpreis von 9,000.000,– Schilling an die Republik Österreich verkauft. Die Republik Österreich sei am 17. Jänner 2001 auch weiterhin Eigentümerin der gegenständlichen Liegenschaft gewesen. 32

Zu den Bestimmungen nach dem Entschädigungsfondsgesetz (EF-G) brachte die Finanzprokuratur vor, dass ein Neuaufrollen bereits erledigter Ansprüche nur in Ausnahmefällen vorgesehen sei. Die in den RStG festgelegten Rückgabemodalitäten bildeten jedoch keine Ausnahmefälle. Eine Entscheidung, die tatsächlich zur Rückstellung des fraglichen Vermögenswertes im Sinne des seinerzeitigen Antrages geführt habe, könne keine extreme Ungerechtigkeit darstellen. 33

Die Republik Österreich habe die gegenständliche Liegenschaft erst 1965 erworben, wobei ihr Vertragspartner nicht die seinerzeit geschädigten EigentümerInnen bzw. deren ErbInnen gewesen seien, sondern ein Dritter, an den diese die Liegenschaft in der Zwischenzeit verkauft hätten. 34

Die Republik Österreich erachtet die Voraussetzungen des EF-G für eine Empfehlung zur Herausgabe der gegenständlichen Liegenschaft sohin als nicht gegeben und stellt den Antrag, die Schiedsinstanz möge den vorliegenden Antrag ablehnen. 35

3. Beweise

Beweise wurden erhoben durch Einsichtnahme in die dem Antrag auf Naturalrestitution beigelegten Dokumente. 36

Folgende Dokumente wurden als ergänzende Dokumentation durch die Schiedsinstanz eingeholt: 37

Falldokumentation der Historikerkommission zur Hohen Warte Z, EZ X, KG Heiligenstadt. (= Edith Leisch-Prost, Verena Pawlowsky, Harald Wendelin, IN REM-Dokumentation. Dokumentation aller am 17. Jänner 2001 im Eigentum der Republik Österreich befindlichen Liegenschaften, Wien 2002.) 38

Auszug aus dem elektronischen Grundbuch zur EZ X, KG Heiligenstadt. 39

Akten des BG Döbling: Historisches Grundbuch EZ X, KG Heiligenstadt; Grundbuch-Urkunde Nr. 3389/65 EZ X, KG Heiligenstadt. 40

Akten aus dem Österreichischen Staatsarchiv (ÖStA), Archiv der Republik, Abteilung 06: Vermögensanmeldung (VA) Nr. 41592 Alfred G.; VA Nr. 35750 Ella G.; Akt der FLD Wien Nr. 17289 Alfred und Paul G., Bände 1–5; Vermögensverkehrsstelle Statistik (VVSt Stat.) Nr. 7954 Garvens-Werke; Abgeltungsfonds (AbgF) Nr. 11.243 Liselotte E.; AbgF Nr. 3052 Liselotte W. 41

4. Established Facts

4.1 Seizure

45   On 13 March 1938, the property EZ X, KG Heiligenstadt, Hohe Warte Z, was under the unencumbered ownership of Ing. Alfred G. and Ella G., each of them owning 50 %. On 15 July 1938, the value of the property amounted to 93,333 Reichsmark.

46   In May 1939, Ing. Alfred G. and Ella G. fled to England as they were considered Jews according to the Nuremberg Laws. Both of their daughters, Liselotte W. née G. and Johanna Maria, also left Austria.

47   On 3 November 1938, Alfred and Ella G. had concluded a five-year lease for the house Hohe Warte Z with their tax adviser Dr. Arthur P., beginning on 15 May 1939. The rent was fixed at 2,400 Reichsmark per year. The landlords also were responsible for paying all taxes and duties connected to the property. They also undertook to meet the costs for the due maintenance of the building's condition. The application of the *Mietengesetz* ("Rental Law") was excluded.

48   On 19 February 1941, the Secret State Police Vienna ordered the seizure of the complete movable and immovable assets of Alfred und Ella G. and their children Liselotte and Johanna Maria. The aim of this order was the later seizure of the assets for the benefit of the German Reich. The lawyer Dr. Stephan L. was appointed as a property administrator by the Secret State Police.

49   Following the request of Dr. Stephan L., Dr. Arthur P., the tax adviser and representative of Mr. and Mrs. G., rendered a report to him on the property Hohe Warte Z. Dr. Arthur P. informed him on 12 May 1941 that he had obtained an approval under foreign exchange law for the administration of this house. According to Dr. P., the taxes and duties which were to be paid by the owners would amount to 208.03 Reichsmark on the basis of a monthly rent of 200 Reichsmark. In his opinion, a settlement of accounts for the benefit of the owners would therefore not be necessary.

50   In July 1940, Dr. P. sued Mr. and Mrs. G. for a claim of 28,567.13 Reichsmark at the Regional Court Vienna. The amount claimed was for the representation in all tax-related issues. In April 1941, the Regional Court Vienna issued the judgment in which it granted the claim of 28,567.13 Reichsmark including costs of 1,590.89 Reichsmark. After the decision had become legally binding, the claim was guaranteed in the land register under property Hohe Warte Z. In June 1941, the ratable value of the property Hohe Warte Z amounted to 64,100 Reichsmark.

51   On 12 June 1941, Dr. P. conveyed "minutes from memory" of 3 November 1938 to Dr. L. The subject of these minutes was the rental agreement which had been verbally concluded with the spouses G. However, Dr. L. refused to recognize this rental agreement as he was of the opinion that taxes and duties still had to be added to the statutory rent of 2,400 Reichsmark. For this reason, he asked Dr. P. to retroactively correct the outstanding debt to 1 March 1941 since the confiscation had taken place on 19 February. Dr. L. also demanded adequate remuneration for the use of the garden. Regarding the invoice of 28,567.13 Reichsmark, which seemed rather excessive to Dr. L., he informed Dr. P. that he refused to recognize the ruling of the Regional Court Vienna. The ruling was only issued after the confiscation order, and in addition, Dr. L. saw an error in the Foreign Exchange Board's approval.

Akten aus dem Wiener Stadt- und Landesarchiv (WStLA): BG Döbling, Abwesen- 42
heitspflegschaft Nr. 1 P 389/40 Alfred und Ella G.; Vermögensentziehungs-Anmeldung
(VEAV) Nr. 19/26 C 69 Alfred G. und Liselotte W.; VEAV Nr. 2/20 1532 Ga.-werke; BG
Döbling, Verlassenschaftakt 5 A 408/47 Ella G.; BG Döbling, Grundbuch-Urkunden
1343/19, 1793/51, 1299/38, 3461/39, 1159/41, 1347/41 und 1793/51 EZ X, KG Heiligenstadt; Meldeauskunft Dr. Arthur P.; Adressbuch Wien „Lehmann" 1938, 1940, 1942.

Burghauptmannschaft Österreich: Akt der Bundesgebäudeverwaltung I Wien, XIX., 43
Döbling, Liegenschaftsnummer W 0417 Hohe Warte Z.

Akt der Magistratsabteilung (MA) 37/19 – Bau-, Feuer- und Gewerbepolizei zur EZ X, 44
KG Heiligenstadt, Hohe Warte Z.

4. Festgestellter Sachverhalt

4.1 Entzug

Die Liegenschaft EZ X, KG Heiligenstadt, Hohe Warte Z stand am 13. März 1938 las- 45
tenfrei je zur Hälfte im Eigentum von Ing. Alfred und Ella G. Der Wert der Liegenschaft
betrug am 15. Juli 1938 93.333,– Reichsmark.

Im Mai 1939 flüchteten Ing. Alfred G. und Ella G. nach England, da sie laut den Nürn- 46
berger Gesetzen als Juden galten. Auch ihre beiden Töchter Liselotte W. geb. G. und Johanna Maria verließen Österreich.

Am 3. November 1938 hatten Alfred und Ella G. mit ihrem Steuerberater Dr. Arthur P. 47
einen Mietvertrag über das Haus Hohe Warte Z auf fünf Jahre beginnend ab 15. Mai 1939
abgeschlossen. Der Mietzins wurde mit 2.400,– Reichsmark pro Jahr festgelegt. Die VermieterInnen hatten auch sämtliche zu zahlenden Steuern und Abgaben, die im Zusammenhang mit der Liegenschaft standen, zu tragen. Sie verpflichteten sich ebenso, die Auslagen für die ordnungsgemäße Erhaltung des Bauzustandes zu bestreiten; die Anwendung
des Mietengesetzes wurde ausgeschlossen.

Am 19. Februar 1941 wurde die Beschlagnahme des gesamten stehenden und liegen- 48
den Vermögens von Alfred und Ella G. und deren Kindern Liselotte und Johanna Maria
von der Gestapo Wien verfügt. Ziel dieser Verfügung war die spätere Einziehung des Vermögens zugunsten des Deutschen Reiches. RA Dr. Stephan L. wurde von der Gestapo zum
Vermögensverwalter bestellt.

Nach Aufforderung von Dr. Stephan L. an den Steuerberater und Bevollmächtigten des 49
Ehepaares G., Dr. Arthur P., ihm Bericht über die Liegenschaft Hohe Warte Z zu erstatten,
teilte ihm dieser am 12. Mai 1941 mit, die devisenrechtliche Genehmigung zur Verwaltung dieses Hauses eingeholt zu haben. Die Steuern und Abgaben, die die EigentümerInnen zu tragen hatten, würden Dr. P. zufolge monatlich 208,03 Reichsmark bei einem monatlichen Mietzins von 200,– Reichsmark betragen. Eine Abrechnung zugunsten der
EigentümerInnen entfalle seines Erachtens dadurch.

Eine Forderung von 28.567,13 Reichsmark des Dr. P. gegenüber dem Ehepaar G. für 50
die Vertretung in allen Steuersachen klagte er im Juli 1940 beim Landgericht Wien ein. Im
April 1941 erging das Urteil des Landgerichtes Wien, in dem der Forderung von 28.567,13
Reichsmark samt Kosten in der Höhe von 1.590,89 Reichsmark stattgegeben wurde. Nach
Rechtskrafteintritt des Urteils wurde die Forderung auf der Liegenschaft Hohe Warte Z
grundbücherlich sichergestellt. Im Juni 1941 betrug der Einheitswert der Liegenschaft
Hohe Warte Z 64.100,– Reichsmark.

52   On 19 June 1941, Dr. L. transferred the administration of the property Hohe Warte Z to the building administrator Franz S. Profits which were not needed to cover the running costs were to be transferred to Dr. L.'s third-party account (escrow account) "kg. 890 Gestapo" held with the *Creditanstalt-Bankverein*, branch office Kärntnerring 1, sub account "Alfred Israel G.". Dr. P. had also been informed that the administration had been transferred to Franz S. Among other things, Dr. L. pointed out Franz S.'s authority to accept the rental payments.

53   On 14 July 1941, after negotiations with Dr. L., Dr. P., as instigating party, directed a land register submission to the District Court Döbling. In this submission he applied for the cancellation of the lien of 28,567.13 Reichsmark, however, only in regard to the sum exceeding 15,000 Reichsmark. On 22 August 1941, the application was approved by the District Court Döbling. On 25 August 1941, the cancellation of this lien with a partial amount of 13,567.13 Reichsmark was recorded in the land register.

54   On 22 July 1941, a new rental agreement was signed between Dr. P. and the German Reich. The annual rent amounted to 2,430.80 Reichsmark, while the payment of running costs and public taxes was still to be added. It cannot be established whether Dr. P. had to later pay the difference to the previously agreed rental.

55   Early in 1942 – at this point in time the entire property of Mr. and Mrs. G. had already reverted to the German Reich – upon the request of the Secret State Police Vienna, attorney-at-law Dr. Stephan L. retired from the administration of Mr. and Mrs. G.'s property. The law office of Dr. Franz Eb. and Dr. Anton Pr. took over the administration; they already administered the assets of Alfred G.'s brother, Paul G., and his wife, Cornelia. Still extant assets were transferred by Dr. L. to the third-party account of the Eb./Pr. office with the account name "Secret State Police – Chief Finance President Berlin – Dr. Alfred Isr. and Ella Sarah G.". It cannot be established to where the rental earnings had been transferred between 22 July 1941 and the end of the war.

4.2 Land Register as at 1945

56   On 7 April 1938, a lien for the personal tax claim of 29,575.98 Schilling for the Austrian Federal Treasury had been recorded. On 6 July 1938, there were no further open personal tax claims regarding Alfred G. However, the lien continued to be recorded in the land register after 1945. It cannot be established why a cancellation had not been carried out.

57   On 25 October 1940, the lien for the enforceable claim of the court cashier Vienna of 12.40 Reichsmark had been recorded for the German Reich (Reich Justice Treasury). This lien also continued to be recorded in the land register after the end of the NS regime.

58   On 7 May 1941, due to the statement of arrears by the tax office Innere Stadt-Ost Vienna of 6 May 1941, the lien for the enforceable Reich Flight Tax claim of 1,956.99 Reichsmark had been recorded for the benefit of the German Reich (Finance Administration) as a subsidiary contribution. This lien had also not been cancelled after Austria had been rebuilt; neither had the lien for the claim of 15,000 Reichsmark of Dr. P.

59   A change of the ownership status for the benefit of the German Reich had never been recorded in the land register. For this reason, until the sale of the property in 1951 to Dr. Gr., Alfred G. and his wife Ella, and after their death their daughter Liselotte W. née G., were registered as owners of the property in sheet B of the land register.

Dr. P. übermittelte Dr. L. am 12. Juni 1941 ein „Gedenkprotokoll" vom 3. November 1938, dessen Gegenstand der mündlich abgeschlossene Mietvertrag mit dem Ehepaar G. war. Dr. L. erkannte diesen Mietvertrag jedoch nicht an, da seiner Meinung nach zum gesetzlichen Mietzins von 2.400,– Reichsmark noch die Steuern und Abgaben hinzuzurechnen seien. Deshalb ersuchte er Dr. P., den Rückstand rückwirkend mit 1. März 1941 zu berichtigen, da die Beschlagnahme mit 19. Februar erfolgt war. Auch für die Benützung des Gartens forderte Dr. L. ein angemessenes Entgelt. Zur Kostennote von 28.567,13 Reichsmark, die Dr. L. weit überzogen erschien, teilte er Dr. P. mit, das Urteil des Landgerichtes Wien nicht anerkennen zu können; dieses war erst nach der Beschlagnahmeverfügung ergangen, und Dr. L. sah außerdem einen Irrtum bei der Genehmigung durch die Devisenstelle vorliegen.

51

Am 19. Juni 1941 übertrug Dr. L. die Verwaltung der Liegenschaft Hohe Warte Z dem Gebäudeverwalter Franz S. Ertragsüberschüsse, die nicht zur Deckung laufender Ausgaben benötigt wurden, waren auf Dr. L.s Anderkonto „kg. 890 Gestapo" bei der Creditanstalt-Bankverein, Zweigstelle Kärntnerring 1, Subkonto „Alfred Israel G[...]" abzuführen. Auch Dr. P. wurde über die Verwaltungsübertragung informiert; Dr. L. wies unter anderem auf Franz S.s Berechtigung hin, den Mietzins entgegenzunehmen.

52

Nach Verhandlungen mit Dr. L. richtete Dr. P. als betreibende Partei am 14. Juli 1941 eine Grundbucheingabe an das Amtsgericht Döbling. In dieser wurde die Löschung des auf der Liegenschaft Hohe Warte Z eingeleibten Pfandrechtes von 28.567,13 Reichsmark, jedoch nur im Hinblick auf den die Summe von 15.000,– Reichsmark übersteigenden Betrag, beantragt. Der Antrag wurde am 22. August 1941 vom Amtsgericht Döbling genehmigt. Am 25. August 1941 wurde die Löschung dieses Pfandrechtes mit dem Teilbetrag von 13.567,13 Reichsmark im Grundbuch einverleibt.

53

Am 22. Juli 1941 wurde zwischen Dr. P. und dem Deutschen Reich ein neuer Mietvertrag abgeschlossen. Der jährliche Mietzins betrug 2.430,80 Reichsmark, wobei noch zusätzlich die Bestreitung der Betriebskosten und öffentlichen Abgaben hinzukam. Ob Dr. P. die Differenz zum vorher vereinbarten Mietzins nachzahlen musste, kann nicht festgestellt werden.

54

Anfang 1942 – zu dem Zeitpunkt war das gesamte Vermögen des Ehepaares G. dem Deutschen Reich bereits verfallen – legte RA Dr. Stephan L. auf Wunsch der Gestapo Wien die Vermögensverwaltung von Alfred und Ella G. zurück. Diese wurde von der Rechtsanwaltskanzlei Dr. Franz Eb. und Dr. Anton Pr. übernommen, die bereits das Vermögen von Alfred G.s Bruder Paul G. und von dessen Ehefrau Cornelia verwalteten. Noch vorhandene Vermögenswerte wurden von Dr. L. auf das Anderkonto „Gestapo – OFP Berlin – Dr. Alfred Aron Isr[...] und Ella Sarah G[...]" der Kanzlei Eb./Pr. überwiesen. Wohin die Mieterträgnisse aus der Zeit vom 22. Juli 1941 bis Kriegsende geflossen sind, kann nicht festgestellt werden.

55

4.2 Stand des Grundbuches 1945

Am 7. April 1938 war auf die Liegenschaftshälfte des Alfred G. ein Pfandrecht für die Personalsteuerforderung von 29.575,98 Schilling für den österreichischen Bundesschatz einverleibt worden. Am 6. Juli 1938 bestand gegenüber Alfred G. keine zu diesem Zeitpunkt offene Personalsteuerforderung mehr. Dennoch blieb im Grundbuch auch nach 1945 dieses Pfandrecht eingetragen. Aus welchen Gründen die Löschung im Grundbuch nicht erfolgt war, kann nicht festgestellt werden.

56

Am 25. Oktober 1940 war das Pfandrecht für die vollstreckbare Forderung der Gerichtskasse Wien von 12,40 Reichsmark für das Deutsche Reich (Reichsjustizfiskus) ein-

57

4.3 Restitution

60 On 20 January 1947, Alfred G. submitted an application for restitution at the Financial Directorate for Vienna, Lower Austria and Burgenland. He claimed the restitution of his fifty percent share of various properties, which had been owned by Alfred G. and his brother Paul G. and which had been confiscated by the Secret State Police. He also applied for the cancellation of the liens of 1,956.99 Reichsmark together with the extra charges for late payment and costs. The liens had been incorporated on the property Hohe Warte Z in the land register in order to guarantee the outstanding debts regarding the Reich Flight Tax. Initially, the restitution of the property Hohe Warte Z itself was not requested in the application.

61 On 8 April 1947, Alfred G. conveyed to the Financial Directorate a certified power of attorney for his lawyer Dr. Harold Se. In this letter he again requested that "the properties listed in my statement be immediately restituted […], the notice of confiscation as well as the liens registered for the guarantee of the outstanding debts regarding the Reich Flight Tax be cancelled."

62 With the restitution decision of April 1948, the Financial Directorate ordered the restitution of all claimed, confiscated properties in accordance with the First Restitution Act.

63 In January 1947, Dr. Arthur P. informed Alfred G. in writing about his difficulties observing the non-recorded lease agreement. Due to the fact that the Hohe Warte Z had been a much sought after property by many officials of the National Socialist Party, he had repeatedly received threats in order to cause him to vacate the house. The claims for fees of 28,567.13 Reichsmark secured in the land register through litigation were justified by Dr. P. to the effect that an appeal could be lodged in the eventuality of a forced sale of the house due to outstanding tax debts. Further, Dr. P. wrote: "In spite of the present judgment of the court, which I had to bring about solely due to your absence, I naturally declare myself willing to discuss with you the amount and payment of my claims for fees upon your expected presence in Vienna." It could not be established how much Ing. G. had paid for the services of Dr. P., or whether they had settled their accounts by another means.

64 The property Hohe Warte Z suffered damages caused by bombings during the war. It cannot be established which of these damages Dr. P. actually had commissioned to be repaired. After the war, the estimate for the repairs totaled 32,072.31 Gold Reichsmark. Between July 1939 and April 1941, various repair costs for the house had already amounted to at least 1,718.20 Reichsmark.

65 In 1947, a judicial notice of termination of the tenancy rights of Dr. Arthur P. for the use of the villa Hohe Warte Z was issued by means of proceedings (no. 63 RK 867/47). Through a legally binding judgment of 23 January 1948, Dr. P. was obliged to hand over the vacated property EZ X to Ing. Alfred G. It cannot be established whether the property was actually handed over at that point in time.

66 On 15 April 1948, Alfred G. and the estate of Ella G., who had in the meantime passed away, filed an application with the Financial Directorate for restitution of the property Hohe Warte Z and for the cancellation of the lien of 1,956.99 Reichsmark including extra charges for late payment and costs. Pursuant to the Eleventh Decree to the Reich Citizenship Law, the property had been reverted for the benefit of the German Reich. Alfred and Ella G. were still recorded as half-share owners in the land register since incorporation into

verleibt worden. Auch dieses Pfandrecht war nach dem Ende des NS-Regimes im Grundbuch weiterhin eingetragen.

Aufgrund des Rückstandsausweises des Finanzamtes Innere Stadt-Ost Wien vom 6. Mai 1941 war am 7. Mai 1941 das Pfandrecht für die vollstreckbare Reichsfluchtsteuerforderung von 1.956,99 Reichsmark für das Deutsche Reich (Finanzverwaltung) als Nebeneinlage einverleibt worden. Auch dieses Pfandrecht war nach der Wiedererrichtung Österreichs noch nicht gelöscht worden, ebenso wenig das Pfandrecht der Forderung von 15.000,- Reichsmark des Dr. P. 58

Eine Änderung der Eigentumsverhältnisse zugunsten des Deutschen Reiches war im Grundbuch nie angemerkt worden, so dass im B-Blatt bis zum Verkauf der Liegenschaft im Jahr 1951 an Dr. Gr. Alfred G. gemeinsam mit seiner Ehefrau Ella bzw. nach deren Tod ihre Tochter Liselotte W. geb. G. als EigentümerInnen der Liegenschaft eingetragen waren. 59

4.3 Rückstellung

Am 20. Jänner 1947 stellte Alfred G. einen Rückstellungsantrag bei der FLD für Wien, Niederösterreich und Burgenland, in dem die Rückstellung des Hälfteanteils verschiedener Liegenschaften gefordert wurde, die Alfred G. gemeinsam mit seinem Bruder Paul G. besessen hatte und die von der Gestapo beschlagnahmt worden waren. Auch wurde die Löschung der zur Sicherstellung für Rückstände an Reichsfluchtsteuer auf der Liegenschaft Hohe Warte Z grundbücherlich einverleibten Pfandrechte in der Höhe von 1.956,99 Reichsmark samt Säumniszuschlägen und Kosten beantragt. Eine Rückstellung der Liegenschaft Hohe Warte Z selbst wurde zunächst nicht beantragt. 60

Am 8. April 1947 übermittelte Alfred G. der FLD nachträglich die beglaubigte Vollmacht für seinen RA Dr. Harold Se. und stellte in diesem Schreiben neuerlich die Bitte, „die in meiner Eingabe angeführten Liegenschaften unverzüglich [...] zurückzustellen, die Anmerkung der Beschlagnahme, sowie die zur Sicherstellung für Rückstände an Reichsfluchtsteuer eingetragenen Pfandrechte zu löschen." 61

Mit Rückstellungsbescheid von April 1948 verfügte die FLD die Rückstellung nach dem 1. RStG sämtlicher beantragter, entzogener Liegenschaften. 62

Dr. Arthur P. schilderte Alfred G. im Jänner 1947 in schriftlicher Form von seinen Schwierigkeiten, den nicht intabulierten Mietvertrag halten zu können. Aufgrund des bei Funktionären der NSDAP sehr begehrten Objektes Hohe Warte Z habe er immer wieder Drohungen erhalten, um das Haus zu räumen. Die im Klagewege grundbücherlich sichergestellten Honoraransprüche von 28.567,13 Reichsmark rechtfertigte Dr. P. dahingehend, bei einer etwaigen Zwangsversteigerung des Hauses wegen bestehender Steuerrückstände Einspruch erheben zu können. Weiters schrieb Dr. P.: „Trotz des vorliegenden gerichtlichen Urteiles, das ich nur aus dem Grunde Ihrer Abwesenheit herbeiführen mußte, erkläre ich mich natürlich bereit, über die Höhe und Abgeltung meiner Honoraransprüche mir [sic] Ihnen anläßlich Ihrer zu erwartenden Anwesenheit in Wien das weitere zu besprechen." Welchen Betrag Ing. G. für die Leistungen von Dr. P. gezahlt hat oder ob sie sich auf eine andere Weise geeinigt haben, kann nicht festgestellt werden. 63

Die Liegenschaft Hohe Warte Z hat im Laufe des Krieges durch Bombeneinschlag Schäden erlitten. Welche dieser Schäden Dr. P. tatsächlich beheben ließ, kann nicht festgestellt werden. Ein Kostenvoranschlag für die Reparaturen belief sich nach Kriegsende auf 32.072,31 Goldreichsmark. Bereits von Juli 1939 bis April 1941 hatten sich verschiedene Reparaturkosten an dem Haus auf mindestens 1.718,20 Reichsmark belaufen. 64

Arbitration Panel for *In Rem* Restitution – Decision No. 28/2005

the land register of the altered ownership situation had not taken place. Further, the claimants for restitution waived "expressly and irrevocably the settlement of the earnings regarding the property villa Vienna XIX., Hohe Warte Z". At the end of the application, the following handwritten comment by the Financial Directorate is to be found: "House is not under official administration! For this reason, no settlement of accounts! Original owners are still the owners listed in the land register."

67   On 22 April 1948, in response to this application, the Financial Directorate called on Alfred G. by letter to present a certificate of inheritance in order to be able to carry out the restitution of Ella G.'s half share of the property.

68   On 18 October 1948, Ella G.'s estate was devolved to her daughter Liselotte W. by the District Court Döbling. The net value of the estate amounted to 32,040 Schilling.

69   On 13 October 1949, on the basis of the certificate of inheritance of 18 October 1948, Ella G.'s ownership of the half share to the EZ X, KG Heiligenstadt was recorded for Liselotte W. née G. Up to that point, Ella G. had been registered in the land register as a half-share owner.

70   On 15 December 1949, Alfred G. and Liselotte W. filed another application with the Financial Directorate. The claims of the preceding application of 15 April 1948 were repeated. Again, the restitution of the property was claimed "with the express and irrevocable waiver of the settlement of the earnings from the property at issue before the Regional Financial Directorate for Vienna, Lower Austria and Burgenland". It cannot be established why the waivers had been declared. It can also not be established whether there had been negotiations regarding the property Hohe Warte Z between the claimants' representative and the administrative body responsible for restitution, the Financial Directorate.

71   On 14 March 1950, the accounting department of the Financial Directorate drew up a final account regarding the EZ X, KG Heiligenstadt. In this final account it says (in handwriting): "Restitution – No settling of accounts, neither with the Chief Finance President nor with the Financial Directorate. Therefore, proceeds 0 – expenditures from Reich or Federation funds 0 – Waiver, see application for restitution."

72   The Financial Directorate's decision on the restitution applications filed regarding the restitution of the property Hohe Warte Z was issued on 1 June 1950. The request was wholly granted. In the explanation it says that the seizure by the German Reich took place on the basis of abrogated Reich regulations (Eleventh Decree to the Reich Citizenship Law of 25 November 1941) without any kind of consideration. On 27 November 1941, the property reverted to the German Reich. Further it states: "This property is presently being administered by a department of the Federation (Financial Directorate for Vienna, Lower Austria and Burgenland, department for property control and restitution matters […])." Until 30 June 1950, no earnings had been registered with the Financial Directorate, and the presentation and examination of the settlement of accounts regarding the earnings had been waived. A request for the cancellation of the Reich Flight Tax claim in the land register could be filed directly with the Land Register Court with reference to para. 1 (5) of the First Restitution Act.

73   On 30 May/7 July 1951, a purchase contract regarding Hohe Warte Z was signed between Alfred G. and Liselotte W. as vendors and Kurt Gr. as purchaser. The house passed into the ownership of Dr. Kurt Gr. for 145,000 Schilling. The property's ratable value had been reduced from 64,100 Schilling to 56,900 Schilling as the house and garden had been

1947 erfolgte eine gerichtliche Aufkündigung des Mietrechtes des Dr. Arthur P. an der 65
Benützung der Villa Hohe Warte Z mittels einem Verfahren (Zahl 63 RK 867/47). Mit
einem rechtskräftigen Erkenntnis vom 23. Jänner 1948 wurde Dr. P. verpflichtet, Ing. Alfred G. die Liegenschaft EZ X geräumt zu übergeben. Ob die Liegenschaft zu diesem Zeitpunkt tatsächlich übergeben wurde, kann nicht festgestellt werden.

Am 15. April 1948 stellten Alfred G. und die Verlassenschaft nach der mittlerweile verstorbenen Ella G. bei der FLD einen Antrag auf Rückstellung der Liegenschaft Hohe Warte 66
Z und auf Löschung des Pfandrechtes von 1.956,99 Reichsmark samt Säumniszuschlägen
und Kosten. Die Liegenschaft war durch die Elfte Verordnung zum Reichsbürgergesetz
zugunsten des Deutschen Reiches verfallen. Da eine grundbücherliche Einverleibung der
geänderten Eigentumsverhältnisse nicht erfolgt war, waren Alfred und Ella G. laut Grundbuch noch immer jeweils HälfteeigentümerInnen. Weiters verzichteten die RückstellungswerberInnen „ausdrücklich und unwiderruflich auf die Abrechnung der Erträgnisse hinsichtlich der Liegenschaft Villa Wien XIX., Hohe Warte [Z]". Handschriftlich befindet sich
am Ende des Antrages ein Vermerk der FLD: „Haus steht nicht in h.o. Verwaltung! Daher
keine Abrechnung! Ursprüngliche Eigentümer noch grundbücherliche Eigentümer."

Als Antwort auf diesen Antrag forderte am 22. April 1948 die FLD Alfred G. in einem 67
Schreiben auf, eine Einantwortungsurkunde beizubringen, um die Rückstellung des halben Liegenschaftsanteils von Ella G. durchführen zu können.

Am 18. Oktober 1948 wurde der Nachlass von Ella G. ihrer Tochter Liselotte W. durch 68
das Bezirksgericht Döbling eingeantwortet. Der reine Nachlass betrug 32.040,– Schilling.

Aufgrund der Einantwortungsurkunde vom 18. Oktober 1948 wurde am 13. Oktober 69
1949 im Grundbuch das Eigentumsrecht an der Hälfte der EZ X, KG Heiligenstadt der Ella
G. für Liselotte W. geb. G. einverleibt. Bis zu diesem Zeitpunkt war Ella G. als Hälfteeigentümerin im Grundbuch eingetragen.

Am 15. Dezember 1949 stellten Alfred G. und Liselotte W. bei der FLD einen weiteren Rückstellungsantrag. Darin wurde das Begehren des vorangegangenen Rückstellungsantrages vom 15. April 1948 wiederholt. Nochmals wurde beantragt, die Liegenschaft „unter dem nochmaligen ausdrücklichen und unwiderruflichen Verzicht auf 70
Abrechnung der Erträgnisse der gegenständlichen Liegenschaft gegenüber der Finanzlandesdirektion für Wien, Niederösterreich und das Burgenland" zurückzustellen. Aus
welchem Grund die Verzichte abgegeben wurden, kann nicht festgestellt werden. Auch
kann nicht festgestellt werden, ob zwischen dem Vertreter der AntragstellerInnen und der
Rückstellungsbehörde, der FLD, betreffend der Liegenschaft Hohe Warte Z Verhandlungen stattgefunden haben.

Am 14. März 1950 erstellte die Verrechnungsabteilung der FLD eine Schlussabrechnung zur EZ X, KG Heiligenstadt. In dieser Verrechnung heißt es (handschriftlich): „Rück- 71
stellung – Es wurde weder mit dem OFP noch mit der FLD abgerechnet, daher Erträgnisse 0 – Aufwendungen aus Reichs- oder Bundesmitteln 0 – Verzicht siehe R.-Antrag."

Der Bescheid der FLD über die gestellten Rückstellungsanträge bezüglich der Rück- 72
gabe der Liegenschaft Hohe Warte Z erging am 1. Juni 1950. Dem Begehren wurde zur
Gänze stattgegeben. In der Begründung heißt es, dass die Entziehung vom Deutschen
Reich aufgrund von aufgehobenen reichsrechtlichen Vorschriften (Elfte Verordnung zum
Reichsbürgergesetz vom 25. November 1941) ohne irgendeine Gegenleistung erfolgt sei.
Das Vermögen sei mit 27. November 1941 dem Deutschen Reich verfallen. Weiters heißt
es: „Dieses Vermögen wird derzeit von einer Dienststelle des Bundes (Finanzlandesdirektion für Wien, Niederösterreich und Burgenland, Dienststelle für Vermögenssiche-

Arbitration Panel for *In Rem* Restitution – Decision No. 28/2005

substantially bomb damaged and this damage had not yet been repaired. Concerning the payment of the purchase price it had been agreed to transfer to the buyer the property free of any liens recorded in the land register. The following liens were still recorded: 29,575.98 Schilling for personal tax debts, 12.40 Reichsmark for a claim by the Reich Justice Administration, 15,000 Reichsmark for the claim by Dr. Arthur P. and 1,956.99 Reichsmark for Reich Flight Tax debts. The vendors undertook jointly and severally, to bring about the cancellation of the liens from the 80,000 Schilling which were to be deposited upon drafting of the contract. In order for the purchase contract to enter into legal effect it had to be approved by the National Bank since the vendors were non-residents. This took place on 26 June 1951.

74 On 6 June 1951, the cancellation of the lien of 15,000 Reichsmark was recorded in the land register. On 23 August 1951 the liens of 29,575.98 Reichsmark, 12.40 Reichsmark and 1,956.99 Reichsmark were cancelled. It cannot be established what amounts were actually paid by the vendors for the release of the debts of the property.

75 On 13/19 July 1965, the property, in the meantime renovated and partially altered, was sold by Dr. Kurt Gr. to the Republic of Austria for 9 million Schilling.

76 On 17 January 2001, the property Hohe Warte Z was under the ownership of the Republic of Austria.

4.4 Applicants

77 Alfred G. was born on 2 May 1877 in Hannover and died in Australia in 1956. He was married to Ella G. née Pi. She was born on 16 September 1889 and died in England in 1946. They had two daughters: Johanna Maria T. née G. was born on 11 February 1919 and died childless on 4 July 1943 during the emigration. The second daughter, Liselotte E. widowed W. née G., was born on 27 March 1914. She died in Australia in 1974. The applicants Ian Thomas E. né W., born on 7 November 1938, and Kathryn Joan D. née E., born on 14 February 1945, are her children. On 29 November 1956, the estate of Alfred G. was devolved to Walter Pi., Hans F. and Liselotte (Liselot) E. On 27 May 1975, the estate of Liselotte Margaret E. was devolved to her children Ian Thomas E. and Kathryn Joan D.

5. Consideration of Evidence

78 The established facts are based on the presented unobjectionable documents, the public land register, the reports by the Historical Commission, archive materials researched by the Arbitration Panel and submissions by the applicants and the Federal Government.

79 The findings regarding the value of the damage which was suffered by the property as a result of bombing are based on the cost estimate presented to Dr. P. by a master builder in July 1945. Dr. P. himself estimated the restoration to cost at least between 200,000 Schilling and 250,000 Schilling if he were to take out a mortgage loan for repair purposes. The restoration of the garden and of the greenhouse – both of these were substantially bomb-damaged – was estimated by Dr. P. to cost between 20,000 Schilling and 25,000 Schilling.

80 Findings regarding the state of the property at issue are based, among other things, on information drawn from a letter of 30 August 1951 by the municipal department 50 (gen-

rungs- und Rückstellungsangelegenheiten [...]) verwaltet." Erträgnisse seien bei der FLD bis zum 30. Juni 1950 nicht angelaufen, und auf Vorlage und Überprüfung der Abrechnung der Erträgnisse sei verzichtet worden. Ein Antrag auf grundbücherliche Löschung der Reichsfluchtsteuerforderung konnte mit Verweis auf § 1 Abs 5 1. RStG unmittelbar beim Grundbuchsgericht eingebracht werden.

Am 30. Mai/7. Juli 1951 wurde zwischen Alfred G. und Liselotte W. als VerkäuferInnen und Dr. Kurt Gr. als Käufer ein Kaufvertrag zur Liegenschaft Hohe Warte Z abgeschlossen. Das Haus ging um 145.000,– Schilling in das Eigentum von Dr. Kurt Gr. über. Der Einheitswert des Objektes war von 64.100,– Schilling auf 56.900,– Schilling herabgesetzt worden, da Haus und Garten durch Bombeneinfall erheblich beschädigt worden waren und diese Schädigungen noch nicht behoben waren. Über die Kaufpreiszahlung wurde vereinbart, die Liegenschaft frei von bücherlichen Pfandrechten dem Käufer zu übertragen. An Pfandrechten waren noch einverleibt: 29.575,98 Schilling für die Personalsteuerforderung, 12,40 Reichsmark für eine Forderung der Reichsjustizverwaltung, 15.000,– Reichsmark für die Forderung des Dr. Arthur P. und 1.956,99 Reichsmark für Reichsfluchtsteuerforderungen. Die VerkäuferInnen verpflichteten sich zur ungeteilten Hand, aus dem bei Vertragserrichtung zu erlegenden Betrag von 80.000,– Schilling diese Pfandrechte zur Löschung zu bringen. Da die VerkäuferInnen DevisenausländerInnen waren, bedurfte der Kaufvertrag zur Entfaltung seiner Rechtswirksamkeit der Genehmigung durch die Nationalbank. Diese erfolgte am 26. Juni 1951.

Am 6. Juni 1951 wurde im Grundbuch die Löschung des Pfandrechtes von 15.000,– Reichsmark einverleibt, am 23. August 1951 die Löschung der Pfandrechte von 29.575,98 Reichsmark, 12,40 Reichsmark und 1.956,99 Reichsmark. Welche Beträge die VerkäuferInnen für die Lastenfreistellung der Liegenschaft tatsächlich bezahlt haben, kann nicht festgestellt werden.

Am 13./19. Juli 1965 wurde die mittlerweile renovierte bzw. teilweise umgebaute Liegenschaft von Dr. Kurt Gr. um 9 Mio. Schilling an die Republik Österreich verkauft.

Die Liegenschaft Hohe Warte Z befand sich am 17. Jänner 2001 im Eigentum der Republik Österreich.

4.4 AntragstellerInnen

Alfred G. wurde am 2. Mai 1877 in Hannover geboren und verstarb 1956 in Australien. Er war verheiratet mit Ella G. geb. Pi., die am 16. September 1889 geboren wurde und 1946 in England verstarb. Sie hatten zwei Töchter: Johanna Maria T. geb. G. wurde am 11. Februar 1919 geboren und verstarb kinderlos am 4. Juli 1943 in der Emigration. Die zweite Tochter, Liselotte E. verwitwete W. geb. G., wurde am 27. März 1914 geboren. Sie verstarb 1974 in Australien. Ihre Kinder sind die AntragstellerInnen Ian Thomas E. geb. W., geboren am 7. November 1938 und Kathryn Joan D. geb. E., geboren am 14. Februar 1945. Der Nachlass von Alfred G. wurde am 29. November 1956 Walter Pi., Hans F. und Liselotte (Liselot) E. eingeantwortet. Der Nachlass von Liselotte E. wurde am 27. Mai 1975 ihren Kindern Ian Thomas E. und Kathryn Joan D. eingeantwortet.

5. Beweiswürdigung

Der festgestellte Sachverhalt gründet sich auf die vorgelegten unbedenklichen Urkunden, das offene Grundbuch, die Berichte der Historikerkommission, seitens der Schiedsinstanz recherchierte Archivalien, die Vorbringen der AntragstellerInnen und jenes der Bundesregierung.

eral and legal housing concerns) to Dr. Harold Se. regarding a locale investigation by the MA 37 (building inspection). This letter states that

> "the entire house (villa) in Vienna 19., Hohe Warte [Z] has been rendered uninhabitable through the effects of war, and for the restoration of the damages expenditures are necessary which are to be regarded as considerable when compared to the number and state of the rooms."

81 The finding that Alfred G. had settled his personal tax debt is illustrated by numerous documents. For example on 6 July 1938, an official certificate by the tax administration, collection department, certified that Ing. Alfred G. had no personal tax arrears. This also can be gathered from a letter dated 26 June 1941 from the attorney-at-law Dr. Victor H. to the attorney-at-law Dr. Stephan L., property administrator of the Secret State Police. It shows that although the property was encumbered with 27,000 Reichsmark in income-tax arrears, according to information by Mr. and Mrs. G.'s tax adviser, Dr. Arthur P., they had, however, already been paid and therefore they were to be cancelled. Also, two letters by the tax office Innere Stadt-Ost dated 5 February 1941 to the Secret State Police and dated 21 June 1941 to Dr. L. established that the personal tax had been entirely repaid and therefore redeemed.

6. Juridical Appraisal

6.1 Eligibility to File an Application

82 Pursuant to Sec. 27 (2) of the GSF Law heirs are entitled to file applications, applying *mutatis mutandis* the provisions of the (Austrian) General Civil Code. The Arbitration Panel assumes that pursuant to the aforementioned provision, evidence of the statutory right to the inheritance is sufficient for the right to file an application, unless stronger reasons can be presented. The applicants Kathryn Joan D. and Ian Thomas E. are descendants of the originally aggrieved persons and thus their statutory heirs. No evidence contradicting this right to inherit was presented. The Arbitration Panel therefore regards the applicants as eligible to file an application on the basis of their proven right to inherit.

6.2 Persecution

83 According to Sec. 27 of the GSF Law, those persons and their heirs are eligible to file applications, if one of the listed grounds for persecution applies, namely persecution on political grounds, on grounds of origin, religion, nationality, sexual orientation, on account of a physical or mental handicap or on account of accusations of so-called asociality, or if they left the country to escape such persecution. In May 1939, Alfred G. left Austria together with his wife Ella and his daughters Liselotte and Johanna Maria. They were persecuted for reasons of origin and religion, since they were all considered Jewish in accordance with the Nuremberg Laws of 15 September 1935.

6.3 Seizure

84 Pursuant to Sec. 28 (1) item 1 of the GSF Law, the property must have been taken from the previous owners between 12 March 1938 and 9 May 1945 on the basis of the aforementioned grounds for persecution. On 19 February 1941, the Secret State Police issued a confiscation order regarding the entire movable and immovable assets of Alfred and Ella G. as well as regarding all their rights and claims. The aim of this order was the confisca-

Die Feststellungen zu der Höhe des Schadens, den die Liegenschaft durch Bombeneinschlag erlitten hat, beruhen auf dem Kostenvoranschlag, den ein Baumeister Dr. P. im Juli 1945 vorgelegt hat. Dr. P. selbst schätzte die Wiederherstellung auf mindestens 200.000,– bis 250.000,– Schilling, bei erforderlicher Aufnahme eines Hypothekardarlehens für Reparaturzwecke. Die Wiederherstellung des Gartens und des Glashauses, beide durch Bombentreffer ebenfalls schwer geschädigt, bezifferte Dr. P. auf weitere 20.000,– bis 25.000,– Schilling.

Feststellungen zu dem Zustand der gegenständlichen Liegenschaft beruhen unter anderem auf den Informationen, die sich aus dem Schreiben der MA 50 (allgemeine und rechtliche Angelegenheiten des Wohnungswesens) an Dr. Harold Se. vom 30. August 1951 bezüglich eines Lokalaugenscheins durch die MA 37 (Baupolizei) ergeben. Dieses sagt aus, dass

„das gesamte Haus (Villa) in Wien 19., Hohe Warte [Z] durch Kriegseinwirkung unbewohnbar geworden und zu deren Wiederherstellung Aufwendungen erforderlich sind, die im Verhältnis zur Anzahl und Beschaffenheit der Räume als erheblich anzusehen sind."

Die Feststellung, dass Alfred G. seine Personalsteuerschulden beglichen hatte, ergibt sich aus mehreren Dokumenten. So wird in einer Amtsbestätigung der Steueradministration, Einhebungsabteilung bereits am 6. Juli 1938 bestätigt, dass Ing. Alfred G. mit keiner Personalsteuer im Rückstand war. Dies ergibt sich ebenfalls aus einem Schreiben des RA Dr. Victor H. an den Vermögensverwalter der Gestapo, RA Dr. Stephan L., vom 26. Juni 1941. Daraus geht hervor, dass die Liegenschaft zwar mit 27.000,– Reichsmark an Einkommensteuerrückstand belastet gewesen war, dass dieser Rückstandsausweis jedoch laut Auskunft des Steuerberaters des Ehepaares G., Dr. Arthur P., bereits bezahlt war und daher zu löschen wäre. Auch zwei Schreiben des Finanzamtes Innere Stadt-Ost, vom 5. Februar 1941 an die Gestapo und vom 21. Juni 1941 an Dr. L., stellten fest, dass die Personalsteuern zur Gänze bezahlt bzw. abgedeckt und somit getilgt waren.

6. Rechtliche Beurteilung

6.1 Antragslegitimation

Gemäß § 27 Abs 2 EF-G sind ErbInnen in sinngemäßer Anwendung der Bestimmungen des Allgemeinen bürgerlichen Gesetzbuches (ABGB) antragsberechtigt. Die Schiedsinstanz geht davon aus, dass nach der vorzitierten Bestimmung der Nachweis des gesetzlichen Erbrechts, wenn nicht stärkere Berufungsgründe dargetan werden, für die Antragsberechtigung ausreichend ist. Die AntragstellerInnen Kathryn Joan D. und Ian Thomas E. sind DeszendentInnen der ursprünglich Geschädigten, somit gesetzliche ErbInnen. Es wurde kein diesem Erbrecht entgegenstehender Nachweis vorgelegt. Damit sieht die Schiedsinstanz die Antragsberechtigung der AntragstellerInnen aufgrund des nachgewiesenen Erbrechts als gegeben an.

6.2 Verfolgung

Gemäß § 27 EF-G sind Personen und deren ErbInnen antragsberechtigt, wenn einer der aufgelisteten Verfolgungsgründe, nämlich Verfolgung aus politischen Gründen, aus Gründen der Abstammung, Religion, Nationalität, sexuellen Orientierung, aufgrund einer körperlichen oder geistigen Behinderung oder aufgrund des Vorwurfes der so genannten Asozialität, vorliegt bzw. diese das Land verlassen haben, um einer solchen Verfolgung zu entgehen. Alfred G. verließ mit seiner Ehefrau Ella und seinen Töchtern Liselotte und Jo-

tion at a later point in time for the benefit of the German Reich. The issue of this order already represents a confiscation as this order itself and not just the registration of the ownership in the land register for the benefit of the German Reich represented the transfer of ownership. This is an exception from the principle of recording the acquisition in the land register.

6.4 Federal Ownership

85 Pursuant to Sec. 28 (1) item 3 of the GSF Law, the notion of "publicly-owned property" includes properties which were owned on 17 January 2001 exclusively and directly by the Federation or any legal person under public or private law that is wholly owned, directly or indirectly, by the Federation. The date of the transfer of property to the Federation is not relevant for the affirmation of this prerequisite. The property only had to be owned by the Federation on the cut off day. The property in question was purchased by the Republic of Austria on 13 August 1965, and from then until the present day has been under its ownership.

6.5 Previous Proceedings

86 A further prerequisite for applications under Sec. 28 and Sec. 32 (1) of the GSF Law is that the property was never the subject of a claim that was previously decided by an Austrian court or administrative body, or settled by agreement, and for which the applicant or a relative has never otherwise received compensation or other consideration. According to the aforementioned law, a prior claim is defined as any proceedings before an administrative body or a court, in the course of which a substantive decision or a settlement by agreement has been reached concerning the property requested in the proceedings before the Arbitration Panel. The restitution proceedings, which were carried out in accordance with the First Restitution Act and through which the property was restituted, are considered prior proceedings in the meaning of the abovementioned regulations, as the proceedings were conducted before an administrative body and the matter was decided in a legally binding manner.

6.6 Extreme Injustice

87 The GSF Law provides for a transgression of the legally binding nature of a decision or the effect of a settlement of disputes only in special cases, namely if an extreme injustice exists. Such an extreme injustice can only be determined by the Arbitration Panel unanimously and only if a previous decision by an Austrian court or an Austrian administrative body is based on a decision-making process that indicates that the statutory basis for the decision was applied in an objectively inadmissible manner to the detriment of the aggrieved party and that, as a result, the aggrieved party suffered a gross disadvantage with regard to his/her restitution or compensation claims. However, it does not fall within the competence of the Arbitration Panel defined by the GSF Law to review the legal provisions, on the basis of which the decision has been made, in regard to a possible extreme injustice.

88 On 19 February 1941, the property at issue was confiscated and then reverted to the German Reich pursuant to the Eleventh Decree to the Reich Citizenship Law of 25 November 1941 without the change in ownership having been recorded in the land register. Due to this reversion, the property Hohe Warte Z was regarded as German Property. It was the then prevailing opinion that assets under the ownership of the German Reich would fall under the administration of the Republic of Austria after the end of the NS

hanna Maria Österreich im Mai 1939. Sie waren sowohl aus rassischen als auch religiösen Gründen verfolgt, da sie alle gemäß den Nürnberger Gesetzen vom 15. September 1935 als Juden galten.

6.3 Entzug

Gemäß § 28 Abs 1 Z 1 EF-G muss die Liegenschaft zwischen 12. März 1938 und 9. Mai 1945 den früheren EigentümerInnen aus den oben genannten Verfolgungsgründen entzogen worden sein. Am 19. Februar 1941 erließ die Gestapo eine Beschlagnahmeverfügung über das gesamte stehende und liegende Vermögen sowie über alle Rechte und Ansprüche von Alfred und Ella G. Das Ziel dieser Verfügung war die spätere Einziehung zugunsten des Deutschen Reiches. Bereits der Erlass dieser Verfügung stellt den Entzug dar, da diese Verfügung selbst und nicht erst die grundbücherliche Eintragung des Eigentumsrechts zugunsten des Deutschen Reiches den Eigentumsübergang bedeutete. Es handelt sich um eine Ausnahme vom Intabulationsprinzip.

84

6.4 Bundeseigentum

Gemäß § 28 Abs 1 Z 3 EF-G umfasst der Begriff „öffentliches Vermögen" Liegenschaften, welche sich am 17. Jänner 2001 ausschließlich und unmittelbar im Eigentum des Bundes oder einer unmittelbar oder mittelbar im Alleineigentum des Bundes stehenden juristischen Person des öffentlichen oder privaten Rechts befanden. Für die Bejahung dieser Vorbedingung ist es irrelevant, wann der Eigentumsübergang auf den Bund stattgefunden hat. Die Liegenschaft muss sich nur zum Stichtag im Bundeseigentum befunden haben. Die gegenständliche Liegenschaft wurde am 13. August 1965 von der Republik Österreich erworben und steht seit damals bis heute in ihrem Eigentum.

85

6.5 Früheres Verfahren

Eine weitere Anspruchsvoraussetzung gemäß §§ 28 und 32 Abs 1 EF-G ist, dass die Liegenschaft niemals Gegenstand einer Forderung war, die bereits zuvor durch österreichische Gerichte oder Verwaltungsbehörden entschieden oder einvernehmlich geregelt wurde, und für die weder die AntragstellerInnen noch ein Verwandter auf eine andere Weise eine Entschädigung oder sonstige Gegenleistung erhalten hat. Als frühere Forderung im Sinne dieses Gesetzes ist jedes Verfahren vor einer Verwaltungsbehörde oder einem Gericht zu verstehen, in welchem bereits bezüglich der in diesem Schiedsinstanzverfahren begehrten Liegenschaft eine materielle Entscheidung beziehungsweise eine einvernehmliche Regelung getroffen wurde. Das nach dem 1. RStG durchgeführte Rückstellungsverfahren, mit dem die gegenständliche Liegenschaft zurückgestellt wurde, ist als ein früheres Verfahren im Sinne der oben erwähnten Bestimmung anzusehen, da es vor einer Verwaltungsbehörde geführt und über die Sache rechtskräftig entschieden wurde.

86

6.6 Extreme Ungerechtigkeit

Eine Durchbrechung der Rechtskraft von Entscheidungen bzw. der Streitbeilegungswirkung von Vergleichen sieht das EF-G nur ausnahmsweise in besonderen Fällen, nämlich beim Vorliegen einer extremen Ungerechtigkeit vor. Eine solche kann von der Schiedsinstanz nur einstimmig und nur dann angenommen werden, wenn die frühere Entscheidung eines österreichischen Gerichts oder einer österreichischen Verwaltungsbehörde auf einer Entscheidungsfindung beruht, die darauf hindeutet, dass gesetzliche Entscheidungsgrundlagen objektiv unvertretbar zu Lasten des Geschädigten angewendet worden sind und der Geschädigte dadurch im Ergebnis hinsichtlich seiner Rückstellungs- oder Ent-

87

regime. However, the Republic of Austria was only regarded as the administrator and not the owner.

89 In July 1945, the *Behörden-Überleitungsgesetz* ("Authority Transition Act") was enacted. Among other things, this law regulated the transition of duties from the German Reich administrative bodies to the Austrian administrative bodies. Hence, para. 28 of the Authority Transition Act determines that the duties of the Chief Finance President are transferred to the Financial Directorate. Furthermore, para. 29 (2) leg. cit. determines that the administration of confiscated and seized properties is also transferred to the Financial Directorate. With the coming into effect of the Authority Transition Act on 28 July 1945, the administration of the property Hohe Warte Z fell to the Financial Directorate as it constituted confiscated property.

90 Accordingly, the application for restitution was filed in accordance with the First Restitution Act as this law comprised the restitution of property which had been confiscated by the German Reich due to, among other things, the repealed Reich legal regulations such as the Eleventh Decree to the Reich Citizenship Law.

91 The First Restitution Act provided that properties which had been confiscated in this manner were to be restituted in the same condition in which they had been at the point of restitution. In addition, para. 1 (2) leg. cit. provided for the possibility of claiming the surrender of earnings from the property that had accumulated since the confiscation. However, these earnings were to be restituted only insofar as they were still located in Austria at the point of restitution.

92 The applications of 15 April 1948 and of 15 December 1949, which had been filed by the claimants for restitution, claimed for the restitution of the property Hohe Warte Z, in accordance with para. 1 (5) leg. cit., as well as applied for the cancellation of the liens for discriminating taxes and costs secured in the land register. The surrender of the earnings had not been requested. They were even expressly waived. Therefore, it can remain open with regards to whom the waiver had been submitted.

93 The Financial Directorate, in its role as a restitution authority, granted the filed application for restitution in its entirety. It restituted the property in question to the restitution claimants pursuant to the decision of 30 June 1950. It also ruled on the requested cancellation of the recorded liens for discriminating taxes (Reich Flight Tax claim, extra charges for late payment) by advising the restitution claimants pursuant to para. 1 (5) of the First Restitution Act to file the relevant applications directly with the Land Register Court.

94 A more favorable decision on the present case was not possible within the framework of the First Restitution Act, as the restitution claimants had legally waived the earnings. Para. 5 leg. cit. established that claims for compensation beyond the restitution could not be asserted until there was further statutory regulation. However, a regulation of this kind, which would have stipulated provisions on a possible compensation or on another form of monetary compensation, did not occur. Therefore, the Arbitration Panel determines that the decision-making body applied the restitution law in a correct and objectively logical manner. A breach of the constitution asserted by the applicants can be disregarded as the Financial Directorate granted the maximum that was legally possible.

schädigungsansprüche grob benachteiligt worden ist. Eine Überprüfung auf eine allfällige extreme Ungerechtigkeit jener rechtlichen Normen, auf deren Grundlage eine Entscheidung gefällt worden ist, fällt jedoch nicht in den vom EF-G festgelegten Kompetenzbereich der Schiedsinstanz.

Die gegenständliche Liegenschaft wurde am 19. Februar 1941 beschlagnahmt und verfiel dann dem Deutschen Reich aufgrund der Elften Verordnung zum Reichsbürgergesetz vom 25. November 1941, ohne dass die Veränderung der Eigentumsverhältnisse im Grundbuch vermerkt worden wäre. Die Liegenschaft Hohe Warte Z galt aufgrund dieses Verfalls als Deutsches Eigentum. Für solche im Eigentum des Deutschen Reiches stehenden Vermögenswerte wurde die Ansicht vertreten, dass diese nach dem Ende der NS-Herrschaft unter der Verwaltung der Republik Österreich stünden. Die Republik Österreich wurde jedoch nur als Verwalterin und nicht als Besitzerin dieses Vermögens angesehen. 88

Im Juli 1945 wurde das Behörden-Überleitungsgesetz (Behörden-ÜG) erlassen. In diesem wurde unter anderem die Überleitung der Geschäfte von den deutschen Reichsbehörden auf österreichische Behörden geregelt. So bestimmt § 28 Behörden-ÜG, dass die Geschäfte der Oberfinanzpräsidenten auf die Finanzlandesdirektionen übergehen. Weiters regelt § 29 Abs 2 leg. cit., dass die Verwaltung eingezogener oder beschlagnahmter Vermögen ebenfalls auf die FLD übergeht. Mit dem In-Kraft-Treten des Behörden-ÜG am 28. Juli 1945 ging jedenfalls die Verwaltung der Liegenschaft Hohe Warte Z, da es sich bei dieser um beschlagnahmtes Vermögen handelte, auf die FLD über. 89

Der Rückstellungsantrag wurde dementsprechend nach dem 1. RStG eingebracht, da dieses die Rückstellung von Vermögenschaften umfasste, die vom Deutschen Reich unter anderem aufgrund von aufgehobenen reichsrechtlichen Vorschriften – darunter auch die Elfte Verordnung zum Reichsbürgergesetz – entzogen wurden. 90

Das 1. RStG sah die Rückstellung der auf diese Art entzogenen Liegenschaft in jenem Zustand vor, in dem sie sich zum Rückstellungszeitpunkt befand. Darüber hinaus sah § 1 Abs 2 leg. cit. die Möglichkeit vor, die seit der Beschlagnahme angefallenen Erträgnisse der Liegenschaft herauszuverlangen. Diese Erträgnisse waren jedoch nur insofern auszufolgen, soweit sie sich zum Rückstellungszeitpunkt noch im Inland befanden. 91

In den von den RückstellungswerberInnen gestellten Anträgen vom 15. April 1948 und vom 15. Dezember 1949 wurde, abgesehen von der Rückgabe der Liegenschaft Hohe Warte Z, gemäß § 1 Abs 5 leg. cit. die Löschung der grundbücherlich sichergestellten Pfandrechte für diskriminierende Steuern und Abgaben beantragt. Die Herausgabe der Erträgnisse wurde nicht beantragt. Es wurde sogar ausdrücklich auf diese verzichtet. Damit kann auch dahingestellt bleiben, wem gegenüber der Verzicht abgegeben worden war. 92

Die FLD als Rückstellungsbehörde gab dem gestellten Rückstellungsantrag vollinhaltlich statt. Sie stellte die gegenständliche Liegenschaft mit dem Bescheid vom 30. Juni 1950 an die RückstellungswerberInnen zurück. Auch sprach sie über das beantragte Begehren auf Löschung der einverleibten Pfandrechte für die diskriminierenden Steuern (Reichsfluchtsteuerforderung, Säumniszuschläge) ab, indem sie die RückstellungswerberInnen gemäß § 1 Abs 5 1. RStG darauf verwies, die entsprechenden Anträge unmittelbar beim Grundbuchsgericht einzubringen. 93

Im Rahmen des 1. RStG war eine günstigere Entscheidung für den vorliegenden Sachverhalt nicht möglich, da von den RückstellungswerberInnen rechtswirksam auf die Erträgnisse verzichtet worden war. § 5 leg. cit. bestimmte, dass Ansprüche auf einen über die Rückstellung hinausgehenden Ersatz bis zur weiteren gesetzlichen Regelung nicht geltend gemacht werden konnten. Eine solche Regelung, die Bestimmungen über einen möglichen 94

Arbitration Panel for *In Rem* Restitution – Decision No. 28/2005

95   The application for restitution of the property Hohe Warte Z, EZ X, KG Heiligenstadt was to be rejected.

Dr. Josef Aicher, university professor, Chairman
Dr.Dr.h c. Erich Kussbach, LL.M., honorary professor and retired ambassador
MMag. Dr. August Reinisch, LL.M., university professor

Schadenersatz oder eine andere Form monetärer Entschädigung vorgesehen hätte, ist jedoch nicht erfolgt. Die Schiedsinstanz stellt daher fest, dass das Entscheidungsorgan in korrekter und in objektiv nachvollziehbarer Weise das RStG angewendet hat. Da die FLD alles zugesprochen hat, was von Gesetzes wegen möglich war, muss auf die von den AntragstellerInnen behauptete Verfassungswidrigkeit nicht näher eingegangen werden.

Der Antrag auf Rückstellung der Liegenschaft Hohe Warte Z, EZ X, KG Heiligenstadt war abzulehnen. 95

o.Univ.-Prof. Dr. Josef Aicher, Vorsitzender
Honorarprofessor Dr.Dr.h.c. Erich Kussbach LL.M., Botschafter i.R.
ao. Univ.-Prof. MMag. Dr. August Reinisch LL.M.

Appendix

The English versions in this volume are translations of the authentic German texts. The English versions printed on the left side of this volume represent legally non-binding translations which merely serve the non-German speaking readers in comprehending these texts.

Federal Law on the Establishment of a General Settlement Fund for
Victims of National Socialism and on Restitution Measures
(GSF Law, original version: Federal Law Gazette I No. 12 /2001),
latest Version 384

Opt-In Dates of Austrian Provinces and Municipalities 412

A Select Bibliography on the Subject of *(In Rem)* Restitution 414

List of Abbreviations 418

Editors 426

Anhang

Von den in diesem Band enthaltenen Texten stellt jeweils die deutsche Fassung die authentische dar. Bei den auf den jeweils linken Buchseiten abgedruckten englischen Fassungen handelt es sich um unverbindliche, lediglich dem Verständnis nicht deutschsprachiger LeserInnen dienende Übersetzungen.

Bundesgesetz über die Einrichtung eines Allgemeinen Entschädigungsfonds für Opfer des Nationalsozialismus und über Restitutionsmaßnahmen (Entschädigungsfondsgesetz, Stammfassung: BGBl I Nr. 12/2001), geltende Fassung 385

Opt-In von Ländern und Gemeinden 413

Auswahlbibliografie zum Themenbereich der (Natural-)Restitution 415

Abkürzungsverzeichnis 419

Herausgeber 427

Federal Law on the Establishment of a General Settlement Fund for Victims of National Socialism and on Restitution Measures (General Settlement Fund Law), as well as on an Amendment to the General Social Security Law and the Victims Assistance Act (NR: GP XXI AB 476 p. 55. BR: AB 6301 p. 672). Original Version: Federal Law Gazette I No. 12/2001.

Amendments:
Federal Law Gazette I No. 40/2001
Federal Law Gazette I No. 58/2001
Federal Law Gazette I No. 114/2002
Federal Law Gazette I No. 108/2004
Federal Law Gazette I No. 142/2005
Federal Law Gazette I No. 20/2007
Federal Law Gazette I No. 2/2008
Federal Law Gazette I No. 89/2008

Latest Version (as at: February 2009). The amendments are set off in italics.

Article 1

Federal Law on the Establishment of a General Settlement Fund for Victims of National Socialism and on Restitution Measures (General Settlement Fund Law)

Part 1

General Settlement Fund

Title 1

Establishment of the General Settlement Fund

Establishment and Purpose of the Fund

§ 1. (1) In order to comprehensively resolve open questions of compensation of victims of National Socialism for losses and damages as a result of or in connection with events having occurred on the territory of the present-day Republic of Austria during the National Socialist era, the General Settlement Fund (in short: Fund) shall be established.

(2) The Fund's purpose shall be to acknowledge, through voluntary payments, the moral responsibility for losses and damages inflicted upon Jewish citizens and other victims of National Socialism as a result of or in connection with the National Socialist Regime. The return of works of art shall be governed by the special legislation presently in force.

(3) The Fund shall be an institution of the Republic of Austria, subject to Austrian law, shall be an independent legal entity, and shall exclusively serve non-profit purposes. The Fund shall have its headquarters in Vienna. It shall be exempt from all federal taxes and duties. The payments provided by the Fund shall be governed by the principles guiding the public administration acting under private law.

(4) The Fund shall be regarded as dissolved once its tasks are fully completed.

Bundesgesetz über die Einrichtung eines Allgemeinen Entschädigungsfonds für Opfer des Nationalsozialismus und über Restitutionsmaßnahmen (Entschädigungsfondsgesetz) sowie zur Änderung des Allgemeinen Sozialversicherungsgesetzes und des Opferfürsorgegesetzes (NR: GP XXI AB 476 S. 55. BR: AB 6301 S. 672.) StF: BGBl I Nr. 12/2001.

Änderung idF:
BGBl. I Nr. 40/2001
BGBl. I Nr. 58/2001
BGBl. I Nr. 114/2002
BGBl. I Nr. 108/2004
BGBl. I Nr. 142/2005
BGBl. I Nr. 20/2007
BGBl. I Nr. 2/2008
BGBl. I Nr. 89/2008

Geltende Fassung (Stand: Februar 2009). Novellierungen sind durch Kursivsetzung erkenntlich gemacht.

Artikel 1
Bundesgesetz über die Einrichtung eines Allgemeinen Entschädigungsfonds für Opfer des Nationalsozialismus und über Restitutionsmaßnahmen (Entschädigungsfondsgesetz)

Teil 1
Allgemeiner Entschädigungsfonds

1. Hauptstück
Einrichtung des Allgemeinen Entschädigungsfonds

Einrichtung und Ziel des Fonds

§ 1. (1) Zur umfassenden Lösung offener Fragen der Entschädigung von Opfern des Nationalsozialismus für Verluste und Schäden, die als Folge von oder im Zusammenhang mit Ereignissen auf dem Gebiet der heutigen Republik Österreich während der Zeit des Nationalsozialismus entstanden sind, wird der Allgemeine Entschädigungsfonds (kurz: Fonds) eingerichtet.

(2) Der Fonds hat das Ziel, die moralische Verantwortung für Verluste und Schäden, die als Folge von oder im Zusammenhang mit dem nationalsozialistischen Regime den jüdischen Bürgerinnen und Bürgern sowie den anderen Opfern des Nationalsozialismus zugefügt wurden, durch freiwillige Leistungen anzuerkennen. Die Rückgabe von Kunstgegenständen ist den bestehenden besonderen gesetzlichen Regelungen vorbehalten.

(3) Der Fonds ist eine Einrichtung der Republik Österreich, unterliegt österreichischem Recht, besitzt eigene Rechtspersönlichkeit und dient ausschließlich gemeinnützigen Zwecken. Der Fonds hat seinen Sitz in Wien. Er ist von allen bundesgesetzlichen Abgaben befreit. Die Leistungen des Fonds erfolgen im Wege der Privatwirtschaftsverwaltung.

(4) Mit der vollständigen Erfüllung seiner Aufgaben gilt der Fonds als aufgelöst.

Capital of the Fund

§ 2. (1) To carry out its tasks, the Fund shall be endowed with an amount of 210 million US Dollars. This amount shall be made available, at the latest, 30 days after all claims in the United States pending as of June 30, 2001 against Austria or Austrian companies arising out of or related to the National Socialist era or World War II have been dismissed. Excepted therefrom are claims covered by the Reconciliation Fund, Federal Law Gazette I, No. 74/2000, claims for the return of works of art, as well as claims for *in rem* restitution against provinces or municipalities, unless or until the latter have availed themselves of the option under § 38. Furthermore, the Fund may dispose of the interest that will accrue at the 3-month Euribor rate from investment by the Fund, starting with the date cited above and continuing for the entire duration of the Fund. The endowment of the Fund shall thus be complete. There shall be no obligation for additional funding.

(1a) A contribution to the Fund of up to 60 million US Dollars may also be made available from those amounts which the Federation [Bund] receives in the financial year 2000 pursuant to § 69 (3) of the National Bank Act 1984, Federal Law Gazette No. 50/1984, as amended by the Federal Law, Federal Law Gazette I No. 60/1998. The amount of 210 million US Dollars as specified in Paragraph 1 remains hereby unchanged.[1]

(2) Contributions to the Fund shall not be subject to inheritance and gift taxes or similar financial burdens having the same purpose or effect. They may be treated as company expenditures.

(3) Yields from the Fund's capital and other revenues shall be used exclusively for the Fund's purposes. This includes the necessary costs for personnel, material and administration of the Fund, including the costs of the Claims Committee, in so far as these cannot be covered by the budget of the National Fund.

(4) The legal transactions necessary for carrying out the Fund's tasks shall be exempt from federal legal fees.

Organs of the Fund

§ 3. (**constitutional provision**) The organs of the Fund shall be the organs of the National Fund of the Republic of Austria for Victims of National Socialism, Federal Law Gazette I, No. 432/1995, as amended, that is, the Board of Trustees and the Secretary General. The Claims Committee specified in § 4 shall take the place of the Committee. Unless the present Federal Law provides otherwise, the administrative tasks of the Fund and its external representation shall be carried out in accordance with the principles of the Federal Law on the National Fund of the Republic of Austria for Victims of National Socialism, Federal Law Gazette No. 432/1995, as amended.

§ 3a. The Fund and the National Fund of the Republic of Austria for Victims of National Socialism as well as their organs shall not be liable for claims for compensation arising from the execution of tasks in accordance with the Federal Laws which establish these Funds.[2]

---

[1] Paragraph 1a was inserted by the amendment to the GSF Law, Federal Law Gazette I No. 40/2001.

[2] § 3a was inserted by the amendment to the GSF Law, Federal Law Gazette I No. 40/2001.

Anhang

Mittel des Fonds

§ 2. (1) Zur Durchführung seiner Aufgaben wird der Fonds mit einem Betrag von 210 Millionen US-Dollar ausgestattet. Dieser Betrag ist spätestens nach Ablauf von 30 Tagen zur Verfügung zu stellen, nachdem alle in den Vereinigten Staaten am 30. Juni 2001 anhängigen Klagen gegen Österreich oder österreichische Unternehmen, die sich aus oder im Zusammenhang mit der Zeit des Nationalsozialismus oder dem Zweiten Weltkrieg ergeben, abgewiesen worden sind. Davon ausgenommen sind Klagen betreffend vom Versöhnungsfonds, BGBl. I Nr. 74/2000, erfasster Ansprüche, Klagen auf Rückgabe von Kunstgegenständen sowie Klagen auf Naturalrestitutionen gegen Länder oder Gemeinden, sofern diese nicht von der Möglichkeit nach § 38 Gebrauch gemacht haben. Weiters verfügt der Fonds über jene Zinsen, welche durch die Veranlagung durch den Fonds ab dem oben genannten Stichtag für die gesamte Laufzeit des Fonds zum 3-Monats-Euribor-Satz anfallen. Der Fonds ist damit abschließend dotiert. Es besteht keine Nachschusspflicht.

(1a) Eine Zuwendung an den Fonds bis zum Betrag von 60 Millionen US-Dollar kann auch aus jenen Beträgen erfolgen, die dem Bund gemäß § 69 Abs. 3 Nationalbankgesetz 1984, BGBl. Nr. 50/1984, in der Fassung des Bundesgesetzes BGBl. I Nr. 60/1998 aus dem Geschäftsjahr 2000 zufließen. Der in Abs. 1 genannte Betrag von 210 Millionen US-Dollar bleibt hiedurch unverändert.[1]

(2) Zuwendungen an den Fonds unterliegen nicht der Erbschafts- und Schenkungssteuer oder ähnlichen bundesgesetzlichen finanziellen Belastungen mit gleichem Ziel oder gleicher Wirkung. Sie können als Betriebsausgaben geltend gemacht werden.

(3) Erträge des Fondsvermögens und sonstige Einnahmen sind ausschließlich im Sinne des Fondszweckes zu verwenden. Dies schließt die notwendigen Personal-, Sach- und Verwaltungskosten des Fonds, einschließlich der Kosten des Antragskomitees, ein, soweit diese nicht aus dem Budget des Nationalfonds bestritten werden können.

(4) Die zur Durchführung der Aufgaben des Fonds erforderlichen Rechtsgeschäfte sind von den bundesgesetzlichen Rechtsgebühren befreit.

Organe des Fonds

§ 3. (**Verfassungsbestimmung**) Die Organe des Fonds sind die Organe des Nationalfonds der Republik Österreich für Opfer des Nationalsozialismus, BGBl. Nr. 432/1995 in der jeweils geltenden Fassung, und zwar das Kuratorium und der Generalsekretär. An die Stelle des Komitees tritt das Antragskomitee gemäß § 4. Die Besorgung der administrativen Aufgaben des Fonds und die Vertretung des Fonds nach außen erfolgen, soweit in diesem Bundesgesetz nichts anderes bestimmt ist, gemäß den Grundsätzen des Bundesgesetzes über den Nationalfonds der Republik Österreich für Opfer des Nationalsozialismus, BGBl. Nr. 432/1995 in der jeweils geltenden Fassung.

§ 3a. Der Fonds und der Nationalfonds der Republik Österreich für Opfer des Nationalsozialismus sowie deren Organe haften nicht für Ersatzansprüche, die auf die Wahrnehmung der Aufgaben nach den Bundesgesetzen, die diese Fonds einrichten, gegründet werden.[2]

---

[1] Absatz 1a wurde durch die EF-G Novelle, BGBl I Nr. 40/2001, eingefügt.
[2] § 3a wurde durch die EF-G Novelle, BGBl I Nr. 40/2001, eingefügt.

Claims Committee

§ 4. (1) An independent Claims Committee shall be set up to decide on claims for payments from the Fund. The Claims Committee shall take its decisions by a majority vote, unless unanimity is specifically prescribed.

(2) **(constitutional provision)** Members of the Claims Committee shall be:
1. one member to be appointed by the Government of the United States of America;
2. one member to be appointed by the Austrian Federal Government;
3. one member to be appointed by the above members as chairperson.

(3) In the event that the members appointed according to items 1 and 2 are unable to agree upon the chairperson within 60 days after the entry into force of the present Federal Law, the Government of the United States of America and the Federal Government [of Austria] will enter into consultations to name a chairperson.

(4) The members of the Claims Committee shall serve in an honorary capacity.

(5) The National Fund shall provide technical and administrative support to the Claims Committee, making use to the greatest extent possible of its administrative infrastructure. The National Fund shall be reimbursed for the resulting additional costs in accordance with the first sentence of § 2 (3).

Title 2

General Provisions

Distribution of Funds

§ 5. (1) Of the funds available for payments to entitled persons one half shall be reserved for payments in the claims-based process, and one half for payments in the equity-based process.

(2) Of the funds available for payments to entitled persons, the equivalent in Schillings of 25 million US Dollars shall be allocated for payments for insurance policies. In the event that this amount is exhausted, and this is certified by the Claims Committee, in consultation with representatives of the plaintiffs' attorneys recommended by the Government of the United States, an amount of up to 5 million US Dollars from the amount allocated to the claims-based process may be used to pay insurance claims.

(3) After expiration of the filing period, the Board of Trustees shall, following consultation with the Claims Committee, calculate the total amount of funds available for payments to entitled persons after deduction of the Fund's expenditures.

(4) After completion of the tasks of the Fund, any remaining funds shall be transferred to the National Fund of the Republic of Austria for Victims of National Socialism. These funds shall be used for programs to benefit victims of National Socialism, including members of the Roma community.

Eligibility

§ 6. (1) Persons (in the claims-based process also associations), who/ which were persecuted by the National Socialist regime on political grounds, on grounds of origin, religion, nationality, sexual orientation, or of physical or mental handicap or of accusations of so-called asociality, or who left the country to escape such persecution, and who suffered losses or damages as a result of or in connection with events having occurred on the territory of the present-

Antragskomitee

§ 4. (1) Zur Entscheidung über Anträge auf Leistungen aus dem Fonds wird ein unabhängiges Antragskomitee eingesetzt. Das Antragskomitee fällt seine Entscheidungen mehrheitlich, sofern nicht ausdrücklich Einstimmigkeit vorgesehen ist.

(2) **(Verfassungsbestimmung)** Dem Antragskomitee gehören an:
1. ein von der Regierung der Vereinigten Staaten von Amerika zu bestimmendes Mitglied;
2. ein von der österreichischen Bundesregierung zu bestimmendes Mitglied;
3. ein von diesen Mitgliedern zu bestimmendes Mitglied als Vorsitzender.

(3) Können sich die Mitglieder gemäß Z 1 und 2 nicht innerhalb von 60 Tagen nach dem Inkrafttreten dieses Bundesgesetzes auf einen Vorsitzenden einigen, nehmen die Regierung der Vereinigten Staaten von Amerika und die Bundesregierung Beratungen über die Ernennung eines Vorsitzenden auf.

(4) Die Funktionen im Antragskomitee werden ehrenamtlich ausgeübt.

(5) Unter möglichster Nutzung seines Geschäftsapparates leistet der Nationalfonds dem Antragskomitee technische und administrative Unterstützung. Daraus entstehende Mehrkosten sind dem Nationalfonds gemäß § 2 Abs. 3 erster Satz zu vergüten.

2. Hauptstück
Allgemeine Bestimmungen

Aufteilung der Mittel

§ 5. (1) Die für Zahlungen an die Leistungsberechtigten zur Verfügung stehenden Fondsmittel werden jeweils zur Hälfte für Leistungen nach dem Forderungsverfahren und nach dem Billigkeitsverfahren verwendet.

(2) Von den für Zahlungen an die Leistungsberechtigten zur Verfügung stehenden Fondsmitteln entfällt der Schillinggegenwert von 25 Millionen US-Dollar auf Leistungen auf Grund von Versicherungspolizzen. Falls dieser Betrag erschöpft ist und das Antragskomitee dies bestätigt, kann nach Konsultationen mit von der Regierung der Vereinigten Staaten empfohlenen Vertretern der Klägeranwälte ein Betrag von bis zu 5 Millionen US-Dollar von dem für das Forderungsverfahren bereitgestellten Betrag zur Zahlung von Forderungen aus Versicherungspolizzen verwendet werden.

(3) Die Gesamtsumme der für Zahlungen an die Leistungsberechtigten zur Verfügung stehenden Fondsmittel wird nach Ablauf der Antragsfrist unter Abzug der vom Fonds zu tragenden Kosten vom Kuratorium nach Anhörung des Antragskomitees berechnet.

(4) Nach Erfüllung der Aufgaben des Fonds verbleibende Mittel fallen dem Nationalfonds der Republik Österreich für Opfer des Nationalsozialismus zu. Diese Mittel sind für Programme zugunsten von Opfern des Nationalsozialismus, einschließlich der Angehörigen der Roma, zu verwenden.

Antragsberechtigung

§ 6. (1) Antragsberechtigt sind Personen (im Forderungsverfahren auch Vereinigungen), die vom nationalsozialistischen Regime aus politischen Gründen, aus Gründen der Abstammung, Religion, Nationalität, sexuellen Orientierung, auf Grund einer körperlichen oder geistigen Behinderung oder auf Grund des Vorwurfes der so genannten Asozialität verfolgt wurden oder das Land verlassen haben, um einer solchen Verfolgung zu entgehen, und die als

day Republic of Austria during the National Socialist era shall be eligible to file an application.

(2) In addition, applying *mutatis mutandis* the provisions of the (Austrian) General Civil Code, heirs of eligible claimants as defined in (1) shall also be eligible to file an application. In case of a defunct association, an association which the Claims Committee regards as the legal successor shall be entitled to file an application as well.

General Conditions for Payments

§ 7. The payments shall be awarded as a final compensation for losses and damages as a result of or in connection with events having occurred on the territory of the present-day Republic of Austria during the National Socialist era. There shall be no legal right to these payments.

Filing Period

§ 8. Applications for payments are to be filed in writing no later than 24 months after the entry into force of the present Federal Law.

Multiple Applications

§ 9. Applications for compensation for damages and losses as defined in § 7 may be filed either under the claims-based or the equity-based process. In the respective processes, only one application may be filed, which may include losses and damages in multiple categories (§§ 14 and 19). Simultaneous applications in both processes based on the same loss or damage are, however, inadmissible. If an application is entirely and finally rejected under the claims-based process, the Claims Committee shall consider the application under the equity-based process.

Consideration of Prior Restitution Measures

§ 10. (1) Unless the present Federal Law provides otherwise, no payments shall be made for claims regarding losses and damages which have been finally decided by an Austrian court or administrative body or which have been settled by agreement.

(2) In the exceptional circumstances where the Claims Committee unanimously determines that such decision or settlement constituted an extreme injustice, a payment may exceptionally be awarded. (§ 15 (1) item 2).

(3) Where a piece of art shall be restituted to a claimant pursuant to the provisions of the Federation [Bund], the provinces and the municipalities regarding the restitution of publicly-owned property pursuant to Part 2 of this Federal Law and where the claimant is already in receipt of a payment for this property pursuant to § 11a, § 16 or § 20, the claimant shall repay this payment to the General Settlement Fund. Such reversal shall be performed concurrently.[3]

Waiver

§ 11. (1) The condition for a payment from the Fund shall be a statement to be made by the recipient of the payment that upon receipt of a payment he or she will, for him/herself and

---

[3] Paragraph 3 was inserted by the amendment to the GSF Law, Federal Law Gazette I No. 20/2007.

Folge von oder im Zusammenhang mit Ereignissen auf dem Gebiet der heutigen Republik Österreich während der Zeit des Nationalsozialismus Verluste oder Schäden erlitten haben.

(2) Antragsberechtigt sind weiters Erben von antragsberechtigten Personen gemäß Abs. 1 in sinngemäßer Anwendung der Bestimmungen des Allgemeinen Bürgerlichen Gesetzbuches. Im Fall einer aufgelösten Vereinigung ist auch eine Vereinigung antragsberechtigt, die vom Antragskomitee als deren Rechtsnachfolgerin angesehen wird.

Allgemeine Voraussetzungen für Leistungen

§ 7. Die Leistungen werden für die endgültige Abgeltung von Verlusten oder Schäden zuerkannt, die als Folge von oder im Zusammenhang mit Ereignissen auf dem Gebiet der heutigen Republik Österreich während der Zeit des Nationalsozialismus entstanden sind. Auf diese Leistungen besteht kein Rechtsanspruch.

Antragsfrist

§ 8. Anträge auf Leistungen sind bis spätestens 24 Monate nach In-Kraft-Treten dieses Bundesgesetzes schriftlich beim Fonds einzubringen.

Mehrfachanträge

§ 9. Entschädigungen für Verluste oder Schäden im Sinne des § 7 können entweder im Wege des Forderungsverfahrens oder des Billigkeitsverfahrens beantragt werden. Im jeweiligen Verfahren kann nur ein Antrag gestellt werden, der Verluste und Schäden mehrerer Kategorien (§§ 14 und 19) umfassen kann. Gleichzeitige Antragstellung in beiden Verfahren auf Grund ein und desselben Verlustes oder Schadens ist jedoch unzulässig. Bei vollständiger und endgültiger Ablehnung eines Antrags im Forderungsverfahren wird das Antragskomitee den Antrag im Billigkeitsverfahren behandeln.

Berücksichtigung früherer Restitutionsmaßnahmen

§ 10. (1) Für Forderungen betreffend Verluste und Schäden, die durch österreichische Gerichte oder Verwaltungsbehörden endgültig entschieden oder einvernehmlich geregelt wurden, ist, sofern in diesem Bundesgesetz nicht anderes bestimmt ist, keine Leistung zu erbringen.

(2) In besonderen Einzelfällen, in denen das Antragskomitee einstimmig zu der Auffassung gelangt, dass eine solche Entscheidung oder einvernehmliche Regelung eine extreme Ungerechtigkeit dargestellt hat, kann jedoch ausnahmsweise eine Leistung zuerkannt werden (§ 15 Abs. 1 Z 2).

(3) Soll an einen Antragsteller ein Kunstgegenstand gemäß den Bestimmungen des Bundes, der Länder und der Gemeinden über die Kunstrückgabe oder öffentliches Vermögen nach Teil 2 dieses Bundesgesetzes restituiert werden und hat er für diesen Vermögenswert bereits eine Zahlung nach den §§ 11a, 16 oder 20 erhalten, so hat der Antragsteller diesen Betrag an den Allgemeinen Entschädigungsfonds zurückzuzahlen. Eine derartige Rückabwicklung hat Zug um Zug zu erfolgen.[3]

Verzichtserklärung

§ 11. (1) Eine Leistung aus dem Fonds hat zur Voraussetzung, dass der Leistungsempfänger eine Erklärung abgibt, mit Erhalt dieser Leistung für sich und seine Erben auf alle Ansprüche gegen Österreich und/oder österreichische Unternehmen, die sich aus oder im Zu-

---

[3] Absatz 3 wurde durch die EF-G Novelle, BGBl I Nr. 20/2007, eingefügt.

his/her heirs, waive any and all claims against Austria and/or Austrian companies arising out of or related the National Socialist era or World War II.

(2) Such a waiver shall not preclude the claimant from bringing an action against Austria and/or Austrian companies for in rem restitution of a specifically identified piece of art or an action for in rem restitution against provinces or municipalities, unless or until the latter have availed themselves of the option under § 38. Such a statement shall not include a waiver of any right in any prior settlement reached in courts in the United States of America.

Initial Payments

§ 11a. (1) The Board of Trustees by consent of the Claims Committee shall be authorized to determine the disbursement of initial payments to an eligible person.

(2) Initial payments shall only be made by the Claims Committee where the requirement of § 44 (1) is satisfied and shall exclusively be made to eligible persons whose claim – with the exception of insurance claims – has been decided and where any filing period for the re-opening of the matter has expired.

(3) Guidelines for the disbursement of initial payments shall be issued by the Board of Trustees requiring that initial payments are determined so as not to exceed the estimated total amount payable to the claimant according to this Federal Law. The Board of Trustees may state in these guidelines that a initial payment shall only be disbursed if its determination according to the guidelines meets or exceeds a minimum amount.[4]

Rules of Procedure and By-Laws

§ 12. The Claims Committee shall issue and publish rules of procedure and by-laws, in particular regarding:
1. relaxed standards of proof;
2. a simplified and expedited internal appellate procedure in the claims-based process;
3. the attendance of observers at individual procedural stages of the claims-based process under strict rules of confidentiality.

Taxes, Fees and Social Benefits

§ 13. (1) Applications to, and payments from, the Fund shall be exempt from all federal taxes and fees.

(2) **(constitutional provision)** Payments from the Fund shall not affect the recipient's claims to any Austrian social benefits.

Title 3

Claims-Based Process

Categories of Property

§ 14. In the claims-based process, applications may be filed for awarding payments for losses or damages in the following categories of property:
1. liquidated businesses, including licenses and other business assets;

---

[4] § 11a was inserted by the amendment to the GSF Law, Federal Law Gazette I No. 142/2005.

sammenhang mit der Zeit des Nationalsozialismus oder dem Zweiten Weltkrieg ergeben, zu verzichten.

(2) Ein derartiger Verzicht schließt nicht aus, dass der Antragsteller einer Klage auf Naturalrestitution eines genau identifizierten Kunstgegenstandes gegen Österreich und/oder österreichische Unternehmen oder eine Klage auf Naturalrestitution gegen Länder oder Gemeinden, sofern diese nicht von der Möglichkeit nach § 38 Gebrauch gemacht haben, erhebt. Diese Erklärung umfasst nicht den Verzicht auf Rechte aus früheren, vor Gerichten in den Vereinigten Staaten von Amerika erzielten Vergleichen.

Vorläufige Leistungen

§ 11a. (1) Das Kuratorium ist im Einvernehmen mit dem Antragskomitee ermächtigt, die Erbringung vorläufiger Leistungen an Leistungsberechtigte zu beschließen.

(2) Vorläufige Leistungen können nur unter der Voraussetzung der Erfüllung von § 44 Abs. 1 und ausschließlich an Leistungsberechtigte erbracht werden, über deren Forderungen, ausgenommen gegebenenfalls Forderungen aus Versicherungspolizzen, vom Antragskomitee entschieden wurde, und nachdem eine allfällige Frist zur Stellung eines Antrags auf neuerliche Entscheidung abgelaufen ist.

(3) Richtlinien über die Erbringung vorläufiger Leistungen erlässt das Kuratorium mit der Maßgabe, dass vorläufige Leistungen so zu bemessen sind, dass sie die voraussichtliche Höhe der insgesamt nach diesem Bundesgesetz an den Antragsteller zu erbringenden Geldleistungen nicht übersteigen. Das Kuratorium kann in diesen Richtlinien vorsehen, dass eine vorläufige Leistung nur zu erbringen ist, wenn ihre richtliniengemäße Bemessung einen Mindestbetrag erreicht oder übersteigt.[4]

Verfahrens- und Geschäftsordnung

§ 12. Das Antragskomitee erlässt und veröffentlicht eine Verfahrens- und Geschäftsordnung, insbesondere über:
1. die erleichterten Beweisstandards;
2. ein einfaches und beschleunigtes internes Rechtsmittel im Forderungsverfahren;
3. die Zulassung von Beobachtern zu einzelnen Verfahrensabschnitten des Forderungsverfahrens unter Einhaltung strenger Vertraulichkeit.

Abgaben und Sozialleistungen

§ 13. (1) Anbringen an den Fonds sowie dessen Leistungen sind von allen bundesgesetzlichen Abgaben befreit.

(2) **(Verfassungsbestimmung)** Zahlungen aus dem Fonds berühren nicht Ansprüche des Empfängers auf allfällige österreichische Sozialleistungen.

3. Hauptstück

Forderungsverfahren

Vermögenskategorien

§ 14. Im Forderungsverfahren können Anträge auf Zuerkennung von Leistungen für Verluste oder Schäden in folgenden Vermögenskategorien gestellt werden:
1. liquidierte Betriebe einschließlich Konzessionen und anderes Betriebsvermögen;

---

[4] § 11a wurde durch die EF-G Novelle, BGBl I Nr. 142/2005, eingefügt.

2. real property, unless in rem restitution pursuant to Part 2 of the present Federal Law has been granted;
3. bank accounts, stocks, bonds, mortgages;
4. movable property, unless such property losses have been compensated by payments based on the Federal Law amending the Federal Law to Establish the National Fund of the Republic of Austria for Victims of National Socialism, Federal Law Gazette I, No. 11/2001;
5. insurance policies.

Conditions for Claims and Standards of Proof

§ **15.** (1) The claimant must show, under relaxed standards of proof according to (2) proof or convincing evidence of ownership of property in one of the categories listed in § 14 or entitlement based on insurance policies at the time of confiscation/Aryanization/liquidation as a result of or in connection with events having occurred on the territory of the present-day Republic of Austria during the National Socialist era, and that
1. such property claim was never previously finally decided by Austrian courts or administrative bodies, or settled by agreement, or
2. such a decision or settlement by agreement constituted an extreme injustice, or
3. such property claim was denied by Austrian courts or administrative bodies because of failure to produce required evidence, where such evidence was inaccessible to the claimant at that time, but has since become available.

(2) The Claims Committee shall review all applications using relaxed standards of proof. In the claims-based process, claimants must as a rule produce supporting evidence to establish eligibility. If no relevant evidence is available, eligibility for payments may also be made credible in some other way. In cases relating to (1) items 1 and 3, if no contradictory evidence is presented, an affidavit, including a plausible explanation for why this claim was never decided or settled, or why the necessary evidence was inaccessible to the claimant, shall be deemed sufficient.

Decisions of the Claims Committee

*§ **16.** (1) If the Claims Committee determines – in case of § 15 (1) item 2 unanimously – that the claimant satisfies the evidentiary requirements mentioned in § 15, the Claims Committee shall establish the total amount of all of the claimant's approved claims (claimed amount). The claimant shall be notified of the claimed amount. The Claims Committee may notify separately the part of the claimed amount regarding insurance claims and the part of the claimed amount regarding all other claims. After expiration of the filing period according to § 8 and decision of all applications, the Claims Committee shall award each claimant a proportionately reduced amount (pro rata) on the basis of the established claimed amounts and according to the funds allocated for the claims-based process pursuant to § 5 (awarded amount). The amount awarded for each application may not exceed 2 million US Dollars. More detailed regulations shall be laid down in the by-laws and rules of procedure.*[5]

(2) In order to ensure that no claimant shall receive payments for those losses or damages for which compensation has been paid on the basis of other measures, the Claims Committee, when establishing the claimed amount, shall take particularly into account the following restitution and compensation measures:

---

[5] § 16 (1) was amended by Federal Law Gazette I No. 142/2005.

2. Immobilien, soweit für diese nicht Naturalrestitution gemäß Teil 2 dieses Bundesgesetzes geleistet wurde;
3. Bankkonten, Aktien, Schuldverschreibungen, Hypotheken;
4. bewegliches Vermögen, soweit derartige Vermögensverluste nicht bereits durch Leistungen auf Grund des Bundesgesetzes, mit dem das Bundesgesetz über den Nationalfonds der Republik Österreich für Opfer des Nationalsozialismus geändert wird, BGBl. I Nr. 11/2001, abgegolten wurden;
5. Versicherungspolizzen.

Antragsvoraussetzungen und Beweisstandards

§ 15. (1) Dem Antragsteller obliegt nach erleichterten Beweisstandards gemäß Abs. 2 der Beweis oder die Glaubhaftmachung des Eigentumsrechts an einem Vermögenswert in einer der in § 14 genannten Vermögenskategorien oder der Berechtigung aus Versicherungspolizzen zum Zeitpunkt der Entziehung, Arisierung oder Liquidierung als Folge von oder im Zusammenhang mit Ereignissen auf dem Gebiet der heutigen Republik Österreich während der Zeit des Nationalsozialismus, und dass
1. die den Vermögenswert betreffende Forderung niemals zuvor durch österreichische Gerichte oder Verwaltungsbehörden endgültig entschieden oder einvernehmlich geregelt wurde, oder
2. eine derartige Entscheidung oder einvernehmliche Regelung eine extreme Ungerechtigkeit darstellte, oder
3. die den Vermögenswert betreffende Forderung durch österreichische Gerichte oder Verwaltungsbehörden aus Mangel an erforderlichen Beweisen abgelehnt wurde, in Fällen, in denen derartige Beweise dem Antragsteller seinerzeit nicht zugänglich waren, aber in der Zwischenzeit verfügbar wurden.

(2) Das Antragskomitee prüft alle Anträge nach erleichterten Beweisstandards. Im Forderungsverfahren sind die Leistungsvoraussetzungen in der Regel durch Vorlage unterstützender Unterlagen nachzuweisen. Sind keine entsprechenden Beweismittel vorhanden, kann das Vorliegen der Leistungsvoraussetzungen auch auf andere Weise glaubhaft gemacht werden. In den Fällen des Abs. 1 Z 1 und 3 wird, wenn keine gegenteiligen Beweise vorgelegt werden, eine eidesstattliche Erklärung einschließlich einer plausiblen Begründung, warum niemals über die Forderung entschieden oder eine Regelung getroffen wurde bzw. die erforderlichen Beweise dem Antragsteller nicht zugänglich waren, als ausreichend erachtet.

Entscheidungen des Antragskomitees

§ 16. (1) Gelangt das Antragskomitee zu der Ansicht, im Fall des § 15 Abs. 1 Z 2 mit Einstimmigkeit, dass der Antragsteller die in § 15 genannten Beweiserfordernisse erfüllt, wird das Antragskomitee einen Gesamtbetrag aller anerkannten Forderungen des Antragstellers festlegen (Forderungsbetrag). Der Forderungsbetrag wird dem Antragsteller mitgeteilt, wobei das Antragskomitee jenen Teil des Forderungsbetrages, der Forderungen aus Versicherungspolizzen betrifft, und jenen Teil des Forderungsbetrages, der alle übrigen Forderungen betrifft, gesondert mitteilen kann. Nach Ablauf der Antragsfrist gemäß § 8 und Entscheidung aller Anträge wird das Antragskomitee den jeweiligen Antragstellern auf Grundlage der festgelegten Forderungsbeträge und nach Maßgabe des gemäß § 5 für das Forderungsverfahren bereitgestellten Betrages eine verhältnismäßig zu kürzende Leistung (pro rata) zuerkennen (Zuerkennungsbetrag). Der Zuerkennungsbetrag je Antrag darf 2 Millionen US-Dollar nicht übersteigen. Nähere Bestimmungen werden in der Geschäfts- und Verfahrensordnung geregelt.[5]

---

[5] § 16 Abs. 1 wurde novelliert durch die EF-G Novelle, BGBl I Nr. 142/2005.

1. Payments based on the Federal Law amending the Federal Law to Establish the National Fund of the Republic of Austria for Victims of National Socialism, Federal Law Gazette I, No. 11/2001;
2. Payments and measures of the German Foundation "Remembrance, Responsibility and Future", German Federal Law Gazette I, No. 38/2000;
3. Settlement of claims under the Insurance Reconstruction Act, Federal Law Gazette No. 185/1955, the Insurance Indemnification Act, Federal Law Gazette No. 130/1958, or on the basis of claims settlement procedures of the "International Commission on Holocaust Era Insurance Claims" (ICHEIC); or
4. Settlement of claims on the basis of the Bank Austria Settlement.

Appeal for a New Decision

§ 17. In the event of a negative decision by the Claims Committee on the claimed amount *or a part thereof*[6], the claimant may file an appeal for a new decision. Such an appeal shall specify the reasons why a revised decision would be justified. In particular, such reasons may include references to new circumstances or errors in fact or in law in the decision of the Claims Committee. More detailed regulations shall be laid down in the by-laws and rules of procedure.

Insurance Claims

§ 18. (1) Within the framework of the claims-based process, the Claims Committee shall decide on all insurance claims (§ 14 item 5) against Austrian companies, unless these claims are directed at companies which
1. are considered "German companies" under the German Law for the Establishment of the Foundation "Remembrance, Responsibility and Future", German Federal Law Gazette I No. 38/2000; or
2. are already covered by ICHEIC.

(2) In taking decisions on insurance policies (§ 14 item 5), the Claims Committee shall apply *mutatis mutandis* the ICHEIC claims-handling procedures, including those pertaining to valuation, standards of proof, and relevant decisions by the chairperson. In doing so, particularly prior compensation measures shall be taken into account according to § 16 (2).

(3) If the Claims Committee determines that all conditions for the approval of an insurance claim are met, it shall authorize in accordance with the principles of § 16 (1) the disbursement of a payment from the capital of the Fund allocated pursuant to § 5 (2). All funds used to pay approved insurance claims shall be distributed on a pro rata basis.

(4) The Austrian Insurance Association shall, to the extent available, make the lists of policyholders who are possible victims of National Socialism as defined in § 6 (1) publicly accessible.

---

[6] These words were inserted by the amendment to the GSF Law, Federal Law Gazette I No. 142/2005.

(2) Um sicherzustellen, dass ein Antragsteller keine Leistung für jene Verluste oder Schäden erhält, für die bereits auf Grund anderer Maßnahmen Entschädigung geleistet wurde, hat das Antragskomitee bei der Festlegung des Forderungsbetrages insbesondere folgende Rückstellungs- und Entschädigungsmaßnahmen zu berücksichtigen:
1. Leistungen auf Grund des Bundesgesetzes, mit dem das Bundesgesetz über den Nationalfonds der Republik Österreich für Opfer des Nationalsozialismus geändert wird, BGBl. I Nr. 11/2001;
2. Leistungen und Maßnahmen der deutschen Stiftung „Erinnerung, Verantwortung und Zukunft", dBGBl. I Nr. 38/2000;
3. Befriedigung von Forderungen durch das Versicherungswiederaufbaugesetz, BGBl. Nr. 185/1955, das Versicherungsentschädigungsgesetz, BGBl. Nr. 130/1958, oder auf Grund eines Anspruchserledigungsverfahrens der „International Commission on Holocaust Era Insurance Claims" (ICHEIC); oder
4. Befriedigung von Ansprüchen auf Grund des Bank-Austria-Vergleiches.

Antrag auf neuerliche Entscheidung

§ 17. Bei ablehnenden Entscheidungen des Antragskomitees über den Forderungsbetrag *oder einen Teil des Forderungsbetrages*[6] kann ein Antrag auf neuerliche Entscheidung gestellt werden. In einem solchen Antrag sind jene Gründe anzuführen, die für eine Abänderung der Erstentscheidung sprechen. Als solche Gründe kommen insbesondere der Hinweis auf neue Umstände oder auf tatsächliche oder rechtliche Irrtümer bei der Beurteilung durch das Antragskomitee in Betracht. Nähere Bestimmungen werden in der Geschäfts- und Verfahrensordnung geregelt.

Forderungen aus Versicherungspolizzen

§ 18. (1) Das Antragskomitee entscheidet im Rahmen des Forderungsverfahrens über alle Forderungen aus Versicherungspolizzen (§ 14 Z 5) gegen österreichische Unternehmen, soweit diese Forderungen nicht gegen Unternehmen gerichtet sind, die
1. nach dem deutschen Gesetz zur Errichtung einer Stiftung „Erinnerung, Verantwortung und Zukunft", dBGBl. I Nr. 38/2000, als „deutsche Unternehmen" gelten; oder
2. bereits von ICHEIC erfasst werden.

(2) Für die Entscheidung über Versicherungspolizzen (§ 14 Z 5) wendet das Antragskomitee die Verfahrensregeln über die Anspruchserledigung der ICHEIC sinngemäß an, einschließlich jener betreffend Bewertung, Beweisstandards und diesbezüglicher Entscheidungen des Vorsitzenden. Dabei sind insbesondere bisher erbrachte Entschädigungsmaßnahmen gemäß § 16 Abs. 2 zu berücksichtigen.

(3) Gelangt das Antragskomitee zur Ansicht, dass alle Voraussetzungen für die Anerkennung einer Forderung aus einer Versicherungspolizze vorliegen, wird es nach den Grundsätzen des § 16 Abs. 1 die Auszahlung einer Leistung aus den dafür gemäß § 5 Abs. 2 bereitgestellten Mitteln des Fonds bewilligen. Alle zur Auszahlung anerkannter Forderungen aus Versicherungspolizzen verwendete Mittel werden pro rata verteilt.

(4) Der Verband der Versicherungsunternehmen Österreichs wird, soweit verfügbar, Listen der Polizzeninhaber, die mögliche Opfer des Nationalsozialismus im Sinne des § 6 Abs. 1 sind, öffentlich zugänglich machen.

---

[6] Diese Worte wurden durch die EF-G Novelle, BGBl I Nr. 142/2005, eingefügt.

Title 4

Equity-Based Process

Categories

§ 19. In case the claimant is not able, under the standards of proof of the claims-based process, to document specific claims or make them credible, applications may be submitted to the Claims Committee in the equity-based process for awarding payments for losses or damages in the following categories:
1. for any of the categories of property mentioned above in § 14;
2. for occupational or educational losses as a result of or in connection with events having occurred on the territory of the present-day Republic of Austria during the National Socialist era; or
3. for any other claims for losses or damages arising as a result of or in connection with events having occurred on the territory of the present-day Republic of Austria during the National-Socialist era, unless those claims are covered by the Federal Law concerning the Fund for Voluntary Payments by the Republic of Austria to Former Slave Laborers and Forced Laborers of the National Socialist Regime, Federal Law Gazette I No. 74/2000, or by the provisions on in rem restitution of publicly-owned property pursuant to Part 2 of the present Federal Law.

Special Conditions for Payments

§ 20. If the Claims Committee has reason to believe that
1. there is a valid case of loss of property in any of the categories of property listed in § 14, or – where such claim was finally decided by Austrian courts or administrative bodies, or settled by agreement – that such a decision or settlement was inadequate;
2. the claimant was not adequately compensated for losses as defined in § 19 item 2; or
3. a claim raised pursuant to § 19 item 3 is justified, the Claims Committee may award an equity-based payment.

Payment per Household

§ 21. (note: repealed by Federal Law Gazette I No. 142/2005)

Exclusion of Appeal

§ 22. Decisions made by the Claims Committee under the equity-based process cannot be appealed.

Part 2

In Rem Restitution

Title 1

Arbitration Panel for *In Rem* Restitution

Establishment of the Arbitration Panel

§ 23. (1) An Arbitration Panel for the examination of applications for *in rem* restitution of publicly-owned property shall be established with the Fund.

4. Hauptstück

Billigkeitsverfahren

Kategorien

§ 19. Falls der Antragsteller nach den Beweisstandards des Forderungsverfahrens nicht in der Lage ist, konkrete Forderungen zu dokumentieren oder glaubhaft zu machen, können im Billigkeitsverfahren Anträge an das Antragskomitee auf Zuerkennung von Leistungen für Verluste oder Schäden in folgenden Kategorien gestellt werden:
1. in jeder der oben in § 14 genannten Vermögenskategorien;
2. für berufs- oder ausbildungsbezogene Verluste, die als Folge von oder im Zusammenhang mit Ereignissen auf dem Gebiet der heutigen Republik Österreich während der Zeit des Nationalsozialismus entstanden sind; oder
3. für alle anderen Forderungen für Verluste und Schäden, die als Folge von oder im Zusammenhang mit Ereignissen auf dem Gebiet der heutigen Republik Österreich während der Zeit des Nationalsozialismus entstanden sind, soweit diese nicht vom Bundesgesetz über den Fonds für freiwillige Leistungen der Republik Österreich an ehemalige Sklaven- und Zwangsarbeiter des nationalsozialistischen Regimes, BGBl. I Nr. 74/2000, oder den Bestimmungen über die Naturalrestitution von öffentlichem Vermögen gemäß dem zweiten Teil dieses Bundesgesetzes erfasst werden.

Besondere Leistungsvoraussetzungen

§ 20. Hat das Antragskomitee Grund zur Annahme, dass
1. ein berücksichtigungswürdiger Fall eines Vermögensverlustes in einer der in § 14 genannten Vermögenskategorien vorliegt, oder - falls die Forderung durch österreichische Gerichte oder Verwaltungsbehörden endgültig entschieden oder einvernehmlich geregelt wurde – diese Entscheidung oder Regelung unzureichend war;
2. der Antragsteller für Verluste im Sinne des § 19 Z 2 nicht ausreichend entschädigt wurde; oder
3. eine gemäß § 19 Z 3 erhobene Forderung berechtigt ist, kann das Antragskomitee eine Billigkeitszahlung zuerkennen.

Zahlung pro Haushalt

§ 21. (Anm.: aufgehoben durch BGBl. I Nr. 142/2005)

Ausschluss von Rechtsmitteln

§ 22. Gegen im Billigkeitsverfahren gefällte Entscheidungen des Antragskomitees kann kein Rechtsmittel eingelegt werden.

Teil 2

Naturalrestitution

1. Hauptstück

Schiedsinstanz für Naturalrestitution

Einrichtung einer Schiedsinstanz

§ 23. (1) Beim Fonds wird eine Schiedsinstanz zur Prüfung von Anträgen auf Naturalrestitution von öffentlichem Vermögen eingerichtet.

(2) **(constitutional provision)** Members of the Arbitration Panel shall be:
1. one member to be appointed by the Government of the United States of America;
2. one member to be appointed by the Austrian Federal Government;
3. one member to be appointed by the above members as chairperson.

(3) The members should be familiar with the relevant rules and provisions of Austrian and international law, in particular with the European Convention for the Protection of Human Rights and Fundamental Freedoms.

(4) In the event that the members appointed according to (2) items 1 and 2 are unable to agree upon the chairperson within 60 days after the entry into force of the present Federal Law, the Government of the United States of America and the Federal Government [of Austria] will enter into consultations to name a chairperson.

(5) The members of the Arbitration Panel shall serve in an honorary capacity. Any expenses incurred by the members as well as the necessary costs for personnel and material shall be borne by the Federation [Bund], making use to the greatest extent possible of the administrative infrastructure of the Fund.

By-Laws and Rules of Procedure

§ 24. The Arbitration Panel shall establish and publish by-laws and rules of procedure, in particular about requirements for applicants regarding burden of proof and rules of evidence.

Liaison with the Historical Commission

§ 25. The chairperson of the Austrian Historical Commission shall appoint a liaison person to the Arbitration Panel.

Title 2

Settlement of Claims

Case-by-Case Examination

§ 26. The Arbitration Panel shall examine applications for *in rem* restitution of publicly-owned property on a case-by-case basis.

Eligibility

§ 27. (1) Persons and associations who/which were persecuted by the National Socialist regime on political grounds, on grounds of origin, religion, nationality, sexual orientation, or of physical or mental handicap, or of accusations of so-called asociality, or who left the country to escape such persecution, and who suffered losses or damages as a result of or in connection with events having occurred on the territory of the present-day Republic of Austria during the National Socialist era shall be eligible to file an application.

(2) In addition, applying *mutatis mutandis* the provisions of the (Austrian) General Civil Code, heirs of eligible claimants as defined in (1) shall also be eligible to file an application. In case of a defunct association, an association which the Arbitration Panel regards as the legal successor shall be entitled to file an application as well.

Publicly-Owned Property

§ 28. (1) For the purposes of *in rem* restitution, the notion of "publicly-owned property" shall cover exclusively real estate (land) and buildings (superstructures) which

(2) **(Verfassungsbestimmung)** Der Schiedsinstanz gehören an:
1. ein von der Regierung der Vereinigten Staaten von Amerika zu bestimmendes Mitglied;
2. ein von der österreichischen Bundesregierung zu bestimmendes Mitglied;
3. ein von diesen Mitgliedern zu bestimmendes Mitglied als Vorsitzender.

(3) Die Mitglieder sollen mit den einschlägigen Bestimmungen des österreichischen und internationalen Rechts, insbesondere der Europäischen Konvention zum Schutze der Menschenrechte und Grundfreiheiten, vertraut sein.

(4) Können sich die Mitglieder gemäß Abs. 2 Z 1 und 2 nicht innerhalb von 60 Tagen nach dem Inkrafttreten dieses Bundesgesetzes auf einen Vorsitzenden einigen, nehmen die Regierung der Vereinigten Staaten von Amerika und die Bundesregierung Beratungen über die Ernennung eines Vorsitzenden auf.

(5) Die Funktionen in der Schiedsinstanz werden ehrenamtlich ausgeübt. Die Auslagen der Mitglieder sowie der notwendige Personal- und Sachaufwand werden unter möglichster Nutzung des Geschäftsapparates des Fonds vom Bund getragen.

Geschäfts- und Verfahrensordnung

§ 24. Die Schiedsinstanz erlässt und veröffentlicht eine Geschäfts- und Verfahrensordnung, insbesondere über die Beweislast und Beweismittel für Antragsteller.

Verbindung zur Historikerkommission

§ 25. Der Vorsitzende der österreichischen Historikerkommission benennt eine Verbindungsperson zur Schiedsinstanz.

2. Hauptstück
Erbringung von Leistungen

Einzelfallbezogene Prüfung

§ 26. Die Schiedsinstanz prüft Anträge auf Naturalrestitution von öffentlichem Vermögen im Einzelfall.

Antragsvoraussetzungen

§ 27. (1) Antragsberechtigt sind Personen und Vereinigungen, die vom nationalsozialistischen Regime aus politischen Gründen, aus Gründen der Abstammung, Religion, Nationalität, sexuellen Orientierung, auf Grund einer körperlichen oder geistigen Behinderung oder auf Grund des Vorwurfes der so genannten Asozialität verfolgt wurden oder das Land verlassen haben, um einer solchen Verfolgung zu entgehen, und die als Folge von oder im Zusammenhang mit Ereignissen auf dem Gebiet der heutigen Republik Österreich während der Zeit des Nationalsozialismus Verluste oder Schäden erlitten haben.

(2) Antragsberechtigt sind weiters Erben von antragsberechtigten Personen gemäß Abs. 1 in sinngemäßer Anwendung der Bestimmungen des Allgemeinen Bürgerlichen Gesetzbuches. Im Fall einer aufgelösten Vereinigung ist auch eine Vereinigung antragsberechtigt, die von der Schiedsinstanz als deren Rechtsnachfolgerin angesehen wird.

Öffentliches Vermögen

§ 28. (1) Für Zwecke der Naturalrestitution umfasst der Begriff „öffentliches Vermögen" ausschließlich Liegenschaften und Überbauten (Superädifikate), welche:

1. between March 12, 1938 and May 9, 1945, were taken from the previous owners whether without authorization or on the basis of laws or other orders, on political grounds, on grounds of origin, religion, nationality, sexual orientation, or of physical or mental handicap, or of accusations of so-called asociality, in connection with events having occurred on the territory of the present-day Republic of Austria during the National Socialist era; and
2. were never the subject of a claim that was previously decided by an Austrian court or administrative body, or settled by agreement, and for which the claimant or a relative has never otherwise received compensation or other consideration; except in exceptional circumstances where the Arbitration Panel unanimously determines that such a decision or settlement constituted an extreme injustice; and which
3. on January 17, 2001 were exclusively and directly owned by the Federation [Bund], or any legal person under public or private law wholly-owned, directly or indirectly, by the Federation.

(2) For the purposes of *in rem* restitution to Jewish communal organizations, the notion of "publicly-owned property" shall furthermore cover tangible movable property, particularly cultural and religious items, which

1. between March 12, 1938 and May 9, 1945, was taken from the previous owners whether without authorization or on the basis of laws or other orders, on political grounds, on grounds of origin, religion, nationality, sexual orientation, or of physical or mental handicap, or of accusations of so-called asociality, in connection with events having occurred on the territory of the present-day Republic of Austria during the National Socialist era; and
2. was never the subject of a claim that was previously decided by an Austrian court or administrative body, or settled by agreement, and for which the claimant or a relative has never otherwise received compensation or other consideration; except in exceptional circumstances where the Arbitration Panel unanimously determines that such a decision or settlement constituted an extreme injustice; and which
3. on January 17, 2001 was exclusively and directly owned by the Federation [Bund], or any legal person under public or private law wholly-owned, directly or indirectly, by the Federation.

Filing Period

§ 29. Applications to the Arbitration Panel are to be filed in writing with the Fund *no later than December 31, 2007*.[7]

Basis of Examination

§ 30. The Arbitration Panel shall make recommendations on the basis of evidence submitted by the claimant and submissions of the Austrian Federal Government, as well as any relevant findings of the Austrian Historical Commission.

Status of Ownership

§ 31. If the claimant asserts that a property is publicly-owned, the Arbitration Panel shall verify in cooperation with the Federal Government whether this is the case.

---

[7] § 29 was last amended by Federal Law Gazette I No. 20/2007.

Anhang

1. zwischen 12. März 1938 und 9. Mai 1945 dem früheren Eigentümer, sei es eigenmächtig, sei es auf Grund von Gesetzen oder anderen Anordnungen, aus politischen Gründen, aus Gründen der Abstammung, Religion, Nationalität, sexuellen Orientierung, auf Grund einer körperlichen oder geistigen Behinderung oder auf Grund des Vorwurfes der so genannten Asozialität im Zusammenhang mit Ereignissen auf dem Gebiet der heutigen Republik Österreich während der Zeit des Nationalsozialismus entzogen wurden; und
2. niemals Gegenstand einer Forderung waren, die bereits zuvor durch österreichische Gerichte oder Verwaltungsbehörden entschieden wurde oder einvernehmlich geregelt wurde, und für die der Antragsteller oder ein Verwandter nicht auf andere Weise eine Entschädigung oder sonstige Gegenleistung erhalten hat; es sei denn, dass in besonderen Ausnahmefällen die Schiedsinstanz einstimmig zu der Auffassung gelangt, dass eine solche Entscheidung oder einvernehmliche Regelung eine extreme Ungerechtigkeit dargestellt hat; und
3. sich am 17. Jänner 2001 ausschließlich und unmittelbar im Eigentum des Bundes oder einer, unmittelbar oder mittelbar, im Alleineigentum des Bundes stehenden juristischen Person des öffentlichen oder privaten Rechts befanden.

(2) Für Zwecke der Naturalrestitution an jüdische Gemeinschaftsorganisationen umfasst der Begriff „öffentliches Vermögen" zudem bewegliche körperliche Sachen, insbesondere kulturelle oder religiöse Gegenstände, welche:
1. zwischen 12. März 1938 und 9. Mai 1945 dem früheren Eigentümer, sei es eigenmächtig, sei es auf Grund von Gesetzen oder anderen Anordnungen, aus politischen Gründen, aus Gründen der Abstammung, Religion, Nationalität, sexuellen Orientierung, auf Grund einer körperlichen oder geistigen Behinderung oder auf Grund des Vorwurfes der so genannten Asozialität im Zusammenhang mit Ereignissen auf dem Gebiet der heutigen Republik Österreich während der Zeit des Nationalsozialismus entzogen wurden; und
2. niemals Gegenstand einer Forderung waren, die bereits zuvor von österreichischen Gerichten oder Verwaltungsbehörden entschieden oder einvernehmlich geregelt wurde, und für die der Antragsteller oder ein Verwandter nicht auf andere Weise eine Entschädigung oder sonstige Gegenleistung erhalten hat; es sei denn, dass in besonderen Ausnahmefällen die Schiedsinstanz einstimmig zu der Auffassung gelangt, dass eine solche Entscheidung oder einvernehmliche Regelung eine extreme Ungerechtigkeit dargestellt hat; und
3. sich am 17. Jänner 2001 ausschließlich und unmittelbar im Eigentum des Bundes oder einer, unmittelbar oder mittelbar, im Alleineigentum des Bundes stehenden juristischen Person des öffentlichen oder privaten Rechts befanden.

Antragsfrist

§ 29. Anträge an die Schiedsinstanz sind bis *spätestens 31. Dezember 2007*[7] schriftlich beim Fonds einzubringen.

Prüfungsgrundlagen

§ 30. Die Schiedsinstanz gibt ihre Empfehlungen auf Grundlage der vom Antragsteller vorgelegten Beweise und des Vorbringens der österreichischen Bundesregierung sowie auch allfälliger relevanter Befunde der österreichischen Historikerkommission ab.

Eigentumsverhältnisse

§ 31. Wenn vom Antragsteller behauptet wird, dass sich ein Vermögenswert im öffentlichen Vermögen befindet, hat die Schiedsinstanz unter Mitwirkung des Bundes festzustellen, ob dies der Fall ist.

---

[7] § 29 wurde zuletzt novelliert durch die EF-G Novelle, BGBl I Nr. 20/2007.

Prior Measures

§ 32. (1) As a matter of principle, the Arbitration Panel shall not have the authority to reopen or reconsider cases that were previously decided by Austrian courts or administrative bodies, or settled by agreement. Neither the claimant nor a relative (in the case of an association also its legal predecessor) must have otherwise received compensation or other consideration for the property in question.

(2) Excepted therefrom are only cases
1. where the Arbitration Panel unanimously determines that a prior settlement constituted an extreme injustice; or
2. the claim was denied because of failure to produce required evidence, where such evidence was inaccessible to the claimant at the time but has since become accessible.

Examination Period

§ 33. The Arbitration Panel shall issue recommendations and rejections within 6 months of the Fund's receiving an application.

Recommendations and Rejections

§ 34. After examination of the application, the Arbitration Panel shall make a recommendation for *in rem* restitution to the competent Austrian Federal Minister, or reject the claim. Where *in rem* restitution, although merited, is not practical or feasible, the Arbitration Panel may recommend, in consultation with the competent Austrian Federal Minister, that the claimant be awarded a comparable property.

Taxes and Fees

§ 35. Applications to the Arbitration Panel and awards based on its recommendations shall be exempt from all federal taxes and fees.

Obligation to Publish Recommendations

§ 36. Recommendations by the Arbitration Panel shall be published.

Disposition of Federal Property

§ 37. (1) If the Arbitration Panel recommends *in rem* restitution or the conveyance of a comparable property, the Federal Minister of Finance shall be authorized, to the extent of the recommendation, to dispose of parts of the immovable or movable federal property irrespective of the estimated value by voluntary conveyance.

(2) If a property is exclusively and directly owned by a legal person under public or private law wholly-owned, directly or indirectly, by the Federation (§ 28 (1) item 3 and (2) item 3), the executive bodies of such a legal person have to comply with the proprietary instructions of the respective competent Federal Minister, in concert with the Federal Minister of Finance, regarding the voluntary conveyance of such property.

(3) (note: repealed by Federal Law Gazette I No. 142/2005)

Frühere Maßnahmen

§ 32. (1) Grundsätzlich hat die Schiedsinstanz nicht über Forderungen zu entscheiden, die bereits zuvor von österreichischen Gerichten oder Verwaltungsbehörden entschieden oder einvernehmlich geregelt wurden. Weder der Antragsteller noch ein Verwandter (im Fall einer Vereinigung auch nicht deren Rechtsvorgängerin) darf auf andere Weise eine Entschädigung oder eine sonstige Gegenleistung für die in Frage stehenden Vermögenswerte erhalten haben.

(2) Davon ausgenommen sind nur jene Fälle,
1. in denen die Schiedsinstanz einstimmig zu der Ansicht gelangt, dass die frühere einvernehmliche Regelung eine extreme Ungerechtigkeit dargestellt hat; oder
2. in denen der Anspruch aus Mangel an Beweisen abgelehnt wurde und in denen diese dem Antragsteller nicht zugänglich waren, wobei die Beweise in der Zwischenzeit zugänglich sind.

Prüfungsfrist

§ 33. Die Schiedsinstanz trifft ihre Empfehlungen und Ablehnungen innerhalb von sechs Monaten nach Einlangen eines Antrages beim Fonds.

Empfehlungen und Ablehnungen

§ 34. Nach Prüfung des Antrages gibt die Schiedsinstanz eine Empfehlung über die Naturalrestitution an den zuständigen Bundesminister ab oder lehnt den Antrag ab. In Fällen, in denen eine Naturalrestitution zwar angezeigt, aber nicht zweckmäßig oder durchführbar ist, kann die Schiedsinstanz nach Konsultation mit dem zuständigen Bundesminister empfehlen, einen vergleichbaren Vermögenswert zuzusprechen.

Steuern und Abgaben

§ 35. Anbringen an die Schiedsinstanz sowie Leistungen auf Grund ihrer Empfehlungen sind von allen bundesgesetzlichen Abgaben befreit.

Veröffentlichungspflicht

§ 36. Empfehlungen der Schiedsinstanz sind zu veröffentlichen.

Verfügung über Bundesvermögen

§ 37. (1) Empfiehlt die Schiedsinstanz die Naturalrestitution oder die Übereignung eines vergleichbaren Vermögenswertes, so ist der Bundesminister für Finanzen ermächtigt, im Ausmaß der Empfehlung über Bestandteile des unbeweglichen oder beweglichen Bundesvermögens unabhängig von der Höhe des Schätzwertes durch unentgeltliche Übereignung zu verfügen.

(2) Ist ein Vermögenswert ausschließlich und unmittelbar im Eigentum einer, unmittelbar oder mittelbar, im Alleineigentum des Bundes stehenden juristischen Person des öffentlichen oder privaten Rechts (§ 28 Abs. 1 Z 3 und Abs. 2 Z 3), so haben die Organe einer solchen juristischen Person Eigentümerweisungen des jeweils zuständigen Bundesministers im Einvernehmen mit dem Bundesminister für Finanzen auf unentgeltliche Übereignung dieses Vermögenswertes zu befolgen.

(3) (Anm.: aufgehoben durch BGBl I Nr. 142/2005)

Provinces and Municipalities

§ 38. *(1)* If and as far as provinces or municipalities provide for *in rem* restitution of publicly-owned property, they may provide for the Arbitration Panel – *after December 31, 2009 with its consent* – to examine applications for *in rem* restitution, applying *mutatis mutandis* the above provisions. The costs incurred therefrom shall be borne by the respective province or the respective municipality.

(2) Notwithstanding Sec. 29, the filing period for cases specified in paragraph (1) shall end on December 31, 2009, however, not earlier than the end of the 24th month after the province or municipality availed itself of the option under paragraph (1). The General Settlement Fund shall appropriately announce these filing periods.[8]

Part 3

Entry into Force and Final Provisions

Publicity Measures

§ 39. Within two months of entry into force of the present Federal Law, the Fund shall assure adequate worldwide publicity of the payments that may be made pursuant to the present Federal Law. Such publication shall, in particular, include information about the Fund, the conditions for payments, filing periods and the necessary examination of data.

Provision of Information

§ 40. (1) The Fund and its organs established according to the present Federal Law shall be authorized to obtain from public authorities and other public institutions all information necessary to fulfill its tasks. Information may only be withheld if prohibited by specific statutory provisions or if the protected interest for secrecy of the affected person outweighs the legitimate interest for information of the Fund and its organs.

(2) (note: repealed by Federal Law Gazette I No. 20/2007)

Data Protection

§ 40a. The Fund shall be authorized to use personal data including sensitive data as defined in § 4 item 2 of the Data Protection Act 2000 to fulfill its tasks prescribed by this Federal Law. In addition, it is legal to provide this data only to the National Fund of the Republic of Austria for Victims of National Socialism to fulfill the tasks assigned to the National Fund. Any use of sensitive data shall be recorded and documented in accordance with § 14 (2) items 7 and 8 of the data Protection Act 2000. The Data Protection Act 2000, Federal Law Gazette I No. 165/1999, as amended, is applicable.[9]

Gender-Related Terms

§ 41. The terms used in the present Federal law relating to individuals apply equally to women and men, wherever this is relevant.

---

[8] § 38 was amended by the amendment to the GSF Law, Federal Law Gazette I No. 89/2008.
[9] § 40a was inserted by the amendment to the GSF Law, Federal Law Gazette I No. 20/2007.

Länder und Gemeinden

§ 38. (1) Wenn und insoweit Länder oder Gemeinden Naturalrestitution von öffentlichem Vermögen vorsehen, können sie die Schiedsinstanz – *nach dem 31. Dezember 2009 mit deren Zustimmung* – zur Prüfung von Anträgen auf Naturalrestitution in sinngemäßer Anwendung dieser Bestimmungen vorsehen. Die dadurch anfallenden Kosten sind vom jeweiligen Land oder der jeweiligen Gemeinde zu tragen.

(2) Abweichend von § 29 endet die Antragsfrist in den Fällen des Abs. 1 am 31. Dezember 2009, jedoch nicht früher als mit Ablauf des 24. Kalendermonats nach dem Zeitpunkt, zu dem das Land oder die Gemeinde von der Möglichkeit des Abs. 1 Gebrauch gemacht hat. Der Allgemeine Entschädigungsfonds hat diese Fristen in geeigneter Weise bekannt zu machen.[8]

Teil 3
In-Kraft-Treten und Schlussbestimmungen

Publizitätsmaßnahmen

§ 39. Der Fonds sorgt innerhalb von zwei Monaten nach In-Kraft-Treten dieses Bundesgesetzes für eine angemessene, weltweite Bekanntmachung der nach diesem Bundesgesetz möglichen Leistungen. Diese beinhaltet insbesondere Informationen über den Fonds, die Leistungsvoraussetzungen, Anmeldefristen und über in diesem Zusammenhang notwendige Datenüberprüfungen.

Auskunftserteilung

§ 40. (1) Der Fonds und die nach diesem Bundesgesetz eingerichteten Organe sind berechtigt, von Behörden und anderen öffentlichen Einrichtungen Auskünfte einzuholen, die zur Erfüllung seiner Aufgaben erforderlich sind. Eine Auskunftserteilung darf nur unterbleiben, wenn besondere gesetzliche Bestimmungen dem entgegenstehen oder die schutzwürdigen Geheimhaltungsinteressen des Betroffenen die berechtigten Informationsinteressen des Fonds und der Organe überwiegen.

(2) (Anm.: aufgehoben durch BGBl. I Nr. 20/2007)

Datenschutz

§ 40a. Der Fonds ist berechtigt, personenbezogene Daten einschließlich sensibler Daten im Sinne des § 4 Z 2 DSG 2000 zum Zwecke der Erfüllung seiner durch dieses Bundesgesetz zugewiesenen Aufgaben zu verwenden. Darüber hinaus ist eine Übermittlung dieser Daten nur an den Nationalfonds der Republik Österreich für Opfer des Nationalsozialismus zum Zwecke der Erfüllung der dem Nationalfonds zugewiesenen Aufgaben zulässig. Alle Verwendungen sensibler Daten sind im Sinne des § 14 Abs. 2 Z 7 und 8 DSG 2000 zu protokollieren und zu dokumentieren. Das Datenschutzgesetz 2000, BGBl. I Nr. 165/1999, in der jeweils geltenden Fassung ist anwendbar.[9]

Personenbezogene Ausdrücke

§ 41. Die in diesem Bundesgesetz verwendeten personenbezogenen Ausdrücke betreffen, soweit dies inhaltlich in Betracht kommt, Frauen und Männer gleichermaßen.

---

[8] § 38 wurde zuletzt novelliert durch die EF-G Novelle, BGBl I Nr. 89/2008.
[9] § 40a wurde durch die EF-G Novelle, BGBl I Nr. 20/2007, eingefügt.

Appendix

International Agreements

§ **42.** International Agreements dealing with the consequences of the National Socialist era or World War II, in particular the State Treaty for the Re-establishment of an Independent and Democratic Austria, Federal Law Gazette No. 152/1955, as well as the Exchange of Notes of 1959 between the United States of America and Austria relating to the Settlement of Certain Claims under Article 26 of the Austrian State Treaty, shall not be affected by the present Federal Law. Thus, there shall be no legal right to payments or awards under the present Federal Law.

Entry into Force

§ **43.** *(note: not applicable according to Federal Law Gazette I No. 2/2008)*

Dismissal of Claims

§ **44.** (1) Payments and awards under the present Federal law may be made only after all claims under § 2 (1) have been dismissed. The Federal Government shall announce that day in the Federal Law Gazette I.[10]

(2) The expression "Austrian companies", as used in the present Federal Law, is defined in the **Annex** to this Federal Law.

Annex
Definition of the Expression "Austrian Companies"

The expression "Austrian companies", as used in the present Federal Law, is defined as follows:

1. Enterprises that, at any given time, had or have their headquarters within the borders of the present-day Republic of Austria as well as their parent companies (past or present, direct or indirect), even when the latter had or have their headquarters abroad.
2. Enterprises situated outside the borders of the present-day Republic of Austria in which Austrian enterprises as described in Sentence (1), at any given time, had or have a direct or indirect financial participation of at least 25 percent.
3. a) An "enterprise" or "company" means any entity, whether organized under public or private law as a corporation, partnership, sole proprietorship, association of business entities, society, community, cooperative, non-profit organization or otherwise as well as any municipality, private or other public law entity. Any enterprise (in the above meaning) incorporated or otherwise organized under Austrian law shall be deemed for all purposes of this definition to have its headquarters in Austria. An company (in the above meaning) includes its successors, predecessors, former parents, assigns, officers, directors, employees, agents attorneys, heirs, executors, administrators, personal representatives, and current or former shareholders. Any branch office, place of business, establishment or place of work of a non-Austrian company or company (in the above meaning) located within the borders of the present-day Republic of Austria shall be deemed to be a company or enterprise (in the above meaning) that had or has its headquarters in Austria, and any such non-Austrian company or enterprise (in the above meaning) shall be deemed to be a parent or former parent as the case may be, with respect to actions or inactions of such branch or place of business.

---

[10] The Proclamation of Legal Closure by the Federal Government took place in Federal Law Gazette II No. 414/2005.

Anhang

Völkerrechtliche Verträge

§ 42. Völkerrechtliche Abkommen, die sich mit den Folgen der Zeit des Nationalsozialismus oder des Zweiten Weltkrieges befassen, insbesondere der Staatsvertrag betreffend die Wiederherstellung eines unabhängigen und demokratischen Österreich, BGBl. Nr. 152/1955, sowie der Notenwechsel von 1959 zwischen den Vereinigten Staaten von Amerika und Österreich betreffend die Regelung gewisser Ansprüche nach Art. 26 des österreichischen Staatsvertrages, werden durch dieses Bundesgesetz nicht berührt. Ein Rechtsanspruch auf Leistungen nach diesem Bundesgesetz besteht daher nicht.

In-Kraft-Treten

§ 43. *(Anm.: als nicht mehr geltend festgestellt durch BGBl. I Nr. 2/2008)*

Abweisung von Klagen

§ 44. (1) Leistungen nach diesem Bundesgesetz können erst erfolgen, nachdem die Klagen nach § 2 Abs. 1 abgewiesen worden sind. Die Bundesregierung gibt diesen Tag im Bundesgesetzblatt I bekannt.[10]

(2) Die Definition des Begriffs „österreichische Unternehmen" im Sinne dieses Bundesgesetzes wird im **Anhang** zu diesem Bundesgesetz festgelegt.

Anhang

Definition des Begriffs „österreichische Unternehmen"

Der Begriff „österreichische Unternehmen" im Sinne dieses Bundesgesetzes wird wie folgt definiert:

1. Unternehmen, die zu irgendeinem Zeitpunkt ihren Sitz innerhalb der Grenzen der heutigen Republik Österreich haben oder hatten, sowie deren Muttergesellschaften (frühere oder gegenwärtige, unmittelbar oder mittelbare), auch wenn diese ihren Sitz im Ausland hatten oder haben.
2. Unternehmen außerhalb der Grenzen der heutigen Republik Österreich, an denen österreichische Unternehmen nach Satz 1 zu irgendeinem Zeitpunkt unmittelbar oder mittelbar mit mindestens 25 Prozent finanziell beteiligt waren oder sind.
3. a) Ein „Unternehmen" oder eine „Gesellschaft" bedeutet eine Rechtsperson, sowohl unter öffentlichem oder privatem Recht als Aktiengesellschaft, Personengesellschaft, Einzelunternehmer, Vereinigung von Wirtschaftskörpern, Verein, Gemeinschaft, Genossenschaft, gemeinnützige Organisation oder auf andere Weise organisiert, wie auch jede Gemeinde, private oder andere Körperschaft öffentlichen Rechts. Von jedem nach österreichischem Recht eingetragenen oder anders organisierten Unternehmen (in obigem Sinne) wird für alle Zwecke dieser Definition angenommen, dass es seinen Sitz in Österreich hat. Ein Unternehmen (in obigem Sinne) umfasst seine Rechtsnachfolger, Rechtsvorgänger, frühere Muttergesellschaften, Einzelrechtsnachfolger/Zessionar, Vorstands- und Aufsichtsratsmitglieder, Angestellten, Rechtsvertreter, Erben, Exekutoren, Verwalter, persönlichen Vertreter und gegenwärtigen und früheren Aktionäre. Jede Zweigniederlassung, Ort der Geschäftstätigkeit, Einrichtung oder Arbeitsplatz einer nicht-österreichischen Gesellschaft oder eines Unternehmens (in obigem Sinne) innerhalb der Grenzen der heutigen Republik Österreich wird als Gesellschaft oder Un-

---

[10] Die Kundmachung der Bundesregierung über das Eintreten des Rechtsfriedens erfolgte in BGBl II Nr. 414/2005.

b) A "parent company" means any company that owns or owned a direct or indirect participation of at least 25 percent in any enterprise that had or has its headquarters in the present-day Republic of Austria.

The definition of "Austrian companies" does not include foreign parent companies with headquarters outside the present-day territory of the Republic of Austria in which the sole alleged claim arising from National Socialist injustice or World War II has no connection with the Austrian affiliate and the latter's involvement in National Socialist injustice, unless there is a pending discovery request by plaintiff(s), of which the United States is provided by the defendant with copy to plaintiff(s), seeking discovery from or concerning National Socialist or World War II actions of the Austrian affiliate.

ternehmen (in obigem Sinne) betrachtet, das seinen Sitz in Österreich hat oder hatte, und jede derartige nicht-österreichische Gesellschaft oder jedes Unternehmen (in obigem Sinne) wird hinsichtlich der Handlungen oder Unterlassungen einer derartigen Zweigniederlassung oder Ort der Geschäftstätigkeit als Muttergesellschaft oder je nachdem als ehemalige Muttergesellschaft betrachtet.

b) Eine „Muttergesellschaft" bedeutet jede Gesellschaft, die eine unmittelbare oder mittelbare Beteiligung von mindestens 25 Prozent an einem Unternehmen innehat oder innehatte, das seinen Sitz in der heutigen Republik Österreich hat oder hatte.

Die Definition von „österreichischen Gesellschaften" umfasst nicht ausländische Muttergesellschaften mit Sitz außerhalb des gegenwärtigen Territoriums der Republik Österreich, bei denen der einzige angebliche Anspruch aus nationalsozialistischem Unrecht oder dem Zweiten Weltkrieg in keinem Zusammenhang mit der österreichischen Tochtergesellschaft und der Verwicklung der Letzteren in nationalsozialistisches Unrecht steht, es sei denn ein Ersuchen des (der) Kläger(s) auf Offenlegung ist anhängig, das die Vereinigten Staaten vom Beklagten mit Kopie an den (die) Kläger erhalten, in welchem die Offenlegung von oder betreffend nationalsozialistische Handlungen oder Handlungen im Zweiten Weltkrieg der österreichischen Tochtergesellschaft begehrt wird.

Opt-In Dates of Austrian Provinces and Municipalities

Applications for restitution of publicly-owned (on the cut off day 17 January 2001) properties or movable assets of Jewish Community Organizations are decided on by the independent Arbitration Panel for *In Rem* Restitution. "Public property" in the meaning of the General Settlement Fund Law (GSF Law) is present if the requested property (the requested movable assets of a Jewish Community Organization) were owned by the Federation or a legal person solely owned by the Federation on the cut off day, 17 January 2001. Furthermore, within the scope of Sec. 38 GSF Law, Austrian provinces and municipalities could and can give the Arbitration Panel jurisdiction to examine applications for restitution of provincial or municipal property (opt-in). The deadlines for the Federation and those provinces and municipalities that have made use of the opt-in are listed below:[1]

Regional Administrative Body:	GSF Law/Date of Opt-In, Deadline Extended on:	Deadline:
Republic of Austria	GSF Law (Federal Law Gazette I No. 12/ 2001), deadline last extended by Federal Law Gazette I No. 20/2007 of 25 April 2007	31 December 2007
Provinces:		
The City of Vienna	**27 June 2001, 1 October 2008**	**31 December 2009**
The Province of Upper Austria	10 April 2002	31 December 2007
The Province of Lower Austria	28 August 2002	31 December 2007
The Province of Burgenland	12 November 2002	31 December 2007
The Province of Salzburg	9 December 2002	31 December 2007
The Province of Carinthia	16 June 2003	31 December 2007
The Province of Vorarlberg	**16 December 2003, 13 January 2009**	**31 December 2009**
The Province of Styria	22 December 2003	31 December 2007
Municipalities:		
Vöcklabruck	**28 September 2001, 13 March 2009**	**31 December 2009**
Stockerau	16 September 2004	31 December 2007
Eisenstadt	27 September 2004	31 December 2007
Bad Ischl	**21 October 2004, 26 February 2009**	**31 December 2009**
Oberwart	7 November 2006	31 December 2007
Rechnitz	18 November 2006	31 December 2007
Kittsee	28 November 2006	31 December 2007
Wiener Neudorf	11 December 2006	31 December 2007
Purkersdorf	12 December 2006	31 December 2007
Mattersburg	**14 December 2006, 19 February 2009**	**31 December 2009**
Grieskirchen	10 December 2007	31 December 2007
Korneuburg	17 December 2007	31 December 2007

[1] This list is regularly updated on the homepage of the General Settlement Fund (www.nationalfonds.org, www.entschaedigungsfonds.at or www.generalsettlementfund.org).

Opt-In von Ländern und Gemeinden

Anträge auf Rückstellung von Liegenschaften oder beweglichem Vermögen jüdischer Gemeinschaftsorganisationen im öffentlichen Eigentum (Stichtag 17. Jänner 2001) werden durch die unabhängige Schiedsinstanz für Naturalrestitution entschieden. „Öffentliches Eigentum" im Sinne des Entschädigungsfondsgesetzes (EF-G) liegt jedenfalls vor, wenn sich die beantragte Liegenschaft (das beantragte bewegliche Vermögen einer jüdischen Gemeinschaftsorganisation) am 17. Jänner 2001 im Eigentum des Bundes oder einer im Alleineigentum des Bundes stehenden juristischen Person befand. Darüber hinaus konnten und können – im Rahmen des § 38 EF-G – auch österreichische Bundesländer und Gemeinden die Schiedsinstanz zur Prüfung von Anträgen auf Naturalrestitution von Landes- bzw. Gemeindevermögen zuständig machen („Opt-In"). Im Folgenden sind daher die Fristen für den Bund und jene Länder und Gemeinden aufgelistet, die ein Opt-In erklärt haben:[1]

Gebietskörperschaft:	EF-G/Datum des Opt-In, Frist verlängert am:	Fristende:
Republik Österreich	EF-G (BGBl I Nr. 12/2001), zuletzt Frist verlängert mit BGBl I Nr. 20/2007 vom 25. April 2007	31. Dezember 2007
Länder:		
Stadt Wien	27. Juni 2001, 1. Oktober 2008	**31. Dezember 2009**
Land Oberösterreich	10. April 2002	31. Dezember 2007
Land Niederösterreich	28. August 2002	31. Dezember 2007
Land Burgenland	12. November 2002	31. Dezember 2007
Land Salzburg	9. Dezember 2002	31. Dezember 2007
Land Kärnten	16. Juni 2003	31. Dezember 2007
Land Vorarlberg	**16. Dezember 2003, 13. Jänner 2009**	**31. Dezember 2009**
Land Steiermark	22. Dezember 2003	31. Dezember 2007
Gemeinden:		
Vöcklabruck	**28. September 2001, 13. März 2009**	**31. Dezember 2009**
Stockerau	16. September 2004	31. Dezember 2007
Eisenstadt	27. September 2004	31. Dezember 2007
Bad Ischl	**21. Oktober 2004, 26. Februar 2009**	**31. Dezember 2009**
Oberwart	7. November 2006	31. Dezember 2007
Rechnitz	18. November 2006	31. Dezember 2007
Kittsee	28. November 2006	31. Dezember 2007
Wiener Neudorf	11. Dezember 2006	31. Dezember 2007
Purkersdorf	12. Dezember 2006	31. Dezember 2007
Mattersburg	**14. Dezember 2006, 19. Februar 2009**	**31. Dezember 2009**
Grieskirchen	10. Dezember 2007	31. Dezember 2007
Korneuburg	17. Dezember 2007	31. Dezember 2007

[1] Diese Liste wird auf der Homepage des Allgemeinen Entschädigungsfonds (unter www.nationalfonds.org, www.entschaedigungsfonds.at oder www.generalsettlementfund.org) laufend aktualisiert.

A Select Bibliography on the Subject of *(In Rem)* Restitution

Allgemeiner Entschädigungsfonds/Josef Aicher/Erich Kussbach/August Reinisch (eds.), *Entscheidungen der Schiedsinstanz für Naturalrestitution*, vol. 1, Vienna 2008 [bilingual, German/English].

Fiorentina Azizi/Günter Gößler, *Extreme Ungerechtigkeit und bewegliches System*. In: Juristische Blätter (JBl) 2006, 415–436.

Stuart Eizenstat, *Unvollkommene Gerechtigkeit. Der Streit um die Entschädigung der Opfer von Zwangsarbeit und Enteignung*, Munich 2003.

Ronald Faber, *Substanzerhaltungspflicht der Bundesforste und Naturalrestitution durch den Entschädigungsfonds*. In: Journal für Rechtspolitik (JRP) 2003, 247–252.

Ronald Faber, *Zwischen Anspruch und Wirklichkeit: Zur Naturalrestitution nach dem Entschädigungsfondsgesetz*. In: Zeitschrift für Verwaltung (ZfV) 2008, 151–167.

Alfred Fehringer, *Ihr müsst hier weg. Die Jüdische Gemeinde Hollabrunn von 1850 bis 1938*, Vienna 2007.

Günter Gößler/Martin Niklas, *Ein konstruktiver Staatsdiener. Eine Erinnerung an den Juristen Heinrich Klang*. In: Wiener Zeitung (24th/25th January 2009), E9 ("extra"-supplement).

Günter Gößler/Susanne Helene Betz, *Ist die Vergangenheit nicht mehr zu bewältigen? Eine Replik auf Graf, Privatautonomie und extreme Ungerechtigkeit*, JBl 2007, 545. In: JBl 2008, 690–707.

Georg Graf, *„Arisierung" und Restitution. Anmerkungen zum Entschädigungsfondsgesetz*. In: JBl 2001, 746–756.

Georg Graf, *Privatautonomie und extreme Ungerechtigkeit. Kritische Anmerkungen zur Entscheidungspraxis der Schiedsinstanz*. In: JBl 2007, 545–554.

Clemens Jabloner, *Juristische Aspekte der Historikerkommission*. In: juridikum 2003, 19–23.

Ursula Kriebaum/Ernst Sucharipa, *Das Washingtoner Abkommen. Die österreichische Restitutionsvereinbarung vom 17. Jänner 2001*. In: Verena Pawlowsky und Harald Wendelin (eds.), *Die Republik und das NS-Erbe. Raub und Rückgabe – Österreich von 1938 bis heute*, Vienna 2005, 164–185.

Hannah Lessing, *„Bei uns werden alle berücksichtigt"*. In: Heidrun Schulze (ed.), *Wieder gut machen? Enteignung, Zwangsarbeit, Entschädigung, Restitution. Österreich 1938–1945/ 1945–1999*, Vienna/Innsbruck 1999, 132–138.

Hannah M. Lessing/Renate Meissner/Nina Bjalek, *„Wir können nur anklopfen, wo die Tür offen ist" – Der lange Weg zu Anerkennung und Entschädigung*. In: Verena Pawlowsky/Harald Wendelin (eds.), *Ausgeschlossen und entrechtet*, Vienna 2006 (= Raub und Rückgabe – Österreich von 1938 bis heute, vol. 4), 241–259.

Hannah Lessing/Richard Rebernik/Nicola Spitzy, *The Austrian General Settlement Fund: An Overview*. In: The International Bureau of the Permanent Court of Arbitration (ed.): *Redressing Injustices Through Mass Claims Processes. Innovative Responses to Unique Challenges*, Oxford 2006, 95–107.

Franz Stefan Meissel, *Unrechtsbewältigung durch Rechtsgeschichte? Zum Begriff der „extremen Ungerechtigkeit"* im Entschädigungsfonds-Gesetz. In: juridikum 2003, 42–46.

National Fund of the Republic of Austria for Victims of National Socialism (ed.), *Business Report 2007 National Fund of the Republic of Austria for Victims of National Socialism and the General Settlement Fund for Victims of National Soicalism*. Editorial contributors: Jür-

Auswahlbibliografie zum Themenbereich (Natural-)Restitution

Allgemeiner Entschädigungsfonds/Josef *Aicher*/Erich *Kussbach*/August *Reinisch* (Hrsg.), Entscheidungen der Schiedsinstanz für Naturalrestitution, Band 1, Wien 2008 [zweisprachig, Deutsch/Englisch].

Fiorentina *Azizi*/Günter *Gößler*, Extreme Ungerechtigkeit und bewegliches System. In: Juristische Blätter (JBl) 2006, 415–436.

Stuart *Eizenstat*, Unvollkommene Gerechtigkeit. Der Streit um die Entschädigung der Opfer von Zwangsarbeit und Enteignung, München 2003.

Ronald *Faber*, Substanzerhaltungspflicht der Bundesforste und Naturalrestitution durch den Entschädigungsfonds. In: Journal für Rechtspolitik (JRP) 2003, 247–252.

Ronald *Faber*, Zwischen Anspruch und Wirklichkeit: Zur Naturalrestitution nach dem Entschädigungsfondsgesetz. In: Zeitschrift für Verwaltung (ZfV) 2008, 151–167.

Alfred *Fehringer*, Ihr müsst hier weg. Die Jüdische Gemeinde Hollabrunn von 1850 bis 1938, Wien 2007.

Günter *Gößler*/Martin *Niklas*, Ein konstruktiver Staatsdiener. Eine Erinnerung an den Juristen Heinrich Klang. In: Wiener Zeitung (24./25. Jänner 2009), E9 („extra"-Beilage).

Günter *Gößler*/Susanne Helene *Betz*, Ist die Vergangenheit nicht mehr zu bewältigen? Eine Replik auf *Graf*, Privatautonomie und extreme Ungerechtigkeit, JBl 2007, 545. In: JBl 2008, 690–707.

Georg *Graf*, „Arisierung" und Restitution. Anmerkungen zum Entschädigungsfondsgesetz. In: JBl 2001, 746–756.

Georg *Graf*, Privatautonomie und extreme Ungerechtigkeit. Kritische Anmerkungen zur Entscheidungspraxis der Schiedsinstanz. In: JBl 2007, 545–554.

Clemens *Jabloner*, Juristische Aspekte der Historikerkommission. In: juridikum 2003, 19–23.

Ursula *Kriebaum*/Ernst *Sucharipa*, Das Washingtoner Abkommen. Die österreichische Restitutionsvereinbarung vom 17. Jänner 2001. In: Verena *Pawlowsky* und Harald *Wendelin* (Hrsg.), Die Republik und das NS-Erbe. Raub und Rückgabe – Österreich von 1938 bis heute, Wien 2005, 164–185.

Hannah *Lessing*, „Bei uns werden alle berücksichtigt". In: Heidrun *Schulze* (Hrsg.), Wieder gut machen? Enteignung, Zwangsarbeit, Entschädigung, Restitution. Österreich 1938–1945/1945–1999, Wien/Innsbruck 1999, 132–138.

Hannah M. *Lessing*/Renate *Meissner*/Nina *Bjalek*, „Wir können nur anklopfen, wo die Tür offen ist" – Der lange Weg zu Anerkennung und Entschädigung. In: Verena *Pawlowsky* und Harald *Wendelin* (Hrsg.), Ausgeschlossen und entrechtet, Wien 2006 (= Raub und Rückgabe – Österreich von 1938 bis heute, Bd. 4), 241–259.

Hannah *Lessing*/Richard *Rebernik*/Nicola *Spitzy*, The Austrian General Settlement Fund: An Overview. In: The International Bureau of the Permanent Court of Arbitration (Ed.): Redressing Injustices Through Mass Claims Processes. Innovative Responses to Unique Challenges, Oxford 2006, 95–107.

Franz Stefan *Meissel*, Unrechtsbewältigung durch Rechtsgeschichte? Zum Begriff der „extremen Ungerechtigkeit" im Entschädigungsfonds-Gesetz. In: juridikum 2003, 42–46.

Nationalfonds der Republik Österreich für Opfer des Nationalsozialismus (Hrsg.), Geschäftsbericht 2007 des Nationalfonds der Republik Österreich für Opfer des Nationalsozialismus und des Allgemeinen Entschädigungsfonds für Opfer des Nationalsozialismus. Redaktionelle Mitarbeit: Jürgen *Schremser*, Maria Luise *Lanzrath*, Richard *Rebernik*, Peter

gen Schremser, Maria Luise Lanzrath, Richard Rebernik, Peter Stadlbauer, Christine Schwab, Claudia Müller, Ingeborg Gratzer und Elisabeth Leeb, Vienna 2008.

Christian Rabl, *Die Erben als Begünstigte der Naturalrestitution nach dem Entschädigungsfondsgesetz (EFG)*. In: ecolex 2006, 374–377.

Walter Rechberger, *Ist Ungerechtigkeit komparationsfähig? Zum Begriff der „extremen Ungerechtigkeit" in § 10 Entschädigungsfondsgesetz*. In: juridikum 2005, 59–65.

Michael Schoiswohl/Marianne Schulze, *Der Entschädigungsfonds – Entstehung und Grundlagen*. In: juridikum 1/2003, 38–41.

Georg Wilhelm, *Zur Naturalrestitution nach dem Entschädigungsfondsgesetz*. In: ecolex 2004, 847–850.

Coming soon:

Nicole Immler, *Restitution and the Dynamics of Memory: A Neglected Trans-Generational Perspective*. In: Astrid Erll/ Ann Rigney: *Mediation, Remediation and the Dynamics of Cultural Memory*, Berlin/New York 2009 (= Media and Cultural Memory, 10).

Stadlbauer, Christine *Schwab*, Claudia *Müller*, Ingeborg *Gratzer* und Elisabeth *Leeb*, Wien 2008.

Christian *Rabl*, Die Erben als Begünstigte der Naturalrestitution nach dem Entschädigungsfondsgesetz (EFG). In: ecolex 2006, 374–377.

Walter *Rechberger*, Ist Ungerechtigkeit komparationsfähig? Zum Begriff der „extremen Ungerechtigkeit" in § 10 Entschädigungsfondsgesetz. In: juridikum 2005, 59–65.

Michael *Schoiswohl*/Marianne *Schulze*, Der Entschädigungsfonds – Entstehung und Grundlagen. In: juridikum 1/2003, 38–41.

Georg *Wilhelm*, Zur Naturalrestitution nach dem Entschädigungsfondsgesetz. In: ecolex 2004, 847–850.

Im Erscheinen:

Nicole *Immler*, Restitution and the Dynamics of Memory: A Neglected Trans-Generational Perspective. In: Astrid *Erll* und Ann *Rigney*, Mediation, Remediation and the Dynamics of Cultural Memory, Berlin/New York 2009 (= Media and Cultural Memory, 10).

List of Abbreviations

The meaning of the German abbreviations can be found in parentheses or in the German list of abbreviations ("Abkürzungsverzeichnis").

AdR ("Archiv der Republik")	Archives of the Republic
AG ("Aktiengesellschaft")	corporation
Baurat	building officer
BGBL/BGBl ("Bundesgesetzblatt")	Federal Law Gazette
BKA ("Bundeskanzleramt")	Federal Chancellery
BlgNR ("Beilage(n) zu den stenographischen Protokollen des Nationalrats")	Addenda to the Stenographic Minutes of the National Council
BMF ("Bundesministerium für Finanzen")	Federal Ministry of Finance
DI ("Diplomingenieur")	chartered engineer
Dkfm. ("Diplomkaufmann")	business graduate
Doz. ("Dozent")	university lecturer
Dris. ("Doktoris")	Ph.D.
ed./eds.	Editor/Editors
EZ ("Einlagezahl")	register number
FLD ("Finanzlandesdirektion")	Financial Directorate
GB ("Gerichtsbezirk" or "Grundbuch")	judicial district or land register
GBlÖ/GBl.f.d.L.Ö. ("Gesetzblatt für das Land Österreich")	Austrian Law Gazette
Ges. ("Gesellschaft")	company
GmbH.	limited company
Gestapo („Geheime Staatspolizei")	Secret State Police
GP ("Gesetzgebungsperiode")	legislative period
GSF Law	General Settlement Fund Law
GZ ("Geschäftszahl")	file no.
HfD JGS ("Hofdekret Justizgesetzsammlung")	High Decree Law Gazette, Collection of Laws
Ing. ("Ingenieur")	engineer
KG ("Katastralgemeinde")	cadastral district
leg. cit. ("legis citatae")	the cited act/law
Lg. ("Liegenschaft")	property
MR ("Ministerialrat")	assistant head of a government department
NS	National Socialist
OGH ("Oberster Gerichtshof")	Supreme Court
ÖJZ ("Österreichische Juristenzeitung")	Austrian Lawyers' Journal
O.Nr. ("Ordnungsnummer")	reference number
Öst. RGBl ("Österreichisches Reichsgesetzblatt")	Austrian Empire Law Gazette
ÖStA ("Österreichisches Staatsarchiv")	Austrian State Archives
OZ ("Ordnungszahl")	reference number
Para.	paragraph
Pg. ("Parteigenosse")	party comrade/member
Prim. ("Primar")	consultant
Reg. Rat ("Regierungsrat")	government counsilor
RGBl/RGBL ("Reichsgesetzblatt")	Reich Law Gazette
RK ("Rückstellungskommission")	Restitution Commission

Abkürzungsverzeichnis

1. BRBG	Erstes Bundesrechtsbereinigungsgesetz, BGBl I 191/1999
3. RStG	Drittes Rückstellungsgesetz (Bundesgesetz vom 6. Februar 1947 über die Nichtigkeit von Vermögensentziehungen), StF BGBl 54/1947
ABGB	Allgemeines bürgerliches Gesetzbuch vom 1. Juni 1811, StF JGS 946
Abs	Absatz
AdR	Archiv der Republik
AG	Aktiengesellschaft
AMS	Arbeitsmarktservice
AMSG	Arbeitsmarktservice-Gesetz (Bundesgesetz über das Arbeitsmarktservice), StF BGBl 313/1994
Anm.	Anmerkung
AÖF	Amtsblatt der österreichischen Finanzverwaltung
Art.	Artikel
ATS/S	österreichische Schilling
AußStrG	Außerstreitgesetz
AV	Aktenvermerk
B-Blatt	Eigentumsblatt des Grundbuchs
Beschl.	Beschluss
Bd.	Band
BG	Bezirksgericht, auch Bundesgesetz
BGBL/BGBl	Bundesgesetzblatt
BH	Bezirkshauptmannschaft
BKA	Bundeskanzleramt
Blg KNV	Beilage(n) zu den stenographischen Protokollen der Konstituierenden Nationalversammlung
BlgNR	Beilage(n) zu den stenographischen Protokollen des Nationalrats
BKA	Bundeskanzleramt
BM	Bundesministerium
BMF	Bundesministerium für Finanzen
BMJ	Bundesministerium für Justiz
BMVS	Bundesministerium für Vermögenssicherung und Wirtschaftsplanung
BWG	Bankwesengesetz
BundesforsteG	Bundesforstegesetz 1996 (Bundesgesetz zur Neuordnung der Rechtsverhältnisse der Österreichischen Bundesforste und Errichtung einer Aktiengesellschaft zur Fortführung des Betriebes „Österreichische Bundesforste"), StF BGBl 793/1996
B-VG	Bundes-Verfassungsgesetz von 1929, StF BGBl 1/1930
BVG	Bundesverfassungsgesetz(e)
CA-BV	Creditanstalt-Bankverein
DAG	Deutsche Ansiedlungsgesellschaft
DÖW	Dokumentationsarchiv des österreichischen Widerstands
Dris	[des] Doktors
dRGBl	Deutsches Reichsgesetzblatt

Rkv	file code used by the Supreme Restitution Commission
RM ("Reichsmark")	Reichsmark
RV ("Regierungsvorlage")	government bill
Sten Prot ("Stenographische Protokolle")	Stenographic Minutes
StGBl ("Staatsgesetzblatt")	State Law Gazette
VEAV ("Vermögensentziehungs-Anmeldungsverordnung")	Ordinance on the Notification of Seized Property
VfGH ("Verfassungsgerichtshof")	Constitutional Court
VfSlg ("Erkenntnisse und Beschlüsse des Verfassungsgerichtshofes")	Collection of Decisions by the Constitutional Court
VwGH ("Verwaltungsgerichtshof")	Supreme Administrative Court
VwSlg	Collection of Decisions by the Administrative Court

E	Entscheidung
EMRK	Europäische Menschenrechtskonvention, StF BGBl 210/1958
EF-G	Entschädigungsfondsgesetz (Bundesgesetz über die Einrichtung EntschädigungsfondsG eines Allgemeinen Entschädigungsfonds für Opfer des Nationalsozialismus und über Restitutionsmaßnahmen), StF BGBl I 12/2001
ErbStG	Erbschafts- und Schenkungssteuergesetz 1955 (Bundesgesetz vom 30. Juni 1955 betreffend die Erhebung einer Erbschafts- und Schenkungssteuer), StF BGBl 141/1955
EvBl.	Evidenzblatt
EZ	Einlagezahl
f	und der/die folgende
ff	und die folgenden
FLD	Finanzlandesdirektion
FN	Fußnote
FVF	Familienversorgungsfonds des Hauses Habsburg-Lothringen
GB	Grundbuch
GBl	Gesetzblatt
GBlÖ (GBl f.d.L.Ö.)	Gesetzblatt für das Land Österreich
geb.	geboren
Gestapo	Geheime Staatspolizei
GP	Gesetzgebungsperiode
GSF	General Settlement Fund, Allgemeiner Entschädigungsfonds
GST	Grundstück
GVO	Geschäfts- und Verfahrensordnung
GZ	Geschäftszahl
HabsbG	Habsburgergesetz (Gesetz vom 3. April 1919 betreffend die Landesverweisung und die Übernahme des Vermögens des Hauses Habsburg-Lothringen), StGBl 205/1919
HfG JGS	Hofdekret Justizgesetzsammlung
HG	Handelsgericht
HRA	Handelsregisterauszug
Hrsg.	Herausgeber
idF	in der Fassung
IKG	Israelitische Kultusgemeinde
inkl.	inklusive
iSd	im Sinne des
iVm	in Verbindung mit
JBL	Juristische Blätter
JGS	Justizgesetzsammlung (Gesetze und Verordnungen im Justizfach)
JUVA	Judenvermögensabgabe
K	Kronen
KG	Katastralgemeinde
KGF	Kriegsgeschädigtenfonds
KGFG	Kriegsgeschädigtenfondsgesetz (Gesetz vom 18. Dezember 1919 über den Kriegsgeschädigtenfonds), StGBl 573/1919
KO	Konkursordnung

Appendix

KVG	Kriegsverbrechergesetz
KZ	Konzentrationslager
LAA	Landesarbeitsamt
leg. cit.	legis citatae (des genannten Gesetzes)
LG	Landesgericht
LGfZRS	Landesgericht für Zivilrechtssachen
LH	Landeshauptmann
lit.	litera (literae)
MA	Magistratsabteilung
Mio.	Millionen
mwNw	mit weiteren Nachweisen
NÖ	Niederösterreich
NS	nationalsozialistisch
OFG	Opferfürsorgegesetz
OFP	Oberfinanzpräsident
OGH	Oberster Gerichtshof
ÖJZ	Österreichische Juristenzeitung
OLG	Oberlandesgericht
ORK	Oberste Rückstellungskommission
Öst. RGBl	(Österreichisches) Reichsgesetzblatt
ÖStA	Österreichisches Staatsarchiv
OSZE	Organisation für Sicherheit und Zusammenarbeit in Europa
OZ	Ordnungszahl
Pkt.	Punkt
PSK	Postsparkasse
RA	Rechtsanwalt/Rechtsanwältin
RAM	Reichsarbeitsministerium
RassDiskrBVG	BVG vom 3. Juli 1973 zur Durchführung des Internationalen Abkommens über die Beseitigung aller Formen rassischer Diskriminierung, BGBl 390/1973
RGBl	Reichsgesetzblatt
RK	Rückstellungskommission
Rkv	Aktenkürzel zu Verfahren vor der Obersten Rückstellungskommission
RM	Reichsmark
RStG	Rückstellungsgesetz
R-ÜG	Rechts-Überleitungsgesetz 1945, StGBl 6/1945
RV	Regierungsvorlage
Rz	Randzahl
Sign.	Signatur
Slg.	Sammlung
SS	Schutzstaffel
SSt.	Sammelstelle(n)
StenProt KNV	Stenographische Protokolle der Konstituierenden Nationalversammlung
StF	Stammfassung
StFROG	Stiftungs- und Fondsreorganisationsgesetz vom 6. Juli 1954, BGBl 197/1954
StGBl	Staatsgesetzblatt

Appendix

StGG	Staatsgrundgesetz über die allgemeinen Rechte der Staatsbürger für die im Reichsrate vertretenen Königreiche und Länder, StF RGBl 142/1867
StPO	Strafprozessordnung
Stv	Stellvertreter
StV 1955	Staatsvertrag vom 15. Mai 1955 betreffend die Wiederherstellung eines unabhängigen und demokratischen Österreich, BGBl 152/ 1955 SZ Entscheidungen des Obersten Gerichtshofes in Zivilsachen
StVDG	Staatsvertragsdurchführungsgesetz
TEG	Todeserklärungsgesetz 1950 (Wiederverlautbarung der Rechtsvorschriften über Verschollenheit und das Verfahren zum Zwecke der Todeserklärung und der Beweisführung des Todes), StF BGBl 23/1951
TZ	Tagebuchzahl
USIA	Uprawlenje sowjetskowo imuschtschestwa w Austrii/Verwaltung des sowjetischen Vermögens in Österreich
VA	Vermögensanmeldung nach der Verordnung über die Anmeldung des Vermögens von Juden vom 26. April 1938, GBlÖ 102/1938
VEAV	Vermögensentziehungs-Anmeldungsverordnung (Verordnung des Bundesministeriums für Vermögenssicherung und Wirtschaftsplanung vom 15. September 1946 zur Durchführung des Gesetzes über die Erfassung arisierter und anderer im Zusammenhang mit der nationalsozialistischen Machtübernahme entzogenen Vermögenschaften vom 10. Mai 1945, StGBl 10/1945), BGBl 166/46
VG	Verbotsgesetz
VS	Vermögenssicherung
VfGH	Verfassungsgerichtshof
VfSlg	Erkenntnisse und Beschlüsse des Verfassungsgerichtshofes
vgl.	Vergleiche
V-ÜG	Verfassungs-Überleitungsgesetz 1945, StGBl 4/1945
VwGH	Verwaltungsgerichtshof
VwSlg	Erkenntnisse und Beschlüsse des Verwaltungsgerichtshofes
VVSt	Vermögensverkehrsstelle
WStLA	Wiener Stadt- und Landesarchiv
WVK	Wiener Vertragsrechtskonvention (Wiener Übereinkommen über das Recht der Verträge), BGBl 40/1980
Z/Zif	Ziffer
Zl.	Zahl
ZPO	Zivilprozessordnung

Editors

Josef Aicher, born on 14 November 1947

Full professor for Corporate and Economic Law at the University of Vienna, honorary professor at the University of Salzburg, visiting professor of the Danube University Krems, corresponding member of the Austrian Academy of Sciences, deputy chairman of the board of the "Austrian Takeover Commission".

1970 University of Salzburg (Dr. iur.).

1975 Professor for Civil Law at the University of Graz, professor for Commercial and Securities Law at the Universities of Linz (1978) and Vienna (1982).

Co-editor of the legal journals "Wirtschaftsrechtliche Blätter" and "Zeitschrift für Vergaberecht und Beschaffungspraxis".

Since 2001, Chairman of the Arbitration Panel for *In Rem* Restitution.

Erich Kussbach, born on 5 May 1931

Former member of the International Humanitarian Fact Finding Commission, founding prorector of the "Gyula Andrássy German-Language University Budapest", ambassador of the Sovereign Order of the Knights of St. John in Hungary, retired Austrian ambassador.

1953, 1958 Universities in Budapest and Vienna (Dr. rer. pol.; Dr. iur.). 1961 Yale University (Master of Law).

Joined Austria's diplomatic service in 1963. Served to Hungary as ambassador and permanent representative with the International Danube Commission as his last posts between 1993 and 1996.

Since 1996, honorary professor for Humanitarian International Law, University of Linz.

Full member of the European Academy of Sciences and the Arts.

Until 2008 professor for International Law at the Catholic Pázmány Péter University, Budapest.

Author of numerous publications in the fields of International Law, Private International Law, Philosophy of Law and Political Science.

Since 2001, Member of the Arbitration Panel for *In Rem* Restitution appointed by Austria.

August Reinisch, born on 29 January 1965

Professor for International Law and European Law at the University of Vienna, Adjunct Professor at the Bologna Center/SAIS of John Hopkins University.

Works as an expert in international arbitration cases, as well as in proceedings relating to International Law and European Law.

1988 University of Vienna (Mag. iur.), 1990 University of Vienna (Mag. phil.).

1991 University of Vienna (Dr. iur.), 1989 New York University (LL.M. International Legal Studies), 1994 Diploma of the Academy for International Law in The Hague.

Co-editor of the journals "International Organizations Law Review", "International Legal Materials" and "Oxford Reports on International Law in Domestic Courts".

Since 2001, Member of the Arbitration Panel for *In Rem* Restitution appointed by the USA.

Herausgeber

Josef Aicher, geboren 14. November 1947

Ordentlicher Professor für Unternehmens- und Wirtschaftsrecht an der Universität Wien, Honorarprofessor der Universität Salzburg, Visiting Professor der Donau-Universität Krems, korr. Mitglied der Österreichischen Akademie der Wissenschaften, stv. Vorsitzender der Übernahmekommission.

1970 Universität Salzburg (Dr. iur.).

1975 Professor für Bürgerliches Recht an der Universität Graz. Professor für Handels- und Wertpapierrecht an den Universitäten Linz (1978) und Wien (1982).

Mitherausgeber der juristischen Fachzeitschriften „Wirtschaftsrechtliche Blätter" und „Zeitschrift für Vergaberecht und Beschaffungspraxis".

Seit 2001 Vorsitzender der Schiedsinstanz für Naturalrestitution.

Erich Kussbach, geboren 5. Mai 1931

Ehemaliges Mitglied der Internationalen Humanitären Ermittlungskommission, Gründungsprorektor der „Gyula Andrássy Deutschsprachige Universität Budapest", Botschafter des Souveränen Malteser Ritterordens in Ungarn, Österreichischer Botschafter i. R.

1953, 1958 Universitäten Budapest und Wien (Dr. rer. pol.; Dr. iur.). 1961 Yale University (Master of Law).

1963 Eintritt in den Diplomatischen Dienst Österreichs. Zuletzt Botschafter in Ungarn und ständiger Vertreter bei der Internationalen Donaukommission 1993–1996.

Seit 1996 Honorarprofessor für Humanitäres Völkerrecht der Universität Linz.

Ordentliches Mitglied der europäischen Akademie der Wissenschaften und Künste.

Bis 2008 Professor für Völkerrecht an der Katholischen Pázmány Péter Universität Budapest.

Verfasser zahlreicher Publikationen auf dem Gebiet des Völkerrechts, des internationalen Privatrechts, der Rechtsphilosophie und der Politikwissenschaft.

Seit 2001 von Österreich ernanntes Mitglied der Schiedsinstanz für Naturalrestitution.

August Reinisch, geboren 29. Jänner 1965

Außerordentlicher Professor für Völker- und Europarecht an der Universität Wien, Adjunct Professor am Bologna Center/SAIS der Johns Hopkins University.

Gutachter im Bereich der internationalen Schiedsgerichtsbarkeit sowie der völker- und europarechtlich relevanten Prozessführung.

1988 Universität Wien (Mag. iur.), 1990 Universität Wien (Mag. phil.).

1991 Universität Wien (Dr. iur.), 1989 New York University (LL.M. International Legal Studies), 1994 Diplom der Haager Akademie für Internationales Recht.

Mitherausgeber „International Organizations Law Review", „International Legal Materials" und „Oxford Reports on International Law in Domestic Courts".

Seit 2001 von den USA ernanntes Mitglied der Schiedsinstanz für Naturalrestitution.